David King Dunaway

HUXLEY IN
HOLLYWOOD

Also by David King Dunaway

How Can I Keep from Singing: Pete Seeger
Oral History: An Interdisciplinary Anthology (with W. K. Baum)

Aldous Huxley
August 2nd
1962

Bachardy

HUXLEY IN
HOLLYWOOD

DAVID KING DUNAWAY

A Cornelia & Michael Bessie Book

HARPER & ROW PUBLISHERS, New York
GRAND RAPIDS, PHILADELPHIA, ST. LOUIS, SAN FRANCISCO
LONDON, SINGAPORE, SYDNEY, TOKYO, TORONTO

Letters of Aldous Huxley used by permission of Laura Huxley and Matthew Huxley.

Grateful acknowledgment is made for permission to reprint excerpts from:
Here Lies the Heart by Mercedes De Acosta, published in the United States by Reynal & Co. in 1960. Reprinted by permission of William Morrow & Co., Inc. and by courtesy of Andre Deutsch, Ltd.; *Garbo* by Norman Zierold published by Stein & Day, Inc. New York, 1972; *This Timeless Moment* by Laura Archera Huxley. Copyright © 1968 by Laura Archera Huxley. Reprinted by permission of Farrar, Straus and Giroux, Inc.; *My Guru and His Disciples* by Christopher Isherwood. Copyright © 1980 by Christopher Isherwood. Reprinted by permission of Farrar, Straus and Giroux, Inc.; *The Hollywood Exiles* by John Baxter. Reprinted by permission from Taplinger Publishing Company; *A Girl Like I* by Anita Loos. Copyright © 1966 by Anita Loos. The Viking Press, Inc., New York; Hamish Hamilton, London. Quoted by permission from Anita Loos Trusts; *Kiss Hollywood Good-by* by Anita Loos. Copyright © 1974 by Anita Loos. The Viking Press, Inc., New York; W. H. Allen, London. Quoted by permission from Anita Loos Trusts; *Fate Keeps on Happening* by Anita Loos. Edited by Ray Pierre Corsini. Copyright © 1984 by Anita Loos Trusts. Dodd, Mead & Co., New York; Harrap Ltd., London. Quoted by permission from Anita Loos Trusts; *Leaves of the Tulip Tree* by Juliette Huxley. Published by Salem House; *Aldous Huxley* by Sybille Bedford. Copyright © 1973, 1974 by Sybille Bedford. Reprinted by permission of Harper & Row, Publishers, Inc.; *Tales from the Hollywood Raj* by Sheridan Morley. Copyright © 1983 by Sheridan Morley. First published by George Weidenfeld & Nicolson Ltd. Reprinted by permission of Curtis Brown Ltd. London; *Success* screenplay by Aldous Huxley from Special Collections Department, The Stanford University Libraries, Aldous Huxley Collection; "The Diaries of Grace Hubble" from The Huntington Library, San Marino, California, The Hubble Collection; and photographs from *Madame Curie* © 1943 Loew's Inc. Renewed 1970 Metro-Goldwyn-Mayer Inc.; *Pride and Prejudice* © 1940 Loew's Inc. Renewed 1967 Metro-Goldwyn-Mayer Inc.; and *Jane Eyre* © 1944, renewed 1972. Twentieth Century–Fox Film Corporation. All rights reserved.

FIRST EDITION

Designer: Barbara DuPree Knowles

LIBRARY OF CONGRESS CATALOGING-IN-PUBLICATION DATA
Dunaway, David King.
  Huxley in Hollywood / David King Dunaway.
  p. cm.
  "A Cornelia & Michael Bessie Book."
  Includes index.
  ISBN 0-06-039095-6
  1. Huxley, Aldous, 1894–1963—Biography. 2. Huxley, Aldous, 1894–1963—Homes and haunts—California—Los Angeles. 3. Authors, English—20th century—Biography. 4. Screenwriters—United States—Biography. 5. Motion pictures—California—Los Angeles—History. 6. Hollywood (Los Angeles, Calif.)—Social life and customs. I. Title.
PR6015.U9Z599 1989
823'.912—dc20
[B]   89-45036

89 90 91 92 93 VB/RRD 10 9 8 7 6 5 4 3 2 1

To my parents

and

To exiled and
emigrant writers
around the world:
*"A great writer creates a
world of his own and readers
are proud to live in it."*

—CYRIL CONNOLLY,
The Enemies of Promise

Contents

Illustrations follow page 140 and page 300

Prologue

I sit on a balcony of D. H. Lawrence's ranch north of Taos, New Mexico, where Aldous Huxley and his family spent their first summer in the United States, in 1937.

In the late-summer heat the Jeffrey pines give off the vanilla-sweet scent of an old-fashioned soda fountain. Black and brown shadows cross the mesa below like stripes dividing a life into eras—until a wind-blown cloud redivides and sorts them. I have come here seeking the spellbinding silence of the Rockies, to the spot where Huxley wrote his first American book, the pacifist tract, *Ends and Means*:

> We are living now, not in the delicious intoxication induced by the early successes of science, but in a rather grisly morning-after, when it has become apparent that what triumphant science has done is to improve the means for achieving unimproved or actually deteriorated ends.

Huxley wrote this at age forty-three, when already considered "one of the most prodigiously learned writers not merely of this century but of all time," as the *Paris Review* wrote.

F. Scott Fitzgerald, in the notes for his Hollywood novel *The Last Tycoon*, wrote: "There are no second acts in American lives." Huxley, one of Britain's most famous twentieth-century novelists, was more fortunate: He had a new beginning, on the eve of World War II. Huxley came to the United States to lecture on pacifism and ended up in Hollywood, writing screenplays with Europeans exiled there, including George Cukor, Zoltán Korda, and Christopher Isherwood.

Huxley's American period was characterized by a dramatic shift in his writing, from the cynicism of his disaffected post–World War I generation to an ardent exploration of mysticism, parapsychology, and Indian religions. A conventional explanation of this shift is that Huxley's work in the studios (or the effects of balmy California) undermined his satirical talents. Writers as thoughtful as Margaret Drabble, in the current *Oxford Companion to English Literature*, continue to disregard his American years.

He had come to California, when he could have written from any place on earth, because he needed the quick and generous rewards of screenwriting and because he appreciated the sinuous beauties of Hollywood and the endless sunlight which allowed him vision.

He fell in love with Southern California, describing it in his science fiction novel, *Ape and Essence*:

> *The sea and its clouds, the mountains glaucous-golden,*
> *The valleys full of indigo darkness,*
> *The drought of lion-colored plains,*
> *The rivers of pebbles and white sand.*

Was there something more to California's appeal, beyond the sybaritic comfort of palms and wooded hills at the continent's edge? Was he fulfilled by his new life among those who befriended him in Hollywood's golden years: Charlie Chaplin and his wife Paulette Goddard, Thomas Mann and Igor Stravinsky, Anita Loos and Christopher Isherwood?

My own interest in Huxley began when I was thirteen, in 1961, with a tattered copy of *Brave New World*. Genetically engineered test-tube babies seemed captivating but preposterous science fiction; I recall rooting for the band of "savages" in these same mountains of New Mexico, the oddballs of the future who bred for love, not eugenics.

Our teacher mentioned, vaguely, that Huxley was one of Britain's angry young men after World War I, that this nearly blind man had somehow overcome his handicap to publish nearly fifty books, including some considered the most brilliant of his generation.

That summer, I devoured *Crome Yellow, Antic Hay,* and *Point Counter Point* in cheap paper editions; their lurid covers promised a high-pitched sexuality the author never quite delivered. By the time I was in high school, I saw what Proust, Woolf, and Eliot had been excited about: the jibing, sophisticated intellect who took no creed on its own terms, war having besmirched them all; who broadly attacked gentility, order, and overintellectualism. Huxley left little room for self-satisfaction.

My generation knew about angry young men, having just found its own among musicians: Phil Ochs, Bob Dylan, and Mick Jagger. If Huxley had been born a generation later, he might have used a guitar to make a point.

The summer I began college, I remember friends discussing people worth writing books about: Huxley was one, Gandhi another. I didn't know anything about Huxley's life except that he'd been blinded by an eye infection at seventeen and learned braille in two weeks: "the only comfortable way to read under the covers," he called his disability. Other writers pushed Huxley out of my mind, though occasionally I sampled his more obscure works, such as *The Perennial Philosophy,* on the common ground among the world's religions.

Then, to my surprise, by the late sixties Huxley came back into fashion. The paper edition of *Island,* his last novel, circulated in dorm rooms for its experiments in education, sexuality, and psychedelics. *Doors of Perception* was read avidly by those hungry for alternatives to booze. Huxley was Hip, having taken mind-altering drugs years before Timothy Leary.

Yet despite its topicality, *Island's* speechifying resembled Ecclesiastes. (Besides, Huxley took mescalin under supervision of a clinical psychiatrist, which didn't sound like fun.) Other, more pressing concerns crowded literature: the draft, the war in Vietnam, our emerging sexuality, and our professional identities.

As the seventies began, Ray Mungo, with whom I had worked as a writer for Liberation News Service, published *The Art of Seeing.* This visual self-help book had a particularly poignant effect on me.

My eyes, which had kept me out of the army, were in steady decline; I outgrew glasses every six months. I tried the eye exercises which had allowed Huxley to cast off his glasses, but they gave me a fearsome headache.

In a used bookstore at Berkeley, where I was in graduate school, I found a copy of *Science, Liberty and Peace*, Huxley's post–World War II hopes for life in small, decentralized communities. This was a different writer from the angry young man of the 1920s. The more I read, the more foresighted Huxley seemed: in 1932 predicting genetic engineering; in 1944 warning of the dangers of nuclear energy, long before "the friendly atom" campaign; in 1947, environmental catastrophes. Huxley appeared a Tiresias, the blind seer to whom antiquity assigned the dubious pleasure of being correct about the most unbearable truths, the one who bore to Oedipus the facts of his parentage.

As Swinburne wrote of Tiresias:

I prophesy of life, who live with death;
of joy, being sad; of sunlight, who am blind;
of man, whose ways are alien from mankind.

Then, in the eighties, I learned two facts which moved me to write: Huxley had spent twenty years in and out of the studios of Hollywood and he had come to America as an absolute pacifist. Sitting in the shade of the tall pines on the Lawrence Ranch, I connected Huxley's anger at weapons sales in 1937 with my own a half century later, as the Reagan administration doubled the nation's debt to devote 63 percent of the budget to defense, the largest percentage ever in peacetime.

I began to study Huxley's career to discover what he offered a generation preoccupied by war and survival. I wondered how the shy, bookish man had become a public speaker for peace. I sensed the melancholy which blindness had brought, "my own spirit's dark discouragement/Deprived of inward as of outward sight," as he wrote in his last book of poems, *The Cicadas*.

The difficulties of writing on Huxley became apparent; acquaintances shifted uncomfortably in their seats when his name came up. All recognized him as a major author, but few had read beyond a half-dozen of his classic works. Huxley taxed readers with allusions people felt silly about not knowing or looking up.

Few friends recognized the parallel between his first American novel, *After Many a Summer Dies the Swan*, and his friend Orson Welles's later *Citizen Kane*. In researching Huxley's send-up of William Randolph Hearst, I came across the meaning of "Rosebud," the *leitmotif* of *Citizen Kane*. I thumbed through hundreds of documents the FBI kept on Huxley. I pored over the originals of Huxley's film scripts, some of them—such as his adaptation of *Alice in Wonderland* and a musical comedy of *Brave New World*—long considered lost.

At last count, there are over 100 books on Aldous Huxley, including dissertations from around the world; only five of these are biographical. One reason so few biographies exist is that virtually all of Huxley's papers perished in a sudden fire in the Hollywood Hills: love letters, manuscripts, annotations to his enormous library—all burned in an hour in 1961. What survived were his published letters—occasionally on his writing, though he rarely discussed works-in-progress—and four boxes of his wife's letters, in French, which sit uncatalogued in the Belgian Royal Library.

These letters, together with surviving backdrops of his life in California, pose unanswered questions of Huxley's American sojourn. *Was* he a coward not to fight for England? What sort of a screenwriter was he—did he sell out to the studios, as some of his readers thought? How did he become involved with mysticism and drugs? Did he ever reach that unitary experience he sought for the last two decades of his life?

To answer such queries, I had to mine living memories; thus, I found myself beginning an oral history in the Hollywood Hills, looking down on what Aldous called the "Metrollopis" of Los Angeles, talking with his widow in the house where he lived last, just below the first "O" in Hollywood's most famous sign.

The day of our first meeting, in 1985, was balmy and luminous—particularly so in this white-walled room with Laura Archera Huxley, former violinist with the Los Angeles Philharmonic and author of a memoir of Huxley and a successful self-help book, *You Are Not the Target*. We talked below a window two stories tall, whose light flooded the room, further reflected by a bone-white shag carpet. Here was a house in which Huxley could see.

To me, Laura Huxley was gracious but reserved. She had met hundreds of Huxley admirers, some reeling with hallucinogens, others privately convinced that Huxley had fried his marbles under the Southern California sun. Widows make detailing their husbands' lives a career, but Laura was a therapist before, during, and after her marriage. Only by chance did I see her in action.

Midway through our discussion, the doorbell rang. Laura frowned, anticipating my disappointment. She wasn't expecting anyone. She flicked her pale hair and smiled; this would be brief.

At the door was a teenager who had lost her dog. Her face was red from crying. She was slightly taller than Laura, with the same thin, delicate figure. But for the intense look in Laura's crystal blue eyes, they might have been waiting for the same school bus.

The girl could scarcely stop sobbing. She had just moved to the neighborhood, her mother was at work, her German shepherd had run off. Laura took her arm and led the girl outside.

Her reminiscences on Huxley derailed, we called for the dog in the canyon in back of the house. Laura held the girl's arm lightly, alternately calling aloud and speaking in soothing tones. She took the girl's phone number, and finally we sat down again. As I was pinning on the microphone, she shook her head.

"You can see the picture. The family moves, over the wishes of the girl; the mother works, the girl's left alone. Obviously by more than her dog." We started up again and parted new friends.

The next day I drove to Beverly Hills to visit Peggy Kiskadden. One biography of Huxley noted his first wife Maria's casual attitude toward sexual fidelity. She selected women Aldous might like, invited them over for lunch or tea; sent an inscribed volume of her husband's work; then booked the restaurant and, in some cases, the motel. Critics suggested that this was either too much or too little to know of the Huxleys' domestic arrangements.

The Kiskadden residence sits on a long, winding alley, once the carriage road of an estate whose present worth is in the tens of millions. In her eighties, immaculately mannered, Peggy is equally at ease discussing Stravinsky or sacred Indian philosophies like the Vedanta, two topics which came up in recalling her days as a hostess to Hollywood's British émigré community of the forties.

Huxley lived with daily bouts of eyestrain, she says, but to visit a museum with him was exciting. He would pull out his magnifying glass and scan every sector of a canvas. His breath would quicken. Then he would move to the next picture, without talking, until he'd had his fill. Kenneth Clark ranked this purblind writer among the great art critics of his time.

At times, Kiskadden became reticent. After the tape recorder was turned off, she told how Maria helped Aldous write letters ending his affairs; why they lived this way she could not say.

In London I interviewed the widow of Sir Julian Huxley, Aldous's biologist brother and the first Director General of UNESCO. After our interview in the library, Lady Juliette asked if anyone had told me anything "unusual" about Maria. What might that be, I inquired of this jaunty octogenarian. "Oh, if no one has said anything, I can't possibly mention it," she said airily, leading me down the staircase.

I learned to expect accounts of the three tragedies which marked Huxley's adolescence: his mother's sudden death from cancer when he was fourteen, his blindness at Eton, and his brother's suicide, as Huxley entered college. Everyone drew attention to these facts, relentlessly. Some suggested them as the cause of his private depressions.

What's most interesting about lives is how they clamber over obstacles, not the obstacles themselves. That his mother's death taught him to accept impermanence, that his blindness made him a relentless seeker of visions and light, that his brother's suicide redoubled his survivor's instinct and created ambivalent attitudes toward sexuality—these were starting points of a life, not its explanation.

Easy causes—even self-declared ones—often become less important as the pieces of a life fit together toward the unexpected whole. Biographers apprehend truth long before they know it.

In the darkly lit Paris salon, one of Maria's sisters offered me another piece of the puzzle: "My sister was a lesbian," Jeanne Neveux said directly. This was news to me. Biographers hadn't mentioned this. Facts fell into place: the Huxleys' unusual marital arrangements; why Maria had nearly committed suicide at the London house of Lady Ottoline Morrell; why their only child Matthew, kept from the fact of his mother's sexual preference, was a stranger in his home. "She and Aldous shared this taste for beautiful women," Aldous's nephew Francis Huxley reflected. "It brought them together."

My tape-recorded interviews echo in the modern log cabin on the ranch, not forty yards from Lawrence's home. The afternoon winds of the last days of autumn are blowing down from the upper ranges, peeling copper gold leaves from the cottonwoods. This is the chill wind of mid-September that announces summer has passed: the same wind which drove Huxley off the mountain toward the sunny glamour of Hollywood.

In the distance, the Jemez mountains rise beyond the silvery ribbon which flows through the Rio Grande gorge. Below, horizontal ranges of desert mountains rasp the firmament; amid all this space the mountains seek still more, and borrow the sky.

In this expanse distance becomes time as the years recede. Back to 1934, in London, to the worst dilemma of Huxley's life, when the tall, frail writer reached the end of his emotional tether. The resolution of that crisis eventually propelled him to America.

HUXLEY IN
HOLLYWOOD

ONE

EYELESS IN GAZA

"What are the fruits of fame-seeking, ambition, desire to excel? Among others, war, nationalism, economic competition, snobbery, class hatred, and colour prejudice." (1936)

Aldous Huxley, at forty, found himself a writer among gentlemen. He lived at Albany, the elegant flats near Piccadilly Circus, founded in 1803 as a *pied à terre* for wealthy bachelors. In the last weeks of 1934, however, Huxley had discovered the disadvantages of swank. Accommodations in the past abode of Byron and William Lamb were medieval: his rooms were dark and ill furnished; the kitchen was underground; and his study faced the covered walk—which gave him the impression of working in a goldfish bowl, he told friends.[1] Worse, neighbors had twice complained about his typewriter; they suspected him of engaging in "trade." He was as discontent here as in the two previous places he'd lived in the last half year.

Huxley's physique was in no better shape than his accommodations. Though 6'4", he weighed barely 170 pounds; clothes hung on him as on a hanger. His greenish pallor suggested a statue in a neglected back room of a museum. Bright, fishy eyes peered out from black-rimmed, bottle-glass lenses. Beneath a broad forehead, his face was lined with worry.

He wrote to friends of a "disquieting sense that I am being somehow punished . . . to lead me deeper into my besetting sin, the dread and avoidance of emotion. . . . I have been working a fair amount, with not much results, as I am in chronic trouble with my book and have been sleeping rather badly." To E. M. Forster he mentioned "a considerable gloom about myself" which lunching with his old friend Bertrand Russell did not alleviate.[2]

According to Sybille Bedford, the German-born novelist who was his wife's cherished friend and who lived in the maid's room at the top of the stairs, Huxley was immensely depressed as he wrote *Eyeless in Gaza*—very scared about money and appallingly worried that he couldn't write, that he might never have the sort of success he had had earlier.[3]

He took pills at night to sleep—Sedobol, or a French concoction of calcium and magnesium called Calsédine. He depended on these for rest, but they left him too groggy to write. His novel *Eyeless in Gaza* waited in his study like a neglected toothache. The less he wrote, the more pressure mounted from his two-book-a-year contract with Chatto & Windus: the year was up, and he had barely finished one book. Huxley was blocked, his son Matthew remembers, his words as tightly bound as his bowels.[4]

Physically, Huxley had always been frail; now he had become a private wreck and a public star. Six months earlier, following the publication of his twenty-sixth book, *Beyond the Mexique Bay*, a two-shilling biography of him had appeared. Huxley made a poor subject for popular biography, the critic for *Life and Letters* decided, because he was the model of a contented man. He had everything—fame, a home in the south of France, "an absolutely happy and prolific marriage."[5]

Huxley had long ago abandoned (if he had ever accepted) conventional marriage. He and Maria had come of age among those bisexual experimentalists associated with London's Bloomsbury Square. Like the rest of these well-documented literary eminences, Huxley liked to shock: "The commonest, one might call it the natural, rhythm of human life is routine punctuated by orgies," he had written in his last book.

In the twenties, such lines had the provocative effect of Tom Wolfe in the 1960s. Millions knew Huxley as the naughty—if not wicked—writer of books best read under the covers of a newspaper or a bed. He understood that outrageousness helped sales; in the last decade, he had been the subject of many profiles. Beverly Nichols, the literary stylist, suspected that the ink in Huxley's pen was clarified and frozen to obtain his icy prose; like most interviewers, he couldn't resist mocking his long, emaciated form: "Quantities of Aldous Huxley reclined on my sofa, spreading over the cushions, and stretching long tentacles on to the floor."[6]

Despite his ill health, the writer had reason to be thankful. He had a supportive wife who not only typed and corrected his manuscripts, but arranged liaisons with admirers—hers or his. Critics had lavished praise on his writing: at twenty-one, before Huxley had published his first novel, Proust had classed him among Britain's most promising writers. In the early twenties, Huxley had fulfilled that promise with his "House Party" novels, as critics called them: *Crome Yellow, Those Barren Leaves, Antic Hay.* Then *Point Counter Point* (1928) and *Brave New World* (1932) placed him among the most famous British postwar novelists. A vast reading public revered him as the picador of Victorian smugness; he was translated into a dozen languages. On his last world tour, hundreds of thousands in India had turned out to greet him, as did crowds of readers from Guatemala to Hong Kong.

Raised in a family of scientists, educators, and literary critics, Aldous Leonard Huxley had surpassed all expectations: scholarships and prizes at Eton, first-class honors at Oxford.[7] He made himself a hard act to follow. By age 30, Huxley had already published sufficient poetry, plays, and novels that his reputation, like Rimbaud's, would have been secure had he fled his problems and traveled around the world, giving up writing altogether. Instead, writing seemed to have given Huxley up. At the nadir of his career, he began the reconstructive direction of his American years.

By the mid-thirties, Huxley no longer prided himself on the cynicism which had been his literary hallmark. Like the alcoholic who stands up before a group and acknowledges his problem, Huxley was painfully self-conscious of his emotional blindness: "I'm a bad experiencer. I've lived most of my life post-humously. . . . As though my existence were a novel or a text-book of psychology or a biography, like any of the others on the library shelves."[8]

As he later described a character, the biographer Chawdron,

I'm decidedly high-brow, and I'm literary; I'm even what the newspapers call a "thinker." I suffer from a passion for ideas. Always have, from boyhood onwards. . . . Personal relationships, I have never been able to manage effectively. Only ideas. With ideas I'm at home. . . .

An awful situation. That was why I've always liked bitches so much, always have been so grateful to them—because they were the only women I ever contrived to have a non-posthumous, contemporary, concrete relation with. The only ones.[9]

He had fallen for just such a vamp a decade earlier, the last time he had lived in London for more than a few months: Nancy Cunard, the steamliner heiress who had entranced fellow writers Raymond Mortimer, Robert Nichols, and Evelyn Waugh, among many others. A decade had passed, he had fashioned her into a half-dozen characters, and still he could not forget.

They had slept together, finally, before she pushed him off, complaining of his hangdog looks. One day he had returned home to find Maria packing; she was moving them immediately to Italy, near Florence. Matthew went off to boarding school: first Frensham Heights, then Dartington.

The brothers Julian, Trevenen, Aldous, and their baby sister, Margaret, were born in Godalming, Surrey. Their father, Leonard Huxley, a schoolmaster at Charterhouse, had married Matthew Arnold's niece Julia and devoted himself to teaching and writing the life of his father, Thomas H. Huxley, known to the newspaper-reading public as "Darwin's Bulldog," the man who marshaled the scientific evidence underlying the great biologist's theories. Leonard had begun compiling this two-volume opus soon after Aldous's birth. Grandpater, as T.H. was called, was as much a household saint as the bones of an ancestor in a Caribbean hut.[10]

The fate of the boys was fixed: Eton, Oxford, then science or medicine. Margaret followed her mother's career into teaching and found herself in the position of Alice James, under the tall shadow of her elder brothers.

While Julian and Trev declined Latin verbs at Eton, Aldous cycled the back roads along the sandy bays of West Surrey. Under his thick brown hair, his face was pale, with full lips and blue eyes which had an inward look. He was an independent boy who rode out further than he should; then he would return wet, doused by a spring storm fragrant of clay and heath.

In those early days, the young man saw clearly, without glasses. His eyes could make out the motes of sunlight which cut the clouds and cast a dazzling trapezoid on the dusty road. Leaves of copper beeches swirled and crunched beneath his tires.

At night, after papers were marked, Julia Arnold Huxley read to her youngest boy, the quiet one given to staring pensively out the window at the rain. She held and rocked him, quizzed him about his studies or his weekends off with her sister, the novelist Mrs. Humphry Ward. Father was the stern presence; Julia was the social pivot for the family, organizing picnics and charades, the solace from children who teased Aldous about his thin body and substantial head: "Ogre," they called him.

Until one moist autumn in 1908, when Aldous was fourteen, Julia's life seemed "suffused with a pleasant glow," as Ronald Clark, the family's historian, reflected.[11] Her husband's transition from schoolmaster to editor of the *Cornhill Magazine* had recently given him new purpose. She was forty-seven, loved her new school, Prior's Field, and looked forward to decades of teaching there. Though she didn't know it, she was dying of cancer.

Creating a family tradition of secretiveness that lasted Aldous's lifetime, neither Julia's husband nor her fellow headmistress would break the news to her. As the long summer evenings darkened, she wasted slowly away without realizing why. Finally she was told. "Why do I have to die; and die—so young," she cried. In the deathwatch which followed, Julian would stare at the light at the top of the stairs, wanting to tell his stricken mother how dear she was to him. He didn't go.[12]

"It was to Aldous the irreparable loss, a betrayal of his faith in life," one of his closest friends wrote later. "He never got over it."[13]

Why her? Why not some other mother, less sure, less kind?

"He hadn't known she was going to die," Huxley wrote in his second novel, *Antic Hay*, "but when he entered her room, when he saw her lying so weakly in the bed, he had suddenly begun to cry, uncontrollably. All the fortitude, all the laughter even, had been hers. . . . She had told him what he was, and what he should try to be, and how to be it. And crying, still crying, he had promised he would try."[14]

Just before she died, worn and hollow-cheeked, she called in her children: "It is very hard to leave you all—but after these weeks of quiet thought, I know that all life is but one—and that I am only going into another room 'of the sounding labour-house vast of Being.' "[15] To Aldous she whispered, "Don't be too critical of other people; love much."[16]

Here was an injunction, as he later wrote in *Eyeless*, "like most, unaccompanied by instructions as to the right way of carrying it out." After his mother's death, Huxley was haunted by the impermanence of human relationships; death teaches injustice like no other emotion.[17]

"This young woman who had stood in a garden at the turn of the century was like a ghost at cockcrow. His mother, Anthony Beavis recognized. A year or two, perhaps only a month or two, before she died."

So begins *Eyeless in Gaza*, perhaps the most autobiographical novel Huxley wrote, mingling bitterness and pathos. This is a book for those who lost a parent as an adolescent. "Poor motherless child. . . ." Huxley wrote fervently: "There's no help for it; it'll always hurt—always. You'll never be able to think of her without some pain. Even time can't take away all the suffering" (*Eyeless*, 41, 109).

The book has an unorthodox chronology, divided into distinct time periods: 1902–1904 (lower school), 1912 (Oxford), 1926 (as a beginning writer), 1933–1934 (as a grown man, struggling out of illness). The intercutting creates a cinematic effect, crisscrossed with flashbacks, as child continually fathers the man. This complex superstructure (and its autobiographical parallels) partly explains why Huxley had more trouble drafting this than anything he had written before and why it weighed on him so heavily in his new flat.

In Huxley's cottage in Sanary, France, *Eyeless* had started well. There was a relaxed gaiety about the house, Sybille Bedford recalled. Maria took prints of visitors' hands for her favorite handwriting expert. Aldous was writing a steady five to seven hundred words per day, relaxing in the late afternoons with expeditions on an inflatable raft or by painting watercolors.

Then, at the end of 1933, his block began. The fragmented time sequence of the novel continued to elude him. A trip to Italy hadn't helped—rain everywhere, costly meals, too many hours on the road. When they returned, Huxley stopped writing altogether. To Eddy Sackville-West, his wife's confidant, he lamented that he couldn't make his plot work.[18]

He and Maria then traveled to Central America to write a travelogue, *Beyond the Mexique Bay*. Returning to France, he still couldn't finish his novel. The Huxleys had taken a small flat on Lower Regent Street, before moving into Albany. The unfresh food bothered Maria, as did the noise. Aldous had hoped London would inspire him, but gray, sooty skies only dimmed his vision. Meanwhile, pressured to keep writing, he floundered in his story.

In *Eyeless in Gaza*, sociologist Anthony Beavis is an amoral gadfly, educated at the right schools, with an independent income. He writes authoritatively on human behavior but is devoid of compassion. When Beavis tires of Mary, the mother-surrogate with whom he has had an affair, he takes her daughter Helen as a mistress. They are lying nude on the roof of a house in the south of France when, in one of Huxley's most memorable scenes, a dog falls from an airplane and lands a few yards away from where they have just made love. They are spattered with blood, which Helen takes as an omen to end the affair. Undaunted, Anthony takes up with the fiancée of his best friend from school, Brian (a character the family resented as being modeled after Trev, down to his stutter).

"Five words sum up every biography," the sociologist notes coolly:

"*Video meliora proboque; deteriora sequor.* I see what I ought to do, but continue to do what I know I oughtn't." Anthony cannot bring himself to confess his seduction to his friend. Brian—who has restrained himself from making the advances his fiancée desires—throws himself off a cliff.

Aldous Huxley lost his vision at Eton when he was sixteen. Over Easter break he'd been in the dormitory; one morning his eyes had turned red and swollen. The school nurse thought it was pink-eye.

She was wrong. He had a strep infection in both eyes, *keratitis punctata*, and he grew blinder by the hour. According to a classmate, the science-minded boy was bemused by what was happening to him, peering into a mirror with a magnifying glass.[19] It must have seemed a grand experiment to the prospective medical researcher.

Then the curtain fell. It was night all day long and night again in the evening; later he would call it "a kind of death."[20]

No records tell us what time he lost his sight. Was it morning and did he wake up blind? Did he fumble at breakfast that first day, reaching for the milk and the spoon? Perhaps it happened in the afternoon—at twilight, when weak eyes are at their weakest. Was he alone outside, fire flashing helplessly beneath his opaque eyes? By day or by night, it was the world that darkened, not he who grew dim.

Where were his books? For years he had hidden among these friends, far from the taunting and at times damnably stupid world of human contact. Now there was only darkness, as far as he could touch. An occasional shadow flickered by, like light falling into a basement from a street-side window.

Meanwhile, life went on as he lay in the infirmary: a healthy boy with withered eyes. He could hear voices as the boys dressed. Familiar sounds reverberated distantly, like voices in a tunnel.

At his aunt's that first week, he walked into a four-poster bed. Then his uncle Henry, one of several generations of Huxley M.D.s, found a surgeon at the Institute for Tropical Medicine; injections over the following year cleared the infection.[21]

His eyes were left virtually opaque, two tiny bluish clouds. He got used to drinking his tea with both hands and learned not to stray near the stove. He taught himself braille in three weeks and then to type, his stepmother Rosalind remembered.[22] He learned to read music in braille and took up the piano, which sounded as if he were walking through the instrument: how deeply the tones of an instrument resonate when visual distractions subside.

Studies resumed full-tilt; reading Macaulay in braille was slow, he complained, "You can't just glance across the page."[23] Tutors came and went. He wrote his first novel, about 80,000 words, and then lost it unread, the manuscript misplaced by unseeing hands; years later he would blame his blindness for propelling him into fiction.[24]

By the time he reached eighteen, blinded for two and one-half years, and entered Balliol College, Oxford, he had only one quarter of normal capacity in one eye. He had to dilate his pupils with Atropine to read his texts. Nevertheless, he won a scholarship, as his grandfather, father, and older brother had before him; but medicine was a dream soured and rechanneled.

The man who did the most to inspire the end of Huxley's writing block was a short, wiry intellectual with red hair and a sonorous Irish voice—Henry Fitzgerald Heard.

Born on October 6, 1889 in London, Heard had expected to follow his paternal grandfather, father, and brother into priesthood in the Church of England but instead became an aide to Horace Plunkett, a founder of Irish agricultural cooperatives.

Heard and Huxley had become instant friends five years earlier in 1929, when Heard had asked Huxley for an article for the free-thinking journal Heard edited, The Realist. Heard later suggested that Huxley had needed someone with whom to exercise his mind, but his body was equally eager.[25] Not for sexual relations—though Heard was a homosexual (and perhaps enamored of Huxley)—but for walks. Heard's short, brisk steps neatly matched Huxley's loping, long-legged gait. They would stroll the shaded alleys of Kew or out along the bright hill overlooking Hampstead, where Huxley had lived while an upstart critic for the literary gazette, The Athenaeum.

Heard was a sought-after dinner guest; he walked into a crowded room and soon had the company roaring attentively at an apparently inexhaustible supply of stories, some supplied by George Bernard Shaw and H. G. Wells. His clear diction—the "r" in "number" trilled like a country church bell—had helped make him a BBC science commentator in 1930.

His great attraction for Huxley was an intellect hewn by the Jesuits and by Gonville and Caius College, Cambridge. His grasp of history, literature, cultural anthropology, and odd facts rivaled Huxley's. (Heard's rival informant was the magnificent eleventh edition of the *Encyclopaedia Brittanica.* Huxley kept an extra set in his kitchen and had a packing case built to carry it on trips.) One always knew which volume Aldous was reading, Bertrand Russell said: "One day it would be Alps, Andes and Apennines, and the next it would be Himalayas and the Hippocratic Oath."[26] Gerald's conversation similarly ranged from Italian Renaissance painters to recent developments in theoretical physics.

Five years older than Huxley, Gerald Heard had already won a reputation as author of a series of books synthesizing history, philosophy, and anthropology. Heard's BBC broadcasts attracted a sophisticated following and a pipeline to information Huxley treasured.

A Heard-like character emerges toward the end of *Eyeless in Gaza:* a "little man, short and spare, but with a fine upright carriage that lent him a certain dignity." (Huxley made him a doctor, one of many medical heroes in his pages.) Dr. Miller offers an elaborate philosophy, combining a Buddhist acceptance of suffering, a pragmatic approach to political reform and pacifism, and a system for reeducating the body (a "principle of perfect functioning," Huxley would later call it). This troika—Indian religion, pacifism, and self-healing—characterized the second half of Huxley's life. Together, they offered a means to write his way free of his dilemma.

Heard hinted at a solution in 1935, in *Science in the Making:* "We have got to relax our whole muscular system. We find we can't. The more we try, the tenser we get. . . . Most people won't give the time necessary to untie the tangle in which their fuss and hustle knots their body and nerves. They haven't the time, they think, to learn real self-control. . . . The only thing which can make man safe against himself . . . is to discover a superhuman purpose."[27]

When Maria summed up Aldous's condition at Albany to friends, she wrote of "insomnia and all that therefrom necessarily follows in the way of gloom, irritation, lack of work and so on."[28] Huxley had reached the point he later attributed to Beavis: "You've got to change if you want to go on existing. And if it's a matter of changing—why you need all the help you can get, from God's to the doctor's" (*Eyeless*, 553).

Melancholia, that nineteenth-century euphemism for mental illness, plagued the Huxley and Arnold families; one of T.H.'s daughters, Marian Huxley, was institutionalized. Leonard, a reserved man without mood swings, largely escaped this dark legacy, as his eldest son, Julian, wrote:

> Though he had great sorrows in his life, I never knew him depressed or ill-tempered. He was not, in this, a typical Huxley, nor was his brother Harry, the surgeon. It seems as if the Huxley genes skipped a generation to assert their particular characteristics, which are perhaps best defined as temperamental.[29]

Julian had first visited a nursing home (the Hermitage, in Kent) as a teenager after a breakdown at Eton:

> Love affairs can be just as devastating between boys, just as romantic, as between young men and women. . . . The boy I fell in love with was really beautiful, with an oval face, fair hair and blue eyes, and a lovely mouth. I was so obsessed by him. . . .
>
> My nervous breakdown in 1912, due to my unresolved conflicts about sex, had inflicted on me "the dark night of the soul," in which all sense of fruitful communion . . . went overboard.[30]

Julian's next crisis occurred at what ought to have been a crowning moment—his first academic appointment, at Rice Institute in Houston, Texas. Just twenty-five, he was about to be married when he changed his mind about his fiancée. He had a nervous breakdown with insomnia, which left him completely incapacitated for six months.

Blond-haired Trev was always the easygoing brother, the one with a ready smile to Julian's scowl. The one who had troubled to help his half-sighted brother study for his scholarship exams. Not quite as tall as his brothers—Aldous had passed 6'1" by fourteen—Trev had a firm, athletic body from mountaineering in the Alps. Though more gregarious than scholarly, he was Aldous's first publisher, in *The Climber's Club Journal* at Oxford.

When the results of Trev's examination were posted, the family was shocked to find a Second class honors degree instead of a First. Trev had already earned a First in mathematics; he had failed to match Julian's feat of double Firsts in science and letters.

Despite Trev's disappointing showing, no one was particularly worried. There was always the civil service. Then a second mishap befell Trev; in the annual competition for twenty high-level administrative posts, Trev was short-rated.

When Julian returned to the rest home from Rice the following summer, 1914, Trev was already there. After a few weeks, Julian's neuroses abated; Trev's troubles did not.

Julian joined Aldous, Leonard, and their new stepmother, Rosalind Bruce Huxley. No one knew how long Trev might remain ill. What Leonard and Rosalind knew—and apparently the boys did not—was that Trev had become "deeply attached" to a parlor maid in his father's home. Trev was secretly trying to educate her, Julian eventually learned, by taking her to museums and plays.

Sarah, the family maid, tried to stop it, threatening exposure. "The girl was village-educated in a mild way. It couldn't have worked," Rosalind commented seventy years later. "His friends could never have been hers; nor hers, his."

Julian reflected the common prejudice of the Edwardian period against falling in love with someone outside one's class when he wrote:

> I considered a little girl living in a humble cottage as belonging to another sphere—like the menservants at Stocks, who, though we enjoyed chatting with them, were kept behind green baize doors, only emerging into the main rooms for their particular duties.[31]

Sarah persuaded the young lovers to part. The girl was sent off to London; Trev had a breakdown. Soon afterward, the girl wrote Trev despondently at the nursing home: she was pregnant.[32]

Trev had options. He could have retaken the civil service exam; the twenty-four-year-old certainly could have been apprenticed with distinction. Instead he went for a walk alone, something prohibited by his doctor. A search party was dispatched, without luck. He was missing for a week before his body was found nearby in the woods.

He had jumped from a tree, fourteen feet up, with a rope around his neck.[33]

"Trev was not strong, but had the courage to face life with ideals. And his ideals were too much for him," Aldous wrote to a family friend in virtually his only published comment.[34]

The affective members of Aldous's family had disappeared. A college friend doubted Huxley could ever be content: "For him, happiness is possible on the animal level; it is possible on the superhuman, timeless level, but not on the human plane of time and craving."[35] Huxley's pain at his brother's death resurfaced in *Eyeless in Gaza* and *Brave New World*.

Twenty years later, as Huxley struggled to extricate himself from his block, he shared a back malady with Beavis, whose slouch was "pressing down on the vertabrae like a ton of bricks. One can almost hear the poor things grinding" (*Eyeless*, 552).

This sounds like the phrasing of Dr. F. Matthias Alexander, the Australian physical therapist known for the self-help books *Constructive Control of the Individual* and *The Use of Self* and for treating John Dewey and George Bernard Shaw (who may have recommended Alexander to Huxley). The Alexander Technique consisted of learning the correct way to sit and stand, relearning how to hold oneself in a straight-spine position.

Huxley's physical treatments soon became a family enthusiasm. "We sat in a straight-backed chair and were told to get up," Matthew recalled. "Then Alexander would say, 'That's all wrong.' He would hold you in position and move you up and down, adjusting the stance of the legs, the way you held your weight."[36]

"There he was, practicing at Albany," Sybille Bedford wrote, "how to place one's feet, how to get out of a chair. It became noticeable that he was holding himself differently."[37] The patient improved slowly, showing the same dedication which he later applied to his eyes, when he took up the Bates Method of visual reconditioning.

Treatment continued on other fronts. Gerald proposed "Yoga with accompanying mental concentration," which Aldous complained of as "frightfully difficult and time-consuming."[38]

In 1936 he wrote to T. S. Eliot:

Meditation itself is just a method of training, comparable to that, on the physical plane, of the athlete. You can train to climb Everest or to become a first-class murderer. . . . [I]t is, I believe, effective—even when practiced, as I do it, rather unsystematically and with difficulty. True, the difficulty grows less, I find, as one persists; one is able to keep the mind directed, focussed, one-pointed more easily, after a few months, than at the beginning.[39]

Life became one long regime; if he wasn't practicing how to walk upright, he would be sitting, legs crossed, trying to meditate; if he wasn't meditating, he was recovering from a colonic irrigation at the hands of Dr. J. R. McDonagh (whose theories on intestinal poisoning later emerged in *After Many a Summer Dies the Swan*).

These practices helped Huxley redesign his body. Yet just as acute as intestinal poisoning was his chronic misanthropy. If the human race appeared "more or less imbecile or odious, the fault is at least as much in oneself as in them" *(Eyeless, 171)*.

Huxley was undergoing a reverse *crise de foi*—fleeing his own lack of faith. The Huxley whom Isaiah Berlin aptly called "God-denying" had belittled religion the way a dog snarls at intruders. Now he was netted in cognitive dissonance: Huxleys weren't religious; the whole country knew them as free-thinkers; his grandfather had coined the term "agnostic." But despite being a professional sacrilegist, Huxley felt a private urge which paralleled T. S. Eliot's decision to convert; Huxley's American years would be spent exploring and accommodating urges to transcendence many might have called religious. The man newspaper editors had headlined ALDOUS HUXLEY: THE MAN WHO HATES GOD had traveled as far as his agnosticism would allow. Only in *Proper Studies*, a few years earlier, had this attitude softened. There *could* be idealistic substitutes for religion, he decided, based on certain characteristics: absoluteness of purpose, leaders of high character, ritual, and sexual abstinence.[40] As his son said, "Aldous was trying to believe." Huxley eventually found that hard-sought substitute for religion—pacifism.

In World War I, Huxley had twice been rejected for the British army because of his eyes. His Oxford classmates—including Lewis

Gielgud (brother of John) and Aldous's cousin, Gervas Huxley—had both joined the Great War. In March 1916, Aldous wrote to Julian that at the war's beginning, he wanted to fight; now, he had decided to be a conscientious objector.

Huxley did his alternative service at Garsington, the noted literary salon near Oxford belonging to Philip and Ottoline Morrell. There he sawed trees and brush alongside John Middleton Murry, Bertrand Russell, and Tommy Earp, staunch pacifists all. Aldous and Julian met their wives at Garsington; Julian eventually marrying the Swiss governess, Juliette, and Aldous a refugee, Maria Nys, eldest of four sisters (Jeanne, Suzanne, and Rose) driven out of Belgium by German armies.

Juliette remembered Maria at eighteen, "small, rather plump, lovely beyond words, with large blue-green eyes matching an Egyptian scarab on her long finger . . . She had the vulnerable and defenseless face of a beautiful child with a mature body."[41]

Aldous, twenty-two, also impressed Juliette: "Wearing straw-coloured jodhpurs and pale stockings with a dark brown corduroy jacket, he looked absent-mindedly but absurdly romantic and beautiful. Even in those early days, he often seemed to be living in a remote and secret world. . . . Some people tire one out by talking too much, Aldous by talking too little; by his detachment, by what could have been his distress—or his defence. . . . One could only retreat, on tip-toes."[42]

In the novel he set at Garsington, *Crome Yellow*, Huxley didn't dwell on the pacifist undercurrent at the house, where Russell (Ottoline's lover), biographer Lytton Strachey, and Earp sparred with pro-war visitors over dinner. (He did create a Reverend Bodiham, for whom war is a prelude to Armageddon.)[43]

After Maria had moved to Italy, Huxley had tried the family tradition of teaching, at Eton. His students included Eric Blair (George Orwell) and Harold Acton, who remembered him "walking down Eton High Street like a juvenile giraffe escaped from a zoo, trailing an orange scarf or dangling a shoelace."[44]

Huxley doesn't seem to have taken either teaching or pacifism very seriously until Bertrand Russell was sent to prison. Russell invited prosecution, and received a six-month sentence for suggesting American troops were to be stationed in England to put down strikes, "not something I'd choose to be sentenced on," Huxley reflected.[45] Russell's *Principles of Social Reconstruction* and, later, *Which Way to Peace?* influenced Huxley enormously. Russell's prison letters evoked a mystic revolt against war, which Huxley would take up thirty years later in *The Perennial Philosophy:*

> There is a possibility in human minds of something mysterious as the mighty wind, deep as the sea, calm as the stars, and strong as death, a mystic contemplation, the intellectual love of God. Those who have known it cannot believe in wars any longer.[46]

Soon after Russell was released, Aldous wrote a saga of a pacifist, "The Farcical History of Richard Greenow," which appeared in his first collection of stories, *Limbo* (1920). This is a tale of a man with a most literary multiple-personality disorder: by day, he writes pacifist tracts for a *Left Review*–type magazine; by night, he falls into a swoon and Pearl Bellairs, a schmaltzy, jingoist novelist, takes over and turns out trite romances. In 1916, Greenow becomes a pacifist, but instead of going to prison, as Russell had, Greenow's alter ego does alternative service. The hero ends up in an asylum, mad.

The twenties were the decade of the great, early Huxley, dark jester to the postwar generation. His erudition and wit won for him the intelligentsia of America, Europe, and Britain, but his literary fireworks were unaccompanied by activism or human sympathy. "He could manage the complications as well as anyone," Professor C. E. M. Joad commented. "But when it came to the simplicities he lacked the talent—that talent which is of the heart, no less than of the head; of the feelings, the sympathies, the intuitions, no less than of the analytical understanding."[47]

In the years between "Richard Greenow" and *Eyeless in Gaza*, pacifism appears occasionally in Huxley's articles for the Hearst papers in America or in his literary journalism in England.[48] Typical of these is a 1930 column on Gandhi for *Vanity Fair;* Huxley rejected the man he later claimed as a hero because "he has failed to notice the distressingly easy passage from non-violence to violence."[49]

In the autumn of 1933, as Huxley first bogged down on *Eyeless in Gaza*, Gerald Heard visited for ten days, prompting a telling letter to Julian: Gerald was "more pessimistic than ever, advising us all to clear out to some safe spot in South America or the Pacific Islands before it is too late. He enjoys his glooms; but the fact does not necessarily mean that the glooms are unfounded."[50]

A few months after this, Huxley wrote his first avowedly pacifist statement, "War and Emotions," included in *Beyond the Mexique Bay*. After quoting Russell's *Which Way to Peace?*, Huxley pointed out that many people enjoy wars. Suicides drop, group solidarity rises; war gives new meaning to individual lives amid the hypnotic chants of government propaganda: "People can get more satisfaction out of hating foreigners they have never seen than out of vaguely wishing them well."[51]

In this first phase of his pacifism, which lasted from the spring of 1934 through the following summer, Huxley still ruled out "a campaign of religious and ethical preaching against war," a predictable omission for a man who had once written, "Any tentative solutions of problems are never, except incidentally, metaphysical solutions."[52]

By the end of 1934, most intellectuals were simultaneously anti-Fascist and antimilitarist. Many saw the imperialist need for colonies and for raw materials as a source of inequalities leading to war.

Behind the Fascist and Nazi uprisings, Huxley found the devilish shadow of nationalism (disguised as patriotism). Pacifism wasn't the only substitute for religion, he had discovered. All barbarisms could be committed in the name of national chauvinism or "national narcissism," as Wilhelm Reich wrote at this time in *The Mass Psychology of Fascism*.[53]

Huxley profoundly understood how symbolic manipulation underlay military solutions to diplomatic crises. With millions of Europeans, he sought an alternative. The contradictory pressures toward stopping Nazism at all costs and refusing to fight a war had not yet become unavoidable.

On October 16, 1934, the Reverend H. R. (Dick) Sheppard wrote to newspapers across Britain, inviting readers to mail in postcards pledging, "I renounce war and never again, directly or indirectly, will I support or sanction another." The canon of St. Paul's Cathedral couldn't be sure how many would respond.

Sheppard's plea reflected a growing public certainty of another war. The previous year, the Oxford Union had debated and, surprisingly, passed a resolution, "that this House will in no circumstances fight for its King and country." Winston Churchill called this statement "very disquieting and disgusting."[54]

The first day, no cards arrived; the next day the postal service rented a van, and the first of 80,000 cards addressed to Sheppard tumbled out of bags.[55] One of these was from an author in distress, Aldous Huxley.

Sheppard held special services for Christian pacifists; as more cards arrived he organized the Peace Pledge Union, with Huxley a founding member.[56] The PPU set up open-air lecture forums, marches, and newspapers (*Peace News,* edited by John Middleton Murry). PPU membership swelled to 140,000. This, the second generation of twentieth-century British opponents to conscription, agreed on taking personal responsibility for stopping war, religious leadership, and an absolute commitment—the very qualities Huxley had noted as central to any substitute for religion. The movement extended beyond previous antidraft coalitions. This "New Pacifism," as Gerald Heard called it, implied a pacifist counterculture.

Sheppard for the soul; Alexander for the body. The spine-straightening exercises and colonic irrigation liberated a pent-up energy in Huxley for writing pacifist pamphlets, attending lectures, even, for the first time, mounting the podium himself—a sudden, midlife flush of energy.[57] Maria noted his recovery with amazement, as Aldous began what might today be called aerobic gardening, digging "every spare inch of the ground, causing havoc, to the despair of the gardener."[58]

Recovery also prompted Huxley's second pacifist phase, "peace on the spiritual horizon": individuals had responsibilities to create peace themselves, for their governments would not, and since man's divinity was obscured by war, as D. H. Lawrence had written, its solution required spiritual armament. Huxley soon grafted this new direction onto Anthony Beavis:

> I agreed to contribute money, prepare some literature and go round speaking to groups. The last is the most difficult, as I have always refused to utter in public. . . .
>   Get well, achieve co-ordination, use yourself properly; you'll be able to speak in any way you please [Dr. Miller tells Beavis]. The

difficulties, from stage fright to voice production, will no longer exist.
(Eyeless, 17)

The silent writer became a born-again pacifist; he approached what Gerald would later call "The Watershed" in an evolution from a descriptive cynic to a prescriptive mystic.[59]

"I'm hard at work on a novel that won't get finished," he wrote to Robert Nichols. "I wish I could see any remedy for the horrors of human beings except religion or could see any religion that we could all believe in."[60] Huxley's attitude toward religion became even more charitable in this pacifist period.

Two months later, he wrote more definitely, as his block finally dissolved from a combination of physical therapy and belief:

I am working at my book and in the interval talking over ways and means, with Gerald, for getting an adequate pacifist movement onto its feet. The thing finally resolves itself into a religious problem—an uncomfortable fact which one must be prepared to face and which I have come during the last year to find it easier to face. . . . Not easy. But I suppose nothing of any value is easy.[61]

War was determined in Europe by the summer of 1935, and nothing Huxley or Sheppard or their adherents could do would have changed it. Germany and France reintroduced conscription. The British White Paper on Imperial Defense marked a turn to rearmament. Pacifists were suddenly squeezed on two sides. Communists, Labourites, and unionists in Britain repudiated pacifism that summer, while Sir Oswald Mosley's British Union of Fascists, the Black Shirts, held rallies where peace demonstrators were roughly handled.[62]

On June 7, 1935, at London's Olympia Arena in Hammersmith, Huxley, Dick Sheppard, writer Naomi Mitchison, and several members of Parliament listened to Mosley; their reactions were recorded in a pamphlet, *Fascists at Olympia*.[63]

The evening started late, as 12,000 people filled the galleries. Mosley's stewards led chants, "We Want Mosley." "We want work," an opponent yelled in response. The spotlights on stage were turned around to the audience, and a group of eight stewards descended on the man, punching him in the jaw while others held his arms.

"Does Hitler allow free speech?" another voice from the audience called out. Mosley stopped, the spotlights again played on the audience, and another disrupter was taken from the hall.

"At last I could stand it no longer," Aldous's family friend Naomi wrote. "I leant over and said to the man in front of me. 'You call yourself a gentleman; do you like this sort of thing?' He turned round. 'Yes, I do, I am enjoying myself! Do you want some of it yourself?' "

A pair of students in their early twenties sat in front of Huxley, two yards away. When they stood up to protest the beatings, a half-dozen men grabbed them. They slammed the boy in the face, more than once, as Huxley watched in horror. The girl was hustled down the stairs and disappeared. (This was the British equivalent of America's Peekskill riots in 1949, when concertgoers at a Paul Robeson concert were led down a gauntlet of rock-throwing Ku Klux Klansmen, who smashed their car windows.)

Planning his first public speech, to be given at the London Society of Friends a few months hence, Huxley was daunted. He incorporated his anxiety into *Eyeless in Gaza,* for now he had decided to end his novel by having Beavis join in his own conversion to pacifism:

> *"Sir,"* [the letter to Anthony Beavis] *began, "we have been keeping an eye on you for some time past, and have decided that you cannot be allowed to go on in your present disloyal and treacherous way. We give you fair warning. If you make any more of your dirty pacifist speeches, we shall deal with you as you deserve. Appealing to the police will not do any good. We shall get you sooner or later, and it will not be pleasant for you. It is announced that you are speaking to-night in Battersea. We shall be there."*
>
> A GROUP OF PATRIOTIC ENGLISHMEN   (Eyeless, 609)

Second thoughts persisted. Huxley wrote of a small voice prompting Beavis with unquiet thoughts, as he prepared his talk:

> *Why do you go and saddle yourself with convictions and philosophies? And why put yourself in the position of being able to betray anyone? Why not go back to doing what nature meant you to do—to looking on from your private box and making comments?*
>
> *"Ring them up," the voice went on. "Tell them you've got flu. Stay in bed a few days. Then have yourself ordered to the south of France by the doctor."* (Eyeless, 611)

Gerald Heard paved the way by speaking to the Quakers a week before Aldous. Heard was not shy of microphones. His voice was an instrument: rich yet serious, as if the Voice of Science spoke that day in lower case:

> War to-day is attempting to put a watch right with a sledge hammer. Peace through threat of war to-day is attempting to make a man moral by blackmailing him.[64]

New Pacifism was his text, its end not merely disarmament, but a fresh relationship among people, "a kinship which will cure their own inner conflict, permit them to live a life of unlimited liability with their company—a true co-operative commonwealth."

Heard's hopes for peace rested on small groups of peace organizers, meditating daily. Such meditations, he continued, are "uniquely restorative, bodily as well as mentally, giving a power to deal generously and with creative initiative with all outside."[65]

A week later, the moderator called the lunchtime crowd at the Friends House on the Euston Road to order. Huxley carried his fistful of pages through a forest of chairs and knees up to the dais. If he swayed that day, like a not very solid tower in the wind, if he squinted at his dimly seen text, having to choose between focusing on the pages or on the audience, he can be forgiven by the power of his words:

> Warlike passions burn most fiercely in minds which think about the problems of peace and war in terms of generalizations and abstractions. To bring oneself to kill individual human beings is not easy; but when those human beings are thought of merely as members of a class which has previously been defined as evil, then killing becomes a simple matter.[66]

Violent means led inexorably to violent ends; to be constructive pacifists, Huxley told the crowd, everyone needed to take individual responsibility for what happened in the name of their governments' Realpolitik. "The only hope lies in the pacifists being better disciplined than the militarists and prepared to put up with as great hardships and dangers with a courage equal to theirs."[67]

He realized it was unlikely that his audience was prepared for such a commitment: "In a vague way, practically everyone is now a pacifist. But the number of those who are prepared to inconvenience themselves for their opinion is always small. Most pacifists will go to the trouble of voting for peace," the blasphemer said, "but it must be a kind of religious order [which] entails devoted and unremitting personal service for the cause. . . . peace is the by-product of a certain way of life."

In the first half of 1936, Huxley finished *Eyeless in Gaza*, wrote an article on pacifism for the London *Star*, produced the first Peace Pledge Union pamphlet, *What Are You Going to Do About It?: The Case for Constructive Peace*, and wrote a preface to a book on training pacifists for civil disobedience. (Huxley's productivity varied according to his emotional commitments.)

The article in the *Star* appeared New Year's Eve: "I am not a prophet," he began. "Let others darkly hint at what may happen when the sun next enters Scorpio or at the conjunction of Jupiter and Saturn. The stars are invisible through our London smoke, and I have not consulted them. . . ."

"To future historians," he nevertheless prophesied, "1936 may come to be known as the crucial year, when the statesmen of Europe definitively made up their minds to have peace, or alternatively (and, alas, more probably) failed to make up their minds and allowed the world to drift towards war."[68]

Huxley advocated a world conference to stop war by resolving "the problems of raw materials, migration, currency, and markets." Redistributing goods and power—before Germany, Italy, and Japan took this process into their own hands—might ward off aggression, Huxley suggested naively—but what other choice was left? In the post–Popular Front, Collective Security period, Huxley was caught between conservatives, who impugned his courage and loyalty for opposing war preparedness, and socialists, antagonized by his unswerving pacifism in the face of Nazism.

In February 1936, Huxley had become so widely identified with militant pacifism that cartoonist David Low caricatured Huxley and Sheppard in the London *Times*. Huxley responded tartly by mail.

"Too often my breakfast would be ruined," Low complained in his autobiography, "by the arrival of some letter like this one, referring to a cartoon of 100% pacifists affirming, 'We won't fight anybody' to two butchers of the weak who answered, 'Anybody includes us, pal.' "[69]

"Dear Low," Huxley wrote on February 12, 1936: "Will you please in the future . . . draw the result of the conflict between three butchers (anti–Fascist Collective Security types) and two butchers (Fascist states). True, these results have already been set down by Callot and Goya, but those artists had the misfortune to live before the age of mustard gas and bombers. So there is still plenty of scope for you."

Collective Security, a term winging its way among the Left intelligentsia in London, meant coalitions of those on the Left opposed to Fascism and Nazism. In such an alignment, anti-Stalinists (often pacifists such as Russell and Huxley) were suspect. In Leonard Woolf's *The League in Abyssinia*, written at the same time as the Low cartoon but from a more radical perspective, Huxley read characterizations of pacifists as ostriches, "those who will have nothing to do with evil."[70]

Woolf's salvo was only an initial barrage in the full-scale bombardment of pacifism mounted by British radicals. Tactical pacifism gave way first to peace through Collective Security, only to be replaced by armed Collective Security. Committed to pacifism, not only as a political solution but as a way of life, Huxley could not abandon it as lightly as those for whom pacifism was merely another tactic.

In the end of March 1936, Huxley submitted the final manuscript of *Eyeless in Gaza*. A clue to how he resolved the agony of its production is buried in a letter Maria later wrote her sister Jeanne: "When he finished *Eyeless*, after my having hesitated [after reading it], and after he had truly suffered from my hesitation, I told him my thoughts. This resulted in a great amplification of the intimate journal [of Beavis], which was valuable."[71] The book's fragmented chronology allowed Huxley to update according to the events of the day.

What Huxley ended up with in *Eyeless* was more a testament

than a novel, a spiritual *Bildungsroman*. Its last pages have a stream-of-consciousness pace reminiscent of Molly Bloom's soliloquy at the end of *Ulysses;* they also forecast a new moralism in Huxley's writing. For Anthony Beavis (and his creator), finding meaning to life "had been an act of the will":

> If it were all nonsense or a joke, then he was at liberty to read his books and exercise his talents for sarcastic comment; there was no reason why he shouldn't sleep with any presentable woman who was ready to sleep with him.
> If it weren't nonsense, if there were some significance, then he could no longer live irresponsibly. There were duties towards himself and others and the nature of things. Duties with whose fulfillment the sleeping and the indiscriminate reading and the habit of detached irony would interfere.(Eyeless, 616)

Sending the galleys of *Eyeless* to Professor Joad, Huxley confessed he "would have liked, if it had been possible, to put it aside and look at it again after two or three years. Wolves at doors imposed immediate publication and I let it go, feeling uncomfortably in the dark."[72]

The same week as he submitted *Eyeless,* Huxley also gave Chatto & Windus a peace pamphlet: *What Are You Going to Do About It?: The Case for Constructive Peace.*

This was Huxley's clarion call: can we say for certain, weighing the suffering it brings, that anyone ever "won" a war other than bankers or arms manufacturers? Has war ever really brought peace? Pacifism had a positive, preventive function, Huxley insisted; even when symbolic, resistance strengthened a nation's moral position.

To a new generation of poets and novelists, these positions made Huxley an occasional hero. Influenced by the Depression into political activism, the post-Bloomsbury generation congregated in each other's flats and in print—in *Left Review* (formerly *Viewpoint*), which Cecil Day Lewis underwrote, and later, Cyril Connolly's *Horizon,* which poet Stephen Spender helped finance.

Connolly found in Huxley a father figure whom he followed to Sanary to study how to make a living as a writer.[73] Christopher Isherwood would follow Huxley and Heard even further, to America, to study Indian religion. Their mutual friend Brian Howard "agreed with Huxley that the things that matter cannot be defended or imposed by force."[74] Thus, Huxley was understandably surprised when Spender, Day Lewis, and others turned on him.

In *Forward from Liberalism*, Spender wrote: "prayers, the kind Huxley recommends, probably assisted Napoleon to take Moscow, Rockefeller to make his pile." The constructive pacifist, Spender feared, "possesses an apparatus which will enable him to withdraw from reality altogether." (Underlying this attack, as noted in a letter to Isherwood, was Spender's concern that W. H. Auden would "fall for" Huxleyan pacifism: "Just in case, I have tried to show it up in my book.")[75]

Yet Spender couldn't help but be touched by Beavis's (and Huxley's) transformation to belief: "[*Eyeless*] certainly made me realize that I, at all events, am, by now, completely bigoted and shut off from most things that people mean by Life, and one certainly ought to be frank enough to realize that and own that."[76]

Cecil Day Lewis answered Huxley's pacifist manifesto with "We're Not Going to Do Nothing." Day Lewis's critique had the unfriendly mood of Jove's army attacking the Titans. He called Huxley's ideas a "big, beautiful idealist bubble [which was] inadequate protection against a four-engine bomber."

"Where was Mr. Huxley when the lights went out in Italy, in Germany?" he asked, knowing full well that Aldous and Maria had watched the rise of Mussolini's *carabinieri* more closely than he had. Political orthodoxy curdled his words: "We are not at that stage of absolute impotence where there is nothing to be done but wile away the time with Mr. Huxley's 'spiritual exercises.' "[77] (Yet Day Lewis's solution—a world union of socialist states waging war for "collective security" was hardly more realistic.)

Day Lewis's attack on "the Prophet of Disgust" was remarkable for its incivility and for its tone of *Götterdämmerung*. The *Left Review* joined the fray. In October 1935, it had editorialized, "Our Business Is to Keep the Peace"; nine months later its position had shifted from "Go Not to War" to "Go Not for Pacifism."[78]

"Are we or are we not willing to call the fascist bluff," Day Lewis demanded of Huxley, "to take the comparatively small risk of immediate war rather than, by letting things slide, increase a hundredfold the certainty of war in the more remote future?" As George Orwell's biographers phrased this development:

Until the summer of 1936, it was possible as a dedicated young man or woman of the Left to declare oneself a socialist, an anti-Fascist, and a pacifist, and not be troubled by a sense of inconsistency in any of these particulars. But Spain changed things. Suddenly reality caught up with one's idealism: it became possible (perhaps necessary) to bear arms against Fascism. And by doing so, did not one bring that much closer the nightmare of war that had haunted the European imagination since 1918, and shaped the generation in England that only three years earlier had sworn never to bear arms for King and Country?[79]

When the June '36 *Left Review* appeared—featuring an editorial on Huxley, a review of *Eyeless*, and an open letter to Huxley from Spender—questioning was replaced by conviction. The English Left adopted a Spanish Republican stance—tentatively at first, then with all the momentum of a brakeless car rolling downhill.

The *Left Review*'s editors had made Huxley's banishment from their circle official, suggesting that he was no more than "a ghost speaking in a vacuum." *Eyeless* was "a tribute to the ability of Fascism to arouse disgust even in so aloof a sensitive mind. It is the task of *Left Review* to draw sensitive minds close to an appreciation of social realities." Spender, in his open letter, gave Huxley no quarter:

In spite of my recognition of your sincerity, I cannot but feel angry. . . . What you propose to do with your conference [on rearmament] is to sacrifice the freedom and even the lives of oppressed pacifists and socialists in Italy, Germany, and Austria on the altar of a dogmatic and correct pacifism. . . .

Your warning that means determine ends is tonic; yet it surely has muddled you into thinking that one kind of violence is as bad as any other.

Spender concluded sarcastically: "We had to wait for Aldous Huxley to propose that prayer is an exercise for the soul, like an elastic exerciser or a dose of Eno's Fruit Salts."[80]

Huxley didn't respond to this provocation, though he answered Day Lewis's attack tartly: "The case as a whole still seems to me absolutely unanswerable, and so far as your pamphlet and other anti-pacifist writings are concerned, unanswered":

"Defending democracy" also sounds fine; but to defend democracy by military means, one must be militarily efficient, and one cannot become militarily efficient without centralizing power, setting up a tyranny, imposing some form of conscription or slavery to the state. In

other words the military defence of democracy in contemporary circumstances entails the abolition of democracy even before war starts.[81]

Huxley was not the only one newly isolated from the mainstream of the intellectual Left; politically oriented Surrealists likewise suffered attacks that their "lyricism is socially irresponsible . . . a particularly subtle form of fake revolution," A. L. Lloyd, the folklorist, asserted in the *Left Review.*[82]

In Sanary for the summer, Huxley responded to attacks by reviewing Russell's *Which Way To Peace?* in the BBC's *The Listener:*

> *There are many people who think we ought not to remain neutral in a conflict, for example, between democracy and fascism. "I confess," says Mr. Russell, "that the old Adam within me boils with rage at the thought of what may happen if we sit still. The matter, however, is too serious to be left to the judgment of old Adam." Considering the question dispassionately, he decides that not even the noblest end can justify anyone in using the means placed at men's disposal by the modern armaments maker.*[83]

It no doubt comforted Huxley enormously to have old friends on his side.

Before returning to London to speak at the vast Albert Hall peace rally in November, Huxley also completed the series of lyric essays later published as *The Olive Tree.* Although Matthew and Aldous enjoyed a summer by the ocean, they had not fared well together since Aldous had pulled his son out of his progressive boarding school, Dartington Hall, where the boy had enjoyed carpentry and manual arts. Considering that his parents didn't tell him of the change until they showed up at school with his trunk, Matthew had taken the move well. He maintained his jaunty, devil-may-care attitude (which sharpened to attention when Aldous spoke), but he felt undervalued. For three years, "poor Matthew," as family friends called him, had been shuttled between Maria's family in Belgium (to learn French and manners) and boarding school. Matthew had been an unexpected product of their marriage—unexpected not only because he and Maria rarely shared a bedroom, but because Maria had never had a period before marriage.

Matthew's new Swiss prep school was strict, without the bohemian ambience he enjoyed. The boy was caught between two Aldouses: one who expected him to maintain family standards and another still vexed at the high-pressure education of Eton and Oxford which Huxley blamed for Trev's suicide.[84] Aldous refused to send Matthew to the schools which would have assured his son's continuation of the Huxley intellectual legacy, yet he couldn't help but be disappointed when academic honors didn't materialize.

All this left Matthew in the position of a distant cousin whom one likes, and feels responsibility for, but wishes lived somewhere else. A photo from this period shows Aldous peering down at Matthew, who is dressed neatly in tie and long-sleeved shirt; his dad towers over him and leans forward slightly, as if examining some unusual botanical specimen.

Aldous took Matthew with him to Holland and Belgium where, in Brussels, they attended the antiwar congress organized by Henri Barbusse. The French writer had declared, "The campaign against war must enter the social plane against the economic, against the permanent causes of war—that is, against the regime of capitalist imperialism."[85] Huxley understood this side of war, but he considered economic solutions to war useless without self-government: "a complete change in the system of ownership is necessary—but I don't think such a change will do much good unless accompanied by decentralization, a reduction of the power of the state, self-government in every activity—in a word, anarchism in the sense in which Kropotkin uses the word."[86]

Anarchism was also how Huxley explained his feelings about Spain to Nancy Cunard, who'd sent out a broadside, "Enquête," later published as *Authors Take Sides*, to build support for intervention. (Of those responding, 126 supported the Republic, 5 favored Franco [Waugh said that if he were a Spaniard, that would be his side], with 16 [including Huxley, Eliot, and Wells] neutral.) "My sympathies are, of course, with the Government side, especially the Anarchists," Huxley's answer began: "For Anarchism seems to me much more likely to lead to desirable social change than highly centralized, dictatorial Communism. As for 'taking sides'—the choice, it seems to me, is no longer between two users of violence, [but] between militarism and pacifism. To me, the necessity of pacifism seems absolutely clear."[87]

Also absolutely clear was the mood of Huxley's fellow writers. At his most engaged period, Huxley found himself overextended and losing ground fast. Politicians ignored even the practical suggestions he and Gerald made: stockpiling Canada's nickel, for instance, to prevent it being turned into shells. "Impractical," British prime minister Neville Chamberlain had answered when the possibility was broached.[88]

Isolated from those he had mentored, caricatured as woolly-headed in *The Times*, Huxley's foray into politics was a painful one. And his isolation extended beyond politicians. His family was irate at the too-telling portraits of Trev and Leonard in *Eyeless in Gaza*; Huxley protested in vain to Rosalind that characters are composites. It got so one had to be careful around Aldous; anything might end up in a book, Sybille reflected.[89]

Huxley's new personality had burst the bounds of the old, leaving his colleagues with a dismay bordering on hostility. Professor Joad warned readers that *Eyeless* was unfunny: "For him to return to the detachment of the ironic philosopher is impossible."[90]

What, then, remained after two years of pouring out his soul in a river of pacifist tracts? Limited options: continue to oppose war in Spain, retreat into art, or seek a clime where his and Gerald's ideas would be more warmly received.

For a pacifist in 1937, the United States held the key to the future European war; if America refused to be drawn into the arms race, sanity might prevail, the pair hoped. Moreover, in the United States, pacifism had not yet fallen from favor. In 1935, a "peace strike" had brought out 150,000 students on 130 campuses; a year later a half-million had participated. In July, James Wechsler had led a peace march in New York during which tens of thousands had signed the same Oxford Pledge Huxley had.[91] As European intellectuals waived pacifism in support of the Spanish Republic, Roosevelt took up neutrality. Isolationism and antiinterventionism were popular sentiments in the United States; why not mount a pacifist lecture tour, Huxley and Heard asked each other. Nonviolent resistance was much less effective once war had begun; high-flying bombers are heedless of human suffering. It was now or never.

If Huxley and Heard deluded themselves on America's neutrality—as export-oriented arms factories opened across the South and West, as those opposing war included the anti-Semitic Father Coughlin and Colonel Charles Lindbergh, this oversight could be attributed to distance and to the intemperate spirit in the air. Who would wish to stay in a community where one was called in print, as Day Lewis had written, ". . . some miserable figure, standing with face averted from the ruin and filth that surround him"?[92]

Huxley continued to draw strength from D. H. Lawrence's views on war. At the opening of World War I Lawrence had written:

> In this war, in the whole spirit which we now maintain, I do not believe. I believe it is wrong, so awfully wrong, that it is like a great consuming fire that draws up all our soul in its draught. So if they will let me I shall go away soon, to America.
>
> Perhaps you will say it is cowardice: but how shall one submit to such ultimate wrong as this which we commit, now, England—and the other nations? If thine eye offend thee, pluck it out. And I am English, and my Englishness is my very vision. But now I must go away, if my soul is sightless for ever. Let it then be blind, rather than commit the vast wickedness of acquiescence.[93]

During the previous five years Maria and Aldous had repeatedly discussed an American visit. The idea was a touchstone to which Aldous returned when gray London shadowed his vision and when the petty scarcities of southern France soured him.

Huxley had stopped in Los Angeles in 1925, toward the end of the round-the-world trip recorded in *Jesting Pilate*. In 1931 he had considered a return, remarking with the acerbity then his trademark, "We are thinking of going to America this Autumn—just to know the worst, as one must do from time to time."[94] The following year Huxley had set *Brave New World* in New Mexico, consulting works on ethnography from the Smithsonian Institution. In 1933, he had hoped his and Maria's trip to Central America would end in the United States.[95] America had rewarded him handsomely over the years; *Eyeless in Gaza* was already on the best-seller list.

Once the decision was made, the chores of planning for the trip to America snowballed. Beyond the usual errands of visas and packing, they had to book lectures.

For Matthew, the trip was a reprieve: "Anything that got me out of school sounded fine to me. There I wouldn't have been picked out as a Huxley." He had a year of high school before beginning an American college and medical school. His parents had settled on Duke University in Durham, North Carolina.

Maria guessed they'd be gone nine months to a year; Aldous wrote Rosalind they'd be back in a half year.[96] In the back of their minds must have been the possibility of a longer journey, something more momentous than their stays in southern Europe.

On November 27, 1936, Aldous Huxley gave one last pacifist speech in England, at a famous meeting at Albert Hall moderated by Dick Sheppard.[97] Matthew, in the audience, was amazed that his father could now lecture. At Christmas, at the end of a year which had brought their world no closer to the peace he had predicted, they returned to Sanary for one last look around. On February 19, the family left for London. Aldous was to lecture in Paris before departing, but a remnant of his earlier weakness returned: he had abscesses and four teeth had to be extracted. It seemed an ill omen, this leaving a piece of himself behind before departure.

They passed the Albany flat to Sybille, who remembers Aldous and Gerald's mood as "very, very discouraged":

> No real chance of making the kind of impact that could push the government into action. There was plenty of fear of war, but it was touched by a fatalistic apathy. Not that Aldous was deserting the PPU. Gerald told him that he had shot his bolt and the most useful thing to do now was to re-state the case of peace by some sustained writing such as he was planning.[98]

Gerald also hinted darkly of how modern technology could wipe out a city in hours. This made Maria distraught at leaving family in France and Belgium. Before leaving, she insisted Aldous write Condé Nast, his publisher at *Vogue*, for a job for Jeanne. Then the Huxleys made final plans—after docking in New York City, they would confirm lecture dates and drive across the U.S., via the South and Southwest, to Lawrence's ranch in New Mexico.

Gerald nearly missed their train to Southampton; he refused to accord departures any particular attention. On April 7, 1937, they boarded the S.S. *Normandie*. There was none of the solemnity of fellow pacifist George Fox's crossing in 1671, bringing Quakers to America.

They had booked third class to save money, but after second thoughts they hinted to the French Line that they wouldn't mind first-class accommodation. In their courtesy staterooms, they appeared déclassé; Maria had brought only a single blue suit. They had no idea there would be a Grill on board. "Oh," Maria sighed to Mainbocher, the dress designer, "this is so stylish."[99] Amid such casual chatter, they did not realize they had embarked on the longest voyage of their lives.

TWO

ENDS
AND MEANS

"We have thought of ourselves as members of
supremely meaningful and valuable communities—
deified nations, divine classes and what not—
existing within a meaningless universe. And
because we have thought like this, rearmament is
in full swing, economic nationalism becomes ever
more fierce, and general war becomes increasingly
more probable."   (1937)

On a hot, dry day in May in 1937, the Huxleys rolled across
south-central Texas in a boxy brown Ford. Summer heat and an
abnormal calm lay on the land like a sleepy giant, cracking the desert's pate and pressing down upon their car. It was the sort of morning when a Texas dirt farmer rises with the dawn, sniffs the wind,
and wishes he lived somewhere else.

Glimpsed from a passing car, the Huxleys made an elegant, distinctly non-Texan family. In front rode Aldous, age forty-three. In
his flannel suit he looked like a very tall dean on holiday. His rimless,
Ben Franklin glasses magnified the eyes beneath—the effect on strangers
was gentle but overbearingly cerebral, like shaking hands with a walking library. Despite this intellectual severity, his lips were sensuously
full, his black hair as fine and close-cropped as his wife's.

Maria sat at the wheel: a tiny, aristocratic-looking, thirty-nine-
year-old woman, with the figure of the ballerina she had aspired to
be. She had a strikingly pale oval face set with large blue green eyes
and dark hair. Barely five feet tall, she sat on a pillow to reach the

wheel and wore goggles to keep out the dust that roared through the open window. In a silk wraparound dress and driving gloves, she seemed ready for an opening-night crowd rather than a roadside inn. An observer would scarcely have guessed that she had driven a racing car for Bugatti in the thirties.

Matthew, age seventeen, rode in the back. His round, guileless face suggested a European Mickey Rooney, fruitlessly yelling requests to the front seat over the noise of the road. Everyone said he was his mother's child—by which they meant that he was, for a Huxley, "normal"—more interested in baseball than Botticelli. Yet Matthew had the broad Huxley forehead. His ears stuck out and his cowlick bounced as the Ford hit a dip in the road.

On the road's shoulder Maria passed parched cows, broken-down trucks, and the Model A's John Steinbeck immortalized in *The Grapes of Wrath*. Farm families took to the road by the millions that summer; their farms had gone to the bankers, their savings to the railroads, and they followed the handbills to the fields of California.

That summer Woody Guthrie headed out for California on the same road. He left Central Texas for Los Angeles about the same week the Huxleys passed by. His trip was more casual: hitchhiking, sleeping in empty gas stations at night, humming his songs of the West:

> *Rain quit and the wind got high*
> *And a black old dust storm filled the sky.*
> *I swapped my farm for a Ford machine*
> *And I poured it full of this gasoline*
> *And I started rockin and a-rollin over the mountains,*
> *Out toward the old peach bowl . . .*[1]

As the Huxleys jounced along through the dust, past the Guthries and Joads with hard, starved faces, they did not stop. There wasn't room in the car: Aldous had the seat pushed all the way back for his legs, and Matthew was crammed into the space left behind.

The family was not having an easy time. The Huxleys had no more of a home than the migrants they passed. The war tailed them like a shadow. "Aldous and Gerald truly have the impression that the situation [in Europe] is getting worse and worse," Maria wrote, "and that before the summer there is a possibility of cataclysm."[2]

Were they to spend the rest of their life in America? They wrote friends that they didn't know—realizing, half-consciously, that if fighting broke out, they faced permanent exile.

Like their fellow travelers, the family had their possessions packed into a cheap car, wondering where they'd stay and what would happen next. On the highway the once-famous writer became the middle-aged father worried with the rest about the cost of gas, the price of roadside meals, the blowing dust.

The wind wrestled with the walnut trees by the side of the road, bobbing the branches up and down. A low whine filled the air, which the Huxleys overlooked as they trundled past. A local boy like Guthrie knew that sound: "spider webs, feathers, old flying papers, and dark clouds swept along the ground, picking up the dust, and blocking out the sky. Everything fought and pushed against the wind, and the wind fought everything in its way."[3]

By the time the Huxleys realized they were headed into a dust storm, it was too late to do anything but drive. Fast. The nearest town of any size was probably a hundred miles away, across the flat prairie that stretched endlessly in swirling dust.

"We didn't stop," Matthew recalled. "We just wanted to get the hell out of there."[4]

Maria was disappointed in the Ford, whose steering wheel sat too high for her; otherwise, the trip so far had been a success. After they had landed in New York on April 7, they had vacationed up the Hudson at Rhinebeck with Eugene Saxton of Harper, Huxley's American publisher. Both Maria and Aldous were impressed with the city: "The immense river [and across in New Jersey], masses of black rock and an astonishing light, which calls to man to build gigantically." Maria's first impression of New Yorkers was wildly improbable: "childish and ingenuous."[5]

For a few days, the Huxleys wandered the boulevards and window-shopped at the great stores. Everything was new and wonderful. They promenaded along wind-swept Riverside Drive, which they loved even as they noticed the city's indifference: "The dead trees drop their branches in an enormous, cold solitude. Nobody bothers to walk here. No one is poor enough to collect the wood nor rich enough to maintain the parks."[6]

A high point of Matthew's visit to New York was his first baseball game. In the days before televised sports, he didn't know the rules and had trouble keeping up with the action. Nevertheless, luck was with him. He saw one of the great ball teams of all time; the Yankees were halfway through their record-setting sweep of the World Series in four consecutive seasons.

The family was taken aback by their reception in America: "You won't believe how famous Aldous is here," Maria wrote to her sister. "Perhaps I'll end up being impressed. Paramount newsreels came to shoot us."[7] Huxley and Heard arranged lectures at a price which partly subsidized their inexpensive but new Ford, with its beige interior and huge trunk.

In a whirl of dust and tread they drove with Gerald to Charlottesville, Virginia, and points south. Maria sliced into turns, almost lofting the car over potholes. Aldous loved her speed—"the only new pleasure since the Pleistocene era," he'd say—and the way she'd pull on her driving gloves and gun across 300 miles in a day on rough, ungraded roads.

They drove and drove, marveling at the immense spaces between spots in America, the great un-filled-in-ness of the Northeastern woods, the roads winding through creekbed and craggy farm, past copses bright and green with early summer foliage.

They arrived at Black Mountain College in Appalachia, that utopian colony of writers and educators, then including Robert Creeley. A remoter version of the Southern labor schools of the thirties— such as Brookwood, Highlander, and Commonwealth College—Black Mountain was a timbered grove of cottages where the primary activity, to the consternation of its neighbors, was sitting inside all day scratching on pieces of paper. The members' children attended equally puzzling "free schools."

Gerald and Aldous held court on the rough-hewn wooden steps, their adherents trailing them through the summer-camp atmosphere. Their literary hegira to America was a reversal of the centuries-old trend where American writers (such as James, Emerson, and Howells) visited England and chose, in Stephen Spender's phrase, between "the European past and the American present [as] a matter of life and death—though they disagreed which was life, which was death."[8]

The arrival of Huxley and Heard (followed by Auden, Isherwood, and Spender) signified more for American letters than a new infusion of vitality and self-respect. Those who stayed explored what had become America's greatest gift to world culture: Hollywood film. In joining the emigration to Hollywood, Huxley reaffirmed the spreading cinematization of modern prose.

At their next stop, in Knoxville, Tennessee, they toured the Tennessee Valley Authority with its director, a friend of Julian's.[9] Finally they reached Duke University in Durham, North Carolina, where J. B. Rhine and the staff of his famous Parapsychology Laboratory awaited them. Instead of following them through the ESP lab (later parodied in the 1984 film *Ghostbusters*), Matthew joined a group of students relieving final-exam anxiety under one of the great arches with a belching contest; the echoes could be heard across campus. His parents had hoped Matthew would appreciate the medical school; he was happier at the belch-fest.

That evening Huxley was honored with a reception at the home of one of Duke's benefactors. He found a collection of beautiful eighteenth-century woodcuts and began examining them closely with his magnifying glass. He moved methodically along a wall, oblivious to the party around him, scanning each picture a few inches away with sweeps of his glass, left to right.

The guest of honor was momentarily forgotten. Then Matthew heard a loud clatter. When he looked up, Aldous had fallen down a flight of stairs no one had warned him about.[10] There had been a great to-do, and he was carefully laid out, but the family had less energy for exploring their next stop, Atlanta, Georgia. From there Gerald Heard traveled to California via the Northwest (where his friend, the playwright Christopher Fry, had investments).

Minus one passenger, the engine leaped forward down the good road toward New Orleans. The Huxleys passed row after row of shanty houses, marking the edge of the old plantations. The tenants bent over the fields, café silhouettes etched in a persimmon-orange sky. This was the land immortalized by Erskine Caldwell and Tennessee Williams, by Walker Evans and James Agee's *Let Us Now Praise Famous Men:* the South before New South, peasantry dotted with urban finery.

In the lobby of a fancy hotel in New Orleans, Matthew and Aldous found a long, shiny box of chrome and black glass in the men's room. "There was a sign that read, 'Pee here. Get your answer there.' We put in our dime and got a little ticket: 'You do/do not have albumin.' That was our introduction to American technology," Matthew remembered.[11]

As they passed from Louisiana into Texas, New Orleans's sleek hotels seemed a distant dream against the dust storm, building steadily around them.

After three weeks on the road, they were tired. Excitement at new sights gave way to the urge to arrive, anywhere, and rest from the heat. "By the time we got to Texas," wrote Maria in a letter, "the desert grew more desertic, the roads dustier, and sun more and more vicious."[12]

The brown Ford held the rutted road lightly; dust blew through the car doors, even through tightly closed windows. Phone wires whistled, hay flew across the sky, and a dark curtain dropped in front of them. "It was fearsome stuff this dust," Matthew remembered. "We didn't see very far. For my mother, who loved to drive fast, it was not funny."

Ever sensitive to dust—which he blamed for his childhood blindness—Aldous covered his face with a handkerchief. The little Ford tracked its way through daytime darkness. The eerie howl of the wind, the gritty dirt beneath their clothes, dust in their throats—all these made an odd portent of their visit. Already they had sampled the major directions of their time in America: education at Black Mountain, parapsychology at Duke, the open stretches of the American West.

After a long day, they stopped for the night in Del Rio, Texas, just across the Mexican border. The worst of the storm had passed. Their Ford, showroom-new when they'd left New York, now looked sorely used. Mud from the South was baked into its rims, and mosquitoes lay in layers across the wind screen. On one side of the car, the paint had been ground away by the wind, exposing bare metal.

The devastation of their car suggested that facing the land they had left behind. In November 1936, a few weeks before they had begun planning their departure, conscription had moved closer to reality in Britain: political leader Earl Stanhope had remarked that "voluntary service is a luxury." Jingoism mounted daily. Military police talked of putting conscientious objectors in prison if they resisted conscription.[13] Huxley was still draft age (though his poor eyesight disqualified him for combat). In Britain, his public protests against war would have provoked hostility, perhaps even the attacks he had witnessed from Mosley's Black Shirts.

"In these days of war and rumors of war, have you ever dreamed of a place where there was peace and security, where living was not a struggle but a lasting delight?" So begins the film *Lost Horizon*, which the Huxleys probably watched, with the rest of America, that summer when they "dashed from one air-conditioned motel to an air-conditioned movie and back," as Maria wrote home. It was a perfect summer fantasy for 1937—swirling snow hiding a valley without soldiers or guns. In the film's uncut version, Ronald Colman promises to abolish the armed forces. Misplaced Horizons, Huxley might have called it, for pacifism emerges finally as a drunken fantasy.

The Huxleys turned their car north to New Mexico, drove the empty highways of New Mexico's southeastern corner, and rode Carlsbad Caverns' famous elevator into the lower caves. As they mounted from the Texan prairie to the higher plains, the air cooled. Hugging the Rio Grande, their road climbed the mile-high plateau of Albuquerque, a city lined on its eastern flank by the first real mountains they had seen west of the Adirondacks, the Sandia range. Albuquerque was a sleepy city of 35,000, which many Americans to this day consider a part of Old Mexico, evoking stereotypes of oversized sombreros and crumbling adobe houses.

The Huxleys continued north, ascending steadily until they reached Santa Fe, at 7,000 feet. They drove the two-lane dirt road to Taos, their pace quickening as they approached their destination of 6,000 miles, Frieda Lawrence's ranch north of Taos on Lobo Mountain, where they planned to summer.

In their weeks traveling the American South and Southwest, they had begun to take the measure of America, finding it endlessly huge, "as if there were no end, and we couldn't get anywhere fast." They had been unprepared for the heat and the open-air poverty of Negroes, Mexicans, and poor whites. Huxley knew Nancy Cunard's epic anthology, *Negro*. In Europe the family had watched American films—gangsters and Ginger Rogers dancing with Fred Astaire across the screen. "But it was so different to see and smell it!" Matthew recalled. "We found the poverty heartbreaking, extraordinary, shocking."[14]

This was the tail end of America's Depression, before the war plants Huxley hated performed a short-term miracle on the American economy. That summer the pages of the papers were filled with news from Britain: the marriage of former King Edward VIII to an American divorcée. A large comet passed through the summer skies, as did Amelia Earhart, on her tragic round-the-world flight. Roosevelt had been sworn in for his second term only a few months before, and his vast public works were well launched. Those who weren't out building bridges or parks with the Works Progress Administration trudged the streets searching for work or fought for their jobs, as the autoworkers were doing in the bloody sit-down strike in Detroit that forced Henry Ford to recognize a union. In Washington D.C., the La Follette Committee's hearings on the railroads disclosed antiunion spies.

Washington was as distant from New Mexico as Europe was from Washington. New Mexico had always been poor, for centuries a neglected corner of the Spanish empire. In 1937, when the Huxleys arrived, New Mexico had been a state only twenty-five years; its inhabitants lived as they had for centuries, exchanging corn, cattle, and water rights. Taos, when they finally arrived, looked not like a town so much as a dusty crossroads. Time had a different measure here, engraved into the foot-thick walls and dry timbers which held up the Taos Pueblo, a five-hundred-year-old apartment house.

New Mexico's great attraction for the Huxleys was the memory of their friend D. H. Lawrence. When Huxley had first met Lawrence two decades earlier, Aldous had given an impulsive "yes" to joining Lawrence's fantasy of a utopian commune, Rananim (then projected for Florida). Over the last decade the Huxleys had drawn closer to the Lawrences. Maria had typed the draft of *Lady Chatterly's Lover*, though Lawrence forbade her to say the four-letter words. Maria and Aldous were at his deathbed, and Lawrence died while Maria was rubbing his hands.

Like Lawrence, Huxley shared a dream of literary exile. His introduction to Lawrence's collected letters could have served as his own epitaph: "He was at once too English and too intensely an artist to stay at home. . . . His travels were at once a flight and a search: a search for some society with which he could establish contact, for a world where the times were not personal, and conscious knowing had not yet perverted living."[15]

The first time Lawrence had returned to New Mexico, he had written: "I must say I am glad to be out here in the Southwest of America. There is the pristine something, unbroken, unbreakable, and not to be got under even by us awful whites with our machines."[16] It was no accident that the Huxleys headed here on leaving Europe.

Perhaps Lawrence had triggered their decision to set out for America, when Huxley had typed passages such as this one while editing Lawrence's letters:

> I know now, finally: (a) That I want to go away from England forever. (b) That I want ultimately to go to a country of which I have hope, in which I feel the new unknown. In short, I want, immediately or at length, to transfer all my life to America. Because there I know, the skies are not so old, the air is newer, the earth is not tired.[17]

Over the years, Lawrence's accounts of his beloved cow, Black-Eyed Susan, and his evocations of the burnt-red mesas and the lion-colored dust had penetrated Huxley's imagination. Now, for the first time, he saw the stark formations he had conjured up as the rebel colony in Brave New World. Huxley had even imagined the road they traveled: "Uphill and down, across the deserts of salt and sand, through forests, into the violet canyons, over crag and peak and table-topped mesa, the [road] marched on and on, irresistibly the straight line."[18] Then he had populated New Mexico with "pumas, porcupines, and other ferocious animals, infectious diseases, priests, venomous lizards."[19]

Maria veered along this steep, long-imagined road. On their right, as they passed north of Taos, rose the Sangre de Cristo Mountains, the southernmost chain of the Rockies. The car then crossed the windy prairie, where the expanse of the earth and sky remind humans of their true size.

To Matthew, the trip was a lark before his last year of prep school, in Colorado. Unlike Aldous or his uncle Julian, Matthew got along with other boys, sharing interests such as carpentry or playing ball; in this geniality, he resembled his uncle Trev. The seventeen-year-old watched with excitement as the car cut off the highway onto the dirt track leading to Frieda's ranch. The open plains receded as they wound up past subsistence farms, crossing the old Kiowa Trail where the Plains Indians traded with the pueblos.

Fragrant Ponderosa pines replaced the scrub pines and sagebrush. They passed the Del Monte Ranch, where Dorothy Brett, their old friend from England, lived. They drove up past the turnoff to San Cristobal, site of the trading post and post office. Finally, at the end of the road, 8,500 feet high, they rested in the log-and-adobe cabins built by homesteaders and finished with Lawrence's own erratic carpentry.

Frieda Lawrence was now living with Angelo Ravagli, an Italian captain in the bersaglieri, whom she later married. Frieda was a sweet and disheveled blonde, too frank for her own good. In 1912, twenty-five years earlier, she had reminded many of a lioness; she still had the roar and mane. Huxley called her Rabelaisian, admiring but distrusting her "hedonistic abandon to the pleasures of the moment."

Frieda's temper also concerned Aldous. Five years before, she had unsuccessfully tried to untangle Lawrence's estate: "Her diplomatic methods consist in calling everyone a liar, a swine, and a lousy swindler, and then in the next letter being charming—then she's surprised that people don't succumb to her charm. . . . I like her very much; but she's in many ways quite impossible."[20]

When she and Lawrence had originally settled on the ranch in the early twenties, Frieda left much of the work to Lawrence, who was more enthusiastic than accurate. As he had banged away at furniture and dug the irrigation ditch in front of what now was the Huxleys' house for the summer, Frieda had often sat inside on her bed, smoking.

Angie, with a peasant's knowledge of animals, adapted better to ranch life. Lawrence's favorite cow did not run from him as she had from Lawrence, who cursed and flirted to get her milked. Frieda had the highest hopes for Angie, telling a friend that she could make a second Lawrence out of him.[21]

Frieda believed Lawrence's spirit haunted the ranch; Lawrence believed it was haunted before they arrived: "A mountain fever got into the blood, so that the men at the ranch, and the animals with them, had bursts of queer, violent, and half-frenzied energy," Lawrence wrote.[22]

The ranch was populated not only by the ghost of Lawrence but by two women who made Taos a Bloomsbury-in-exile: Dorothy Brett and Mabel Dodge Luhan. All three had loved Lawrence, though only Frieda had full possession. Bitter rivalries among the women continued while the Huxleys stayed and for decades afterward. They even fought over Lawrence's ashes.

Brett was born in 1883, daughter of Viscount Reginald Esher (a close adviser of Queen Victoria) and a playmate of Kings Edward VII and George V. A shy, socially retarded girl who didn't learn to tie her shoelaces till she was twelve, Brett remained a virgin till forty and an eccentric all her life. During her art school days in London, she had visited Garsington (and shared Maria's crush on Lady Ottoline Morrell). The crowd there included an odd mix of conscientious objectors and writers: Virginia Woolf, Lytton Strachey, Katherine Mansfield and her husband John Middleton Murry. Murry had been the lover of both Brett and Frieda, and this rivalry continued as each fell under the spell of Lawrence.[23]

Lawrence had accepted the hospitality of American art patron Mabel Dodge, first visiting New Mexico in 1922 to set up his utopian commune. Of Lawrence's London friends, only Dorothy Brett followed—more a menage à trois than a commune.

As the years went by on the ranch, Frieda grew less tolerant of her live-in shadow. Brett was banished down the mountain and required to blow a staghorn whistle on arrival so that Lawrence could rush out with news of whether her visit was welcome. Brett bitterly resented Frieda's possessiveness, once telling Lawrence in a burst of Old West vitriol, "If Frieda starts her spinster and curate and asparagus nonsense again, I will rope her to a tree and hit her on the nose until she really has something to yell about."[24]

Mabel was little more restrained. Dynamic and loud, her mood varied from magnanimous (she gave Taos its first hospital) to wily (as she plotted to alienate Brett or Frieda from Lawrence).[25] Huxley had referred to this two-sidedness as Mabel's Higher Unlearning in *Those*

Barren Leaves. "Mabel was born bored," Brett wrote in her memoir, *Lawrence and Brett.* "She had an insatiable appetite for tasting life in all its aspects. She tasted it and spat it out."

Once Lawrence asked Mabel to trim his beard. The next time Mabel visited, she asked Lawrence for a haircut. Lawrence ignored her, but Brett was ready. Seating Mabel in a chair, she went at the task so energetically that she snipped off a piece of Mabel's ear.

"She hated me," Mabel later wrote: "and she was deaf, and she tried to mutilate my ear! That seemed so interesting that I forgot to be indignant."[26]

"We saw Brett," Aldous wrote to his brother a few days after their arrival. "She has not been on speaking terms with F since she (Brett) and Mabel Luhan made a plot, two years ago, to steal Lawrence's ashes out of the little chapel that F has built for them. Deafer and odder than ever, in a Mexican ten-gallon hat, with a turkey's feather stuck in it, she has sky blue breeches, top boots, and a strong American accent."[27] Brett had become one of Taos's curiosities: she strode the countryside in a paint-flecked pullover, easel under her arm, with an Indian knife in one of her boots.

Soon after their arrival, Matthew demonstrated his practical skills (to the near amazement of his parents, who had dwelled on his lack of success in school). He hooked up water and a sink to the old cabin, which dated from the previous century. Maria helped Frieda with the chores.

This was the first time Maria had baked a loaf of bread. "My mother had been instructed in what you might call domestic economy," Matthew pointed out. "My grandmother had sent her into the kitchen for a few weeks as a girl to let her know what sort of work went on there. In her first years of marriage with Aldous, in the days when they lived near Hampstead Heath and Aldous worked as a literary journalist, she had taken care of the house, not very well."[28] Ever since, she'd had a cook and house cleaner, as her own family had always had.

In a three-room log cabin 300 miles from the nearest city, her life-style altered dramatically. They ate all their food on the same plate; they had no laundry service, and water was scarce. Maria wore the same clothes day after day. Pumpkin blossom omelets sounded exotic, but the pantry was a hole of mud or dust, depending on the weather, and the ranch was literally timeless.

"Time ceased to exist because our watches suffered from the altitude," she wrote to Jeanne. "Frieda has a clock that advanced only an hour yesterday."[29]

Maria was overtired and overworked. Most of the time everyone left Aldous alone at a table near where Lawrence used to write with his thick-barreled pen. Aldous perched there all day, staring out across the mesa, struggling with a new book, *Ends and Means*. Once Angie walked by their house at night and heard Aldous typing in complete darkness.

After the first month, Maria calmed down and ceased her petulance at being thrust into this earlier version of Walt Disney's Frontierland. She decided baking bread was easy; she wrote Jeanne to find out how bread was made in Belgium. She served tea and eased Aldous out for his walk at his regular time. They crossed the mountain while Matthew visited friends in Colorado and Frieda and Angie worked the ranch. Their path overlooked Taos mesa, where Lawrence wrote *St. Mawr*:

> *The desert swept its great fawn-colored circle around, away beyond and below like a beach, with a long mountainside of pure blue shadow closing in the near corner. . . . And on the desert itself, curious puckered folds of mesa-sides. And a blackish crack which in places revealed the otherwise hidden canyon of the Rio Grande . . . later the sun would go down blazing about the shallow cauldron of simmering darkness.*[30]

As the sky foamed orange and crimson, the Huxleys climbed slowly back up the hill. Maria reported wide-ranging talks: where they would go, what they were doing on this distant mountain, so far from England. They traveled for economy of living, in southern France or Italy, and to bask in the brilliant southern sun, which relieved Huxley's private darkness. He had always been one of those British writers who spent more time out of England than in. Before, however, they had always had the option of boarding a train or boat for England to visit friends and family. Now the Atlantic separated them by what would soon be a dangerous distance; if they were serious about returning, they should have to decide soon. Yet summer days languished, high above the mesa's floor, a Godlike distance from earth.

Both took their fears a different route. Maria was preoccupied with bringing over as many of her family as possible, before the bombs came. She pleaded for her sisters and mother to come.

Aldous submerged his anxieties over living hand-to-mouth in *Ends and Means*. By rights, the book should have reflected his anxious, unknown future, yet its tone is a ringing call to forsake arms, in his most measured, direct prose.

*E*nds and Means is a series of connected essays on humankind's ability to resist the temptations and dangers of war. The foibles of the species are roughly exposed, one by one, leaving the reader in the position of an ant scurrying when its rock is overturned.

"Why have war?" Huxley began. "The causes of war are not solely economic or psychological. People prepare for a war, among other reasons, because war is in the great tradition; because war is exciting and gives them a certain personal and vicarious satisfaction; because education has left them militaristically minded; because they live in a society where success, however achieved, is worshipped and where competition seems more 'natural' than co-operation" (*Ends and Means*, 51).

While others focused on the economic incentives to militarism for arms manufacturers and nations—which he did not deny—Huxley insisted that contemporary warfare was a predictable outgrowth of mass psychology and collective miseducation. Any passing dictator could flog nationalism, patriotism, and ethnic supremacy into war.

The previous spring, when Aldous had first mentioned this book to his publisher, he had anticipated controversy, calling it "a short philosophico-psychologico-sociological book on the various means which must be employed if desirable social changes are to be realized—pointing out the folly of the idea that there is a single cause to our troubles and a single panacea."[31]

Still smarting from Cecil Day Lewis's assault, Huxley attacked the purge trials in the Soviet Union where seven generals had just been shot as traitors: "We are asked by the supporters of Stalin's government to believe that the best and shortest road to liberty is through military servitude; the most suitable preparation for responsible self-government is a tyranny employing police espionage, legalized terrorism and press censorship. . . . The dictatorship of the pro-letariat is in actual fact dictatorship by a small privileged minority" (*Ends and Means*, 69).

Comments like these won Huxley few friends among those still eyeing the Soviet experiment with hope. But even those who shared his distrust of Stalinism could not abide his absolute pacifism. Emma Goldman and her fellow anarchists—who had also opposed World War I and Soviet centralism—broke ranks with him over his opposition to an anti-Franco army. In a single book Huxley managed to alienate both Communists and anti-Fascists.

At least he was consistent, refusing to spare his own country: "The English and the French are sated militarists whose chief desire is to lead a quiet life, holding fast to what they seized in their unre-generate days of imperial highway robbery" (*Ends and Means*, 40). Such harsh, unmincing words would later explode in his face.

Huxley blamed war fever on defects in popular education rather than on individual villains such as Hitler. When people are educated to take as heroes Napoleon and Alexander the Great, militarism can only spread: "Future wars will be as ferociously ideological as the old wars of religion," he predicted (*Ends and Means*, 114).

Fifty years after these ideas were written, Huxley's analysis seems far-sighted. In his framework, religious wars of Islamic fundamental-ism in the Mideast—Iran and Iraq, Israel and Lebanon—could have been anticipated. Nor would Huxley have been surprised by Christian fundamentalism which has, via Pat Robertson, Jerry Falwell, and their associates, speeded arms production in Western nations.

As to the causes of war, a half century later his comments stand unchanged. The United States displays pomp for the soldiers annihi-lated in Lebanon; Britain honors those who died retrieving the Falk-land Islands. In both cases, leaders' war spending has mortgaged their nations' future to satisfy those hungry for the sword and the military contract.

War as vicarious satisfaction? Matters have developed beyond Huxley's imagination. Toys, video games, and movies have made war the biggest entertainment phenomenon in the world. Huxley would be stunned by the awesome cinematic destructiveness of the *Rambo* films—or even the gratuitous violence offered daily on television po-lice shows.

Education for the military-minded? Huxley lived in an era where war was a gentlemanly occupation (except for the horror in the actual trenches). In World War I, Huxley's Oxford classmates joined up, as did that era's best-educated and best-bred. Today the U.S. Junior Reserve Officers' Training Corps (JROTC) recruits students before they finish high school. America's contemporary mythology comes not from tales of Washington crossing the Delaware but from copyrighted war epics set in outer space; *Star Wars* and its ilk have replaced the *Odyssey* or biblical adventure in the collective consciousness of America.

Huxley saw this Armageddon Army rising from the world's failure to curb scientism, an exaggerated trust that technological innovation solves present dilemmas (this concern surfaced in many of his American works, particularly the macabre *Ape and Essence*).

Yet *Ends and Means* offered hope—hints of a solution Huxley would elaborate in *Island*, at the end of his life. We *can* change human nature, he insisted, by reeducation, by social reforms—not by revolution, whose violence bred further violence and reaction—but by decentralization and cooperative ventures. Lasting social change came from small groups at the margin of society personalizing ideology via long-term commitments to reform, sacrificing profits for ideals.

One of the most moving passages of this book—which influenced Matthew "as much as anything he wrote"—is a brief confession. Characteristically reticent, Huxley's autobiographical sliver occupies only four paragraphs out of 382 pages: "Like so many of my contemporaries," he avowed, "I took it for granted that there was no meaning [in life]. This was partly due to the fact that I shared the common belief that the scientific picture of an abstraction from reality was a true picture of reality as a whole; partly also for non-intellectual reasons. I had motives for not wanting the world to have a meaning. . . . [Any rational world would have had to account for his mother's and Trev's sudden deaths and his own blinding.]

"For myself as, no doubt for most of my contemporaries, the philosophy of meaninglessness was essentially an instrument of liberation. The liberation we desired was simultaneously liberation from a certain political and economic system and liberation from a certain system of morality. We objected to the morality because it interfered with our sexual freedom; we objected to the political and economic system because it was unjust. . . . There was one admirably simple method of confuting these people and at the same time justifying ourselves in our political revolt: we could deny that the world had any meaning whatsoever" (*Ends and Means*, 312–16).

A world without meaning was where satirist Huxley had joined company with the postwar Dadaists (and, in theory, with the later Existentialists). Now, twenty years later, he rejected his early nihilism. He had run out of meaninglessness.

Huxley's life had reached a Continental Divide: henceforth he would define liberation not as political or sexual alternatives but as nonattachment. The nonattached man or woman was for Huxley a model of calm: bodily fit but not self-preoccupied, self-sufficient without lust or wealth or other projections of the self, disinterested but moved by passion and charity.

Ends and Means encompasses the phases of Huxley's later intellectual development. In his American period, he would venture along a path friends and readers considered eccentric: mysticism, meditation, psychoactive drugs. Critics would urge their familiarly sardonic writer to put aside these quests, which Angus Wilson called "the adolescent dream that gradually turned into a yogi trance."[32] Huxley could not. The pursuit of nonattachment was, paradoxically, his way of seeing around the corners of his personal and physical handicaps.

These directions lay in the future; in the present there was only confusion as to where he was going and why. Huxley understood the dangers of rising above the world to see it more clearly. He had criticized Lawrence's own work for this reason, commenting:

> Those who take the bird's eye view of the world often see clearly and comprehensively; but they tend to ignore all tiresome details, all the difficulties of social life and, ignoring, to judge too sweepingly and to condemn too lightly.[33]

Yet this same isolation had crept into his writing on Lawrence's ranch. From his pigeon's-eye view of the world there, he guessed at the aftereffects of a war not yet begun.

Among his guesses, 1937 A.D.: a dramatically increasing birth rate in the Third World (with Britain unable to sustain its empire due to relative population decline); chaos in family life, tied to increasing use of birth control in industrialized nations; China as "an aggressive imperialist power" in two generations; television, once perfected, as an agency of propaganda; the arrival of cable, "a controlled teletype service," in every house; the move of politics to the silver screen; and, most ominously, the fact that "in any future war, [noncombatants] will be exposed to risks almost, if not quite, as great as those faced by fighting men" (*Ends and Means*, 107).

Into these projections, Huxley incorporated bits of his *Encyclopedia of Pacifism*. The work showed the encompassing range of Huxley's mind, a critic wrote, "his drive toward a theory of all of reality."[34] Gerald had never seen him work so fast: "All hesitation was gone."[35]

While his father wrote *Ends and Means*, Matthew explored the ranch. He poked his way past the raspberry fields up the mountain to Bear Canyon and the abandoned mill. At night, he'd step out of the cabin and see pine hogs—as the locals called them—dining, their quills vibrating in the clear, silvery light. Lawrence had hated the porcupines, because they killed pine trees by gnawing their bark. On walks with his parents, Matthew watched the brown-winged scrub jays or the all-blue piñon jays dart through the low trees whose pine nuts filled their casseroles and whose logs spiced the evening sky.

"After a while, there wasn't much to say to Frieda," Matthew recalled. The Huxleys' attention turned to others, including the poet Witter Bynner, Mabel, Brett, and the visitors who dropped by to visit Frieda, Woman of the Man of the Mountain. Frieda was patient with such pilgrims, one remembered: "We had visited them earlier, as part of a world-long trip, including visiting Lawrence's birthplace. Then one night we were invited back for a party. Mabel had brought up her husband Tony's friends and a crowd from the Taos pueblo. They danced in a circle under the dark, starry sky, though it was cold." Aldous looked on, tall and somewhat stiff.[36]

Maria wrote to Jeanne and Suzanne often and at length, alternating descriptions of sweeping with a broom made of cedar branches with her pleas to emigrate. By August, Jeanne had agreed to visit, and arrangements were made: sometime that autumn, Maria would drive back east (2,500 miles) to meet Jeanne's boat, while Aldous and Gerald carried on their tour. Jeanne should eat lightly on board and not drink too much liquid, Maria wrote in her big-sister manner.

Mountain life became more supportable, but the electricity in the air bothered her: "At night, when I go to bed, the rustling of my silk camisole sets off a miniature fireworks."[37]

By the end of August, Aldous had almost finished *Ends and Means*; the book's last chapters, scarcely rewritten, wandered from pacifism to metaphysics to biology. Because the manuscript was due on the first of September, Maria typed ceaselessly.

The Huxleys were considering California, where, they heard, writers made royal sums in the movies. The first mention of this occurs in a letter of Maria's on August 20, 1937: "Aldous will perhaps go to work in California—that is, if he's wanted and they pay him enormously. . . . This latest book is the best thing he's ever done, in one sense. It's a treatise on philosophy, politics, sociology, all viewed morally. . . . It's not that it's better written, in the literary sense. But better spiritually, a practical continuation of *Eyeless in Gaza*."[38]

Money had resurfaced as a problem. The private school they had chosen for Matthew in Colorado was expensive. Frieda already had agent Jake Zeitlin selling Lawrence's work. Aldous wrote, authorizing Zeitlin to sell his film rights, and Frieda invited Zeitlin out for a visit.

September began, and the nights froze. Electric storms swept in with flashes from gray, impenetrable clouds on the valley floor. For a fraction of a second, lightning exposed the vast crack in the mesa where the Rio Grande churned.

As the storm approached, the lightning seemed to climb the mountainside as a bar of light, trailing thick blue ropes of rain. The pause between lightning and thunder shortened, and the rumble became a low clatter. Firewood was brought in, supper hurriedly finished, and the Huxleys closed up the windows as the storm leaped in behind them.

From down the mountainside the thunder echoed in the dark, wooded canyons. The jays cawed at the whistling wind, hopping for cover in the branches. It began to rain. Then another Crack! and the air pulsed with electricity; the room turned blindingly bright and Aldous could make out the furniture and the worried expression on Maria's face all the way across the room.

Then, almost as quickly as it came, the rumble faded and the rain passed. Turquoise shone through the edges of the clouds amid prismatic flashes of sun. The mountain ranges emerged one by one from the clouds, leaving the air cleansed and freshened.

By the time Jake Zeitlin left his book shop in Los Angeles to visit the ranch, the good weather had passed: he remembers only clouds. Maria impressed him right away: "Decisive yet not aggressive—you took her into account, because her concern for Aldous was continuous.

"Aldous wasn't doing well financially; he couldn't make a living in England and there was very little money around. He had pale, transparent skin; you could see the veins. I could tell he'd been ill."[39]

Zeitlin told Huxley of the distinguished writers working in Hollywood: Fitzgerald, Faulkner, Agee.[40] Maugham had had three films made of his books in the past two years; Wells had similar luck with *Things to Come, The Man Who Could Work Miracles,* and *War of the Worlds.* Julian had just won an Academy Award for the best one-reel short subject, his *Private Life of the Gannets.* Surely it was Aldous's turn.

The salaries and the perks all sounded wonderful. Heard, who looked forward to exploring Southern California in the company of his lover, Christopher Wood, an independently wealthy pianist, agreed: the place was an Eden, its gentle climate warmed by an omnipresent sun, brilliantly reflected off the sea. They could re-create the old times in Sanary: writing, a bit of painting, and then a walk through the hills or down to the ocean. The lecture tour was about to begin, and no definitive decision to stay or return to Europe could be made until its end. The prospect of going back now, as war news continued, alarmed them.

They decided to go for a visit, for Matthew to see Los Angeles, for Jake to see if he could sell Aldous's books to the studios. At worst, they could return to England at the end of winter, when the tour was over.

At any rate the book was done, and the weather was fast growing too cold for comfort. The storms reduced Aldous's vision. Gray, diffuse light made him more dependent on Maria, even to find his fork at dinner.

One visitor to the ranch remembers coming upon him after supper, as dusk gave way to a clear, star-studded night. There was Orion and the Dippers and the constellations of the autumn sky. Aldous craned his neck to stare at them, but he just couldn't make them out: "Even with his glasses they were all a blur. 'I just wish I could see them better,' he said and went inside."[41]

At the end of the first week in September 1937, they packed the little brown Ford and headed west, across the real Continental Divide.

THREE

SUCCESS

"He launches out into a lyrical
paean in praise of advertising.
Throwing up the window he points
to the city spread out below.
Millions of human beings—all
blindly craving, all gullible, all
ignorant, all stupid. What golden
opportunities, what a rich field for
an intelligent man to work in!"
(*unpublished screenplay*, 1937)

In the days when the Huxleys set out for California from New
Mexico, the road was hard-won: four days, at best, on roads
potholed and washed-out, with gas stations a hundred miles apart,
across immense stretches of red rock etched sharply against a transparent blue sky.

After driving down the copper and sage-green mesas, past Taos
and Santa Fe, the Huxleys joined Route 66 west in Albuquerque. They
were enveloped in a hot, dry cloud of gasoline fumes and dust—dust
which had blown across the pueblos for a thousand years. New Mexico had some of Route 66's worst-paved segments, now clogged with
the human tide leaving the dust bowl.

A few hours west of Albuquerque, the car began its slow climb
into Navajo country. Sheepdogs guarded their brown-and-white flocks.
Clouds rose out of the mountains ahead like huge, inverted pyramids
which turned burnt orange in the sunset.

Huxley's spirits rose, as they always did when he'd sent off a manuscript. "Maria always knew that when he finished a book he wanted to go somewhere," a friend related. "She'd say, 'Sweetums, give me five minutes.' She'd throw some things into a suitcase and off they'd go."[1]

"Aldous had been working, therefore, his mood was better; there was no question about that," Matthew said. "He could not *stop* writing. It was when he couldn't write that he became terribly depressed."[2]

September brought thunderstorms to the high mesas. In the afternoons, clouds gathered from behind the ridges until, blowing across the distant strip of road, the air shook with thunder. Toward nightfall, the cloudbursts hit as roadside gullies flooded the road. Rusty-brown water sloshed against the car.

At Flagstaff, Arizona, the sky darkened to gray and stands of tall pine lined the road's steep grade. At the summit the road bent downhill to the California line; every mile the air thickened and the heat rose until another storm broke, swords of lightning flashing through an ink-blue fringe of rain. Afterward the air smelled of moist sage.

Matthew relished the drive across the Old West. Every mile down Route 66 brought a new distraction: the Petrified Forest, the Painted Desert, the Grand Canyon. They were heading for Hollywood, land of the two-gun Western and the six-lane highway.

Of course, Matthew didn't worry about the bills. At gas station after gas station, in motels and restaurants, his parents watched their funds dwindle. Los Angeles had sounded luminous when Jake had described it at the ranch: high-priced screenwriting jobs, houses by the beach, beautiful women. Zeitlin claimed to know producers who wanted Huxley's books for films.

As they closed the 700 miles of desert and mountains which separated New Mexico from the coast, a new world beckoned: the promise of wealth, light, and ocean breezes.

Despite growing financial straits, their intention on arriving in Hollywood—then in its fiftieth anniversary year—was to accept film work only if "it's fabulously well paid." At least that's what Maria wrote Jeanne: "Even then Aldous is horrified, though fascinated, by the prospect of being tied to this horrible [studio] life."[3]

They entered California by crossing the Colorado River and the Mojave Desert—15,000 square miles of sand valleys and spiny peaks. No other part of the United States would so appeal to the land-loving grandson of a ship's doctor.

Near Redlands, they gazed down across that vast, dry basin of Southern California. The hot Santa Ana winds blew grit across their cheeks and clothes. From the heights where they stood, a crosshatch of fine silver lines appeared, trolley tracks glinting in the sun all the way from Santa Monica.

Closer to Los Angeles, they smelled the orange groves of San Bernardino. The sweet odor filled the car but was overpowered by the stench of oranges rotting by the roadside. Around them trudged migrant laborers, gazing bitterly at the piles of putrefied oranges and the vast haciendas behind them. The contrast between California's abundant land and the impoverishment of those who worked it had radicalized writers over the last century: Norris, London, Steinbeck. Huxley was similarly moved and recorded this scene in his first American novel, *After Many a Summer Dies the Swan*. The memory of those rotting oranges still haunts Matthew.

A month before, when Huxley had journeyed from the ranch to L.A. to meet his new agent, William Morris, Jake Zeitlin had booked him into the swank Roosevelt Hotel. He had almost as much difficulty paying the bill as the young David Niven—whom a hotel clerk had given a maid's room—but the view was impressive.[4]

His room looked down on one of the glamorous streets of the world, Hollywood Boulevard in the 1930s. Between La Brea Avenue and Vine Street, the boulevard boasted more movie theaters than anywhere on earth. Its architecture was an outdoor temple to the Spanish hacienda and art deco styles. Best of all, here one sauntered. Stars mingled unnoticed until tourists surrounded their favorite restaurants.

Below, amid the bustle, were the men who could make a most delectable life possible. The person on whom Huxley's chances principally rested, Jacob Zeitlin, had been part of Hollywood's literary and book-collecting scene since 1925, when he had hitchhiked to L.A. from his native Texas. Poet, art critic, and reporter, Zeitlin trailed electricity as he swept into a meeting room; his black bushy eyebrows bounced when he was excited.

Zeitlin savored the avant-garde; he was just finishing an exhibition of work by the maverick German artist Käthe Kollwitz. If overly enthusiastic about Huxley's prospects, he was at least a friend in a strange town. The meetings with "Billy" (William Morris, Jr.) had gone well, and Huxley had returned to New Mexico with memories of palm trees and ocean beaches. Huxley didn't realize the William Morris Agency wouldn't expect many outright sales after they discovered he no longer controlled film rights to *Brave New World*.

Hollywood was then a dry suburb of L.A., with 153,000 people in its craggy hills and canyons. The surrounding towns were growing like spring corn. "Only a retired Iowan farmer would think of Los Angeles as a metropolis," J. B. Priestley wrote. "It's a kind of boomtown that has gone mushrooming itself for scores of miles."[5] Not a city so much as a collection of lost tribes, Los Angeles and its one and one-quarter million people had resources metropolitan enough for the Huxleys: excellent museums, book shops, a respectable orchestra or two, and fascinating restaurants where any European gourmet could feel at home.

Their first nights in Hollywood, the Huxleys put up at an auto court typical of California in the late twenties: tiny, self-contained cabins with arched doorways in a halfhearted Spanish style. The Huxleys next joined S. J. Perelman and F. Scott Fitzgerald at the lush Garden of Allah apartments. The Huxleys required less expensive accommodation, however, if they wanted to stay in America.

It wasn't clear they did. They were broke, but Huxley's (and Heard's) first priority was to lecture on disarmament. As a friend remembered their mood, "They had both worked very, very hard in England immediately preceding their coming to America, and I think it was a sense of despair over the impossibility of arousing a really significant segment of public opinion that influenced their decision to leave England."[6]

Nineteen thirty-five had been a splendid, hopeful year for pacifists. Europe and America agreed on resisting war; the fragile League of Nations debated world peace.

Nineteen thirty-six had been less propitious: in London, the government set up ARPs (Air Raid Precautions) in secret.[7] Then Franco's attack on the democratically elected Spanish Republic had reminded humanity that the dilemma of life in Eden was the fault of man, not of Eden.

Nineteen thirty-seven was still worse, a vice grip for those who, like Huxley, hoped war wasn't inevitable. Politicians piously rearmed "for defensive purposes." Few friends volunteering to fight in Spain understood Huxley's absolutist fervor. Yet pacifism had given him what he had lacked since the tragic deaths of his brother and mother: something to trust, a credo.

Only one God, and to many, a false one: but in Huxley's turmoil he didn't doubt that pacifism was right; what was wrong was the world. The more others would try to discredit pacifism as impractical or inhumane in the face of Nazism, the more tightly he would hold to it.

That summer of 1937, in the sultry heat near Villa Huxley in southern France, Cyril Connolly cautioned writers who promoted pacifism and political involvement: "Such activity leads to disillusion."[8] Also that summer in Madrid, shoot-outs between Communist- and anarchist-allied factions taught Orwell a painful fact: politics, art, and moral imperatives do not mesh. Huxley, barreling past cactus and bluff, hadn't heeded these European auguries.

Peggy Bok had the Huxleys over for dinner their first week in Los Angeles: "Maria had dark hair and very blue eyes—very vivacious. She would chatter and make everybody feel comfortable and at home. Then Aldous would feel comfortable and he'd talk. That was fine, because if you can't see very well, and you're English, you just don't chatter."[9]

A tall, leggy blonde raised on Philadelphia's Main Line (her mother an Adams and grandmother an Alden), Peggy had married the writer Curtis Bok, from a similar background. She had originally met the

Huxleys when her children attended Dartington with Matthew. Now remarried to a film producer, she had time to drive Huxley around; this relieved Maria, still fatigued from the long drive from New Mexico.

As Peggy got to know Huxley, she learned how to work around his blindness. She never broached the subject directly, would never exclaim over the oversized letters on his typewriter: "You took care not to look too closely because you never wanted him to feel that you were being intrusive; I never wanted him to think I noticed that he didn't see well."[10]

Being blind in one eye brought periodic shame for Huxley; there was a day at Oxford when he'd knocked over a beaker of acid left in the hallway by a careless lab assistant. After leaving Professor Haldane's laboratory, he'd found the shoe half-burned off his foot, his skin stained bright yellow. The faint but nauseating smell of chemical and peeling flesh embarrassed him before his classmates.[11] Thus, "Ogre" played Oedipus with swollen foot and blinded eyes.

In approaching the mighty engine behind his famous sarcasm, Peggy tread lightly, for she trod close to his dreams. "He wouldn't say anything, but you'd know you had intruded. Usually you just walked quite close to him and waited [crossing the street]. He moved with you. I never took his arm."[12]

Invitations besides Peggy's soon followed, including one from Anita Loos, author of *Gentlemen Prefer Blondes*.

Anita Loos had grown up in San Francisco and San Diego, an actress at sixteen. Her grandfather was a successful gold miner, but her father was the sort she later chose to marry: a man who attracted women but couldn't hold a job, money, or anything except a drink.

By the time Loos left high school, she had reached her full 4'11" height and weighed 92 pounds. The first thing one noticed about her was her size and the second, her hat. Standing up, Loos matched the height of a tall man sitting down—and, for some reason, she chose to be surrounded by tall men. Huxley once said he'd like to keep her as a pet.

As a teenager, Loos had decided that if men were to keep her, they might as well be millionaires. She tried out beaus—one she jilted committed suicide—until, like many precocious women, she married to escape the clucking of the nest (in Loos's case, to become the movie industry's first staff writer). She left her husband after the wedding night; romance appeared as laughable as the silent films she wrote for D. W. Griffith and others.

Loos had written her first screenplay, *New York Hat*, in 1912. By the time Huxley arrived, she was one of the old-timers hanging on, despite shifts in studio personnel: now her nest was MGM, a superb place for Huxley to launch his new career.[13]

Through Griffith, Loos had met her second husband, Broadway actor John Emerson, a tall, dark-haired hypochondriac with a fragile air. Loos must have wanted someone to take care of. Her husband's maladies increased steadily until Loos got the picture: "I failed to realize that John suffered from a very dangerous pathological insecurity. . . . Until the day he died he resented me."[14] She paid for his love in screen credits and hospital and liquor bills.

Emerson dated widely. Loos didn't seem to mind; as she wrote of attractive women like her bosom buddy Paulette Goddard, "They learn too early that married men are cheaters and those who don't cheat aren't real men."

In the twenties, Anita and John (who called her "my bug" and plundered her work) left Southern California for New York, where she had written *Gentlemen Prefer Blondes*, an enormously successful novel (eighty-five printings and fourteen translations and later a musical and a Broadway play).[15] They had returned to Hollywood in the early thirties, when unfortunately—or fortunately, for Loos's career and eventual peace of mind—Emerson became a classic manic-depressive. On Sundays before company came for brunch, she would pick him up at the hospital and hope his medication prevented an outburst.

Loos lived in a beach house on that precious strip of Santa Monica sand called the Gold Coast. To her north lived Louis B. Mayer of Metro-Goldwyn-Mayer and nearby his chief assistant, Irving Thalberg; a few houses south stood the mansion where William Randolph Hearst kept his mistress Marion Davies. Loos's shouting distance of Hollywood's moguls was no accident; by now, she had close to a hundred film credits.

When she first saw Huxley, Loos was struck by his statuesque shape, the long body with a harmonious Greek column for his head. "Faulty sight even intensified Aldous' majesty, for he appeared to be looking at things above and beyond what other people saw," she wrote.

"It was after I came to know [her] well that I learned the real meaning of the word 'fey,' for Maria lived a life of pure fantasy. She studied palmistry, believed in the stars, and even in the crystal gazers of Hollywood Boulevard. At the same time, she had practical virtues. . . . As well as being Aldous' best companion, she was his housekeeper, secretary, typist, and she drove his car in California. She protected him from the swarms of bores, pests, and ridiculous disciples who try to attach themselves to a great man."[16]

She was also a most peculiar cook; once Maria invited Anita over for a dinner worked out to include all the nutrients for an evening meal: "It consisted of a platter of string beans at room temperature surrounded by cold sliced bananas. When Aldous diplomatically insisted on leading us off to the Farmer's Market for a banquet, Maria's wide blue eyes grew misty with chagrin."[17]

The Huxleys were comfortably settling into Hollywood's longstanding British colony. One of the first Englishmen to sample Los Angeles's cultural attractions was Oscar Wilde, in 1882 (traveling with the D'Oyly Carte production of *Patience*): "A sort of Naples," Wilde had called the city. "I am feted and entertained to my heart's content . . . orange trees in fruit and flower, green fields and purple hills, a very Italy without its art."[18]

This was four years before the name "Hollywood" was conferred on a ranch in the Cahuenga Valley and long before a twenty-one-year-old Charlie Chaplin began his film career there, grumbling at "an ugly city, hot and oppressive; the people looked sallow and anemic."[19]

By the thirties, Hollywood had become a switchyard of British letters. In 1937, novelists Anthony Powell and J. B. Priestley also arrived in Hollywood; P. G. Wodehouse left the month after the Huxleys came.

Powell sought screenwriting work at MGM; unfortunately, just before his arrival, his agent dropped dead on Hollywood Boulevard; local gossip to the contrary, this did not help his career.[20] He soon returned to England.

Priestley thought Los Angeles besotted: "a sprawling city which somehow suggests this new age of ours at its silliest. . . . Once in Hollywood, after crossing mountains and deserts, you must get into films, stay in films, or perish. You are, as it were, wrecked on an island that does nothing but make films."[21]

Of this trio P. G. Wodehouse had the worst time; he circulated and toiled, but after eighteen months he had virtually no credits. He did collect anecdotes and meet Jake Zeitlin's friend, child actor Freddie Bartholomew, who later incited him to a kidnapping in a Hollywood novel, *Laughing Gas*. Typically, Wodehouse saved the best lines for the butler: " 'There's the heartache of the exile, sir. There's the yearning to be away from it all. There's the dull despair of living the shallow, glittering life of this tinsel town where tragedy lies hid behind a thousand false smiles.' . . .'Ah Hollywood, Hollywood,' said the butler, who seemed not to like the place."[22]

It was no accident British authors now thronged the film community, including Huxley's friends Hugh Walpole and H. G. Wells. The American magazine-reading public's hunger for British culture had transferred to film. Hollywood capitalized on this old-country nostalgia; by Huxley's arrival, the studios were exporting British drama to Britain, complete with stars from Chancery Lane. Producers desperately sought scenarists whose knowledge of Britain extended beyond London's fog and Dover's cliffs—and they paid royally for names such as Huxley's.[23] So keen was the competition that William Morris offered Jake Zeitlin all of its 10 percent commission if he brought Huxley to the agency—just so they could say they represented him.

Thoughtful writers such as Walpole, however, were quickly disaffected: "No wars, no politics, no deaths make any effect here. We are all on a raft together in the middle of the cinema sea and nothing is real here but the salaries."[24] Yet the fantasy-ridden atmosphere which satisfied hundreds of millions of picture-goers was just what Huxley most enjoyed (or needed) from Hollywood. The studios' eerie unreality fascinated British writers. As Wodehouse noted:

> In Hollywood, nothing is what it affects to be. What looks like a tree is really a slab of wood backed with barrels. What appears on the screen as the towering palace of Haroun-al-Rashid is actually a cardboard model occupying four feet by three of space. The languorous lagoon is a smelly tank with a stage hand named Ed wading about in a bathing suit.[25]

"Wealthy Californians began to look on the English writers in their midst as advisers or adult nannies," a film historian noted, "guides to a world of social protocols which their sudden movie wealth had thrown them into unprepared."[26] Falling into this role was a persistent fear of Aldous and Maria, a pair of highly improbable nannies. "Americans want above all else to be amused," Maria had written in New York, "which could make life difficult and tiresome, if it's by amusing them that you earn your living."[27]

Evelyn Waugh noted the same tendency on his visits to Hollywood: "They are a very decent, generous lot of people out here and *they don't expect you to listen.* Always remember that, dear boy. It's the secret of social ease in this country. They talk entirely for their own pleasure."[28]

Huxley's wonder at arriving in California was soon recorded in *After Many a Summer Dies the Swan:*

> At every corner there was a drugstore. The newspaper boys were selling headlines about Franco's drive on Barcelona. Most of the girls, as they walked along, seemed to be absorbed in silent prayer; but he supposed, on second thought, it was only gum that they were thus incessantly ruminating. Gum, not God.
>
> Then suddenly the car plunged into a tunnel, and emerged into another world—a vast, untidy suburban world of filling stations and billboards, of low houses and gardens, of vacant lots and wastepaper. . . .
>
> The car was traveling westward; the sunshine, slanting behind them as they advanced, lit up each sky sign and billboard as though with a spotlight. EATS. COCKTAILS. OPEN NIGHTS. JUMBO MALTS. DRIVE IN FOR NUTBURGERS—whatever they were. . . .
>
> Once more the traffic lights turned red. A paper boy came to the window: "FRANCO CLAIMS GAINS IN CATALONIA." [29]

Despite the author's initial exuberance at landing in an adult toy palace, where pretty women queued up to shuttle him about, Huxley had a fit of the family melancholy, "a black uncomfortable devil of doubt," as he had called it earlier.[30] Perhaps it was the arrogance of brilliance: he had expected success too quickly. Jake was beginning to resemble that agent S. J. Perelman had taken on a few months earlier while also staying at the Garden of Allah apartments:

> There was nothing to worry about. The studios were crying for writers, he declared buoyantly; in a week or two at the utmost, he would have us established, at a princely salary, with one of the titans of the industry. The week had grown into nine, and the manager of the hotel bubbled like a percolator every time he saw us. . . .[31]

"The first two weeks we were both extremely depressed and I was despondent to the point of tears," Maria wrote Jeanne. Nothing had come of the proposed film sales, "The fact is, he has the sensation no one wants him and he's worth nothing."[32] A new acquaintance sensed this, calling Aldous "a blasted angel in a place that is somehow wrong."[33]

This, the first of Huxley's major depressions in America, was typical of recently arrived writers. As Budd Schulberg wrote in *What Makes Sammy Run?*:

> Those first few months in Hollywood were the loneliest I've ever known. You'd think a writer on contract to one of the biggest studios in Hollywood would be thrown into that merry-go-round of social life the fan magazines and the columns like to tell you about. Unless you have an unusual talent for knowing everybody, it isn't so.[34]

Impatient to hear good news from his agent, Huxley drafted a scenario, "Success," a Vonnegut-like fable of how American advertising techniques turn a humble sausage-maker into a national figure. Huxley was simultaneously brash and naive in his choice of subject; he had noted that American preoccupation with tycoons he would develop in *After Many a Summer Dies the Swan*, after he met William Randolph Hearst.[35] "Success" includes equal parts of P. T. Barnum, *Babbit*, and Gumbril of *Antic Hay* (who once advertised pneumatic trousers to protect nerve centers of the spine).

While "Success" shows Huxley's first, flawed efforts at film writing—he hadn't even learned to divide a scenario into scenes and shots—its true value lies in recording the writer's initial impressions of American values in the thirties: "money, sex, and good health," pursued relentlessly and with the worst possible taste. Advertising had been a prominent part of the American scene since the misleading campaigns which lured English colonists to these shores.

Advertising tycoon John Crackenthorpe bets a wealthy college chum that he can turn the proprietor of a small sausage factory, Sam Sims, into a household name. Crackenthorpe places Sims's ads in the papers, then has models and society figures photographed eating Sims's sausages. "People are stupid enough to accept anything if it's properly publicized," the advertiser smiles wanly. Soon the whole country breakfasts on these wieners and Sims, Distinguished Industrialist, grows as stuffed up as his sausages. Crackenthorpe wins his bet.

Unfortunately when Mr. Sausage becomes a factory owner, his friendships with his workmen deteriorate. He's called a "blood-sucking capitalist" and is surrounded by bodyguards: wealth, the scenarist suggests, makes little men into little prisoners.

Overall, Huxley's first American fiction is dreadfully stereotyped, suggesting a land of dour accountants, social-climbing wives, and impractical playwrights. He imagined that an industrialist's wife would be embarrassed at seeing her name on a newspaper ad, whereas many Americans yearn to see their name in print; some actually commit multiple murders to make the news.

The writing lacks Huxley's characteristically elegant digressions: no puns, no neat stylistic thrusts. His metaphors were obvious: "Larger and larger herds of pigs rushing toward the slaughter house. They dissolve into a crowd of human beings going down into the subway."

In April 1938, Maria confided her opinion of the scenario to her sister Jeanne: "I don't find it very good, frankly . . . neither original nor particularly amusing."[36] She was right. Huxley didn't realize that his drama of human vanity set in the Chicago stockyards was so bad that both his agent and Jake agreed never to show it to anybody: "It was just no good at all; we thought it better not to sell it, to leave a better impression."[37]

His agent was selling his reputation, not his books—nor, at least in the beginning, any screenwriting talent. By the end of the thirties, there were plenty of famous names writing in Hollywood, including Faulkner and Dreiser. Some even knew how to write films. "I don't know what the hell you imagine you're doing here," Isherwood would later ask. "Selling your soul, I suppose? All you writers have such a bloody romantic attitude. You think you're too good for the movies. Don't you believe it. The movies are too good for you. We don't need any romantic nineteenth-century whores. We need technicians."[38]

Heard complained about Huxley moping around; days would pass without his writing, ever since the scenario had been unsuccessful. "For Aldous not to work for a whole day is the worst," Maria told friends.

Strange, this sudden lack of confidence in Britain's most famous novelist of the twenties. As 1937 ended, the problem eased, though it didn't disappear. His recurrent melancholy faded before the bright, reassuring California sun.

"There, in the annihilating sunshine," Huxley wrote, "among the enormous, and for northern eyes, the almost unreal beauties of that mythological landscape, [life] had seemed as remote and as unimportant as everything and everybody else in our life. . . . Expose a northern body to the sun and the soul within seems to evaporate."[39] Aldous had written this about Italy, yet the words suggest the deliverance he sought in the sun-filled climates which allowed him sight.

In 1925, when Huxley had first visited Los Angeles, he had poked fun at California's flashy religious sects in *Jesting Pilate:* "Dr. Leon Tucker, with the musical messengers, in a Great Bible conference. ORGAN CHIMES, GIANT MARIMBAPHONE, VIBRAPHONE . . . JAZZ IT UP, JAZZ IT UP. KEEP MOVING. STEP ON THE GAS."[40]

It was one thing to mock California and quite another to set up shop there. One of his early attacks on America was written to Julian in 1925, as Aldous had discussed plans for syndicating articles via the Hearst papers: "Golden lures. I have a sad feeling that it's all too good to be true and that I shall never make the money out of these devils."[41]

His emotional reaction then had paralleled that of his great-uncle, Matthew Arnold, whose celebrated essay "Civilization in the United States" argued that in spite of America's material prosperity, the country lacked "what is elevated and beautiful . . . what is interesting. . . . In truth, everything is against distinction in America."[42]

This was the view of someone bent on taking America seriously, which Maria and Aldous did not intend to do. "We Huxleys especially have a tendency not to suffer fools gladly," Aldous once admitted to Matthew.[43]

Something had to be done about finances, however. Though reviewers like Henry Seidel Canby of *The Saturday Review of Literature* praised *Ends and Means*, advance sales were not large, and if war finally occurred, British royalties would be jeopardized.[44] Finding studio work had become unfortunately urgent, yet "Success" sat in a file drawer at William Morris.

Learning of their financial straits, Anita Loos decided to act. After a few calls, Huxley was invited out to the studio by MGM executive Bernie Hyman.[45]

MGM wanted the luster of Huxley's fame—"the name alone was impressive, indicating that Hollywood could buy anything it wanted—a human equivalent of the Spanish cloisters and the French baronial halls from which Hearst pieced together his fantasy castle."[46] Nevertheless, Huxley turned down the first project offered, a short-term contract adapting John Galsworthy's *The Forsyte Saga*: "Even the lure of enormous lucre could not reconcile me to remaining closeted for months with the ghost of the late poor John Galsworthy. I couldn't face it, "Aldous ended plaintively.[47]

If Huxley had been reading *The Saturday Review of Literature* on arriving in America, he would have had a more realistic picture of what awaited him. In the article "Writer in Hollywood," writers' film work was always trivial: "The texture of average conversation is 'I've got a swell twist to break into the running action,' and 'I can't get a good dissolve off the scene of the murder.' " (Had Huxley realized shop talk was expected, he might have remained in New Mexico.) The worst effect of Hollywood, the article concluded, was the cinematization of a writer's style:

> *After two years or even less of dissolves, cuts, fades, irises, montage, tempo, pace, rhythm, zooms, sterilized dialogue and situations, wipes, trucks, sound, scenery, and all the rest, a novelist's style and approaches are almost certain to be impaired and probably ruined. Few, if any, respectable novels have ever come out of Hollywood or from people who have spent much time there.*[48]

"Hollywood is like a permanent international exhibition," Maria wrote to friends in Europe: "In hot weather, the women wear fancy *undress* costume." They'd already visited the "only Chinchilla farm in the world, the largest hogs, the making of the Mickey Mouse films, and. . . . the best and largest private collection of French modern pictures in the house of a nice madman [Hearst]. In fact, now we want to have a rest."[49]

And rest they did, after Matthew departed for boarding school in Colorado and Aldous corrected the proofs of *Ends and Means*. Around him echoed the inescapable contrast between his family's roots at Oxford and Eton and the icons of Southern California: restaurants in the shape of a hat or a hound, a real estate office done up like an Egyptian temple—zoomorphs, Aldous called them. Hollywood made him seem more English than ever. He had only to order a cup of tea or ask the way to the lavatory for people to stare, curious and amused at his high, well-modulated baritone.

After a day of shopping, Maria would visit Aldous's study with a morsel of film-industry gossip or a new discovery (chili sold by a shop shaped like a chili bowl). "Phe-nom-e-nal," Aldous would answer, stretching out the syllables one by one, lifting his eyes from the page. Aldous relished these tidbits. "Mother always was his hearing- and seeing-eye dog," Matthew said.

Before they left L.A. on the lecture tour, Huxley tried to gauge prospects for work on his return. He soon discovered, as Hollywood-goers have before and since, that social connections bred professional ones.

On October 9, 1937, Anita Loos invited the Huxleys to the first of many brunches at the beach. A low fog hung over the sand; the sea hissed quietly in the sand, calm enough for swimming. Guests lounged in Anita's split-level living room or looked out to sea from a balcony, designed by architect Richard Neutra to resemble a ship's railing.

Anita had one of the sharpest tongues in Hollywood: D. W. Griffith had asked her to subtitle *Intolerance*. Today she was in fine form, presiding over the table with the sad, bright eyes of a puppy and the wisecracks of a stand-up comic. She told everyone that King Edward's recent abdication speech reminded her of a barroom drunk talking about his mother.

Grace Hubble, wife of the prominent astronomer Edwin Hubble, met the Huxleys that morning: "Mrs. H. spoke of her belief in palmistry. I said, innocently, how surprising it was that the future was revealed by lines in the hand. Anita shot a wicked glance at Edwin."[50]

Destined to be the chronicler of the Huxleys' Hollywood set, Grace Burke Hubble kept a detailed journal of her meetings with the Huxleys from 1937 to 1953. Grace had grown up in San Jose and Los Angeles, attending the fashionable Marlborough School and graduating Phi Beta Kappa from Stanford. She was slim, attractive yet austere, the sort who involuntarily pursed her lips at an off-color joke. Yet Grace knew the peccadilloes of men, particularly of her ideal: tall, angular, Anglo-American intellectuals like Aldous and Edwin Hubble.

A bulky, solemn-looking giant, Hubble's droopy eyelids suggested fatigue from nights of star-gazing. He was as Anglophile as they come—a Rhodes scholar who had played soccer with Aldous's brothers at Oxford. At his Mount Wilson Observatory post, he wore only London suits: brown tweeds, dark blue serge, or, like Aldous, gray flannels.

At 6'5", Hubble matched Aldous physically and intellectually, though Edwin never told a funny story, Grace insisted, "and he listened to them with politely concealed impatience. . . . he quoted the long-suffering man who exclaimed, when James Joyce was about to read a long piece of his prose, 'Do you absolutely insist upon giving us the pleasure?' "[51]

Grace and Edwin were each forty-eight, five years older than Aldous. She was California Irish-Catholic, he Kentucky Anglican with an Oxford accent. Their hobbies were congruent: Grace favored her horse tackle, Edward his fishing creel. Neither was gregarious, though both were schooled in high-society politesse: a stranger could drop raspberry soufflé on the rug without hearing a murmur.

Edwin had attended the University of Chicago on scholarship and studied law at Oxford but gave up his practice for astronomy after the first year: "The Hound of Heaven caught up with him," Huxley wrote later.[52]

In Grace Hubble's world, the only clouds on the horizon were those at the observatory which prevented Edwin from working. Mornings, returning from work, Edwin glided his roadster smoothly through the curves of the Angeles Crest Highway, down to their home in San Marino adjoining the famous Huntington Library and Gardens. Their black cat, Nicolaus Copernicus, would be waiting at the door.

While Aldous had tea with Gerald and Edwin—sometimes dining afterward with a starlet at a restaurant which his wife had booked—Maria had her own affairs. She entered Hollywood's underground lesbian community, its so-called Sewing Circles.[53]

Such groups kept to themselves—homosexuality was still against the law, even among consenting adults. Fringe members of this community included bisexuals (known as "Gilette Blades" because they cut both ways) such as Salka Viertel and holdovers from actress Alla Nazimova's Sapphic Circle of the twenties. Two or three bars along Sunset Boulevard in Hollywood, a few in Santa Monica Canyon, stores catering to the mannish woman—these were the haunts of the film community's female "inverts."

In the afternoons, Maria frequently dropped Aldous at a book shop or museum, while she met Mercedes De Acosta, an independently wealthy Argentinian poet who was as short and stylish as Maria.[54] While Mercedes had a husband, she was also one of Hollywood's most visible lesbians, often sporting a tuxedo as her friend Marlene Dietrich did in *Morocco* (where, dressed in trousers, Dietrich became one of the first women in Hollywood film to kiss a woman squarely on the lips).

De Acosta was Greta Garbo's long-time companion. Garbo's penchant for privacy may thus be more understandable. "A certain mysticism characterized both Garbo and Mercedes," according to Garbo's biographer Norman Zierold. "Mercedes was a faddist—a vegetarian, a student of Oriental philosophies, full of odd ideas about the arts. Garbo has always liked faddists." The two owned houses near one another and vacationed together in America and abroad.[55]

(Documenting the goings and comings of Hollywood's homosexual and lesbian communities requires a respectful and ingenious historiography. Ex-members of the Communist Party will admit membership before a Hollywood lesbian will come out of the closet. As the director of Hollywood's International Gay and Lesbian Archives puts it, "You have to read between the lines, use evidence of asterisks. Identities are protected at all cost"; the result is gay cryptography.)

To date, no books and only a few articles reveal the underground gay network; the most common references are cutesy asides: "Marlene Dietrich and Greta Garbo are gentlemen at heart."[56] In De Acosta's autobiography describing her relationship with Garbo, her most explicit image was a thunderstorm swelling across a beach where they lay.

Lesbian actresses routinely married, often amid studio fanfare; many of their husbands were homosexuals, "cover-ups for an adoring public."[57] During Prohibition, lesbians would gather at the Big House on Hollywood Boulevard or the Lakeshore Bar off Westlake (today MacArthur) Park—convenient to cruising spots. At the Lakeshore no heterosexuals were allowed, though at gay bars along Channel Road (The Golden Bull, S.S. Friendship), Hearst and Marion Davies sometimes appeared. At these clubs, producers' wives whispered of film roles to actresses in slacks and cropped hair. A select few were invited back to "open houses" offered by the semianonymous Flos and Freddies, who would take the guests off to the beach or to the hotels on Figeroa where rooms were let by the hour. The latter spots catered primarily to lesbian rough trade, the bottle-breakers and prostitutes who patronized the If Club or the Open Door.

Mercedes, Salka, and Maria were more likely to visit the Hotel Brevort for a poetry reading or a séance. More literary types worked on Hollywood's short-lived lesbian paper, Vice-Versa, in the late forties. In Hollywood, as long as a woman could show she was married or occasionally available to men, lesbian affairs were more acceptable and in some circles avant-garde.[58]

The portrayal of lesbians in Hollywood had changed dramatically since the tolerant twenties. Will Hays, enforcer of Hollywood's Production Code administration, was overly protective of Hollywood's image following sex scandals in the 1920s and '30s. Call Her Savage (1932) had shown the first Hollywood gay bar: "a smoky nightclub filled with cartoonish bearded revolutionaries and artists, the only people willing to tolerate the other patrons of the club, who are pairs of neatly dressed men and slightly tweedy women sitting in booths with their arms draped around each other."[59] Hays let nothing like this on screen after 1934—this was not Berlin.

Mercedes was not the first woman in Maria's life. That had probably been Costanza Fasola, an Italian professor's daughter whom Maria loved after the Nys sisters left Belgium for Italy during World War I. Jeanne first fell in love with Costanza, but Maria took the slim Italian away.

Then, returning to England after a stay in Italy, Maria had fallen under the spell of Ottoline Morrell, Bloomsbury's flamboyant (and bisexual) hostess. They may never have consummated this attraction, but Maria attempted suicide when she thought Ottoline had abandoned her. D. H. Lawrence rebuked Ottoline for leading Maria on.[60]

Another of Maria's lovers, Eva Herrmann, was now coming to the United States; Maria was to see her in New York on the lecture tour. Herrmann later became a regular at the Huxley quarters in L.A.—the way she'd been in Sanary, where she'd occasionally shared a bed with both Aldous and Maria. Eva or another nubile girl would lie face-down on a mirrored coffee table, while onlookers photographed or stroked her.

Though Maria's lesbianism was private, some glimpsed it after meeting her friends. "Maria—like a whole generation of European women of sophistication—never saw the connection between sex and marriage," Peggy Kiskadden commented. "She paved the way for Aldous with other women. She once told me, 'I always knew when Aldous was tired of someone, ready for the break.' Looking back on that period of Aldous's infatuation with Nancy Cunard, she said, 'I always knew that I was his wife.'

"As to Maria's relations, this is something I kept out of. She might have told me except that I never evinced an interest. I remember meeting Eva Herrmann: dark hair, pale complexion, dignified, rather reserved. She let me know she was Maria's friend, not mine.

"What Aldous made of this, I can't say. On one level, he clearly disassociated himself with gayness. When he spoke of Gerald's crushes on boys, he did so with a detached humor."[61]

Heard was "a very beautiful man to look at," wrote Christopher Isherwood. 'He had the most wonderful pale blue eyes that seemed almost sightless."[62] Heard underwent a physical transformation in America; while his lover, Chris Wood, merely looked sunburned after coming over from London, Gerald became prototypically Californian, according to Isherwood: "The London Gerald had been a characteristically clean-shaven type. The Los Angeles Gerald wore a beard. . . . It gave his face an upward, heaven-seeking thrust which was disconcertingly Christlike.

"And whereas the London Gerald had been neatly and even elegantly dressed, the Los Angeles Gerald wore jackets with ragged cuffs and jeans which had holes or patches in the knees. The London Gerald had struck me as being temperamentally agnostic, with a dry wit and a primly skeptical smile. The Los Angeles Gerald was witty, too, but he had the quick eager speech and the decisive gestures of a believer."[63]

Head-to-head, Gerald and Aldous made a matched pair, conversationalists people would pay money to hear—and they were about to get the chance, in their peace lectures.[64] Their conversation leaped from Italian Renaissance painting to the direction a nebula turned, to a ghoulish interest in weapons systems. Theirs was a competitive, recondite friendship. Zeitlin said that Aldous was Gerald's disciple; in this phase, "intellectual partner" would be more appropriate. Even in his Bloomsbury days, Huxley had difficulty finding peers. Heard's encyclopedic interest in scientific trends and history attracted him the way Russell and Lawrence did.

Departure for the tour neared; in lighter moments Maria called the lectures their Mutt and Jeff act. Aldous resented Gerald's pressure to rehearse; he hated public speaking since he couldn't see beyond the first row of his audience. "Gerald convinced him," Maria wrote home, "that this was the moment or never to say what they had to say." War *might* be averted through diplomatic channels; he could at least try.

Nevertheless, in moments of stress—when Aldous felt put upon to do something he didn't like—he would fall silent, in a "bilious state, turning slightly greenish," his nephew Francis said. He awaited an opportunity to speak, sitting "on the outskirts of a conversation until he found that he was well-placed to drop one of his long-playing records upon his turntable. Then he would pick up remarkably."[65]

At their best, Gerald drew Aldous out in this way: "Aldous would start with that moonlike expression, accentuated because of the eyes which didn't look quite normal, and Gerald would just ply him with questions, get him going," Peggy said.[66] When Aldous caught fire, Gerald would chime in with his own carefully tailored remarks. The effect was like birds in an aviary, chirping at each other and fluttering their wings in display, Grace Hubble observed.

Maria's reaction to their first lecture, on October 18 at the Los Angeles Philharmonic Auditorium, was mixed: "Aldous so slow and calm and passive; Gerald vehement and busy and coercive."[67] Aldous read his talk, holding the pages a few inches from his nose. Gerald spoke fluidly from notes. Their text was drawn from their London lectures to the Quakers. The resulting publicity brought even more invitations, which Maria enjoyed: they were to meet Charlie Chaplin and Greta Garbo.

This was a time when lecturing was a public entertainment second only to live music. In its heyday at the end of the nineteenth century, when Mark Twain and journalistic crusaders like Lincoln Steffens and Ida Tarbell toured, lecturers had the following of such TV personalities as Phil Donahue or Mike Wallace. The public expected information and showmanship, not always in that order; at question time, they leaned forward in their seats. Gerald was practiced at deflecting barbs; Aldous stood off to one side. Their strength lay in the reasoned delivery of their appeals against rearmament: arms build-ups historically are followed by wars; arms-makers love a good fight. Their lilting accents and their refined discourse provided that comforting edification for which people attend lectures, but they lacked the common touch.

Once afire, however, Aldous could be more outspoken than he looked:

Our world is lousy with armaments and we are so utterly lost to all reason and decency that we complacently accept our verminous state. A couple of pennyworth of commonsense and insecticide would rid us for ever of all our loathsome parasites. But we prefer to remain verminous. We prefer to run the risk of being killed by the party insects we ourselves have fashioned.[68]

"This might have been acceptable enough in the early 1930's," observed biographer Ronald Clark, "but the idea began to lose its cogency for the Left when the alternative to arms was seen to be the concentration camp. The Left was naturally unwilling to forgive Huxley for sticking to his lack of guns."[69]

The Los Angeles *Times* didn't mention the lecture, though its pages trumpeted war news: Japan marching into Manchuria, Italy building an African empire in Libya and Ethiopia, Germany converting peacetime industry to armament. Eleven days before the first Huxley-Heard lecture, Roosevelt had given his famous quarantine speech; though attacking "terror and international lawlessness," he avoided commitment to Spain or a declaration of who the "terrorists" were.

To Huxley, it didn't matter whom Roosevelt censored. Huxley worried not about quick fixes but about nations ready, in the name of patriotism or nationalism, to sacrifice millions of lives to bring about the New Jerusalem.[70]

He had found political disarmament just as he discovered what might be called emotional disarmament: the realization that our individual egos, collectively manipulated, were vulnerable to the advertising techniques parodied in "Success." He had taken up pacifism at the same time as meditation and blended them to suit his needs. At times, he seemed to conflate the two. The former was a matter of geopolitics, the latter of conscience and consciousness.

Huxley's pursuit of disarmament was contradictory. On the one hand, he believed earnestly in pacifism—and with it, the necessary reforms to make it universal; on the other, he couldn't shake his cynicism of humanity. "Aldous has a lot of rancor to get out of his system, like D. H. Lawrence. He is somehow cold-blooded," Grace noted after her initial meetings. "Aldous has read too much."[71]

These contradictions left Huxley in the position of a Christian Scientist with appendicitis (in the phrase of satirist Tom Lehrer). One way to resolve this conflict lay in downplaying the horror of Nazism, like those who later could not acknowledge Hitler's concentration camps. Another lay in upholding his right to reject the kill-or-be-killed situation of former pacifists in Spain. People fight wars because of their horror at brutality and inhumanity, and they become brutal in the process. Huxley tried both alternatives: repression and idealism.

Maria understood his repression in a personal context, as she confided to Jeanne: "Because of me, he's constantly brought to face life naked and raw. The conflict is enormous. We have trouble understanding how he lives in the abstract and, in sum, very serenely; because, I'm sure, he has trouble facing daily circumstances and often, humanly painful ones. Perhaps it's too much to ask. And yet I don't believe it's good to encourage him to soar. It's too easy to soar."[72]

Huxley's idealism can be read in his vivid preface to *White Corpuscles in Europe*, a now obscure volume on European pacifists: "Among the nations of the Old World, the drift towards destruction and insanity is not unanimous. The masses, as always, have fatalistically accepted the politics of their rulers, as they would accept the weather. . . . they honestly desire to cure the world's disease, but all they can do is to prescribe more of the poison which brought it on."

Resolving this situation was the job of "a minority of energetic and well-intentioned individuals who do not conform to the standard orthodoxies of right-wing and left-wing politics. . . . These individuals do not believe that organized evil can be remedied by the organization of more evil."[73] Reform proceeds from the outskirts of society inward, Huxley concluded, from the efforts of dedicated, clearheaded individuals. (He was now sketching such a character, based on Gerald Heard, for *Swan*.)

Not all his emigrant friends could accept Huxley's pacifism. Those fleeing Europe for their lives hated Nazism and Fascism more than they shared Huxley's hatred of war. For these, "exile" was far more appropriate than "émigré"; and ignoring Hitler was an impossible luxury.

Maria felt this way. Nearly every letter home reveals her obsession with getting her relatives out of Europe before it was too late; the fate of Maria's family eventually forced Aldous to stop his soaring and confront the war.

It was appropriate that Huxley's family dragged him into the general fray, for can we really be said to be pacifists before we are tried? Before we see perish something we care about passionately? Huxley made such an easy target in the following years precisely because his pacifism came without apparent sacrifice or effect. As one English critic would bitterly complain, "It was all very well to say [with Auden] 'We must love one another or die' three thousand miles away when the bombs were dropping here."[74]

Huxley kept rewriting his unread scenario "Success"; for inspiration, he visited the Paramount studio. A chatty correspondent for the *New York Times* wrote the visit up as "Mr. Huxley at the Zoo." Huxley appeared "shilpit," as a Scot might say: "school-boyish, frowsy-haired and stalky, with owl-like glasses."[75] Ironically, Huxley found that many at the studio knew his work, from an actor who admired his essay on Shanghai ceramics to the guard at the gate, who lamented that he'd left his copy of *Crome Yellow* at home.

He erred in refusing to talk to the Los Angeles *Times*'s film industry reporter, Philip Scheuer. After the *New York Times* ran its interview, Scheuer retaliated by calling Huxley "An Artist who Condescends." In an "intelligentsia item," the journalist snidely wrote that Huxley "didn't think Hollywood any too hot" and mocked him for circulating his scenario under a new name, "It Pays To Advertise," when there was already a play by that name.[76]

The first week in December, Aldous and Gerald left by train for Chicago, the Midwest, and the Eastern seaboard, "both in leather coats, small grey hats, and umbrellas. In spite of feeling very sad, which I was," Maria reported, "I laughed."[77] In hindsight, their timing wasn't ideal; while Huxley and Heard urged alternatives to militarism, the Spanish Republic floundered, having lost thirty-seven towns in the twenty-four hours preceding their first lecture in L.A. Yet the amphitheaters were crowded by collegians—those still keeping the Oxford Pledge and members of the International Relations Club, whose 806 chapters were committed to "a definite attempt to find substitutes for war." Huxley and Heard were by no means alone.[78]

The tour went smoothly until Iowa, where Gerald slipped in a snowbank and broke his arm, forcing Aldous to carry on by himself.

He did so desultorily, meeting Maria in New York City. There he told a reporter—carried away by his own lectures, perhaps—"If you're hopeful, you finally end by creating the things you hope for."[79] Such optimism remained a possibility in 1937.

The visit to New York stimulated Maria, who savored the grand shops of Fifth Avenue and indulged her taste for silk. Sweetening the visit further, on December 12 Huxley's picture filled the cover of the *New York Times Book Review* alongside a lengthy review of *Ends and Means*. The reviewer, Henry Hazlitt, expecting a sequel to *Point Counter Point*, found the book perplexing. He correctly noted that the book heralded a major shift in Huxley: "The intellectual libertine has become a holy man. The cynic has turned messiah." Huxley's arguments against capitalist greed, war, torture, and press censorship were casually ignored, as if a novelist had no business commenting on political matters.

Reviews in the English press were harsher, a sign of things to come. Kingsley Martin wrote: "I recognize in *Ends and Means* the valiant effort of a sincere and brilliant writer to find an objective justification for exactly that attitude to life which for at least one day in each week I long to take myself." Evelyn Waugh all but called Huxley a fool: "There is no reason to suppose that in ten years' time he will hold any of the opinions he holds today."[80]

Maria stayed in upstate New York (on Jacob Astor's former estate) while Huxley finished off his lectures. Jeanne went off to Washington, D.C., for a job but soon returned to Paris. This and the icy New England weather put them out of sorts. What was next?

"Well, the Hollywood adventure is over," Maria had written to her mother in November. "We were very amused . . . yet we are leaving it because it does not seem the place for us to settle down in."[81] They considered moving to Maryland or Virginia. Huxley suffered from the very freedom writing provided: able to write anywhere, he couldn't decide where to live. Still hoping for a movie sale, he urged Zeitlin to work harder; unless prospects were good, "I probably should go back to Europe when my lecturing is over."[82]

Was this a bluff? Perhaps the Huxleys never intended to leave the United States; at any rate, they took Jake's noncommittal response as reason to drive west, stopping at the Lawrence ranch in New Mexico before returning to California on January 18, 1938.

"We're deciding to stay in the West," Maria wrote to Jeanne in half apology, "maybe Santa Barbara. I couldn't leave Matthew." She continued in an improbable burst of maternal feeling: "If he needs me, I can fly to him." They rented a stunning town house in Hollywood at 1340 North Laurel Avenue, barely a half block from Sunset Strip. Enormous wooden doors opened into a courtyard with a blue-tiled fountain and a patio. Light streamed through the tall windows of their duplex with its bright, very quiet living room and bedrooms.

They had hardly unpacked when Aldous caught a chill. "I don't think he had any idea it could get cold in California," Jake Zeitlin said. "I told him to wear a coat."[83] The cold became bronchitis. By the end of March, he was back from the hospital and slowly resuming his working routine. He didn't know where his next check was coming from, but the Huxleys were hooked on California.

Surrounded by mimosas, orange trees, and palms, Maria would rise first, eat breakfast, and tend her beloved flowers; then she'd wake Aldous with tea and toast or a soft-boiled egg. Maria made the beds, vacuumed, and, while Aldous wrote, ran to the post office and bought fresh food for lunch, their main meal of the day.

This was life as Aldous loved it, as they'd lived it under the equally balmy skies of the Mediterranean. When writing was going well—perhaps the day after Maria had arranged a sexy encounter—his lazy, waking smile thrilled her: "Every morning I can't believe he's going to smile that way, and then he does," she wrote her sister; "then I remember those dark days in Albany, when I didn't dare ask how he'd slept, the rages of insomnia in his eyes."

The maid Hazel arrived by 12:30, and they prepared "a true, good lunch," as Maria liked to say, for 1:30. By that time Aldous had written his customary six to ten pages; after lunch they took a long walk in the Hollywood Hills. Tea at five, and Aldous returned to work until his eyes gave out. Maria bathed, heated up a bit of supper and, assuming they were at home that evening, readied the evening's entertainment: reading aloud. She had developed a way of reading to Aldous for hours using only half her voice.

An eavesdropper passing their window might well have wondered what this couple was up to: Aldous stretched out full-length, his feet raised on the couch's edge, with a tiny woman whispering by his head. In fact, they were reading Herodotus.

Despite this domestic calm, they lived in the health fanatic's twilight of ill health—Maria with her migraines, Aldous with his bronchitis. Their diets varied wildly: one month they ate wheat and no fish; the next, vitamins, fish, and no bread. Occasionally Maria glimpsed the underlying cause of Aldous's and Gerald's lingering illnesses: "Gerald is fatigued and sick as well. He believes it's because we're subconsciously concerned with what's going on in Austria. Even though we're far away, there's no doubt we can't forget."[84]

The deterioration of peace haunted the Huxleys quietly, like the pain of an extracted tooth after the anesthetic wears off. That spring of 1938, Hitler occupied Austria, Nazi sympathizers ransacked Vienna, and every week more of Spain fell before Generalissimo Franco. Confronted by this gloomy picture, Aldous Huxley began writing *After Many a Summer Dies the Swan*—the novel which stimulated the later Orson Welles–Herman Mankiewicz classic, *Citizen Kane*.

Huxley based his story on the career (and neuroses) of William Randolph Hearst, one of the richest men in America; he was worth today's equivalent of $2 billion in real estate and media chains. A tall, portly man with small, piercing eyes and worry lines, he dressed in loose three-piece suits and bustled into a room "as though propelled by a hurricane," Huxley wrote in *Swan*.[85]

Anita Loos probably introduced him to Hearst, for she was a fixture at the opulent New Year's Eve parties thrown at Marion Davies's 110-room mansion a few doors down the beach. A country club with a wide verandah overlooked "two swimming pools, one heated, the other at air temperature like certain wines. A tall hedge separated the grounds from the beach, beyond which gleamed the phosphorescent surf of the Pacific," Loos wrote.[86] Hearst also owned a 400,000-acre ranch, San Simeon, America's largest private zoo. Writers were often taken to meet its keeper. In these encounters, Hearst emerges as a victim of his own ego. One writer described "a dinner party at which twenty-one waiters marched into the room each bearing on his head a huge block of decorated ice cream fashioned into a letter of the alphabet, so that when the waiters were ranged round the walls you could read out in great ice-cream lettering the words WILLIAM RANDOLPH HEARST."[87]

When P. G. Wodehouse visited San Simeon, he wrote a friend about the dining arrangements: "The longer you are there, the further you get from the middle. I sat on Marion's right the first night, then found myself being edged further and further away till I got to the extreme end, when I thought it time to leave. Another day, and I should have been feeding on the floor."[88]

H. G. Wells and Hugh Walpole made the pilgrimage in the company of Paulette Goddard (like Marion, a former Ziegfeld girl): "Magnificent tapestries," Walpole wrote in his journal, "and everywhere marble statues, sham Italian gilt, and a deserted library where the books absolutely wept for neglect."[89] They might also have mentioned Hearst's Neptune pool, holding 250,000 gallons, or the castle's main room, stretching eighty-four feet with a ceiling three stories high.

Swan picked up speed after Huxley abandoned efforts to revise "Success." Through Anita Loos, MGM had tentatively suggested a treatment of Marie Curie's life. Visiting the MGM lot, he ran into Davies, whose career was shamelessly trumpeted in Hearst's papers. (Hearst's publicizing was so known that Beatrice Lillie, on her first view of Los Angeles's lights, told Chaplin: "How wonderful! I suppose later they all merge and spell MARION DAVIES.")[90]

Davies brought out a dangerous side in Hearst, one Huxley might have heeded. Hearst was mortally jealous. In the twenties, one of Hollywood's better-known rumors concerned the death of silent film director Thomas Ince, formerly Marion's lover. On a cruise aboard Hearst's yacht, Ince had taken violently sick and had to be put ashore; three weeks later he was dead. Whether or not Hearst slipped something into his consommé is irrelevant; few were better positioned to get away with murder—a fact Huxley duly noted for the climax in *Swan*. After Ince's death, becoming Marion Davies's lover grew less fashionable.

Aldous didn't venture out much that spring, but he did dine at the Hubbles'. In her journal, Grace devoted three pages to the night she fell for his wordy charms: "He had left off his thick eyeglasses and his eyes had a tragic blinded look. His face without the glasses was quite beautiful and youthful-looking, very white, the mouth large and sensitive, the mass of thick dark hair."

Aldous knew what lay ahead; he'd written about the uneasy chemistry of love affairs in "Two or Three Graces," before loving and losing Nancy Cunard:

> One can very agreeably and effectively act the part of 'lover' in the restricted and technical sense of the word, without being wildly in love. And if both parties could always guarantee to keep their emotions in a state of equilibrium, these little sentimental sensualities would doubtless be exquisitely diverting.
>
> But the equilibrium can never be guaranteed. The balanced hearts begin sooner or later, almost inevitably, to tilt towards love or hatred. In the end, one of the sentimental sensualities turns into a passion—whether of longing or disgust it matters not—and then, farewell to all hope of tranquility.[91]

This was by no means the first time a married woman had fallen in love with him. Usually he spotted the prey and sat quietly in his blind. In this case, he did more. He loaded his gun for bear, challenging Grace at an outdoor dinner party: "It would be more sensible if Americans practiced more adultery instead of having easy divorces and held the families together as the French do."

"The thought of the West, my boy, lies against the double-cross and this extends to marriage," Grace answered hotly.

"Americans are too optimistic and full of illusions," Aldous replied, "like adolescents about skies of blue and always true, waiting for the predestined mate."[92]

The morning after this exchange, Grace awoke in a bad humor. "Every morning when I wake up," she complained to her journal, "I am humiliated by the mental and moral lowness of my subconscious mind."

Poor Grace: one wonders at what "lowness" meant to a woman so selfless and faithful to her husband that she stopped keeping her journal when he was out of town. She was caught between the cosmopolitan, European flair she admired in Maria and the way girls were raised to be in the upper class of turn-of-the-century San Jose.

Soon Grace and Aldous were sitting together in a swing at the edge of the Hubbles' vast English-style lawn. The thermometer inched up into the sweaty nineties; outside, on the long, slow evenings, the only entertainment was conversation floating up to the stars and a bottle or two of vintage Bernkasteler in a silver bucket. Slowly they rocked hip-to-hip, the warm breeze stirring Grace's skirts. Maria knew how trouble begins, when a married woman fights the urge to give herself to a man (or woman). She warned Grace, "You can keep on doing a thing on condition that you never flirt with the possibility of letting go: for once, then for twice, and then constantly. As for flirting itself; it is easier never to flirt than to sometimes and sometimes not and trying to resist it . . . Don't you find that too?"[93]

While Grace fretted over her dangerous attraction, Huxley's attentions returned inexorably to work. In late July, just as he had roughed out the plot of *Swan*, he received a call inviting him to a meeting on the Curie project from MGM. "You will have enough to set yourself up for life," Anita Loos told Maria, "and I'll protect him at the studio."[94]

Aldous dropped his novel temporarily. *Swan* was not entirely forgotten, however; it had become his way of mastering this new land: "a wild extravaganza, but with the quality of a most serious parable."[95]

The Huxleys' financial problems vanished, at least temporarily. It wasn't as though Huxley had sat in his room counting his pennies; rather, poverty had become a low drone, heard often enough to distract him from writing or truly relaxing. Maria understood this: "For Aldous, I know that financial security would be a very, very great tranquility." The contract was worth $1,800 per week, if it came through; in eight weeks, he would earn more than he had from his last two books!

For Maria, the sad-eyed refugee with the large family, raised on hand-me-downs, the contract meant fine clothes and dinners at Musso & Frank's or at Romanoffs where, as actor George Jessel remarked, a man could take his family out for a nice 7-course dinner for $3,400.

A new, unexpected treasure arrived at their door, for almost accidentally Aldous found himself in the company of the foreign intellectuals rapidly making Hollywood resemble the Medicis' Florence; every month a Mann or an Eisler or a Brecht arrived. Hollywood's German community—arriving later than the British immigrants, via

France or Italy—included Lion Feuchtwanger, Franz Werfel, Otto Preminger, Bruno Walter, and Kurt Weill.

"America": one historian noted, "For many this exotic word carried a thousand overtones: gangsters and flappers; boxing and the latest dance steps; Prohibition and Charlie Chaplin films; auto racing and labor violence; jazz and Wild West films . . . For Brecht and his contemporaries, America of this period stood for a mode of modern experience rather than for a geographical location."[96] In his play on Hollywood emigrants in the 1940s, British playwright Christopher Hampton admirably summed up their response: "I loved gullibility, cheap religious mementos, plastic, superstitions, pornography with spelling mistakes, girls dressed as mermaids, streets without end, the ethics of the fairground. . . . In short, after two years in Los Angeles, I knew I was home."[97]

The new arrivals permanently shaped Hollywood's aesthetic by bringing with them European expressionism and futurism, which molded the emergent film noir of the forties. The German peasant drama of Hauptmann was transformed into mass culture; Fritz Lang's shadowy sets were shoveled into Loew's formidable distribution system.

Among Huxley's European colleagues, there was no Germany, no England. Aldous assembled the floating salon he'd enjoyed at key points in his previous life—in Italy in the twenties, in southern France in the thirties. Best of all, this new setting was brighter and the air more bracing: a long-time aficionado of the beach, Huxley had fallen in love with the Pacific.

Walking along the beach and eating fried clams, riding the empty freeways (before they became a dirty noose around the city), feasting on aged sirloin and ripe conversation with visiting dignitaries, Huxley was an exile in paradise.

FOUR

AFTER MANY A SUMMER DIES THE SWAN

"If you want to make the world safe for animals and spirits, you must have a system that reduces the amount of fear and greed and hatred and domineering to their minimum, which means that you must have enough economic security to get rid at least of that source of worry. Enough personal responsibility to prevent people from wallowing in sloth. Enough property to protect them from being bullied by the rich, but not enough to permit them to bully. And the same thing with political rights and authority—enough of the first for the protection of the many, too little of the second for domination by the few." (1939)

One bright July afternoon in 1938, Aldous Huxley, director George Cukor, and writer Salka Viertel sat beside a pool at MGM executive Bernie Hyman's beach house, thrashing out a treatment for *Madame Curie*. A sea breeze rattled in the nearby palms; the temperature hovered in the eighties. The table was set for lunch, silverware glinting in the sun. The absence of a hostess indicated that this was business, one of those poolside meetings-of-the-greats from Hollywood folklore.

Salka was a short, Polish-born woman whose left-wing politics and bisexuality kept her from the mainstream of studio life. Friends described her as "Handsome, witty, worldly . . . predatory in search of life."[1] An intimate of Greta Garbo's, Salka was prized as an intermediary when Garbo chose to rest incommunicado. In turn, Salka helped émigré writers; Huxley owed his participation in the Curie film to an Old Girls' network of Anita Loos and Greta and Salka—and now Maria.

Salka had met Huxley only a week before. She was struck by how extremely tall and fragile he seemed: his "distinguished head with its soft brown hair bent forward; [Huxley] listened with an absent expression in his strange eyes." (However abstracted he appeared to Viertel, Huxley could earn enough on this picture to live for a year, and the contract wasn't yet signed. He paid close attention.)

Hyman asked Cukor to tell Huxley "how we see the Curie film," Salka wrote. "After a few rather vague sentences he interrupted himself: 'It is much more important to hear what Mr. Huxley thinks about the idea.'

"Huxley said that he did not go much to the movies but that he was very much in favor of a film about the Curies. The discovery of radium was very photogenic and dramatic: the glowing glass tubes, the dark shack." Cukor nodded his agreement; Bernie was less committal. At the end of the meeting, Salka and Aldous went for a walk on the beach. The surf was thick and creamy, and a new moon rose in a hard blue sky.

"You see," Salka shouted over the roar of the incoming waves, "the greatest problem is that Bernie does not understand the complete disinterest of the Curies in fame and personal profit. Poor as they were, they refused one million dollars to patent their discovery."

"Now, how could they?" Huxley laughed, one European intellectual to another. "Of course, [to Bernie] this does not make sense."

"My great hope is that you will compel Bernie to curb his imagination and stick to facts."[2] Huxley intended to do just that, given the chance.

Favoring Huxley was Louis B. Mayer's uncomplicated formula for success: "Grab onto a top man any time you can; maybe you don't need him right that minute, but you can always make use of him."[3] Never mind that the prospective screenwriter had to sit twenty feet from the screen in order to see the picture; he was a Huxley.

If Huxley wrote *Madame Curie*, he would bring to it his family's gift for communicating science to a popular audience. The project suited him enormously—being simultaneously literary and scientific. To his amusement he uncovered an erotic dimension: Madame Curie chose lab assistants partly on their looks and made love to them in a bed over which hung a picture of her husband, Pierre.

Huxley's struggle, as Salka predicted, was how to fit accurate scientific information into the studio formula. At MGM, writers were asked to rely on "polish, a well-structured dramatic plot, the semblance of literacy and (above all else) a star."[4] This was entertainment, not an essay. "A bit of titillation was acceptable," one historian of MGM wrote, "but there must be nothing lewd or blasphemous, nothing that abused the sanctity of marriage and motherhood, nothing that challenged the virtues of wholesome living." (How the industry has changed in the last half century!)

Anita Loos kidded Huxley about the job in her mock autobiography, *A Mouse Is Born:* "In Hollywood we realize that those Scientists keep right on discovering better and better things all the time, but emotions like Madame Curie had for Monsieur Curie can never be improved on. So when we made the Movie of it, we placed the emphisis [sic] where it should be."[5]

All this can't have surprised Huxley: the year before he had excoriated Hollywood films as the visual equivalent of mass narcotics:

> *Nor are poverty and powerlessness [moviegoers'] only troubles; it is more than likely that they are also plain, have an insufficient or unromantic sex life; are married and wish they weren't, or unmarried and wish they were; are too old or too young; in a word, are themselves, and not somebody else. Hence those Don Juans, those melting beauties, those innocent young kittens, those beautifully brutal boys, those luscious adventuresses. Hence Hollywood.*[6]

Huxley had no illusions about the film industry's shallowness. He knew what he was getting himself in for. By now he had waited a year for a contract, and, though he disliked executive types like Bernie Hyman, he badly needed their financial support. Maria had plans to bring her sister and mother over from Europe; she wanted to give Matthew a car, and then there was his college tuition. "The contract is not yet signed," Aldous wrote Julian nervously on July 22. "It is still of course in the cards that they may change their minds— which seem to have the characteristics of the minds of chimpanzees, agitated and infinitely distractable."[7]

Before Huxley arrived in Hollywood, he had written enough negative comments about America to embarrass him mightily—if any studio head cared to track them down. On his first visit in 1927, he had complained that, for Americans, "existence on the lower, animal levels is perfectly satisfactory. Given food, drink, the company of their fellows, sexual enjoyment, and plenty of noisy distractions from without, they are happy." About Los Angeles, the place he called the Joy City of the West, he had complained, "Its light-hearted people are unaware of war or pestilence or famine or revolution, have never in their safe and still half-empty El Dorado known anything but prosperous peace, contentment, universal acceptance."[8]

He'd been even more lancing about American mass culture ("the same interminable balderdash about high-minded principles and ideals, couched in the same verbose, pseudo-philosophic, sham-scientific, meaningless language").[9] In previous writings only the huckstering and self-indulgence of America captivated him.

Now that he had prospects of film work, however, he fantasized about running up MGM's travel account to visit places where radium was found, such as the Belgian Congo. This mixture of high-minded derision, bewilderment, and greed characterized many German and British arrivals to American film: "Your fame had taken you among other elite of the world to the moon," a historian of this migration wrote, "and there were short men chewing on dead cigars who ruled the planet."[10]

From the air, Santa Monica Canyon resembles a tiny green crack in the foothills north of Los Angeles. The gorge extends from Rustic Canyon in the woodsy Santa Monica Mountains, down to the grandiose beach houses on the Gold Coast. Here many European emigrants lived, for its cover of sycamore and oak gave the canyon a Mediterranean air. Even the street names echoed Europe: Mabery Road, where Salka lived—with Garbo asleep in her upstairs bedroom and Brecht typing away in a converted garage in back; Amalfi Drive, where Mann, Garbo, and the Huxleys lived, and Adelaide Street, where Christopher Isherwood finally settled.

Two roads run along the upper rim; houses, including the Huxleys', gave on to the canyon's interior, where palm fronds protrude from darker corners. A stream leads down to the ocean, past a tin-shacked Mexican settlement, past the gay bars which to this day line Channel Road.[11]

Near the bottom of the canyon, Santa Monica's pier led walkers out to dine on fish caught off the wooden jetty; its Ocean Avenue hosted beach bungalows for wealthier residents of Los Angeles. Misty vistas of the Pacific made the city one of those photographic black holes which manufacturers of film treasure: no matter how many photos of swaying palm trees were snapped, another shutter arrived behind.

Santa Monica Canyon hosted the most distinguished exile literary community the west coast of the Americas ever saw. "With the influx of the refugees in the thirties," wrote S. N. Behrman, "Hollywood became a kind of Athens. It was as crowded with artists as Renaissance Florence. It was a Golden Era. It has never happened before. It will never happen again."[12]

What Hollywood liked most about the arriving Continentals was their theatricality: "bizarre, grotesque, exotic."[13] These artists with thick accents and unruly haircuts angled for the same fish Huxley did, a studio contract. As they developed power in the studio system, Europeans helped others get started; many had dreamed back home of meeting writers like Mann or Huxley. At the same time, however, they despised those who thought themselves too good for films, and they rarely forgave a slight; a few words too cynical (or not cynical enough) and Huxley's needed job might vanish. "Anyone gambling on a career in movies," commented Thomas Mann—advice which Huxley might have heeded—"was dependent on Satan's mercies."[14]

Ambitious or not, Aldous didn't care for those emigrants who'd collar him to discuss the coming war. "We didn't talk very much about the war," Matthew said defensively. "Aldous was so appalled by it. He came out of a generation when two out of three of his peer group at Eton were killed in the war—very, very close friends. The folly, the asininity, the disgust that was generated in him was quite clear—to have another thing like this coming again—how can one even talk about it?"[15] After such confrontations, Maria would come to his rescue "like a little dachshund saving a St. Bernard," said Peggy Kiskadden: "She'd do it so charmingly that the people wouldn't realize that they'd been just cut out. She would say, 'Oh, I'm so glad to meet you, too,' and then speak for a minute or two, and then say, 'I'm sorry, we have to go; we have another engagement.' She'd just take him right away."[16]

Many of Europe's greatest artists (as well as egos) had come to L.A. to escape Hitler—but not to escape the war: "Some were Jews, of course, but many, like Mann and Stravinsky, were not. Some were quite left-wing; others were conservative," wrote Lionel Rolfe.[17] Thomas Mann and his wife Katia, were a special case, received at the White House and given an honorary degree (alongside Einstein) at Harvard.

The previous Easter, 1938, the Huxleys had gone for a walk with the Manns, then considering whether to join the "new Weimar" in California. The couples packed a picnic lunch and wandered out on an expanse of beach. Mann stared into the ocean, exclaiming how the scene reminded him of the Baltic, then walked briskly ahead.

Thomas Mann was as remote and as tall as Huxley; both left deep impressions in the sand. Mann's deep-set eyes had looked on too much sadness; his books and citizenship had been formally repudiated by the Nazi government in 1936—long after others, including his elder brother, Heinrich, had had their royalties seized. Mann was a classic exile without a home—though his Nobel Prize left him in far better straits than most. *Death in Venice* had taken up the Huxleyan theme of a writer who falls prey to an uncontrolled sexual passion, weakens, and dies.

In 1933, Mann had left Germany voluntarily, first for Switzerland then Sanary, after finishing *Mario and the Magician*, an allegorical attack on Fascism. He had written a correspondent of his pleasure meeting Huxley, "one of the finest flowerings of West European intellectualism, especially in his essays."[18] Huxley, however, had privately called Mann and his associates "a dismal crew, already showing the disastrous effects of exile."[19] They brought war too close for comfort.

Maria and Katia Mann walked along the sand behind the two writers, peering down at the shells and debris. Maria noticed some long shapes, "white and vaguely suggestive." She stared at them and suddenly realized thousands of condoms were spread across the otherwise deserted beach. She guffawed. "I was polite, but then I couldn't hold it in anymore."[20] She told Katia and then relayed her discovery to the men, locked fast in discussion. They stopped and looked around; Huxley saw only flowers blowing in the wind.

No one could figure out how all those couples could have gotten together at the same time—or why the condoms seemed inflated. Aldous finally guessed they were at the outflow of a sewage line and that gas from the decaying sewage caused some to appear to stand at attention. "I do hope they had fun," he chuckled.

The condom-filled beach fascinated Huxley for years; a decade later in *Ape and Essence*, he would write:

> . . . *the glory that was Queen Victoria*
> *Remains unquestionably the W.C.;*
> *The grandeur that was Franklin Delano*
> *Is this by far the biggest drainpipe ever—*
> *Dry now and shattered, Ichabod, Ichabod;*
> *And its freight of condoms (irrepressibly buoyant*
> *Like hope, like concupiscence) no longer whitens*
> *this lonely beach with a galaxy as of windflowers*
> *Or summer daisies.*[21]

Mann struck many emigrants as tough and disturbingly formal, yet this very toughness was what allowed the tightly knit German community to survive, overcoming barriers of language which British émigrés did not suffer. In fact, many Germans resented the term "émigré"; they saw themselves as "exiles" driven from their land.

This influx met a mixed reception. Only those with international reputations had an easy time in Hollywood. Already established American writers, like James Agee, felt threatened: "They were, many of them, the spoiled children of Hollywood, in the thrall of a medium that they all treated with the utmost condescension."[22] Others, such

as Lillian Hellman in *Pentimento,* scrutinized their political creden-
tials: "We took for granted that they had left either in fear of perse-
cution or to make a brave protest. They were our kind of folks. It
took me a long time to find out that many had strange histories. . . .
Two of the perhaps eight or nine that I met turned out to have unexpected reasons for emigration: both had been Nazi sympathizers."[23]

Sometimes refugees rejected the émigrés vehemently. Once Brecht
sneered: "Isherwood is a Buddhist (a little ersatz-monk, standing
barefoot in his cowl in the incense of a Hollywood monastery that is
really a boarding house), Auden an Anglican, and Huxley a hazy kind
of deist."[24]

Huxley didn't respond to cracks like this, but this hostility
promised trouble for a pacifist in a house of war-ravaged exiles.

That summer of 1938 was the last season of Huxley's innocence: he was faced with sudden wealth, famous stars as friends, discreet and gorgeous companions, a reading public awaiting his next
work. The trip to Hollywood seemed a victory—particularly after the
MGM contract came through in late July.

Before Huxley began work at the studio, Matthew arrived home
on vacation, admitted to the University of Colorado for the fall. There
remained between them that admiration mixed with distance which
characterized Victorian fatherhood. Matthew would leave the house
quickly after breakfast so as not to disturb Aldous's work. His father's
desires came first in all arrangements; if a guest bored Aldous, Maria
would dismiss him. Matthew seemed at times a guest in his parents'
home. "I pity his suffering for being Aldous's son," Maria wrote
Jeanne. "He wants to change his name. If war breaks out he will, or
leave for England or be a conscientious objector."[25] No matter how
well Matthew did, it was never enough; compared to the stars, even
the mountains seem low.

Maria unexpectedly found herself the mother of a typical American teenager; he was lazy, she complained, uninterested in anything
except cars and girls: "He's negative, as Aldous used to be." At least
Aldous had the excuse of all-engrossing work.

Matthew was born into the wrong family. He was caught between his father's rejection of his Eton–Oxford education and Aldous's desire to produce another generation of doctors. With an ultraintellectual father, uninvolved in life around him, and a lesbian mother often uninterested in parenting, Matthew was lucky to have any home life at all. (Most of the Huxleys' close friends in California—Gerald and Chris, Edwin and Grace, Anita and John, Isherwood—had no children.)

In August, as Matthew left for Colorado, the family moved to a house decorated with yellow and red tiles in the flatlands of Beverly Hills, on North Linden Avenue. Aldous spent his mornings working outside the walled-in patio, his shirt off, traffic buzzing impatiently on Santa Monica Avenue, three blocks south.

In her journal, Grace Hubble noted Huxley's rising mood; at a lunch with Helen Hayes, he was sniffing flowers, staring into people's eyes, telling off-color stories poking fun of monogamy. Aldous and Grace hadn't consummated their attraction, though the feelings lingered. Was Aldous's good humor a product of his new contract or was it Grace? In any case, Aldous became so relaxed one afternoon that he lay on the Hubbles' lawn, singing his favorite folk song, "Green Grow The Rushes-o."[26]

The Huxleys were finally freed from shuttling between southern Europe (where he wrote comfortably in the light) and London (where he published his work). California answered both needs. Besides, they had tired of moving: "We can't go on like Lawrence, keep running off in search of the perfect place," Maria wrote to friends. "It doesn't exist, and it seems to me that at our age we ought at last to have found the tranquility to stay where we are."[27]

Beyond personal satisfactions, a world of action opened before him. Huxley remained in vogue as a public opponent to rearmament. Of course, Hitler had already moved into Austria, but nearly 90 percent of German-speaking Austrians had welcomed him. "What's happening in Europe?" people asked each other innocently. "Why don't we know more about it? Why doesn't somebody do something?"[28]

Huxley had not yet suffered for "abandoning" England. George Orwell wrote that criticisms of *Ends and Means* as self-righteous were "beside the point. Anyone who helps to put peace on the map is doing useful work."[29] To his former student, Huxley remained a hero.

Fortunately for Huxley, the studios where he hoped to work also remained neutral, fearing the loss of lucrative overseas markets. Instead of protesting Nazi censorship, Hollywood studios took shelter under the prevailing isolationism.

"The trenchant *March of Time* documentary series used its 'Nazi Germany, 1938' to show an industrious, apparently happy and well-cared-for people," film historian John Baxter wrote. "Despite this placating policy, Germany continued to ban American films—Fox's *My Weakness* in 1934 because 'the lace panties on the girls would contaminate the morals of New Germany,' *Country Doctor* (1936) on the grounds of Jean Hersholt's alleged Jewish birth. Too greedy to protest, the studios acquiesced, even entering into correspondence with the German censors to prove that Hersholt had no Jewish relatives for three generations."[30] That first- and second-generation Jewish producers would go to such lengths reveals how isolated American anti-Fascists were in 1938.

Of course, Hollywood film had its own pacifist tradition, dating back to the early days before U.S. involvement in World War I. Griffith's *Judith of Bethulia* (1913) and Ince's *Civilization* (1916) had shown films could make biting antiwar statements; *All Quiet on the Western Front* (1930) confirmed this. Message films made studio heads uncomfortable, however, and anyway, in Hollywood, war news arrived slowly. More real to Huxley and his friends was the festive and self-congratulatory spirit pervading the film colony. An emigrant service industry had emerged, providing everything from English cake shops to genuine Devonshire cream.[31] Exquisite clothes, lavish dinners awaited the Huxleys—now that they could afford them. The royalties of *Ends and Means* and the studio checks made the Huxleys wealthier than ever before.[32] They ran around trying to do everything at once: upgrade their wardrobe, buy a new Ford, persuade Maria's family to emigrate—before it was too late. Tangible pleasures abounded, provided the quiet, nagging voices of guilt over leaving family, friends, and country were stilled.

When she wasn't chauffeuring Aldous around, Maria enjoyed her life as Wife of the Famous Writer. She wrote home about the role; how not to nag about philandering, how to stage an effective dinner for the stars (cater it on someone else's account!). She and Aldous had separate bedrooms and separate partners, very discreetly;

she wrote to Jeanne about her gratitude for the freewheeling life-styles of California and Hollywood.

Maria treasured her svelte figure and European fashions: one evening Grace Hubble commented on her "grey slacks, sandals, red socks, and short leopard-skin coat." She looked like a very thin mouse.[33] A small-boned woman, Maria would eat lettuce in the kitchen before guests came, then nibbled at the table, according to her cook.[34]

The longer they stayed in Hollywood, the more fascinating and famous people they met. One riotous evening, Aldous and Maria dined at Harpo Marx's house with the Hubbles. The living room was large, and pine-paneled, with plum-colored quilted silk, harp, and grand piano. On the walls hung a phony Rembrandt of the four Marx Brothers, a Gainsborough of Harpo as the Blue Boy, another portrait of Harpo by Hals or Vandyke.

Conversation ranged from tea to drugs, to publicity, to Gertrude Stein, to pictures, to British eighteenth-century portraits, to George III. All the while Huxley heard butlers and cooks arguing in the kitchen and dropping dishes. At one point he stuck his hand in the salmon mayonnaise.

Huxley's vision could be selective, like someone who turns up a hearing aid during a juicy conversation. At dinner, lubricated by champagne, Harpo digressed about work. Maria noticed her husband's attention drifting. He was staring at another guest, a young woman with apparently enormous breasts. Maria looked again, and saw that the girl was wearing falsies. Fascinated and baffled, Huxley couldn't pull his eyes away.

Over dessert, Huxley suggested they make a picture about the real Marx Brothers: Groucho as Karl Marx, Chico as Bakunin, Harpo as Engels. The mime thought he was serious: "They don't do films like that here, Aldous," Harpo answered nervously.[35]

Hollywood in the late thirties had a freshness and vitality which British journalist R. J. Minney captured: "In the glorious sunshine I saw, for all its crudities, a picture-postcard town with mountains at hand as well as the sea. . . . A pervading air of holiday is not confined to Sundays but persists through the week. Girls go to work in beach pyjamas." (Minney remains famous in Hollywood for his re-action to the insanity clause in his studio contract: "My wonder was how they would be able to distinguish me from the rest. But perhaps it was a sort of trade union precaution to prevent there being more than a limited number of lunatics in employment?")[36]

Meanwhile Anglophilia spread, which assisted Huxley considerably, though 1938 proved a terrible year to break into the movies. "The only picture that made money recently," Mae West quipped, "was *Snow White and the Seven Dwarfs*, and that would have made twice as much if they had let me play Snow White."[37]

On a sweltering August day, the Huxleys drove up to the marbled gates of Metro-Goldwyn-Mayer in Culver City. Maria sat at the wheel, smartly dressed and gratified at their studio contract.

The MGM gate sat under the office of Louis B. Mayer, tyrant or genius, depending on who tells the story. Tall rococo arches adorned the entrance along Washington Boulevard, where hangers-on and prospective extras milled noisily by the large turnstile. Mayer, above, liked to keep an eye on passers-by.

The studio operated twenty-four hours a day, seven days a week, producing as many as forty pictures at the same time. A broad alley divided the main lot, with a constant parade of actors in costume and producers followed by an entourage of yes-men. On the enormous back lot stood the outdoor sets: a village square with homes, shops, and a church (where the Andy Hardy series was filmed in the late 1930s), and a block of brownstone fronts for New York exteriors.

Activity swirled around Huxley as he received his grand tour. The twisting crowds, the exotic noises, the clouds of dust were more than he could take in at once. Nathanael West recorded the scene in *The Day of the Locust*: "He could see a jungle compound with a water buffalo tethered to the side of a conical grass hut. Every few seconds the animal groaned musically. Suddenly an Arab charged by on a white stallion. He shouted at the man, but got no answer. A little while later he saw a truck with a load of snow and several malamute dogs. . . . Throwing away his cigarette, he went through the swinging doors of the saloon. There was no back to the building and he found himself in a Paris street."[38]

Aldous plunged into a velvet-lined trap that writers of his quality rarely resisted. West, Faulkner, Fitzgerald, and Agee had their checkered-but-stimulating Hollywood periods, usually driven by poverty, soured love, or both. "None of them ever could make as much any other way," Fitzgerald wrote succinctly.[39]

Earning vast (if brief) salaries turned many a writer's head. Film historian Fred Guiles noted in *Hanging On in Paradise:* "If you were a Metro star, director, producer, or writer, you were given the sort of snob status accorded a Vanderbilt or a Van Rensselaer in New York society."

Huxley entered a Hollywood in transition. Only ten years before, the talkies had transformed the Capital City of Romance. Some silent stars—like Garbo's public love, John Gilbert—lacked a sexy voice; their appeal plummeted, and a generation of Americans lost their sex objects. Sound films also required more skilled technicians, which eventually prompted the tight professional guilds and craft unions. The new technology made movies a stockholder's business; capital to retool studios and theaters poured in from Wall Street.[40] The era of the studio mogul slowly gave way to that of the stockbroker.

Hollywood's changes in the midthirties extended beyond economics and technology. The screen guilds and craft unions, prompted by the New Deal's Labor Relations Act, were growing in numbers and power; the year Huxley arrived strikes broke out in several unions. Organizations like the Hollywood Anti-Nazi League—in which Salka Viertel was active—publicized Spanish war relief.

MGM in the thirties and forties became one of America's rare literary colonies. Robert Benchley, Stephen Vincent Benét, Scott Fitzgerald, Moss Hart, Ben Hecht, Charles MacArthur, Dorothy Parker, and S. J. Perelman all wrote in the MGM writers' building at one time or another. As Fitzgerald recorded in *The Last Tycoon:*

"Why, you can hire anyone!" exclaimed his visitor in surprise.
"Oh, we hire them, but when they get out here, they're not good writers—so we have to work with the material we have."
"Such as what?"
"Anybody that'll accept the system and stay decently sober."[41]

That wasn't particularly easy given the celebrating going on at MGM, which in 1937 had steamed toward its greatest profits ever, despite the death of Mayer's chief of production, Irving Thalberg, the previous year. As Huxley began work, the studio's creative zeitgeist faltered, due to Thalberg's demise, but the elaborate management structure Mayer put in place kept the studio rolling forward. In fact, MGM (and the studio system in general) had peaked by Huxley's arrival, though this was noticeable only in retrospect; in its stable of talent, MGM was unexcelled.[42]

Today the legend of MGM has fallen prey to revisionism and counterrevisionism. Mayer's first biographer, Bosley Crowther, undervalued his financial shrewdness and organizational acumen. Later Gary Carey, biographer of both Anita Loos and Mayer, recalled MGM as "the Tiffany of Hollywood studios . . . the poshest and most glamorous, the one with the most incandescent stars."[43] Otto Friedrich concluded in his masterly *City of Nets*, "MGM was in the business of producing rubbish. That was its function, its mission, and its nature."

Both assessments are extreme: MGM thrived in the mainstream of American film, only with a more Anglophile profile than other studios, having produced *The Barretts of Wimpole Street* and *David Copperfield* in 1934, followed by *A Tale of Two Cities* in 1935.

By the end of August 1938, Huxley began work in the new Thalberg Building, known unofficially as the Iron Lung. "The building offered a spectacular view of a mortuary establishment," one wag noted; "the studio had been unable to buy out the undertaker, so it build around him."[44]

Previously, MGM writers had worked in small cottages, but, "Irving didn't have a great deal of respect for us scribblers," Anita Loos wrote. "We irritated him as a sort of necessary evil. 'Damn it' he told me one day, 'I can keep tabs on everybody else in the studio and see whether or not they're doing their jobs. But I can never tell what's going on in those so-called brains of yours.' "[45] This attitude made corralling strays into the Thalberg Building all the more attractive.

"In every studio in Hollywood," P. G. Wodehouse once wrote, "there are rows and rows of hutches, each containing an author on a long contract at a weekly salary. You see their anxious little faces peering through the bars. You hear them whining piteously to be taken for a walk. . . . There are authors on some lots whom nobody has seen for years. It is like the Bastille."[46]

In quiet moments at the studio, Huxley took notes for *Swan*. Like Dorothy Parker, he crossed paths with Hearst's comely mistress, Marion Davies. Her bungalow at MGM, with its figure of the Virgin over the door, inspired one of Parker's most acerbic rhymes:

Upon my honor
I saw a madonna
Sitting alone in a niche
Above the door
Of the glamorous whore
Of a prominent son of a bitch.[47]

Ironically, Huxley and Hearst not only found themselves on the same lot, invited to the same gatherings, they seemingly shared a political perspective—an accidental alignment of isolationists who agreed in practice, though not in theory, on pacifism. Hearst (a staunch Republican then supporting Roosevelt) and Charles Lindbergh were both friends of Louis B. Mayer; all played key roles in opposing U.S. intervention in Europe.

Hearst shared Gerald Heard's and H. G. Wells's apocalyptic vision of war. As Hearst wrote for William Wanger's 1933 *Gabriel Over the White House*:

> *The next war will depopulate the earth. Invisible poison gases, inconceivably devastating explosives, annihilating death rays will sweep to utter destruction not only the men but the children . . . the race of man shall perish from the earth and the world will be left to the less destructive, less cruel and less stupid wild animals.*[48]

Huxley may have chosen Hearst to symbolize American materialism precisely because the tycoon also opposed rearmament for World War II. His send-up of Hearst thus distanced his pacifism from Hearst's right-wing isolationism. To Huxley, the difference was as clear as that separating ends and means; to others, movies and politics made strange bedfellows.[49]

Since Huxley was scriptwriting in Culver City, he and Maria decided to move back to the busy neighborhood south of Hollywood's Sunset Boulevard. Isolated in Beverly Hills, he was tired of having to ask Maria every time he needed anything. They rented a place on North Crescent Avenue, only a block from their previous town house on Laurel.

There they led a surprisingly quiet life. In the hot September evenings after returning from the studio, Huxley would walk up into the Hollywood hills through wooded canyons. Orange poppies and weeds flowering purple, blue, and yellow clung to the cliffsides as he trod slowly upward, out of the city's noise and cars, up to where the vast shelf of ocean blue glistened. The view recalled the serenity of Lawrence's ranch, where mesas shimmered in the dust.

As night fell, the tall, fragile figure climbed slowly down the trail, watching the lights on the horizon fade into the streetlights' glare. Across town, Nathanael West made a similar journey up the end of Vine: "The edges of the trees burned with a pale violet light. . . . The same violet piping, like a Neon tube, outlined the tops of the ugly, hump-backed hills, and they were almost beautiful."[50]

His walk done, Aldous would find Maria waiting with supper and the promise of a good book. Jake had asked him for an essay for a book exhibit to celebrate reading, "The Most Agreeable Vice":

> *Myself a reading addict, I can claim a first-hand acquaintance with this delightful vice, for which men have been known to sacrifice health and wealth, their nearest and dearest, their duty and what the rest of the world regards as pleasure. . . . reading can be as intoxicating, as reality-destroying as wine, and one can be as fatally obsessed with books as with women.*[51]

When his eyes ached from book reading, Aldous enjoyed sexual encounters with his literary admirers and women he met at the studio. Though their names have vanished, his approach remained consistent, according to biographer Sybille Bedford: "The cure by affairs . . . Maria thought that he enjoyed such distractions, needed the change and his mind taken off his work. They amounted to very little, the distractions, and were either short or intermittent over the years. Aldous was never in the least involved. The women concerned were always very attractive in one way or another. Some were beauties. Aldous had no fixations as to type or age. It might be a fluffy blonde just as soon as someone middle-aged and amusing. What Aldous offered, apart from the essential thing that he *liked* making love *and* made no bones about it, was friendliness, good humour, a measure of affection. What he did not offer was courtship. He would have grudged the *time*.

"Aldous seriously pursued only two women in his life—Maria and Nancy. So it was dinner and bed, or nothing. . . . The logistics were largely Maria's. 'You can't leave it to Aldous,' she would say, 'he'd make a muddle.' She did it with tact, unbreachable good manners and a smile (ironic). She sent the flowers. Maria did up the parcel. She did more than that. In a very subtle way she prepared the ground, created opportunities, an atmosphere, stood in, as it were, for the courtship."[52]

Nor was this arrangement uncommon by Hollywood standards. Clearly the Huxleys lived in a free-moving set; their friends had pets instead of children (Grace and Edwin's Nicolaus Copernicus, Anita's dog Cagney, Maria's Loulou, a baby-sized Pomeranian which she swung in her arms). The Viertels had their sexual independence, alongside the Chaplins, George Heard and Chris Wood, Mercedes and her friends. Anita felt sex was overrated: "Sex attraction, being entirely a matter of chance, has to be accepted where one finds it. Frequently, its victims have nothing else in common and the whole affair dwindles into a matter of chemistry. There's nothing colder than chemistry."[53]

The Huxleys had parity in their unusual domestic economy: Maria did her own entertaining in a town accustomed to sexual alternatives. At least Huxley was used to them. In *Swan*, he made the Marion Davies character bisexual: "In all these months she hadn't yet given him any reason for being jealous—unless you counted Enid and Mary Lou; which she didn't; because she really wasn't that way at all; and when it did happen, it was nothing more than a kind of little accident" (*Swan*, 44).

Maria had her own friends. She would meet Mercedes and Greta in the morning or afternoon, while Aldous was at the studio or a museum. "Garbo tends to be attracted to strong women," her biographer wrote, "particularly when they are intellectual and artistic as well."

Viewers of Garbo's classics today see her as a heterosexual vamp, but in her own time, as Fredric March remarked, "women were more attracted to her than men."[54] A story circulated in Hollywood of a bridegroom on his wedding night who vowed that he would be faithful—with one possible exception. If he had an opportunity to make love to Garbo, he would no doubt succumb. "Me too," said the un-perturbed bride.[55]

W̲hat sort of a job had Huxley done on *Madame Curie* for Garbo, now between *Camille* and *Ninotchka?* The script remains in the MGM script vaults: an unpublished 145-page novel (which he considered a treatment), its first draft dated August 26, 1938.

He hadn't yet mastered basic cinematic language and structure. As in "Success," the text lacks visual cues; the "treatment" is plotted rather than laid out cinematically. Yet as a lost novel by Huxley (following the biography of Marie by her daughter, Eve Curie) the work is fascinating. In a scene from Huxley's own youth, Marie Curie accidentally breaks a beaker, spilling acid.

His Curie is a protofeminist, a scientist moving from a one-room studio to become the first woman lecturer at the Sorbonne. The studio apparently barred mention of her extramarital life; the result is Marie the obsessed scientist, "stony, like a statue."

With personal elements muted, the treatment became an unreconstructed hymn to scientism. Unlike his later writings on science, which would dwell on its failure to address imminent crises, Huxley has a character "amazed at the results Science has given; its record in the past justifies us in looking to a future no less richly productive." Like "Success," his characters and asides are strangely wooden, as if he had scraped them from a casting office notebook on a bad day: "It's a law of nature. Man minus woman equals pig. Woman minus man equals lunatic." Perhaps Huxley—who never was a moviegoer—thought such clichés obligatory. In his revisions, he showed signs of learning cinematic craft, recasting the work as an extended flashback from the end of Curie's career.[56]

After Huxley finished, he awaited the studio's response. Nothing. His contract expired without a renewal, and he returned to the welcome privacy of his desk unsure if he had a future in film. To his brother Julian, he reflected on writing *Curie*: "a rather amusing job—tho' I shan't like too many of the kind [he omits the financial necessity which led him to the studios], since this telling a story in purely pictorial terms doesn't allow any of the experimentation with words in their relation to things, events and ideas, which is, *au fond*, my business. . . . It now remains to be seen whether the studio will preserve anything of what I've done."[57] Huxley told a *New York Times* reporter that the project's greatest challenge was to picture the discovery of radium rather than describe it; he also compared Hollywood to the court of Louis XIV—"because people are always losing their heads."[58]

F. Scott Fitzgerald, then Salka Viertel, worked next on the Curie script. Viertel recorded what happened to Huxley's work:

> It was instantly forgotten. . . . I was surprised that no one mentioned the Huxley script, and on the next occasion, I asked Bernie what happened to it. Embarrassed, he admitted that he had had no time to read it but had given it to Goldie, his secretary, who told him "it stinks."[59]

Just as Aldous was packing up his desk at MGM, a series of events in Europe began to transform his California haven: the Munich crisis of September 1938, as Hitler annexed Czechoslovakia's Sudetenland.

British politicians, desperate for time to arm—and, like Huxley, loving peace so much that they were willing to buy it any price—flew to Germany to discuss Hitler's plans. By September 23, when no agreement was reached, mobilization began in England.

Christopher Isherwood was in London during the Munich crisis, already planning to leave England and study with Gerald and Aldous. Isherwood had returned a pacifist from a journey to the war in China. "The papers talk as if we were at war already," he complained. "They weigh up our chances—our side has so and so many planes; theirs so and so many. Conscription is to be declared tomorrow. This afternoon I got fitted for a gas mask."

Amidst the screams of children thrust into masks and the grinding of trench-digging machines in Hyde Park, Isherwood had an epiphany: Looking back on calmer days he wondered,

> Why wasn't I simply content to enjoy each moment of my newsless paradise? . . . The idea of running away is meaningless. Because in a sense, we are all mad here—the crisis is our madness—and, if you ran

away to some land where there is sanity and joy, you couldn't help bringing your madness with you. But I hereby make a bargain with fate—if, by some miracle, we do get through this [Munich] without war, then I am going back to America. For a long time. Perhaps for always.[60]

The week of Munich, Bertrand Russell—who'd known Aldous and Maria since they were all teenagers—disembarked in New York City on his way to teach at the University of Chicago. Like Huxley, he struggled with adapting his pacifism to a post-Munich world. In *Which Way to Peace?* he'd written: "Having remained a pacifist while the Germans were invading France & Belgium in 1914, I do not see why I should cease to be one if they do it again. . . . You feel 'they ought to be stopped.' I feel that, if we set to work to stop them, we shall, in the process, become exactly like them, & the world will have gained nothing."

Interrogated by reporters at boatside, Russell refused to condemn the Munich accord: "Even if we win, after the war I am afraid we would be just as mad as Hitler is. . . . I was glad of the settlement, bad as it was."[61]

This was the moment Matthew realized that his parents weren't going back to Europe soon.

Ln the autumn of 1938, one way the Huxleys distracted themselves from war news was through social engagements, and their friends now included Charlie Chaplin and his new (but secret) wife, Paulette Goddard. "We were a little snooty," Anita Loos confessed. "We weren't interested in actors. . . . Our little group never invited any of them except Chaplin. We only wanted amusing people around with wit and intelligence."[62]

Chaplin was five years older than Huxley and poised between the making of his two most political films, *Modern Times* (1936), which Northrop Frye called "an allegory of the impartial destructiveness of humor," and *The Great Dictator* (1940).[63]

On November 30, 1938 (soon after Berlin's Crystal Night, when Jewish shopkeepers were attacked), Aldous and Maria invited Anita Loos, the Chaplins, and the Hubbles over for dinner. Loos sat in the corner; her fine, silky hair hung in a bob across her forehead. She clothed her thin, mannish build in blouses and skirts; tweeds marked her as a professional woman.

Chaplin ended the evening by announcing the subject of his next picture: "a wretched little Jew mistaken for Hitler—satire and propaganda for a joyous world."

Although his former circus buddies complained that Charlie now "didn't mingle with the bunch," even in his most democratic moods, Chaplin yearned for aristocratic privileges such as those of his friend W. R. Hearst. Chaplin—who had once slaved with his family in a public work house—had been making phenomenally successful short films; by 1917, he was earning $1 million a year. Huxley and Chaplin had grown up at opposite ends of Edwardian England's rigid class system, yet in Hollywood they met as equals.

More than equals: friends—though Aldous at times found tiresome the same qualities film critic James Agee also disliked: "a blend of conflict and sensitiveness with icy coldness."[64]

Aldous and Charlie were drawn together in late 1938 by a common abhorrence of war. "How soon we forgot the First World War," Chaplin wrote in his autobiography, "and its torturous four years of dying. How soon we forgot the appalling human debris: the basket cases—the armless, the legless, the sightless, the jawless, the twisted spastic cripples. . . . Like a minotaur, war had gobbled up the youth, leaving the cynical old men to survive."[65] This stance did not win Chaplin favors. He didn't need them; he had his own studio.

Charlie and Paulette weren't getting along, though he still enjoyed watching how every man's eyes followed his "natural-born honeypot," as another of Anita's (gay) friends, British actress Constance Collier, described her. One night Matthew and Aldous dined with Goddard, who was attired in a black velvet dress with a high waist, a thin white bodice cut square, very low. Father and son each told Maria later how the other had fallen for Paulette.

Like Charlie, Paulette Goddard had grown up poor: she and her mother scrounged and picked potatoes on her native Long Island. First a model, then a precocious show girl, she had married young and begun a lifelong collection of precious stones. She had met Chaplin several years before on film financier Joe Schenck's yacht; Chaplin was between pictures and honoring his reputation as Hollywood's best-endowed male. Goddard met Chaplin's requirement that his women be young, malleable, and gorgeous, ready to learn at his hands. In return, Chaplin made an instant sensation of Paulette as the little tramp's companion in *Modern Times*. Charlie and Paulette splashed across *Variety* when the film appeared in February 1936.

Two years later, when Paulette got to know the Huxleys, she'd been waiting for Chaplin's next film for a year and a half. Though the Chaplins did not require marital fidelity, Paulette's wrenching affair with George Gershwin hadn't helped their marriage.

Then Paulette lost the part she'd been angling for—Scarlett O'Hara in *Gone With the Wind*—because she could produce no marriage license (she now claimed to have married Chaplin at sea or on Catalina Island).

The loss affected Goddard profoundly, and she began visiting the Huxleys alone, for, in the genteel phrase of her biographers, "She and Charlie often kidded each other to diffuse potential explosions."[66] Huxley abhorred such scenes as much as he enjoyed going out on the town with Goddard, whose smooth complexion rivaled Garbo's and whose slim, well-proportioned figure and bedroom eyes may have inspired Anita's sequel to *Gentlemen Prefer Blondes, But Gentlemen Marry Brunettes*. According to Mary Anita Loos, Anita's niece, the luscious female vamp in *After Many a Summer Dies the Swan* was drawn from Paulette Goddard.

*S*wan is modeled after the myth of Tithonus, to whom the Greek gods had given eternal life, though not eternal youth.

The opening sequences of the novel are a joy ride through mythotypical Southern California, out to the pleasure dome of a modern Kublai Khan. Many details Maria and Aldous noted in their letters appear: scenes of farm workers ("Transients . . . Come to pick our navels"), descriptions of Forest Lawn Cemetery (the place Waugh later called "a Tivoli garden for the dead" in *The Loved One*), and cynical plotting for war ("the rearmament boom had sent his aircraft shares up another three points").[67]

The murder story begins as a visiting Englishman arrives in California to catalogue papers which Jo Stoyte (a Hearst-like tycoon) has purchased. The Englishman, Pordage (his name reflecting the weight of the older civilization he carries), meets a strange cast: Virginia (Marion Davies) in a white bikini; Obispo, a cynical scientist experimenting with longevity; Pete, an idealist back from the Spanish Civil War; and Propter, a Gerald Heard-like hero. For a subplot of greed and sex, Huxley used L.A.'s Owens Valley water development scandal (later filmed as *Chinatown*) and film-maker Thomas Ince's murder—which gave the novel a docudrama aura similar to John Dos Passos's *U.S.A.* trilogy. (Huxley's literality almost got him in trouble; in his first draft, he actually used Davies's maiden name, Douras, changing it only after Anita Loos insisted.)

By the novel's end, Pordage accidentally uncovers the secret of eternal life (carp intestines!) in a dusty journal; Obispo succeeds in seducing the Davies character; and Pete is shot at Hearst's swimming pool by the jealous magnate, who mistakes him for Obispo. When the remaining characters visit the Fifth Earl of Gonister (the only human to live eternally), they discover that he has devolved into an ape, Aldous's (and T. H. Huxley's) persistent metaphor for men without souls.[68]

In *Swan*, Huxley's ambivalence to the coming war approached schizophrenia. One side of him remained the reformist of *Ends and Means:* a man struggling to learn compassion and to redirect his species away from war, toward practical solutions of decentralization and self-help. Another side, influenced by Heard (and, soon, Isherwood), emphasized a timeless, nonattached transcendence. The Huxley of *Swan* wanted both to be a part of—and apart from—the human predicament, as critic Milton Birnbaum observed.[69]

In writing *Swan*, Huxley inserted himself in three characters, all representing paths not taken.

Pordage is a desiccated, public-school caricature, incontinently fond of esoterica—the academic Huxley might have become. This character had Huxley's habits: "Why on Earth couldn't people live their lives in a rational, civilized manner: breakfast at nine, lunch at one-thirty, tea at five." He shared his early cynicism toward mysticism, his taste for old masters, even his impossibly bad eyes.

Propter, the ex-scholar, embodied the nonattachment Huxley

admired but was unready to embrace. Earnest and robust, he becomes a mouthpiece for Huxley's pronouncements. Thomas Merton uncharitably called him "the dullest character in the whole history of the English novel."[70]

Pordage represents the Huxley who would not sit still for talk of religion; Propter, the quasireligious pacifist Huxley became in desperation, following the crisis of *Eyeless in Gaza*.[71]

Pete represented the modern reformist. "Gee, they were swell guys," the ex-pacifist comments ingenuously about his fellow fighters in Spain, ignoring how their anti-Fascist bullets killed mothers' sons just as dead as those sons killed by Fascist bullets.

Critics have remarked on the novel's wordiness, its fantastic plot, its violent contrasts between wealth and poverty, evil and ingenuousness, but few have explored how the novel embodied *Ends and Means* or why Huxley wrote it at this time.

Swan marked a transition for Huxley. In *Ends and Means*, he had sat on Lawrence's mountain and issued edicts: humanity must ready itself for pacifism and a spiritual awakening, which might take a century. In *Swan*, he applied this credo to modern times. He wrote the book for several practical reasons: the material was rich and at hand, he needed to reassert his Englishness by burlesquing America's myth of success. He had to redeem his reputation in England, where his royalties were sinking as fast as a torpedoed U-boat.

Beyond practicalities, however, Huxley had to write a novel where an idealistic Spanish War vet (Pete) is proved hopelessly naive and a middle-aged cynic (Pordage) incapable of action. For he'd now glimpsed a third way: not optimistic idealism to remake humanity, not repression or cynicism about people's inability to follow the course they knew was right, but a path to the higher ground which united men and women more profoundly than their nationality, gender, or ethnicity.

In *Swan*, Huxley insisted that the quest for immortality by physical means is as pointless as the quest for fulfillment by possessions—in both cases, the end product is reversion to the ape (a theme to be expanded in *Ape and Essence*). Huxley stressed the futility of spontaneous action: whether amassing wealth, appeasing sexual appetites, unlocking nature's secrets, or using violence to achieve nonviolent ends.

Superficially, Huxley had resurrected his well-known satirical voice, perhaps to mollify English critics who were wondering if he'd abandoned it. "Satire," he noted in *Swan*, "was much more deeply truthful and, of course, more profitable than a good tragedy."[72] On a profound level, *Swan* shows the author's struggle for direction. Just as Huxley's phototropism had propelled him relentlessly in search of the sun—along the Italian and French coasts, eventually to California—so now his search for peace led him first into politics and then past political solutions. His glimmer of a solution, which Propter spins out tiresomely, gave him a responsibility beyond satire. That unmelting iceberg at the center of Huxley—what Mann called "his cold attitude toward everything that burns under our skin, the things we love and hate"—had begun to melt.[73] When Huxley reached back for that cynical fillip his readers expected, he found it missing.

When Huxley speared a character like Obispo, he wriggled off the barb. Times had changed. The antiwar salvos of *Eyeless in Gaza* now met a world hoping Nazism and Fascism would miraculously halt in Spain. Huxley saw only the militarism, not the anti-Fascist heroism of events in Spain. His short-sightedness soon isolated him from friends.

"It's good to be cynical," Propter says. "That is, if you know when to stop." Huxley had reached that point by the end of 1938, even if his readers had not.

In the winter of '38 and the subsequent spring, Huxley submerged himself in *Swan* with the reluctance of a writer who yearns to be engaged but regrets the constant burden of carrying around characters and story. "Aldous talked of technical problems of the novel he's writing," Grace Hubble wrote in her journal. "Said he had a passion for the words, the temptation to use them for the pleasure of it. Says he thinks it might be better to write in a plain flat style of narrative, and raised the question of major and minor characters— why should some be minor? I said that was true in life."[74]

Though Huxley rarely discussed works-in-progress, he did so with Grace, once confessing the limits of *Swan* at a dinner party:

"My last novel got away from me and went on developing regardless."[75] Huxley could control speechifying less and less as the years passed.[76]

Throughout the book, Huxley's self-rage boiled over: that pessimism which had darkened his life after his blindness and the sudden deaths of his mother and Trev. Huxley was mad—at Spain, for distracting pacifists from opposing rearmament; mad at others (such as Bertrand Russell and George Orwell), for committing themselves to Spain's defense, at himself, for having opened a door in the wall through which his all-too-vulnerable pacifist sincerity could be seen. Thus not Germany but Spain became the enemy in *Swan*.

Writing *Swan*, Huxley again incorporated contemporary events which threatened his balancing act between pacifism and denial. Pordage complains that "in these last months, since the *Anschluss* and Munich, one had found that the political discussion was one of the unpleasant things it was wise to avoid" (*Swan*, 89). This ostrichlike stand couldn't help but isolate Huxley. When Zeitlin asked him for a statement deploring the treatment of Jews in Nazi-occupied Europe, he declined:

> I used at one point to do a lot of writing letters to the press and signing statements; but recently have been coming to the conclusion that it is better not to do these things, unless there is some specific and concrete piece of good to be gained by doing so—as there was, for example in the case of the Spanish children, where my preface [to They Still Draw Pictures] might serve to raise a little extra money.[77]

Huxley raised funds for Spanish war relief but condemned the fighting; unwilling to sign Zeitlin's appeal, he nonetheless sent his limited funds to Germany to help two political exiles emigrate.

Politics was not his most productive field of action. As he had anticipated in his first political fiction, "The Farcical History of Richard Greenow," he had enjoyed "rousing the passion of the crowd to enthusiastic assent":

> It all seemed tremendously exciting and important at the time. And yet when, in quiet moments, he came to look back on his days of activity, they seemed utterly empty and futile. What was left of them? Nothing, nothing at all. The momentary intoxication had died away, the stirred ants' nest had gone back to normal life.[78]

By March 1939, as the first draft of *Swan* neared completion, Europe looked even grimmer: Madrid had fallen, and Hitler occupied the rest of Czechoslovakia, proving worthless the guarantees of Munich.

As war closed in on them, the Huxleys' work and social lives quickened, blotting out the news. Outings were their favorite relief, Anita remembered:

> Both Aldous and Maria loved picnics; the thought of one made them happy as little children. I recall one particular outing with dramatis personae *so fantastic that they might have come out of* Alice in Wonderland. There were several Theosophists from India, the most prominent being Krishnamurti. The Indian ladies were dressed in saris which were elegant enough, but the rest of us wore the most casual old sports outfits. Aldous might have been the giant from some circus sideshow; Maria and I could have served as dwarves, but with our tacky clothes the circus would have been pretty second-rate. . . .
>
> Greta was disguised in a pair of men's trousers and a battered hat with a floppy brim that almost covered her face; Paulette wore a native Mexican outfit with colored yarn braided into her hair. Bertrand Russell, visiting Hollywood at the time, Charlie Chaplin, and Christopher Isherwood all looked like naughty pixies out on a spree. Matthew Huxley was the only one of the group who was a mere normally disheveled teenager.
>
> The picnic gear was as unusual as the cast of characters. Krishnamurti and his Indian friends, forbidden to cook their food or eat from vessels that had been contaminated by animal food, were weighed down with crockery and an assortment of clattering pots and pans. Greta, then strictly a vegetarian, was on a special diet of raw carrots which hung at her side in bunches. The others could and did eat ordinary picnic fare, but Paulette, to whom no occasion is festive without champagne and caviar, had augmented the equipment with a wine cooler and Thermos cases.
>
> We had started out in several motor cars, with no definite objective except to find a spot where a fire could safely be built. . . . Krishnamurti and the Indian delegation set about cooking their rice. And while the remainder of us were unpacking sandwiches, Greta's raw carrots, and Paulette's caviar, we were shocked by a gruff male voice ringing out with, "What the hell's going on here?"
>
> Stunned into silence, we turned around to face a Sheriff, or some reasonable facsimile, with a gun in his hand.

"Don't anybody in this gang know how to read?" he demanded of Aldous.

Aldous meekly allowed that he could read, but still no one got the man's implication until he pointed out the [No Trespassing] sign. . . . Then Aldous played his trump card. He indicated the presence of Miss Garbo, Miss Goddard, and Mr. Chaplin. The Sheriff's measly little eyes squinted only briefly at the group.

"Is that so?" he asked. "Well, I've seen every movie they ever made," said he, "and none of them stars belong in this outfit. So you get out of here, you tramps, or I'll arrest the whole slew of you."

We folded our tents like the Arabs, and guiltily stole away. It was not until we were in the garden at the Huxley house where the picnic was resumed that we began to think about the titillating headlines . . . "Mass Arrest in Hollywood. Greta Garbo, Paulette Goddard, Charlie Chaplin, Aldous Huxley, Lord Bertrand Russell, Krishnamurti, and Christopher Isherwood Taken into Custody."[79]

California remained a movable feast for Aldous and Maria, sweetened monthly by the arrival of more distinguished expatriates. Bertrand Russell was one of these, taking a post at UCLA after his hoped-for professorship at the University of Chicago vanished. Isherwood was another: a short, square-shouldered novelist with the mind of a de Sade in the body of a football player.

Isherwood, thirty-five, took to Maria immediately. He loved the way her silks rustled as she walked and her hair, which she clipped like Anita's, to frame her piercing eyes. Isherwood found her supremely protective of Aldous and worldly, the kind of woman who smoked in public without apology: "She was unflappable, confident, and nothing I said or did came as a surprise."[80] That was saying quite a lot, as anyone who knew Isherwood would agree.

Isherwood's best-known novels were drawn from his adventures in the early thirties, when he had reveled in Berlin's after-hours sex clubs, producing *Mr. Norris Changes Trains* and *Goodbye to Berlin*. A few years later, he and his lover W. H. Auden boldly covered the China-Japanese war in Manchuria. Following the Munich crisis, he kept his "bargain with fate" and traveled to the United States, "perhaps for always."

"Traveling makes us sadder but wiser," Thomas Jefferson is credited as saying, and worldliness overtook Isherwood's political and sexual radicalism. On the eve of his departure for America with Auden, he remembered, "I was empty because I had lost my political faith. My leftism was confused by an increasingly aggressive awareness of myself as a homosexual and by a newly made discovery that I was a pacifist. . . . What I now needed to learn were positive pacifist values, a pacifist way of life, a Yes to fortify my No . . ."

Christopher had known Gerald Heard and Chris Wood in London; he'd read *Ends and Means* and knew "that Heard and Huxley had become involved in the cult of Yoga, or Hinduism, or Vedanta—I was still contemptuously unwilling to bother to find out exactly what these terms meant. Hindus I saw as stridently emotional mystery mongers whose mumbo jumbo was ridiculous rather than sinister. That Heard and Huxley could have been impressed by such nonsense was regrettable."[81]

Adrift in California, Isherwood was given $2,000 by Chris Wood to launch himself in film. Heard and Isherwood grew particularly close. (Isherwood later portrayed Heard as Augustus Parr in another of his autobiographical docudramas, *Down There on a Visit*.) "To become a true pacifist," Heard told Isherwood, "you have to find peace within yourself; only then could you function pacifistically in the outside world."[82]

Gerald had now begun a drastic program of three daily two-hour periods of meditation. (In the 1980s, movie stars like Shirley MacLaine casually collect omens of previous lives; Heard set out on his spiritual journey with a knapsack full of devotion.)

Unfortunately, Heard's sacrifices demanded the participation of others. Refusing to drive or to maintain a telephone, he nevertheless visited friends and kept appointments as less holy personages do. This meant Maria picked him up to shop or to drive him over to the Hubbles' in Pasadena for tea. She kept his phone messages; besides ferrying her blind husband, she found herself accommodating a mystic who had to be home promptly at six for the evening's sitting.

On the other hand, Gerald could be sweet and attentive, in just the ways Aldous couldn't. When guests came, it was Gerald who poured, who hovered with the hors d'oeuvres, who kept the assembled company laughing. Grace Hubble, who thought him "a bit donnish and ascetic," could never resist one of his parlor tricks: he would stop the guests before tea to insist the leaves steep just the time it takes to recite the Jesuit penitential chant—which he then proceeded to do.

When just the three of them were at home, Gerald could be as devastatingly silent as Aldous. He'd sit at the edge of his chair, motionless but alert with his long, tapering fingers pressed together—a pose which often reminded Isherwood "of a radio operator with headphones over his ears, receiving a message which the people around him couldn't hear. And meanwhile, his pale, brilliant blue eyes would appear to lose focus and go blind—at least to the outside world."[83] When she wasn't irritated about the demands on her time, Maria saw in Gerald "an unknown serenity without egotism."[84] The Huxleys had a guru.

Actually, they had two. Over the last year, both Gerald and Aldous had been meeting with Jiddu Krishnamurti, former world teacher of the Theosophists. Krishnaji's life had been a fascinating one, from his discovery in 1909 on the banks of the Adyar River in Madras, India, by Annie Besant, to his being groomed for his role as a successor for Christ, to his renunciation of all titles and separation from the Theosophists.

Huxley had long suspected the Theosophical Society, crowded as it was with Madame Blavatsky's celestial maildrops and the scandals which one wag eventually summarized as "disturbances in the Mahatmamosphere."[85]

Thus Krishnamurti's renunciations of the Society in 1929, coupled with a lifelong belief in the power of humans to free their spirits from psychological blinders, meshed with Huxley's own drives of the 1930s. For the next two decades, the pair saw each other frequently, often in the company of Krishnamurti's associates, the Rajagopals.

The spring of 1939, so turbulent for Europe, proved a quiet one for Huxley. He was so engrossed in *Swan* that he cut back on visitors and kept largely to himself. Doctors treating him for a relapse of his earlier bronchitis required that he sleep ten hours a night and two per day; his strength returned slowly.

Restless in their new country, the Huxleys moved a fourth time in thirteen months, this time to Amalfi Drive in Pacific Palisades, halfway up Santa Monica Canyon. The house was eccentrically furnished: "The first thing to greet one on entering the hall," Anita Loos laughed, "was . . . a larger than life-size facsimile of King Kong, the Ape Man, in whose hairy arms a sparsely dressed cutie was struggling. . . . The remainder of the decor did Kong full credit; there was a bar that was an Arabian night's dream of dowdy grandeur; red lights revolved and blinked down on a large, stuffed crocodile."[86] Stores were distant, but now that he had all of Hearst's castle to roam in his imagination, this mattered less.

Since Loos's and Salka Viertel's houses stood at the foot of the hill, on Sunday the Huxleys had their choice of brunches and get-togethers. One typical day the gang met at the Chaplins' for lunch: "Tables set in a crescent-shaped arbor by the swimming pool," Grace reported; "guests included Constance Collier, Charlie MacArthur, and Helen Hayes, Lillian Gish." This was company Aldous enjoyed—Maria didn't worry about sudden declarations that he was too sick to dine.

The repast began with Pernod cocktails in shaved ice and continued through curries, salads, and pineapples filled with sherbet, angel cake, and champagne. After lunch, Helen Hayes and Paulette delicately tore apart Norma Shearer, popular MGM actress. Hayes: "She worked too hard to get laughs in *The Women*." Paulette: "I wouldn't laugh at her if she blacked herself all over. Norma is getting a little bunchy around the middle, isn't she?"

This cattiness was catching; as the Hubbles and Huxleys departed at 5:00 P.M. (a long lunch, Hollywood-style), they were walking across the terraced lawn when Aldous laughed out loud: "Isn't it the ugliest house you ever saw?"[87]

Of course, clouds sometimes obscure even the sunniest paradise. Something was happening to Huxley's vision by 1939: he bumped into things; his headaches from reading were more frequent. He learned of a Dr. Bates, whose visual exercises were said to restore sight.

To begin treatment, however, Huxley would have had to give up writing and reading for months. He gave it a try, but the teacher proved inept and Huxley was too keyed up for the exercises to work.

There the matter lay. It took a man at peace, seeking a spiritual grail, to learn the art of seeing.

Previously, Huxley's attitude toward the life of the spirit had been everything one could expect from a smug Oxford intellectual of the 1920s. Now, in *Swan*, Huxley made light of this attitude: "He had read [the literature of Eastern mystics] and been moved by them into wondering whether he ought to do something about them; and, because he had been moved in this way, he had taken the most elaborate pains to make fun of them . . ." (*Swan*, 89, 102).

Yet as Gerald extolled the virtues of meditation and Christopher enthusiastically followed him into classic Hinduism, Huxley looked again. Huxley visited the Southern California Vedanta Society and met its founder, Swami Prabhavananda, a Hindu guru his age.

Grace Hubble quickly noted this new direction: "Aldous and Gerald seem to me, in this pursuit of religion, like two small boys working over a conjuror's box of parlor tricks. No, that isn't quite it, they are looking for magic and power, for the secret word, the open sesame that rolls back the door."[88]

Huxley's changing orientation emerged in letters as he drafted *Swan*. Following the Munich crisis in November 1938, Aldous wrote Julian:

> All this [mysticism], of course, seems rather like fiddling while Rome burns, in view of what's happening in the world. But, then, what is happening in the world, is happening, among other reasons, because people have neglected that side of the psychological problem. Rome burns because it has not been sufficiently fiddled over.[89]

By the time he finished *Swan*, seven months later, Huxley had become more of a believer; he wrote Eva Herrmann:

> For individuals there remain enormous potentialities, both physical and psychological—potentialities which, in the ordinary course of events, remain completely unrealized, but which, if one knows how and is prepared to take the trouble, one can realize. . . . this seems to be about the only sensible and constructive thing that one can do in this lunatic asylum we've got into.[90]

Aldous found himself in the position of Humphry Bogart in *To Have and Have Not:* a cynical, worldly man barely able to dodge the shadow of his own dark vision of humanity.

Fourteen years earlier, Huxley had forecast his current direction in a letter to a friend:

> For me the most vital problem is not the mental so much as the ethical and the emotional. . . . because men are more solitary now than they were, all authority has gone; the tribe has disappeared and every at all conscious man stands alone. . . .
> What's to be done about it? That's the great question. Some day I may find some sort of an answer. And then I may write a good book.[91]

Was *Swan* that book? Not quite, though as he finished the final chapters, he naturally had his hopes. Maria was more ambivalent.

In January, she had sensed the emotional tumult which resulted from Huxley's partition among his characters, but it didn't worry her: "It's good for him to empty himself of these things from time to time. The Great Novels only gain for waiting and ripening."

By June 1939, as the novel was half done, she became apprehensive. Aldous was uncharacteristically hesitant to give her the manuscript to type: "He waited as long as he could, afraid, I believe, that I'd criticize the cynicism with which he described stupidity, mother of all vices and all misfortune. . . . It's pornographic with a vengeance, but there's another side to the book . . . an explanation of theories of *Ends and Means*."[92]

What accounts for this "vengeance" Maria read between the lines, a vendetta not only against believers in idealistic wars but in casual sex?

Despite his enjoyment of female sexuality, Huxley's books require a patient scholar to unearth joyous heterosexuality. The devastating final scene of *Brave New World* may hold the key to his virtually pathological resentment of unmarried sex; there, John the Savage (a man born of woman, instead of a test tube) flagellates himself like a New Mexican *penitente* for his sexual thirsts. He holes up in an abandoned lighthouse only to find himself spied upon via helicopter-mounted cameras and finally seduced into an orgy. When he awakens, the only course left after his sexual transgression is to hang himself: "Slowly, very slowly, like two unhurried compass needles, the feet turned towards the right; north, north-east, east."

Almost twenty years earlier, it was his brother Trev's feet which had turned thus, dangling from a tree in the dark wood after he killed himself for loving (and impregnating) the family maid. "It couldn't have lasted, don't you see?" their stepmother, Rosalind Huxley, intoned later: "Their friends couldn't talk to each other. She wouldn't have been welcome. We sent her off into London somewhere."[93]

Was it sex Huxley never forgave, or was it Trev, his smiling, blond-haired brother—so good with people, so shy in academic competition? Huxley's novels—except the last, *Island*—offer hundreds of instances of the destructive power of sex and the emotional poison of affairs. In person, Huxley was susceptible to cleavage and a sense of humor; in his writing, he mounted a dark campaign against sexual vulnerability.

He fundamentally distrusted the sexual impulse and its accompanying responsibilities. When *Brave New World* appeared, he had written to a friend: "I share with you a fear of the responsibilities of relationships—have only one that counts at all, with my wife—nothing else that commits me in any serious way. [How must Matthew have felt to read this?] It's awful to be committed—but at the same time if one isn't, one gets very little in return."[94]

His best friends in California, his wife, his brother Julian (as a teenager), his sister Margaret—all were homosexuals.[95] Yet no one has found evidence that he himself was gay.

"Aldous was surrounded by homosexuals," Peggy Kiskadden noted. "Why, I don't know. Except that he was interested in the unusual; from books way back he was interested in the odd, and homosexuality may be the most intimate oddness."[96]

War was in the air, even in far-off California. More in touch than Aldous, Isherwood smelled the war panic hovering over the exile community:

> Like all my friends, I said I believed that a European war was coming soon. I believed it as one believes that one will die, and yet I didn't believe. For the coming war was as unreal to me as death itself. It was unreal because I couldn't imagine anything beyond it; I refused to imagine anything; just as a spectator refuses to imagine what is behind the scenery in a theatre. The outbreak of war, like the moment

of death, crossed my perspective of the future like a wall: it marked the instant, total end of my imagined world.[97]

This wall extended to conversation topics. One teatime in January 1939, Frieda Lawrence and Dorothy Brett were visiting California. The latter needled Huxley, as old friends will, asking his feelings about the war. Huxley virtually lost his temper (something his son never remembers him doing), calling Brett "very malicious, like a woodpecker, tap, tap, tap on your sensitive spot." After Heard and Huxley left, the talk turned again to war; few of Huxley's friends made the mistake of discussing the war with him a second time.[98]

Some of Huxley's countrymen in Hollywood tolerated his pacifism no more than they accepted his German friends: "The really disgusting thing at that time, before Pearl Harbor," one English patriot complained, "was that Hollywood was full of Germans. I remember one at a cocktail party proposing a toast to the fall of France, so I threw a lot of glasses at him; they told me to behave because America was still supposedly neutral."[99]

On July 30, 1939, in their new house in Pacific Palisades, the Huxleys awaited a dozen guests for lunch and tea. This was already their third celebration of his birthday. The previous night Aldous and Matthew had gone out on dates wearing boutonnieres Maria had bought; they'd returned at 3:00 A.M.

The hot July sun was tempered by breezes from the nearby ocean; eucalyptus scented the air, and a hockey-stick palm swayed gently: a perfect day for a picnic. The new home had a rambling garden in back, overlooking the canyon. In front, a long redwood picnic table offered drinks and food. Many guests arrived on foot from houses in Santa Monica Canyon, a delicious thought to a lifelong pedestrian. (Greta Garbo lived a few minutes' walk away, as did Eva Herrmann, Salka Viertel, and Mercedes De Acosta.)

First to arrive were the Hubbles; while the astronomer helped Maria set up, Aldous and Grace sat in the swing "being controversial about adultery," as Grace dryly put it.

Aldous had much to rejoice: surrounding him were his good friends, the academy he most enjoyed; it was like having volumes of his precious *Britannica* over for cocktails.

The previous week he'd finished *Swan* after ten months of intense work. By now, he'd virtually forgotten that Hearst had given him a job as a correspondent during the thirties, when he had needed the money badly in southern France. Maria didn't think *Swan* was his best work ("not quite . . . quite," she told Peggy Kiskadden), but its wryness would show readers that he hadn't lost his touch.

Maria was also in good spirits. Aldous had completed his novel, and there was time for a jaunt up the coast to Big Sur. Maria had also completed arrangements to have her mother and her niece, Jeanne's daughter Sophie, come to California. Perhaps in time all her family would be reunited here, where she'd be Queen Bee.

"The rest of the party [arrived] bit by bit till we sat down to lunch in the garden," Grace wrote. "Charlie Chaplin and Paulette Goddard, Charlie MacArthur & Helen Hayes, Constance Collier, Gerald and Peggy, Christopher Isherwood (dark and slight), Matthew and his friend."[100] Paulette brought an eight-pound cake from an English pastry chef: all white, with *"mon coeur"* in red icing. Charlie brought a case of Mumm's Cordon Rouge.

Chaplin launched into high gear, competitive in Huxley's presence: this time it was a story of being threatened by three fierce clams near Monterey. He almost split his throat in the effort.

Amid the general laughter, Huxley relished his latest good fortune: next week he was invited back to work at MGM. Aldous had finally asked Anita if she thought he could return to the studio. "Amused at his humility, I told Aldous nothing could be easier than to find him a job. Next day at the studio, I learned that the outline of *Price and Prejudice* had been finished and it was ready for dialogue. I informed the producer, Hunt Stromberg, that the great British writer was available, and he immediately set up an appointment to see Aldous the next day.

"Soon after their interview my phone rang. Aldous was calling, with Maria on an extension, and their mood was one of gloomy resignation.

" 'I'm sorry,' Aldous said, 'but I realize now that I can't take that movie job.'

"I wanted to know why not.

" 'Because it pays twenty-five hundred dollars a week,' he answered in deep distress. 'I simply cannot accept all that money to work in pleasant surroundings while my family and friends are going hungry and being bombed in England.'

" 'But Aldous,' I asked, 'why can't you accept the money and send it to England?'

"There was a moment of silence and then Maria spoke up.

" 'Anita, what ever would we do without you?' "[101]

As usual, Chaplin did bits from his pictures over coffee and brandy, imitating a sheik ("Chaplin thinks old pictures stand aging") and performing a dance with a balloon from *The Great Dictator*. The comedian's face rippled like a pool in a breeze as he passed from one role to another. Beneath watchful blue eyes, Chaplin was high-strung, about to take an impulsive interest in unpopular causes.

"Then talk went on," Grace continued, "C.C.'s accent and mannerisms became more & more British, until he remained the compleat Englishman; I do not even know whether he realized this chameleon-like change. After lunch we all sat under the eucalyptus tree, and Orson Welles arrived and then Lillian Gish.

"Paulette was ravishingly beautiful, the deep blue brilliance of her large eyes, the silky curling wave of glossy hair, the full red lips, white teeth, and very good nose, and the smoothest skin. She wore a pair of short slacks and a wisp of a brassiere narrowed in the middle by a large square jewel that may have been a sapphire."[102] Huxley chatted with Welles, newly arrived in Hollywood to work at RKO; six months later, Welles would begin *Citizen Kane*, his film on Hearst. The guests thinned out by 7:00 P.M. with Grace and Edwin among the last to leave.[103]

The party was over for the Huxleys and their friends. In five weeks, Poland would be invaded by Nazi soldiers; two days later, England and France would be at war. While Europe bled, the sun still shone in California and Angelinos ignored the war until they saw it in a newsreel. Tea would still be served in the Huxleys' garden, but the Hubbles would host fund-raisers for war bonds.

FIVE
GREY EMINENCE

"For the radical and permanent transformation of personality only one effective method has been discovered—that of the mystics. It is a difficult method, demanding from those who undertake it a great deal more patience, resolution, self-abnegation and awareness than most people are prepared to give, except perhaps in times of crisis."   (1941)

On a stifling August afternoon in 1939, Aldous and Maria drove up the cinder driveway of Edwin and Grace's roomy, white house in Pasadena, whose orange roof tiles were imported from southern Italy.

The day had that paralyzing stillness of the San Gabriel Valley in late summer. Clouds hung in the sky as if pasted on; no wind disturbed the silence. Even the perfume rising from the nearby Huntington Botanical Gardens seemed to float in midair, unable to reach noses sniffing at the flowers.

In the late dusk of August 23, 1939, Aldous and Maria carried in some of the Mumm's Charlie Chaplin had brought to the party celebrating the completion of *After Many a Summer Dies the Swan*. In leisurely fashion, talk turned to contemporary poets—Auden, Spender, and C. Day Lewis; Aldous disavowed them, still smarting at Day Lewis's earlier attack on his pacifism. He considered their contemporary admiration "a curious passing phase."[1]

He spoke with amazement at how wealthy people went through £ 40,000 a year. (Wealth was particularly on his mind. For his work on *Pride and Prejudice* MGM had finally offered half the sum he'd earned on *Madame Curie*, with no guarantee of the number of weeks. He could be terminated on a day's notice.)[2]

The evening ended warmly, with plans to meet the following week. They would talk again the next morning, when they read the headlines. Aldous Huxley and that odd coalition opposing American entry into the war were about to meet unlikely allies.

Hᴜᴛʟᴇʀ ѕɪɢɴѕ ᴘᴇᴀᴄᴇ ᴘᴀᴄᴛ ᴡɪᴛʜ ѕᴛᴀʟɪɴ. The headlines mocked the quiet gathering of the night before. "We could never see the logic of the Hitler-Stalin pact except as a way for the Russians to prepare for the war," Matthew said, pointing to the 1936–1937 purge trials in Russia. "They were knocking off about one third of their officer corps, so they couldn't run an army."[3] The West's efforts at forging an anti-Nazi alliance with Russia had been halfhearted; politicians hoped Hitler would take on the Bear before the Bulldog.

Huxley's private reaction must have been mixed. He distrusted allies who had seesawed between the Oxford Peace Pledge and Collective Security, but for the first time pacifists, Communists, and isolationists had joined ranks to demand political rather than military solutions. (Throughout the period before the war, a bewildering stream of words arrive and vanish as United Front becomes Popular Front, isolationism becomes noninterventionism, pacifism becomes nonbelligerency.)

For pacifists, the pact warmed faint chances of postponing conflict: with Russia refusing to fight, perhaps Britain and France would seize on negotiation. The arguments of Huxley's *Ends and Means* catapulted into vogue. Kurt Weill's *Johnny Johnson* was newly topical; Hollywood brimmed with antiwar plays. Peace singers like the Almanac Singers in New York sang "The Yanks Are ɴᴏᴛ Coming."

Britain naturally viewed the pact as a sign of imminent hostilities. First-aid posts were set up in shops, warehouses, and schools. Windows were boarded, walls sandbagged. After years of listening to apocalyptics like Heard, the British government expected the worst: a quarter of a million casualties in London in the first three weeks of the war. The Ministry of Health distributed a million burial forms to local authorities and stacks of paper shrouds.[4]

Americans continued to hope their country could provide help but somehow escape a fight. This mood cut across parties, classes, regions, from the pacifist War Resisters League to the business-oriented National Council for the Prevention of War. Many still sought Fortress America, proud and on its own.

Citizens of Hollywood reacted to the Hitler-Stalin pact with as much confusion as indignation. Even staunchly pro-British J. B. Priestley asked himself:

> Now what is happening in the real world? . . . Europe is bristling with armaments and gigantic intolerances, Asia is stirring out of her ancient dream, America is bewildered and bitter . . . some men are marching in column of fours, shouting slogans, and making ready to kill and be killed; some men—many of them in exile because their minds are honest and not without distinction—are arguing in a melancholy circle.[5]

Few were more melancholy than Huxley; characteristically, his eyes chose this moment to trouble him. In the past he had made the most of what sight he had. He scanned paintings with a magnifying glass, taught himself to notice sudden flares of color on a forest walk.

Unfortunately, over the last years his one seeing eye had required progressively stronger correction, from six to eight to ten and now to fifteen diopters of correction. Huxley was legally blind and getting blinder.

The connection between exterior visual perception (sight) and interior (vision) has long perplexed physiologists. No one showed the two categories of sight more clearly than Huxley, Kenneth Clark asserted: "The efficient functioning of the physical organ in carrying messages to the brain, and the reception of those messages by a prepared intelligence."[6]

At times, those with apparently perfect sight suffer blindness due to trauma or neural misconnection or to a chemical disorder in the brain. Yet others, with defective eyes, see beyond medicine's ability to explain their talent.

In Huxley's case, direct, undiffuse sunlight determined the sharpness of what he saw. But physiology is only one factor in sight; mood and tension affect perception. The steadily worsening news from

Europe in the thirties coincided with Huxley's gradual but deeply depressing loss of sight.

Aldous Huxley published no autobiography, except via indirect references in fiction and essays. He did, however, publish *The Art of Seeing*, a history of his sight, a telling way to slice a life. Pain and fear rattle beneath his dispassionate tone:

> At sixteen I had a violent attack of keratitis punctata, *which left me (after eighteen months of near-blindness, during which I had to depend on Braille for my reading and a guide for my walking) with one eye just capable of light perception, and the other with enough vision to permit of my detecting the two-hundred foot letter of the Snellen chart at ten feet.*
>
> *For the first few years my doctors advised me to do my reading with the aid of a powerful hand magnifying glass. But later on I was promoted to spectacles. With the aid of these I was able to recognize the seventy-foot line at ten feet and to read tolerably well—provided always that I kept my better pupil dilated with atropine, so that I might see round a particularly heavy patch of opacity at the center of the cornea. . . . I was overcome by that sense of complete physical and mental exhaustion which only eye-strain can produce. Still, I was grateful to be able to see as well as I could.*
>
> *Things went on in this way until the year 1939, when in spite of greatly strengthened glasses I found the task of reading increasingly difficult and fatiguing. There could be no doubt of it: my capacity to see was steadily and quite rapidly failing.*[7]

How much is a hand worth to a painter? What price a foot to a professional soccer player or an arm to a bus driver? Only one quarter of one eye linked Huxley directly to print, helped him visualize the sounds words make on a page. He was forty-five, with many more books to write and a desperate readiness to try anything to hang on to his sight.

Throughout the fall of 1939 and into the winter, Aldous worked at MGM, alongside Christopher, Anita, and Salka. *Pride and Prejudice* (Pee and Pee, everyone called it at the studio) originally starred Norma Shearer and Robert Donat, with George Cukor directing. The film was produced by Hunt Stromberg, about whom Dorothy Parker once complained, "If a physician should tap one of his knees, both of Mr. Stromberg's feet would fly into the air at once, kicking off his shoes."[8] (Parker was unhappy in Hollywood, believing herself "living in Babylonian captivity and working for cretins.")

Huxley's first week passed in an airless cubicle waiting for a phone call from Stromberg to rough out the plot. "They also serve who sit and wait," he joked when Jake Zeitlin stopped by. The furnishings consisted of a desk and a rumpled couch; the windows didn't open, legend had it, so that Thalberg's ghost couldn't get in to see what the writers were up to.[9] The worst problem was that Huxley's cubbyhole lacked sufficient light for him to read—and he found forty earlier scripts piled before him: "It gave one the most peculiar feeling—all this wasted energy, this huge pile of pulp that no one looked at."[10] (Huxley returned to this scene when he savaged the studios in *Ape and Essence*.)

To stretch his legs, he would wander through the empty fifty-foot-high sound stages, big enough to hold a dirigible and cool on the hottest September days. Thick power cables tangled the floor; he stepped among them gingerly in the Godlike atmosphere of the lot, where cities were built in a day and crowds of workmen and extras milled in the alleys like Hebrew slaves at the pharaoh's door. "There is neither day nor night, [only] a kind of Pompeii, but more desolate, more uncanny, because this is, literally, a half-world, a limbo of mirror images, a town which has lost its Third dimension," Isherwood wrote in *Prater Violet*.[11]

Trying to reconcile his simultaneous fascination with Hollywood fiestas and yogic discipline, Isherwood mulled the changes war would bring: "I had better admit to myself that the situation is worse than ever before. It is so serious that I must force myself to be interested in it, to observe it step by step, instead of just staring at it in horror. If the ship really is sinking, one ought to be sending out wireless signals. But to whom?"[12]

Working alongside MGM senior writer Jane Murfin, Huxley struggled to turn out a screenplay divided by scenes and shots, not a novelistic treatment such as *Madame Curie* or a sketch like "Success." There was no room to fudge; either their script was filmable or not. If not, he could be dismissed overnight.

Huxley learned his filmic art on this script, as much as he ever did:

> I work away at the adaptation of Pride and Prejudice for the moment—an odd, cross-word puzzle job. One tries to do one's best for Jane Austen; but actually the very fact of transforming the book into a picture must necessarily alter its whole quality in a profound way.
>
> In any picture or play, the story is essential and primary. In Jane Austen's books, it is a matter of secondary importance (every dramatic event in Pride and Prejudice is recorded in a couple of lines, generally in a letter). . . . the insistence upon the story, as opposed to the diffuse irony which the story is designed to contain, is a major falsification of Miss Austen.[13]

Actually the film would turn out to be a classic (with Greer Garson and Laurence Olivier, directed by Robert Z. Leonard), though Huxley couldn't have guessed this from his daily grind. While he struggled with Austen's saga of class and character, tanks rolled across Germany's border with Poland; England and France declared war.

"LONDON, SEPTEMBER 3RD. ON THIS MORNING'S DECLARATION BY CHAMBERLAIN, DOUGIE CABLES 'ENGLAND TO WIN, FRANCE TO PLACE, RUSSIA TO SHOW.' " So begins a racetrack commentary on World War II from one of F. Scott Fitzgerald's Pat Hobby stories. (Fitzgerald, like Salka Viertel, remained embroiled in the rewrites of Madame Curie.)

As Huxley looked at the world after September 3, 1939, it was neither brave nor new. He had already lived with this war in his imagination for nearly a decade. He was unsurprised by its outbreak and sure of his response: no matter how evil another nation's deeds, fighting with arms was counterproductive. His absolutism led him to refuse to take part in any army, navy, air force—or any group whose purpose was to kill, destroy, or pacify in the name of defense or patriotism.

The day the war began in Europe, the star of Pride and Prejudice, Laurence Olivier, who was finishing his appearance opposite Joan Fontaine in Hitchcock's Rebecca, sat on a yacht near Catalina Island as the news came through the radio. When Olivier finally arrived on the set, confusion reigned. "That autumn morning," recalled Joan Fontaine, "calls to the British Consul in California were placed from every bedside phone before the morning tea . . . should every male and female born under the British flag take the next plane home? Were we needed, expected, commanded?"[14]

Nobody, least of all the British government, had an answer. Calls from Hollywood were eventually answered by a cable from Britain's ambassador, Lord Lothian, urging expatriates to remain, "because the continuing production of films with a strong British tone is one of the best and subtlest forms of British propaganda." If this news had been as widely publicized in England as it was in California, "a lot of ensuing unpleasantness might have been avoided," Sheridan Morley noted.[15]

At home in Britain, talk of the California expatriates conjured up images of starlets on palm-strewn beaches. Commentators in London debated if the Hollywood British would "Do the Decent Thing" or whether they were "Gone With the Wind Up."

Within the expatriate community, distinct groupings emerged: those who, like Olivier, planned immediate departure; those definitely staying, like Aldous; and those with regrets but no immediate plans to leave.

The first group, the departing, were easily understood. Their integrity was unmistakable, even if their tactics for persuading others to return were unorthodox:

> Nigel Bruce would creep up on film sets behind unsuspecting young British actors not yet in uniform and murmur, "Going back to do your bit? Jolly good show. You'll join the RAF, I suppose? Or the RN, what? Or the Army, perhaps? By the way, here's your ticket to London. Nothing to pay. It's the least we old-timers can do, what? About the picture you're making now? Not to worry, old boy; we've organized an immediate release for you. Goodbye, old fellow, and good luck."[16]

The second group, the stayers, were likewise understandable, though the internal pressure required to distance themselves from the war increased steadily until they were mummified in Hollywood's peculiar cloak of unreality. As John Gielgud once heard an assistant director cry on the set of *Julius Caesar*, "All right, kids, it's hot, it's Rome, and here comes Julius."

The third group, those who stayed with regrets, had a minefield of conscience to walk. The ever candid Isherwood noted his "self-accusation, because I'm not in England. . . . I only wish to return because I care what the world thinks of me."[17]

On January 27, *Picturegoer* published a hard-edged piece by Maurice Cowan, suggesting that all British writers, actors, and directors working in Hollywood "be forcibly repatriated, regardless of age, to work in British studios for army pay."[18] Aldous was past draft age, and he couldn't have hit a barrel at ten paces. Even in the last war, before his eyes had weakened, he had been rejected more than once by the War Board. Few were of less direct use to Britain's defense. Nevertheless, a vindictive (and hard-pressed) government could take steps: cutting off royalties, invalidating passports, harassing relatives.

Huxley reacted to the declaration of war with resignation—as if it were already history. It brought the saddest of memories—his lonely days at Oxford while his friends were at the front and his bitter despair at those wounded or dead. "Soon we'll be reduced to writing Hymns of Hate—then we'll be lost," he had written in 1916.[19]

More and more, the words of old friends were newly relevant, such as Ottoline Morrell's comment: "Why is it that yesterday we called death by another man's hand murder or manslaughter, but now it is called glorious bravery and valour?"[20]

Huxley avoided the war talk broadcast through his emigrant community. "News," Huxley wrote, "is one of the great distractions, separating the mind from reality. For this reason the aspiring contemplative must practice self-denial in regard to curiosity, just as he does in regard to any other craving or intellectual dissipation."[21]

At what point does denial turn to outright repression and blind the soul? The declaration of war caught Aldous in a trap every bit as real as the foxholes in central London. While he could not partake of the never-ending patio buffet of patriotism, each defeat for Britain brought a quiet sadness; he was unable either to cheer her wins or mourn her losses. The loudest defenders of nonintervention were also the most anti-European and anti-English; their harangues were more than he could bear. Stymied by opposing sympathies, Huxley's cynicism returned as thickly and suddenly as his bronchitis.

Some suspected Huxley of being anti-Semitic. Salka told of inviting over a young Jewish writer who fawned on the British author; uninterested, Huxley had left.

"Was Aldous Huxley anti-semitic," Isherwood has a student ask in *A Single Man*. " 'No . . .' he repeated loudly and severely, 'Mr. Huxley is *not*.' "[22] The era in which Aldous was born (that of the Dreyfus affair) was institutionally racist, Hugh Kenner remarked: "In those years middle-class Englishmen were wary of intrusions into a social system as sensitive as a Calder mobile, and could be anti-Semitic the way they're still often anti-American."[23] Huxley resented European Jews the way he blamed the Spanish Republic for melting the resolve of pacifists; in both cases he blamed the victims.

Huxley struggled against this legacy. In "Cruelty," an essay written in the early 1930s, Huxley had commented explicitly on Nazism—the sort of statement Zeitlin had hoped for.

> The gusto with which tens of thousands of young Germans have taken to the pastimes of Jew-baiting and Communist-hunting, and the approval with which a majority of the general population regards their beastly activities, are painfully significant in this context. . . . The Nazi movement is a deliberate rebellion against the standards of Western civilization.[24]

In *Ape and Essence*, he gave the dullest character an anti-Semitic hue. And, of course, Huxley satirized more than Jews, consistently roasting clerics, Christians, and Catholics; he was anti-British, anti-Nazi, anti-American (not to be confused with un-American), perhaps even antihuman.

"There's something dismally fixed, stony, sclerotic about most [humans]," Huxley reflected in a letter. "A lack of sensibility and awareness and flexibility, which is most depressing. There seems to be nothing much to be done, beyond . . . making oneself into a little window through which at least some light can be admitted; keeping oneself alive and aware so that at least some point in the vast stony structure shall be in a position to grow and respond."[25]

In this last quote Aldous Huxley pictures himself as an eye—a little window through which light could pass. This metaphor seems appropriate for someone obsessed with the World of Light, as he had called his first published play. When Aldous decided to take the Bates Method seriously, he went through a horrific period of three months when he could not see, read, or write. Giving up his glasses, he plunged into a private twilight. Perhaps this too was denial. Huxley tuned out of his time, sinking into his handicap in order to overcome it. Reaching for his spectacles he found nothing—except that panic of a world unglued.

How infuriating to lose—worse, to give up voluntarily—so much control over life, to accept that a task as simple as making a pot of tea could take a half-hour. Almost against his will, his cranelike arms would reach out for his cup, for a pencil, for anything if not his glasses.

Huxley's glasses were weighty objects, probably half a pound, with inch-thick lenses—or even thicker when he allowed himself the luxury of large frames. Huxley treasured his seeing aids, never setting forth without a plentiful supply of optical glass: on his trip to Central America, he carried two clear, two black, and one green pair of glasses. When he came to the United States, he wore a design John Lennon later popularized: so-called Ben Franklin glasses, with silver-dollar-sized lenses. In Huxley's prescription, the lenses' thickness gave him a hawklike look; as if some tall, predatory bird looked down on the rest of humanity—particularly in an elevator, where his head extended a half foot over the rest of the riders.[26]

If any human being knew what he could and couldn't see, it was Maria. She casually moved objects out of his way, pulled the shades or flicked the switch when they walked into a room. She knew what Aldous needed to feel comfortable—and she made sure he got it, grasping his arm and saying something like "It's Miss Fidgit, dropping by. What a surprise."

When Aldous lacked direct sunlight, a dizzyingly indistinct canvas stretched around him wherever he turned. On winter days, when the fog blew a few hundred feet over the ground, Aldous kept reaching for his glasses like an ex-smoker does for his pack. Walls lost their color until the sun brought its searching rays; patches of color bloomed. He had to hold a flower close enough to kiss to see its dainty heart.

Putting aside his glasses was the first step in the time-consuming exercises developed by oculist Dr. W. H. Bates of New York, who researched ways of reeducating those with defective sight. His theory, elaborated in *How to Improve Your Eyesight*, reads like a television pitch for a rowing machine. Huxley elegized his rather straightforward exercises into Buddhist self-awareness.

For him, the heart of the Bates Method rested not only on breaking bad visual habits (which allowed eye muscles to atrophy) but on committing oneself to several hours per day of exercises and meditations to calm "the interference of the conscious I, whose fears, worries, whose craving and griefs and ambitions are forever interfering with the functioning of the physical origins [of sight]."[27]

To see clearly, he concluded, he had to modify his personality through spiritual, as well as ocular, exercises. When people learned to use their eyes and mind in a relaxed way, vision was improved and refractive errors tended to correct themselves, he wrote in *The Art of Seeing*.[28]

In one stroke, Huxley joined the twin struggles of his life—his burning hunger to see and his quest for inner clarity. Every action taken toward the one brought progress for the other. His overarching drive to improve his sight was only part of a unitary quest for vision which characterized his California years. The Bates Method would finally lead him into that arena between eternal darkness and the midway of spirits.

Cynics wondered if Huxley's self-help experiments with sight didn't show soft-headedness. Huxley missed the irony that Bates's training helped remediate naval recruits past their eye exams.

Few friends appreciated to what lengths Huxley went to salvage his sight. Many heard him retail Bates's arguments against optometry, for treating visual defects with glass (which, Bates was convinced, simply froze eyes in their weakness). In all these accounts, Sybille Bedford noted, "What Aldous did not mention were the hours spent on learning those simple practices, the vigilance, the submission, the tough perseverance. Not to strain, not to stare, is as hard to learn for an urban adult as turning cart-wheels; harder. It needs a patience which, as Maria said, we could only understand if we ourselves had been half-blind."[29]

Just as Dr. Alexander's physical reconditioning helped him out of a nervous breakdown in the midthirties, the art of seeing guided him through the personal crises of world war. In times of great stress, Huxley attempted truly radical self-development.

No one knows what occurred behind his closed eyes, but his published descriptions of meditation suggest what it did for him. In his next book, *Grey Eminence*, he would write:

> The cloud drifted away; he was exposed once more to the light. Patiently, delicately, he opened himself to its purifying and transforming radiance.
>
> Time passed, and a moment came at length when it seemed to him that he was fit to go on to the next stage of contemplation. The mirror of his soul was cleansed; the dust and vapours that ordinarily intervened between the mirror and that which it was to reflect had been laid to rest or dissolved. . . .
>
> Tenaciously he held the beloved image behind his half-closed eyelids; and this time he permitted himself the happiness of that adoration, intense to the point of physical pain, that boundless bliss and agony of compassion. (Grey Eminence, 12)

Huxley could not remain entranced for two hours, as Gerald Heard could. But the more he learned of mental relaxation and discipline, the lengthier his sits became. The more relaxed, the more open he was to the exercises of his teacher, Mrs. Margaret Corbett.

The spiritual discipline to which Huxley turned to bolster his sight was Vedantism (literally, followers of the *Veda*, the ancient scriptures of Hinduism). Vedantists believe the phenomenal world surrounding us is illusion, as are our individual selves; ignorance of our profound unity with a larger spirit, Brahman, condemns us to an unceasing cycle of death and rebirth. Realization of our union with Brahman is *samadhi*, roughly equivalent to Buddhist *nirvāna*, a foretaste of the final state of spiritual emancipation.

To approach this goal, Huxley had only to cross safely Hollywood Boulevard, the same street which had earlier glowed with promise, to Ivar Avenue. There stood that improbable minaret, impossibly white, of the Vedanta Society of Southern California—tucked away a sandal's throw from Hollywood's main street. Gerald and Christopher and Aldous—the three English "beacons" of Vedanta, local residents called them—would meet for the afternoon, meditating in the onion-domed chapel or discussing a translation of the *Gita* with the chain-smoking, westernized Swami. Lotus incense lingered on Huxley's suit like a woman's perfume.

When he returned home, he felt refreshed, his step was looser—and he claimed he saw better. "Vision is not won by making an effort to get it," Huxley decided. "It comes to those who have learned to put their minds and eyes into a state of alert passivity, of dynamic relaxation."[30] His double-edged progress toward sight and insight became an extended—if sometimes mixed—metaphor in his writing:

> *where there is no vision, the people perish. . . . The mystics are chan-nels through which a little knowledge of reality filters down into our human universe of ignorance and illusion. A totally unmystical world would be a world totally blind and insane.* (Grey Eminence, *103*)

At Thanksgiving 1939, the first copies of *Swan* arrived from Harper's bindery. Aldous sent one to Grace Hubble on November 24, thanking her for proofing galleys he could no longer read, since he had stopped wearing his glasses. Fallout from the book was mild, con-sidering Huxley had lambasted one of America's most powerful finan-ciers. The president of Occidental College recognized himself in the acquisitive Dr. Mulge and fired off hostile letters to Jake Zeitlin. He had been ready to dedicate a Huxley-Heard Library of Peace at the college, he said, "and now this . . ."[31] After *Swan's* publication, Huxley was probably also unwelcome at Forest Lawn and at Hearst's dining table—but the mystery is why he never suffered the fate of Orson Welles and Herman Mankiewicz after *Citizen Kane* appeared in 1941, when Hearst blocked the film's distribution and attacked Welles's career. The press baron threatened to publish the sex lives not only of the twenty-five-year-old Welles (who was having a secret affair with married movie queen Dolores Del Rio) but of his distrib-utors. He forbid any Hearst paper to run ads for the film and asked Louis B. Mayer to buy and destroy the film's prints.

If Hearst would be this furious at *Citizen Kane*, how did Huxley get away with *Swan*—particularly while working on Mayer's lot? The answer lies in a fortuitous political coincidence. By the late thirties, Hearst and Mayer had a falling out—over, of all people, Herbert Hoover, whom Mayer unaccountably backed as the savior of the Republican party. Thus, in lampooning Hearst in 1939, Huxley actually tickled Mayer; his job was safe. Had he written *Swan* a few years earlier or later, he might never again have worked in American film.[32]

In England, the publication of *Swan* marked open season on Huxley. An anonymous reviewer for *The Times Literary Supplement* detected "a graveyard aroma of the flesh" about the book; Anthony West excoriated the novel in *The New Statesman* as "Huxley's petition in moral bankruptcy." David Daiches, the critic, revaluated Huxley: "His novels are either a series of character sketches or simple fables or tracts." *Nature* was less kind: "Retreat to mysticism is a poor prescription for the millions who already, through the turn of political fortune, have to face a violent death."[33]

Better news arrived from France: after four years of urging, Jeanne's daughter, Sophie, was leaving for America, where she would live with the Huxleys for two years. Julian was also scheduled to visit in late December.

Aldous had a younger brother's respect for Julian, his senior by seven years—the vulnerable years when Julian brought home the results of his formidable intellectual and athletic prowess. "It must have been impressive to a youngster at prep school to see Julian getting the Brackenbury Fellowship," Julian's wife reflected, "the Newdigate Prize, the Oxford Blue, the brilliant First in his final exams. Julian, nevertheless, always recognized in Aldous a superior quality, with some greater dimension to his mind."[34] Aldous and Julian had been competitors since Aldous's days at Garsington, when Julian had married black-haired and bright-eyed Juliette, a beautiful Swiss governess hired by Ottoline. Julian's intimidating successes brought Trev self-rejection; how fortunate that Aldous was only briefly in Julian's shadow.

Now director of the London Zoo, Julian had received a grant to lecture at Stanford and stopped en route in L.A. There was family business to discuss: Julian and Juliette's marriage was severely tried after Julian had adopted his brother's nonmonogamy.

Difficulties had started when Julian had been sent to East Africa to study biology education, leaving Juliette at home with their two sons. On board ship, he had fallen dizzily in love with a scintillating, headstrong American girl of about eighteen. His letter to Juliette stated his intent to pursue the affair and "his entire right to do so, while he swore his continued devotion to me, from whom he was taking absolutely nothing," Juliette wrote. "I found myself instantly deprived and lost, an empty shell, aware only of my total deadlock and immense sense of failure."

When Ottoline heard what had occurred, she took Juliette off to a shop in Knightsbridge and bought her a red dress. "But I took it back the next day, not even unpacking the tissue papers wrapping it. I often think of that dress, and my obscure rejection, rejecting in so doing also a renewed self.

Julian had made it quite clear that the freedom he demanded for himself was mine in equal measure, that I could take a lover if I chose, and that he would, implicitly, accept the situation. I was too far gone into an obsessive neurosis to find this funny or to resist the advice of a woman doctor I was taken to see, who told me: 'Take a lover, and I will give you the contraceptive.' . . .

"So, in a kind of desperation, I broke my taboo and took the lover as a sort of medicine: a kind man, whose grave honesty appealed to me."[35]

This saga unfolded in the hectic week Julian was in town. While Julian's (and Juliette's) new friendships were unconventional—and unconcealed, for Julian couldn't be bothered—Aldous's forays were motivated by perhaps the best excuse a husband has.

Huxley called his affairs "brief candles." In a short story, "After the Fireworks," he wrote the *modus amandi* of a famous novelist with a smitten admirer. First came the initial attraction:

> *You love the celebrated man, who was not only unsnubbing and attentive, but obviously admiring. Even before you saw him, you vaguely loved his reputation, and now you love his odd confidences. You love a kind of conversation you haven't heard before. You love a weakness in him which you think you can dominate and protect. You love— as I, of course, intended you to love—a certain fascinating manner.*

Then the sexual self-revulsion so characteristic of Huxley's characters appears (the hero comes down with hepatitis after his first sexual encounter):

> For a time will come when the freshness of young bodies, the ingenuousness of young minds will begin to strike you as a scandal of shining beauty and attractiveness, and then finally as a kind of maddeningly alluring perversity, as the exhibition of a kind of irresistibly dangerous vice. The madness of the desirer—for middle-aged desires are mostly more or less mad desires—comes off on the desired object, staining it, degrading it. (Brief Candles, pp. 319–320)

"Maria told me she had to write Aldous's good-bye letters; he never would," said Peggy Kiskadden. "She said it was obvious when Aldous began to lose interest, but he didn't know how to stop."[36]

If Julian shared Aldous's attraction to other women, he also shared its dark side—both had lost their brother to unbridled passion. Julian's autobiography is studded with asides like "Why is sex both an inspiring blessing and primal curse, inflicting guilt as well as joy?"[37]

The brothers Huxley toured Walt Disney's studio of 1,200 employees on December 21, 1939, talking their way in to see *Fantasia's* rushes. Julian lectured at the California Institute of Technology, then ate Christmas dinner at the Chaplins'. Christmas lights bobbed on the hedges outdoors. The next night, Aldous and Maria hosted a dinner in Julian's honor, inviting Ronald Colman, George Cukor, Grace and Edwin, Anita and John, and Bertrand Russell.

Russell had visited Huxley after arriving in the United States to lecture at the University of Chicago. Now that he taught at UCLA, where his two children were enrolled, he was often included in gatherings. If conversation over cocktails touched on pacifism, controversy was guaranteed. The Hubbles were vocally interventionist—and Russell had begun to lean in this direction. The nonaggression pact infuriated him, for if he detested any leader more than Hitler, it was Stalin.

Russell became an American oddity rather quickly. *Time* poked fun at the earl's offbeat appearance: "Bertrand Russell has bright blue eyes, a big nose, very little chin and looks like Alice in Wonderland's Mad Hatter. . . . [His] married life has been unconventional." His first wife, a Quaker, divorced him in 1921 because he was about to have a child with another woman. His second wife shared his view that people should 'indulge in infidelity to preserve their homes.' In 1933, she announced that she had a child by a British journalist. . . . Next year, at age 64, Earl Russell married his former secretary."[38]

One guest omitted from the gathering was Gerald Heard. Julian passionately disliked Aldous's closest friend: "Gerald was a strange character. Behind his secretarial efficiency there was a strong strain of mysticism, which I am sure influenced Aldous when they both went to live in California. Gerald even went so far as to found a new church with its own ritual and prayers. I later attended one of the services and found the whole thing ridiculous."[39] Big brother resented the captivating Irishman for his predominance over Aldous.

All this entertaining strained Huxley's fragile constitution and dampened his enthusiasm about returning to the studio. On January 14, 1940, Aldous wrote Julian: "No news here. Pee and Pee drags on—not through any faults of the writers and directors, but because we cannot get to see our producer without whom nothing further can be done. If he does get round to seeing us, it will all be finished in a few days."[40] (Huxley was asked back on half salary through February.) By this point he had seen enough of what biographer Bosley Crowther called Mayer's "expensive vulgarity." Huxley had been required to shift Austen's novel forty years ahead to justify more elaborate costumes, the plot had been simplified, and, in revision, some favorite bits of dialogue had been dropped as too literary. One significant scene remained, however, one he reworked more than any other. At a key juncture in the movie, a friend of the wealthy local squire Darcy discloses how a match across classes was prevented.

"Darcy's taken an infinite amount of trouble to save the young man from an impossible marriage," Fitzwilliam says, not realizing that he's speaking to the sister of the girl involved.

"Impossible? In what way impossible?" she answers ingenuously.

"I understand there were some very strong objections against her family. Common, vulgar people . . . *you* know."

This passage, reworked in pen, pencil, and Huxley's extra-large type, parallels his own family tragedy. He had not forgotten his stepmother Rosalind's handling of Trev's affair with the family maid; Austen's anger at strangling class prejudice avenged a private sorrow.

"We have had a great disappointment several days ago," Maria wrote Jeanne soon after revisions on Pee and Pee ended. "You know Aldous is paid a regular stipend from his publishers. This isn't large and only once have we fallen in debt, and then not by much. . . . When the accounts arrived the day before yesterday, Aldous discovered that he owed them 9,000 dollars."[41] No matter how much they saved from MGM, they would always have this "enormous sum" hanging over them. The shock saddened them, for they had counted on studio earnings to set them up in America.

Then more bad news: Huxley's longtime agent, Ralph Pinker, was suddenly found to be bankrupt—after he had siphoned funds from his writers' accounts to keep afloat. Royalty checks to Huxley's London account simply stopped arriving and he didn't find out until his checks bounced. By the time the matter was settled, he had lost nearly $3,000. This loss, on top of their withheld British income, effectively marooned them in the United States.

Part of the problem, Maria guessed, was that Aldous should have relied on *new* books to generate income; back sales were insufficient. And then, Huxley's productivity had declined in the United States— one book for 1937, none in 1938, one in 1939—from an author who used to meet a three-books-per-year contract.

Huxley's experience with debt was Sisyphean; he rolled his typewriter up the mountain, turning out books with the nagging sensation that they could have been improved with more time. Yet rushing his work never kept him ahead of debt, no matter how modestly he lived (the age-old dilemma of free-lance writers). Bills for the oculist—four times weekly—and the doctor—twice weekly—threw Aldous and Maria into the financial situation they most disliked: daily economies. They weren't much ahead of where they had started when they married in 1920, back in Hampstead when Maria had heated soup on the pilot of their kitchen hot-water heater.

The financial setbacks touched off a sickness unresponsive to medical care. "Meanwhile, I have been unable to do any work," he wrote Julian, "an inability enhanced by the situation of the world, which is singularly unpropitious to the production of works of art.

. . . I wish one could see much hope even in the event of the best possible outcome of the war—that the future will be anything but a descending spiral."[42]

Huxley's own life spiraled downward in the spring of 1940. Recurrent illness, financial disaster, the trauma of giving up glasses, attacks in Britain—all took their toll. Waugh was wrong: Huxley had held to his opinions past the new year. He did so even when this cost him attacks from Britain. "Huxley's mood darkened," remarked David Fine, a literary historian of Los Angeles. "His long-shot hope that individual Propters on the margins of society would somehow rescue mankind on the brink now faded."[43]

Of course he wasn't the only one disappointed in the war's course: April 9, the Nazis invaded Norway; May 10, Amsterdam; May 10, Brussels—and Maria's family were again forced from their homes, traveling by foot for France alongside German infantry. In Hollywood, cars of British drivers displayed a new medium, the car sticker: a Union Jack with words written across it, ALONE AND AFRAID.

In the 1936 film *Things to Come*, based on the H. G. Wells work, the author imagined the voices of American isolationists as saying, "The horrors of war—don't we rather overdo that song?" and "This little upset across the sea doesn't mean anything—they're crying wolf." Reality soon overtook this scenario. Explosions cracked and whined across the continent, plaster puffed from falling walls, and blood stained the rubble a hideous tomato red.

In Britain, the pressure to attack those left in Hollywood increased. On April 2, 1940, Harold Nicolson dined in London with Kenneth Clark, W. Somerset Maugham, Mrs. Winston Churchill, and actor Leslie Howard. He wrote, "We all regret bitterly that people like Aldous Huxley, Auden, and Isherwood should have absented themselves. They want me to write a *Spectator* article attacking them. That is all very well, but it would lose me the friendship of three people whom I much admire."[44]

By April 19, however, Nicolson was persuaded. In *The Spectator*, he wrote, "How can we proclaim over there that we are fighting for the liberated mind, when four of our most liberated intellectuals refuse to identify themselves with those who fight?"[45]

This was followed in *The Spectator*, a few tense weeks later, by an epigram from the Dean of St. Paul's:

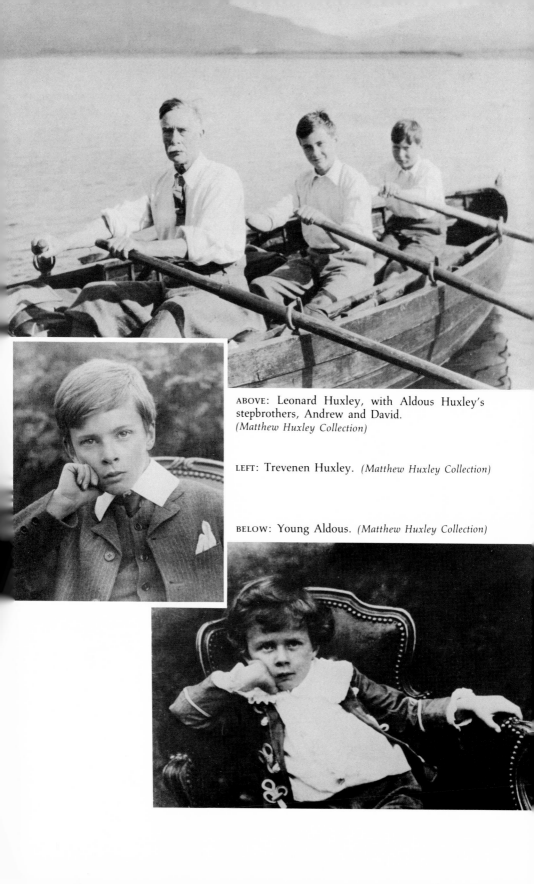

ABOVE: Leonard Huxley, with Aldous Huxley's stepbrothers, Andrew and David. *(Matthew Huxley Collection)*

LEFT: Trevenen Huxley. *(Matthew Huxley Collection)*

BELOW: Young Aldous. *(Matthew Huxley Collection)*

RIGHT: Maria Nys (Huxley), at Garsington (near Oxford), 1914. *(Matthew Huxley Collection)*

ABOVE: Aldous Huxley with son Matthew, approximately 1923. *(Matthew Huxley Collection)*

RIGHT: Huxley family portrait, early 1930s. *(Matthew Huxley Collection)*

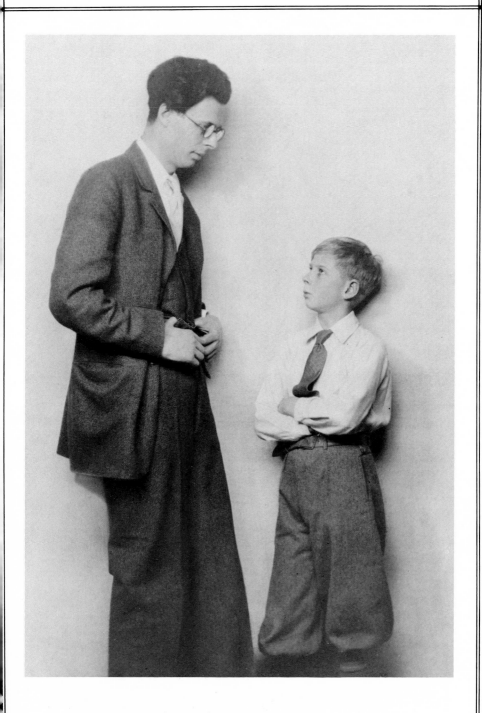

Aldous and Matthew Huxley, early 1930s. *(Matthew Huxley Collection)*

ABOVE: Publicity still
for *Point Counter Point*, 1928.
(The Huxley Family)

RIGHT: Aldous and
Maria Huxley, early 1930s.
(Matthew Huxley Collection)

RIGHT: Drawing by
David Low, portraying
Aldous Huxley and the
Reverend Dick Sheppard
saying, "We won't
fight anybody" to
Mussolini and Hitler,
who answer "Anybody
includes us, pal."
1936. *(Tate Gallery)*

ABOVE: Mabel Dodge Luhan, Frieda Lawrence, and Dorothy Brett, near the Lawrence ranch, New Mexico, 1935. *(Photograph by Cady Wells, Courtesy of The Great Southwest Books)*

RIGHT: Aldous Huxley and Gerald Heard at Black Mountain College in North Carolina, at the beginning of their drive across the United States, 1937. *Matthew Huxley Collection)*

LEFT: Entryway to Huxley's cabin on the Lawrence ranch, San Cristobal, New Mexico.
(David King Dunaway)

RIGHT: Oceanside house and pool of Anita Loos, Santa Monica, California.
(David King Dunaway)

LEFT: Huxley house in Llano, California.
(David King Dunaway)

RIGHT: Behind the Huxley house: swimming pool, water tank, and San Gabriel Mountains.
(David King Dunaway)

ABOVE: Thalberg Building, Metro-Goldwyn-Mayer lot, Culver City, where Huxley, Loos, and Isherwood wrote in the mid-1930s. *(Photograph by Bob Plunkett. Courtesy of Jim Heimann.)*

BELOW: Gerald Heard, Christopher Isherwood, and Swami Prabhavanda, early 1940s. *(Photograph by William Caskey. Courtesy of Don Bachardy.)*

This Europe stinks, you cried, swift to desert
Your stricken country in her sore distress.
You may not care, but still I will assert,
Since you have left us, here the stink is less.[46]

Not only was Huxley savaged for keeping to his pacifism; word of his, Heard's, and Isherwood's Hinduism prompted cheeky comments: "Mr. Huxley and his ally, Mr. Heard, will be lucky if they do not wake up some morning to find themselves transformed into yogis and installed in one of those Wizard of Oz temples that puff out their bubble-like domes among the snack bars and the lion ranches."[47]

Swan's satire was welcome, but by 1940 Huxley wasn't as funny from a far-off shore. His metaphor of an English earl struggling to preserve his life span was poorly received in a country fighting for survival. Heard, Huxley, and Isherwood seemed to be boycotting Europe, customers waiting for new management before returning to a restaurant.

Even if his agent hadn't embezzled them, Huxley's royalties from English sales dropped to an all-time low. The man widely considered Britain's foremost novelist after World War I seemed disturbingly foreign to the generation which had idolized him only a decade before.

The downward spiral continued, as it had at the time of *Eyeless*. The more his royalties dropped, the deeper he fell into debt. The more deeply in debt, the more depressed and ill he grew. Strain brought swellings all over his body, "alternated or accompanied by intestinal upsets and bronchial flare-ups . . . I'm trying to deal with the beastly thing before it deals with me," he wrote to Julian.[48]

This new, inexplicable illness blocked his writing. He gave up on a book he'd started, about

> a man who offers himself as a corpus vile *for a prolonged exper-*
> *iment in the hibernation treatment which they are now using for can-*
> *cer and heart disease—and who is kept on ice for a couple of centuries,*
> *when he is woken up, and finds himself in a different and better kind*
> *of world.*[49]

With this idea, Huxley mined an American literary-prophetic tradition: the man who escapes the current world to wake in another, better one. Storytellers in New England had such a character in Rip Van Winkle; Twain wrote similar stories, notably *A Connecticut Yankee in King Arthur's Court*. Edward Bellamy's *Looking Backward*—for which Aldous had written a preface—also used a similar plot (and spawned forty imitations in the decade it appeared). Why did Huxley abandon this project? In the best of times, his imagination would have strained at such a world; he always was better at dystopia than utopia. As war closed in, he was even less able to hope for humanity.

Huxley might have borne his difficulties more lightly had he had more confidence in the industry on which he depended to meet family responsibilities. He was beginning to agree with Dreiser: "This region is stuffed with hard-boiled savage climbers. . . . arrogant, insolent, and contemptuous."[50] As Budd Schulberg commented sardonically at this period: "What we need is more men out here who think of pictures as a commodity like any other—and forget this prestige business.

" 'That's exactly what I've been saying,' Sammy jumped in. 'After all, pictures are shipped out in cans. We're in the canning business.' "[51]

In the early forties, the studios underwent a slump and retrenchment—caused by the sudden wartime loss of up to 90 percent of their overseas revenue; at the same time the industry moved toward an endorsement of U.S. intervention in Europe. There are at least three ways to read this last development: as the erotic and patriotic attraction of any war, as the Hollywood film industry finding its conscience, or as an after-the-fact effort to cash in on growing anti-Fascist sentiment.[52]

Salka Viertel and others had unsuccessfully tried to make anti-Nazi films before major European markets had closed; the best that could be done was to set up a program to resettle exiled writers and artists fleeing Nazism by hiring them as inexpensive skilled labor. One writer included in this program was Heinrich Mann, Thomas's elder brother.

The Manns had finally made America their new home. Thomas had excellent connections and did not rely on Anita, Salka, or Aldous for help: after all, *Life* had run a story on him in 1939, and he'd just completed a novella, *Lott in Weimar*, while a visiting professor at Princeton. Strangely enough, Mann kept a permanent distance from American culture; though he wrote a half-dozen volumes during his time here, none were set in America.

"I have what I wanted," Mann declared of Southern California, "the light; the dry, always refreshing warmth; the spaciousness compared to Princeton; the holm oak, eucalyptus, cedar, and palm vegetation; the walks by the ocean which we can reach by car in a few minutes." Also, they had friends—the Bruno Walters, the Leonhard Franks—and two of their children, Klaus and Erika.[53] Mann treasured not only the climate but the opportunity to live again at the nexus of German art—even in America. "He hazarded that not even Weimar in its Goethe-Schiller heyday could have boasted such an array," according to one of Brecht's biographers.[54]

Stravinsky also arrived in May 1940, just as the Germans were closing in on Paris (where he'd lived since 1934). Now a double refugee—he had been on blacklists of both Stalin and Hitler—Stravinsky had sailed for America the week war had been declared to lecture at Harvard. By December, he had the opportunity to see what Walt Disney had done to his *Rite of Spring*, which the film-maker had used as part of the score for *Fantasia*. (The studio had offered him $5,000 for it, pointing out in typical Hollywood fashion that since the work was not copyrighted in the United States, it intended to use it anyway.) In March of 1940, the composer married again and moved to the coast, attracted, like the Huxleys, by the warmth and dryness, which he hoped would help him avoid the fate of his first wife and daughter—tuberculosis.[55]

Bertrand Russell too had settled in California. He had passed a cozy evening with Aldous at Christmas 1939, when Julian was in California; then everyone had sat on the living room floor and discussed astronomy with Edwin Hubble. As the summer of 1940 began, however, Aldous and Bertie grew less chummy. With German soldiers twenty-five miles from Dover, Russell's attachment to England melded with his distrust of the German-Russian accord, and he finally committed himself to Britain's war effort. "I am still a pacifist in the sense that I think peace the most important thing in the world, but I do not think there can be any peace in the world while Hitler prospers," he wrote to Elizabeth Trevelyan. He summed up his change of heart somewhat limply: "Being away from home makes one more patriotic."[56]

Russell's position gave Huxley the most exquisite intellectual indigestion. Rather than argue the point, however, he found himself defending his friend against a vile blacklisting campaign.

Russell had been offered a professorship in logic by City College of New York and had submitted his resignation to UCLA—before the offer was official. Soon the letters columns to the *New York Times* filled with wild denunciations of Russell's provocative book *Marriage and Morals*. The Jesuit periodical *America*, in a hysterical outburst of consonance, called Russell "the desiccated, divorced, and decadent advocate of sexual promiscuity . . . who is now indoctrinating the students of the University of California." Another opponent of Russell's telegrammed Mayor Fiorello La Guardia, "Quicksands threaten! The snake is in the grass! The worm is busy in the mind!"[57]

When a Catholic judge revoked Russell's appointment as "in effect establishing a chair of indecency"—as if Russell was hired to teach foreplay, not logic—Huxley wrote: "Sympathy, I'm afraid, can't do much good; but I feel I must tell you how much I feel for you and [Russell's wife] Peter in the midst of the obscene outcry."[58] That Huxley expressed his support—at the very time Russell published his defection from pacifism—shows character. There were few allies in pacifism Aldous would rather have kept. Huxley and Russell met at the Hubbles the following month and talked about everything but war, Grace recorded. At dinner, Aldous expounded on the migration of eels. "I don't believe a word of it," Bertie good-naturedly challenged.

Huxley attributed his friend's troubles to "anti-foreign sentiment growing increasingly stronger in America as the war continues."[59] Russell provoked an ugly streak in American consciousness— as common as a snake, as virulent as a shotgun rack in a truck, as knowledgeable as the Know-Nothings of the nineteenth century. Americans in the forties could no more appreciate the British philosopher's sexual unorthodoxy than they could accept a pacifist in wartime. The House Committee on Un-American Activities (HUAC) was barely two years old and eyeing Hollywood, but fears of un-Americanism predate the Declaration of Independence.

Meanwhile the flow of British citizens to California continued; Hollywood teemed with expatriates. The *New York Times* suggested that while the situation was not yet at the alarming stage, it was "nevertheless giving some concern to certain people."[60] (One of these was Hearst, who, according to Welles biographer Barbara Leaming, threatened "an attack on [Hollywood's] widespread employment of aliens at the expense of American labor.")[61]

Meanwhile, in Britain, the controversy over errant artists continued, with E. M. Forster defending and J. B. Priestley and Louis MacNeice attacking. *Picturegoer* reported that studios were "bribing" actors not to return to Britain and thereby "sabotage" films worth millions of dollars.

At every step in his deepening spiritual crisis—being of, but not in, Britain—Aldous Huxley had a choice: he *could* have gone back. His return would have provided only moral support, but that might have been sufficient. Instead, Huxley continued his denial and distancing from war:

> To become ill with sympathy and anxiety is the one sure way of widening the scope of the war—to carry the devastation into a region which physically should be spared. One creates evil in oneself and in one's surroundings and one can then do no good for those who suffer far away. The possibility of curing the evil depends on our own strength at the moment when the opportunity to intervene is offered. It is, therefore, absolutely necessary to conserve and nourish this strength; not to dissipate it in allowing one's sympathy to overwhelm our health and our morale.

Other emigrants chose to return. The religious philosopher Dietrich Bonhoeffer, for example, had come to the United States with excellent prospects for staying safely through the war. Yet a month after arriving in New York, he was on a ship back to Germany, planning to refuse the draft and thus be sent to prison and death. "I have come to the conclusion that I made a mistake in coming to America," he wrote Reinhold Niebuhr. "I will have no right to participate in the reconstruction of Germany after the war if I do not share the trials of this time with my people."[62]

Maria shared the same worry: "When it is over, we cannot possibly make up [for being absent]; there will be an uncommunicableness that only a long, long time can make up. I went through it after the last war."[63]

What might Huxley have faced as a wartime pacifist in Britain? The diary of pacifists Frances and Ralph Partridge offers clues. As the war began, the Partridges' friends were interrogated by the army and local police on charges of having "signaled the enemy" with a flashlight. Then on April 3, 1940, the Partridges learned of Hitler's long-dreaded "spring offensive":

> We were jerked back into the war like fish that have forgotten for a bit that they are on the end of a hook. . . . Air-raids, invasion, refugees—one's body reacts with a taut restlessness, as though one had a lump of lead for a stomach and sensitive wires from it reaching to toes and fingers.[64]

Like Huxley, the Partridges were also angry with Russell: "Bertie should not (as a pacifist who has recanted after fleeing from the war to the security of the U.S.A.) tell all of us who are still 'in' it that he finds war less terrible than he expected and has therefore decided we must go on with it."[65]

By June 1940, Continental Europe (except France and Switzerland) was in Nazi-Facist hands; an air attack and invasion of Britain loomed. The fall of Paris was particularly frustrating to the Huxleys: Paris had symbolic weight for Aldous. Two years earlier, he had characterized its downfall as proof of evil: "Life in what the Christians would call a 'fallen world' entails the siege of Paris, etc., just as it entails the simple pleasures of sensuous, instinctive, and emotional satisfaction. . . . The only alternative is Reality, the Kingdom of Heaven, Nirvana, etc."[66]

These "alternatives" may have preoccupied Huxley as he trudged down the hill to Anita Loos's at dusk on the night Paris fell. Tiny points of light glistened on the edge of Santa Monica Bay. The wind blew a dark, moist breeze from the ocean, with the menacing face it turns to a soul in torment.

Dinner was laid in Loos's seaside dining room. "I remember the night when Paris fell," she wrote. "A number of our group came to dine at our house. When Aldous arrived his face was dead white, he bore the expression of someone who was peering into hell; but the talk was mostly some sort of scientific discussion between Aldous and Edwin Hubble. Nobody mentioned Paris."[67]

A few British pacifists, including Huxley's friend Desmond MacCarthy, thought Britain should sue for peace to make the best terms possible with Hitler. Senator Key Pittman of Nevada, chairman of the Senate Foreign Relations committee, felt it futile for Britain to resist; it would be more sensible, he suggested, if the population emigrated to Canada and left the British Isles to their new owner.[68] In Britain, members of the Peace Pledge Union were called cowards, disloyal, treacherous—even treasonous. Soon after this interview with a Ministry of Information spokesman was published, leaders of the PPU were successfully prosecuted for interfering with recruiting. The focus of the case was a poster: WAR WILL CEASE WHEN MEN REFUSE TO FIGHT. WHAT ARE YOU GOING TO DO ABOUT IT?[69] Huxley—who'd borrowed this slogan for a pamphlet—might have met the same fate as Russell in World War I.

After a direct appeal from Maria, Jeanne left Paris before German troops streamed in. Panic-stricken crowds jammed the roads out of the city, an incredible confusion of cars, taxis, ambulances, and bicycles. Most people slept along the road, *Time* reported, with water scarce and the smoke from battle turning white blouses gray. From all directions, Jeanne heard the drone of sirens and the unearthly low rumble of armed tanks. "Our main anxiety is for Maria's mother and sisters," Aldous wrote to Julian in July. "Her mother and [her sister] Rose, with baby daughter Olivia, got out of Brussels and, after frightful days on the road, got to Bordeaux [just as Marshal Petain was forming his surrender cabinet there]."

"We were making arrangements to get money through," Aldous continued, "when the curtain drops again. Goodness knows where they are now." Maria hoped they had been repatriated to Belgium; Aldous, that they had found a safe farmhouse. A wave of powerlessness surged over the Huxleys: what could they do? Letters and checks weren't arriving; and if the war went on, Aldous finished, "there will be famine conditions in Belgium by the winter."[70]

The fall of Paris splintered the Huxleys' community like hairline cracks across a windscreen.

He and Gerald Heard began to see less of each other. "Gerald no longer quotes Aldous when one asks him questions or defers to him," Grace noticed. "Gerald is very much on his own road, with no side roads."[71] The split had begun earlier, perhaps out of Aldous's effort to placate his older brother's disapproval. Julian had criticized Heard's new book, *Pain, Sex, and Time;* two weeks before Julian's last visit, Aldous had agreed, calling the book—on the anthropological basis for aggression—"a quite unnecessary confusion of issues."

Personal rather than intellectual reasons underlay their falling-out. Heard was getting on their nerves. Maria particularly disliked his directives on when to pick him up for shopping, when to bring Aldous. He went for walks on his own schedule, and only near his house. He refused to vary his outfit of blue jeans, work shirts, and sneakers. He would look sharply at his watch when it was time for his meditation and make Aldous wait outside—even if Maria hadn't returned for him. Maria called him "a dictator—spiritual—but the danger is the same. . . . He makes no effort to see us, complains about where we live . . . he won't even come visit because he can only leave the house two hours at a time because of his meditations."[72]

The same spiritual competitiveness undermined Huxley's friendship with Isherwood, who had thrown himself in the Vedanta Society as Huxley never could, for Huxley and Prabhavananda were "temperamentally far apart": "Prabhavananda was strongly devotional. Aldous was much more akin to his friend Krishnamurti, who expounded a philosophy of discrimination between the real and the unreal."[73]

Isherwood submerged himself in the Ivar Avenue monastery, editing its publication, *Vedanta and the West,* and amazing himself with his reverence. As part of his obligations, he renounced sex—active sex, at least, if Tennessee Williams's word can be taken. The playwright visited Ishyvoo—as friends began calling him—at the monastery; immediately attracted, Williams declared himself. Isherwood suggested that his vows said nothing about passive participation in sex.[74]

Aldous visited Christopher and the swami regularly but was more an intellectual seeker than someone comfortable at the alter. Outflanked spiritually by Heard and Isherwood, Huxley also withdrew from the Hubbles.

Grace never was persuaded—as many of Maria's friends were—that taking Aldous to bed would be a delightful experience. Huxley wasn't one to force an issue. Unfulfilled attraction often sours friendship, but not in this case. Nor was the problem Edwin, who apparently didn't notice his wife's attraction.

Unlike the schisms with Heard and Isherwood, what forced the Hubbles and the Huxleys apart was neither personal nor intellectual but political. Grace and particularly Edwin vehemently opposed any delay in supporting the war. Of course, even Edwin could be cynical on the subject, as in one lecture to local dowagers: "The younger men will go to war like a shot because they won't want to miss the show; the older men will go to get away from their wives." ("This was not well received," Grace noted icily.)[75]

There were no heated arguments, no ruptures. The Huxleys still enjoyed Edwin's fishing stories and the telescopes on Mount Wilson, but war had opened a fissure. The Hubbles worked on William Allen White's Aid the Allies drive; on July 3, over tea, Grace and Anita Loos talked about the approaching rally, but "Aldous is silent when war is discussed. Maria tells us she makes an *examen de conscience* every night in bed before she goes to sleep. . . . Good time, but talk spotty."[76]

The Huxleys even had a tiff with the Manns over America's treatment of exiles: "Thomas was peaceful and pacifying; she [Katia] was hating and violent and we would not discuss it; besides—to be rude about America while you have to remain in it."[77]

In Britain, producer Michael Balcon continued a self-interested crusade against Hollywood expatriates: "When things become tough here they desert the country and take cover in America. . . . I maintain that they should return at once to this country instead of cavorting about on the dance floors of Hollywood." (Not that Huxley did much cavorting.) A *Picturegoer* reader urged a ban of films made by "these Hollywood deserters": "Loyal Britishers can do without looking at the mock heroics of a bunch of cowards. The failure of their pictures over here would mean a salary cut and possibly end their miserable careers."[78]

In July, Sybille Bedford visited California. She was shocked to find the Huxleys "under the greatest possible strain, submitting themselves to some rigorous process of repression. . . .

"The ease had gone, the lack of tension . . . Maria's protectiveness, that had been so discrete, was now compulsive. There were a number of taboos. 'Don't talk war to Aldous.' One had to accept everything American, never show longing for Europe. . . . once I maneuvered our mutual English friend into asking him, 'Aldous, don't you want England to win? Wouldn't it be better if England won?' Aldous remained mute for a second, then he said in a colourless voice, 'There won't be any England as we knew it.' "[79]

Sybille was unimpressed with Aldous's new visual ability, "because of his looking so drawn and strained, like a man with great burden of unhappiness severely locked away. I had often seen him look ill or withdrawn or quietly sad, but even during the great insomnia of 1935 he had always kept his air of equanimity. And poor Maria was so thin, so worn, so nervous—and so resolutely cheerful. One felt that everything was too much for her, physically too much, every minute."[80]

Though beleaguered, Huxley kept hunting film work. His hope was that if he and Anita collaborated, they would have more artistic control. He proposed *Othello*. Finding little interest at MGM, Anita asked what else Huxley was interested in. He came up with an unlikely property: *Lady Chatterley's Lover*, which Frieda was anxious to have adapted to the screen. Huxley was forty years early.[81]

After these long shots failed, Huxley turned from film to biography. His approach combined narrative skill and intellectual curiosity. *Grey Eminence* (alongside his studies of Pascal and Maine de Biran) suggest that in biography Huxley made excellent use of his talents: his vivid characterizations fused with nonfictional exposition more smoothly than they did in many of his novels. He also had a reflexive interest in the genre itself; a dozen years before, he had pondered:

> the borderland between biography and autobiography. Which is more real: you as you see yourself or you as others see you? You in your intentions and motives, or you in the product of your intentions? You in your action, or you in the results of your actions? And anyhow, what are your intentions and motives? And who is the you who has intentions?[82]

In *Grey Eminence*, Huxley embarked on the tragic story of Father Joseph, the sixteenth-century *éminence grise* of Cardinal Richelieu, "the only power politician of note who started life as a mystic and continued to the very end to make a desperate effort to make the best of both worlds."[83]

He had first mentioned the idea a year before, as he wrote to Kingsley Amis of his frustration with political activism: "Religious people who think that they can go into politics and transform the world always end by going into politics and being transformed by the world (e.g., the Jesuits, Père Joseph, the Oxford Group)."[84]

Huxley claimed the book had "oblique topical interest, for Joseph was as much responsible as anyone for prolonging the Thirty Years War, which is on the direct line of ancestry to the present disasters," but this may explain his marketing strategy rather than his private imperative.[85] The book became a cautionary tale for his time, half reminder, half justification, to alert pacifists like Russell to the danger of substituting the right end for the right means.

When the war began, Huxley had been adapting a nineteenth-century novel to the screen; now, after a year which included the blitz and the fall of Paris, Huxley retreated still further in time—as if *he* were the time-traveler he had started to write about. There were many figures Huxley could have chosen to demonstrate the spiritual hazards of political involvement: Becket or Frederick II, King Saul or Karlstadt. In choosing Père Joseph, he selected a life parallel to his own in fascinating ways.

François Leclerc du Tremblay was born into a highly placed family in 1577. Prodigiously bright, at age ten he delivered a funeral oration in Latin. A master of Greek as well, he attended private schools, where he was bullied as much as the young narrator in *Eyeless in Gaza*, but holding his own in intellectual discourse. His older brother had set François a pattern of intellectual achievement; then the boy's father died:

> *His grief on this occasion was profound; and when the first paroxysm was past, there remained with him, latent at ordinary times, but always ready to come to the surface, a haunting sense of the vanity, the transience, the hopeless precariousness of all merely human happiness.* (Grey Eminence, 26)

The most significant of these parallels was also the most poignant. The young friar had just begun his career as a theologian when it was cut short, "after only a year, by an aggravation of the progressive defect of vision which advanced throughout his life, until, at the end, he was nearly blind" (*Grey Eminence, 107*).

After practicing Bates's exercises for the first few months, Huxley detected a slight clearing of the opacity of his eyes, the same phenomenon his friend, the actress Constance Collier, had noticed with her cataract after using the Bates Method.

Huxley spent several hours a day "sunning" (letting sunlight flood his closed lids) and "palming" (cupping closed eyes). Unlike those who were congenitally blind, he had memories of sight to motivate him. One of Bates's favorite techniques for relaxing the eyes was to have his subjects palm and recollect vivid scenes of childhood. This Huxley could do, for he had logged a whole bright world before losing his sight.

In college, Huxley had dilated his pupils with atropine to peer around the opacities in his eyes—only with a drug could he read. Yet a year after beginning Bates's exercises, he was seeing beyond what lenses offered. On January 14, 1940, he had written to Julian of a breakthrough of major proportions:

> *Yesterday for the first time I succeeded, for short stretches, in getting a single fixed image from both eyes together—a thing I never have had. This is a very encouraging advance; for anything that can be got*

momentarily like this can be built up by proper exercise into a permanent acquisition.

Perspective would not come to Huxley so easily. "No eyes in your head, nor no money in your purse?" asks Lear. "Your eyes are in a heavy case, your purse in a light."

During his recent physical/emotional breakdown, he had slid backward, but never given up. He practiced in the backyard on Amalfi Drive, out of sight of people who might find his palming and sunning ludicrous. Steadily, images grew stronger; even his bad right eye registered more light. By early fall, he was emboldened to give away his extra-large-print typewriter. The same day he did, September 29, 1940, Grace lunched with the Huxleys; talk was of *Grey Eminence*. Maria told her Gerald had suggested he write about Père Joseph.[86]

Huxley became so entranced with the Bates Method that when a bill formally legalizing it was introduced into the California Senate, he went to Sacramento and dined with Governor Culbert Olson, "who will look after the bill if necessary."[87]

The Bates Method remained controversial among his friends; some were unconvinced of his visual progress. Mary Anita Loos, Anita's niece, whom she had virtually adopted, heard Aldous bragging about Bates and how his eyes had improved so completely that he no longer needed glasses. Then, as they reached her house, Aldous reached for the car door and missed, falling into the street.[88]

After his precocious childhood and near blindness, Father Joseph served as an aide to Cardinal Richelieu and the expansionist aims of Louis XIII. In doing so he changed from a contemplative to a foreign secretary whose missions annihilated not egos but hundreds of thousands of peasants caught in the crossfire of the Thirty Years War. Father Joseph hoped to launch a new crusade against the Turks; his last moments were spent listening to a chronicle of those bloody and contradictory wars for religious freedom.

Huxley underlined the moral. "Anyone who has any desire for sanctity," he wrote in self-justification, "can do far more good by sticking to his curious activities on the margin of society than by going to the centre and trying to improve matters there. Instead of raising politics to his level, he will always be pulled down to the level of politics."[89]

In the end, politics could no more contain Father Joseph than the ministry had. In the grey eminence's last days he, like Huxley, turned from his political activism. He had sacrificed his spiritual gifts by rendering them unto Caesar rather than to Jesus:

> Abandoning seership for rulership, he gradually, despite his most strenuous efforts to retain it, lost the mystical vision which had given him his spiritual authority. . . . In a very little while, the last vestiges of Father Joseph's spiritual authority disappeared, and he came, as we have seen, to be regarded with general horror, as a man capable of every crime and treachery. (Grey Eminence, 316)

As Huxley wrote the depressing saga of Grey Eminence, he found a few bright islands in his sea of despondency. One of these was watching the final edit of Pride and Prejudice. "Stromberg sat for weeks, night after night, cutting here, putting in there, like a jigsaw puzzle," Aldous told Grace.

"I should think he would go quite mad, like taking Chinese water torture," Grace answered.

"He *is* mad," said Aldous. "They all are quite mad, you can't blame them when you see it done. . . . I should have liked Cukor. I barely stopped my director from having Bennet fight a duel with Wickham! The principals were *so* bad; the supporting cast was very good."[90]

There were amusing interludes as the book progressed, keeping pace with spring. Once, the Huxleys joined Krishnamurti and the Rajagopols for a picnic in a sunny eucalyptus grove. After a walk in the woods, they sat down to a gala lunch with Chris and Gerald and Peggy on a field of sweet-smelling grass surrounded by dogs and a baby goat they had brought.[91]

Another bright spot was that Charlie and Paulette had stayed together long enough to finish The Great Dictator.

In November 1938, a Munich exhibition called the "Eternal Jew" had featured a picture of Chaplin with the caption, "An Englishman? No, a Jew." Chaplin may have heard about this; the next month he began *The Great Dictator* in earnest. By January 1939, Maria and Aldous had seen Chaplin's bits become so polished that "we were sick with laughter," Maria wrote. "We have seen the film develop since the beginning of the summer; now it is ripe." Shooting the film further strained the Chaplins' relationship, however. Charlie Chaplin, Jr., remembered Paulette coming home in tears, with his perfectionist father saying, "Your stepmother worked very hard today, and I had to tell her a few things about acting, which isn't easy." "You're just a slave driver," Paulette would burst out, lying down on a couch to cry.[92]

Chaplin had polished and repolished the script; the final stenciled copies were completed the day England declared war on Germany. This had added urgency; a week later shooting had begun, running straight through March 1940.[93] Finally, on October 3, 1940, Chaplin completed the fine cut and invited Aldous, Maria, Anita, John Steinbeck, and a half dozen others to see the film. It was obviously brilliant; if Aldous and Maria had reservations about the film, they did not mention them to friends. (The film is not prowar so much as anti-Hitler.)

"Chaplin was understandably nervous about the reaction to *The Great Dictator*," biographer David Robinson reports. After all, America's schizophrenia on war had been evident from the outset, and there was no predicting whether Americans were ready to laugh at Hitler. A Gallup poll at the outbreak of war in Europe had shown 96 percent opposed to America's entry into the war (yet 84 percent favored an Allied victory).[94]

The one mistake Chaplin made with *The Great Dictator* was opening it in New York City; when he returned to L.A., local critics were ready to roast Chaplin and his film. They soon had their chance.

Throughout the fall of 1940, Huxley worked at *Grey Eminence* with the breakneck speed of a man trying to clear his conscience. Writing always pulled him into himself. The less he was involved with war news, the more immersed he could be in the dominions of his imagination, so far removed in time and space from his physical surroundings. By March, Huxley finished with an athletic burst: a

550-page manuscript in under five months. "My book seems to have entered the last lap, thank goodness—for I shall be glad to be done with it," he wrote to Julian.[95]

At the same time, Isherwood went to Pennsylvania to work with the pacifist Quakers resettling European exiles in Pennsylvania. The fundamental difference between Isherwood and Huxley was really not between the organizationally devout and the individual transcendentalist. Isherwood was more adventuresome, molding events into semiautobiographical fiction; Huxley more cerebral, with a fiction unrepentingly grounded in ideas.

Huxley had evolved from a reformist disenchanted with politics to someone enchanted by spiritual reform. But could he keep the world in perspective as a Buddhist wise man, a *bodhisattva*, does? Hindus teach various paths to salvation: via devotion or faith, sacrifice, community service, and knowledge. Of these, the latter *(Jnana Marga)* came the most easily to Huxley.

Isherwood chose service. He had tested his pacifism first by joining a religious community and now with the Quakers. How active was Huxley's commitment? He could have tried his beliefs as a medic amid the decay of the battlefield—if he'd had sight enough to dodge the bullets and mortar. (The closest Huxley came to actual violence was the 1935 riot at the Olympia Arena.) "Seer is not the same as a mere spectator," Huxley wrote of Father Joseph; the problem was once again how to "see."

While Huxley withdrew from the twentieth century to the sixteenth, America moved toward war at a quickening pace. Isherwood noticed this as he got off his train in Philadelphia: " 'Out there on the Coast,' someone declared, in the group nearest to me, 'you just don't know what the score is. Why, back East, we're practically in the war already.' Someone else agreed that F.D.R. would get us in as soon as he could find an excuse."[96]

In 1940, Roosevelt was campaigning against Willkie with promises like "you boys are not going to be sent into any foreign wars"; many disbelieved him, especially after September, when he signed the Selective Service Act.

On September 7, 1940, German aircraft began to bomb London's docks and East End. By evening, warehouses and timber yards were aflame; smoke and soot blacked out the sunset. The blaze burned all night, killing 500 civilians and injuring 1,600. That month the "London After Dark" broadcasts began, hosted by Edward R. Murrow. Grace Hubble tuned in for the first program, where Murrow described searchlights piercing London's sky against a backdrop of air-raid sirens and patrons stranded at Hammersmith's dance hall by night-flying bombers. The documentary closed with J. B. Priestley, patriotically returned from Hollywood to help defend "this great rock that's defying the dark tide of invasion that has destroyed freedom all over Western Europe."[97]

War reports on radio affected the public the way later Vietnam-era telecasts would: sounds of explosions created what Isherwood called "the terrible psychic restlessness which a war-situation generates."[98] This disquiet manifested itself in America by restless, gratuitous violence. Crowds in Illinois mobbed a Jehovah Witness motorcade, overturning cars. In Maine, 2,000 people sacked and burned the pacifist Witnesses' headquarters.

Back in Hollywood, Jack Warner was forbidding employees to speak German at his studio. Though powerful anti-Nazi films at last appeared—*Underground, The Mortal Storm*—they played to small audiences, with picture-goers preferring *Strike Up the Band* and *Rebecca*. Isolationists upset at *The Mortal Storm* held a Senate hearing on propaganda in American film. Formerly accused of being callously neutral, the film industry was now investigated for taking sides. It was too late for the studios to turn back. Having lost their European markets to the Nazis, producers were forced to concentrate on domestic, Latin American, and English markets. The German decision to ban Hollywood imports forced the studios into the Allied camp.

At first, Hollywood cast the conflict in historical dress—just as Huxley had in *Grey Eminence*. In *The Sea Hawk*, Philip of Spain (in the time of the Armada) complains, "We will never keep Northern Europe in submission until we have a reckoning with England."[99] Then producers and writers focused on the privations of war-torn countries.[100]

Producers worried whether the war would end before pictures in the pipeline could be released, given the six-month lead time for a feature. The first round of war films were approved in the summer and autumn of 1940; the public preferred musicals. Not till the spring of 1941 did the first anti-Nazi blockbuster catch on, *Sergeant York*, (where a pacifist [Gary Cooper] converts to fighting).

As the industry's interest in war peaked, the Huxleys plummeted: "For us, the cinema no longer exists," Maria wrote. "We never go and have lost all interest." Yet by the following March, they were growing increasingly dependent on studio work at the moment war films boomed. The picture of Hollywood and of America Maria offered her younger sister, Rose, had become significantly less rosy:

> *There's a petty, sordid side to American life. But you'll have plenty to eat and it won't be cold. We dare count, more than anything, that Aldous will find a film as soon as his book's completed. All my hopes for you are based on this.*[101]

Other friends also similarly bucked the trend. Greta Garbo refused to read war scripts and began planning to leave Hollywood for the duration.[102]

Garbo was still friendly with Mercedes De Acosta, whose husband had asked for a divorce: "That we could no longer make a success of our sexual life seemed to me no reason to separate," Mercedes wrote. "I was too European to feel, as Americans do, that the moment the sex relation is over one must fly to the divorce courts."[103] Despite Garbo's unwillingness to act in Mercedes's script of Joan of Arc, she and Mercedes spent afternoons in the seaside homes of absent friends, drinking champagne and dancing to "Daisy, You're Driving Me Crazy."

Garbo shunned gala parties, and Aldous and Maria attended them only when given by good friends. There was something distasteful about these social extravaganzas while the *Luftwaffe* dive-bombed London. Dislike of fancy-dress affairs—the Huxleys called them "granders"—had become a moral device to manifest their allegiance and their compassion for war victims.

Some parties were obligatory, however. On January 9, 1941, Edwin and Grace Hubble joined the Huxleys at Anita Loos's, then they all drove over to George Cukor's place for a party in honor of Lady Elsie Mendl and Tallulah Bankhead.

"All of Hollywood was there," Grace remarked tritely. Elegant and daring dresses pressed against more scruffy writers' garb; people glanced over each other's shoulders for someone more notable. Aldous heard the tinkle of ice in glasses and the practiced musical laughter of a screen temptress.

Tallulah was sitting by the pool when she heard Cukor walking up with Lady Mendl, the world-famous interior decorator. Tallu, a bisexual, quickly doffed her clothes and grabbed a bunch of violets. (In a current New York play, *The Captive*, these flowers served as a means of communication between two lesbians.) Mendl understood. George shouted at her to put her clothes on.

"One of her guests remarked that *The Captive* had been raided in New York and closed by the police," Anita wrote of a party given by Lady Mendl. "Her Ladyship pretended ignorance of the reason why. 'What is a lesbian?' she asked, slapping the tea table briskly with a characteristic gesture. 'Tell me what they do!'

"Now for years Elsie had had a very close relationship with a Broadway play agent, a lady of width and heft who wore her hair in a crew cut, sported ground-gripper shoes, and was given to shooting her cuffs in a manly gesture. And when Tallu heard Lady Mendl's questions, she asked, in her gruff *sotto voce*, 'If Elsie doesn't know what lesbians are, who does?' "[104]

The first months of the new year had more sobering moments. Two weeks after Cukor's party, Edwin Hubble appeared on NBC's "I Disagree" program to debate representatives of the America First movement, who attacked America's "hereditary enemies" (the British) while arguing, "We could do business with Hitler."

The next day, so many crank calls arrived that the Hubbles brought the phone downstairs to the kitchen and took turns answering. "Some were complete pacifists and didn't believe in the manufacture of guns, bullets, or powder. 'How do you feel about burglars?' Grace asked.

" 'That's all hooey,' was the response.

" 'Whatever the Germans do,' another partisan said, 'I'll always be grateful because they've given the world the most marvelous love story: *Tristan and Isolde*.'

" 'They got that out of Britain,' Grace acidly pointed out: 'Chaucer.' "[105]

"Others called Edwin to threaten him for his disloyalty. 'Talk while you can, because you aren't going to have much time.' "

The Huxleys and the Hubbles continued to drift apart. The previous October, when Edwin had addressed the Aid to Britain rally, Anita and Grace had sat together; the Huxleys were noticeably absent. Phone contact dwindled. Where they had once seen each other weekly, a month now passed before Maria would appear at the Hubbles', bringing red lettuce, fresh fennel, and tiny round carrots from the farmer's market.

Nineteen forty-one was one of the rainiest springs on record in Los Angeles. Darkness without meant darkness within—optimism drained from Huxley like sand from an hourglass:

> The accounts I get of London now have a strange similarity to those which Homer gives of Hades—a place of diminished life, of vagueness and uncertainty and sub-acute despair. . . .
> I see no hope except in a reversal of existing trends and a deliberate return to a more decentralized form of society with a wider distribution of land and other property.[106]

Then, on June 22, 1941, the Soviet Union was invaded. Richer by the three republics she had occupied (Estonia, Latvia, Lithuania), Russia was finally in the war. Few in Hollywood discussed pacifism anymore—only how and when war would come. Hitchcock portrayed pacifists as spies in *Foreign Correspondent*. The only allies left to Huxley were the rather unpleasant America Firsters and the German-American Bund, already guilty of spying.

With Christopher off in Pennsylvania and Gerald ensconced in his remote religious community in the Laguna Hills, Trabuco College, Aldous Huxley was as isolated from friends and country as one could be. The next step was physical isolation, once America entered the war.

SIX

THE
PERENNIAL
PHILOSOPHY

"The politics of those whose god is beyond time are always pacific; it is the idolators of past and future, of reactionary memory and utopian dream, who do the persecuting and make the wars." (1944)

Except for the war in Europe, hovering off-camera, it was business as usual for America that December of 1941: New England college boys suited up for the end of the football season; smoke from late-burning leaves swirled over suburban streets; the first breath of winter froze the green tidal flats of Maryland, where Edwin Hubble worked in his ballistic weapons laboratory.

In Hollywood, studios began to churn out pro-Ally features. L.A. darkened with the soot of steel rolled in Torrance and ships built in Long Beach. The smoke of factories complicated the Huxleys' delicate health and drove them toward a place of light and calm. They finally found such a haven in the Mojave at Llano del Rio (literally, "the river's plain"), population fifty, fifty miles north of L.A. There the Huxleys bought a forty-acre ranch.

On December 3, 1941, Julian disembarked in New York, on his way across the United States to California to promote Anglo-American solidarity. At the dock, the scientist met angry questions from representatives of Hearst's papers opposed to intervention:

The man from the Evening Telegram *was particularly insistent . . .*
"Did I hope that America would come into the fighting?" I said, rather
incautiously: "Yes, under certain conditions," and named them. . . .
On returning to my hotel, I suddenly found myself . . . on the front
page of the Telegram *. . . with the caption* HE WANTS WAR *in block*
lettering—nothing, of course, about my conditional phrase.[1]

(Apparently no reporters made the connection that Julian's famous brother did *not* want war.)

For the last five years, Julian had headed the London Zoo. This position, alongside his phenomenally popular "Brains Trust" broadcasts, made him a national figure in Britain. Now he'd become an unwilling prowar celebrity; offensive letters from anti-interventionists arrived at his New York hotel, some containing human excrement. Such antagonism soon became moot.

I n Steven Spielberg's film *1941*, Los Angeles drifts along pleasantly on December 7: big band jazz on the car radio, a fresh breeze off the ocean, a blue sky above. Across the Pacific in Hawaii, fishermen waded in Honolulu's harbor, and midshipmen slept in on a warm Sunday morning. Suddenly 360 Japanese planes appeared on the horizon with a rain of bombs, followed by submarines, torpedoes, and the hideous whine of dive bombers. Over 2,400 Americans died, with 18 ships and 170 planes destroyed.

That day, Aldous and Maria were picnicking at their new ranch. The sage-covered plains of the Antelope Valley stretched below on one of those clear, windy afternoons when the shadow of the metropolis fades before the fenceless splendor of the West.

Peggy Kiskadden had brought along her son Ben, fourteen: "We were walking out in that high desert, a few hundred yards from the Huxleys' new house. I remember sitting under a greasewood tree eating sandwiches when an old man came over. 'Pearl Harbor has been bombed,' he shouted. 'We're at war.' "[2]

In Pasadena, Grace and Edwin (home on leave) were also out on a walk; when they returned, they found a message from the cook: "Peggy says to turn on the radio."

"First reports coming in," Grace wrote. "The Philippines & Hawaii attacked. Then local announcements—all firemen to their stations, police ditto, do not use telephones more than necessary, keep off the streets, Japanese aliens rounded up by the F.B.I., police guard at Little Tokyo. Bulletins coming in throughout the afternoon, with C.B.S.—Ed Murrow . . . Eric Sevareid, Major George Fielding Eliot, & the rest. Edwin said, 'Well, I'm glad it's come but too bad it had to come this way.' "[3]

The night bombs fell in Hawaii, a blackout was in force for L.A. All night the air sirens wailed, with nervous citizens firing at specks in the air. Southern Californians anticipated an invasion: the United States had never fought a world war on its soil.

A Japanese submarine fired shells north of Santa Barbara. Californians demanded the Japanese pay for their impudence; in the next week 1,300 "Japs" and 1,000 Germans were arrested, more or less at random. In Nashville, Tennessee, a state agency request for hunting licenses for six million Japanese was turned down by the Game Department: "Open Season on Japanese—no license required."

An eerie dusk hung over a Los Angeles deserted of cars, its streetlights extinguished. The Huxleys tar-papered their windows. The war had finally arrived, though not everyone believed it, according to expatriate actor Cedric Hardwicke:

> A group of us used to meet at my house in those days for Sunday brunch and bridge. Kippers were on the menu that December Sabbath. I lay abed anticipating the pleasure of eating them when I heard on the radio the first incredible news. . . . because there were no pictures as yet of Pearl Harbor in flames, Hollywood as a whole simply did not care what was happening. If, later in the war, Japanese troops had landed on Santa Monica Boulevard, not a soul in town would have believed it until you showed them a photograph or a film of the event. Then they would have jumped around like fiends.[4]

Pearl Harbor put paid to Huxley's hopes of peace in the United States. There was no more talk of negotiations and tactical support— only of bigger and better arms: who could kill the most enemy soldiers the most efficiently. The Japanese attack curtailed most nonreligious pacifism in the United States. Since most of his close friends had already left L.A., all that was left for Aldous was hermitage or art.

In discussing the function of writers in a time of crisis, John Berger has suggested that they must remind those living within the walls of their own time that other possibilities exist, outside that wall; they must "describe the world we live in as not being inevitable."[5]

Unfortunately, Huxley's depression following the fall of Paris made any wall seem too high to scale. To make himself a window through which a permanent solution to war could be seen he had to find hope within himself.

At the end of 1941, Huxley was working on a new novel based on an idea which had haunted him—the story of a man whose consciousness persisted once his body had died, *Time Must Have a Stop*. The idea turned out to be an excellent one, but not for Huxley, at least not then. He started, then thrust *Time* aside. As the year turned, he had trouble finishing anything longer than a letter. The usual confusion of moving affected him, but there was something more, he confided to Isherwood. He couldn't work:

> *a state partly due to my having slightly strained my heart at the ranch, with resultant chronic fatigue, partly to having reached an impasse in my writing, where I don't know whether I can achieve what I want to achieve, or how exactly to do it. I would like to do something else altogether for a little; but my physical condition makes it difficult for me to do anything but the usual sedentary work.*[6]

As Huxley was putting aside *Time*, Grace recorded a melancholic conversation. She asked Aldous why, for a change, he didn't create some *positive* characters (she had just finished reading the proofs of *Grey Eminence*). "I am not good enough myself to create good characters," he answered.[7]

Weeks passed and still Huxley could not write. He moped around the house, helping with the packing as best he could. Maria drove him to the oculist for his lessons and on to the doctor for his bronchitis. Neither relieved his gloom. "Now Aldous's breakdowns were not like Julian's," Juliette reflected. "But I don't know how you describe them. I know he had more than one; I think Maria had some very difficult times with him. You see, these Huxleys were fragile people. Genius is a fragile quality. And if it's strained to a point where

it doesn't seem to give the kind of reward, or the kind of enlightenment, something cracks."[8]

Huxley's first reaction to Pearl Harbor, according to Maria, was
to consider departure. But leaving the country wouldn't solve his
problems now any more than it had when he first came to America.
The *Wanderjahr* he needed was interior.

Huxley was at a crossroads, emotionally and physically. He had
to make a peaceful man out of an agitated pacifist, an optimist of a
cynic. Huxley was creating an antiself, as Yeats had: specifying the
qualities he lacked in order to acquire them. The inspiration fueling
this transformation was not purely philosophical; it seemed the only
way out of this, his second American writer's block. Just as his inability to believe positively had paralyzed him while writing *Eyeless*,
so now he had to pierce his carapace of aloofness and feel with his
emotions instead of his brain.

In the early forties, the drive to Llano was a long one, via
the sinuous one-lane Sierra Highway which twisted off from the
San Fernando Valley into the San Gabriel Mountains. The intrepid
traveler wound up through passes as high as snowy Mill Creek Summit,
4,910 feet, before descending into the brown, wind-swept valley
beyond.

From the back of the San Gabriels, the Antelope Valley tilts
downward, "dotted with isolated buttes and rimmed, in the far distance, by other ranges of mountains," Huxley wrote. "The ground is
carpeted with plants and bushes which have learned to adapt themselves to a land where it rains eight or nine inches during the winter
and not at all from May to November."[9]

Ever since that first summer in New Mexico, Maria had wanted
a place of her own in the wilderness, she had told Frieda. Lawrence
would have appreciated the Mojave's all-encompassing sky, a perfect
setting for its fiery sun. The Huxleys may have heard of the place
from contacts in the film community. For decades the Mojave hosted
troops of the French Foreign Legion; rustlers and singing cowboys
had waltzed by on trick ponies.

Since November 1941, the Huxleys had been remodeling the place, starting with the main house—Anita Loos said it looked like the shack where Huck Finn's father died. They built an extra story on the front building and added a hexagonal apartment, self-contained, where Aldous slept and worked. Painted white, the place had a cozy, ramshackle appearance. (Amateur carpentry was all they could afford, with the packages of food and clothes sent to Europe and the expenses of supporting Maria's mother, her sister Rose, and niece Sophie's acting lessons.)

Tall trees marked their oasis for miles: apple and almond, grapevines, pears; an irrigation ditch ran through their place. In the autumn, when they had fallen in love with the house, the temperature hovered between seventy and eighty; now, as they unpacked their belongings under a cloudless winter sky, the daytime temperature rested in the sixties.

Matthew and Maria moved out with the moving van on February 11, 1942, leaving Aldous at Eva Herrmann's. They hired a caretaker and quickly hired another, for the first burned up their precious pump. Thereafter, for luck, they placed a bust of Heard on the wellhead, calling it Gerald's Tomb.

Besides its isolation and quiet, Llano del Rio came with an engaging legend: it had been the site of a utopian socialist community, which Huxley christened Ozymandias, after Shelley's poem of the ruins of the Egyptian statue. In 1917, hundreds of colonists had left Los Angeles to set up a cooperative farming and publishing enterprise, a hotel, a quarry, and craft workshops. The community burgeoned, then overextended itself, remedying shortages of capital by accepting anyone who applied. A periodic drought shattered the last of their hopes. By 1942, all that remained were pillars and a silo Huxley treasured: "On the fringes of what had been the colony's land. . . . gleaming in the morning light or black against the enormous desert sunsets, that silo was like a Norman keep rising, against all the probabilities, from the sagebrush."[10]

By April the Huxleys had settled in, far from the warring world. Many of the world's mystics have turned to deserts for their pure air, lack of distractions, and, Huxley noted, "because God seemed nearer there than in the world of men. . . . The desert's emptiness and the desert's silence reveal what we may call their spiritual meanings."[11] "Mysticism has the enormous merit of being concerned with the eternal present," he wrote to Julian, "and not, as humanism is, with the future."[12]

Matthew returned to their Doheny Drive flat. Maria took to Llano, proud of its intense light (which had considerably restored her husband's sight) and the fifty-mile view from the front porch. "There is everything to do, it is true," she wrote Grace:

> But if there is repeated sink standing, there is, above the sink, an immense view of the mountains and the snowy outlines with ever-changing clouds.
>
> If there is a continual sweeping [and] running to Aldous's house . . . the way lies under the blossoming apple tree, over the running ditch and past the comic kittens. The desert is immense and calming. So you see, I do feel very happy even if my hands ache . . . it is tiring enough to make me sleep ten hours a night.[13]

Throughout the moving and unpacking, Huxley had managed without his glasses. There were many little traps in his new home, unseen dips which could pitch him forward, misplaced logs over which he might stumble. Day after day, he felt his way through the world, gingerly but with deliberation. His long arms stretched in front of him like antennae as he entered an unfamiliar room. He continued to fumble for his glasses. Anyone who has given up smoking or drinking knows the feeling. The bottle beckons like a friend come to play. He knew if he were going to live without glasses, he had to persevere.

The Bates exercises relieved his eyestrain, that persistent, sawing pain which receded only to whine loudly when he again picked up print. Yet reading material kept arriving: new books of friends, requests to write prefaces, correspondence.

Twice Huxley had reconditioned his body when it failed him. Each reconstruction coincided with a major philosophical shift and a rebirth of hope. F. M. Alexander's back-straightening exercises had shaken Huxley from his 1935 depression—and inspired his pacifism. Bates's exercises similarly set the stage for his serious study of mysticism.

Huxley's bodily transformations liberated energy for contemplation and action; his belief in physical perfectibility, even starting from defective organs, brought a corresponding faith in spiritual perfectibility. Could the scion of a family of evolutionists conclude otherwise? His contribution to this tradition was to chart the world within; to this end he read and reasoned and measured.

He had Maria read aloud autobiography after spiritual autobiography—even *Lives of the Saints*—anything which proved that a body and a contemplative mind could fuse into a willing spirit. He would rest his eyes and listen to these accounts of triumph, when the self-conscious mind dissolved and the spirit rose up into the everlasting blue. The realm of the mystic is a land of uneven surfaces, where roomfuls of light blind the sighted (but illuminate the blind). It is a hotel where egos find no room, where mortification and humility—virtues neglected in Huxley's training at Eton and Oxford—count more than intellect. On nights in Llano when the crickets were silent and the ranch dogs weren't howling to their wild coyote cousins in the foothills, the silence within swelled. Sounds echoed like coins in a metal vat.

In the mornings, Huxley would rise, select a text to ponder, and sit for a prolonged meditation. Eugen Herrigel, author of *Zen in the Art of Archery*, offers a good introduction to these sessions:

> The soul needs an inner hold, and it wins it by concentrating on breathing. This is performed consciously and with a conscientiousness that borders on the pedantic. The breathing in, like the breathing out, is practiced again and again by itself with the utmost care.
>
> One does not have to wait long for results. The more one concentrates on breathing, the more external stimuli fade into the background. They sink away in a kind of muffled roar which one hears with only half an ear at first, and in the end one finds it no more disturbing than the distant roar of the sea, which, once one has grown accustomed to it, is no longer perceived.[14]

Not the roar of the ocean but the relentless breeze of the prairie whistled outside Aldous's book-lined study as he sat, fixing the infinite with an unlidded inner stare. Behind closed eyes, Huxley's vision was as good as anyone's. Years before, he had complained to T. S. Eliot that his meditations were unsystematic and difficult; "true, the difficulty grows less as one persists; one is able to keep the mind directed, focused, one-pointed more easily, after a few months, than at the beginning."[15]

At times, frustrated by his slow spiritual progress, he strained at his meditations, "never overcoming his all too natural desire to take the kingdom of heaven by violence"—the very sin of which he had accused Père Joseph.[16]

Huxley set out on his spiritual search in earnest, joining it to the struggle to quiet his personality so that exercises might improve his sight.

The quest for enlightenment is a continuing motif in the West, as old as Jason and the Argonauts and as recent as Woody Allen's films.[17] Ours is an age of the Drive-in Church of Rapid Enlightenment, when Hollywood stars find samadhi watching the surf outside their Malibu condominiums.

Mysticism literally refers to closing the distance between humans and God and Nature; all religions, Huxley discovered, share a vital principle of mystical transcendence. His current contribution to peace—inner if not outer—lay in outlining this Higher Ground. Soon after completing Grey Eminence in 1940, Huxley had begun a collection of mystical texts: "He did it with the efficiency which is possible only to those who possess, as well as the highest intellectual abilities, an extraordinary strength and fixity of resolution," as he wrote of Father Joseph in Grey Eminence.[18]

The goal of the mystic, regardless of denomination, is that intuitive union with a god or a spirit which puts daily life into perspective. Such an epiphany, William James suggests in The Varieties of Religious Experience, expands our field of consciousness beyond the margins of daily thought. Other students of mysticism, such as Frits Staal in Explaining Mysticism, write not of a sudden flash but of "a property of the mind" manifest only in a mystical state and founded on a superstructure of spiritual discipline.

While the rewards are large, the dangers of mysticism are equally great, and not obvious. One danger is that those who develop mental powers cheapen their knowledge by performing spiritual parlor tricks of the spoon-bending variety. Beyond this temptation, the possibility of spiritual failure of nerve looms; after years in an ashram, the initiate seeking relief from alcoholism might remain an addict.

The ascent of a spiritual ladder extends beyond contemplation, as any novice learns. The annihilation of the self—in favor of unity with some larger spirit—takes place both passively ("when God actually makes himself present to us in contemplation") and actively ("dwelling inwardly in eternity while outwardly operating in time," according to Huxley).[19]

(Nonattachment does not mean indifference. Many misassociate the search after enlightenment with escapism, yet for millennia Hindu and Buddhist mystics have taught the importance of bringing enlightenment back down to earth through compassion and charity. Buddhists include this in their Eight-fold Path, where monks abstain from, among other practices, manufacturing arms or alcohol and perform selfless service to the community.)

Another danger of the mystical undertaking lies in becoming so nonattached that one *loses* perspective instead of gaining it. The mind's purchase on reality dwindles; supposedly freed from distractions, it dwells on piffle instead of Eternal Harmony. Such a mystic is of no use as a spiritual guide to family, friends, or society.

Ironically, the greatest pitfall of mysticism is temporary success: reaching a plain of understanding that no reading or study can offer—only to lose it, beyond recall. This notion of a long, dark night of the soul haunted Huxley. Soon after coming to the United States, he'd noted different varieties of the "Dark Night": "One due to the loss of a sense of the personality of the godhead, as described by St. John of the Cross; another due to the sense of unworthiness; another to 'dryness' or the inability to transcend personality and perhaps another due to a kind of temporary psycho-physical disintegration."[20] Huxley's writing blocks during personal crises were only one symptom of this affliction.

Isherwood knew this peril as well as any of Huxley's friends. In Pennsylvania, among the Quakers, he continued his own search for inner peace: "infinitely faint, how distant, like the high far glimpse of a goat-track through the mountains between clouds, I see something else: the way that leads to safety.

"For a second, I glimpse it. For an instant, it is even quite clear.

"Then the clouds shut down, and a breath off the glacier, icy with the inhuman coldness of the peaks, touches my cheek. 'No,' I think, 'I could never do it. Rather the fear I know, the loneliness I know . . . for to take that other way would mean that I should lose myself. I should no longer be a person. I should no longer be Christopher Isherwood.' "[21]

Huxley could accept this loss of ego better than Isherwood, as he didn't fashion his art out of autobiography. Nevertheless, as anyone who has tried it knows, meditating for hours at a time takes tremendous effort. "If a man would travel far along the mystic road," he had written in *Grey Eminence*, "he must learn to desire God intensely but in stillness, passively and yet with all his heart and mind and strength."[22]

Gerald Heard, already a master of contemplation, turned his attention to organizing: "Humanity is failing. We are starving—many of us physically, all of us spiritually—in the midst of plenty. Our shame and our failure are being blatantly advertised, every minute of every day, by the crash of explosives and the flare of burning towns." In his familiarly apocalyptic voice, Heard framed a prospectus for a new spiritual community, Trabuco College, set high in the rolling hills overlooking the Pacific at Laguna Beach.

There Heard gathered a few disciples for "a slow hard lifetime of study, prayer, and disciplined ascetic living."[23] Once again Gerald and Aldous were moving in parallel (but literally opposite) directions, Aldous sixty miles to the north of L.A., Gerald to the south. Heard had taken on the role of Mr. Propter in Huxley's *After Many a Summer Dies the Swan*.

Reconciliation between the two friends was not made easier by the way readers blamed Heard for Huxley's conversion to mysticism. Richard Chase, in the essay "Yogi-Bogey," attacked Heard's "rather flaccid and uncritical intellectualism."[24] Not everyone was as direct as critic William Tyndall ("the trouble with Aldous Huxley is Gerald Heard"), but his sentiment spoke for many. Tyndall mourned the younger Huxley: "Master and disciple retired to California where," Tyndall concluded, "when not working with Greta Garbo or writing for the cinema, they eat nuts and lettuce perhaps and inoffensively meditate."[25]

At Trabuco College, they did a great deal more than munch on nuts. Construction on the site of the 392-acre orange ranch began in the summer of 1942 with materials purchased immediately before America entered the war. By the end of 1943, Aldous had visited three times, impressed as Gerald's dreams rose in stone around him. The place resembled a tile-roof Italian cloister largely inhabited by English intellectuals: tea at four, brilliant conversation, fog hanging over green meadows. Maria noticed Aldous's happy, unselfconscious laugh when reunited with Gerald: "I realized how English he is, how good for him to be with his own."[26]

Though Aldous admired Gerald's dedication, the Huxleys weren't ready for monastic life. Before leaving the city completely, they intended to enjoy their remaining friends: Anita, Greta, and Mercedes.

Mercedes and Greta continued their romps: "Shortly after Christmas it began to pour in such torrents that the drops seemed like eggs. . . . we would rush to the highest peak overlooking the sea to watch the lightning break through the sky like great cracks of fire, and hear the thunder crashing down on us. We were always happy and stimulated in a storm."[27]

Unfortunately, as friends watched, Greta's career unraveled. To increase her appeal to American audiences, MGM had retailored Garbo, cutting her hair and trading her silken gowns for a ski instructor's outfit in *Two-Faced Woman* (1941). Neither true comedy nor sultry drama, the result was "almost as shocking as seeing your mother drunk," wrote *Time*.[28] One of the great fiascos in movie history, this film drove Garbo from the screen.

Garbo's message had become steadily antimale throughout the thirties. "That's men again," she quipped in *Anna Christie*. "How I hate 'em, every mother's son of 'em." "I will die a bachelor," she says in *Queen Christina*. More sophisticated European audiences accepted such badinage; Hollywood studios, however, sold wholesomeness. Film portrayals of lesbians were "freak products of imaginary worlds gone haywire, the result of tampering with the natural order," noted one film historian.[29]

The upshot of *Two-Faced Woman* was that the Huxleys lost another friend in Hollywood. Mayer called Garbo into his office and told her that MGM had no films for her until the war was over. She refused his offer to continue her salary and left for New York.

Mercedes remained behind, fond of both Maria, whom she thought "fragile and charming-looking," and of the sexually responsive Eva Herrmann: "a German painter well known in Berlin for her caricatures, lovely and sensitive." With these companions, Maria had her own "sewing circle" in walking distance.

Mercedes also found Aldous very attractive. "We used to go for walks together just before or after sunset. When I was alone with Aldous, I always felt he knew so much that I shouldn't spend a second with him without digging some rare piece of information out of him."[30] Doubtless Aldous appreciated her attentions as he struggled free of his block. "During work, women never interested me," Chaplin wrote. "It was only between pictures, when I had nothing to do, that I was vulnerable." H. G. Wells agreed: "There comes a moment in the day when you have written your pages in the morning, attended to your correspondence in the afternoon, and have nothing further to do. Then comes that hour when you are bored; that's the time for sex."[31]

Finally, in the spring of 1942, "just as I was wondering apprehensively what on earth I should do, if reading were to become impossible,"[32] Huxley's meditations paid off in a breakthrough, the calm which allowed him to resume his writing. The first thing he wrote was his book on sight, *The Art of Seeing*, "this little book of pure utility." He wrote it, without glasses, in three months.

Huxley's blindness remained a source of shyness, he confessed in *Art:* "The disability tended to reinforce my natural tendency towards solitude and away from practical matters."[33] The sighted could drive a car, read signs, recognize faces, pick items off a shelf by their label. The blind ones, the "four-eyes," were at others' mercy.

Frustration at his disability had emerged in print for perhaps the first time in *Swan*, when he made Pordage a resentful bearer of heavy glasses:

> He took off his glasses. Deprived of their six and a half diopters of correction, his eyes were instantly reduced to a state of psychological despair. Curved crystal had become their element; unspectacled, they were like a pair of jellied sea creatures, suddenly taken out of water. Then the light went out; and it was as though the poor things had been mercifully dropped, for safe keeping, into an aquarium.[34]

Two years after writing these lines, Huxley had found a way to relieve this resentment and pain.

"Aldous has recovered from the shock of the Japanese war," Maria wrote her sister Suzanne, now in New York with her Dutch husband, painter Joep Nicolas. "The moment his work gets going he is so absorbed that he forgets the world. He forgets Mère [Maria's mother], he forgets Noel [his infant niece in Paris] and Matthew, and the house and our bank account, and to take his medicine and not to tire himself and to answer his letters. I believe that he is outside life more than he ever was."[35]

The war years were the making of Aldous Huxley as a stylite, marooned by gas and tire shortages. In 1920, he had written a poem, "From the Pillar," about those solitary ascetics who dwelt on columns to approach God: "And the saint from his high fastness of purity apart cursed them and their unchasteness. And denied them in his heart."[36] Unlike the hero of Luis Buñuel's film *Simon of the Desert*, Huxley struggled to believe in, not curse, humanity. In Llano, Huxley perched in the desert, surveying (and rejecting) the ways of a world he no longer felt he could change.

A dozen years before, another of Huxley's characters had bleakly confessed agnosticism:

> "I'd like to be able to think and live in the spirit of God. But the fact remains that I can't."
> "Can't you?" said Pamela with a polite sympathy. She was more interested in the opium.
> "No, no, you can't entirely disintoxicate yourself of mysticism and the tragic sense."[37]

Huxley had reconsidered: mysticism was a method, not a toxin. His earlier objections—that the benefits of mysticism were untranslatable, that mystics confused austerity with holiness, that the texts lacked intellectual coherence—faded as he read widely: Shankara, the great eighth-century Hindu interpreter; Saints Bernard, Aquinas, Augustine, and Catherine of Siena; Meister Eckhart; the anonymous author of *The Cloud of Unknowing*; Lao-tzu; Chuang-tzu. Research disconnected Huxley from his time as completely as adapting Jane Austen.

This wasn't the first time Huxley had felt out of touch with his era: "I was born wandering between two worlds, one dead, the other powerless to be born [here Huxley quotes his great-uncle Matthew Arnold], and have made, in a curious way, the worst of both. For each requires that one should be whole-heartedly there."[38]

There-ness was exactly what Huxley sought in Llano. "The Hindus reckon four ages," he explained to a friend:

> that of the schoolboy; that of the married man living in the world; that of the mature man who withdraws into the forest and tries to understand nature, things and his own essence; that of the aged man who detaches himself completely from desire and, though living bodily, dwells in the eternity which he perceives even in temporal things. As for myself, I begin to penetrate the forest.[39]

Before Aldous could do much more than pierce the thickets, however, he was called back to Movieland. David O. Selznick had offered him another literary project, *Jane Eyre*, at Twentieth Century-Fox.

The previous July, at the project's beginning, Huxley had spent a few weeks outlining it with director Robert Stevenson and producer William Goetz. Huxley's friend Orson Welles also sat in, lending a characteristically strong voice to the scenario. Maria wrote Sybille Bedford that Aldous was doing "some sort of nonsense for Fox and Fox is nice. They don't expect him to go there and sit everyday"— thus sparing her the drive into L.A.[40]

The English Tudor–styled Writers' Row at Twentieth Century-Fox was edged by a profuse garden which suggested a country club down on its luck. Here writers did as they were told, which gave Huxley an opportunity to test his new-found self-abnegation:

> The first thing a successful writer learns is to lose any self-conceit as to his abnormal abilities. When William Shakespeare, sitting in Bungalow No. 1, has sent in his story to the supervisor, the latter, if not immediately satisfied—a very, very rare occurrence—will pass it on to Ibsen in Bungalow No. 2 or Maeterlinck in Bungalow No. 6.[41]

Selznick, one of Hollywood's classic Anglophiles, had Huxley brought in for tony dialogue; while not Brontë's sort of novelist, he spoke like an Oxford don. Selznick was then riding one of film's all-time great successes, having just produced *Gone With the Wind* (and

Rebecca, featuring Joan Fontaine, who was to play opposite the moody Welles in *Jane Eyre*). The novel was a guaranteed success, having already been filmed successfully four times. The cast was right—and director Stevenson actually belonged to the Brontë Society. He, Huxley, and John Houseman provided "a high-class Hollywood shellacking," a critic for *PM* wrote.[42]

Now that he was back from Llano in the flat on Doheny Drive, he visited Anita Loos, still at MGM, who remembers, "We went for almost daily excursions either on the beach or through the firebreaks plowed across the crackling, dry hills that surround Hollywood."[43] Loos's spirits were buoyed by a temporary remission of her husband's illness. She somehow continued to enjoy her martyred marriage: "John treated me in an offhand manner, appropriated my earnings, and demanded from me all the services of a hired maid. How could a girl like I resist him?"[44]

Loos commiserated with Huxley's difficulties in working with tycoons: "That incredible man [Selznick]," Huxley told her, "frequently phones me at three A.M. to say 'My car is at your door. Get right over to the studio.'"[45]

Hollywood gossip had ceased to amuse Huxley. He found himself agreeing with family friend Val Gielgud, who, on his second visit, found Hollywood full of "fake values, talent wasted or misused, physical beauty exploited and degraded. . . . To leave Hollywood was for this traveller one of his most satisfying experiences."[46]

Associates of Louis B. Mayer cracked jokes at expatriate writers who "earned their keep as window dressing."[47] Such slurs were particularly unacceptable to Huxley as the studios denounced and fired its few conscientious objectors, such as Lew Ayres of the 1940s *Dr. Kildare* films, who said, "I'll praise the Lord, but I'll be damned if I'll pass the ammunition."

This treatment mirrored the widespread wartime hostility to pacifists, now accused of everything from cowardice to outright sabotage. Across town, Grace Hubble recorded a conversation with a major: "As for appeasers . . . we'll hang 'em, as we hung people in vigilante days." British pacifists he compared to "pukka sahibs in the colonies."[48]

America had tolerated conscientious objectors since colonial days. Like Huxley, the first C.O.'s came as immigrants: the Quakers first in 1656, the Dutch Mennonites in the 1680s.[49] These early American colonists were pilloried as heretics and publicly whipped. At best, they paid a tax or found substitute work for military service; at worst, they were pierced with bayonets or hung by their thumbs. Nonetheless, nineteenth-century peace churches such as the Rogerenes, Huterites, and Shakers proliferated.

In the Mexican and Civil wars, absolutist pacifists like Huxley won exemption from military service. As long as the United States was a rural, small-town nation, pacifists won a respect based on solid citizenry. As the country grew, however, their qualms were ignored in favor of a national defense. Nonetheless, the United States has produced major theoreticians of nonviolence, including two who influenced Gandhi, Adin Ballou and William Lloyd Garrison. Thoreau's "Civil Disobedience" (1849) was based on principled resistance to the Mexican War.

If Huxley had been a citizen of California thirty-five years earlier, during World War I, he might have been sent for "rehabilitation" to the Sierras; Isherwood's current lover, Denny Fouts, now worked in such a camp for C.O.'s.

During the First World War, C.O.'s were lined up twenty-five at a time and blasted with fire hoses—to test their commitment. The force of the water broke bones and dislocated backs. At Fort Riley in Kansas, C.O.'s had ropes put about their necks, "hoisting them off their feet until they were at the point of collapse. Meanwhile officers punched them in their ankles and shins."[50] Only one out of several hundred withstood this treatment to end up among 20,000 classified as C.O.'s. The rest received an average of twenty years in prison; seventeen were sentenced to death. By World War II, such abuse had been corrected; but only those classified as "religious," unlike Huxley, could claim C.O. status.

Huxley worked on *Jane Eyre* through March 1943, earning a writing credit. Huxley's script closely followed the novel's text, taking transitions from close-ups of pages of the book.[51]

How did Huxley feel about film writing once the first flush of wealth wore off? Few knew better than Isherwood, who commented:

"He found it harder [as time went on]. It embarrassed him somehow, I always felt. I say this with total authority because I not only worked with him, but we were intent on earning our livings. We always got interested, of course; the only real side of total 'no-goodness' is when you aren't interested in your work.

"He could live with it. You see, wise, braver, nobler people than any of us were doing it, and hating it far more than we did." [52]

Some of these writers had to register as enemy aliens; the Manns had to leave the Huxleys' dinner table by the 8:00 P.M. curfew: "Thomas Mann and Albert Einstein appealed to the President," Salka Viertel wrote. "The earliest and most far-sighted adversaries of the totalitarian governments . . . are not subjected to a humiliating treatment." [53]

Hollywood was infinitely more gracious to German refugees *before* war was declared; now some were rounded up for using a flashlight in the backyard at night. Lion Feuchtwanger's wife remembered the day the telephone went out of order, "and then suddenly came back. Then they came and said the whole house had to be rewired. At first I didn't think about that. I let them do it. I joked with them and said they were bugging the house. Then America got into the war, the curfew was started, and the Japanese were relocated. We stopped joking then." [54]

Though British, Chaplin also suffered from attacks on the refugee community. In his case, they focused on charges of living in sin with Paulette Goddard. When *The Great Dictator* had premiered in New York eighteen months earlier, Charlie had surprised the audience by introducing "my wife Paulette." If he had hoped this would patch things up with her or his critics, it didn't work. Before Charlie could make his way back to the coast, Paulette had moved out, to a house near Anita Loos on the beach.

Paulette had found celebrity outside the Chaplin studio; she had started dating Burgess Meredith, whom she had met on the set of *Second Chorus*, in which she costarred with Fred Astaire.

Disappointed but not crushed, Chaplin dated sex sirens Carole Landis and Hedy Lamarr. He was working on *Shadow and Substance,* a never-completed film about an Irish girl whose religious visions are quashed by local orthodoxy. For the lead Chaplin had in mind a girl he'd just met, Joan Barry. After Chaplin's new flame cracked up the

Cadillac in the driveway, he sent her east with her mother, hoping to see the last of her.

Chaplin began to dabble in politics, making speeches calling on Roosevelt to open a second, Western front to support Russia (a demand supported by the U.S. Communist Party). These activities proved his downfall, though he little imagined this at the time. He was more concerned about getting Barry off his coattails, so he could court his new love Oona, the eighteen-year-old debutante daughter of Eugene O'Neill.

O f the Huxleys' close friends, only Anita Loos was writing war films. Beginning in 1942, Hollywood became a converted war propaganda factory, working under the semisupervision of the Office of War Information (OWI). OWI's heavy-handed directives read as if cribbed from a textbook—Propaganda, How to: "Suppose there was a love scene in a cafe," Lowell Mellett of the OWI argued. "The girl could say to the boy, 'I only want half a spoonful of sugar. It's not only patriotic—it's good for my figure too.' "[55]

This was prior censorship, as subtle as Russian cultural commissar Andrei Zhdanov's directives to Soviet writers on the importance of writing socialist-realist romances on dairy farming. Commercial film-makers had shunned controversy and censorship. Yet by 1942, the Hays Office was limiting the number of bullets and blanks used on a set (the cowboy had to fall after a single shot; the bank robber accelerated slowly, so as not to be a bad example of tire wasting).

Hollywood's response to wartime pressure was obeisance to each service: MGM made *Salute to the Marines, Stand by for Action* (the navy), *Keep Your Powder Dry* (the WACs), *Cry Havoc* (army nurses), *They Were Expendable* (torpedo crews), and *Thirty Seconds Over Tokyo* (the air force).[56] In the obligatory "Buy War Bonds" trailer, Fortress America—proud, independent, invulnerable—was refurbished to a hands-across-the-sea spirit.

Hollywood films made during the war can be divided into four phases. The first, after Pearl Harbor, struggled to make defeat glorious in films like *Wake Island* and *Bataan.* The second phases emphasized Europe's anti-Nazi courage.[57]

By 1943, Americans had wearied of war; Hollywood's third phase of films returned to the extravaganza of the 1920s. *The Gang's All Here,* the all-black *Cabin in the Sky,* Ernst Lubitsch's *Heaven Can Wait,* and horror classics *(Cat People* and *I Walked With a Zombie)* offered diversion from casualties. By the war's end, in a fourth phase, epics of insanity and gangsters proliferated in film noir.

In American war films, anti-Fascist sentiment was sometimes transmuted to a racist hatred of the Japanese that bordered on genocide: the more killed, the better. "I'll hook a Jap, with tartar sauce," one navy man tells another in *Destination Tokyo.* "I'll take mine boiled in oil," came the reply. (The working-class internationalism embedded in films about ally Russia did not extend to Asians.) Audiences eating popcorn and mints cried with joy at newsreels of bombs leveling a city. Such films were pornographic to Huxley. Hollywood soured further. Humor and despair were the only responses to an industry in which a publicity agent put fifty parrots in a room with a record that played the name of a motion picture over and over, intending to release the birds over L.A. By the time the birds learned the title of Mae West's film *It Ain't No Sin,* the studio had changed the name to *I'm No Angel.*[58]

Huxley couldn't divide himself the way Isherwood did: chat on the telephone with a prominent secretary at MGM, meditate, nap, run errands, translate a verse of the *Bhagavad-Gita,* and indulge in too many peppermint drops.[59] For better or worse, Huxley had declared war on distractions, and his heavy artillery was massing for the attack on the Self.

"Contemplatives have compared distractions to dust, to swarms of flies, to the movements of a monkey stung by a scorpion. Always their metaphors call up the image of a purposeless agitation," Huxley wrote.[60]

He met many such distractions at his small ranch, tending the pump or obtaining electricity, meat, sugar, or eggs. Aldous and Maria adopted a stylite's diet, "meatless, milkless, saltless, so that a minimum of strain may be thrown on the eliminatory processes. . . . Beans and other legumes are now my main source of proteins—a bit boring, especially without salt; but one gets used to anything."[61]

Though their clapboard house in Llano had few creature comforts, he and Maria returned to the quiet life they had in the south of France: breakfast at ten, work through the morning, lunch and a siesta, with the afternoon for hiking and painting, followed by reading aloud in the evening. Bucolic pleasures took the place of city life: hunting wild asparagus for lunch, jouncing on a tractor through their orchard. Aldous cultivated his goat Spike, as Lawrence had his cow Sally. Grapefruit rind kept Spike out of the radishes and potatoes.

Afternoons Farmer Huxley worked his victory garden, the desert wind leaving a scaly dryness on his hands. He struggled to be self-sufficient in his sight and spirit—which is why the disease which eventually robbed him of this oasis was so pernicious. He divided his time between chores and reading, "a queer fellow of an author wearing blue jeans and thinking he can grow radishes—but Aldous waters them from such a height and with such gusto that the heads get buried and the tails stand in the air as if they were doing yogi exercises and so all we get are dry roots and laughs," Maria joked to Grace.[62]

Guests were welcomed, if ill nourished, by Maria's cooking. One Thanksgiving dinner, Mary Anita Loos ate a chicken Maria had roasted for five hours ("Americans undercook chicken terribly," she told her), with a side dish of Maria's "earth potatoes," baked with soil clinging to the outside "for all those nutrients."[63]

(This was actually an improvement over Maria's earlier culinary attempts, particularly the evening she served Matthew's teenage friends skimpy portions of roast chicken because she had cut off and thrown away the drumsticks. Using an Elizabethan pet name by which they addressed each other, Aldous asked, "But, Sweetins, why didn't you cook the drumsticks?" "Because, Sweetins, they looked so *gross* in comparison with their dainty little wings."[64])

Guests arrived rarely, for roads winding through cactus might puncture an all-precious tire. Maria asked Grace to visit before departing for the East Coast: "You stimulate Aldous almost as much as Gerald. Might almost say, 'Mrs Hubble and Aldous Huxley scintillating at one another.' "[65]

Huxley had curtailed his "brief candles," however, in favor of male continence, an ideal raised in *Ends and Means*. Perhaps he'd gotten this idea from Gandhi, perhaps from Heard. In *Pain, Sex, and Time*, Heard had announced that if pacifism was grounded on self-control, sexual abstinence was excellent practice: "Yogis who are real researchers would as lief suffer pain as experience organsm."[66] (There's no record of what Gerald's lovers thought of this remark.)

Perhaps Huxley's renunciation was pragmatic; he didn't work as intensely when in love. As he had once written Priestley, when a man (or woman) becomes involved in affairs, the attention paid to other matters slackens.[67] Huxley was no Alfred de Musset or George Sand, nineteenth-century writers who unabashedly turned to affairs to nurse their poetic fires.

Old flames such as Mercedes De Acosta braved the journey to Llano out of friendship and curiosity: "I managed to go there once and Aldous took me for a walk on the desert. We came to an old Indian cemetery and sat down on one of the graves where we discussed the Christian mystics and Aldous told me a lot about Catherine of Siena. He said he hoped to write a book about her. He was eating, then, only food cooked in a manner which he called 'natural.' This meant by the sun's reflection in a mirror."[68]

In November 1942, Matthew fell seriously ill with appendicitis—fortunately, studying at UCLA, he had been quickly operated on. The twenty pounds he had lost he regained in Llano, eating his mother's porridge-and-cream breakfasts. Then, on March 8, 1943, Matthew received his draft notice.

Out of filial loyalty, Matthew had planned to be a C.O. One of Edwin Hubble's many radio speeches, however, changed his mind: now he sought only noncombatant status. Since he'd done premed at Colorado, the army obliged by posting him to the medical corps, where he nearly perished after a severe attack of measles. "One can only hope," Aldous wrote Julian, "that the army doctors aren't merely pumping him full of toxic sulpha drugs for lack of knowing any other treatment." Unfortunately, this was exactly what happened. The twenty-one-year-old remained in bed for seven weeks; by the time he had left the army, he'd lost forty pounds, returning to Llano as weak as when he had left. The experience only confirmed Huxley's bitterness against armies and orthodox medicine.

Nineteen forty-two had been dismaying to pacifists and war supporters alike. The blitz had stopped temporarily, after killing 1,436 people in a single raid, but German armies had pierced the Ukraine. In North Africa, General Rommel repulsed Allied attacks and drove their troops to the sea. The German army hoped to enclose the entire Mediterranean and Near East in an enormous vise while Japanese forces were approaching India. The Japanese took Singapore and sunk the British ships *Prince of Wales* and *Repulse*. In occupied Paris, life for Maria's sister Jeanne continued grimly: Nazi street patrols, motorcycle police guarding the trains, collaborators in cafés.

The thread of Allied survival had been stretched thin, which increased ill feeling against pacifists (who had never wanted to fight in the first place). The journalist Malcolm Phillips suggested that British actors still in Hollywood should be filmed only in black and white, "since Technicolor would undoubtedly show up the yellow of their skin."[69]

Though Britain's treatment of pacifists was far more tolerant now than in World War I, when three out of ten were jailed (instead of World War II's three out of a hundred), regional wartime tribunals were anything but friendly to C.O.'s.

Pacifism in wartime is not a matter for debating societies. British philosopher G. C. Field, who served on wartime tribunals, disputed Huxley's *Ends and Means* by name, insisting that ethical dilemmas cannot be settled by arguing that good is unobtainable by evil means, which ignores the necessary choice between two evils in a less-than-perfect world. Pacifists must consider the consequences of *not* fighting.[70]

If a universal morality applies across situations, differences in degree or purpose of warfare are irrelevant: every war, without exception, is unjustified. Gandhi and Huxley assumed this position. Gandhi's last wartime campaign for the Congress Party was based on passive resistance to invaders; in 1942, he had led his fellow believers in *Satyagraha* in pacifist civil disobedience: fourteen thousand were jailed over the right to speak out against the war.[71]

Once this absolutist position is modified, however, *some* wars might be justified, and what higher priority than an anti-Nazi, anti-Fascist war? Can't the imbalance between two evils force us toward an action unpalatable but nonetheless justified, even mandatory?

Justifying particular wars, however, puts C.O.'s in the uncomfortable position of having to judge whether the actions of a particular country are sufficiently evil that they must be resisted by force—if this is the only way.[72]

Fortunately for anti-Nazi pacifists in World War II, by November 1942, American and British troops were triumphing over Axis troops in Algeria and Morocco; by May 1943, the Allies had taken North Africa. The French Resistance began winning its skirmishes. Germans lost the battle of Stalingrad—but to a pacifist, the Russians can hardly be said to have won, losing more casualties there than the United States did in the entire war.

Six thousand miles from these horrors, the farmers of Llano little suspected their stalky, middle-aged Englishman was a world-renowned advocate of pacifism. They saw him hike their fields, book in hand, his wavy brown hair streaked with gray. A thin, determined fellow, he pecked away at weeds with a hand tool or sat cross-legged in a field, humming quietly to himself with his eyes closed. Here war was distant and peace the urgent quest, as Huxley pored over accounts of mystics and pacifists.

The war years in Llano blurred. Property improvements demarcated the passage of time: the year they dammed the irrigation ditch into a concrete swimming pool, the day they had running water in the main house from a working windmill, the summer they had a grape harvest and made their own wine squishing grapes barefoot in a metal tub, jeans rolled up to their knees.

Llano brought out a surprising domesticity in Maria, but she worried about the changes farm life brought: "Physically, I am now a walking advertisement for the boy's department of Sears Roebuck which at 45 is not exactly correct or perhaps even wise. But I am very satisfied and there is no full-length mirror in the place." A harmony emerges in her letters—as if by withdrawing from the everyday world she and Aldous unblocked their response to the natural world. They noted the migrations of local birds, and how at dawn the hares endlessly wash their face and ears.

Maria and Aldous were bathed in quiet contentment. Life slowed to where Maria imagined she could watch flowers emerge from the desert floor. She would get up in the middle of supper to watch the sunset. When she switched off the light, the cries of crickets filled the cool night air, a bittersweet sound. "But sometimes—often—," she wrote, "the sadness of the world made me distant and lost. Wouldn't it be the greatest egotism to live while forgetting the sadnesses which could be helped."

If Aldous was haunted by such thoughts, he did not express them as freely or frequently as Maria did. Probably he should have, for silence whetted the hostility of critics. George Orwell, for one, no longer forgave and forgot Huxley's absence:

> The thing that is common to all these people, whether it is Petain mournfully preaching "the discipline of defeat" . . . or Huxley advocating non-resistance behind the guns of the American Fleet, is their refusal to believe that human society can be fundamentally improved. Man is not-perfectible, merely political changes can effect nothing, progress is an illusion. The connection between this belief and political reaction is, of course, obvious. Other-worldliness is the best alibi a rich man can have.[73]

Hypocrisy—a simple statement in support of Britain's war effort—would have suited Huxley's critics more than intellectual explanations. Instead, the writer perversely asserted his freedom of thought: "One is accused, if one takes this point of view [pacifism]—which, incidentally, is that of all the men to whom humanity looks up as the founders of religions—of practising escapism. One might as well accuse of escapism the mathematician who does not continually spend his talents and energies on the problem of squaring the circle."[74]

Huxley wrote three books after the writing block which followed the outbreak of war: *The Art of Seeing* (autobiography and essay), *Time Must Have a Stop* (novel), and *The Perennial Philosophy* (anthology). All three were first published in the United States. He finished *Art* in July 1942; by January 1944, he'd returned to and finished *Time*. Just over a year later, *Perennial* was published. These works are a complementary trilogy whose unity is evident only in retrospect.

Of the three, *Time Must Have a Stop* was by far the most Christian; its undercurrent of redemption joins *Grey Eminence* and *The Perennial Philosophy* as the closest Huxley could ever come to religious writing.

Time takes place in Florence in 1929. The Barnack family consists of Uncle Eustace, a wealthy voluptuary, and his seventeen-year-old nephew, Sebastian, a poet with a hunger for evening clothes. The uncle promises to buy them, then dies, and the boy decides to steal a painting (for which he is eventually caught).

Along the way, the young poet has a typically dark sexual encounter with a typically icy Huxley siren (yet another Nancy Cunard clone, in finer-cut clothes). As usual, out-of-wedlock sex is the only sort portrayed, with Huxley cheerfully comparing the lovers to twin cannibals in bedlam. The book's most fascinating section is its thirteenth chapter, where Huxley whimsically provides a character so nonattached he faints away dead in his bath. The uncle has a prolonged out-of-body experience, suggestive of *The Tibetan Book of the Dead*, a work central to Huxley's ideas of death.[75]

Time's epilogue was finally finished in 1944, after the end of Huxley's block. The nephew, now the same age as Huxley (but in wartime London), laments man's destructive impulses but finally makes a separate peace, a state he wills to persist, "in spite of the infernal racket of the guns, in spite of my memories and fears and preoccupations. If only it could persist always."[76]

In *The Art of Seeing*, Huxley documented how physical discipline could perfect vision; in *The Perennial Philosophy*, he asserted that spiritual discipline could perfect insight. For the first time he made explicit this connection between sight and insight: through meditation and mysticism, humans could see beyond their limits.

This trilogy neatly illustrates Huxley's genius, for in three genres and dramatically different contexts he makes the same point. In each book, Huxley explored self-abnegation; in *Time*'s epilogue he wrote:

> The more there is of I, me, mine, the less there is of the Ground.
> . . . People love their egos and don't wish to mortify them, don't wish
> to see why they shouldn't "express their personalities" and "have a
> good time." They get their good times; but also and inevitably they
> get wars and syphilis and revolution and alcoholism, tyranny. . . . In
> the long run we get exactly what we ask for.[77]

In *The Art of Seeing*, he took up the same point on the physiological level:

> The more there is of the "I," the less there is of Nature—of the
> right and normal functioning of the organism.[78]

In *Perennial Philosophy*, he posed this issue as mortification, quoting Saint John of the Cross:

> The soul that is attached to anything, however much good there may be in it, will not arrive at the liberty of divine union. For whether it be a strong wire rope or a slender and delicate thread that holds the bird, it matters not, if it really holds it fast; for, until the cord be broken, the bird cannot fly.[79]

Thus, in these three key works, did Aldous soar over his generation's great tragedy. All three lack Huxley's earlier humor. The mysticism he now embraced had earlier been parodied in *Crome Yellow*, where the character Barbecue Smith writes *Pipelines to the Infinite:*

> "Get into touch with the subconscious and you are in touch with the Universe. Inspiration, in fact. You follow me?"
>
> "Perfectly, perfectly," said Denis. "But you find that the Universe sometimes sends you very irrelevant messages?"[80]

Christopher Isherwood returned from his alternative service with the Quakers to a very different town: "By this time. . .Hollywood Boulevard was crowded with servicemen wandering in and out of the newly opened pinball joints and the roaring bars. It was like a fun fair, but hideously sad."[81]

Particularly depressing were the racial tensions World War II highlighted in L.A., of which the 1943 Zoot Suit riots—when several thousand soldiers rampaged through east L.A.—are only the best known. While Gerald Heard was writing intellectual detective stories at Trabuco, a hundred Mexican-American youths were arrested for a single crime.

On Isherwood's return, he did not have to choose sides between Huxley and Heard—they had ended the competitive "lull" (Sybille Bedford's term) between them: "Aldous, to put it bluntly, could neither believe in or approve of Gerald as a Guru figure," she wrote.[82] Yet Heard's devotees treated him as one, and he protested it less than Krishnamurti did. "It's funny," Isherwood once told Heard, "how these people invariably write to you airmail and special delivery, when all their questions are about eternity."[83]

Aldous's horror of sanctimony had led him to withdraw; Gerald assumed Aldous was unable to commit himself. In any case, both Heard and Isherwood were amazed at the changes hermithood had wrought: Aldous's nut brown color, his clearer vision, the grace with which he sat unfidgeting through the thrice-daily meditations at Trabuco.

Christopher, now immersed in writing *Prater Violet*, was particularly impressed by *The Perennial Philosophy*, which they discussed for hours: "What he really wanted to try and do was to say, 'Look. You think there are endless religions—and so there are, but don't imagine that they are just freakishly hitting on new gods, or new beliefs—new creeds.' It all has a kind of organic unity. All it's about is man trying to answer the question, 'Who am I?' "[84]

In a fascinating but neglected preface to the Prabhavananda-Isherwood translation of the *Bhagavad-Gita*, Huxley first presented his synthesis of the "organic unity" joining the world's religions:

> 1. *The phenomenal world of matter and of individual consciousness. . . . is the manifestation of a Divine Ground.*

> 2. *Human beings can realize the existence [of the Divine Ground] by a direct intuition, superior to discursive reasoning.*

> 3. *Man possesses a double nature, a phenomenological or eternal self, which is the inner man . . . a man, if he so desires, [can] identify himself with the spirit.*

> 4. *Man's life on earth has only one end and purpose: to identify himself with his eternal self.*[85]

Huxley's saints for *The Perennial Philosophy* were intellectual seekers, those who tried to find God with their head, the William Laws and Meister Eckharts: sages following a yoga of reflection. (The English mystical tradition stretches well back into the fourteenth century, in ballads and the poetry of Rolle de Hampole; the earliest sage Huxley quotes in *The Perennial Philosophy* is Francis Quarles of the seventeenth century.[86])

To emulate these models, Huxley had given up the Encyclopedists' scientific materialism for its mirror image: the mystic's intuitive, transforming flash of understanding. T. H. Huxley's grandson turned away from his courageously unorthodox (but essentially negative) tradition. Huxley became an unholy mix of mystic, atheist, communitarian, and pacifist.

This synthesis, later elaborated still further with psychedelics, prompted wartime critics to accuse him of obscurantism: "What has happened to turn Huxley the clear-headed objective intellectual into Huxley the symbolist-mystic with a bias towards Yoga and occultism?" asked one reviewer.[87] "To a world at war," Huxley answered, the perennial philosophy "stands pointing, clearly and unmistakably, to the only road of escape."[88]

Not all critics were disaffected with Huxley's odd theology, of course. The physicist Erwin Schrödinger called *The Perennial Philosophy* a "singularly fit" explanation of "why [mysticism] is so difficult to grasp and so liable to meet with opposition."[89] In 1944, Somerset Maugham noted that mysticism had transformed the subject matter of Huxley's writing, making him "one of the few spiritual torches left burning in the blackout."[90]

It also remade the man, as Maria noted: "Aldous is completely happy. You wouldn't recognize him. So serene and sweeter than ever, closer to material life. He helps now with housework, tries to do the washing up while the phono plays *Don Juan*."[91] Huxley may not have made the world understand his notion of peace, but he had certainly become peaceful.

Visiting Llano, Isherwood was touched by Huxley's rapport with local farmers: "Aldous was not in the very least bit superior. He, who seemed like the most elevated being in some ways, was nevertheless perfectly charming. The neighbors would come when they were in their little house out in the desert. And they would start talking about all kinds of things to do with wildlife, and crops, and problems—Aldous just as much or more than any of them."[92] This was no minor breakthrough. All his life Huxley had bridged the barriers separating him from others—sight, intelligence, education (and height!)—only on the printed page.

His isolated years in Llano had given him a new self-confidence, tempting him to activities of which he could once only have dreamed. He learned to drive a car. Out on the remote desert roads, where only a half-dozen cars a day passed, he would take the wheel without his glasses. For the first time in his life, he was auto-mobile, and self-sufficient. He not only raised and cooked carrots, he drove the extras to a friend's house.

"Even the cattle stare in wonder," Maria wrote Sybille proudly, "when he drives through them and our gate neatly into a crowded garage. And he smiles and his cap is always on one side or the other for the setting sun, and you know how comic and rakish and adorable he looks then. Also like a little boy because he is very preoccupied to do it well—and does."[93]

He took the daunting step of applying for a driving license—and, coached on what to expect, he passed. Southern California had rarely seen a blinder driver. "Few men will anything very strongly," he had written in *Grey Eminence*, "and out of these few, only a tiny minority are capable of combining strength of will with unwavering continuity."[94]

Huxley and Isherwood's reunion went so well they decided to collaborate on a script on faith healing, *Jacob's Hands*.[95] Between Huxley's anger at his son's medical mishaps and Isherwood's peevishness at not seeing enough of his lover, Denny Fouts (now premed), the script had a distinctly antidoctor bent. In April 1944, Huxley finished his part; he wrote to Matthew: "Let's hope that when Chris has added his quota, we shall be able to sell the thing and live in cultured ease for a bit."[96]

This was an odd comment for a man who had chosen a cabin at the edge of the desert, with rabbits and birds for neighbors. But Huxley was turning fifty; even a stylite wearies. They celebrated his fiftieth birthday, July 26, 1944, with a picnic. Aldous and Maria hiked up the mountain and spread out an old blanket by the irrigation ditch. Below, the buttes huddled on the horizon "like kneeling elephants and beyond them, far away, the blue ghosts of mountains."[97]

Their self-segregation in Llano became a time for family. For his five-year-old niece, Olivia, Rose's daughter, Huxley wrote his first (and only) published children's story, *The Crows of Pearblossom*.[98] Matthew, invalided out of the army, was welcomed back to the ranch. Maria beamed as her boy fixed the broken-down phonograph. Mother and son sat under the shade trees and talked till they ran out of words, and still they sat, gazing across the horizon to the snowcapped mountains.

Maria tried to repair her earlier neglect as a mother, but misgivings surfaced continually. When their dog LouLou died in 1943, she wrote to Grace: "I pray to fate never never to have children thrust at me like that little dog was. I am much too conscientious to be given responsibilities."

Aldous also grew closer to Matthew, even if he never could unconditionally accept a boy so different from himself. "Be a bit more directed, less disintegrated and drifting," he advised. Parenting was for Aldous synonymous with good advice—drop a postcard to a friend, fix the phono (again), type up this idea for a film on art.[99]

Like Matthew, Julian was at loose ends. Returning to England after his stormy visit before Pearl Harbor, he had found himself sacked. In his absence, the secretary of the London Zoo had suspended Julian's position for the duration (the Zoo having been largely emptied in fear of wild animals released during a bombing). The situation triggered another of Julian's breakdowns, following a case of hepatitis he brought back from Nigeria: "My illness became a real ordeal . . . I was moved to the London Hospital. However, the blitz was at its worst, and one large flying bomb fell on a corner of the building. The inmates had to be evacuated, and I was taken in an ambulance to a private nursing home near Harrow Weald" for electric shock through the brain. In those days electroshock was "new, potent and quick" and, "like most promising scientific discoveries, it was overextended."[100] Sometimes patients were subjected to "regressive" treatments, receiving as many as 100 jolts.

"I shall never forget the doctor's eyes peering into mine as he fixed the electrodes on my skull, nor the horrible moment of threshing about before I fell into unconsciousness."[101] Better a mystic, on the fringes of society, than a prominent scientist strapped to an electroshock chair.

From time to time, Aldous Huxley accepted speaking engagements to send funds to victims of the bombing of Britain; once, he chose the Quakers as a topic for a broadcast to be aired in Britain, sponsored by Jell-O.

"Pacing Sunset Boulevard en route, Aldous, in a state of euphoria, became almost lyrical," wrote Anita Loos, who drove him to the studio. " 'Just to think that sound had made it possible to reach listeners who never heard of Quaker philosophy and their manner of living!' Aldous declared. . . . 'We are approaching a new Utopia!'

"But on our way home, Aldous became rather distrait. It had transpired that his broadcast was frequently interrupted by commercials touting the sponsor's gelatin as a cure-all for any disease known to mankind.

" 'I hope the British critics won't think I set myself up as a swami or some sort of faith healer,' he fretted.

"As I tried to assure him," Anita continued, "that no intelligent person took commercials seriously, we passed a supermarket. Suddenly, Aldous halted. 'D'you mind stopping in here a moment?' he asked. 'I think I'll buy a box of that gelatin and give it a try.' " [102]

A touching story, but to redeem himself in the eyes of compatriots, a gesture considerably larger than sampling Jello-O was required. [103]

By August 1943, Mussolini had resigned, and Allied troops marched north across Italy. The following summer, the Allies invaded Normandy and then Provence, the German army proved vulnerable, and Paris was liberated by August 1944. *La libération* wasn't exactly the liberation Huxley had sought. He feared war's legacy. The problem was "not how to get rid of the enemy but rather how to get rid of the last victor," pacifist Niccolò Tucci said. "For what is a victor but one who has learned the lesson that violence works. Who will teach him a lesson?" [104]

"The whole dreadful business grinds on," Huxley wrote morosely, "producing precisely the kind of political, economic and moral results that were anticipated. Sausage machines produce sausages, calculating machines produce calculations and war machines produce what they were made to produce, namely misery, chaos, and more war."[105]

If *Grey Eminence* was Huxley's *Inferno*, as war was declared, then *The Perennial Philosophy* was his *Paradiso*, at war's end. Some will call Huxley's efforts to envision peace indirection rather than courage. Yet the ultimate heroism in wartime may lie in imagining a world without war, for no matter how good the cause, war is uncomfortably close to mass murder.

Realizing that millions of humans had died in religious wars exactly like the one now ending, Huxley saw the process recurring infinitely, until its root causes (in defective psychology and education) were resolved. In his search for long-range solutions, Huxley was most at peace in the middle of war, in precisely the way Camus characterized Sisyphus, rolling his rock up the hill: "The struggle itself toward the heights is enough to fill a man's heart. One must imagine Sisyphus happy."[106]

The Perennial Philosophy was a paradox not only because Huxley's readers had little time for mystical pursuits amidst the smoldering ruins of their lives, but because an anthology of mysticism is self-contradictory—one can't read one's way to enlightenment, as he had acknowledged in *Swan:*

> What they know is only the literature of mysticism—not the experience [and not worth talking about]. . . . There is a way between the horns. The practical way. You can go and find out what it means for yourself, by first-hand experience.[107]

A further paradox was pointed out by George Woodcock, editor of the British wartime pacifist journal *Now*. The pursuit of selflessness, ironically enough, requires exercise of individual will, a great deal of it: thus one must first be self-conscious to rid oneself of self-consciousness.[108]

As *The Perennial Philosophy* neared release, Huxley worried how the book would be received. After jacket copy arrived, he wrote to his publisher to tone down its claims: he was neither a great novelist nor a philosopher, "but an essayist sufficiently ingenious to get away with writing a very limited kind of fiction." Glad that his publisher had included a line about his not wanting to start a religion, he hoped this would "take the winds of the sails of some of the ecclesiastical critics who will want to say that I am another Mrs. Eddy [founder of Christian Science]."[109]

In 1910, H. G. Wells had written "The Door in the Wall," a short story about mysticism which loomed large in Huxley's private mythology.[110] A London man is haunted by a childhood vision of a garden he once discovered behind a door; there panthers sported, and sunlight poured in through the surrounding rain. The rest of his life the man searched for that door, but it appeared only at the worst times—when he was taking his college exams, when he was speeding to a ministerial meeting in a cab. Each time he passed by until the last—when, on a foggy evening, he walked through the door. He was found the next morning at the bottom of an excavation.

After seven years in Hollywood, Huxley sought not the polished wooden door overseen by the comely receptionist at MGM's Thalberg Building, but the mystical portal of *The Perennial Philosophy*.

The enchanted garden behind that door was flooded with light. There he could see again, could be a bit less tall, less intimidating, less burdened by the sorrows of the deaths of his mother and brother: more kind. If a Mahayana Buddhist acceptance of suffering was the walkway to that door, he was finally ready to enter.

SEVEN

APE AND ESSENCE

The City of the Angels . . .
More rubber goods than Akron,
More celluloid than the Soviets,
More Nylons than New Rochelle,
More brassieres than Buffalo,
More deodorants than Denver,
More oranges than anywhere,
With bigger and better girls—
The great Metrollopis of the West. . . .

    [In 2108] a ghost town, what was once
the world's largest oasis, is now its greatest
agglomeration of ruins in a wasteland.
Nothing moves in the streets. Dunes of
sand have drifted across the concrete . . . .

                (1948)

Ape and Essence opens with a 1947 Buick convertible careening across the desert floor, raising mushroom clouds of dust at eighty miles an hour.

The Mojave Desert, north of L.A., stretches wide-angled across the screen. Two mussy-haired screenwriters jerk to a stop by an outpost straight out of *The Petrified Forest:* red, old-fashioned gas pumps in front of a country store. In the clear, high-desert air, the San Gabriel Mountains shimmer with snow.

They are looking for a mysterious writer, one William Tallis. All they know of him is the address on his script, which fell at their feet from a studio truck on its way to the dump.[1] Fascinated by this vision of Los Angeles after World War III, the two veterans set off in search of its author.

"Why a man in his senses should choose to live at the end of a road like this, I can't imagine," says the jaded one. On the desert floor jagged buttes rise, "like islands, out of the enormous plain." Then, suddenly, the buttes which had looked black and dead, like the protruding skeleton of a dinosaur, came to life as the clouds opened. Their bright foreground stood out dramatically against the shadows.

"Now do you see why Tallis chooses to live at the end of this road?" the Huxley-like narrator murmurs (*Ape and Essence*, 12).

They pull up at a white frame house, very like Huxley's in Llano, only to find that the misanthropic screenwriter had died six weeks before. Tallis—his name echoing the shards of civilization left after the war—had gone. He left only a sign by the gate, creaking in the wind: "Do you like the human race: no, not much. THIS MEANS YOU. KEEP OUT."

It was no accident this drama took place in the Mojave—or that no one was at home. Like Tallis, the author of *Ape and Essence* had vanished. A fearsome, freak accident—really more of a nightmare— had driven Aldous and Maria from their desert garden at Llano. The grapes still waved gently in the hot, dry breeze; the cottonwoods' spring blossoms shone with tiny bright emeralds, but Aldous was not there to bear witness.

It had happened one day late in the war, as he was gardening out back. He had been jabbing at the earth with his trowel, working the soil too hard, as men unaccustomed to exercise sometimes will.

Suddenly his hand grasped a burr weed, one of those prickly, hoary growths in the desert which, in wet years, bloom in late spring and summer. The tiny thorns pierced his hand, but as the day was still and beautiful, he continued to work in the plot behind his octagonal study. His hands and arm had swollen; his skin flared an ugly red. Maria called it "a ridiculous accident . . . a poisoning of the skin comparable to poison ivy. Not knowing anything about it—except that there is no poison ivy here—we neglected it."[2]

As the days passed, his symptoms worsened. A local doctor diagnosed blood poisoning. Huxley was driven all the way to a hospital in L.A.

There he recuperated, then returned to the ranch. Before the day was out, however, the problem flared up badly. Inconvenience turned to anxiety, and soon he had trouble breathing. Maria drove him back to L.A., this time for allergy shots. His spirit was at peace, as it had been for the last year; the flesh, however, was angry.

Throughout the summer of '44, he saw doctor after doctor. Some had given tests and shots and sent him off cured—only to find him back the following week, fairly howling in frustration. To make matters worse, that summer was particularly rainy and overcast, which caused an extensive bloom.

The culprit was probably horehound—the stuff of old-fashioned cough drops—a short, prickly weed with a sturdy trunk; uprooted, it resembled a miniature tree. They tried ridding the land of the weed; airborne particles dispersed the toxicity. The first attack had heightened his sensitivity to where the very ghost of the substance affected him grievously.

Doctors kept him from the desert until November. By the following June 1945, the irritating cycle had recurred: flight, inoculations, hopeful return, and flight again. The rash and pain grew so intolerable that on a drive up the neighboring mountains to escape the heat, they had purchased "quite suddenly and vaguely, the most hideous little house at Wrightwood," Maria wrote her sister.[3]

Their bright cabin in the desert looked as restful and attractive as ever, but their peace was unexpectedly shattered. Huxley had lost more than his home. The desert's help in seeing had vanished and, with it, his hard-won balance.

The war in Europe had ended a month earlier, at Reims; now the world wondered how long Japan would hold out. Armistice brought Huxley little relief. Even with the Allied victory, there was cause for pessimism—if one looked ahead. Huxley imagined possibilities he thought "really blood-curdling":

> On the Continent a chaos so frightful that, to millions of people,
> the war years would seem in retrospect a time positively of prosperity.
> . . . Too many people, too little arable land. Thanks to technology and
> the Pax Britannica, Malthus's nightmare had become, for a sixth of
> the human race, their everyday reality.[4]

Peace took some getting used to. "Maybe it's suddenly not having any enemies to hate anymore," characters in the postwar movie *Crossfire* told each other. "For four years we've focused our mind on a peanut. The Win-the-War peanut . . . then all at once, no peanut."[5]

Long before its end, the war had worn out its patriotic welcome. The V-2 rockets, Cyril Connolly wrote, "have made London more dirty, more unsociable, more plague-stricken than ever. The civilians who remain grow more and more hunted and disagreeable, like toads each sweating and palpitating under his particular stone."[6] Churchill called Europe "a rubble heap, a charnel house, a breeding ground for pestilence and hate."[7]

After V-E Day, as Allied troops occupied the ruins of Germany, concentration camps ceased to be rumors: Auschwitz and Treblinka exposed the final depths of the already ragged human soul. Soon afterward, the most prosperous nation in the world unleashed the most destructive moment in the history of its species: the atomic bombing of Hiroshima and Nagasaki. In three days, more than 100,000 Japanese died.

"Thank God, we are to have peace very soon," Huxley wrote the day after Nagasaki was vaporized. "But peace with atomic bombs hanging overhead." The bomb and the grisly revelations of the Holocaust intensified the loss of Huxley's sanctuary; together they plunged him into a five-year trough culminating in his most macabre works, *Ape and Essence* and *The Devils of Loudun*.

The change did not come about at once. His stored capital of contentment ebbed slowly, starting with paranoia and dread of postwar Europe: "Not much news from England," he wrote Frieda Lawrence, "and what comes is unutterably drab and weary. . . . Luggage is stolen at the station if you leave it unguarded for a minute; every parcel has to be registered, or else it won't arrive: people swipe the electric light bulbs out of railway carriages by the hundreds of thousands."[8]

However exaggerated this picture was—the ultimate conflagration predicted by Wells and Heard never had occurred—it reflects Huxley's dour spirits.

In the postwar years, Huxley's writing captured the twin moods of his era: optimism in humanity—for triumphing over the seemingly irresistible Nazi and Fascist armies—and pessimism at the human race's passive victimization before militarism and technology.

His pessimism would emerge in *Ape and Essence*, but first, carrying forward the calm of his wartime contemplations, he wrote a steadfastly optimistic, though now forgotten book, *Science, Liberty and Peace*. Huxley sought something in the postwar period that was if not cheering, then resolutely full of potential. Grasping for the hopeful spirit of those organizing the United Nations in San Francisco, he returned to youthful ideals of the model scientist, leading humanity from its gruesome addictions: patriotic chauvinism, racism, and gigantism.

His immediate task, he decided, was "to unlearn the dirty devices of adult humanity," as he had written in *The Perennial Philosophy*:

> *Seen through the dung-coloured spectacles of self-interest, the universe looks singularly like a dung-heap; and as, through long wearing, the spectacles have grown on to the eyeballs, the process of "cleansing the doors of perception" is often, at any rate in the earlier stages of the spiritual life, painfully like a surgical operation.*[9]

The eighty-six-page *Science, Liberty and Peace* was a Tolstoyan survey of how applied science ill served humanity and why, in the future, every advance in technology would only further the unequal distribution of power and property around the world.

The book is addressed to scientists, who might still profit from it. Huxley's search for a positive direction for science again led him to forecast the future: nuclear proliferation by 1950, eventual wars over oil, development of solar and wind power ("strangely only in the experimental stage"), small farming turning into agribusiness, centralization in corporations and labor unions, the rapid reindustrialization of Asia and its technological superiority. Even Gerald Heard was amazed by these predictions: "After three years of a 'peace' of unparalleled tensions, Huxley is back on earth viewing mankind, and he is prophesying."[10]

Huxley insisted in 1946 that humanity's future was inextricably bound to ecology—a notion pioneer ecologists Aldo Leopold and Henry Fairfield Osborn were having trouble publicizing. Ecological devastation was not widely understood by the public until Rachel Carson's works in the early fifties. For Huxley, the crisis was a product of spiritual, as well as scientific, ignorance: "Our present economic, social and international arrangements are based, in large measure, upon organized lovelessness. We begin by lacking charity towards Nature, so that instead of trying to co-operate with Tao or the Logos on the inanimate and subhuman levels, we try to dominate and exploit, we waste the earth's mineral resources, ruin its soil, ravage its forests, pour filth into its rivers and poisonous fumes into its air."[11]

These prophecies had the decentralist leanings of William Morris's 1891 *News from Nowhere* and H. G. Wells's 1901 *Anticipations of the Reaction of Mechanical and Scientific Progress upon Human Life and Thought*. The concentration of capital and industry (capitalist or socialist) led only to tyranny and war. The alternative? Self-sufficiency through economic democracy and deinstitutionalization.[12] Instead of weaponry, scientists should research practical self-government: small-scale technology, alternative energy supplies.

How could scientists believe they worked for the good of all, Huxley asked, "while applying the results of disinterested research in ways which demonstrably increase the power of the ruling capitalist or governmental minority at the expense of personal liberty and local and professional self-government?"[13]

The casual reader might think Huxley's argument is Luddite, a reversion to a preindustrial cottage industry; it most emphatically is not. He struggled to inspire scientists to commit themselves to Right Livelihood, the Buddhist notion of serving humanity before serving oneself. Huxley turned over his royalties from the book to the pacifist Fellowship of Reconciliation.

Science, Liberty and Peace was his positive vision of what could be done to right a wrongward drift of his species—mustered, surprisingly, immediately following the detonation of the worst weapon in the history of the planet.[14] When his hopes did not prevail, his optimism soured.

"Huxley seems to have experienced, in the late 40s and early 50s," one biographer wrote, "so intense an onset of pessimism that his mystical beliefs became almost irrelevant to the world in which he and his contemporaries were forced to live."[15]

The melancholy streak which had sent his brothers and grandfather into asylums hovered not far below the surface. The Huxley boys were Type A characters, with Julian particularly high-strung and irascible. So far Aldous had managed to escape the clinical depressions and suicide of his brothers—yoga and meditation had helped. Yet his breaking point—physically and psychically—was never distant.

After Huxley's allergy banished him from Llano, he and Maria returned to their flat in town, at 145 1/2 Doheny Drive, at the junction of Beverly Hills and Los Angeles. Their squarish, distinguished-looking house was cozy rather than large; while by no means Albany, the Huxleys could receive there.

In town they often saw Paulette Goddard and her new husband, Burgess Meredith. Over dinner, conversation frequently turned to *Brave New World*, in which Burgess wanted to act and Paulette to finance. (She was now a multimillionaire from her divorce settlement—"I even got the yacht," she boasted to a friend.)

Paulette, thirty-three, and "Buzz" Meredith had married in 1944, a third time for each. Paulette had become pregnant—but miscarried. Even Anita Loos's friendship and Meredith's kidding could not reduce her despondency. The miscarriage was among the major events of her life, propelling her forcefully into her career and her wealth. Goddard's name was everywhere, on patriotic pictures like *I Love a Soldier* and *So Proudly We Hail*. In 1945 *Kitty* heightened her fame as a tough and sexy character.

Though Huxley and Greta Garbo refused to participate in the win-the-war films, Anita and Paulette had no such qualms. Paulette was sent to sell war bonds, improbably enough, to Quakers, Amish, and Mennonites in Pennsylvania. Her rallies took her within a few miles from where Christopher Isherwood had worked as a C.O.

$\mathbb{B}$y the war's end, Huxley really had two separate reputations: his literary identity, in which he was still regarded as among the brightest novelists alive, and his reputation as a screenwriter, on which he depended for his family's support. Throughout the forties and fifties, literary critics struggled to untangle Huxley's development. Whether scolding and ill tempered, such as William Tyndall's "What's Wrong with Aldous Huxley" in *The American Scholar* in 1947, or adulatory, such as Charles Rolo's 1947 essay in *The Atlantic Monthly*, critics tied each successive work to previous ones, with mixed success.

Rolo unearthed mystic leanings in early characters such as Calamy (in *Those Barren Leaves*) who declared he would "burrow a way right through mystery [to] some kind of truth, some explanation."[16] (The problem with such exegesis is that opposite, antimystical sentiments occur in early novels. "Mysticism or Misty Schism," one critic titled an essay on the difficulty of interpreting Huxley.)[17]

Since his arrival in the United States, Aldous Huxley had vacillated between literary fiction designed to amuse (and palliate) his regular readers and nonfiction of an explicitly philosophical or didactic cast *(Ends and Means, The Art of Seeing, The Perennial Philosophy, and Science, Liberty and Peace)*.

His nonfiction was optimistic, replete with solutions; his fiction, relentlessly doubting. Of the two, his fiction was sold and reviewed more positively. *The New Yorker* called *Time Must Have a Stop* "brilliant" in its "essentially rather dismal and dark-brown way."[18] Novels no longer interested Huxley (though he had enjoyed drafting the out-of-body passage in *Time*, he later acknowledged in a *Paris Review* interview). Not until his last years would he publish another full-length novel. Giving up fiction was a gamble, however, since earnings from nonfiction were insufficient to keep his family, particularly if Matthew was to finish college.

It was as a screenwriter that Huxley had prospects. In fact, if the old Hollywood adage "You're only as good as your last picture" held, 1945 was Huxley's year. *Madame Curie* had recently appeared, to excellent reviews. The *Hollywood Reporter* had called his script for *Pride and Prejudice* "superb"; *Variety* had tagged *Jane Eyre* with its highest compliment ("a picture geared for heavy grosses") while praising the script's articulation.[19] The *New York Times* called the Welles-dominated film "grimly fascinating." The New York *Sun* singled out Huxley's screenplay as "a splendid piece of work." The fifty-one-year-old writer was "hot."

Huxley's shunning of war films had made advancement difficult for the last few years, but now new projects surfaced continually. Disney asked him to script *Alice in Wonderland;* Zoltán Korda (who had previously asked Huxley's help in dramatizing Kipling's *Jungle Book*) wanted to film an old short story, "The Gioconda Smile."

Huxley's new approach to film was to find a friend as a producer or coauthor. This hadn't worked on his and Isherwood's script, *Jacob's Hands,* but Aldous and Anita discussed reviving Goldsmith's *She Stoops to Conquer;* Aldous and cash-rich Paulette eagerly planned their film of *Brave New World.* (Paulette got so carried away that she told reporters both Aldous and Julian would work on the scenario! This improbable idea would have been one of the few times the brothers collaborated.)

One problem with *Brave New World* was deciding how to present the story. "Audiences may be confused and worried, if we plunge straight into the twenty-seventh century A.D. as is done in the book," he wrote to Anita in October 1945.[20] Out of these conversations came a new preface to the book, which glosses Huxley's postwar mood. Originally, the unnoble Savage faced "an insane life in Utopia, or the life of a primitive in an Indian village," two impossible alternatives which Huxley thought "the most serious defect in the story."

"Today," Huxley wrote, "I feel no wish to demonstrate that sanity is impossible":

> If I were now to rewrite the book, I would offer the Savage a third alternative. Between the utopian and the primitive horns of his dilemma would lie the possibility of sanity.[21]

Film was becoming a family affair. Matthew, following his recovery from his army illness, had cast about for a way to enter the movie industry. The twenty-three-year-old found a reader's job at

Warner's, where he went through women's magazines for story ideas, a dreary job, but a start. He was caught up in one of Hollywood's most famous strikes: a battle by the Conference of Studio Unions (CSU) against corrupt union boss Roy Brewer, who was secretly arranging with studio heads to lock out other unions. When the CSU's painters, publicists, and cartoonists went on strike, they took the readers—including Matthew—out with them.

A showdown took place on October 5, 1945, amid a month of 4,600 strikes across America. That day, CSU pickets congregated at the old Warner lot in Burbank.[22] By midmorning 750 were on line, singing and jeering at the scabs. Outside the gates stood the Burbank police and the Warner studio force, armed and ready. A CSU picket captain, Matthew bragged to his cousin Sophie how he coordinated signs and pamphlets: "never in my life have I sweated so both mentally and physically."[23]

Brewer's scabs arrived, and their cars were overturned. Broken glass lined the side streets where the company union men milled. According to Alvah Bessie (later one of the Hollywood Ten), thugs armed with tire irons and baseball bats awaited a signal to lay into the pickets—one of whom was stabbed in the forehead; a woman was hit in the eye by a police tear gas grenade. Then the Burbank police waded into the fray with clubs; they doused strikers with fire hoses.[24]

Working the line that day was Aldous Huxley, alongside his son. "Aldous was totally uninvolved with matters like labor disputes until his son got involved in the dispute at Warner's," Jake Zeitlin recalled. "He thought differently after he got knocked down. It damn near killed him—he's blind and here, suddenly, this jet of water comes and hits him."[25] The next day the studio was shut down and Matthew was arrested and jailed for several hours. Reading the *Ladies' Home Journal* for movie plots paled; Matthew left Los Angeles soon afterward to finish his B.A. at Berkeley.

Father and son had a front-row view of the antilabor, anti-Communist hysteria arriving in Hollywood. Aldous had just signed a contract for *Alice in Wonderland* with Disney—who was bitterly opposed to the CSU.[26]

If this was to be Huxley's year in Hollywood—and his declining revenues from Britain made this a necessity—he had to produce extravagantly good material to follow his earlier successes. As he began work at Disney Studios, he wrote Anita excitedly of fantasies like a visit of Queen Victoria to Oxford, where she insists on having the author of *Alice* presented to her, "in preference to all the bigwigs." Huxley planned to explore the life of *Alice*'s author, Charles Dodgson, an Oxford lecturer on logic and mathematics whom his mother and aunt (Mrs. Humphry Ward) had known as girls. "This is the first movie he really likes doing," Maria told Jake.

All too soon, however, familiar problems in film writing resurfaced: his taste for wordplay and for the complexity of history were flattened by the demands of writing to a mass audience. He hoped to reconstruct the university of the period, "with its long-drawn struggles between Tory High Churchmen and liberal Modernists":

> But, alas, there is not time in an hour of film—and even if there were time, how few of the millions who see the film would take the smallest interest in the reconstruction of this odd fragment of the forgotten past! So I have to be content with . . . preventing producer and director from putting in too many anachronisms and impossibilities for the sake of the story.[27]

Huxley worked on *Alice* at the end of 1945; his script, dated December 5, incorporates a series of unusual prefaces to the action, including one prurient scene where Dodgson, in his photography studio, helps a young friend out of her dress and Victorian underclothes into a costume. Instead of a rabbit hole, Alice finds a false front to a cabinet—a door in the wall, as it were. Before she can plunge in, Dodgson warns her, in Huxleyan tones, "You've got to find the little door inside your own head first." Huxley's adaptation concentrated on Dodgson and his world over the story's famous incidents (which he retells laconically).

"Mr. Dodgson's influence on children is thoroughly pernicious," a priggish nanny complains. "He encourages the wildest flights of fancy and caprice."[28]

Alice had already been filmed in 1915 and again in 1933, but Disney wanted a new, lavish production, recruiting Ed Wynn as the voice of the Mad Hatter and Jerry Colonna as the March Hare. When the film was finally released in 1951, it had become an uncomplicated (though memorable) cartoon based on John Tenniel's original illustrations. In the final credits, *thirteen* people received "story" credits—but not Aldous Huxley, by then on a graylist of suspect writers.

In the forties, Chaplin had similar troubles with the film industry. The actor-director who, thirty years earlier, had averaged four films a year would turn out only two pictures in this decade.

When Charlie and Paulette split up after the opening of *The Great Dictator*, Chaplin went into a spin from which he barely recovered: "Maybe Chaplin realized for the first time," Otto Friedrich commented, "that he had lost someone valuable. He was now 53, not a good age to be divorced for the third time."[29]

On February 10, 1944, Chaplin had been formally indicted under the Mann Act for transporting across state lines the unstable Joan Barry, who sued Chaplin for the paternity of her daughter, Carol Ann. Though blood tests conclusively demonstrated that Chaplin could not have been the father, the judge allowed Barry's suit to continue. The first trial ended in a hung jury; the self-righteous actor did not accept an out-of-court settlement and insisted on exoneration, engaging only two witnesses for his defense and an unaggressive attorney. In a retrial the blood tests were ruled inadmissible, and Chaplin lost.

Fortunately, Charlie's child bride, Oona O'Neill, encouraged him to keep working. Soon Geraldine Chaplin, their first child, was born—the same year as Chaplin's two boys entered the army.

Another misfit in the postwar world was Garbo. The glamorous star had waited out the war in New York and Europe. Greta and Salka Viertel saw less of each other. Friends reported that Salka's earlier feelings for Garbo had cooled.

Scripts were sent to her first by the studio, then via friends; they went unacknowledged or unanswered.[30] The characters proposed to Garbo ranged widely: Madame Bovary, Talleyrand, Cyrano de Bergerac, Joan of Arc, and Salome. "Even St. Francis entered the lists," a biographer noted. "When he did, Garbo's friend Aldous Huxley asked, 'What? Replete with beard?' "[31]

Rather than boycott the industry, other friends of Huxley's such as Isherwood balanced script writing and personal priorities—in his case, Vedanta. Isherwood slept, most nights, in Brahmananda Cottage, a stone's throw from Hollywood Boulevard. No longer confined to "passive" sexual activity, he dated until he found a man with whom he settled down: William Caskey, a rangy Irish-Indian, ex-Catholic. In hours left over from movie work, Isherwood translated a Hindu mystical work, Shankara's *Crest-Jewel of Wisdom.*

In 1946, Isherwood was laid off at the studios and left California. Despite his usually compulsive candor, he never explained his departure. He told friends he would be gone only a few months while he visited family in England, but a few must have suspected it would be longer. He ended up in New York, where Caskey joined him. Then he left for South America (to write *The Condor and the Cows*), returning directly to Europe. Isherwood didn't visit L.A. until July 1948, thus missing some of Huxley's darkest hours.

Soon after Huxley returned to the country after scripting Disney's *Alice in Wonderland,* his hopes for filming *Brave New World* were dashed. Ralph Pinker, the British agent who had gone bankrupt on Huxley, had sold the film rights to RKO for the pitiful sum of £750. RKO wanted $50,000 to resell the rights, and the project had to be dropped.[32] The loss bitterly frustrated an author ever more dependent on film revenue. As Mann had warned, dependency on script writing was dangerous for a writer; it happened gradually, without forethought. Like so many other Hollywood writers, Huxley had concluded that scenarios were the fastest way of earning money. The industry had changed during the war, however, and the writer was out of touch with its currents.

Aesthetic and technical developments opened a window of opportunity in the postwar period for the hard-edged creativity of film noir. Chaplin thought his new film, *Monsieur Verdoux,* would have a major impact; Paulette Goddard rested her hopes on her new temptress look in *Kitty*; even Isherwood was childishly optimistic, before being laid off: "One can foresee a time when quite a large proportion of Hollywood's films will be entertainment fit for adults, and when men and women of talent will come to the movie colony not as absurdly overpaid secretaries resigned to humouring their employers but as responsible artists free and eager to do their best."[33]

If 1946 inspired Isherwood's confidence, the year was also the making of the Hollywood Faulkner, who had previously written limp scripts like *The De Gaulle Story*. Now—almost by accident—Faulkner had a string of successes and a director with clout who believed in him: Howard Hawks. Faulkner's guardian angel assigned him such classics as *To Have and Have Not* and *The Big Sleep*. There seemed no limit to the opportunities for a shrewd writer with backing in high places.

And that, finally, was what Huxley had in the Hungarian director Zoltán Korda, who had recently made *Sahara* with Humphry Bogart and *Counter-Attack* with Paul Muni.

Korda had read "The Gioconda Smile" years before, and the plot stuck with him: a wealthy banker, sick of his invalid wife, takes a young but shallow mistress. His wife's closest friend also adores him and poisons the wife to get him. When the friend's declaration of passion fails, however, she spreads rumors that the husband was the murderer. The protagonist, already reduced to a Huxleyan "abyss of stinking mud" by his infidelity, cannot stay away from his mistress, thus cinching his apparent guilt. The picture is riddled with darkness, rain, and lightning, its atmosphere matching the prevailing moodiness of postwar films.[34]

Huxley started Korda's script in July 1946 and completed it by September. His mood was exuberant; his revulsion at the atom bomb and the Holocaust faded temporarily before ambitious plans for a script and a play simultaneously (John Van Druten helped him with the visualizations now that Anita was in the East). If the film went well, Korda wanted *Point Counter Point* and other stories. Huxley distinctly enjoyed working with Korda. Intelligent and competent, Korda combined producer and director. Huxley wrote, "We were able to co-ordinate our respective specialties of writer and director without the interference of a producer. Consequently the work was done quickly and efficiently, without being held up by retired button-manufacturers using the Divine Right of Money to obstruct the activities of those who do the actual work."[35]

Peacetime hadn't brought Hollywood the disaster many producers had feared; 1946 was, in fact, film's most financially successful year: three fourths of America's filmgoing population went to the movies weekly. As a character commented in the 1946 blockbuster *The Best Years of Our Lives*, "Last year it was 'Kill Japs.' This year, it's 'Make money.' "[36]

Returning GIs anticipated a land of washing machines and convertibles, where a soldier should find a home and a decent job with decent pay. Reality turned out otherwise: 1946 probably had as many industrial strikes and as low a housing vacancy rate as any previous year in American history.

The result was a period of latent insanity for America, a more genteel version of the trauma suffered by the returning Vietnam veterans in the 1970s. Films mirrored this trauma back into popular consciousness even before Americans understood it. Hollywood exploited new themes: fear that the war wasn't really over—that the defeated genie wouldn't stay in its bottle; horror films which shivered with psychological tension; gangster movies.

Films from this period are marbled with the era's quiet paranoia. In *The Stranger*, Nazi Orson Welles escapes and infiltrates a small New England town to restart the war. *The Blue Dahlia*, based on an unfinished Raymond Chandler work, features a war-weary vet accused of killing his unfaithful wife. In *A Double Life*, the postwar world is a bad dream from which the hero, a Shakespearean actor, cannot wake. "It's a blue, sick world," Humphry Bogart and Lizabeth Scott tell each other in *Dead Reckoning*, as a returning vet blazes away with his pistol and uses napalm (made in Japan) to kill mobsters. In these classics, an enemy waits just over the hill, out of sight, ready to strike.

This was a war popular imagination could not leave behind. Sometimes the bad guys had pictures of Hitler hidden in their office, as in *Brute Force*; sometimes they were Jew-killers, as in *Crossfire*. Dramas of Nazi spies ranging the metropolis *(The House on 92nd Street)* were refashioned for the cold war, with Russians substituting as villains.

Some changes in postwar American film were celluloid-deep, others fundamental. The B films of singing cowboys and dancing couples in tuxes dried up, victim of war rationing and increasing demands for realism. More important, Anglo-American film had become a two-way street, as English flour magnate J. Arthur Rank began buying chains of theaters in the United States. Hugh Dalton, Chancellor of the Exchequer, initiated a stiff import tax on American film to encourage British production. Finally, there was television; though reaching only several dozen cities, it grew as fast as radio had in the 1920s.

Of course, this period was not all grimness; wags like P. G. Wodehouse unceasingly mined memories of Hollywood: "You ever been cornered by a wounded studio executive, Phipps? . . . How well I remember the day when I was wandering through the jungle on the Metro-Goldwyn lot and Louis B. Mayer suddenly sprang out at me from the undergrowth. He had somehow managed to escape from the office where they kept him, and I could see from his glaring eyes and slavering jaws that he had already tasted blood. Fortunately I had my elephant gun."[37]

Restlessness ran through Hollywood's émigré community after World War II. Hollywood's isolation from Europe had only increased after the war. "The world outside is considered mainly in terms of box office," Hortense Powdermaker, the sociologist, noted.[38]

Now that travel was possible, should they return? Some, in Sheridan Morley's phrase, "were too old, too rich, too comfortable or sometimes just still too nervous."[39] Others simply did not wish to return. Perhaps they had drunk of California's River Lethe and forgotten friends and family; perhaps the prospect of returning to a Europe so devastated and disappointing didn't appeal.

"Those who had not already gone home for the war were beginning to become uneasily aware that for the 1950s, it was no longer enough in Hollywood just to be British," Morley wrote.[40]

The British weren't the only emigrants who felt a chill. According to Katia Mann, un-Americanism threatened the exile film community almost as much as the curfews of the war had. The interrogation of Hanns Eisler and Bertolt Brecht at the 1947 HUAC hearings in Hollywood disconcerted many:

> Brecht's speech in his own defense before the Committee on Un-American Activities was broadcast on the radio, and I heard it [Katia Mann wrote]. Brecht was very sly indeed: he pretended to be stupid, and the others were stupid. The whole business of loyalty checks was a great disaster, and today it's almost as bad again. We experienced the whole so-called McCarthy era; during it my husband was continually attacked as a Communist, which he never was in his life.[41]

If Thomas Mann—former guest of Roosevelt, recipient of honorary doctorates and the Nobel Prize—faced such attacks, who among the exiles was safe?

(Apparently no one. Mann visited Germany in 1949, surveying a return from exile; his brother Heinrich was in the tricky position of having received an invitation to host the East German Academy of Letters; if Heinrich accepted, Thomas could count on further problems in America.)

Anita Loos joined those departing Hollywood. She and Helen Hayes had a play, *Happy Birthday*, opening in Boston on October 3, 1946. Gerald Heard's beloved Trabuco College was on the ropes, facing bankruptcy as students wandered off. Maria thought the problem was that Gerald played favorites off against each other. He turned Trabuco over to the Vedanta Society and withdrew into yet another career, as H. F. Heard, mystery writer.

His first novel, *A Taste for Honey*, had concerned a hardened misanthrope involved in a murder by killer bees. Then *Harper's* published Heard's macabre story, "The Great Fog," in which a superhumid fog prevented technology from functioning, initiating a new Dark Age over California. (Heard's science fiction was based on obscure wonders of the animal world which he, Aldous, and Julian avidly collected: bees' territoriality, how crayfish balance themselves.) Heard's detective, Sydney Silchester, was an unlikely cross of Sam Spade and Madame Curie.[42]

For Huxley, the summer of 1946 was lonely: not only were Isherwood, Garbo, and Loos gone, he felt increasingly distant from those who remained, such as the Hubbles. Edwin's speech to L.A.'s Sunset

Club had given Huxley pause: "War can be stopped when and only when we are ready to use physical sanctions—when we are ready to use a police force."[43] Huxley abhorred this "we bombed the dickens out of them" belligerence. Grace recorded no outright disputes in her journal, but visits and calls dwindled. Huxley and Mann similarly parted company over Huxley's wartime pacifism. In October 1944, Mann had written a friend:

> Little or nothing can be said against your Huxley criticism, sharp as it is, and I am glad that I too have decidedly sought distance from the spirit and sentiment of [Time]—and even of the man in general . . . the fact that America rejects him can only be applauded. It would not be desirable for this mystical defeatism to find acceptance here.[44]

In June, Huxley left Wrightwood in the Sierra Madres to work on "The Gioconda Smile" with Korda at Universal for $1,500 a week. The time passed with painful slowness. Even with Zoltán Korda acting as producer and director, problems arose. First, Charles Boyer decided that he could only be photographed so as to show the right side of his face (their female lead was less truculent: Jessica Tandy, who would star in the Broadway premiere of Tennessee Williams's A Streetcar Named Desire the next year).

Next, Joe Breen, Will Hays's successor at the Production Code Administration, bowdlerized their script. The mistress's premarital pregnancy had to be illustrated by "becks and nods and wreathed smiles," an instruction which nauseated Huxley: "The tag which you like will probably have to go," he wrote Anita Loos, "as the censors cannot permit anyone who has ever committed adultery to be shown as happy! This is something which even Tartuffe and Pecksniff could never have imagined."[45] Even in the best of circumstances, with a literate and well-heeled backer, on the first (and only) project on which he would have solo screen credit, film-making was still agonizing. He tired "of the endless jig-saw puzzle and carpentry work that has to go into a play and, still more, into a scenario. Also, I find, one gets tired in a play of having to express everything in terms of dialogue."[46]

The story he most enjoyed telling about "The Gioconda Smile" concerned Claude Rains, whom Huxley and Korda had originally wanted for the male lead before settling on Boyer. Rains had asked for more money, but Universal's casting director was firm: "In this studio," he told Korda, "not even Jesus Christ could get a raise in salary." [47]

When Huxley used this incident in *Ape and Essence* to settle scores, he made Louis B. Mayer the antagonist:

> The tone was friendly; but when Bob tried to insist, Lou had banged his desk and told him that he was being un-American. That finished it.
> "What a subject, I was thinking, for a great religious painting. . . . It would be one of Rembrandt's favorite themes, drawn, etched, painted a score of times. Jesus turning sadly away into the darkness of unpaid income tax, while in the golden spotlight, glimmering with gems and metallic highlights, Lou in an enormous turban still chuckled triumphantly over what he had done to the Man of Sorrows." (Ape and Essence, 40)

As the Huxley-Korda picture was about to be released, studio executives suddenly decided that no one had ever heard of the Gioconda. *Time* reconstructed what happened next:

> The studio, advising him that this title was "too obtuse," asked him to try again. Huxley cheerfully suggested another he has used successfully: Mortal Coils. After a good deal of considering, U-I rejected that one on the grounds that people might mistake it for Brooklynese for "curls" or "girls". . . .
> Huxley, beginning to breathe hard, offered the Macbeth tag, Sleep No More. When U-I still wasn't satisfied, he gave up. Then the studio went to work on the problem. How about The Unguarded Heart? Huxley winced. How about Art of Murder? Huxley shuddered. Or Black Velvet? Huxley beat his temples. Well, then: Vengeance? Or Woman of Vengeance? Huxley's wife tried to calm him down. All right, A Woman's Vengeance it is. [48]

All this irritated Huxley to distraction. His mood paralleled that of his friend Orson Welles, who said, "I'm working on a new disappearing act. When I perfect it I'll just give one wave—and Hollywood will disappear." Or as Chaplin put it, less jocularly, in 1947, "Hollywood is now fighting its last battle, and it will lose unless it decides, once and for all, to give up standardizing its films—unless it realizes that masterpieces cannot be mass produced in the cinema like tractors in a factory." [49]

"The wave of post-war optimism which buoyed us up was soon to break," wrote Christopher Hampton, the British playwright. "All over Hollywood, supporters of liberal causes, of War effort and our glorious Ally began to discover, often to their own amazement, that they were in fact premature anti-Fascists, fifth columnists, Red stooges, subversives, or even Communists!"[50]

In the fall of 1946, Aldous Huxley turned a dark corner and found himself in a hallway of desperation; *Ape* was at the end of that long, dark corridor.

"Suddenly to realize that one is sitting, damned, among the other damned—it is a most disquieting experience," he had written in *Grey Eminence*. "So disquieting that most of us react to it by immediately plunging more deeply into our particular damnation."[51]

Huxley shared Father Joseph's fate:

> *He came to be possessed, in spite of his daily practice of mental prayer, by a sense of bitterness and frustration. Visions, it was true, and pro- phetic revelations were still vouchsafed to him; but the unitive life of his early manhood was at an end; he had the dreadful certainty that God had moved away from him. It was a dark night of the soul—but not that salutary dark night described by St. John of the Cross, not the dark night of those who are undergoing the final and excruciating purgation from self-will; no, it was that much more terrible, because fruitless and degrading, dark night, which is the experience of those who have seen God and then, by their own fault, lost him again.*[52]

At the heart of Huxley's notion of the long dark night of the soul was the attainment of enlightenment and its subsequent, piercing loss—Wordsworth losing the attentive spirit of his youth, Faust fi- nally realizing his devilish choice.

In *Time Must Have a Stop*, such a divine abandonment occurs; Huxley confided his deepest feelings only to his fiction. At the end of the novel, the hero loses his spiritual aplomb:

> *The grace had been withdrawn again . . . Sebastian sadly shook his head. Dust and cinders, the monkey devils, the imbecile unholinesses of distraction.*[53]

Whether caused by the loss of Llano, his disgruntlement at movie-making—even in the best of circumstances, the breakup of his circle of friends, or his despair at the anticommunism threatening liberals in the film colony, Huxley was despondent. What separated this depression from his earlier ones was that now, instead of stopping his writing, he vented his disappointments in a savage attack on the land he had adopted, Southern California.

A similar sense of loss permeates "Dromenon," a story Heard wrote about an architectural historian, who, while visiting an obscure chapel, uncovers pagan and Celtic iconography. He slips into a mystical state, similar to that "one experiences in large high-powered cars when the top gear slips in smoothly and one forges ahead on a wide-open road":

> Almost at once I felt come over me again the strangely significant, soothing effect. . . . this amazing direct sense of wholeness, of the lack of any conflict or striving, not to step back into the old throbbing, knocking, thwarted flutter and thump of life.
> Now that I knew, with a profound kinesthetic intuition, I must— it was my one ordinarily conscious thought, my one contact with my old acquisitive-defensive self—hang on to this knowledge. I simply must not lose this.[54]

Yet lose this Huxley did, according to Matthew, who cites both *Grey Eminence* and *Time Must Have a Stop* as examples. "Somewhere along the line Aldous must have had some kind of contact— once or twice. Maybe that started him on his interest in compiling the accounts in *The Perennial Philosophy;* but I have a horrid feeling that he lost it somewhere. . . . Did Aldous ever achieve [transcendence] or not; that's the question I'm raising. Or is it all intellectualized, put down in technical terms and other people's words as in *The Perennial Philosophy?*"[55]

No autobiography remains to resolve this mystery, but others were convinced Huxley had visited, at least briefly, higher ground. Reviewing *Time Must Have a Stop* for *The New Yorker*, Edmund Wilson wrote that Huxley's descriptions of mystical states "have a certain sound of authenticity and convince one that they are based on experience."[56]

If Huxley did reach *satori*, or sudden enlightenment, he had probably done so at the Vedanta Society or in Llano during 1940–1945. Thus the last stage in Huxley's *Walpurgisnacht* coincides with the sale of their desert hideaway—at the time he began *Ape and Essence*.

As the winter of 1946 approached, Aldous, Maria, and his in-laws Joep and Suzanne Nicolas moved back to L.A. from Wrightwood. "Beautiful abandoned Llano was passed on the way, with its gardens brimming with fruit," his niece wrote of the oasis Huxley could never again possess.[57]

"We are in the process of getting out of our ranch," Huxley wrote to a friend, "very sadly, but feeling that it is the sensible thing to do, in view of the difficulties and the troubles it involves."[58] Ironically, the "troubles" were what had made the place so adventuresome originally: water shortages, variable electric supply, the summer heat. All that had changed was his interminable allergy. In L.A.'s smog, he could at least work, even if he saw poorly.

Selling their ranchito affected Maria probably more than she had expected, and for her, too, a dark period began. She yearned for Llano as for few other places; Aldous's own nostalgia was particularly hard to bear, since leaving was not *her* fault. "There is no immensity," she complained of Wrightwood. "The beautiful desert is out of my life though it will never be out of my inner eyes."[59]

The road up to Wrightwood from Llano rises sheerly from the desert in one of those storybook straight lines which allow the traveler to see a destination hours before it is reached. Eventually the hiker arrives at a serpentine forest track, winding like an apple peel through dappled knolls and meadows, past tall, arching Coulter pines.

The road marks the western edge of Sumner Wright's spread in the 1880s. The town had a general store, a gas station, a chapel (not much use to Huxley), and a café. Wrightwood's only evidence of culture was the monthly visit of a wooden station wagon sent by the San Bernardino County Library.

Matthew was enchanted by their new place, "set in a large, heavily forested valley with a little torrent running through it." Unfortunately, Maria came down with what Matthew called "mountain sickness": "At first she felt terribly shut in after Llano, but now has found the walks making up for it. . . . When one gets to the crest of the range, one can look down over the whole colossal expanse of the Mojave, with its polished, platinum-like dried lakes."[60]

This Alpine retreat was snowbound five months a year, and, lacking a study, Aldous worked in a silver trailer on a sunny patch under the trees. Maria disliked the mountains' remoteness and took every precaution not to feel isolated. She persuaded Peggy Kiskadden and Krishnamurti to buy plots nearby. Salka Viertel likewise bought a house there: "In a remote way Wrightwood reminded me of the Carpathian Mountains. . . . Instead of the smell of wild berries and mushrooms, one was rewarded with dry whiffs of sage, which the wind blew from the desert."[61] Thus, unbeknownst to the local ranchers, the Huxleys created an improbable gathering spot for European intellectuals.

At night, the only sounds were the yelps of foxes and coyotes drifting into their uninsulated bungalow, where they sat by the tiny heater. There was no electricity, and windows were so scarce they had to strip some from the house in Llano.[62] February 26, 1947, was their first night in Wrightwood as their only home; Maria remained sad, despite the arrival, finally, of costly central heating. For the first time, her letters complain about Aldous in a tone which suggested divorce: "If only Aldous would take a secretary. Or perhaps a taxi every once in a while . . . Aldous *will* not have anything to do with practical or financial matters. He doesn't want to talk about them, he doesn't want to *think* about them."

Maria's eyes began to trouble her—perhaps a sympathetic reaction to Aldous's problems, caused by the shadowy forest. Her migraines returned, joined by constant fatigue—like a cancer victim who, in the early stages, looks healthy but can barely stir. To Jeanne she confided: "I have the sensation that if I were pushed a little further, or a little faster, I would go mad. . . . you must not say a word of this to *anybody*, so don't even refer to it in your letters. . . . I arrange things to cure myself in secret."[63]

Why didn't she mention to Aldous the pains in her chest? No doubt she didn't wish to worry him, or perhaps he was becoming increasingly difficult.

Huxley had just had a further setback. Prospects for an American theatrical production of "The Gioconda Smile" were slim; theater owners didn't want the play unless they could resell the film rights— which Korda already owned. Six months' work was for naught, at least in America.

The discovery made him tired and more irritable; in combination with the physical strains of moving, it threw him into a sitting-in-bed grouch. His lethargy progressed to where he abandoned a novel on Saint Catherine of Siena he had worked on desultorily for nine months. He had hoped to evoke fourteenth-century Italy: the age of the *Decameron*, Petrarch, Sienese painting, and the Black Death. The work was to have been another *Grey Eminence*.[64]

Now, he suggested to Anita, "I may write something about the future instead . . . about a post-atomic-war society in which the chief effect of gamma-ray radiations had been to produce a race of men and women who don't make love all the year round but have a brief mating season."[65]

Revealingly, Huxley set the introduction of *Ape and Essence* in Llano, where the mysterious screenwriter Tallis lived, rather than in Wrightwood. Like Maria, Aldous could not get the desert out of his inner eye.

In his dyspeptic mood, Huxley's efforts to write the book "straight" (rather than in the form of a scenario) failed, he told science fiction writer Philip Wylie: "the material simply wouldn't suffer itself to be expressed at length and in realistic, verisimilitudinous terms. The thing had to be short and fantastic, or else it could not be at all."[66] Huxley eventually divided the work into two parts, a contemporary introduction (in which the scenario and its desert-rat author, Tallis, are introduced) and a fantasy, set in 2108, of the destruction of Los Angeles.

In fiction, Los Angeles has been burned, destroyed by atomic bombs, comets, and earthquakes, roiled with environmental decay, and plagued with microscopic bacteria. Southern California writers do violence to it on a massive scale. Nathanael West wanted to incinerate the place, "to show the city burning at high noon. . . . He wanted the city to have quite a gala air as it burned, to appear almost gay.

And the people who set it on fire would be a holiday crowd."[67] Ross MacDonald's *The Underground Man* has a more sinister fire. "The City burning," wrote Joan Didion, "is Los Angeles's deepest vision of itself."[68] In *Ape and Essence*, Huxley brought World War III (a plague of glanders and postapocalypse radiation) to Southern California.

Ape and Essence contains his most explicit comments on Hollywood; given his present anger, the portrait is savage and bizarre. The work is written in the form of a film script, complete with narration. The scenario opens in a parody of the present, at a picture palace packed with baboons, all staring glassy-eyed at a baboon in a shell pink evening gown who raises her "bedroom contralto" to sing:

> Love, Love Love—
> Love's the Very essence
> Of everything I think, of everything I do
> Give me, Give me, Give me,
> Give me detumescence
> That means you.

At this point, the new plague descends.

The only survivors of World War III's biogenicide are in Equatorial Africa and in New Zealand, which sends an exploratory schooner to rediscover California, a crew of Balboas traveling backward in time. One of their number, the biologist Alfred "Stagnant" Poole, is captured by the savages; he learns the new creed of Belial from the Arch-Vicar, Bishop of Hollywood, and his assistant, the Patriarch of Pasadena. History, these postapocalypse sages conclude, is the product of diabolical possession, which began in the Victorian era of T. H. Huxley. (Huxley had propounded this theory earlier to John Middleton Murry: "to account for the seemingly possessed demonic behaviour of our rulers at the present time, I don't think we need go beyond the products of our own past behaviour."[69])

Humans are reduced to robbing graves for clothing. Birth defects are so common that Spartan purgation ceremonies are held at the Los Angeles Coliseum. The coffee shop at the Biltmore Hotel becomes the site of a new cottage industry: fashioning cups of skulls; Pershing Square becomes a communal oven where cretins bake bread with fuel from the nearby Los Angeles Public Library: "In goes *The Phenom-*

enology of Spirit, out comes the corn bread. And damned good bread it is."[70]

"The trouble about being a satirical writer," Aldous complained to Julian as he began *Ape,* "is that plain facts outdo anything an ironist could concoct."[71] Nevertheless, Huxley's ironic instincts worked overtime: from the tawdry film he imagines made of his never written book on Catherine of Siena to his send-up of his family's heritage of evolutionism.

By 2108 the species has tumbled down the ladder charted by his grandfather and Darwin. War reduces two and a half million Angelinos to skeletons. "Consciousness might be an evolutionary mistake," Aldous once told Edwin Hubble.[72]

In *Ape and Essence,* Huxley created a world of devolution where humans no longer have the biological distinction of breeding when they choose. Instead, the race reproduces in an annual two-week "orgy-porgy"; here, "ends are ape-chosen/Only the means are man's." Huxley reinvents original sin. Man's Fall is due to his inability to see far enough into the future to stop "the squalid disintegration of the very substance of the species," an occurrence as likely "the product of atomic industry as of atomic war" (*Ape and Essence,* 75).

In *Ape and Essence,* Huxley savaged science as earnestly as he had earlier hoped to reform it with *Science, Liberty and Peace.* The apocalypse resulted from scientists casually ignoring the ends which their daily means created:

> To see that all shall die has been the task of some of those brilliant D. Sc.s now in the employ of your government . . . Here they are after a hard day at the Lab, coming home to their families. A hug from the sweet wife. A romp with the children. . . . And in the morning, after orange juice and Grapenuts, off they go again to their job of discovering how yet greater numbers of families precisely like their own can be infected with a yet deadlier strain of Bacillus Mallei. (Ape and Essence, 32)

Such behavior brought humanity to ecocatastrophe:

> Everywhere erosion, everywhere the leaching out of minerals. And the deserts spreading, the forests dwindling. . . . Yes, Belial foresaw it all—the passage from hunger to imported food to booming population and from booming population back to hunger again.[73]

Huxley's antiscience diatribes could be explained as frustration at the blindness which had prevented him from joining those bright D. Sc.'s in the first place. Yet despite his physical disabilities, Huxley had become a scientist and his demifictional characters his laboratory. Many scientists read him avidly—including, irony of ironies, those he now attacked in *Ape and Essence*, that brilliant Hungarian quartet of doom (physicists Szilard, Wigner, Von Neumann, and Teller) who worked on the Manhattan Project.[74]

In *Ape*, Huxley tore at the bowels of L.A. the way Tiresias prophesied from the bird entrails thrown at Oedipus's feet. The closest parallel is Aldous's other California novel, *After Many a Summer Dies the Swan*. In both, events unfold at Forest Lawn Cemetery; only now the fate of the Fifth Earl (whom longevity had devolved into a protoape) belongs to the human race.[75]

Huxley's depression cannot alone explain the ghoulish tone of *Ape and Essence*. He had always balanced hope and distrust for his species; now loathing entered the equation. A dissertation written about the younger Huxley had captured this attitude in a close reading of the twenty-six-year-old's poems: "Men are born, suffer pain, and die— all to no purpose whatsoever . . . What of the human world? Huxley's answer was that it is the counterpart of the mad cosmos outside man."[76]

Thirty years later, Huxley no longer blamed a mad cosmos. Was there time to salvage the race? Huxley doubted it. The solution, spiritual and psychological retraining for peace, was one few chose to tackle.

The genesis of *Ape and Essence* lies in Huxley's reading of early English, French, and American science fiction—Matthew vividly remembers reading and discussing Wells and Verne in Sanary—and in one of the most popular science fiction films ever made, *Things to Come* (1936), an example of eschatological science fiction, a subset of what scholars call "future histories."[77]

Huxley never claimed to write science fiction, though *Ape and Essence* and *Brave New World* fit the genre's parameters: "the more or less scientific basis, real or imaginary, theoretical or technical, on which the writer predicates a fantastic state of affairs."[78]

In this imaginative writing, Huxley drew not only on the Anglo-French tradition extending back to Francis Godwin's *Man in the Moone* (1638), he tapped perhaps the only American literary genre which influenced his writing. Before and after Mark Twain's *Three Thousand Years Among the Microbes* (1905)—whose hero is named Huxley—American writers have speculated on the changes science would write on society. Huxley knew this literary tradition, having written a foreword to Edward Bellamy's 1888 *Looking Backward*.

Other examples of the "future history" are the wry *Penguin Island* of Anatole France, Olaf Stapleton's *Last and First Men*, Robert Heinlein's "Lost Legacy," and, later, Isaac Asimov's *Foundation* trilogy.[79]

Just before Aldous had left for the United States, Maria had noted how impressed he had been by *Things to Come*. A decade later, unconsciously or not, Huxley's *Ape and Essence* borrowed scenes from Wells.

Things to Come concerned the long-term effects of world war, a subject which preoccupied Huxley in 1936. As in *Ape and Essence*, the principal cause of destruction, once the bombers had run their course, was a biological weapon, a fever of mind and body called the "Wandering Sickness." Zombies and golems stalk a ruined Europe until a Chief (Ralph Richardson), not unlike the one in *Ape and Essence*, takes command Mussolini-style by shooting the victims.

Later, an aviator (Raymond Massey) arrives. The Chief greedily fantasizes about using this remnant of the Mechanical Age to conquer his enemies. Crowds riot against the scientists whose Progress produced the race's downfall. In the end of the film, the Chief is subdued by a Gas of Peace, as convenient a *deus ex machina* as the bacteria which subdued Martians in Wells's *War of the Worlds*.

*A*pe and Essence is an unrecognized predecessor of science fiction films on the environmental destruction of Los Angeles and human devolution. The most popular of these is the series begun in 1968 with *Planet of the Apes*. This society of the future, where apes rule humans, is based on the same reverse evolution which character- izes *Ape and Essence:* archeological finds reveal that the earlier the ape artifact, the more advanced. "The proper study of Apes is Apes," says one actor, parodying Huxley's *Proper Studies* (which took its title from Pope, "The proper study of mankind is man").

Los Angeles's future decay is also the subject of Hollywood films such as *Blade Runner.* In 2817, Los Angeles is raining all the time, an Asian city where sophisticated robots whom genetic engineering has failed run amok. As in *Ape and Essence,* human technology out- strips the race which created it. In *The Omega Man,* a man immune to World War II's plague prowls through an abandoned L.A. for an antidote.

A more primitive version parallel to *Ape* is *Them!* (1954), in which nuclear explosions bring mutations—in this case, giant ants who make their way from New Mexico to Los Angeles, where they live in the sewers that so fascinated Aldous.

Unlike these films, Huxley's present mood allowed no happy ending for humanity. At the end of *Ape,* the scientist and his young lover escape L.A. by crossing the San Gabriels via the ruins of the Angeles Crest Highway (the same route Maria advised Grace and Edwin Hubble to use in visiting Llano). The pair bed down in a pine forest similar to Wrightwood—then descend to Llano and out across the Mojave, probably to perish on their way to indepen- dence.

Huxley poured out the spleen of Los Angeles into his new work. But even vitriol needs replenishment, and in September 1947, midway through *Ape and Essence* and after the filming of "The Gio- conda Smile" ended, Aldous and Maria decided to leave California for the first time in nearly a decade and travel to New York. Having just graduated from Berkeley with a major in Latin America studies, Mat- thew was moving into an apartment there. His parents, for once proud of the new graduate, helped him settle into his new job at Elmo Ro- per's polling company.

They visited the Lawrence ranch in New Mexico and enjoyed the autumn smells of roasting chilies and burning leaves. New York was at first "horribly disappointing," and their sublet apartment a dilapidated flat.

Once used to the fast-paced, East Coast life, however, the visit proved a tonic for Maria, uncharacteristically bitter at their recent past: "I have an absolute horror of California. I would not mind if I never went back. . . . Nothing holds me, nothing invites me back. . . . It seems quite a mad life. Not the years at Llano. Those were peaceful."[80]

If Maria was seduced by Bloomingdale's and their proximity to Europe, Aldous's depression continued. "Even during the war, you could hope that things were going to be O.K.," he told *The New Yorker*. "Now the whole social order is running down in the most hopeless way, with no prospect for amelioration in the immediate future."[81]

A few weeks later they left New York. "Aldous has a novel to finish, and after all I have a house to run," Maria wrote Jeanne. By the beginning of December, unable even to visit Wrightwood because of mountain snows, they were back in L.A. Aldous fell ill with bronchitis and had to see the doctor every day, in addition to taking his daily Bates lessons. Maria resignedly resumed her life as chauffeur, typist, and maid, roles her mother never anticipated but gladly availed herself of now that she, too, needed driving around from her small apartment nearby. (Mrs. Nys had moved to L.A. from Mexico City in 1942.)

By the end of February, Huxley was back in Wrightwood, finishing *Ape and Essence*. An occasional truck whined by on the road next to his house. The sun peered down through the giant pines, its radiance making brilliant shadow of the thick trunks. Cries of the birds and the occasional rustle of a squirrel made a gentle mountain music.

Fueling his activity was the political assassination of his greatest living hero: on January 30, 1948, Mahatma Gandhi was shot on his way to prayer. Gandhi had heartened Aldous and Gerald by his refusal to compromise his means (Satyagraha, nonviolent resistance) to his end, independence for India. He was the leading example of the 100 percent pacifist; he even turned his back on former associates when he felt they had embraced pacifism purely out of political expediency. Gandhi, too, believed in decentralization and male continence; his speeches could have come out of the mouth of Mr. Propter in *Swan*. The first sentence of *Ape* begins, "It was the day of Gandhi's assassination . . ."

> *Gandhi was a reactionary who believed only in people. Squalid little individuals governing themselves, village by village, and worshipping the Brahman who is also Atman. It was intolerable. No wonder we bumped him off. . . .*
>
> *In that symbolic act, we who so longed for peace had rejected the only possible means to peace and had issued a warning to all who, in the future, might advocate any courses but those which lead inevitably to war.* (Ape and Essence, 6, 7)

Gandhi understood that as we damage others, we ourselves are damaged; as we silence the lives of others, we are numbed. After finishing *Ape*, Huxley wrote "A Note on Gandhi," published in *Vedanta and the West*. His restrained words had the ring of a man who weeps his tears in words:

> *Gandhi's body was borne to the pyre on a weapons carrier. There were tanks and armoured cars in the funeral procession, and detachments of soldiers and police. Circling overhead were fighter planes of the Indian Air Force. All these instruments of violent coercion were paraded in honour of the apostle of non-violence and soul-force. It was an inevitable irony.*
>
> *The men and women who had led the non-violent struggle against the foreign oppressor suddenly found themselves in control of a sovereign state equipped with the instruments of violent coercion. The ex-prisoners and ex-pacifists were transformed overnight, whether they liked it or not, into jailers and generals.*[82]

Much had happened in the last year, as Huxley had retreated to Wrightwood to finish *Ape*. For one thing, he had again become famous—at an improbable juncture, for in the last decade he had produced only two novels, a play, several film scripts, and a few obscure works of nonfiction. Fame here refers to that peculiarly American mass visibility: picture essays in the great mass-circulation magazines of the American forties and fifties—*Vogue, Life,* and *Time*—similar, though weightier than London's *Picture Post* (which also did a 1948 story on Huxley) and *Paris Match*.

Vogue commissioned twin pictorial features on Isherwood and Huxley from Suzanne's daughter, Claire. (This may have been Maria's idea, for she helped launch several members of the family in journalism through features on her husband.) For a twenty-one-year-old, Claire's prose was professional and set in the Llano she, too, loved: "a lean 52-year old, his abundant hair lightly greying. The full mouth and the large mobile nostrils remind one of the placid, good-natured look of a camel [an insider's joke—the family kidded Aldous about the way he puffed his cheeks when bored or impatient]. . . . Huxley is not optimistic about the world."[83]

Following Julian's election as Director General of UNESCO, *Life* ran a four-page story on the Huxley brothers. Their treatment posed a superficial opposition: Julian "the materialist, denying the need for religion or God. At the other pole stands Aldous the mystic, preaching the faith that all religions are one and God is everywhere." Never mind that Aldous's "faith" would fit precious few religious establishments; never mind that Julian, no materialist, lived modestly in Belsize Park and had half a dozen times given up stable careers to carry out independent researches. To *Life*—as conservative as the "U.S. out of the U.N." billboards which finally *did* drive the U.S. out of UNESCO in 1985—Julian was a godless atheist, a phrase his grandfather would have chuckled at, one which in 1947 reverberated with connotations of evil and communism.

For a brief week, every newsstand, every barbershop, and dentist's waiting room from sea to shining sea sported Aldous's picture. The grocer, the service station attendant, the electrician realized a great man was in their midst. The image looking out at the camera was a classic blind man's gaze, the flash's blue bomb reflected in his pale, sightless blue eyes.

If *Life* constituted the highest accolade America's emergent mass cult offered, *Time* was its brightly penned cousin. *Time* ran twin features on *A Woman's Vengeance*, as Huxley's film was finally titled, and on Edwin Hubble and the new 200-inch telescope at Mount Palomar. *Time*'s review of *A Woman's Vengeance* was negative (as were others) and unfortunately focused on Huxley's story or script. The enormously influential Bosley Crowther of the *New York Times* found "something insufficient about the dramatization . . . the lack is in the story Huxley has commercially prepared. For one thing, it's much too slow starting and getting into dramatic high gear."[84]

Reviews like this, which can chill a film career overnight, further contributed to Huxley's prolonged depression. In 1945, he had been a film writer with glowing notes for *Jane Eyre* and *Pride and Prejudice;* then, after wrestling for maximum control over the finished product, he and Korda were prominently panned.

By coincidence, Paulette Goddard was pictured in the same issue of *Time* as the lead in *An Ideal Husband,* and the week the Huxley-Korda film was released, Paulette and Burgess's new film, *A Miracle Can Happen,* also received poor reviews. Salt in the wound, Huxley's old friend George Cukor—whose commercial instincts were sounder than Korda's—released *A Double Life* (with Ronald Colman) to the most laudatory reviews of the year. Well, kiss Hollywood good-by, as Anita Loos later titled her autobiography of this period. What Huxley would do for funds after this fiasco, nobody knew. His publisher had just informed him that his new anthology, *The World of Aldous Huxley,* was selling at only a third of what had been expected.

At least he was not alone in his disappointments. Not only had the Burgess Merediths taken a shellacking in their new film, but Charlie Chaplin's recent *Monsieur Verdoux* had gone down in ignominy.

By any age's standards, *Verdoux* is strangely troubling. The plot is straightforward: an honest bank clerk is dismissed after thirty years. With no assets other than a handsome mien, he makes his living marrying and executing spinsters. His justification is the support of his crippled wife. The resulting film, based on a Bluebeard named Landru, remains a puzzle. In the few existing notes for *Verdoux,* a curious phrase appears: "A reputation is the concern of cooks and butlers."[85] Perhaps it should have been Chaplin's concern as well.

The film opened in New York to a confused reception; the press conference the next day turned into a shouting match with reporters. Yet the film, before a national boycott by the American Legion, did moderately well.[86]

Chaplin then staged a private showing for friends in Hollywood. Though Mann and Feuchtwanger gave him a standing ovation, Huxley was shocked: "What an aesthetic mess! He passes from a mime about murder which depends on *not* being taken seriously, to attempts at serious psychology . . . not conceivably a subject for comedy. One feels terribly sorry for Charlie—such talents, such a mess—in art no less than in life."[87]

Chaplin's last three films have an odd sequence: one was bitter (*Verdoux*, 1947), one touching (*Limelight*, 1952), and one a light, anti-anti-Communist farce (*A King in New York*, 1957). Instead of becoming more bitter at his Red-baiting, Chaplin's films became more sentimental. Because Chaplin had been one of the first Hollywood targets of anticommunism—during World War II—*Verdoux* was a bitter reaction to a phenomenon only just starting to paralyze the studios. If Chaplin had not been attacked in the early forties, he might logically have reversed the order of his last films, first taking on anticommunism before moving on to romances.

In any case, just as he was editing *Verdoux*, he learned that HUAC was planning its investigation of Hollywood and that he could expect a command performance.

The U.S. marshal interrupted Chaplin at his editing bay; HUAC may have heard rumors about the political trial at the film's end. Chaplin outfoxed the committee: for their convenience, he volunteered in a published telegram that he was not a member of any political party, much less the Communist Party. The investigators decided to fry smaller fish, nineteen of them; ten were subsequently tried. The nefarious hearings began in October 1947, producing a real-life counterpoint to *Ape and Essence*.

Huxley had been conscious of HUAC's presence as he drafted the book. As he first explored locations for the novel, he had set the Arch-Vicar's pulpit in the Biltmore's old lobby—then hosting HUAC; he imagined a "mass crucifixion of Conscientious Objectors and the skinning alive, in full color, of the seventy thousand persons suspected, at Tegucigalpa, of un-Honduran activities" (*Ape and Essence*, 100–101).

HUAC's spectacle has often been described: a smarmy circus to intimidate the few committed radicals in Hollywood. The committee received testimony from Ayn Rand that no one in Russia smiled anymore and that people there "ate human bodies." Their session with

Brecht "resembled a zoologist being cross-examined by apes" (a comment Aldous would have relished).[88] Dalton Trumbo shouted self-righteously that this was the beginning of American concentration camps, ignoring the wartime detention of Japanese-Americans.

On November 2, Thomas Mann announced that he had the honor to expose himself as a hostile witness. This was the start of many difficulties for Mann: afterward his lecture at the Library of Congress was canceled; when he attempted to speak in Hollywood, several hotels refused to rent him a room. After the HUAC hearings, not everyone left town as quickly as Brecht, but the world of the Hollywood exiles was definitely waning.

Looking down on these events from his woodland perch at 6,000 feet, Huxley may also have felt the urge to flee; his income, however, would not sustain a trip of any length. Fortune made her appearance in the person of a bright-eyed blond Italian violinist for the Los Angeles Philharmonic, Laura Archera.

Laura Archera had been in the United States for six years, studying at the Curtis Institute in Philadelphia and traveling with her companion, Virginia Pfeiffer. Archera was one of many seeking the Huxley name for a project—in her case, for a film about the Palio races at Siena—but she was more persistent. When her letter went unanswered, she tried to call. There were only two telephones in Wrightwood, neither of them the Huxleys', but she passed a message.

When she arrived at their house, it wasn't clear who found her tanned, leggy, Rita Hayworth look more attractive, Maria or Aldous. They greeted her warmly, in Italian, with that *bonhomie* any European emigrant appreciates in a small American town. They politely heard her ideas out (never mentioning that Aldous knew all about the Palio, having written a lengthy and profound essay on the horse race a dozen years earlier). Afterward, Laura and Aldous retired to his study to listen to records and fantasize over the soundtrack.

As she was leaving, Maria took Laura aside and asked where she was going to get the money. An assistant editor, Laura said she'd heard that studios had funds frozen in Italy for which they were seeking projects with an Italian setting.[89] That was enough for Maria: the Huxleys began planning their first return to Europe as expatriates. The timing was excellent; his play *The Gioconda Smile* was to open in London, and a visit might extend its run. Huxley was between projects, considering a nonfiction film with Burgess Meredith on hypnotism (the beginning of a long-term interest of Huxley's).[90] Alexander and Zoltán Korda agreed to use foreign reserves to pay the Huxleys' expenses in exchange for rights and a scenario to an old story, "The Rest Cure." They were to leave as soon as the last revisions on *Ape and Essence* were finished.

In L.A. over the last year, the Huxleys had replaced old friends who had left with new ones, most notably Igor Stravinsky.

Maria's nieces Claire and Sylvia had recognized Stravinsky and introduced themselves at the old Town and Country Market, where the Huxleys weekly indulged their taste in health foods. Stravinsky, twelve years Aldous's senior, was striking: a short, bald, slightly bent man, whose eyes flashed with intensity and whose beak nose gave the impression of sternness. Stravinsky took an immediate liking to the Huxleys. Maria wrote to Matthew of delightful evenings with the composer and his wife Vera, discussing his recent Symphony in Three Movements and music in general: the Stravinskys even made a vegetarian dinner of which Maria approved. The conversation switched between French and Italian, a polyglot style Aldous and Maria cherished but rarely found in America.

According to Stravinsky's amanuensis, Robert Craft, Huxley sought in Stravinsky the same creative élan he had found in Lawrence. Huxley had suggested W. H. Auden as a suitable librettist for *The Rake's Progress*. When the two artists clicked, and Stravinsky wrote to thank him, Huxley replied in French: "At most I am only the go-between who happily arranged the meeting of those two eminent Lesbians, Music and Poetry, who, for these past thirty centuries, have stuck together so notoriously."[91]

It's odd that Huxley and Stravinsky hadn't met before. Since 1940, Stravinsky had been such a well-known part of the Hollywood émigré community that the young Susan Sontag's favorite game concerned "How many more years of life for Stravinsky would justify our dying now, on the spot."[92]

Maria found Stravinsky gracious. As one evening flagged, he offered champagne. They refused, but he opened it anyway, and they drank each other's health in a genial way. Marie remembered, "I believe they have real friendship for us. We like them very much.

"And who do you think has come back into our life," she continued to Matthew. "Gerald. Not only physically (he has bought a house in the [San Fernando] valley) but he has actually already asked Aldous twice to go for walks with him. . . . There is so much of the old Gerald in him without the old tension in the hands and eyes."[93]

Not only was the reunion moving—Gerald had been terribly torn by the breakup of Trabuco and had withdrawn from old friends—they discovered parallel projects. While Aldous had written *Ape*, Gerald had been at work on his own postapocalypse novella.

Gerald imagined World War III arriving in 1975, after China annexed the Soviet Union; in "The Thaw Plan," the ice of Antarctica is melted via nuclear energy (an idea Julian was then discussing at UNESCO). Once begun, the process was irreversible; waves lapped Manhattan. In retaliation, the United States melted the Arctic and moved to the now warm climate of Greenland. (As in Huxley's fantasy, misuse of atomic energy caused humanity's downfall and a pre-technological society.[94])

All the while Aldous had drafted *Ape and Essence*, Maria had only seen the fragments she typed and retyped. One night Aldous walked into the kitchen in Wrightwood and blurted out, "I think I finished the book!" Maria wrote to Matthew,

> . . . I decided I would read it all night. Take coffee and then take the manuscript to bed. Of course Aldous said no and silly and so on. But after dinner he asked me, "We might read it aloud if you like." This is the first time he allowed me to read anything aloud. . . .
>
> Aldous gave in easily and we finished at one thirty. I read for four hours and a quarter without a lag of interest. . . .
>
> My feeling was awe when I had finished. Not fear and horror . . . that was coming in waves during the reading; but awe at the possibilities and at Aldous. . . . Though he so often looks old now he looked young and a bit shy and pleased: you [Matthew] know his air of a little boy. Honest, innocent, humble and so clever and knowing so much. . . .
>
> When we had finished I was dazed of course, I had . . . a violent head-ache in the eyes . . . All I could say was, "Well, I am impressed."
>
> But when I came up with my hot-water bottles he was walking

around still in his blue jersey and asked, "What do you think of it?
Must I change anything?" "No!" Most emphatically.[95]

The Huxleys sent off the typescript to his publishers and drove east. A feverishness marked their return, as if they had suddenly remembered they were Europeans and they were going home.

California never would be the same for them. It had become a land not of infinite potential but of broken promises. Driving across town, Huxley could sense the ghosts of projects never completed, all those bright ideas, thrown out after a few fingers of Scotch, blown away in the wind.

Isherwood, more deeply involved in the film industry than Huxley, had called this ghostly sensation "a kind of psychological dankness which smells of anxiety, overdrafts, uneasy lust, whisky, divorce and lies. 'Go away,' a wretched little ghost whispers from the closet, 'go away before it is too late. I was vain. I was silly. They flattered me. I failed. You will fail, too. Don't listen to their promises. Go away. Now, at once.' "[96]

And off to Italy they went, exiles returning from paradise. Maria had wanted to sell Wrightwood before leaving, but Aldous kept forgetting. In the end, they left plenty of ballast behind in California.

EIGHT

THE DEVILS
OF LOUDUN

"If we experience an urge to self-transcendence, it
is because, in some obscure way and in spite of our
conscious ignorance, we know who we really are.
This is liberation, this is enlightenment, this is the
beatific vision, in which all things are perceived as
they are 'in themselves.' "   (1952)

"We should be in France by the end of the month," Aldous
wrote to Julian on June 3, 1948, as the Huxleys motored across
their beloved Mojave. For years, Huxley had considered (and post-
poned) returning to Europe. He was a victim of his own morbid foreboding: "What Europe must be like now, after the Fall, is hard to
imagine. And of course it must get much worse, politically, socially,
and personally, as the hunger grows more intense."[1]

Among friends, Huxley had repeatedly conceded his fear of returning, of the craters in the streets, of the "physical destruction which
has made almost the entire population dependent for everything—
food, shelter, clothes, transportation." This was the dreary gloom-
and-doom refrain Huxley and Heard had sung earlier.

He and Maria were soon steering across the Atlantic, toward the
remains of former lives: what had become of their villa in Sanary?
Of Julian and Juliette and Maria's sisters? They sailed on a Cunard
liner.

On his visit a year earlier, Isherwood had scouted the territory:
"During my re-exploration of London, I got two strong impressions;

of shabbiness and of goodwill. The Londoners themselves were shabby . . . and their faces were still wartime faces, lined and tired. But they did not seem depressed or sullen." The bomb damage shocked him, as did the unrepaired façades—paint and plaster littered once-mannered squares. "Several Londoners I talked to at that time believed it would never recover: 'This is a dying city,' one of them told me."[2]

His homecoming was mixed: enthusiasm from many who filled him in on the war he had missed; others insisting pointedly how far away Isherwood and his friends had been:

> Huxley and Heard were very definitely regarded as out of the battle. They were far too old for military service, and their pacifism had been publicly stated years before in their writings. . . . There were the people who said that Aldous and Gerald and I had run away. That was said quite a lot. It was a most complicated thing. Somebody might write a marvellous book about that someday—the whole spectrum of attitudes. On the one hand it is the sort of plain old Hemingway thing, "Am I a coward?"[3]

After a few days in Paris with Jeanne and her husband Georges Neveux on the rue Bonaparte, they traveled together to Rome, where Huxley spent July and August preparing *The Rest Cure* scenario for Korda. This was a ghost-filled trip: Costanza Fasola, Ottoline Morrell, Aldous's parents—specters of their European past.

At one juncture, they found the carnage they dreaded. Arriving in Siena in mid-July 1948, Maria was caught in crossfire between police and Communist militants at a funeral procession. She ducked into a nearby house, barely out of range of the bullets.

Sanary they found lovely but primitive. Their former house had been sold and their goods moved to another, La Rustique. Poking through the attic, they discovered a few cherished books, Aldous's watercolors, and their old walking sticks. To Matthew, Maria fantasized about buying a Ford and scouting out a new place to live, "Sanary most probably." She, more than Aldous, considered staying in Europe. Friends insisted Aldous hadn't had as many health problems as he now suffered in California (of course, he was also a dozen years older).

In one of his last stories, "Things," D. H. Lawrence projected a variant of the Huxleys' dilemma: two American expatriates leave Europe for the United States. Like the Huxleys in their first year in

America, they wander the vast continent, unable to settle down. After revisiting Europe to bathe in Old World civility, however, they return to America in relief: "Europe's the mayonnaise, but America supplies the good old lobster."[4]

Huxley's mind increasingly turned toward predicting the future. For the last several months he had labored over a lengthy essay, "The Double Crisis," a modern reinterpretation of the Malthusian dilemma. The twin emergencies of rising population and declining agricultural productivity (added to ecotastrophy) could wreak havoc within the next half century, he concluded. The long-range effects of nuclear energy particularly incensed him, as they had in *Ape and Essence:*

> Because of some unfortunate little event that occurred at an atomically operated power plant in the later twentieth century, the men of the fiftieth century may find themselves wrestling with the problem of what to do with hare-lipped imbeciles, five-legged calves, non-viable chickens and stunted apple-trees.[5]

Clearly the curmudgeon in Huxley had reasserted itself, as it had in *Ape and Essence.* In his midfifties, Huxley made numerous such predictions, some preposterous (he had half of Europe living in barracks at war's end) and some correct (nuclear proliferation by the 1950s).

In *Brave New World*, he had projected a world in 632 After Ford; writing a new preface to the book in 1946, he decided that mass genetic engineering would occur far sooner, within the century. Predictions offered hope by warning others of long-term trends such as overpopulation and missile warfare:

> One can be safe in betting that, within ten years, there will be rockets . . . capable of flying any distance up to five thousand miles, and travelling along a radio beam precisely to their destination. Five thousand launching stations, firing off twenty robot [missiles] each—and that would be the end of any metropolis in the world. . . .
> And the whole of history is there to show that the possession of large stocks of efficient armament constitutes an almost compulsive temptation to use them.[6]

Huxley drew inspiration for such statements not from mystical understanding, but from clearheaded calculation. His guesses about the future were a structured game he played with himself. Following current trends to their outer limits did not require clairvoyance:

Prophecies of the future, if they are to be intelligent, not merely fantastic, must be based on a study of the present: for the future is the present projected. The prophet must make a selection of the facts that are most significant, that will have the greatest effect on the greatest number of future human beings.[7]

In Huxley's imagined future, he saw a technocratic, centralized tyranny based not on armed oppression but on a "narco-hypnosis more efficient, as instruments of government, than clubs or prisons." He suggested to Orwell that governments will find less arduous ways of governing than brute force; "these ways will resemble those which I described in *Brave New World*":[8]

An all-powerful executive of political bosses and their army of managers control a population of slaves who do not have to be coerced because they love their servitude [due to] a greatly improved technique of suggestions—through infant conditioning and, later, with the aid of drugs.[9]

Huxley arrived in London for the first time in eleven years on October 2, 1948; he put up at Claridge's on the Korda expense account. He brooded about Europe like a prophet upheld. He found himself in the position of Americans during the Vietnam war who immigrated to Canada or Scandinavia scornful of a war that couldn't be won; no one likes an I-told-you-so.

Huxley was barred from the fellowship of war survivors. Of all places to weather those terrible years, Huxley had passed them in California; his former readers knew of the attacks on the British in Hollywood and of the gorgeous stars in the movies he had written: Greer Garson, Maureen O'Sullivan, Joan Fontaine, Jessica Tandy— quite a company in which to sit out the war! The Huxleys found an overcast England and an uncheering crowd. Huxley had written brilliantly in the twenties and thirties, but to many, his mysticism and his refusal to support Britain during the war made him an unwelcome prodigal son. As Anthony West jibed in the *New Statesman and Nation*, "Gods are like old prize-fighters, They Never Come Back."[10]

Symptomatic of the ambivalence Huxley met were the disaffected reviews of *Ape and Essence*. George Orwell wrote a friend:

You were right about A's book—it is awful. And do you notice that the more holy he gets, the more his books stink of sex. He cannot get off the subject of flagellating women. Possibly, if he had the courage to come out and say so, that is the solution to problems of war. If we took it out in a little private sadism, which after all doesn't do much harm, perhaps we wouldn't want to drop bombs, etc.[11]

Orwell missed the point of *Ape*—Huxley understood sadism as the work of countries rather than individuals—but the literary barrage against the book swelled. The reviewer for the *New York Times Book Review* called *Ape* "a claptrap vehicle . . . Form and content maintain a separate existence; the catalyst which would fuse them never takes place."[12]

Nor was Huxley exclusively a remembered phenomenon; theatergoers could judge his current work from *The Gioconda Smile*, which had opened in London to mixed reviews. Curiosity must have outweighed the public's antipathy, for this became the most successful play he ever wrote.

Friends saw a different Huxley than critics did. To Sybille Bedford, Aldous was a man transformed; he had developed a godlike assurance, a serenity. He gave a sense of peace and a natural sweetness mixed with an Olympian calm: a saint without the unctuousness.[13] Huxley's evolution from an agitated pacifist to a calm, clear-minded mystic—Lawrence would have enjoyed this—was noticed by others. When Cyril Connolly interviewed Huxley for *Picture Post*, he remarked, "What is much more remarkable . . . is the radiance of serenity and loving-kindness on his features; one no longer feels 'what a clever man' but 'what a good man,' a man at peace with himself."[14]

O n the morning of February 10, 1949, the man at peace sipped tea outside a cabin in Palm Desert, a tiny resort town twelve miles west of Palm Springs. As he sat in the morning shade correcting a draft of a dramatic adaptation of *Ape and Essence*, it was easy to forget how low his morale had sunk on his return from Europe a few months before. The weeks in England had flown by in a haze of interviews and theatergoing, yet he had left feeling hollow; England was no better for his eyes and lungs than it had been two decades earlier.

They had hurried back to New York City to try a new therapy for his eyes: a Dr. Erlanger had developed a method to clear the eye of cataracts by running a mild electrical current through metal plates to the cornea; this was said to change the chemical composition of the eye.

Like a stamp collector returning after a vacation to a new find, Aldous couldn't wait. "I took some treatments with him," he wrote his brother, "and think they did result in a slight clearing up of the old opacities."[15] Before he could finish, however, his painful, rasping bronchitis had returned, leaving him marooned among the sand dunes and cactus.

Aldous and Maria had checked in to the Sage and Sun Motel the previous December, following the severest attack yet of bronchitis. For weeks he had sat in an oxygen tent.

Palm Desert was the warmest, driest resort in a state ravaged by the wettest winter in memory. Deep snow covered the Mojave. Icicles hung over the eaves of their former house in Llano; their place in Wrightwood had disappeared under a drift.

For an enforced three-month invalid's exile, Palm Desert had much to offer. This new, poorer suburb of Palm Springs—a few trailer courts on a crust of irrigated desert—offered palm trees and sand as far as the eye could see. Short, fat pineapple-shaped palms alternated with spindly thin ones; the spines cast sharp shadows in the sand.

The Huxleys had rented a neighboring cabin for the Hubbles. "Maria, with her generous thoughtfulness, had filled our refrigerator—fruit, honey, cream and eggs. Breakfast and tea in the cottages, lunch and dinner at an excellent Italian restaurant next door," Grace wrote.[16] The foursome were looking forward to hikes through the foothills, where the first wildflowers bloomed.

At the same time, America was suffering from a disease as debilitating as the one which laid Huxley low: anticommunism. A social psychiatrist would recognize this as a subtle virus chronic to America's body politic. Its present form dated from the anti-Red campaigns immediately following World War I—the so-called Palmer raids against emigrants, pacifists, and socialists—which had launched J. Edgar Hoover and his FBI to prominence.

While Huxley recuperated, the appeals of the Hollywood Ten were under consideration at the U.S. Supreme Court; Charlie Chaplin and other of his film-industry friends had signed an amicus curiae brief on their behalf. *American Legion Magazine* was readying a feature on Hollywood: "How Communists Make Stooges out of Movie Stars."

Only in retrospect can one appreciate how the campaign to harass Hollywood liberals as Communists misrepresented the industry. Of thirty thousand employed, a total of 324 were eventually found to have belonged to the Communist Party. (And membership in a legal political party was not the same as subversion.) The most comprehensive analysis of Communist influence in American film—a survey of 159 films from the thirties and forties—found not one instance of pro-Communist propaganda. Even HUAC did not belabor its investigation once the shades were pulled. In its annual report following the Hollywood Ten hearings, HUAC devoted only one sentence to subversion in the film industry.[17] Yet while the Hubbles and Huxleys hiked in Palm Desert, the anti-Communist menace kept pace.

With Edwin and Grace leading the way, the foursome scrambled over boulders at the foot of a cliff, crossed a mossy stream, and climbed out on a mesa overlooking the town. To the south and east loomed craggy peaks iced with snow. Drips of water cut into the steep rock faces and echoed in the canyons below.

As usual, the Hubbles jotted down sightings of birds and unusual plants. Coming upon a bush he didn't recognize, Edwin suggested they drive into Palm Springs and look it up in the museum. Grace noted in her journal what happened next:

> When we reached the museum it was growing dusk and the lights were lighted. Aldous was welcomed cordially by the curator and one of the trustees. They had written asking him to speak at the museum. . . .
>   There was a sudden stillness, which they did not notice. E put away the book and walked across the room. "Where," he asked abruptly, "did you get that stuffed wildcat?" It had appeared nearby, they said,

and they shot it because they thought it might hurt some of the children.

"Since there are so many children," he said casually, "and so few wildcats, I can only deplore your decision."

Hurriedly Aldous made graceful leavetakings. When we were outside he gasped, "Edwin—and I told them you were my friend!"

But driving in the dark, on the road back to Sage and Sun, Aldous was happily considering many other things. . . . He and Edwin were alike in this way. They never descended to argument; it was not worth the effort.[18]

The Hubbles returned home soon after that, while the Huxleys stayed until late spring, as the snows melted in Wrightwood. With Aldous and Maria in the mountains and the Hubbles back in Pasadena, the two couples remained out of touch—though the disagreements of the war years had largely healed. The next time they heard from Grace was when she told them Edwin had nearly died from a heart attack while fishing in the mountains of Colorado.

H uxley had missed a great deal in the year he was away in Europe and Palm Desert. He continued to hunt film work in a low-key fashion—including another proposed script with Isherwood[19]—but he was out of touch with two major developments in Hollywood: the breakup of the studios' control over booking and the effects of the upstart medium, television.

For nearly a decade, theater owners had lobbied Washington to end the advantages studios enjoyed as simultaneous producers, distributors, and exhibitors of their films. The previous summer, the Supreme Court had finally decided this was monopoly: Paramount, Loew's, Fox, RKO, and Warner's would have to divest themselves of 1,400 theaters.

In combination with the growth of television, the loss of theater chains eclipsed the studios' empire. By the end of World War II, according to Otto Friedrich, there were only 6,500 TV sets; by 1948, Americans had a million sets. This number quadrupled in 1949, then tripled again in 1950. Meanwhile the Federal Communications Commission froze the number of stations, creating an emergent TV monopoly at the very time the film studios' ended.

These developments subtly affected Huxley's prospects in the film industry. Television steadily eroded film attendance, which dropped by 10 million weekly admissions in 1950. In Hollywood, furrier Al Teitelbaum made good money covering TV sets in skunk for film producers, "not the screens, of course."[20]

Though much of the new medium's programming was warmed-over radio—amateur hours, sports, comedians, and a few high-toned dramas—advertisers were getting ready to drop radio "like bones at a barbecue," Fred Allen said, making TV the freeway of popular culture. The sort of picture Huxley had worked on—literary, researched features drawing on the classics—no longer served a studio as evidence of culture. Competing with TV required less sophistication and more pop culture. Alertness was the watchword in Hollywood; those at the edge of the industry, marginal writers such as Huxley, needed to be ever vigilant to HUAC and new developments.

Visits with Stravinsky continued to highlight Huxley's stops in town. Stravinsky relied on occasional film work to live like a prince (as Auden once dryly remarked, "With the old boy, obviously the mother figure is money").[21] In Los Angeles in the mid- and late forties, Stravinsky's music and personality flowered—so much so that he took out American citizenship in 1945. He found the city endlessly fascinating: rummaging through a book shop, he discovered some Mozart masses and decided to compose his own mass.

On July 27, 1949, the Stravinskys had the Huxleys over for dinner; Robert Craft sat in on these get-togethers. In the diminutive Stravinsky house, Huxley crouched under low ceilings, ducked through doorways, flinched by a chandelier, "until we feel as though it may *really* be unsafe for him here. . . ."

> At table we are more precisely aware of his visual limitations: he feels for his knife, fork and plate, with the palpations of the blind. His wife helps him to find the food, and she continues to direct him throughout the meal in almost unnoticed sotto voce asides. "Un tout petit peu a gauche, cherie," she whispers when his knife fails to find a hold on the meat, and in the same voice she advises him how long to uptilt the salt shaker . . . he would . . . resent any sign of solicitude from another source.[22]

For Huxley, Stravinsky's gifts "seem in the highest degree mysterious and inexplicable," he noted in a brief biographical essay: "What does it actually feel like to think in terms of melodies and harmonic progressions?"[23]

For Stravinsky, Huxley was equally fascinating, "a kind of handy, neighborhood university . . . I.S., like a radio quiz master, is forever wanting immediate answers to random matters of fact . . . If Mr. H. is in town, however, I.S. need only pick up the telephone, as he did yesterday, when he wanted a run-down on the history of scissors."[24]

The Huxleys in turn had the Stravinskys over to their new house on North King's Road at the edge of Hollywood's city limits, "in that curious country lane between Santa Monica and Melrose," Aldous wrote Matthew. They had moved there in May 1949, just after arriving, healed and in good spirits, from their sojourn at Palm Desert. The $23,000 house was large—to Craft it seemed baronial and empty—with a garden, privacy, and plenty of shade trees, so Aldous could again work outside. After a final summer in Wrightwood, they planned to sell their cabin and rent places in the mountains; the strain of maintaining two houses was too much for Maria, now suffering from unexplained fatigue.

Aldous and Maria introduced Stravinsky to Isherwood, who quickly became a close (and considerably more informal) friend. On his first visit to their home, Isherwood fell asleep when someone played a recording of his host's music, "which is when Stravinsky claims his affection began."[25] Thereafter, Isherwood and Stravinsky went to the beach once a week and got drunk in the sand, often in that strip of beach at the bottom of Santa Monica Canyon known as "Queer Alley," where gay bars predominated.

In his postmonastery period, Isherwood was struggling hard to balance his Vedantism and his unfailing delight in the fleshy extremes of the city:

> To live sanely in Los Angeles (or, I suppose, in any other large American city) you have to cultivate the art of staying awake. You must learn to resist (firmly but not tensely) the unceasing hypnotic suggestions of the radio, the billboards, the movies and the newspapers; those demon voices which are forever whispering in your ear what you should desire, what you should fear. . . . the least wandering of the attention, the least relaxation of your awareness, and already the eyelids begin to droop, the eyes grow vacant, the body starts to move in obedience to the hypnotist's command. Wake up, wake up.[26]

Wrightwood was a charming relief from the smoke and noise of the city. The Huxleys marveled at the birds attracted by pools of still melting snow, their cries echoing through the thick woods by the cabin. Maria would rise early, exercise and bathe, write letters, and dally by the flower garden. From 11:00 to 12:30 she would do her Bates exercises, then make Aldous a late lunch at 1:30.

Aldous's afternoon walks were brightened by bolts of color as the mountain wildflowers burst forth. While Maria remained listless, Aldous was "better than he's been in three years," Maria wrote in a letter: "he's gained weight."[27] His spirits were buoyed by walks with Krishnamurti, who was living nearby and teaching both Aldous and Maria new Yoga exercises. These and the rest cure in the desert had worked wonders. Unfortunately, *The Rest Cure* script hadn't fared as well; after the treatment was submitted, the project was lost at Universal.

Before resuming his hunt for studio work, Huxley turned his attention to the essays later published as *Themes and Variations*. Essay writing relaxed him; he could let his encyclopedic interests range without the anxiety of tying together loose ends of plot and characterization.

The longest piece in *Themes* was his second biography, of eighteenth-century French philosopher Maine de Biran. (While revisiting Sanary the year before, Huxley had come across his annotated copy of Biran's *Journal intime*.)

Physically, Biran was a weak specimen who suffered from overly sensitive nerves, indigestion, and chronic bronchitis; moreover, like Huxley, he was an extreme cerebretonic (according to a classification of Dr. W. H. Sheldon) who lived inside himself. He represented his region in the Chamber of Deputies before retiring to metaphysics late in life, after politics had drawn him fruitlessly out of his study once too often.

Biran's life served as a starting point for intellectual wanderings. Huxley's discursiveness makes this work a catalogue of his current concerns. His commentary ranged from the history of human digestion to humans' digestion of history.[28] (Creative interpolation of asides into dramatic narrative, buttressed by rapid and intriguing transitions, was one of Huxley's greatest gifts and one reason many critics consider him a novelist of talent but an essayist of genius.[29])

Yet, as critic George Woodcock pointed out in *Dawn and the Darkest Hour*, by the end of the 1940s Huxley had lost his belief that destiny could be swayed by skillful words. "Huxley came to regard literature as a lesser art; he felt that words . . . emphasized the separateness of things."[30]

"Variations on a Philosopher" was long enough to have been published on its own; one reason it was not may have been its unconventional embrace of alternative-spiritual healing—the first of Huxley's published works to acknowledge the importance of faith healing (animal magnetism), extrasensory perception, and hypnosis. "We may expect to see in the West an increasing concern with the techniques of yoga," he predicted in 1949; "they'll be scientifically studied, improved, then applied for the purpose of purely mundane and even diabolic ends."[31]

At the risk of being called a "crank," Huxley had decided to alter his public profile of bemused tolerance of parapsychology. Using a trick of narrative—exploring what Biran did *not* write about—Huxley presented a parenthetical history of the experiments of Mesmer, Deleuze, and other experimenters in hypnosis. He took his first public step along the byways of psychic science, but this remained cerebral, an intellectual exploration, until a second, devastating blindness befell him.

His enthusiasm for hypnosis had developed as a way out of his depression following the loss of Llano; it blossomed as Huxley unearthed a connection between sight and hypnosis.[32] Typically, he tracked down the works of a nineteenth-century experimenter to guide his search; he had little patience with secondary sources. "The soul can in certain states receive ideas and sensations without the mediation of the organs," Huxley quoted the naturalist Deleuze. In other words, the eye can see even through darkness, if the mind is trained.[33]

Just as Huxley had associated progress in his sight (through Bates's exercises) with his simultaneous study of Vedanta, so he now saw hypnotism (and mesmerism) as his salvation.

Hypnotism, christened by James Braid in 1842 with the Greek term for being put to sleep, was the preferred nineteenth-century treatment of hysterics and psychosomatic illnesses; Freud used the technique in his early treatments. Yet Franz Mesmer was actually hounded out of Vienna for his experiments, which seemed like witchcraft to his contemporaries, for he cured without drugs, by passing his hand over the sick to correct "currents" of electricity.

In nineteenth-century America, the mesmerizer was a carnival attraction, winning laughs by making subjects behave like chickens. Samuel Clemens wrote about a visit of a mesmerizer to Missouri in 1850. As a young boy, Clemens stared at the magic disc but could not fall under its spell—until one performance when he decided to see visions, even if he had to manufacture them himself: "I saw more than was visible and added to it such details as would help. . . . in case I failed to guess what the professor might be willing me to do, I could count on putting up something that would answer just as well."[34]

The prospect of entering one's unconscious without time-consuming analysis provoked American prurience. In the 1950s, hypnotism was in mild disrepute, associated in the popular imagination with fantasies of girls sexually dominated while under its influence—similar to the stories of early witchcraft in the American colonies. In a 1951 Abbott and Costello film, a big-city hypnotist takes out his watch to hypnotize Abbott; as he murmurs "Sleep, sleep," a dozen people topple over asleep.[35]

Ever the frustrated self-doctor, Huxley visited the reigning hypnotist of the time, Milton Ericson, and Leslie Lecron and members of the UCLA psychology department. He developed a state of Deep Reflection "to summon my memories, to put into order my thinking . . . but I do it solely to let these realizations, the thinking, the understandings, the memories seep into the work I'm planning to do without my conscious awareness of them."[36] These trances via self-hypnosis helped his meditations and opened him up to parapsychology.

Another reason Huxley now explored hypnosis was that he dwelt in his writing on its mass form, when a group shares a hallucination—as, for instance, in the possession by devils.

Hypnotism also served his continuing drive to transcendence. "A hypnotized person," he wrote in his biography of Biran, "seems to be in a kind of contemplation or *samadhi*."[37] Though Huxley often repeated the warnings of Hindu scholars that those seeking enlightenment are tempted to misuse supernormal powers *(siddhis)* for fun and profit—Huxley was ready to elevate a therapeutic technique to metaphysics when it suited an urgent need.

Aldous and Maria returned from their last summer at Wrightwood to the house on North King's Road in October 1949 and began planning another European trip. He looked forward to visiting Dr. Erlanger's clinic now that his bronchitis was in temporary abeyance. He had the usual publishing business to attend to in New York City, and he wanted a longer stay in England than last time.

Partly this was to renew ties; partly to visit yet more eye doctors for experimental surgery to remove the opacity covering his eyes once and for all. He had in mind "an unorthodox eye man called Brooks Simpkins [from Eastbourne] and a German doctor, Luftig, who uses light therapy."

As a further experiment, Huxley had recently adopted "Chinese glasses" (black cellulose goggles); these relied not on glass lenses but on pinhole openings which force the pupils to move stroboscopically and consequently prevent visual fixation. To an outsider, the effect was disconcerting—he looked like a frail carnival barker with trick glasses.

The Huxleys had another reason to travel: Matthew was to be married. Ellen Hovde was a film-maker and daughter of the president of the New School for Social Research. From what they could gather from mutual friends, she was an extraordinary person, just the sort to help Matthew settle into a career.

They also arranged to meet Anita Loos, now polishing the musical comedy version of *Gentlemen Prefer Blondes* at the Ziegfeld. Her husband, John Emerson, was listed as coauthor and director, which suggests that he was in a period of remission. Anita found theater more stimulating than film. As soon as *Blondes* was launched, she planned to do a stage adaptation of *Gigi*, from Colette's novel. Her interest in the theater may have been what animated Aldous's closet interest in plays and musicals in the late forties and fifties.

Anita had not neglected her California friends entirely; on New Year's Eve 1950, she went as usual to Hearst's residence. The mogul was near death. Marion Davies led a group of friends to visit: "He can't t-t-talk so don't ask h-h-how he is. Just m-m-make conversation as usual—you know, b-b-be idiotic." Anita left "vastly shaken."[38] The immortality-seeking protagonist of *After Many a Summer Dies the Swan* was ready for death. He died the following year at eighty-eight, leaving most of his $300 million estate to two vast foundations.

Also injured was Edwin Hubble. Edwin had been under considerable work pressure following the opening of the 200-inch telescope at Mount Palomar in 1948; he was the first researcher on the telescope. In the summer of 1949, he took a badly needed fishing vacation. He and Grace took a train to a favorite lake near Grand Junction. During a thunderstorm, Edwin was wading up a creek with his creel when he was hit by lightning. He was hospitalized with damage to his heart but recovered and returned home wearily. His great discoveries were behind him.

"Once more Biran turns his eyes inwards," Huxley wrote before leaving the United States. "Horrible things were happening in Paris [during the Terror] but the young man kept his attention firmly fixed on the events of his inner world."[39] Huxley admired this stance; he was similarly struggling with a new Terror in his adopted country.

Susan Sontag has warned against "decade-mongering," but the 1950s may have been as decisive to the United States as any. The opening of this turbulent decade began in tragicomedy, at the trial of Alger Hiss. In the first week of 1950 Burr Tillstrom, producer of the popular TV children's show *Kukla, Fran & Ollie*, declared, "The moment I saw TV I knew it was made for puppets," a remark whose epic irony was missed at the time.

"McCarthy made people believe Stalin was the only example of Socialism in the world," musician Billy Bragg later remarked. "That's like saying that the Spanish Inquisition is the only example of Christianity."[40] As the year proceeded, anti-Communist headlines announced the duck-and-cover decade, when the baby-boom generation learned that hiding under one's seat would be protection from nuclear attack—unless one had a fallout shelter, equipped with water, soda, crackers and a radio.

Hollywood again prepared to do its bit. A film on Hiawatha was dropped despite six months' work, because "the message of peace could be misconstrued."[41] While producing some fine films—*Father of the Bride, Sunset Boulevard,* and *All About Eve*—the studios were eager not to appear soft on communism. In 1949–1950, they produced a half-dozen films with titles like *I Married a Communist,* anti-Communist film noir. Producers couldn't act fast or patriotically enough.

Traitors in our midst, Truman declared, despite the meager results of his massive loyalty investigations. His solemn duty, he declared, was to develop a hydrogen bomb to fight an enemy no more visible than the wind.[42] Americans revered generals like MacArthur and Eisenhower, who hadn't yet let go of the last war and doggedly planned another.

Soon this came to pass. In July 1950, Truman sent troops into North Korea. Of course, Korea was not a war, but a "police action" to rout "bandits," the president said, reflecting the hear-no-evil, speak-no-evil mentality which *Our Weekly Reader* promulgated to American youth. Nevertheless, casualty lists made Communists into America's mortal enemies. Julius and Ethel Rosenberg were arrested and executed for allegedly selling atomic secrets to the Soviet Union.

In April 1950, the Hollywood Ten lost their appeal to the Supreme Court (probably due to the appointment by Truman of two conservative justices); by June, they were saying good-bye to their families and packing for federal penitentiaries. On his way to jail, Alvah Bessie visited Charlie Chaplin in hopes of selling him a modern version of *Don Quixote.* Chaplin declined, having already started scripting his next film, *Limelight;* he showed Bessie a version more bitter than the one filmed. He treated Bessie with a respect few others in the industry dared. On his way out the door, Chaplin slipped him $100, which meant three weeks' food for Bessie's family.[43]

While compassionate to most friends, Chaplin was deeply suspicious of Huxley's psychic explorations, as the song in *Limelight* parodying reincarnation demonstrates. Chaplin had reason to be bitter. As the national pastime for Red-hunting swept the entertainment industries, his sins against anticommunism were catching up with him.

In 1947, former HUAC chairman J. Parnell Thomas had urged Chaplin's deportation. In 1948, when Chaplin yearned to take Oona to England to show her his birthplace, the U.S. Immigration and Naturalization Service had interrogated him on everything from membership in the Party to adultery (he looked the word up and claimed he had never slept with another man's wife). Chaplin gave up the trip.

By the fall of 1949, old accusations of Party membership returned; J. Edgar Hoover retrieved a review of Chaplin by *Pravda* (dated 1923) and passed it to gossip columnist Hedda Hopper. Senator Harry Cain of the Senate Judiciary Committee complained that Chaplin was "perilously close to treason" and should be deported.[44] Ex-Communist Louis Budenz slipped Chaplin's name into the four hundred he named as "concealed members" of the Communist Party. In November 1949, the FBI opened a "Security R" file on Chaplin but concluded, just as Huxley packed his grips for New York and Europe, that no witnesses could testify that Chaplin had ever joined or directly supported the Communist Party.

What did the FBI finally turn up on Chaplin? The agency discovered he had attended a Shostakovich concert, a Soviet film, praised Roosevelt's stand against racial discrimination. His FBI file was stuffed with clippings from columnists, poison-pen letters, results from clandestine mail covers and phone taps: sound and fury signifying nothing.[45] Meager as these results were, they were more than the FBI had unearthed on Aldous Huxley.

The first mention of Huxley in the FBI's files dated from four weeks after his arrival in the United States, May 28, 1937; the FBI wasn't letting grass grow under its feet. Huxley's name turned up under investigations of pacifists in the War Resisters League and, nine months later, of the Fellowship for Reconciliation: both groups distributed his pamphlet on pacifism, "What Are You Going To Do About It?" The FBI's file name for its investigation of American pacifist groups was SUBVERSION.

During the war, Huxley's name appeared in numerous files, some still classified. In April 1943, the Special Agent in Charge (SAC) of the Newark office discovered a copy of *Brave New World* with some suspicious markings: someone had underlined pages and made wavy lines in the margin. The Bureau filed this under the unfriendly title of INTERNAL SECURITY/ALIEN ENEMY CONTROL and sent the volume to its cryptography division. The cryptographers pointed out that such markings were often used by students. Nonetheless, the FBI asked for a background check on Huxley.

The Bureau occasionally took seriously Huxley's antipathy to Stalinist communism; one agent actually bought a copy of *Science, Liberty and Peace* to give to a left-leaning scientist. By the end of the 1940s, however, the FBI was scrutinizing virtually any independent thinker. A 1950 espionage investigation of one of Huxley's close friends—possibly Salka Viertel—mentions his name. Over the next few years, in files on internal security, Aldous Huxley appeared regularly.

In April 1949, *Themes and Variations* appeared, the same week Matthew married Ellen. Stephen Spender reviewed the book for the *New York Times*, noting how Huxley's writing—particularly the Biran biography—had become cinematized, particularly the opening shot of Biran taking a cure in a spa: "an exquisitely skillful, intelligent and delightful performance."[46] Spender also acknowledged the prophetic quality of "The Double Crisis," with its long-range implications of environmental devastation.

Just before boarding their ship to Europe in May, Huxley was interviewed by a reporter for the *New York Times Book Review*. His scenario offers a glimpse of how Huxley's reputation intimidated even a representative of one of America's premier literary institutions.

At first, the reporter could only sit in silence, marveling at Huxley's immensely long legs. Huxley waited politely. The reporter squirmed, thinking: "Huxley knows so much. There is nothing to talk to him about."

At length, comfortable in his own silence, Huxley broke the ice. He reminded the interviewer of his own days on a literary supplement, *The Athenaeum*: "People who review books feel an extraordinary kind of self-congratulation. They feel they're much more important than the people who write books." He warmed up, discussing literary life in ancient Alexandria and the still contemplated novel on Saint Catherine of Siena. The historical novel was an "impossible job" because one must "indicate that people are always the same and awfully different." When the interviewer asked, like an aging fan of a pop musician, if he could hope for another *Antic Hay*, Huxley smiled: "That was rather fun . . . No, I don't think so. One is, after all, thirty years older."[47]

The Huxleys departed for Paris on May 9, having previously secured reentry permits (they never knew that the Immigration and Naturalization Service commissioned a background check before granting them).[48]

They visited their favorite cities: from Paris to Siena, Rome, a stop at Sanary—where Matthew and Ellen were honeymooning—then to central France for Maria and on to London for Aldous. As he headed north to Paris, he stopped in central France at the little town of Loudun, where in the seventeenth century a priest had been burned to death, charged with diabolical possession. Aldous spoke and wrote French with complete fluency; he used his skill to unearth 400-year-old memoirs and fashion a riveting drama from the bizarre episode.

Maria sent him to Juliette in London with precise instructions on what he could and could not eat—which her sister-in-law disregarded in order to put some weight on her former flame. Housing two geniuses under one roof proved a strain:

> At first these visits left me disturbed and disconnected. I was suspended between these two singular creatures, brothers steeped in their heredity, in the exclusiveness of their predestination. It seemed that the common ground between them could only be that of learned discussions or intellectual matters: fascinating to listen to, but leaving no room for the small coin of everyday topics, of affectionate exchanges.[49]

Juliette found herself caught between "a competition of sharply informed minds, equal in quality and scholarliness and range." Yet she sensed "a higher reach in Aldous's visions." Apparently Julian also felt this and disparaged himself despite having just finished his term as first president of the first world scientific agency. It wasn't easy being a Huxley, as Matthew and his children often reflected.

"England is much more cheerful than it was two years ago," Aldous wrote Christopher Isherwood. In London, he mended fences with Spender, "white-haired and wonderfully distinguished looking," dined with T. S. Eliot, and mingled at a reception with twenty-seven Huxleys in the same room: "not a bad lot at all," he wrote to Peggy Kiskadden.[50]

Aldous joined Maria in Sanary to sell the house; with rehearsals for *The Gioconda Smile* going poorly in New York, they returned prior to its October opening. The director, Shepard Traube, had made unauthorized changes in the script. Huxley feared the play was doomed, despite Basil Rathbone in the lead role. Notices were indeed poor; five weeks later the play closed. "A bore," he wrote Anita from North King's Road the following month, "because I would have enjoyed making some easy money. Now I must settle down . . . to some dishonest work in the movies, if I can find it, which isn't so easy nowadays."[51]

The failure of his play in America left a bitterness he could not quite shake. Maria assured him that he could always earn his living with lectures and articles. This suggestion was only logical, for now that *The Rest Cure* had been abandoned—with Rank-Universal recouping its expenses by taking rights to another story, "Young Archimedes" (filmed entirely without Huxley's help), work in film seemed a lost cause. Nothing had come of the scenarios he and Isherwood had done. Worse, Huxley's efforts to find scripts met with lack of interest. Maria confessed to Matthew: "He has been trying in vain to get a job since we are back and *nothing* turns up. Anita tried."[52]

I n this mood, at the end of 1950, the fifty-six-year-old writer began *The Devils of Loudun.* The idea was not new; nearly a decade before, Huxley had written to Chatto & Windus about "one of the most fantastically strange stories in all French history":

The story of the demoniac possession of the nuns of Loudun, which begins with fraud, hysteria, malicious plotting; goes on with the commission of a monstrous judicial crime, the burning of Urbain Grandier, as the supposed author of the possession; continues posthumously with more diabolic manifestations and the bringing on to the scene of Father Surin, one of the most saintly ecclesiastics of his age, who tries to exorcise the Abbess of the convent, responsible finally for all the mischief and thoroughly enjoying the enormous publicity which the possession had given her. In the course of his exorcisms . . . Surin, by a kind of psychological infection, himself succumbs to possession.[53]

Fascinating as this saga was, in 1940 Huxley had instead turned to another of the same era, *Grey Eminence;* Père Joseph's story held more direct parallels to World War II.

Huxley may understandably have hesitated before the descent into hell which writing *Devils* posed: a priest burned alive because a woman he had never met claimed he flew through a wall into her bedchamber. Huxley could treat this story only with satire or foreboding: as a humorous example of human capacity for ignorance or as a withering object lesson of the darkness and pestilence of which the human soul is capable. In his present mood, pestilence won out.

Three years later, Arthur Miller would conjure similar vileness and fear in his anti-anti-Communist play about spirit possession, *The Crucible.* Miller's work, set in the Salem witch trials of 1692, succeeded in a way Huxley's did not. Miller created a transparent allegory to the anti-Communist witch hunts of the time (one of the few artistic attacks on the Red hunt to have survived the period). "Any man who's not reactionary in his views," Miller wrote, "is open to the charge of alliance with Red hell."[54] Huxley's stage was larger, grimmer—and hence more diffuse. Yet both works shared an unpleasant fact of human psychology: "When, as in Salem, wonders are brought forth from below the social surface, it is too much to expect people to hold back very long from laying on the victims with all the force of their frustrations."[55]

Huxley began his saga with the arrival of the proud, cosmopolitan priest, Grandier, to his new parish. Huxley netted his subject tightly, showing in Aristotelian fashion Grandier's defects of character: his arrogance to fellow ministers, his hypocritical enjoyment of material comforts, his compulsive seduction, during Latin lessons, of the daughter of one of his local defenders. Month by month we watch Grandier kindle his pyre.

His downfall arrives from an unexpected quarter: an abbess proclaims him the author of diabolic possession. His trial grinds on, just as John Proctor's does in *The Crucible*, and ancient slights and real (but irrelevant) sins discredit him until he burns at the stake. (When filmed in 1971 by Ken Russell as *The Devils*, the burning made particularly lurid cinema.)

The possessed Ursuline nuns succumb to buffoonery, pulling up their chemises and thrusting their pelvises suggestively against the floor, all the while praising Lucifer. This made for the best show since the twin dwarfs and the dancing bear had visited the previous year, locals agree.

A test of their possession, Huxley delighted in pointing out, "was made by a visiting nobleman who handed the exorcist a box in which, so he whispered, there were some exceedingly holy relics. The box was applied to the head of one of the nuns, who immediately exhibited all the symptoms of intense pain and threw a fit. Much delighted, the good friar returned the box to its owner, who thereupon opened it and revealed that, except for a few cinders, it was completely empty.

" 'Ah, my lord,' cried the exorcist, 'what sort of a trick have you played on us.'

" 'Reverend Father,' answered the nobleman, 'what sort of a trick have you been playing upon *us?*' " (*Devils*, 196)

Jake Zeitlin remembers that winter as a quiet, intense period for Huxley: he would drop by Zeitlin's bookstore with requests and stop for tea, especially on Tuesday, his day in town.

Huxley scoured the UCLA Library, making its interlibrary loan office work overtime collecting books in late Medieval French. Winter disappeared like a sheet of paper under piles of seventeenth-century court records and memoirs. Robert Craft dropped by for "an afternoon with Universal Knowledge," and found Huxley typing his witchcraft book in the den at the end of a darkened corridor.[56]

Then, in February 1951, just as HUAC prepared for its third

investigation of Hollywood, Huxley came down with a bad flu. History wouldn't record this ailment of a writer of delicate constitution except for its dire consequences: settling in his eyes, the disease blinded him. By March, he was Eyeless in Gaza, all over again.

HUAC's second Hollywood hearings began March 8, 1951; this time its chairman, Congressman John S. Wood, had a single-minded goal: producing the maximum number of names possible. Thirty ex-Communists named three hundred others, giving new meaning to the term "talkies," as cold war historian David Caute wrote in *The Great Fear*. Among those attacked were Will Geer, a mainstay of the musical and dramatic Left, and screenwriter Waldo Salt (whose *Midnight Cowboy* capped a distinguished career). Huxley hardly needed to underline the parallels between Loudun and more contemporary moral dramas. If the public could believe that top diplomatic secrets were found, miraculously, in Whittaker Chambers's pumpkin, they might in a more animistic time swallow a tale of a preacher changing himself into a devil, flying into a nunnery, and staging a mass seduction of nuns he'd never met.

Witchcraft, that period stretching from the papal bull of 1320 to the Salem trials of 1692, held potent reference to HUAC's method of operation. R. H. Robbins's *Encyclopedia of Witchcraft and Demonology* suggests direct analogies: secret proceedings, where charges were withheld and cheap rumor heeded; where persons of dubious character were allowed unchallenged testimony while witnesses for the accused were presumed guilty.[57]

As in Huxley's period, witch hunts were a self-serving industry, with places for the scaffold builders and the courts' scribes. In Loudun and Hollywood, what masqueraded as righteousness was actually a device for redistributing jobs and assets to the loyal. Actor John Wayne, president of a Hollywood anti-Communist group, cut right to the heart of matters: "Bankers and stockholders must realize their investments are imperiled."[58]

Why was Huxley so fascinated by the seventeenth century, and why did he keep returning to it for morality plays for the twentieth century?

There was much in the seventeenth century to excite Huxley: the founding of the Academy of Science in Paris and the Royal Society (on which both his grandfather and brother served); dramatic breakthroughs in science, literature, and philosophy; Shakespeare and Bacon, Lope de Vega and Molière; the Baroque music he so enjoyed. Pascal situated humanity's place in the universe as somewhere between the smallest joint on a bug's leg and the vast distance between the stars; only a belief in God could join the two. But after more than a century of bloodshed between Protestants and Catholics, during which many an iconoclast ate fire, faith was subject to proof. By 1650, though English courts had discredited hearsay and confessions obtained through torture as evidence, the rest of Europe had not. In the France of Loudun's devils nothing stood between an individual and damnation but the gilded scepters of the church.

The seventeenth century held distinct contemporary parallels. Sounding surprisingly like John Foster Dulles on the bomb, a seventeenth-century Polish king warned England's Queen Elizabeth about providing Western technology to Russia; with this, he warned, they might become invincible. Instead of anti-Communist committees, the seventeenth century offered the groans of the Inquisition; in 1950, a similar "crusade" against communism was organized by citizens of Los Angeles, led by a thirty-two-year-old veteran, to ambush auto workers coming off shift at a Chrysler plant.

"In medieval and early modern Christendom," Huxley wrote, "the situation of sorcerers and their clients was almost precisely analogous to that of Jews under Hitler, capitalists under Stalin, Communists and fellow travelers in the United States. They were regarded as the agents of a Foreign Power, unpatriotic at the best and, at the worst, traitors, heretics, enemies of the people. . . .

"Today it is everywhere self-evident that *we* are on the side of Light, *they* on the side of Darkness. And being on the side of Darkness, they deserve to be punished and must be liquidated (since our divinity justifies everything) by the most fiendish means at our disposal" (*Devils*, 133, 192). Here were sentiments both sides of the cold war might have endorsed in 1951.

A few years after the incidents at Loudun, Europe plunged into the Thirty Years War, fomented by Cardinal Richelieu and his Grey Eminence, the monk turned power-monger. Brutal as the Inquisition had been—in Spain burning as many as a hundred witches in a day— Europe eventually tired of the witch hunting. The devils then moved to Massachusetts, where they met burnings and torture in 1692.[59]

Did Huxley take diabolical possession seriously? He was of two minds, alternately spoofing the idea—"The truly surprising thing was not the fact of an occasional possession, but the fact that most people could go through life without becoming demoniac"—and asking himself if devils could exist:

> If the evidence for clairvoyance, telepathy, and prevision is accepted (and it is becoming increasingly difficult to reject it), then we must allow that there are mental processes which are largely independent of space, time and matter. And if this is so, there seems to be no reason for denying a priori, that there may be nonhuman intelligences, whether completely disincarnate, or else associated with cosmic energy in some way of which we are still ignorant. (Devils, 189–90)

This open-mindedness irritated his brother, Julian, who prided himself as a debunker of matters spiritual. Julian enjoyed suddenly switching on the lights at a séance; once he'd caught a charlatan pretending to be the spirit of Saint Teresa and pressing moist heavenly kisses on participants in a séance.[60]

The saga of Loudun did not end with Grandier's death at the stake. The nuns' earlier possession continued. In contemporary terms, the nuns' show—twice a day, and already drawing crowds from all over Europe—was too hot to close; witch hunting was also a big business, R. H. Robbins noted.[61]

The nuns perversely enjoyed their notoriety. A master exorcist was called in, Father Surin, a mystical philosopher of the variety Maine de Biran and Huxley appreciated. Then the spiritual wrestling began in earnest. The spectacle of humans degrading themselves so energetically suggested a race of apes yearning for apedom. Though different in style, The Devils of Loudun continues Huxley's obsession with diabolical possession from Ape and Essence.

As the book ends, Father Surin himself becomes half mad, with lucid intervals. For two decades this continued, until in his old age Surin began writing tracts on mysticism. The abbess fell out of fashion once her devils departed; she acted the part of a contemplative saint with the most horrible skill before dying a long, slow death from cancer.[62]

The epilogue of *Devils* hinted of Huxley's next preoccupation. Drugs (including tobacco and alcohol), sexuality, crowd intoxication— all these shortcuts to transcendence only simulate the mystic experience, Huxley asserted, reverting to his constant metaphor, sight:

> *The unregenerate are more or less completely blind to the inner light and more or less completely deaf to inspiration. By mortifying his self-regarding impulses, by setting up a witness to his thoughts and "a little sentinel to keep an eye on the movements of the heart," a man can sharpen his perceptions to the point where he becomes aware of the messages coming up from the obscure depths of the mind—messages in the form of intuitive knowledge, of direct commands, of symbolic dreams and phantasies.* (Devils, 93)

This statement maps Huxley's world in the next decade. Typical of the reconstructive impulse of Huxley's American period, he found possibilities for spiritual renewal even in a story of innocents burned at the stake. He would cease to call parapsychology and drugs "downward transcendence" when they allowed him new sight.

Huxley's flu was one of those which periodically surface in L.A. from Asia. This one began normally enough—stomach cramps, fever, and headaches—until it passed to his right eye. Seven days after the flu began he was cured, but he was also one-eyed. The disease struck the weaker, blind eye, which barely made out objects in profile against a bright light.

For a decade now, Huxley had struggled for stereoscopic vision. This had come to him, momentarily, in 1939, after his first round of Bates exercises. In the ten years of daily exercises which followed (for two and three hours a day), he had scarcely recovered that moment. Most of us take for granted stereoscopic vision, the parallax or depth of field which allows distance to be judged relative to surroundings. Remove one eye, and the world is a flat canvas, no matter how one turns one's head. Huxley had been conscious of this inability, frequently referring to his lack of perspective in metaphorical terms: "I must have a two-angled vision on all of my characters."[63]

The Ogre had become Cyclops. Even with his hard-won remnants of stereoscopic vision, Huxley had achieved only a fraction of the sight he sought. He had an occasional coordinate image of the world but still couldn't recognize a friend at five paces. It frustrated him continually. He didn't know how much he had lost until he lost what little he possessed.

It was as if he had been playing a child's game of holding a hand over one eye at a time to watch objects jump from side to side. Only this time, the game had gone dreadfully wrong: his eyes had gotten stuck, with only the left side of the world remaining. Peggy Kiskadden's husband Bill, a surgeon, met with another doctor and approved the use of cortisone drops.

The worst part of the current crisis was its déjà vu aspect. Just as it was at sixteen, his eye was red and swollen. Pain rattled him. He stumbled into furniture and missed the vegetables in his soup. The world lacked color as it lacked depth. He lived in a darkened room, unable to tolerate the light, "hoping and praying that there would be no recurrence"—that the infection would not spread to his remaining eye. "The Inner Light was intense beyond her capacity to bear it and for a time her body suffered excruciatingly" (*Devils of Loudun*, 97).

The hardest part of pain is not knowing if (or when) it will end. As spring turned to summer, it became obvious that the eye drops he had been taking were doing him more harm than good. Huxley apparently had an allergic reaction to the cortisone; the drops brought a severe mood change, peevishness. "Psychologically it was the worst thing I ever got through in my life," Maria wrote to Matthew.[64] Her husband paced the floor in his suit, his necktie awry; in black, he would have resembled a sick crow, his long arms bent upward holding his head. Grandier, too, lost his sight; was it after he was aflame?

"I couldn't finish that chapter on torturing the priest," Matthew said. "It was just too much. My mother had a terrible time with that. It was terrifying."[65]

By June 1951, Aldous still couldn't see. Maria began to call for "hard orthodox medicine," Peggy Kiskadden recalled. Huxley even snapped at Bill, who had grown nervous about his role as medical supervisor: "Not because it was dangerous, but because one never knows. Once in a while these things do turn out badly and Aldous is so evidently a *personage difficile*."[66] Eye doctors hesitated. One advised Maria to operate, removing the right eye entirely for fear that the infection would become glaucoma and spread to his "good" left eye.

On his desk, unused, lay thick volumes bound in vellum: hand-copied seventeenth-century manuscripts that Huxley in the best of times needed his magnifying glass to read. Afternoons he sat in his darkened room, shades pulled so that the bright California sunlight—formerly his friend—would not set off another headache. Maria would read to him in French, her cultured Flemish accent whispering lurid stories of twenty-year-old nuns flagellating themselves. Outside, the sounds of life continued: a truck rumbled by on Melrose Avenue, a passing bird chirped its tribute to the Pacific, ten miles west.

There is a legend in Scotland, from the area where Maria and her family lived before she moved into Garsington, that second sight comes to those who are blinded—a tradition which has circulated since the time of Loinneach Odhar in the seventeenth century. This prophecy is "said to be the result of weakness in the visual organs." Such seers were said to be possessed of minds "of a melancholy cast."[67]

Whether or not Huxley had second sight, he certainly had the melancholy and the defective visual organs. By July, the doctors told Maria that they thought the problem was cured; but then he had a relapse from his extreme nervous tension. On July 27, the day after Aldous's fifty-seventh birthday, Maria wrote to Matthew that his gift—a pocket telescope—was "wildly welcome but sadly so." Huxley's condition had finally been diagnosed as iritis, possibly a complication of his childhood blindness. Doctors put him under sedation for extreme pain. He and Maria ventured out only at night. She noted Aldous's "enormous fear" of having an operation on his eyes.

According to Huxley's cousin Renée Haynes, sudden blindness can trigger episodes of psi-phenomena, such as prevision.[68] Whether or not this can be proven, the times Huxley had the most trouble seeing were followed by his most intense explorations of parapsychology.

Actually, someone with Huxley's visual handicap might have sought extraretinal vision, or "eyeless sight" as French novelist Jules Romains called it: the ability to sense colors and read via fingertips or cheeks. In the midthirties an Indian, Koda Bux, read books and bicycled through Times Square blindfolded (this was a man who had studied Yoga for many years); in 1964, a Russian who worked with blind children read magazines and newspapers merely by running her hand over them—dermooptic sight.[69]

By August 1951, when Huxley had been blinded for five months, an antibiotic diminished the infection to where his doctors decided against an operation: "Poor Aldous, we shall never quite know what he went through. . . . I am *sure* that he was afraid of going blind," Maria wrote.[70]

Then, throughout the autumn, his eyes began to improve steadily, and by December he was finishing *Devils*, whose epilogue was written at the turn of the year. Buoying up his spirit was the birth of his grandson, Trev (Mark Trevenen), on October 20. His recovery was spurred by plans to work on a new film, the first offered him in two years—on Gandhi.

At the end of the year, the spotlight shifted from Aldous to Maria, who had a cyst and entered the hospital for an operation. (Aldous finished the typescript of *Devils* while Maria was in the hospital.)

"I shall recover 100%," Maria wrote to Matthew and Ellen, "and there shall be no recurrence."[71] Despite her imperious tone, the cyst behind her right breast was malignant. Maria had cancer and the operation was unable to remove all of it. "Her cancer has gone into the prelymph nodes," Bill Kiskadden told Peggy. "I'm afraid it's going to be very bad."[72] Maria was dying, and she had decided *not* to tell Aldous.

NINE

THE DOORS OF PERCEPTION

"Some are born with a kind of bypass . . . in others,
temporary bypasses may be acquired either spontaneously, or as
a means of deliberate spiritual exercises, or through hypnosis, or
by means of drugs . . . the eye recovers the perceptual
innocence of childhood."   (1953)

"Maria is back at home and is getting on remarkably well," Aldous wrote to Jeanne on January 26, 1952. "The doctors are confident that there will be no recurrence as the trouble was taken in good time and got rid of very thoroughly. . . . In a few more weeks I think that Maria will be back to normal."

While Aldous exulted in imagined good fortune, Maria reflected on her private tragedy. Only fifty-four, she faced more operations and possibly a painful death in the next years. She had no one to support her. "Maria, always reticent about herself," Juliette noted, "was operated on for a cancerous growth. Absolutely no one was allowed to know. Above all not Aldous."[1]

One of those who did know was their new French cook, borrowed from the Stravinskys, Marie Le Put. Marie began work at the Huxleys right after Maria's operation, yet the attention of the household focused on Aldous: "He was awfully white and pale, as if he never went out into the sun. Sickly."[2]

The previous year's blindness had taken a severe toll. Huxley wrote friends that his insomnia had returned; he lived in fear that the blindness would recur.[3]

When Huxley worried most about his eyes, he turned toward a faculty of inner sight. As his physical limits loomed, he could not help himself. In his essay on Maine de Biran, he had fantasized about receiving sensations and ideas unaided by sensory organs; Huxley was ready for any way of peering into the beyond. (And, if he was losing Maria—a possibility his conscious mind apparently refused—he would need some new bulwark, a new faith, to continue.)

His attention shifted from the world outside his shuttered windows to ways of seeing which did not tax his undependable eyes. When his iritis was at its worst, he suggested an anthology on parapsychology to J. B. Rhine.[4]

Even before his second blindness, Huxley had been curious about this subject. Though many attributed this interest to his sojourn in California—even then known as a haven for the occult—Huxley had quietly experimented with such notions for nearly forty years.

The first such exploration recorded in his letters came at a party at Oxford in 1915, where a "telepathist" read his thoughts. The man succeeded sufficiently to shock the young scholar: "It seems to be a kind of smelling out of the thought, of detecting it in the atmosphere. Altogether it was most interesting. I have never seen anything like it before—it is a wonderful gift to possess."[5]

The subject recurs in his letters at the outset of his worst physical impairment, at the time of *Eyeless in Gaza*. In 1934, he wrote a feature article for *Nash's Magazine* "on the subject of psychical research . . . evidence for and significance of supernormal states of consciousness such as telepathy."[6] His interest then ran underground, like a stream beneath a road, eroding his scientific skepticism. Aldous had sat through séances and the palm readers Maria fancied—apparently with limited enthusiasm. One of the first places Aldous and Gerald visited in the United States, significantly enough, was J. B. Rhine's Parapsychology Laboratory at Duke University. Rhine's experiments in ESP and telekinesis (predicting or controlling dice) took place under controlled conditions, which allowed Huxley to take them seriously.

It was to Rhine that Huxley first stated his opinions on psychic research, following the fears of losing his vision recounted in *The Art of Seeing*:

Your work will finally compel those who suffer from "voluntary ig-norance" to reconsider the anecdotal evidence and to accept a good deal of it as valid. . . .

[There is] a "psychic" world of mental forces, either completely immaterial or else making use of forms of energy akin to those ob-servable in the ordinary space-time world, but more subtle. Under suitable conditions, the mental activities of individuals and groups re-lease forces sufficiently powerful, if not to move mountains, certainly to cure serious lesions and even perhaps to multiply food.[7]

By the 1950s, long before activist Rennie Davis found the guru Maharaji, before Shirley MacLaine's belief in reincarnation took her out where the buses don't stop, before Seth and other channelers were as common as face-lifts in Hollywood, Aldous Huxley had become one of the first New Age explorers.

As a species, humans had evolved for millennia, Huxley re-flected, yet their mental and spiritual sides were untutored. Some had talents or ways of seeing that others didn't. If developed and system-atically studied, perhaps these could spur the race to spiritual evolu-tion, as Ouspensky and Gurdjieff had hoped.

In his 1935 book, *Science in the Making*, Heard had suggested that human evolution had taken another, unnoticed leap. Though we operate on a fraction of brain cells, "these crushed and stunted appre-hensions may expand" as evolution proceeds. If natural selection ap-plied to psychic abilities, for example, the passage of generations might bring more prophets, visionaries, and mediums. "We can, it seems already proved, see much which we have up to the present disre-garded."

Following such suggestions, Huxley had read the original exper-iments of Mesmer on animal magnetism, quoting them extensively in *The Devils of Loudun*. Now he began trying out hypnotic passes to relax Maria and their guests. Some thought it odd, to say the least.

Yet his increasing involvement in parapsychology seemed to generate a personal renewal. Friends told him he looked more re-laxed; he chatted amicably with the UCLA students who followed him around the library.

Huxley's mystical period had not ended; he continued to visit the Vedanta Society now and again, but a subtle transformation had occurred. He maintained a classic spiritual hierarchy, with contemplatives occupying the upper ranks and the "infinitely less valuable intuitions of psychics" assigned to the lower depths (because of the earthly application of their powers). Only now he seemed more interested in the lower deck.

This can be seen in his contribution to a 1951 "What Vedanta Means to Me" symposium. In contrast to Heard's and Isherwood's more elaborated contributions, Huxley's seems tight-lipped, even Puritan:

> *People love their egos and don't wish to mortify them, don't wish to see why they shouldn't "express their personalities" and "have a good time." They get their good times; but also and inevitably they get wars and syphilis and revolution and alcoholism, tyranny. . . . Unutterable miseries! But throughout recorded history most men and women preferred the risks, the positive certainty, of such disasters to the laborious whole-time job of trying to get to know the divine Ground of all being. In the long run we get exactly what we ask for.*[8]

Huxley's terseness is understandable. For fifteen years, since *Eyeless in Gaza*, he had restated the fundamental human problem as he saw it: "I know what I ought to do but continue to do what I oughtn't."[9] This was Huxley's most consistent message of his American period; it applied to Jeremy Pordage in *Swan*, unable to steer his taste for the esoteric into the pursuit of truth; to Mr. Hutton in *The Gioconda Smile*, who could not leave his mistress alone at the cost of death; it applied even to a saint, Father Joseph, unable to forsake power politics to return to his cloister. Huxley might have communicated his points better to spirits; they at least saw lives from a truly nonattached perspective.

The Victorian period of Aldous Huxley's birth was a time of enormous interest in parapsychology. Belief in the power of spirits to affect the living—an idea which had always found little support among "college-bred gentry," despite "a public no less large [which] keeps and transmits it from generation to generation," as William James wrote, was challenged in the test-it-all mood of an era only grudgingly accepting the evidence Aldous's grandfather had marshaled in favor of Darwin's theory of biological evolution.[10]

One of T. H. Huxley's associates in supporting Darwin, Alfred Russell Wallace, was among the new breed scientifically testing psychic powers, alongside Nobel laureate William Crookes, F. W. H. Myers (author of the classic *Human Personality and Its Survival of Bodily Death*), and James himself. Their efforts to develop rigorous tests of mediums, telepathy, and materializations led to the founding of the Society for Psychical Research, the Theosophical Society, and their American branches.

This was also an era of great mediums. Whether scientific investigation burgeoned because of talented channelers or the other way around, their names are known to students of the spiritual arts: the Fox sisters, Florence Cook, Douglas Home, the Italian Eusaphia Palladino, and the American Leonora Piper. This group demonstrated a veritable cloudburst of supernormal endowment. Some recognized, out of hundreds introduced, a dozen who had known their "control" in a previous life; they caused the usual thumps and raps at séances, even while held down by observers; they caused spirits to materialize (and not just in the dimly lit rooms skeptics imagine), read sealed envelopes, guessed private thoughts at a distance, and foretold disasters.

As Aldous was born in July 1894, Myers and French physiologist Charles Richet were on Richet's private island watching levitations and ghostly apparitions, a *son-et-lumière* of the spirits. None of the scientists assembled found evidence of trickery, even when the experiments were repeated at Cambridge.[11] (Naturally, many other mediums *were* debunked, such as Madame Blavatsky, many of whose "miracles" were proved fraudulent by a circuit-riding ghost-buster, Dr. Richard Hodgson, one in a line of skeptics extending back to Hippolytus in the second century A.D.)

Aldous's grandfather was one of those ardent disbelievers. William James called him one of the "hard-headed subjects, disgusted by the revelations' contemptible contents, outraged by fraud, and prejudiced beforehand against all 'spirits.' "

"I take no interest in the subject," T. H. Huxley wrote after attending a séance with Darwin. "The only case of Spiritualism I have ever had the opportunity of examining was as gross an imposture as ever came under my notice.

"But supposing these phenomena to be genuine—they do not interest me . . . Better live a crossing-sweeper, than die and be made to talk twaddle by a 'medium' hired at a guinea a séance."[12] Such statements left T.H.'s grandson with internal battles every bit as fierce as those encountered in challenging the family's agnosticism. To make this leap of faith Huxley needed a guide. He found one in an old friend, Eileen Garrett.

Garrett had grown up in Ireland, considering a career in acting. Moving to London, she opened a tearoom in Hampstead fashionable among literati; Lawrence and Huxley were regulars. In post–World War I London, Garrett found a second generation of spirit-testers, including Conan Doyle (Sherlock Holmes's creator was then a well-known spiritualist). She attended Aleister Crowley's infamous "black masses." Finally, at the College of Psychic Science, she discovered her control, "Uvani"; and unlike the devils of Loudun, her spirits had manners.

Though her ESP faculty, as tested by Dr. Rhine, was weak, her reputation as a medium spread. In Hollywood, she impressed Cecil B. DeMille by telling him, in the voice of his mother, to cut two scenes out of his latest film. Just before the war, she moved to New York and started *Tomorrow*, America's first psychic magazine. Aldous was a close enough friend that when Matthew was job hunting, he was sent to her. "She has excellent contacts," Aldous commented wryly.

In February 1952, as Maria recovered from her mastectomy, the Huxleys toured the Arizona desert. In an expanse of wildflowers they found a needed analogy for survival:

> The tenacity of [life] in the face of the most adverse circumstances, the patience (the lilies will lie dormant for as much as ten or fifteen years, if there is a drought, and then come bursting through the sand at the first moisture . . .)[13]

Around them spread square miles of color—purple verbena, blue lupines, red pentstemon, apricot-colored mallows. On Huxley's return, he lunched with Robert Craft:

*As always after a spell in depopulated regions he is refreshed and in
high spirits. I drive him, later, to the summit of Doheny Hill, the start
of his favourite rambles (but definitely not one of mine; though only
three minutes from the centre of Beverly Hills it has a reputation for
rattlesnakes).*

*We follow rutted tracks into a wilderness, the daddy-longlegs
easily ahead. But the intellectual pace is faster, and here he keeps a
good sprint in front, without trying, which makes my pursuit feel
mentally pigeon-toed—and I am trying very hard.*[14]

"Out there, in the eternal lazy morning of the Pacific, days slip
away into months, months into years; the seasons are reduced to the
faintest nuance by the great central fact of the sunshine; one might
pass a lifetime, it seems, between two yawns."[15] Isherwood wrote
these lines to warn British expatriates of what he considered their two
great dangers: sloth and greed.

After a self-imposed two-year exile from California, with trips
to Ecuador and England, Isherwood had shared quarters with photog-
rapher Bill Caskey, first at Salka Viertel's in Santa Monica Canyon,
in hailing distance of the gay bars, and then in Laguna Beach, not far
from Gerald and Chris Wood. In the late forties and early fifties he
was writing *The World in the Evening,* interspersed with shifts at
MGM *(The Great Sinner)* and his juggling act with the Vedanta Society and Swami Prabhavananda, for whom he was finishing up a translation, *The Yoga Aphorisms of Patanjali.* His economic mainstay during this period was reviewing books for Eileen Garrett's *Tomorrow.*

Isherwood's financial break had come from a fellow Vedanta en-
thusiast, playwright John Van Druten, who agreed to write a scenario
of Isherwood's Sally Bowles stories. *I Am a Camera* opened on
Broadway under Van Druten's direction at the end of 1951 with Julie
Harris.

Before this took place, however, Isherwood had a run-in with
Heard. The Swami had asked Isherwood to become a monk at Trabuco; Christopher had tea with Gerald to ask his advice: "Gerald said
that I should obey Swami and go to live there. He said that he knew
Swami was 'deeply disturbed' about me, and that he was disturbed
himself."[16]

Two days later, Isherwood met with Prabhavananda and told him he could not be a monk, that his heart wasn't in it. Disappointed, the swami said both Gerald and Aldous had come to him "and told him things about the way I am living, and asked him to remonstrate with me. Swami had answered, 'Why don't you pray for him?'

"I was touched and delighted by Swami's reaction, which I interpreted as a rebuke to Gerald and Aldous. Wasn't he telling them, in effect, 'You'd do better to love Chris more and criticize him less'? That was what I wanted him to have meant. It did annoy me that the two of them had spoken to Swami behind my back. . . . When I asked Swami what it was that they had told him, he said vaguely that I'd been seen 'in some bad place'—the nature of the place didn't seem to interest him. It could only have been a homosexual bar. . . .

"I found it much easier to forgive Aldous for his interference than Gerald. Aldous didn't know any better, he was essentially a square." [17]

These days Huxley was most likely to run into Isherwood at the Stravinskys'—on the floor, drunk: "At an immense altitude above me [was] Aldous, who I think was rather fond of me, looking at me rather curiously as much as if to say, 'Aren't you going a little far?' " [18]

Huxley wasn't the only person who thought Isherwood had gone "a little far." By the middle of 1951, some in England who had never forgiven Auden or Isherwood for leaving suspected that he was hiding Guy Burgess and Donald Maclean, two recently discovered Soviet spies in Britain's Foreign Office. Two FBI agents interrogated the apolitical writer (now an American citizen).

The noose was closing in on many of the intellectual émigrés from Hollywood's Periclean Age; a few more turns and Huxley would be caught. Brecht had left for Switzerland and East Berlin after his HUAC interrogation. Mann had moved to Switzerland before anyone could subpoena him. Salka Viertel, who had amicably divorced Brecht, was named as a Communist before HUAC; this didn't help a career which had faltered after Garbo's retirement. When Viertel tried to visit Brecht in Europe, she was denied an exit visa. The list of her sins was as thick as the Manhattan phone directory.[19]

In this same period, Chaplin also met travel barriers, but unlike Viertel, Isherwood, and Matthew Huxley, he had not taken out American citizenship.

Throughout 1951, Chaplin had been writing the novel-length treatment for *Limelight,* his nostalgic tale of an aging comedian who helps a young ballerina after her suicide attempt. By the winter of 1952, he had finished shooting the film and hoped to premiere it in London. Chaplin was assured by the Immigration and Naturalization Service that there would be no problem with his reentry. In September 1952, Oona and Charlie and their five children boarded the *Queen Elizabeth.*

Had Chaplin known that the Vice President–elect, Richard Nixon, had privately promised Hedda Hopper: "You can be sure I will keep an eye on the case," he might have scrutinized his reentry permit more closely.[20] His ship had not been out to sea two days before U.S. Attorney General J. P. McGranery renounced Chaplin's reentry permit, considering him inadmissible because of "morals, health, insanity or advocating communism" (the attorney general doesn't seem to have been particularly choosy). His evidence was as vague as most anti-Red charges of the period: newspaper reports, anonymous letters.[21]

When Chaplin arrived in London, enormous crowds greeted him. The British press scorned the U.S. charges; Foreign Affairs Secretary Anthony Eden was asked in Parliament to guarantee Chaplin's freedom of travel. Chaplin secretly sent Oona back to wind up his business affairs in a hurry.

Showings of the apolitical *Limelight* were hounded by American Legion picketers, who forced three major theater chains to withdraw the film. The FBI interrogated anyone connected with the Chaplin household or studio; they may have driven Chaplin's half brother mad. At least Chaplin was out of reach of congressional committees, unlike Huxley, who had been named as a Communist fellow traveler on May 23, 1951.

HUAC's 1951 Hollywood hearings had been far more professionally staged than the 1947 sessions. If a friendly witness had no names of subversives to recite, he was handed a few, like so many tokens at an amusement park.

One cooperative witness vividly mixed metaphors in calling himself "the real daddy longlegs of a worm when it came to crawling"; he took dozens of roles from less "loyal" colleagues "in an effort to cash in on my new status as a sanitary cultural hero." The only ones in Hollywood exempt from this pressure were Lassie and Rin-Tin-Tin.

Listening to the broadcast HUAC hearings in a federal penitentiary, a jailmate of Hollywood Ten screenwriter Lester Cole told him, "If you *are* a Communist, you better get the hell out. Any group with that many finks is no damn good."[22]

By the early fifties a "graylist" had emerged at the studios. The blacklist left out too many people; HUAC couldn't be everywhere at once:

> The blacklist was a kind of professional cancer, but at least the afflicted person knew what he had done—and what he must do to "cure" the disease. The great frustration of the graylist was that it seemed to many sufferers to be an ailment which had no origin, diagnosis, or treatment. One simply stopped hearing the telephone ring.[23]

A few star writers were exempted from this scenario. Studio executives considered them so valuable that they were cleared whether they liked it or not. Huxley was not one of those; though opposed to Soviet communism since the purge trials of the thirties, he persisted in signing the occasional petition.

Purely commercial writers of Hollywood—the Sammy Glicks of Budd Schulberg's *What Makes Sammy Run?*—led untroubled careers while former radicals either recanted or went bankrupt. To inform or not to inform, that was the question which split an industry as bitterly as the studios' earlier hesitancy to denounce Nazism. The "Time of the Toad," as Dalton Trumbo called it, lasted for the next decade and beyond. Unreconstructed toadies eventually elected one of their own—former Screen Actors Guild president Ronald Reagan—to the

California statehouse and then to the White House. "Communists claimed they were victims of a blacklist when actually they were working members of a conspiracy directed by Soviet Russia," the cowboy actor declared.[24]

The Hollywood guilds outdid each other in Red-hunting. The Screen Actors Guild notified unfriendly witnesses that they were on their own; the Screen Directors Guild not only adopted a loyalty oath, they considered a proposal (by DeMille, when he wasn't listening to spirits) to file reports after each picture on political opinions expressed by crew and cast. The Screen Writers Guild—because of its reputation as a base for active Party members—went one better: not only did they let unfriendlies dangle in the wind, they volunteered to turn over notes of internal debates and meetings to HUAC.[25]

The SWG Awards dinner for 1952 was a gala affair, with George Jessel, Barbara Stanwyck, and other major stars. Aldous Huxley announced the awards on the spotlit stage. A columnist for the *Saturday Review* in the audience reflected on Huxley's "strangely obscure and relatively unproductive existence in the film capital."

After explaining Huxley's rejection of glasses, the columnist continued: "I, along with twelve hundred other guests, watched with astonishment while he rattled glibly on with an announcement of the various awards. Then suddenly he faltered—and the disturbing truth became obvious. He wasn't reading his address at all. He had learned it by heart.

"To refresh his memory he brought the paper closer and closer to his eyes. When it was only an inch away he still couldn't read it and had to fish for a magnifying glass in his pocket to make the typing visible to him. It was an agonizing moment."[26]

The battery of lights had blinded him temporarily, Huxley irritably explained to the reviewer. Besides, having written ten books since his arrival, his California stay could hardly be called unproductive. Nevertheless, this uncomfortable moment was not exactly a reference for his professional fellows in film. Later that year, when he found himself attacked on the cover of the right-wing magazine *Counterattack* as a Communist dupe, his film career collapsed.

In November 1951, the *New York Times* announced Huxley was to write on a film on Gandhi. The opportunity was most welcome; ever since Rank had made *Prelude to Fame* from his short story "Young Archimedes"—without hiring him for the script—the writer had itched for another film.[27] The producer was Gabriel Pascal, a Hungarian the same age as Huxley, famous for persuading George Bernard Shaw to allow his plays to be filmed. For several reasons— because Gandhi was a personal hero, film jobs were scarce, and the producer a rogue elephant in the studio system—Huxley's letters provide the most detailed case study of his involvement in the movie industry.

As usual, the *idea* of the product seduced his imagination; the script reeled with dramatic and political quandaries. He confronted the problems faced by later scenarists of Gandhi's life, as an unpublished letter to Pascal shows:

> *What about the female elements in the story. . . . Miss Slade can scarcely be introduced realistically. When I saw her, twenty-five years ago, she was one of the most unprepossessing English spinsters I ever saw, and fussed around Gandhi in an entirely preposterous way—feeding him with a spoon, pulling up his loin cloth when it showed signs of slipping, and, in general, behaving like a very possessive nanny. In our treatment we are told about an American girl . . . whose admission that she had been a little loose affected the mahatma so much that he felt it necessary to fast, by way of vicarious reparation. Can this incident be recorded? Or would it arouse in Western audiences a mixture of indignation and laughter?*[28]

Then came the actual contractual negotiations, and in these, Huxley sounds increasingly sophisticated—perhaps because he now had separate agents for film, theater, and literary rights:

> *There is something* simpatico *about Pascal. . . . But he has the Bohemian's horror of being pinned down to black and white, of having to commit himself definitely to anything. Hence the difficulty of writing a satisfactory contract—particularly one which calls for conditional payments out of future earnings. The haggling had been going on since February and is as far from a conclusion as the Korean armistice negotiations.*[29]

Huxley's refusal to travel to India for the shoot aggravated Pascal and posed problems for ad-libbing dialogue on the set:

> India presents two dangers so far as my eyes are concerned—dust as a direct irritant and as a possible source of allergic symptoms which can bring on iritis at one remove; for the condition often arises as a reaction to trouble somewhere else in the system. All this may sound very fussy and timorous; but I have had this eye handicap for more than forty years now, and know on what an exceedingly narrow margin I operate. This summer's experience proved how very little it takes to abolish that margin altogether and reduce me to complete incapacity.[30]

In the end, Huxley fell victim to the childlike restlessness of producers he had observed while writing *Madame Curie:* Pascal abandoned the project. "After wasting four months of my time," Aldous wrote to Matthew in June 1952, "Pascal, on my demand that he compensate me for the loss by doubling his initial payment, has called off the Gandhi business."[31]

The year 1952 marked the end of the great television freeze, a four-year period when the Federal government stopped issuing TV licenses. New stations now clamored for lowbrow crime series. Filmed literary classics were money-losers, unless they had the sanitized, epic look of DeMille's biblical dramas. Like so many veterans of Hollywood, Huxley was known by a peg: the brainy writer who worked on literary projects. Even if Huxley had written an old-fashioned mystery—as *A Woman's Vengeance* started out to be—producers would have been leery of it.

Huxley's next offer came from director Frank Capra, whose reputation rests on comedies of American myths *(Mr. Smith Goes to Washington, It's a Wonderful Life).* The American Telephone and Telegraph company wanted a new TV series on science. Fearing a dull documentary, the ad agency, N. W. Ayer, commissioned a pilot one-hour program on the sun from the commercial director.

Capra's first stop was science fiction writer Willy Ley; over coffee, Capra offered him $5,000 for a treatment. His second stop was North King's Road: " 'Aldous,' I said to the fabulous Huxley over a drink in the patio . . . 'if a network like CBS asked you to produce an hour-long filmed program on the sun, what would you say?' " (Capra obviously enjoyed hobnobbing with an author he considered

"Aristotle, Aquinas, Newton, Buddha, and P. T. Barnum all mixed up into one incredible character."[32] Could Huxley have worked successfully with anyone capable of such bombastics?)

Capra neglected to mention to his two writers that he would be competing with them. His "showman's version" included cartoon characters like Thermo the Magician and Chloro Phyll.

While Huxley complained about the intensity of his reading ("one must read 100% in order to be able to leave out 99% . . . for a TV audience"), Capra was whittling his treatment from an astronomer's book, *Our Mr. Sun*. Huxley told friends he was giving "a great deal of thought to the ways information may be conveyed in photographic and animated-cartoon images."[33] Capra's assistants turned out a script with the dialogue of a twelve-year-old.

In his autobiography, Capra offers a neatly fifties peroration: he told his sponsors that "the anti-moral, the intellectual bigots, and the Mafias of ill will may destroy religion, but they will never conquer the cross."[34] In the battle of the scripts, Capra's work won out; who could resist a cute character named Chloro Phyll? The shrewd producer received contracts for four films, all the while protesting his unworthiness.

By the fall of 1952, the only film project Huxley had left were short sketches he hoped to adapt for his compatriots Vivien Leigh and Laurence Olivier.

One reason for his dearth of work is found in the November 7 headline of *Counterattack: Facts to Combat Communism:* LEADING AUTHORS STILL BELIEVE IN "PEACEFUL COEXISTENCE" HOAX. Huxley's name appeared first on the list.

Right-wing magazines such as *Alert* and *Counterattack* regularly touted "Stalin's Stooges in Hollywoodland." At twenty-four dollars per subscriber, *Counterattack* netted a hundred thousand dollars yearly. Senate and House committees flew in ex-Communist "consultants," paying by the day to stretch out testimony. On the side, the editors operated a "clearing house," American Business Consultants, which specialized in loyalty investigations to shake down corporations.

The editors of *Counterattack* would call a TV sponsor and say they had heard actress Y, of questionable background, was employed on its television series. As a public service, the editors would study her loyalty and that of the supporting cast—for $1,000. If the offer was refused, three weeks later the editors would run a story about how actress Y was not a Communist but a fellow traveler—almost as bad. Using these tactics, *Counterattack* drew in General Motors, Du Pont, Woolworth's, and Reynolds Tobacco—at a considerably greater fee than the good sisters of Loudun charged their audiences.

Huxley's trouble had started when, at the request of old friend Naomi Mitchison, he had signed this statement: "We believe that differing political and economic systems can exist side by side on the basis of peacefully negotiated settlements . . . We condemn writing liable to sharpen existing dangers and hatreds." Co-signers included C. M. Joad, Edith Sitwell, Christopher Fry, André Maurois, and Albert Camus.

"These deluded authors have helped Stalin," the professional anti-Communists yelped. To an industry which saw nothing undemocratic about John Wayne's monthly expense account of $13,000, talk of internationalism sounded red; this was definitely graylist material. Despite *Counterattack's* note that the statement's sponsor, The Author's World Peace Appeal, was an "assertedly non-Communist group of 750 famous writers," a small, neat check was added to Huxley's growing file, alongside another petition he had signed on behalf of Friends of International Freedom.

The background to this hysteria was a war that wasn't a war, whose guns nevertheless rumbled on the radio newscasts and whose bullets killed 54,246 U.S. soldiers. By 1952, the "police action" began to sound like Orwell's never-ending war in *1984*. Each year Americans were promised victory was near, and if not, well, "Better Dead than Red," as the popular saying went. A people bred on a Hollywood diet of war-hero films and film noir detectives thought peace as wimpy as body-builder Charles Atlas's famous ninety-seven-pound weakling.

"What a world!" Huxley wrote a friend. "And who knows if, ten or twenty years from now, the survivors may not be looking back at 1952 nostalgically, as to a lost Golden Age."[35]

An unexpected result of working with Pascal was reacquaintance with Laura Archera. One night Pascal seated Archera (his assistant editor) next to Huxley at dinner. Like many a Hollywood couple after them, they discovered a shared interest in metaphysics. Aldous launched an extensive disquisition on the nineteenth-century medical hypnotist Dr. James Esdaile, who in India had conducted operations without anesthetic. From there he segued into the praises of Mesmer's magnetic passes. As a part-time therapist, Archera was fascinated. "Are these passes difficult to make?" she asked. (Across the table, a guest sat agog at the author telling the slim-legged blond how to make a pass.)

"Nothing is easier," Huxley answered: "just have your client lie down . . ."[36]

Laura saw the Huxleys a few days afterward at a going-away party for Matthew, Ellen, and their baby Trev, who were visiting for a few months. Matthew had fallen on hard times. After several years at Fairfield Osborn's Conservation Foundation, he had been promised a post with the U.N. Environmental Program. He quit his job, only to be stymied by a hiring freeze. Though he never knew it, an extensive loyalty investigation may have squelched his prospects; Matthew's picket-line captainship was enough to raise hair on the neck of a professional Red-sniffer. The young couple were broke—with a new child on the way. Aldous had asked Robert M. Hutchins of the Ford Foundation to find a spot for Matthew, but nothing had materialized.

That night, Laura met Edwin and Grace, Peggy and Bill, Gerald and Christopher. Maria's cook from Brittany had made a meal of crêpes with mushrooms, a veal roast, and creamed spinach, with a Grand Marnier soufflé for dessert. When Gerald was asked a question about his current writing on flying saucers, he put his finger to his lips, glanced at Edwin, and whispered, "Hush, the grown-ups will hear us!" Grace reported.[37]

Maria asked Laura for a therapeutic consultation. A week later, she drove up the hill to Laura's studio and told her of her illness. Maria's reaction was fatalistic: "To me, dying is no more than going from one room to another." Maria then sank into a trance, where she recalled walking along the desert, feeling the hot sand prickle on her feet. She asked Laura to help Aldous, now struggling to recover memories "of a two year period around the age of eleven."

After tea the next week, Laura sat with Aldous, trying to help him visualize the "lost years" before his mother died.

Huxley had been sent away to school at nine, where the "pale and apparently fragile child with a big, high-browed head poised unsteadily on a very long, thin body" was bullied.[38]

According to his cousin Gervas Huxley, who attended boarding school with him, Aldous never much respected his father, Leonard: "Aldous thought his father was silly. He *was* silly. He wasn't the kind of father one looked up to, or went to when one was in trouble." At pen and paper games, twelve-year-old Aldous regularly bested his father, who retaliated by inventing words not in the dictionary. Aldous jibed with the callousness of the precocious, "Father, cheating again?"[39]

As Laura listened, Aldous tried to recapture such memories, stretched out on the couch in his hushed, book-walled study. The writer recalled his past fitfully, then abandoned the attempt for chat on their mutual interest in dianetics, L. Ron Hubbard's earliest, most thoughtful, version of what was eventually marketed as the Church of Scientology:

> We have been experimenting with dianetics [Huxley wrote to a doctor friend]. Up to the present I have proved to be completely resistant . . . there is a complete shutting off of certain areas of childhood memory, due, no doubt, to what the dianeticians call a "demon circuit," an engrammatic command in the nature of "don't tell," "keep quiet," etc.
>
> Maria, meanwhile, has had some success. Whether because of dianetics or for some other reason, she is well and very free from tension. Hubbard, the author of the book, is a very queer fellow—very clever, rather immature, far from being a "clear" himself (he says he has never had time to undergo a thorough auditing) and in some ways rather pathetic; for he is curiously repellant physically and is probably always conscious of the fact, even in the midst of his successes.[40]

The next therapy which caught the Huxleys' fancy—like cloaks discarded when a change in emotional weather made them unsuitable—was Entelechy Therapy.

Though the couple were faddists of psychological lore, the reader would be mistaken, however, in thinking these concerns casual. Sybille Bedford noted "an escalation in his interests" in psychic concerns at this time. She also found more conviction behind his explorations, "a change from curiosity to conviction."[41]

E-therapy was a synthesis of early Buddhist texts and modern autohypnosis by A. L. Kitselman, a scholar of Indian religion who had known the Huxleys for a decade. Kitselman urged Huxley to probe his deeper self "with requests for help or enlightenment," which often arrived in an intuition, a symbol, a repressed memory, or in a physical release of tension.[42] This fragrant combination of hypnotism and spiritual classics apparently helped Huxley more than other therapy.

Over the last two years, he had progressed from being a student of hypnotism to becoming a practicing mesmerist. E-therapy required such hypnotic training and, above all, a Wordsworthian willingness "to recapture the experience of the peace experienced under hypnosis during the hours of daily living, through the closing of the eyes for a moment and the repetition of some word like Peace."[43]

Huxley clearly meant something different by "Peace" than he had two decades earlier, as a pacifist. He now considered that ending the Korean War, for instance, was more the business of politicians than philosophers. The focus of E-therapy was inner balance rather than détente. To Kitselman's approach, Huxley added one of Hubbard's better ideas, psychological first aid.[44]

During previous hypnosis sessions, Huxley had engraved a subconscious message which allowed him to regain a deep trance upon repeating a few words to himself. He used this autohypnosis to launch extremely deep meditations in which his ego finally let down its intellectual ramparts. The thin figure sat with crossed legs, his eyes shut and bobbing, his graying hair motionless over his broad forehead. Seen from afar, he seemed to withdraw from life to break free of the pain and visual frustration which bedeviled him.

He used autohypnosis to cure his insomnia and to stimulate visualization simultaneously:

I imagine-remember running along a beach, then walking into the sea, feeling the impact of the cold water as it rises up the legs and body, then swimming, and finally riding the waves on a surf-board and running out again, with the waves breaking against my body, and re-

*peating the ride several times. Then one imagines drying, sun-bathing
and going into the house for a nap. After which one can turn over
into one's normal sleeping position.*[45]

Maria was enthralled: "Aldous, who could never say the right thing,
now cannot say the wrong thing . . . in fact," she emphasized, *"he
runs himself."*

The afternoon session with Laura Archera yielded little information. Reversing roles—and reverting to her original interest—she
asked Aldous to make passes over her. She fell into a relaxed, hazy
state, in which condition she went home. Her housemate, Virginia
Pfeiffer—sister to Pauline, one of Hemingway's wives—demanded she
call the Huxleys to find out what had happened. "Maria was quick to
understand," Laura recalled. " 'Did Aldous give you the waking-up
passes?' . . . 'Aldous,' she repeated, brimming with fun and mock-
ingly reproachful, 'Aldous! You forgot to wake up Laura!' "[46]

Mesmerism was no longer first in Huxley's pantheon; once the
floodgates of skepticism opened, in washed a baggage room of psychic
ephemera.

Huxley distinguished between therapies, such as dianetics, E-
therapy, and hypnosis, and parapsychological phenomena, such as telepathy (communication among minds), clairvoyance (impressions or
perceptions received at a distance), and precognition (vision of the
future). Both promised ways for humans to wrest control over a world
they barely understood, either on an individual level (therapy) or on
a race-wide level (psychic evolution).

The underlying context for both, of course, was the religious
mysticism Huxley had studied during the war.[47] He considered the
growth of scientific research in parapsychology inevitable, but he worried about its results in a society ungrounded in spiritual goals:

> *Psychic powers without humility and without the guiding insights of
> spirituality will lead astray even more fatally than material powers,
> similarly unguided, are doing at present.*[48]

To prevent this, Huxley proposed parapsychological research
through a nondenominational postgraduate institute "to establish contact
with that part of the mind which lies beyond language," to search for

"the best techniques for getting out of one's own light and collaborating with the not-self."[49]

Of course, being a writer and not a trained scientist, his explorations could only be theoretical. Still, he regularly read the *Journal of Parapsychology* and the *Bulletin of Parapsychology*. Starting in the early fifties, he began his own informal laboratory of explorations, his Tuesday evenings, where friends stopped by after dinner to watch hypnotists or mediums at work.

At times, he even credited himself with mentalist powers, though he rarely discussed this. (One such incident occurred in 1947, when his old friend Cyril Connolly had visited California. After lunching together, Connolly dreamed about Huxley "appearing to him in a blue light." Aldous replied, "Yes, I thought about you a good deal. I felt you were unhappy.")[50]

Few old friends were invited to the Tuesday nights: the Hubbles, once, but not Peggy or Stravinsky (who continued to see the Huxleys weekly). Not Anita, who lumped psychic and spiritual approaches into one big joke.[51])

Tuesday night participants had broad interests: "They would flash bright lights, make magnetic passes, turn on records of strange sounds, put the visiting medium or hypnotist through his paces . . . with passionate interest but also critically, accepting that there might be fraud or multiple explanations," according to Sybille Bedford.[52]

Paulette and Burgess Meredith were regulars; at a gathering after the war they witnessed a man under hypnosis "travel forward in time."[53] After Paulette and Burgess divorced in 1951, she too stopped coming by. Her career had eclipsed, once her features from the late forties (*Hazard* and *Anna Lucasta*) proved box office and critical disappointments. Yesterday's glamour girl regularly made films through 1954, but she never recovered the splash of *Kitty*—nor her $5,000-a-week salary. In 1952, she and Anita left for Europe on a junket sponsored by *Life*, a Goddard's Guide to London which seemed to boil down to "Take your jewelry case—empty."

Heard and Isherwood appeared occasionally for the Tuesday nights. Belief in psychic powers "can permit oneself to be set apart as a little 'queer,' " Eileen Garrett wrote.[54] In the 1950s, the underground homosexual population sought out fringe groupings. "California gays in the Fifties appeared as bohemians, artists, joined the Vedanta Society and Esperanto Clubs—anything which challenged the prevailing morality. Many of them were married and apparently heterosexual, with children," gay historian Jim Kepner suggests. "With people like these, gays felt more comfortable in their own 'oddness.' "[55]

Heard had now moved to Santa Monica Canyon, at 545 Spoleto Drive in Pacific Palisades—a one-story house overlooking the ocean, thick with eucalyptus trees. His move coincided with his reentry into the now tightly knit circle around the Huxleys. Again he became a regular for tea and dinner parties, and he and Isherwood had regained their closeness. They would go together to the gay beach at the bottom of the canyon near Anita's house. One day Isherwood got lucky. "A whole bunch of us used to go down there. Naturally, we put our towels where the nice-looking boys were, and one thing led to another." The forty-eight-year-old writer met an eighteen-year-old, Don Bachardy, "full of life, a perfect darling."[56]

Some were shocked at the thirty-year gap between them—as they would probably have been shocked if Aldous started seeing a twenty-five-year old; Isherwood was older than Don's father. "It was illegal," Isherwood noted later. "People were quite scandalized. It went around town that Christopher had brought a 12-year-old with him."[57]

Gerald accepted Don, realizing Christopher had fallen deeply in love. "He spoke of our relationship as if it were a daring pioneer research project of great scientific importance," Isherwood recalled with pride, "urging me to keep a day-to-day record of it. He had now begun to discuss publicly the problems of the 'intergrade,' meaning the homosexual, and the role which homosexuals might play in social evolution. . . .

"All this was only part of an astonishing and mysterious transformation. For Gerald's health had greatly improved, and he seemed less dyspeptic, less puritanical, warmer, merrier. He could now be persuaded to accept an occasional glass of sherry and would sometimes even eat meat."[58]

Not everyone took to this winter-spring relationship. Peggy Kiskadden, who had given Isherwood a birthday party every year he was in California, invited him once again, but asked if "that boy" had to come along. It was a slight Isherwood never forgave.

In October 1952, *The Devils of Loudun* was published by Harper. After she had sent the galleys to Grace Hubble for proofreading, Maria appended a note: "The end chapter [an epilogue Huxley wrote after her operation] I find very beautiful; it explains why everything else. To me, it is pure Aldous, such an adorable Aldous. He always must go through these wallowings."

By "wallowings" Maria must have meant his misanthropic glorying in human perverseness. *Devils* is brilliant in the manner of his other American works—mordant, watchful, and wise.

The most distinctive aspect of Huxley's post-iritis writings of the early 1950s—the biography of Maine de Biran and *Devils*—is his overbearing use of metaphors of light and vision.

> *Biran had never thought to look for light outside the confines of his own mind.*

Or:

> *The words were like lamps, suddenly illuminating a mind that had been darkened by too much brooding over past hurts, too much relishing of future pleasures or imaginary triumphs,* he wrote in *Devils*.

Huxley complained that ordinarily we are "more or less completely blind to the inner light" and how "we all imagine ourselves to be simultaneously clear-sighted and impenetrable; but, except when blinded by infatuation, other people see through us just easily as we see through them."[59]

This tendency was only accentuated in *Doors of Perception*. British critic Angus Wilson insisted that *Devils* revealed Huxley's multiple personalities: the Swiftian hater of the flesh, the popular historian with the personality of a sixth-form master, the lover of scandal, the teacher of religious truth, and the stern moralist watching noble ends destroyed by ignoble means.[60] Faced with so many Huxleys in the same volume, Wilson considered the author unable to decide which was most important. (Huxley was all of these personalities, of course; "Do I contradict myself?" Whitman asked; "yes, I contain multitudes." A better question might be which *persona* came to the fore of any given work, and why.)

"His discovery of what he wanted to say was like the conquest of Mexico," Huxley wrote of Joyce in 1952. "It began with the islands, touched the mainland, climbed to an astounding vision of pyramids and feathered warriors and ended in the triumphant capture."[61]

The autumn of 1952 was devoted to family matters. First Maria's mother sprained her shoulder and, in the resulting medical care and commotion, drained the energy of Rose and Maria; she intimated she wouldn't mind moving in with Aldous and Maria. "In no circumstances would I think of installing her in this house," Aldous wrote Matthew heatedly. "She would drive Coccola [a pet name for Maria] to death or madness in a few months."[62]

Then Julian's boy, Francis—a brilliant anthropologist who worked with Eileen Garrett—visited. He remembered Aldous keeping to his classic schedule on North King's Road: work after breakfast with everyone out of the house, lunch, and another round of solitary work. To his nephew, Aldous was not chatty. Francis remembers, "I used to try to get him to talk; he would keep his knife and fork while he was considering my remark—whether it was worth saying anything about. His blind eye would be gazing off to some invisible star or planet. Then his gaze would fall back to his plate; he would say nothing."

"How is Matthew?" Francis was asked by Aldous.

" 'Well,' I said, 'he's complaining that you've never been a father to him.'

" 'Oh, is he still going on about that?' he replied. He was obviously the last man to be a father to anybody."[63]

For Huxley this was an unbusy time—his film projects languishing, a new book still selling. His next project took him by surprise; his letters offer no anticipation of its enormity.

On a bright and balmy Monday morning in May 1953, Aldous Huxley took mescaline for the first time.

Huxley had read of experiments with the drug by an English psychiatrist living in Saskatchewan, Dr. Humphry Osmond, the man who would coin the term "psychedelic" (mind-revealing). Huxley wrote and, by chance, found a fan who regularly traveled with *Texts and Pretexts*, Huxley's witty anthology. Soon Osmond was invited to stay with the Huxleys while in Los Angeles for the meetings of the American Psychiatric Association.

Osmond felt nervous visiting Aldous and Maria. He saw before him a tall, fragile-looking man, whom the doctor knew as a controversial figure: would his conversation be up to par? On first impression, Huxley seemed to float before him. "His head was massive, finely shaped, with a splendid brow. His gaze, from his better eye, was keen and piercing, but seemed to be focused a little above and below me. His handshake was shaky and uncertain, as if he did not enjoy the custom."[64]

Osmond invited his host to the APA conference, an experience the doctor was unlikely to forget. Throughout the lectures, Huxley was at his most mischievous: "crossing himself devoutly every time Freud's name was mentioned" and kidding his host loudly in the foyer: "But Humphry, how incredible it is in a Marxist country like this . . ."[65]

After the sessions, Huxley brought up mescaline; he had asked Osmond to bring the drug. Humphry agreed, somewhat reluctantly, to the experiment.

At eleven o'clock on May 4, Osmond stirred four tenths of a gram of white, needlelike crystals into a glass of water. Huxley drank and sat back to await whatever inspiration brought with Maria, Humphry, and a Dictaphone.

Mescaline, "the only naturally occurring psychedelic in this family of adrenaline-related drugs," was isolated from peyote in the late 1890s, according to Dr. Andrew Weil, an internationally known researcher. Among psychoactive drugs such as lysergic acid (LSD), yohimbine, psilocybin, and more recent hybrids (such as MDMA or "ecstasy"), it is among the most hallucinatory. Weil writes, "The pure drug may cause initial nausea, though not as frequently as peyote. Its effects last up to twelve hours and generally resemble those of the whole cactus."[66]

Though both peyote and mescaline were legal—and in use by Indians of the Southwest since at least the Civil War—peyote's bitter taste had been enough to make William James complain after choking down half a button, "Henceforth I'll take the visions of trust." Mescaline was easier to swallow.

Osmond was studying the drug for its chemical similarity to adrenochrome, a substance produced by the body and linked to insanity. In 1940, a doctor had noted that "the characteristic effect of mescaline is a molecular fragmentation of the entire personality"; Nazi scientists experimented with the drug as a truth serum. Later, two scientists observed that "mescaline reproduced every single major symptom of acute schizophrenia."[67] To many, all this evidence would have been a sign to stay away, but to Huxley, the frustrated medical researcher, self-experimentation in the name of science made the drug even more appealing. "The remotest discoveries of the Chemist, the Botanist, or Mineralogist, will be as proper objects of the Poet's art . . ." Wordsworth wrote in the Preface to *Lyrical Ballads,* "if the time should ever come when these things shall be familiar to us."

Huxley had read of previous mescaline experiments: Havelock Ellis, in the nineties, and Henri Michaux, the French poet, in the twenties, had both taken the drug without ill effects. Ellis had given peyote buttons to William Butler Yeats, who had seen "the most delightful dragons, puffing out their breath straight in front of them, like rigid lines of steam."[68]

No wonder Huxley had expected to shut his eyes and be dazzled by visions, "of many colored geometries, of animated architectures, rich with gems and fabulously lovely, of landscapes with heroic figures, of symbolic dramas trembling perpetually on the verge of ultimate revelation" (*Doors,* 15).

In conjuring this visual fantasy, he again hoped to transcend his weak faculties of sight and visualization: "For as long as I can remember, I have always been a poor visualizer. . . . Only when I have a high temperature do my mental images come to independent life" (*Doors,* 15). Thus Huxley's difficulties in writing scenarios; his examination of canvases with a magnifying glass, as if every work were a forgery until proven innocent to his weaker eyes. His way of seeing was "a poor thing but my own."

If necessity is the mother of invention, then psychological need must be the father of creative risk. In his pursuit of visions—those ever elusive flashes of the celestial light he had documented in his biographies of visionaries—Huxley was prepared to take a drug which mimicked madness.

Huxley's interest in mind-altering chemicals was not new. He had almost certainly tried cocaine or hashish at parties when these enjoyed a brief vogue in the twenties. He had used drugs like tobacco and alcohol, smoking cigarettes and a pipe at Oxford and enjoying a sherry or a claret with dinner. Drugs which dulled the mind (barbiturates, tranquilizers, hard liquor) and those which left a craving (such as Mary Amberly's morphine in *Eyeless in Gaza*) he had no use for.

An early reference to drugs, from 1930, occurred in the short story "After the Fireworks":

> "Everybody has his own favorite short cuts to the other world. Mine, in those days, was opium."
>
> " 'Opium?' She opened her eyes very wide. 'Do you mean to say you smoked opium?' She was thrilled. Opium was a vice of the first order.
>
> " 'It's as good a way of becoming supernatural,' he answered, 'as looking at one's nose or one's navel, or not eating, or repeating a word over and over again, till it loses its sense and you forget how to think. All roads lead to Rome.' "[69]

A year later he speculated poignantly on a new "world-transfiguring drug" to offer humans "a novel paradise" and (in a remark which anticipated his later interest in mysticism) to "abolish our solitude as individuals."[70] In *Brave New World*, he had invented that insouciant cure-all Soma, named after an ancient Hindu elixir—"A gram is better than a damn."

Long before he sampled any psychedelic drugs he aptly imagined their effect. One instance comes from the Disney *Alice in Wonderland* script, again framed visually. [Dodgson:] "Why, in Wonderland I've looked at turnips till they changed into balloons. And I've looked at balloons till they changed into elephants. And I've looked at elephants till they just weren't there at all." (He lowers his voice.) "Once you've looked at things in the Wonderland way, they're never quite as bad as they were before."

His moment of transfiguration was overdue. For the last fifteen years, Huxley had read the sacred texts. Study and meditation, whatever peace they brought, had not delivered the visual vortex he sought. In *The Perennial Philosophy*, he'd written of the ardors of making oneself worthy and ready for enlightenment, borrowing a phrase from Blake: " 'cleansing the doors of perception' is often . . . painfully like a surgical operation."[71]

The search resembled his grandfather's: "the resolute facing of the world as it is, when the garment of make-believe, by which pious hands have hidden its uglier features, is stripped off."[72]

Aldous Huxley was about to make his boldest strike at the frontiers of knowledge, using the scientific observation techniques of his ancestors. After his five dozen books were reduced in public memory to two or three, he would still be remembered for what he boldly pioneered on this unseasonably warm day in Los Angeles.

In the beginning, the experience was an anticlimax. After a half-hour, he reported a slow dance of golden lights. Gradually, surfaces began to swell and expand; blue spheres floated in his mind's eye. Queasiness grounded him in his body, dragging him down from the light he sought. Movement became less attractive—any movement—and he leaned against a tabletop, supported on his elbows. He felt he was going to be sick.

It might not have been the wisest thing, this experiment. Huxley was almost fifty-nine, his hair steadily silvering and his joints aching in a manner he would rather ignore. His liver was strong; his doctor had agreed to the experiment, but what if the dose was wrong? What if, as Osmond also worried, he went permanently crazy?

Only a year before, in *The Devils of Loudun*, Huxley had denounced drug-induced transcendence:

> There are probably moments in the course of intoxication by almost any drug, when awareness of a not-self superior to the disintegrating ego becomes briefly possible. But these occasional flashes of revelation are bought at an enormous price. For the drugtaker, the

moment of spiritual awareness (if it comes at all) gives place very soon to a subhuman stupor, frenzy or hallucination, followed by dismal hangovers . . .

This is a descending road and most of those who take it will come to a state of degradation, where periods of subhuman ecstasy alternate with periods of conscious selfhood so wretched that any escape, even if it be into the slow suicide of drug addiction, will seem preferable to being a person.[73]

Harsh words. Harry Anslinger, the man most responsible for outlawing psychoactive drugs in America—who as a U.S. government administrator in the 1950s classified such substances alongside heroin—could not have presented the *Reefer Madness* stereotypes more blatantly. This was the propaganda which, in the fifties, led Americans to believe students became heroin addicts once they smoked a marijuana cigarette.

After an hour and a half, Huxley still sat in his study, now staring intently at a glass vase with a hot pink rose, a magenta-and-cream-colored carnation, and a pale purple iris. Suddenly he was not looking at flowers but seeing what Adam had seen on the morning of creation—naked, unmediated existence. Wavy patterns swirled the air.

"Is it agreeable?" his guides asked. Huxley could only laugh: "It just *is.*" The holes in his cane chair seemed enormous, large enough to fall through.[74] "Shortly after this, a sense of special significance began to invest everything in the room. . . . A plain wooden chair was invested with a 'chairliness' which no chair ever had for me before." Plato had made a mistake in separating his idealized Universal Essence from the process of its realization, Huxley mused: "He could never, poor fellow, have seen a bunch of flowers shining with their own inner light." The obscure exchanges of Zen disciples acquired a new meaning: "The blessed not-I, released for a moment from my own throttling embrace" shimmered before him.

His daily concerns slipped away: worries of Matthew's future now that his U.N. job hadn't materialized, fears of a relapse of his iritis, sorrow over the recent death of his oldest friend in Britain, Lewis Gielgud.

The books in his study began to glow in gemlike color: rubies and emerald bindings, books of yellow topaz and aquamarine.

(Did Heard's influence extend even to Huxley's hallucinations?

Huxley's impressions parallel a passage on enlightenment from "Dromenon": "I saw the massive stone altar first begin to glow like a ruby; then it was a heart of liquid gold [which] intensified into ice-cold emerald and passed into the dark sapphire of an arctic sky.")[75]

A lassitude spread over Aldous, limb by limb, as he grew indifferent to spatial relationships, to measured time, even to the rational questioning of his guides. Their questions seemed to trail off into the air—how long *was* a foot?

To the external view of friend Betty Wendell that day, "Aldous was really out of it. He kept saying how bright everything was, how a child's eyes totally differed from an adult's."[76]

Outside the house, the early summer sun heated the streets of Hollywood, prompting gardeners on the stars' estates to peel off their shirts or linger in the shade of a cypress: another Monday morning.

Agents continued to huddle with their phones, producers continued to lunch with actresses, cleaning ladies dialed up the submerged water jets in the lawns. Hissing droplets from sprinklers broke waist-high rainbows over some of the wealthiest real estate in the United States. On a day like this, Eisenhower, the new president, yearned to be out on the golf links. The war in Korea seemed endlessly remote, a small speck on the edge of California's consciousness—unless one read the papers.

There the reader saw pictures of bombs setting fire to civilian targets: "We will smash anything we want up here," said the head of the U.S. Fifth Air Force in that day's *Los Angeles Times*. Americans were fuming over the released British POWs who had called the Korean War "useless and stupid." This didn't convince Secretary of State John Foster Dulles, who liked the Korean War so well he was already preparing another Asian venture, in Indochina, to which he was speeding "critically needed military items." (The French had asked only for cargo planes, but Dulles, denouncing Communist "aggression," insisted on sending weapons.)

Under normal circumstances, Huxley would have registered his disgust at such news with the disappointed sigh he reserved for the collective folly of his species. In Hollywood, however, the war meant loyalty oaths—and not just to the studio bosses who had signed Huxley's paychecks. The effects of black- and graylists surrounded him, even in his beshrouded condition.

The day before, on the Great Red Way (as blacklisters liked to call Broadway) big band leader Artie Shaw had explained how he had been duped into disloyalty. Other musicians refused the bait.[77] Three months earlier, at Decca's recording studios, one of the most popular singing groups in the country, the Weavers, had been forced to disband. *Variety* awarded the singers of "Goodnight Irene" the dubious honor of the first group blacklisted out of a New York night club.[78]

Next month the Rosenbergs were to be executed following unsuccessful appeals in their sensational atom-spy case. Their supporters in Los Angeles received an anonymous note: "These 2 *rats* (and you) should have been hung long ago."[79] Not even Lucille Ball's "I Love Lucy," with its multiyear, $8 million contract, was exempt from scrutiny. "There's nothing red about that girl except her hair," Desi Arnaz quipped defensively. "And even that isn't legitimate."[80]

Out in New Mexico, where Frieda Lawrence was preparing the ranch for summer, blacklisters haunted the production of *Salt of the Earth*, directed by one of the Hollywood Ten, Herbert Biberman. Biberman's cutter was secretly turning in daily reports to the FBI on the progress of the film which magnate Howard Hughes had vowed to prevent.[81]

In that day's paper Huxley, whose astrological sign was Leo, was advised to "control that urge to go off on a tangent," advice he was destined not to heed.

On North King's Road, among his glowing books, Aldous Huxley found the drug wearing off—he thought—and he was ready to explore the shiny world of cars and buildings. He sought the air-conditioned comfort of the World's Biggest Drug Store, showcase of the Owl Drug (Rexall) chain, a fancy spread of plastic and chrome on the corner of Beverly and La Cienega Boulevards, seven blocks from his home.

In those days, Hollywood was locked in a drugstore war. The

California drugstore of the fifties was more a palace of consumerism and a social watering spot than a supplier of shaving cream. Schwab's had the celebrity trade to themselves until the swank Beverly Wilshire Hotel began selling $500 hairbrushes and staying open twenty-four hours a day. Papers covered the rivalry. Rock Hudson picked up his mail at the Wilshire; Schwab's threw an autograph party for Italian actresses at their soda fountain. Some attributed the prominence of drugstores to a lack of interest in night clubs; others, to a need for All-American homeyness which the film colony, in its isolation, missed.[82]

In any case, drugstores were fashionable, though the one Huxley frequented did not boast numbered booths or sundaes at the price of a week's rent. Huxley delighted in the wall-to-wall kitsch of the huge, L-shaped World's Biggest Drug Store. He had become a regular at the lunch counter, munching toasted cheese sandwiches on Tuesdays, the cook's night off.

The World's Biggest Drug Store was a temple of American materialism, or rather, to a Vendantist, a palace of māyā (the cosmic illusion of material reality). Objects on sale on that fateful May afternoon in 1953 are today collector's items: red, boxy Coca-Cola coolers; corrugated Dixie cups complete with dispensers; lipstick in the lascivious red Marilyn Monroe popularized.

According to *Owl Hoots*, the chain's newsletter, the previous month at the store had been turbulent—a nearby Max Factor building went up in a "spectacular blaze," as Owl druggists hopped across the roof, sloshing water until the fire department arrived.[83]

Why the Huxleys visited the World's Biggest Drug Store that day is at first a puzzle. Perhaps the name suggested inspiration appropriate to the mescaline trip; perhaps Aldous, his mind careening, had felt the first pangs of hunger. In any case, improbably dressed in blue jeans, he made his way unsteadily across a floor crowded with toys, greeting cards, and comics—Humphry and Maria beside him. As Huxley threaded through the gravy boats and Bakelite dishes, he stumbled upon a row of art books.

"Aldous Huxley had always been interested in light," his nephew Francis recalled. "When he was painting in the south of France, his work was full of light. He was most interested in those painters themselves interested in light, Piero della Francesca, Tintoretto, Piranesi.

Aldous tried to translate what he saw in [artistic] terms, but once he took mescaline, the innate quality of light in his own mind just beamed out."[84]

Huxley had already written extensively on the Italian Renaissance masters. That he should find them here, amid Southern California's laminated fantasies, seemed providential and a tribute to the diversity of twentieth-century Americana.

First he browsed through Van Gogh, then Botticelli. Huxley found his attention shifting unexpectedly, to the painters' portrayal of clothing. His eye slid down to his own clothes; even folds of denim seemed rich and mysteriously sumptuous. Botticelli's brushstrokes on a purple dress finally opened that long-awaited door in the wall, and Huxley unhesitatingly charged through: "Poring over Judith's skirts, there in the World's Biggest Drug Store, I knew that Botticelli—and not Botticelli alone, but many others too—had looked at draperies with the same transfigured and transfiguring eyes as had been mine that morning" (Doors, 34).

"In Vino Veritas," Huxley's cousin Renée Haynes wrote in her study of ESP. "And perhaps in peyotyl." Speaking of the training a visionary must undergo, she quotes a 1775 account: "He must absorb . . . the splendours of the aurora borealis, that ardently sought occasion for 'drinking in the light' until he at last sees his own genius which says 'Behold me, what dost thou desire?' "[85]

For the first time in years, Huxley saw with the stereoscopic vision he had lost as a teenager. For a fleeting moment, the one-eyed writer looked around with new eyes, no longer inertly two-dimensional. These were better, powerful new organs, ranging proudly over the banal landscape, submerging content to perspectives of light and shadow.

The visual epiphany overcame him with raw force. "This is how one ought to see," he repeated numbly: "These are the sorts of things one ought to look at."

In Religions, Values, and Peak-experiences, psychologist Abraham Maslow described the physiological effect of such a moment: "The percept is exclusively and fully attended to. . . . There is the the truest and most total kind of visual perceiving or listening or feeling."

"It is not my ideas that grow clearer," Maine de Biran wrote of his moments of mystical illumination, "it is my inner light that becomes brighter and more striking, so that the heart and mind are suddenly illumined by it."[86]

Was this enlightenment (literally) or a parlor game which Huxley's mind, set loose, was playing with him? Even as gratitude rose within him for vision in perspective, "more clearly than I had ever seen it before," the world grayed. Asked to turn from Cézanne to his internal landscape, he found himself barren, surrounded by trivial images of plastic or enameled tin.

Just as he was reaching beyond it, human pretension weighted him back. A salutary lesson. Outside he saw a world of shiny depth, colors bright as a fresh palette. Inside, he saw the gearbox of his own mind, not the Dharma-body of Buddha. The doors of perception had been "cleansed," in Blake's phrase, but Huxley could only see out.

"This is how one ought to see," he kept saying, realizing, in some compartment of his mind, that there had to be still more: looking endlessly was not enough. What of the people who surrounded him? He suddenly noticed that he had withdrawn from Maria and Humphry, as he delved into the art books. "How could one reconcile this timeless bliss of seeing as one ought to see with the temporal duties of doing what one ought to do and feeling as one ought to feel?" (Doors, 35).

He could not resolve this quandary, so central to integrating religious philosophy and daily life. His in-depth vision took him away from humanity into the Not-self; people seemed enormously irrelevant. He looked out at his wife and his medical guide and realized he had begun to avoid their eyes. "Both belonged to the world from which, for the moment, mescalin had delivered me—the world of selves, time, of moral judgements . . . of self-assertion, of cocksureness, of overvalued words and idolatrously worshipped notions."

This was a dangerous tack. He had cut himself off from those around him, as he had at his mother's death. Maria, still weak from her mastectomy, had momentarily become a specter. This was Kunstschadenfreude, plunging into art so deeply that sorrow overtakes joy.

His mind slid out of control, into paranoia: "Suddenly I had an inkling of what it must feel like to be mad. . . . I found myself all at once on the brink of panic." Schizophrenia "never permits [a man] to look at the world with merely human eyes, but scares him into interpreting its unremitting strangeness, its burning intensity of significance. . . . once embarked on the downward, the infernal road, one would never be able to stop." That, now, was only too obvious.

"If you started in the wrong way," I said in answer to [Osmond's] questions, "everything that happened would be a proof of the conspiracy against you. It would all be self-validating. You couldn't draw a breath without knowing it was part of the plot."

"So you think you know where madness lies?"

My answer was a convinced and heartfelt, "Yes."

"And you couldn't control it?"

"No, I couldn't control it."[87]

Huxley ended up in a drugstore on a busy corner of La Cienega Boulevard for his moment of enlightenment. This was neither an accident nor poor timing. The setting of Huxley's samadhi was prototypically American with its geegaws: yards of sugar lay in neat heaps—colored, packaged, wrapped—alongside doggy treats and oak toilet seats. Surrounding him was the butterfly rhythm of shoppers moving from one object to the next. The drugstore was the epitome of purposefulness in American culture, a place where people meet and become more themselves by what they purchase. I shop; therefore, I am.

Huxley went to the World's Biggest Drug Store precisely to be purposeless in a world of function: to find not majestic views but the hard-edged dross of life. A drugstore was something to laugh about only on a trip, as others went through their paces in grim earnest, diaper after diaper. In a place unlovely of itself, internal loveliness flowered.

He needed that redirection which comes of indirection. He used mescaline as a gilt-edged invitation to meet the American moment, to enjoy being a bit silly, as he staggered by in his blue jeans. For so many years he had successfully carried off the burden of being a Huxley—a burden which drove one brother periodically mad and another to suicide and eventually discouraged his grandson from attending college. This legacy was a restless pulsing in his blood. It had propelled him around the world (when he wrote *Jesting Pilate* in 1926). Huxley's forays from England show a wanderlust so vast not even the globe encompassed it.

"Our goal is to discover that we have always been where we ought to be," Huxley wrote in *Doors of Perception*. This succinct summary—part Taoism and part Buddhism—captured what Huxley had really gone to a drugstore for. One must conclude that he felt—and had now proved—that epochal moments could occur anywhere, any time.

A parable of James Thurber's is relevant here, the story of the moth who fell in love with a star. Every evening the moth would fly toward it while his brother and sister moths went about their mothly business of battering against windows and streetlights and sooner or later incinerated themselves against the flame. Night after night until he grew old, the moth flew up into the sky and at dawn flew back down again. Eventually he was convinced that he'd reached the star, and in a ripe old age, he bragged to his great-great-great-nephews and nieces about what it was like to visit it. Thurber's moral: "He who flies afar from our sphere of sorrow is here today and here tomorrow."

Huxley was a fellow to this moth. Whether or not he ever had his moment without a "chemical vacation," by the time he grew old he too was convinced he had visited with a star. Thurber's point is contained in the "hereness" of the moral. In those down-to-earth surroundings, for an all-too-brief moment, Huxley found "the extraordinary in the ordinary," in Stanley Cavell's phrase, a Thoreau-like revelation that beauty is in the eyes of the beholder. Even when those eyes were defective, the beauty they saw was not.

Huxley's presentiment of madness gradually gave way to an unprecedented poignancy. It flowed over him in sweaty waves as he tired: "Until this morning I had known contemplation only in its humbler, its more ordinary forms—as discursive thinking, as a rapt absorption in poetry, or painting, or music. . . . But now I knew contemplation at its height" *(Doors,* 41). At its height, but not yet at its fullness. Mescaline had given him this long-sought gift, but it was a contemplation incompatible with action—and even the will to act. He had seen clearly—just as he had envisaged, before World War II, the destructiveness of science applied to creative weaponry—but foresight was not enough. Mescaline could not solve the problem of activity and egoless thought: it only posed it, apocalyptically.

For Huxley, the drugged state was the true—or at least a dimension of the truth. These were not hallucinations he experienced but deliberate visions, which opened at least one clear pane in an otherwise muddy door.

As the descendant of the most eminent Victorian scientists and essayists tottered home, he was already planning *The Doors of Perception*, his narrative of the event:

> *That humanity at large will ever be able to dispense with Artificial Paradise seems very unlikely. Most men and women live lives at worst so painful, at the best so monotonous, poor, and limited that the urge to escape the longing to transcend themselves, if only for a few moments, is and has always been one of the principal appetites of the soul. . . . For unrestrained use, the West has permitted only alcohol and tobacco. All the other chemical Doors in the Wall are labeled Dope, and their unauthorized takers are Fiends.* (Doors, 62)

His prose is visual and laboratorylike, with a graphic sense of place—qualities often lacking in his writing. The book's precise observations show the scientist Huxley might have become:

> *If I had been able to go through with the medical and biological education, which was interrupted in my youth by a period of near-blindness, this is what I should have liked to become—a fully qualified striker at the joints between the separate armour-plates of organized knowledge. But fate decreed otherwise, and I have had to be content to be an essayist, disguised from time to time as a novelist.*[88]

Doors of Perceptions and *The Art of Seeing* together comprise his most extended autobiography. Only visual revelations were important enough to overcome his studied disinclination to write about his own life.

"Perhaps the sixty-odd pages of *The Doors of Perception* reveal more of the seeking, questing Aldous than all his books put together," Juliette Huxley reflected; they capture "the unfathomable Mystery—which haunted him all his life."[89]

After the threesome returned home they listened to Mozart and madrigals, which Huxley found surprisingly flat, after all his visual inspiration; the dissonant Berg earned only giddy laughter.

After the music and a vivid tour of the flower garden, they sat down to eat. "Somebody who was not yet identical with myself fell to with ravenous appetite. From a considerable distance and without much interest, I looked on," Huxley wrote. Then they drove up and out of the city. As Huxley watched, Betty Wendell threaded through what seemed like a Red Sea of traffic. He found himself fatigued and inexplicably convulsed with laughter.

The pictures from that day show him staring down with amazement and hunger written on his features. With a sweet smile, he advanced, arms outstretched, toward the vista which had transfixed Nathanael West: "He could see the reflection of [the city's] lights, which hung in the sky above it like a batik parasol . . . a deep black with hardly a trace of blue."[90]

The view disappointed Huxley. He saw only roads, cars, housing developments, and swimming pools, gleaming in the first reflection of the moon. So far as he was concerned, transfiguration was inversely related to distance: "The nearer, the more divinely other," a not unexpected insight from someone who focused on the world at two inches.

"Poems are made by poets, and chemical reactions by chemicals"—so went a popular saying in the late 1960s, when Huxley's *Doors of Perception* was discovered by a new generation and touted at drug parties. The book had become such a cult object that it inspired the name of Jim Morrison's rock group, The Doors.

Should Huxley be blamed for the aftereffects of bad trips in the sixties? Huxley sought a new drug for transcendence and mass social education, but the millions who followed his path sought only a passing good time. Huxley, like Galileo, would find himself excoriated for seeing too much of the heavens.

Huxley would have been saddened at teenagers on LSD or mescaline watching *Summer Lovers* at the drive-in. In the coming years, paying for his candor, he consistently refused to comment on psychedelic drugs outside of scientific meetings. (And, unlike Michaux and the French Surrealists, Huxley did not try to compose under mescaline's influence.) When he did speak about the vision which had allowed him to see past painting, canvas, subject to a moral luminescence, he spoke discreetly.

Looking out across the vast stretch of Los Angeles, did he wonder if he would need more mescaline to see as he had that morning? Did he yearn for another taste the next morning, tired but delighted that he had no hangover?

In the next years, when he again took mind-activating substances, he did not become addicted. Could anyone be addicted to a self-study this painful and intense? Schizophrenics might share this same transcendental lucidity, but few wish to see permanently with the mind-at-large unlidded.

At the same time as Huxley rejoiced at his visual inspiration, he realized that seeing was only half the battle: the trick was to find words and images to portray what is seen. This dilemma hindered mystics who experienced that celestial light but could not explain it to their eager followers. This frustrated drug takers across the ages who, like the mystics, were told that their experience had to make sense in orderly fashion, under public scrutiny in the hot light of day. That exhumation of the inexpressible, that pressure to editorialize the unspeakable—this is what keeps most of us from accepting our own, momentary insights which fly beyond the rational and the real.

"Our normal waking consciousness, rational consciousness we call it, is but one special type of consciousness," William James wrote fifty years earlier, after a similar mystical experience with nitrous oxide (laughing gas).

"Whilst all about it, parted by the filmiest of screens, there lies potential forms of consciousness entirely different. We may go through life without suspecting their existence; but apply the requisite stimulus, and at a touch they are there in all their completeness."[91] Huxley might not have wished his new vision to come via chemistry, but he accepted it however it arrived.

Mind-altering drugs offer astringents to wipe clear humanity's mental slates. Society reforms its social structures, provides mobility, and improves access to education—yet the need remains for frequent chemical vacations from intolerable selfhood, as Huxley put it.

If humanity will always take alcohol, caffeine, nicotine, and other drugs, it may be because it is not wholly at peace. Alienation from work, from ecology, from biology and a lack of physical intimacy or spiritual unity—these are splintering products of today's age and political systems—of all ages and politics.

What is needed, Huxley concluded after his memorable experience with mescaline, is a new drug to "relieve and console our suffering species without doing more harm in the long run than it does good in the short." He imagined this drug as potent and synthesizable—so that land used for its production does not replace land used for food. "It must be less toxic than opium or cocaine, less likely to produce undesirable social consequences than alcohol or the barbiturates, less inimical to heart and lungs than the tar and nicotine of cigarettes" (Doors, 65). He might also have added that it should be easily and efficiently produced (grown) anywhere, like a weed. Huxley was convinced that he had found this in mescaline or LSD; to the end of his days he took these several times a year.

Unconscious of the controversy he would stir, Aldous began proselytizing for hallucinogens, urging them on Julian, on Matthew, on Maria—on anyone who'd listen, as Freud had done in his early enthusiasm for cocaine. Maria had a different concern. After a series of tests she had found out she had little time left, a year at most.

RIGHT: Anita Loos and Aldous Huxley, hiking in Southern California. *(Matthew Huxley Collection)*

ABOVE: Grace and Edwin Hubble, 1940s. *(The Huntington Library)*

BELOW: Aldous Huxley, British actress Constance Collier, and Maria Huxley, on a picnic, 1940s. *(Matthew Huxley Collection)*

RIGHT: Paulette Goddard
in *Modern Times*.
(UCLA Theatre Arts Library)

LEFT: Greta Garbo, publicity
still, mid-1930s. *(Academy of
Motion Picture Arts and Sciences*

ᴏᴠᴇ: Greer Garson and Laurence Olivier in *Pride and Prejudice,* 1940. ʙᴇʟᴏᴡ: Greer Garson d Walter Pidgeon in *Madame Curie,* 1943. *(Academy of Motion Picture Arts and Sciences)*

RIGHT: Mr. and Mrs. Charles Chaplin
(Paulette Goddard) in Hollywood.
(Academy of Motion Picture Arts and Sciences)

BELOW: Maria Huxley and
friend, Los Angeles, April 1940.
(Matthew Huxley Collection)

OPPOSITE: Orson Welles a
Joan Fontaine in *Jane Eyre*, 194
(Twentieth Century-Fox Film Corporatic

ABOVE: Aldous Huxley during his first mescaline experience,
above Hollywood, May 1953. BELOW: Huxley home in
Hollywood the day after the fire, May 1961.
(Laura Huxley Collection)

LEFT: Huxley Street,
near Griffith Park, Los Angeles.
(David King Dunaway)

BELOW: Aldous Huxley, circa 1962.
(Matthew Huxley Collection)

TEN

HEAVEN
AND HELL

"Heaven entails hell, and 'going to heaven'
is no more liberation than is the descent
into horror. Heaven is merely a vantage
point. . . . For those who, for whatever
reason, are appalled, heaven turns into hell,
bliss into horror, the Clear Light into the
hateful glare of the land of lit-upness."

(1956)

*Following Huxley, one might imagine a person who had gone all the
way on mescaline, who had had the doors of his perception completely
cleansed. Such a person would look at his book covers instead of reading the books; he would be indifferent to Botticelli so long as he could
see his trousers.*

So ran a review of *The Doors of Perception* in the British journal
The Twentieth Century. The bitterness triggered by Huxley's
account of mescaline exceeded any previous criticisms he had received,
even those of his pacifism. Huxley is "bogged up neck-deep in his
mystical dreams and fantasies," opined *The Indian Review*.[1] "The Witch
Doctor of California produces another prescription for his suffering
tribe," wrote Alistair Sutherland.[2]

Though Humphry Osmond answered such slurs, calling Sutherland "a Peeping Tom at a knothole in the Doors of Perception," for
many of Huxley's British readers the author had grown dotty.[3] An

article entitled "The Menace of Mescaline" proclaimed him a virtual criminal.

The Doors of Perception brought Huxley reactions ranging from mild reproof to hostility. Betty Wendell asked why, in his retelling, his blue jeans had changed to gray flannels: "Maria thought I should be better dressed for my readers," he replied.[4] Other friends were less understanding. "I was appalled by his drug taking," Peggy Kiskadden said. "It's the wrong thing to do, jacking yourself up like that. It isn't real what you see. The stuff is nonsense."[5]

Jack Zeitlin went further still: "Not only was experimenting with drugs rash, it was inconsistent with the very idea of mysticism that he admired . . . I told him I felt this was the wrong path. It sanctioned all the people who wanted to indulge."[6]

Comfortably settled in Switzerland, Thomas Mann called *Doors:*

> . . . *the most audacious form of Huxley's escapism, which I could never appreciate in this author. Mysticism as a means to that escapism was, nonetheless, reasonably honorable. But that he now has arrived at drugs I find rather scandalsome. . . . encouraged by the persuasive recommendation of the famous author many young Englishmen and especially Americans will try the experiment . . . an irresponsible book, which can only contribute to the stupefaction of the world and to its instability to meet the deadly serious questions of the time with intelligence.*[7]

Other reviews were either more charitable, or bored, such as the one in *The New Yorker:* "Most of it is the old, weary dance of abstractions named Not-Self, Eternity, Mind at Large, Suchness, and the Absolute."[8]

Was it courage or naiveté that prompted Huxley to include the world in his experimentation? "Some excellent persons seem to think it is a propaganda for dope-taking," Huxley ruefully wrote a reader. He assured his British publisher that his swallow-and-tell book did mention that trips can go awry. Of a review in *Pravda*, denouncing him as a drug-crazed pleasure seeker, he remarked, "It is like a parody of a Dialectical Materialist denunciation written, not by Orwell, but by someone a good deal less clever, less capable of giving the devil his due. Heavily funny—but how extremely depressing."[9] Despite such attacks, he had already begun a new—and far less personal— essay on the visionary instinct, *Heaven and Hell.*

Huxley's mescaline-induced vision continued the unfolding begun through therapy the previous year. The man who comes back through the Door in the Wall will never be quite the same as the man who went out, Huxley confessed in *Doors*. "He will be less cocksure, happier but less self-satisfied, humbler in acknowledging his ignorance." [10] These hopeful words rang true to Maria, who wrote Matthew:

> . . . *You do know for how many years we've loved Aldous and known his goodness and his sweetness and his honesty—but you also know how tiring, in spite of all this, he was to live with—sad to live with. Well, now, he is transformed, transfigured.*
>
> *What I mean to say is that this change has been working in an intangible way and for a very very long time but that the result has suddenly exploded—and I say exploded. Aldous no longer looks the same, his attitude is not the same, his moral and intellectual attitude, his attitude to animals, people, the clouds, to the telephone ringing (and that's going very far). . . .*
>
> *His search for this road, we know, did not only come out of his philosophical interests; he helped himself by psychological experiments, by spiritual exercises. . . .*
>
> *My illness, which might have muddled and blackened and exhausted everything, has been both the starting point and the arrival of this development.* [11]

Maria was undergoing her own transformation. A second operation, in 1953, hadn't improved her condition. She drew an inner readiness from her own meditations (and from mescaline, which she first took a few months after Aldous). She had visions, she told a friend interested in psychic matters: "I have two lights. One very white and intense and so diffuse . . . then there is the other, the golden, which is always like a sheath, a direct ray which comes directly to and through one." [12]

Peggy Kiskadden was one of the first to know Maria was dying. Doctor Hawkins at Good Samaritan Hospital had called Bill Kiskadden directly: "The cancer is on the *inside* of the breast. The lymph glands are affected. I don't know if she will tell her husband. Someone near her has to know."

"I don't know what Aldous knew," Peggy said. "I don't know what he was *willing* to know. . . . It's stupid, but I didn't want to increase his burden. And there was always room for a miracle. In 1954, when she began to complain of a back-ache, I was extremely worried. I knew that meant trouble."[13] Convinced of new sight, Aldous Huxley was most blind.

"In those days Maria had taken to wearing a loose blouse because of her mastectomy," the cook Marie Le Put said. "When her wrist began to swell, the blouses were long-sleeved."

"I saw her suffer so much. . . . She knew she had cancer but she would never talk about it. She never complained. Soon, it spread all over, and she would go to the hospital for treatment. . . . There were no chemicals in those days. My husband took her to the hospital to have those burning [radiation] treatments. She was in pain. I remember once they had a big luncheon, and Maria came into the kitchen and said, 'Marie, I can't stand it any more. Only you understand what I'm going through.' "[14]

Maria wrote Ellen, her daughter-in-law, weekly, her handwriting wider and loopier as the months passed: how much she treasured seeing her grandson, Trev, how glad she was at the birth of her granddaughter, Tessa, in October. One birth, one death: Edwin Hubble died that fall, of cerebral thrombosis.

In May 1953, while Huxley had his epiphany on mescaline, Hubble had visited England to give a lecture honoring Darwin; his friends in the Royal Astronomy Society politely overlooked how the timing of the fisherman's lectures coincided with the rise of the mayfly. Hubble returned with plans for new observations at Mount Palomar.

Maria and Aldous had last seen Edwin at Aldous's birthday party in July. It had been a warm, hazy evening, with a silvery western light at dusk. The Hubbles, Eva Hermann, Vera Stravinsky and Bob Craft, Rose (Maria's sister), Gerald and Chris Wood chuckled as Aldous recounted a recent journey through the Northwest and his reaction to the Mormon Cathedral in Salt Lake City: "Inconce-e-eivable. Utterly lacking in originality yet like nothing else."

On September 28, 1953, Grace was driving Edwin home, as she

had since his last major heart attack in 1951. Entering their driveway, she noticed Edwin suddenly breathing "in an odd little way." "Don't stop," he gasped. "Drive on in." In their courtyard, he fainted in the car. That was the end for the man who had discovered how galaxies turn. "Love remains," Aldous wrote Grace solicitously. "For that is what moves the sun and the other stars, which is something Edwin knew even better than Dante."[15]

A month later, the Huxleys took a step Edwin would have endorsed: after fourteen years as resident aliens, they applied for American citizenship. Matthew urged his parents to go through the formality, perhaps hoping it would help him with the U.N. job, which he still awaited.

On November 3, 1953, they drove to the Rowan Building in downtown L.A. to be sworn in, accompanied by Betty Wendell and another friend, Rosalind Rajagopal. Maria dressed for the occasion in a dark blue suit and hat, with white gloves. Betty gave them monogrammed red, white, and blue handkerchiefs. Maria had boned up for her American history exam; Aldous had ignored the notes prepared for them.

"Aldous, are you *sure* you know American history?"

"Reasonably sure," he smiled.

"They'll see how intelligent *you* are and they won't question you the way they'll question *me*," Maria groused. They and their witnesses were interrogated. All went well.

Then, just as in Arlo Guthrie's song "Alice's Restaurant," they encountered one last form. On it was the question: "Are you prepared to serve in the U.S. armed forces?" When Aldous Huxley answered "No," the near blind author of a half-dozen works on pacifism was summoned into a courtroom:

THE JUDGE: *Mr. Huxley, would you not bear arms in the United States Army?*

ALDOUS: *No.*

THE JUDGE: *Would you not drive an army truck transporting armaments?*

ALDOUS: *No.*

J: *If the enemy were approaching your home, in defense of your wife and in self-defense, would you not pick up a gun and stand by your front door, ready to fire?*

A: *I would not have a gun in the house.*

J: *Would you be willing to make bandages for the wounded?*

A: *Yes.*

J: *Would you serve in the Red Cross, as an ambulance driver?*

A: *If the question applies to my willingness, yes.*

J: *It does, Mr. Huxley.*[16]

In the Southwest, Edward Abbey was writing of a draft resister in a similar fix in *The Brave Cowboy:* "The draft board wanted me to register as a conscientious objector. 'Conscientious objector to what?' I asked them. . . . 'I object to slavery,' I said; 'compulsory military service is a form of slavery.' 'But there is no provision in the law for such an objection,' they said."[17]

In the fifties, committed pacifists were a fringe tarred with the anti-Communist brush. To many Americans, "peace" meant capitulation to the Commies. The majority of pacifists in the United States were still religious; the waves of "selective" pacifists opposed to the Vietnam War had not been heard from. The War Resisters League and the Fellowship for Reconciliation—-both active in L.A.—kept American pacifism alive as a philosophy exterior to religion.

Back in the courtroom, the administrative judge scrutinized the reedy writer, who looked as if a strong wind would topple him: here was an unlikely candidate for military service if he ever saw one. The judge sighed and asked Huxley whether his objection to bearing arms was based on religious views. "On philosophical convictions, your honor, though at 59 I don't expect to be drafted," the writer answered, and his wife followed suit.

"Religio-philosophical?" the judge coaxed. "No, on philosophical grounds only." His interrogator had clearly not read *Ends and Means.*

Unfortunately, the judge explained, the 1952 McCarran-Walter Act—a statute which also authorized detention camps for leftists—denied citizenship to anyone refusing to bear arms "for any reason other than *religious beliefs.*"

"The judge then gazed at Aldous with the deep respect to which he was accustomed," Betty recorded, "asking if he wasn't a religious man?" Huxley answered stoutly that he was religious; his opposition to war, however, was entirely philosophical.[18] "Aldous," Maria finally whispered, "do say it's for religious reasons, let's get it over with."

Instead, Huxley waded into the fray, succinctly explaining that *his* pacifism was based on a revulsion to violence, not on any pretailored credo. A special hearing would then be necessary for naturalization, the judge informed them. When they left the building, Aldous's face was white. "They don't want us here!" he said in an uncharacteristic outburst.[19] On the drive back to Betty's, where champagne and fresh crab awaited, Aldous declared he wanted to go home to bed.

Their situation was unenviable. At the special hearing, their lawyers advised, they would no doubt be rejected—which would make obtaining a reentry permit difficult. Yet Huxley had already accepted speaking engagements in Europe for the next summer.

Their attorney dropped off a deposition: Huxley declared that his opposition to killing other human beings "for any reason whatsoever" had begun in 1933 or 1934. His unpublished statement is worth quoting, as proof that his pacifism hadn't faded as he involved himself in mysticism and parapsychology. In fact, Huxley credited mysticism as the *basis* for his pacifism:

> *I was brought up as an agnostic and continued to reject the religious approach to life until about twenty years ago, when I started to feel an ever deepening concern with religious mysticism. My beliefs and practices were modified by two main influences—Christian mysticism, culminating in that non-dogmatic religion of the Inner Light, which is the essence of Quakerism; and oriental mysticism, culminating in Vedanta and the higher forms of Buddhism. . . .*
>
> *The killing of a fellow being is the breach of a cosmic law, and the question whether it is justifiable in certain circumstances to take life becomes more than a political problem, involving loyalties to a Being superior even to the most highly honored of human institutions.*[20]

The United States Immigration and Naturalization Service was unimpressed, according to documents recently released under the Freedom of Information Act. The administrative judge "contemplated DENIAL because of their unwillingness to bear arms and their desire to take only that part of the oath . . . with added qualifications of their own. . . . It is also noted that they do not claims [sic] any particular religious training or belief but have only their personal belief for wanting to avoid bearing arms."[21]

By February 1954, they had heard nothing. "If papers come through, well and good; if they don't, well and good also," he wrote Matthew. "Still, I wish we hadn't let ourselves in for this bother and confusion."[22]

A few days later they withdrew their application, renewed their British passport, and quietly resumed resident alien status. They had no difficulty obtaining reentry permits.

They sailed for Europe on the *Queen Elizabeth* on April 7. Huxley worked on a novella in his stateroom: *The Genius and the Goddess*, based on Frieda Lawrence's ability, beyond the powers of conventional medicine, to revive her husband.[23] Begun casually, the work would eventually be mounted as a play and cause him untoward grief.

The returning expatriates had a familiar itinerary: first Paris, where they met the press and stayed with Jeanne and Georges Neveux. Then the south of France, where Huxley lectured at Eileen Garrett's parapsychology conference; then to Egypt, where they stayed with Roger Godel, chief doctor for the Suez Canal Company, with whom they improbably hoped Matthew would intern. From there, they visited Lebanon, Greece, Cyprus ("incessantly on the go," Maria wrote), and then Rome. There they found Laura Archera. She and Maria discussed what would happen to Aldous; rumors spread later that Maria had told the young violinist to take care of Aldous.

Of course it was Maria who needed care and Aldous who was careless, handicapped by the same denial which made him cling to pacifism in the face of Nazism. This denial was at best mutual. No one mentioned Maria's sickness that tragic summer of 1954, until a crisis caused her to leave a country house they had rented—where Aldous had happily typed away in the garden—for Paris. "The panicked departure was wrenching," wrote Georges Neveux.

In Paris, Maria visited a noted authority on cancer; Jeanne called him for the diagnosis, and for the first time learned her sister had cancer. Maria came for dinner the next night, alone, and explained her situation. She could resume her treatments, the doctor had told her, but added, "I am afraid it's final."

"You must tell me," Maria answered the doctor. "You must *not* tell my husband." In Paris she visited relatives and friends while awaiting passage home. Aldous went on alone to England. "I have no links to England," Maria wrote, "in fact not many links at all."[24]

At a party Julian gave in his house in Belsize Park, Aldous and Bertrand Russell discussed psychic research. "Its findings," Russell said, "particularly in precognition, were incredible." The brothers Huxley agreed, though doubtless Julian did so reluctantly.[25]

Despite Maria's illness, Aldous struck old friends as seeing better than before and in radiant health. Sybille Bedford was living in Rome when they passed through:

> I had not seen them since Sanary in 1950. Aldous had changed. . . . Never before had I seen Aldous look less vulnerable. He was as gentle as he had been in all his phases, yet behind it one felt authority. There was a sleekness, a smoothed-outness; he was glowing with it, as it were, and this had an extraordinary peace-inducing effect as though one were sitting at the feet of a large and benign cat.[26]

"We were sitting in the garden," Juliette reminisced, "and I said, 'How is Maria?'"

"Well, she's got little nodules coming out."

"Aldous, that's frightening."

"No, no. It's quite all right. It's normal," he told Juliette.

"How serious is it?" she asked nervously.

"Oh, no, it's not serious at all," he replied.[27]

"Aldous did not want to know that Maria was dying," Juliette decided in retrospect. "And Maria did not want him to know. Of course he knew. But he pushed it away. Didn't want to talk about it. He was protecting himself from a truth which was unbearable."[28] Friends worried. In his efforts to convince himself that Maria was actually well, he might exhaust her declining strength.

Throughout the long autumn which followed their return to California, Maria weakened. The radiation treatments continued. Other than continue his magnetic passes, all her husband could do was write out his grief in *The Genius and the Goddess*: "She was his food, she was a vital organ of his own body. . . . When she was absent, he was like a cow deprived of grass." Some part of him understood and could not let her go; fear of another breakdown clotted his emotions. Even if he could not bring himself to talk about it, grief for Maria rimmed his eyes with black circles. Passages in *Genius* rippled with controlled emotion: "Have you ever seen anyone die? It's the cutoffness that's so terrible. You sit there helplessly, watching the connections being broken, one after the other. The connection with people, the connection with language, the connection with the physical universe. They can't see the light, they can't feel the warmth, they can't breathe the air. And finally the connection with their own body begins to give way. They're left hanging by a single thread—and it's fraying away, fraying away, minute by minute."[29]

As Maria's decline proceeded, Huxley did his best to make peace with the transformation he steadfastly denied. Maria was his eyes, his compassion, his tunnel to the world. When the wife of Maine de Biran died, the philosopher knew he ought to accept his loss with the resignation of a Stoic. "But what can philosophy do when the soul is utterly broken," Huxley wrote. "When the mind, bent under the weight of grief, has lost all its energy and activity? With his conscious mind he can think the consolations of philosophy, he can will them to take effect. His unconscious mind pays no attention to these thoughts and his body disregards the will's commands."[30]

Huxley glided along the surface of his life in the autumn of 1954—meeting article deadlines, helping Matthew retool for a career, lecturing at Duke for J. B. Rhine and at the University of North Carolina. Underneath, a more urgent task awaited him: "to make sense of the queer, chaotic phenomena of the inner world."[31] Maria's death would, like his loss of vision in 1951, cast him into the swimmy waters of the occult.

Throughout the fifties, the Huxleys had broadened their contacts with Eileen Garrett. Both Matthew and his cousin Francis now frequented her establishment, as did Humphry Osmond. Aldous

Huxley's deepening commitment to parapsychology in the midfifties could be likened to that of William James in the 1880s, who concluded: "There is a continuum of cosmic consciousness, against which our several minds plunge as into a mother-sea or reservoir."[32]

There was a distinct resurgence of this mother-sea in the American fifties (and eighties), ranging from Gerald Heard's UFO sightings to the burgeoning astrology industry in Hollywood. Huxley was certainly not alone in his explorations of the psyche. Of parapsychology in Los Angeles in 1953 Robert Heinlein wrote:

> "Don't you find that most of that stuff can be explained in an ordinary fashion?"
>
> "Quite a lot of it, sure. Then you can strain orthodox theory all out of shape and ignore the statistical laws of probability to account for most of the rest. Then by attributing anything that is left over to charlatanism, credulity, and self-hypnosis, and refusing to investigate it, you can go peacefully back to sleep."[33]

"Back to sleep" is many people's retrospective impression of America in the middle of the century, a period for which the crowd is the dominant metaphor—in sociologist David Riesman's classic study, The Lonely Crowd, and among "crowders," American college students comfortable with submerging individuality in contests of how many people could stuff into Volkswagen "bugs" or telephone booths. Critic Dwight Macdonald wrote of mass culture and midcult. Even America's trickle-down economic policy, propounded by Secretary of Health, Education and Welfare Oveta Culp Hobby, purportedly favored the crowd.

Popular sociology also took up this theme. In letters, Huxley remarked on Vance Packard's The Status Seekers, and William Whyte's The Organization Man, surveys of mass life and America's new secular religion, conspicuous consumption. Urban growth bred suburbs, towns gave way to exurbs, and exurbs to malls. America was a land of institutionalized group rituals—Sunday barbecues and PTA meetings, bowling leagues and bridge nights.

Sin stalked such gatherings. Main Street gave way to Peyton Place. Falsies and drive-in cinemas promoted sexual fantasy to a still straitlaced society groaning over the gyrations of Elvis Presley's hips. The scene in Rebel Without a Cause in which a neglectful father picks up his juvenile delinquent son (James Dean) at a police station encapsulated the danger of straying too far from the norm.

Yet hidden in the crowd of Boy Scouts marching behind the American Legion car on the Fourth of July were a few rebels with a cause: atheists and beleaguered radicals who survived right-wing attacks, blacks who refused to sit at the back of the bus, Hispanics who insisted on speaking their native language in school, the James Deans and Jack Kerouacs who, for differing reasons, never fit the procrustian rack of popular culture. From these petri dishes of sixties' revolt came antiheroes and nonconformism; instead of stuffing telephone booths, many stuffed envelopes for the nascent ban-the-bomb and civil rights movements.

Schoolchildren read one of the ten most popular school texts of the 1950s, *Brave New World*, in its new paper edition. Bernard Marx's struggle for individuation paralleled the energetic cross-country revels of Allen Ginsberg, Kerouac, and Cassady. This crew excited the same horrified fascination which *Doors* evoked, when Huxley's book and *On the Road* circulated in the midfifties. Intellectuals sought out such passageways in a culture walled in by TV's "Father Knows Best." Jazz and rhythm and blues transformed American popular music. As Aldous was taking his second mescaline trip in 1954, Norman Mailer was writing, in his Hollywood novel, *The Deer Park*, of marijuana:

> *Now and again it placed him in deep mental states. If a thought came up which should be written down—something for example which could seem as clear at night and as mysterious in the morning as "The three eyes of love"—he would discover that his brain watched the thought and the thought watched his hand, and his hand the pencil, the pencil the paper, until the paper stared back at him with a hostile grin, "You're flying, man."* [34]

Similarly, homosexuals and lesbians challenged their characterizations. Ginsberg and Cassady made a pilgrimage to visit Gerald Heard. Again, Mailer forced the issue, parodying Louis B. Mayer's confrontations with gay actors:

> *In a quiet voice, Teddy said, "Mr. Teppis, you know very well I'm a homosexual."*
> *"I didn't hear it, I didn't hear it," Teppis screamed.*
> *"That's the way I am," Teddy muttered. "There's nothing to be done about it. What is, is."*

"Philosophy?" Teppis shouted. "You listen to me. If a man sits in . . . shit, he don't know enough to get out of it?"[35]

Popular magazines made homosexuality a bogeyman similar to communism. In 1950, *Coronet* termed homosexuality "the new menace" in unmistakably anti-Red terms; in 1954, *Commonweal* called the homosexual "a freak of nature as is the albino or the midget." In 1956, *Time* quoted a psychiatrist who asserted, "The full-grown homosexual wallows in self-pity . . . covering his guilt and depression with extreme narcissism and superciliousness."[36] The pain, fear, and misunderstanding of such pronouncements parallels the more obvious Cold War oppression of liberals and radicals.

Yet life for the Hollywood gay community improved, ironically enough, in the frightened fifties. In times of overt cultural repression the radical and the iconoclast thrive. Courageous writers banded together to produce *One: The Homosexual Viewpoint* and *Homophile Studies* with support from older gay organizations, such as the Mattachine Society and the Daughters of Bilitis.

The portrayal of the homosexual had evolved in film, though the celluloid closet hadn't ended. Homosexual stereotypes passed through well-defined stages: his or her invisibility, elimination, transformation into something slightly less offensive (such as a Jew), difficult death or suicide, and, later, to sniggering or circumscribed acceptance.[37]

Images of gay women were no longer impossible to film. Gay relationships were still commonly shorn from scripts by the adapters or the Motion Picture Code Office—as was done in *Cat on a Hot Tin Roof* and *A Streetcar Named Desire*—but in 1953, Otto Preminger released a picture without a code seal—*The Moon Is Blue*. In *The Strange One* (1957), *Tea and Sympathy* (1956), and Kenneth Anger's early underground classic, *Fireworks* (1947), Hollywood directors visualized male homosexuals not as mental patients but as "men who wouldn't run with the pack."[38] This was at least some improvement over sappy films like *Glen or Glenda?* (1953), based on Christine Jorgensen's transsexual operation.

Isherwood made a significant contribution to sexual ambiguity in film. Following the success of the Broadway play, Henry Cornelius filmed *I Am a Camera* in 1955. Isherwood's characters were as provocative as anything the studios made in this culturally antediluvian era. (Isherwood protested, unsuccessfully, at the producers' insistence that the Bowles character have at least one heterosexual romance.)

Buoyed by this success, Isherwood authored *The World in the Evening*, a romantic novel of homosexual love, no mean feat in this period. Isherwood was entering the period a biographer called "The Return of Self-confidence."[39] His finances stabilized and his love for Don Bachardy grew as the couple moved from Sunset Boulevard to a house in Santa Monica Canyon. At a party in their early courtship, talking and drinking on a warm summer evening, they fell head-over-heels out a window.

Though Isherwood maintained more ties to the Vedanta Society than Heard or Huxley, he, too, was drawing away. One cause of the split was drugs. Once, when Isherwood visited the swami, Aldous and Gerald's experiments were discussed. Prabhavananda had a horror of mescaline, suspecting those too lazy to reach enlightenment by meditation might turn to drug-induced transcendence—a heresy, so far as he was concerned. "Swami said that drugs could never change your life or give you the feeling of love and peace which you got from spiritual visions. Drugs only made you marvel—and then later you lost your faith.

"I wasn't ready to accept Swami's condemnation [of drugs] without experimenting for myself," Isherwood continued.

"I had asked both Aldous and Gerald to let me join in a drug session and had got evasive answers. Then I was told, by a third party, that they had agreed I was too unstable emotionally to be a suitable subject. I was indignant, and at once decided to try mescaline on my own. In 1955 . . . about four months after this, in London, I took one of the mescaline tablets, alone; we had agreed that Don should remain an objective observer. . . . I felt exhilarated. My senses, particularly my sight, seemed extraordinarily keen. Certain patches of color were almost scandalously vivid. Faces on the street looked like caricatures of themselves, each one boldly displaying its owner's dominant characteristic—anxiety, vanity, aggression, laziness, extravagance, love.

"I told Don that we must take a taxi to the Catholic cathedral in Westminster, 'to see if God is there.' God wasn't. . . . I had to go into a dark corner and stay there until I could control my giggles. The Abbey's old rock-ribbed carcass was greatly shrunken; I felt I was inside a dead dried-up whale."[40]

At this time Isherwood was writing a film on the early life of Buddha. Sorrow and the end of sorrow, he reflected: "Shortly before Maria Huxley's death in 1955, she told a woman friend, 'Always wear lipstick.' This was a remark which beautifully expressed Maria's particular kind of courage—take care to look your best, even when you are sick and afraid of dying, in order to spare the feelings of those who love you."[41]

As the weeks passed, Maria Huxley became like a well-dressed shadow presiding over her household, reminding Marie to put up a nice roast and Yorkshire pudding for Aldous's Sunday dinner. Maria and Aldous lipsticked over the truth even as radiation treatments tore her insides.

Aldous persisted in attributing Maria's condition to anything other than its source. On January 10, 1955, he wrote that Maria had "recurrent and very painful lumbago," for which she was receiving X-ray treatments. Most of the letter described his second mescaline experience, when he, Gerald, and psychotherapist Leslie LeCron experimented in "group mescalinization." In this psychedelic session, Huxley's attention was focused on people rather than vision.[42]

Two days later Huxley wrote to Humphry Osmond, "Poor Maria still has the lumbago. We [sic] have begun an ultrasonic treatment . . . I hope very much this will do the trick."

But "the trick" was not so simply done. Instead of recognizing the unrealizable, he decided her problem wasn't lumbago after all, but "some infection in the intestine or kidney and I hope they will be able to put their finger on it and get rid of it," he wrote to Osmond petulantly.[43] The rest of the letter discussed another drug experiment, in which he, Gerald, and Al Hubbard of Vancouver tried carbogen, a mixture of carbon dioxide and oxygen.

A week later, January 23, Huxley wrote of Maria's "vaguely arthritic condition" about which he hoped "all will be well within a short time." By the end of January 1955, he was writing Matthew—who knew better—"I hope that, when x-rays are over next week, she will really start to get better." [44]

Maria returned to the hospital. Aldous was kept busy by Betty Wendell, adapting *The Genius and the Goddess* to a play. Maria called Betty from the hospital. She said to let her talk without interrupting, because it was the last time she would speak to her. Betty remembers, "The last thing she said to me was 'Always have a fresh ribbon on your typewriter so Aldous won't have trouble reading.' "

Seeing Maria in the hospital, so pale, Peggy Kiskadden felt a wave of bitterness: "I got tired of my role [in not telling Aldous] but we went right on with it. She wouldn't have given it up for anything. Finally, when she knew she was dying, she said, 'If Aldous can get on without me, he will,' and accepted the fact that she could do no more." [45]

Throughout Maria's illness, Huxley had progressively submerged himself in what he called the Other World. This was the subject of *Heaven and Hell*, whose earliest incarnations were an essay for *Esquire* (for whom Huxley wrote regularly in the early fifties) and various lectures.

In *Heaven*, Huxley set himself a task halfway between the proselytizing of *The Doors of Perception* and the religious gravity of *The Perennial Philosophy*. In the latter volume, he had charted the common ground of mysticism; now he documented humans' search for the Visionary Experience—through colors, art, jewels, anything which brightened humdrum existence:

> There may also be a kind of visionary element. Shiny objects remind the subconscious of what is there, at the mind's Antipodes, and, being so reminded, the subconscious turns away from the ordinary world towards the visionary world, falling into trance in the process. [46]

Over the years, Huxley had redefined his search for transcendence. No longer did he seek self-abnegation; he had lost about as much ego as he needed. Hypnosis, therapies, and drugs had opened private doors. Now he targeted cognitive categorization—the process by which bits of daily existence form a patina over a person's active intelligence, prompting stereotypes which shape his life the way a camera's frame shapes the image it presents. As the moonlit harper of Blake's "Marriage of Heaven and Hell" reminds us: "The man who never alters his opinion is like standing water & breeds reptiles of the mind."

"It's a very salutary thing to realize that the rather dull universe in which most of us spend most of our time is not the only universe there is," Huxley told an interviewer.[47]

Huxley considered visionary and mystical experiences as different, but wrote, "but the first is apt to lead into the second." Perhaps the swami was right: the propensity to marvel among takers of psychedelic drugs caused, if not a loss of faith, then at least a loss of will to erase the ego. Marveling as an activity is passive; it presupposes an individual willingly going along for the ride. The trip ends, and the transcendentalist requires a new supply for a return to Shangri-la.

By virtue of reputation and funding contacts, Huxley was at the center of an American network of researchers: Dr. Henry Puharich, who had set up a foundation in upstate New York to explore psychoactive mushrooms (those containing psilocybin or belladonna); captain Al Hubbard of British Columbia, an eccentric uranium mineowner with enormous stocks of Swiss LSD; and, soon, Richard Alpert and Timothy Leary, trained psychologists at Harvard.

Huxley contributed to this research as an inspirational fulcrum, but some specific questions puzzled him: what if someone with previous hypnotic experience took mescaline with a master hypnotist, who during the session implanted a posthypnotic suggestion which allowed psychedelic impressions to be recaptured after the drug wore off. (Huxley complained that he had raised this probability for three years without anyone trying it, perhaps because of its terrifying totalitarian potential.)

The second idea Huxley quietly posed to Osmond, by now one of his closest correspondents (his wife Jane offered to fly from Canada to nurse Maria): "Have you ever tried the effects of mescaline on a congenitally blind man or woman? This would surely be of interest."[48]

At the root of Huxley's long march through mysticism, spiritualism, hypnosis, E-therapy, and psychedelics was his curiosity and insatiable drive for visions. As with any polymath, different concerns come to the fore by turns. Now he rediscovered Buddhism, of the Mahayana school. By his early sixties, he had become more Buddhist than Hindu and, naturally enough, rediscovered *The Tibetan Book of the Dead,* that manual of dying well which guides the everlasting self across the threshold of consciousness into a roomful of light. He had need of it now: "There is a consciousness of the Pure Truth, like a light 'moving across the landscape in springtime in one continuous stream of vibration.'

"Be not afraid. For this 'is the radiance of your own true nature. Recognize it' . . . the sound of your own real self."[49]

On February 5, 1955, Huxley was finally briefed by doctors on his wife's illness. He immediately wrote the "news" to Matthew and Ellen: "I try not to cry when I see her, but it is difficult—after thirty-six years."

On February 7, she was helped out of bed, dressed, and she drove herself home from the hospital to die.

That afternoon Leslie LeCron put her under with hypnosis; Aldous repeated his magnetic passes. The next day Matthew arrived, and Maria roused herself. "Matthewkins," she said weakly. "I knew you would come." The following day her sister Suzanne came; Maria recognized her but soon lost consciousness.

Aldous spent most of each day sitting by her side. "In the desert and, later, under hypnosis, all Maria's visionary and mystical experiences had been associated with light," Aldous wrote in a long account of his wife's death:

> Light had been the element in which her spirit had lived, and it was therefore to light that all my words referred. I would begin by reminding her of the desert she had loved so much, of the vast crystalline silence, of the overarching sky, of the snow-covered mountains at whose feet we had lived. I would ask her to open the eyes of memory to the desert sky and to think of it as the blue light of Peace, soft and yet intense, gentle and yet irresistible in its tranquillizing power.
>
> And now, I would say, it was an evening in the desert, and the sun was setting. Overhead the sky was more deeply blue than ever. But in the West there was a great golden illumination deepening to red, and this was the golden light of Joy, the rosy light of Love. And

to the South rose the mountains, covered with snow and glowing with the white light of pure Being. . . .

And I would ask her to look at these lights of her beloved desert and to realize that they were not merely symbols, but actual expressions of the divine nature—an expression of pure Being; an expression of the peace that passeth all understanding; an expression of the divine joy; an expression of the love which is at the heart of things, at the core, along with peace and joy and being, of every human mind. And having reminded her of these truths . . . I would urge her to advance into those lights, to open herself up to joy, peace, love and being, to permit herself to be irradiated by them and to become one with them. . . . And I kept on repeating this, urging her to go deeper and deeper into the light, ever deeper and deeper.

So the days passed and, as her body weakened, her surface mind drifted further and further out of contact, so that she no longer recognized us or paid attention. And yet she must still have heard and understood what was said; for she would respond by appropriate action, when the nurse asked her to open her mouth or to swallow. . . . Addressing the deep mind which never sleeps, I went on suggesting that there should be relaxation on the physical level, and an absence of pain and nausea; and I continued to remind her of who she really was—a manifestation in time of the eternal, a part forever unseparated from the whole, of the divine reality; I went on urging her to go forward into the light.

At a little before three on Saturday morning the night nurse came and told us that the pulse was failing. I went and sat by M's bed and, from time to time, leaned over and spoke into her ear. I told her that I was with her and would always be with her in that light which was the central reality of our beings. I told her that she was surrounded by human love and that this love was the manifestation of a greater love, by which she was enveloped and sustained. I told her to let go, to forget the body, to leave it lying here like a bundle of old clothes, and to allow herself to be carried, as a child is carried, into the heart of the rosy light of love. . . .

And then there was peace. How passionately from the depth of a fatigue which illness and a frail constitution had often intensified to the point of being hardly bearable, she had longed for peace! And now she would have peace. And where there was peace and love, there too would be joy and the river of the coloured lights was carrying her towards the white light of pure being. . . .

The breathing became quieter, and I had the impression that there was some kind of release. I went on with my suggestions and reminders, reducing them to their simplest form and repeating them close to her ear. "Let go, let go. Forget the body, leave it lying here; it is *of no importance now. Go forward into the light. Let yourself be carried into the light. No memories, no regrets, no looking backwards, no apprehensive thoughts about your own or anyone else's future. Only the light. Only this pure being, this love, this joy. Above all this peace. Peace in this timeless moment, peace now, peace now." When the breathing ceased, at about six, it was without any struggle.*[50]

Peggy thought Aldous misguided when he kept up his recitation after Maria's coma: "Maria was already gone." But Aldous knew hearing was one of the last senses to pass, and, besides, the exercises in the *Bardo Thodol* are designed to greet the departing spirit at and immediately after the moment of death.

According to Dr. W. Y. Evans-Wentz, editor of *The Tibetan Book of the Dead:*

> *Occidental man will, as he grows in right understanding, recognize . . . that worlds and suns, no less than he himself and every living thing, repeatedly come into the illusory manifestation of embodiment, and that each of these many manifestations is rounded by what the Lamas of Tibet call the Bardo, the state intervening between death and rebirth.*[51]

"Those last three hours were the most anguishing and moving hours of my life," Matthew recalled. "Aldous was whispering to her the lesson of *The Book of the Dead* . . . but framed in such a moving and personal way . . . illustrations of their life together. . . . It was over so quietly and gently with Aldous with tears streaming down his face with his quiet voice not breaking."[52]

As Aldous quoted Shelley, at the end of *Ape and Essence:*

> *Why linger, why turn back, why shrink, my Heart?*
> *Thy hopes are gone before: from all things here*
> *They have departed, thou shouldst now depart.*[53]

"After Maria died, Aldous would walk around the house upset," Marie le Put remembered. "We had to be very careful. He would feel along the walls to find the doors; we had to keep them closed [or he would fall through]. For several weeks he was like that."[54]

Yet his feared disintegration (which had led him to deny her illness) did not occur. Huxley did flounder, however, like a man who had lost his glasses; he told friends he felt amputated. To his niece Claire he wrote that insofar as he had learned to be human—"and I had a great capacity for not being human"—it was thanks to Maria. His grandmother had been the same wife to T.H., "interpreter and communicator, explainer or deepener of experience."[55]

Huxley was soon surrounded by women anxious to help out. The family debated who could take Maria's place and discovered that to do so they needed a staff of three: a driver, a secretary, and a house-cleaner. Fortunately, Marie continued cooking. She noticed Huxley's appetite had doubled, only later guessing that meals she left in the refrigerator were eaten by two. Audrey Hepburn, one of Maria's close friends, would drop by with her dog Famous, and the case of the disappearing entrée continued. Aldous asked the family to let him take care of himself. Yet he was restless, lonely. "The silences got to him," Stravinsky told Marie.

Soon after Maria's death, Huxley planned a trip east. Rose was to take Maria's place at the wheel along the route the Huxleys had taken in 1937, driving via Frieda Lawrence's winter home in Port Isabel, Texas. Members of the family hoped Rose would fill in for her sister in ways other than driving. Suzanne openly admonished her to make the most of her cross-country opportunity.

They left California in mid-April, driving what would become Interstate 10 along the Mexican border. The heat scalded them as they threaded a needle-straight line through sagebrush and bluff. When they arrived in Yuma, Arizona, surrounded by marriage chapels, Aldous proposed. Rose joked him out of it.

"They were hoping that I would be the second wife," Rose said. "But I just couldn't. Because of Maria—she was sitting between us in the front seat. The way she had made all of us [Nys sisters] treat him with so much respect [meant] that I could never have fallen in love with him."[56]

They continued across New Mexico to El Paso, and then south toward Corpus Christi. They traveled at Aldous's pace, just as Maria had: stopping for meals, an air-conditioned movie, and walks, wherever they found a wooded stretch. One night in a motel, Rose found a scorpion seven inches wide walking toward her bed. "Go under the door," she whispered. "Go visit someone else." Then, knowing Aldous would never see the creature, she ran to his room: "Put your shoes and clothes up high!" she cried with a vigor worthy of Maria.[57]

In Washington, they were received at the Indian Embassy; Huxley attended a concert with the Indian ambassador sitting on his right and the Pakistan ambassador on his left. "I never felt like such a miserable border before," he joked.

On May 11, 1955, Huxley addressed the American Psychiatric Association in a session on LSD and mescaline research:

> *"Here I am in this Dome of Pleasure, floating midway on the waves, where is heard the mingled measure of the Electric Shock Boys, the Chlorpromaziners and the 57 Varieties of Psychotherapists."*[58]

In New York, he settled into George S. Kaufman's penthouse on Park Avenue, loaned complete with butler and cook. What better place to visit Anita and help Betty revise *The Genius and the Goddess* for the stage?

This was to be a family summer: first Julian and Juliette arrived in New York on business (Julian giving the first Alfred Sloan lecture on cancer). One night, at a party with old friends, Aldous told Juliette that Eileen Garrett said Maria had "been through." "Her message for Aldous was of deep acceptance of his guiding her in her last days. She heard all he said as she lay dying, especially about 'Eccot' and the 'Todi.' Eileen could not make out what it was and feared it was nonsense, but Aldous knew at once. 'Eccot' was Meister Eckhart, the great mystic of the Middle Ages, and 'Todi' was the *Bardo Thodol*," Juliette wrote in her memoir.[59]

Garrett further told him that she had been in her car at the time of Maria's death. She perceived a presence in the car and heard a voice say: "It's Maria. I'm safely over."[60] At this vulnerable time, these "communications" proved as decisive to Huxley's conversion to spiritism as the famous moment when William James encountered the American medium Leonora Piper: "For me the thunderbolt has fallen."[61]

In January 1954, Huxley published his longest article on parapsychology, "A Case for ESP, PK, and PSI," in *Life*. Huxley pointed out that until 1650, parapsychological events were accepted by "practically everyone in the Christian world." He credited Dr. Rhine with spearheading research since 1930; accepting telepathy and clairvoyance as real depended on having a nonmaterialist orientation, he wrote.

In *Heaven and Hell*, he went a step further, announcing his belief in an afterlife. "Of those who die an infinitesimal minority are capable of immediate union with the divine Ground, a few are capable of supporting the visionary bliss of heaven, a few find themselves in the visionary horrors of hell and are unable to escape; the great majority end up in the kind of world described by Swedenborg and the mediums."[62]

Aldous summered with Matthew and his family. For years, Aldous and Maria's only child had borne the Huxley name without the obsessive drive to achieve which accompanied it. The long wait for the U.N. job (which never materialized) had frustrated him profoundly; posts at the Ford and Rockefeller Foundations likewise never appeared. Finally, at a professional meeting in 1953, he met an old friend, now in public health, who advised him to try this field. "What, and go back to school?" Matthew asked in horror. "Yes, otherwise you'll be a shitworker." The scion of the Huxleys glumly agreed.

Matthew wasted no time finding a fellowship and winning acceptance to Harvard where, in 1954, he earned a master's degree in public health. Now, as Aldous arrived, a post had conveniently opened up at the American Public Health Association in New Haven, and Matthew was house-hunting. They found temporary quarters in Guilford, Connecticut, where Aldous, Ellen, Trev, now four, and Tessa, two, lived summer-camp style.

"There wasn't a breath of air that summer," Ellen said. "Incredibly hot. I made Aldous a pair of pedal pushers out of an old pair of shorts. He looked like a stork because his legs stuck out." To Grace Hubble, Aldous wrote on his sixty-first birthday, "The climate is like Borneo; by comparison L.A. seems like a paradise."[63]

That hot, rustic summer Aldous Huxley did fall in love—but not with Rose. He grew extremely close to Ellen, deeply moved by her sympathy. Ellen had been, in that trite expression, the daughter he and Maria never had. Francis Huxley spent a great deal of time that summer with Aldous and Ellen.

Julian's younger son was the same age as Matthew, but he resembled Aldous more than Matthew did, with a mellifluous voice, dreamy blue eyes, and fair hair he wore long and swept back over a typically high Huxley forehead. Formerly a lecturer at St. Catherine's College, Oxford, he was an able writer with a rugged, restless streak. Like his elder brother, Anthony, he loved travel in exotic spots— Gambia, Haiti, Brazil.[64] Now he and Ellen proposed to make a documentary film on Darwin.

Aldous would work until lunch. He had provided funds for a cook ("It took me about twenty minutes to get used to that!" Ellen laughed) so that they could take off with the kids for walks or the beach in the afternoon. Despite the loss which hung in the air, Huxley had an impish light-heartedness for his grandchildren: "We had rabbits," Trev remembered, "and he used to go out to the cage and pull their hair. He would gleefully tug on their feet and they'd leap around in a most dramatic style. This was one of my sister's favorite pastimes."[65] He drew pictures of animals in the sand or organized tin-can races; Trev and Tessa squealed with delight.

By five, they would return, with Huxley working until seven, when he reemerged for dinner. After supper, Ellen would read to him: that summer, the life of the early Buddhist scholar, Milarepa, and the history of the Light Brigade.

Already Huxley was thinking about remarrying. "He went to visit Eileen in New York that summer," Ellen said. "He came back and told me, over lunch, 'You know I went to see this medium. She went into a trance and said, "Coccola is here." What she wanted to tell me was that it would be good if I married again—that would make her happy.' He was letting himself know in very oblique ways that he was ready to accept something else."[66]

"In spite of the steamy heat, I manage to do a good deal of work," he wrote. He was finishing the appendices to *Heaven and Hell*, yet as he piled up pages he plunged into a different sort of task: self-healing. Something in the all-accepting bosom of his son's family encouraged him to do what he never had done before, to exhume his sorrow about his mother's death when he was fourteen.

"He took LSD some time after Maria died. We were together and he said, 'It was the first time I could really cry.' He cried and cried [about his mother]. It showed him, in the old Zen way of a kick in the ass or a blow on the head, what he didn't know before. He couldn't even remember his mother—no memory of her at all. He could block those things out. LSD usually hits you where you live— where you're most blocked. It hit him hard, and he was most grateful."[67]

That gratitude surfaced in letters to Humphry Osmond and in *Heaven and Hell*. Later, at the suggestion of Cass Canfield of Harper, *Heaven* was reissued in a single volume with *Doors*; this led to subsequent confusion about the two. Only the latter was primarily concerned with drugs; the canvas of *Heaven and Hell* was stretched more broadly. Far less personal than *Doors*, the work ultimately fails to move the reader: there are too many words for moments which must be experienced, not debated.

Though the book could be read as an elaborate justification for his personal need for vision-inducing drugs, Huxley intended it as a documentary of the transcendental impulse, as produced by techniques ranging from diet to self-flagellation:

> It is a matter of historical record that most contemplatives worked systematically to modify their body chemistry, with a view to creating the internal conditions favorable to spiritual insight.
>
> When they were not starving themselves into low blood sugar and vitamin deficiency, or breathing themselves into intoxication by histamine, adrenalin and decomposed protein, they were cultivating insomnia and praying for long periods in uncomfortable positions in order to create the psycho-physical symptoms of stress. In the intervals they sang interminable psalms, thus increasing the amount of carbon dioxide in the lungs and the blood stream, or, if they were Orientals, they did breathing exercises to accomplish the same purpose. (Heaven, 155)

Huxley divided the vision-stimulating process into process and artifact. From the Cro-Magnon period onward, humans had devised objects to evoke a world most knew only instinctively: paintings, fireworks, flower arrangements, gemstones—all stimulated visions in varying degrees. Gems, Huxley insisted, were precious not necessarily because of their rarity, but for their hypnotizing, luminous reflections.

Huxley's *Heaven* is a blind man's paradise, a land "of curved reflections, of softly lustrous glazes, of sleek and smooth surfaces. In a word, the beauty transports the beholder, because it reminds him, obscurely or explicitly, of the preternatural lights and colors of the Other World."[68]

Our problem, Huxley fretted, was that we have grown jaded:

> *Familiarity breeds indifference. We have seen too much pure, bright color at Woolworth's to find it intrinsically transporting. . . . The illumination of a city, for example, was once a rare event, reserved for victories and national holidays, for the canonization of saints and the crowning of kings. Now it occurs nightly and celebrates the virtues of gin, cigarettes and toothpaste.* (Heaven, 115)

The only solution was to seek, actively, windows into a different consciousness.

In *Heaven*, Huxley acknowledged more explicitly the dangers of drug-induced transcendence—perhaps a by-product of meetings such as one described in Anaïs Nin's diary. Nin had complained of massive disorientation following an LSD session; Huxley told her she had been given too strong a dose.

"He was rather indignant about that because, as he said, anyone could see I would react sensitively to a light dose.

"I also ventured my opinion that if we had been properly trained to appreciate music, painting, poetry, meditation, dreams, we would not have needed drugs, for I had reached such 'states' just listening to music, looking at certain paintings, reading certain books, or in nature at times."

"You happen to have direct communication with your unconscious; that is rare, most people do not and for them drugs are necessary," Huxley said vehemently.[69] Yet throughout *Heaven*, Huxley took care to remind readers that psychedelic drugs could bring hell *or* heaven.

Huxley's argument for the universality of the visionary experience contained major, unexplored paradoxes. If a painter's palette and a monk's hymn are transcendental, then what isn't? If the flickering light of a stroboscope engenders visions, as Huxley insisted in one appendix, why not television, regardless of its stale plots and used-car ads? Is content irrelevant, as Marshall McLuhan asserted? Can we find visions on the back of a cereal box as readily as in an equally bright Picasso?

Huxley mistook visual sightseeing for transcendence. The Huxley of 1944 would have insisted that seeking transcendence without a spiritual goal was like strapping on a seat belt on an airplane—that alone brought a destination no closer. Now Huxley suggested that transcendence *was* the destination. From afar, Huxley's intellect seemed to drift aimlessly. There was no telling what he might try next: flying saucers or hashish.

At summer's end, Aldous surrendered his pedal pushers and returned to his lonesome house in California. "How we shall miss him," Ellen sighed. "Even his silences were more eloquent than most people's conversations." He stopped in New York to visit Anita at the Plaza, where she worked on three productions simultaneously. Loos also was about to lose her partner, though Emerson remained hospitalized on money he had embezzled from her. Loos and Huxley agreed to disagree about drugs.

By the time *Heaven and Hell* appeared, in 1956, Huxley had taken psychedelics nearly a dozen times. He had tried not only LSD and mescaline, but ergine from morning glory seeds (which had given Maria visions "of a Monkey trying to climb up heaven on his own tail"), carbogen, and others. The rate of these excursions was increasing. All who remember this period stress the seriousness with which he approached these sessions, and there's no reason to doubt their accounts. As a friend put it, "There was no 'let's have LSD' any more than there was 'let's have whisky and soda.' "[70] "My father relaxed over good conversation at dinner, with perhaps a glass of sherry beforehand and an evening of listening to Mozart afterwards," Matthew said. Yet few reading *Doors* or *Heaven* imagined a man so temperate. Huxley unwittingly set in motion an international movement of drug experimentation involving millions of American and European youths; not accidentally did Timothy Leary and Richard Alpert later dedicate their adaptation of the *Bardo Thodol, The Psychedelic Experience,* to Aldous Huxley.

How had Huxley, who began as a serious religious mystic, become a promoter of better living through chemistry? Part of the answer lies in specific stages of mysticism which adepts often experience, as noted by William James (in *The Varieties of Religious Experience*) and by William E. Hocking, the philosopher.

Most who mount the mystic path do so with enormous will and energy, derived from frustration with church-oriented religions or with the generally dismal state of the world. Entry-level involvement in mysticism is characterized by soul-searching and reading in the abundant literature of mysticism. This is what Huxley underwent in the first flush of his interest in Vedantism, just before World War II.

A common second phase is the period scholars of mysticism refer to as "aridity," the barren period of emptying oneself of fears and ambition—self-abnegation in the positive sense of the word. Since this is harder done then said, at this point many turn back or settle for outward trappings. "The individual not rooted in any tradition uses an alien and thus exotic religious tradition as a screen upon which to project all that one seeks yet finds lacking in one's own world," wrote J. E. Brown. "One is too easily satisfied merely to 'touch the earth' . . . and to hope thereby that somehow some mystic vision of ultimate meaning will automatically and easily come through."[71]

For the few who persevere, decades of meditation may yield a taste of what was to Huxley the Clear Light. Bereavement often follows the mystical moment, that long dark night of the soul Father Joseph suffered; all that remains is a memory of enlightenment. The ethereal nature of ego-transcendence leaves the experiencer feeling responsible for his own fall from grace. Yet as Plotinus noted: "only now and then can we enjoy this elevation."[72] One simply cannot lasso enlightenment.

"Aldous must not have ever had that moment before drugs," Peggy Kiskadden asserted, "else why would he continue to seek it so resolutely?"[73]

In his use (and justification) of psychedelic experiments, Huxley did not nullify fifteen years of arduous religious study. If he had not undergone this spiritual rigor, he would never have had his "gratuitous grace" from drug-induced visions. In hot pursuit of the visionary experience, however, Huxley did not anticipate his moral responsibility for what happened to those less able (or less willing) to ground drug explorations in a religious or secular-mystical tradition. Huxley's visions differed dramatically from the neutral hallucinations others may experience under mescaline or LSD. Thus, Huxley and the CIA could each experiment simultaneously with mind-altering chemicals: one toward liberation, the other for brainwashing. Neoconservative Herman Kahn would use LSD to help him plot bombing strategies against mainland China.

In England, the publication of *Doors* and *Heaven* triggered public debate on psychedelics. The Honorable Christopher Mayhew, M.P., was filmed live by the BBC taking mescaline in the company of Humphry Osmond; literary critic Raymond Mortimer—who had introduced Aldous to Gerald Heard twenty years earlier—reported negatively in *The Times* on his own experiments. A philosopher, R. C. Zaehner, was so exercised over Huxley's equation of mysticism and drugs that he launched a public campaign to refute him—just as the antievolution champion Bishop Wilberforce did to Aldous's grandfather. Zaehner called Huxley "both incoherent and self-contradictory" in his book *Mysticism Sacred and Profane*.[74] Small wonder Huxley hesitated to lecture on drugs after *Doors* appeared!

The attitude of his family in Britain was scarcely more enthusiastic. Though Julian was fascinated, he steadfastly refused to touch hallucinogens, fearing their effects on his depressions. Others in the family thought Huxley an embarrassment, as Laurence Collier had during World War II.

Only his cousin Renée Haynes was on the same wavelength. For many years a member of the Society for Psychical Research, Haynes was writing a book on ESP. Her discussion of psychedelics was positively florid: those who take mescaline "dive deeply down from individual consciousness into the green subaqueous levels of collective being where telepathic currents flow."[75]

In America, drug experiments shared the stigma of communism and homosexuality. Only a few films, such as Preminger's *The Man with the Golden Arm* (1955) and Fred Zinnemann's *A Hatful of Rain* (1957) relayed anything like an honest portrayal. More typically, viewers found suggestive hints of an Other World in passages such as this from *All About Eve*: "I was in a dentist's office and the anesthetic made me feel strange. I couldn't say what I meant. . . ."

In Los Angeles, people hostile to drug experimentation denounced Huxley publicly. He found himself in a position anticipated by science fiction writer Robert Heinlein:

> *Still rarer is the man who thinks habitually, who applies reason, rather than habit pattern, to all his activity. Unless he masks himself, his is a dangerous life: he is regarded as queer, untrustworthy, subversive of public morals; he is a pink monkey among brown monkeys—a fatal mistake. Unless the pink monkey can dye himself brown before he is caught.*
>
> *The brown monkey's instinct to kill is correct; such men are dangerous to all monkey customs.*[76]

Matters got out of hand; Huxley received baskets of letters on his drug-related writings. One was from a man in Mauritius who, "according to himself, has now written the most extraordinary book in the world's history, and will I please write an introduction and secure him a fellowship at the Ford Foundation's Institute for Advanced Studies in the Social Sciences, or failing that a job on an American newspaper! And I say nothing of the gentleman in Chicago who has discovered the Absolute Truth and sends letters and telegrams about it to President Eisenhower and Bertrand Russell; nor the Mexican dermatologist who thinks that mescaline may be good for eczema, and will I tell him where he can procure the drug, nor the young man from Yorkshire who ate a peyote button supplied by a cactus-growing friend and for three days heard all music one tone higher than it should have been."[77]

Asked to appear on a television program on mescaline with Osmond, Huxley refused:

> *One gets a great deal of most unwelcome publicity, with people stopping one in the street, to say how much they liked, or disliked, what you said. This unwelcome publicity would be particularly annoying after a TV show on mescaline. . . . Mescaline, it seems to me, and the odder aspects of mind are matters to be written about for a small public, not discussed on TV in the presence of a vast audience of baptists, methodists and nothing-but-men plus an immense lunatic fringe . . .*[78]

If Huxley had become a crusader for drug-induced visions, he might have attacked the hypocrisy, then and now, which classifies psychoactive substances as "drugs." In *Doors*, Huxley had asked why we ban mind stimulants not found to be physiologically addictive (such as LSD, mescaline, and marijuana) while tolerating demonstrably addictive substances (such as cigarettes, alcohol, and caffeine) and mind-numbing tranquilizers such as Valium and Librium. After all, the first drug to be outlawed in America was alcohol (1919), followed by opiates (1922). (Marijuana was not criminalized until 1937 and psychedelics not until 1966.)

Huxley might have added television to a list of dangerous substances. Psychiatrists have diagnosed TV psychosis on an individual and mass level. The drug is ingested daily, produces withdrawal symptoms, creates measurable changes in brain and neural activity, confuses children as to what is real.[79] Could this be a drug potentially more harmful than nature's pychoactive weeds and mushrooms? Taking such a stance publicly would have made Huxley even more of an outlaw in his times.

In the third week in October 1955, Aldous invited Laura Archera over to the North King's Road house to guide a mescaline session.

"I would love to stay with you all day," Laura told him. "Is there anything I should know or do?"

"Nothing, just be as you are," Huxley answered.

This time Huxley was not searching for the Clear Light of the Void or for more visions. When Laura arrived in the large, empty house—with Maria's furnishings still scattered around—Aldous handed her a note: "I want to know, and constantly be, in the state of love." Even if Huxley meant Love rather than love, such an invocation must have seemed faintly amorous.

He took half of a 400 mg capsule at 10:00 A.M. and the other half forty minutes later. As the mescaline was absorbed in his bloodstream, Huxley began staring at Laura's hair, which she had tinted the day before. Despite his goal for the session, Huxley could not resist visual distractions: "If you could only *see* your hair!"

Again, Archera probed his blocked memory unsuccessfully. After an hour or so she stopped trying as he was swept into transcendence:

> . . . what came through the closed door was the realization—not the knowledge, for this wasn't verbal or abstract—but the direct, total awareness, from the inside, so to say, of Love as the primary and fundamental cosmic fact. The words, of course, have a kind of indecency and must necessarily ring false, seem like twaddle. But the fact remains . . .[80]

Some of the scenes that he wrote about later in *Island* occurred that day, Laura remembered, such as when they sat in leather armchairs in his study, listening to Bach's Fourth Brandenburg Concerto. The notes floated in midair ("undifferentiated awareness broken up into notes and phrases and yet still all-comprehendingly itself").[81] Outside, the day warmed and the traffic buzzed comfortingly on the boulevards. Inside, time had become asynchronous. Aldous kept repeating a key Vedantic insight, that there was no separation between object and subject—Atman and Brahman were joined.

Laura had hoped that Aldous would talk about Maria and his obvious pain at her loss. With the perverseness of writers who save their therapy for their books, Huxley kept that pain contained—until *Island*. Yet when Laura tried to spare him the phonograph's harsh "click" at the end of a record (a Maria-like gesture), Huxley noticed that she was walking like his former wife. At her fourth step, Aldous said firmly, "Don't ever be anyone else but yourself."

Afterward, he tried to retain the intensity of his experience, but it faded as quickly as a flower out of water. His connection to Laura, however, blossomed (though he never mentioned her by name in a long letter about the trip he wrote to Humphry).

Five months later, a most uncharacteristic event occurred—perhaps connected to this trip. Following Aldous's encounter with Love, he and Laura had seen a lot of one another. Laura recounts a night in January 1956, when Aldous invited her to join him on a speaking engagement in Washington. "Well now," he concluded, "what about plans—shouldn't we decide the date we are going to marry?"[82]

Laura had spent the last decade or so living with Ginny Pfeiffer. According to Hemingway's biographers, Pfeiffer was a lesbian. The two were independent, but vacationed and entertained together. Laura had never married, though she had occasionally dated men. She feared losing her independence, she told Huxley. "You know, darling, I love others," she said. To which Huxley replied with characteristic sangfroid, "It would be awful if you didn't."

What made Huxley's courtship of Laura odd is that he never mentioned it to family or friends. The only mutual friend they had was Gerald Heard, who wasn't close to Laura. Thus, virtually all the information on the couple comes from Archera's memoir, *This Timeless Moment*. To Peggy, Grace, Betty, Anita, and Paulette, she was a stranger. This makes even more peculiar the events of a hot Friday afternoon in mid-March 1956.

Aldous had spent the week working with Betty Wendell on their forthcoming stage adaptation of *The Genius and the Goddess*. On March 18, he told her he would call that weekend about getting together. He spent the morning walking with Gerald and returned home to meet Laura. On the spur of the moment, they got in her car and drove to Yuma, Arizona. There, at the Drive-In Wedding Chapel, near where Aldous had a year earlier proposed to Rose, they were married.

This was a common way of tying the knot in the film community: Louis B. Mayer eloped to Yuma; Anita Loos, in her satire *A Mouse Is Born*, also mentioned the possibility.

Huxley told none of his family or friends. Then TV cameras descended on them, "two minutes after signing the license," he wrote Matthew and Ellen. "I had a sense of being unfaithful to [Maria's] memory, but tenderness, I discovered, is the best memorial to tenderness. She is twenty years younger than I am, but doesn't seem to mind."[83] He and Laura repeatedly mentioned to his friends—who heard of the marriage on the radio, after the story broke via wire service—that Maria and Laura had been close. For all the privacy he had, Aldous complained to Humphry Osmond, "we would have done better to have had a slap-up affair at St. Patrick's with Cardinal Spellman officiating and Clare Luce as bridesmaid."

The hasty marriage created a rift among Huxley's friends. Aldous wrote Peggy, "Of course it is not on with the new love and out with the old," but to many that is the way it seemed.[84] Anita, now widowed, may have hoped to marry Huxley herself. She was in any case furious, though she generously offered the newlyweds her apartment in New York.[85]

On July 16, 1956, just before his sixty-second birthday, the Huxleys moved into a new home a few hundred yards from Virginia Pfeiffer's, "high up in the Hollywood hills, and yet only five or six minutes from the thick of things—with virtually no smog and an incredible view over the city to the south and over completely savage hills in every other direction, hills which remind me a little of Greece by their barrenness, their steep-sided narrow valleys and the unsullied sky overhead."[86]

From the beginning, Laura and Aldous lived together differently than he and Maria had. Laura did not take care of him. "If anything, Aldous took care of her," a niece reflected. On occasion Laura would drive him places, but most of the time he relied on cabs or friends for transport. Gone were the multihour reading sessions after dinner. Though Laura shared his interest in hypnotism, psychedelics, and spirit life, her own career as a therapist and her relationship with Ginny and her children made considerable demands.

Old friends watched in wonder as Huxley fended for himself. Each event became a test; the bus ride to Santa Barbara to lecture reintroduced him to his fellow species.[87]

"Aldous liked Laura because she had a darting, kingfisher mind. She would talk, and then a little ripple upon the conversational stream would attract her. She'd plunge into it and come up with a minnow and swallow it, go and perch on a bough and 'kingfish' to herself. . . . She kept him well-supplied with small talk," Francis Huxley said.[88]

Soon after their marriage, Huxley published an important collection of essays, *Tomorrow and Tomorrow and Tomorrow* (in Britain, *Adonis and the Alphabet*), culled from prose meditations in *Esquire*. John Atkins, a critic, called it "his triumph as an essayist."[89] Since 1952 he had planned such a book, "essays about and around this strange and fascinating country, the American West—from the forests and mountains of Washington to the deserts and date palms of southern California. . . . a series of soliloquies having far Western places as their source and excuse."[90] After Maria's death, the project held a special poignancy—it contained journals of his last travels with her.

The title—Shakespearean, like that of most of his books—comes from *Macbeth* where the hero demands a prophecy from the weird sisters. Thus, *Tomorrow* is Huxley's most self-consciously prophetic work.

Prophecy is the most gratuitous form of error, George Eliot wrote in *Middlemarch*, and Huxley was not exempt, as his writings on drugs attest. He lacked the visionary imagination of the prophetic writers he admired, such as Verne, Wells, and France (the last two predicting, for example, the atomic bomb a half century before its creation).

Prophecy was no longer a game Huxley played with himself; it had another dimension: "In the perfectly organized world of the future, most of our ethical difficulties will be non-existent. But I believe that there will be other and subtler cases of conscience, struggles with as yet unsuspected embodiments of evil. Men are not satisfied with mere happiness; or rather their idea of happiness is a good deal queerer and more complicated than most of our contemporary prophets care to admit."

Huxley's mode of predicting the future, according to Richard Lewinsohn's *Science, Prophecy, and Prediction*, involved "creative foresight" based on cyclical trends in human history and sociology.[91] Huxley wrote:

> We are living like drunken sailors, like the irresponsible heirs of a millionaire uncle. At an ever accelerating rate we are now squandering the capital of metallic ores and fossil fuels accumulated in the earth's crust during hundreds of millions of years. How long can this spending spree go on? Estimates vary. But all are agreed that within a few centuries or at most a few millennia, Man will have run through his capital and will be compelled to live, for the remaining nine thousand nine hundred and seventy or eighty centuries of his career as Homo sapiens, strictly on income.[92]

Here he repeated warnings against the relentless danger of nuclear waste; he forecast 8 billion inhabitants of the earth by 2050 (a figure now considered low). He decried the "economic censorship" of the modern publishing industry where "books are subjected to an ever more rigorous ordeal of economic selection," which he considered a subtle but insidious form of totalitarianism.

The most moving essay was "The Desert," which illuminates the complex blend of compassion and ire which characterized his last writings. Jake Zeitlin had arranged for Huxley to join librarians touring a naval weapons laboratory in the Mojave. The tour offered Huxley a venue for chastising the military desecration of the part of America he most cherished—the high desert:

> In its multi-million-acred emptiness there is room enough to explode atomic bombs and experiment with guided missiles. . . . . In brand-new Reservations, surrounded by barbed wire and the FBI, not Indians but tribes of physicists, chemists, metallurgists, communication engineers and mechanics are working with the co-ordinated frenzy of termites.

Jacques Barzun, reviewing the work, effectively characterized its stance: "He does not press, he presents. He scorns our ways but loves us well enough to lure us into changing them": [93]

> The boys in the Reservations are doing their best; and perhaps, if they are given the necessary time and money, they may really succeed in making the planet uninhabitable. . . . . But I am still optimist enough to credit life with invincibility. . . . . For our survival, if we do survive, we shall be less beholden to our common sense . . . than to our caterpillar-and-cicada-sense, to intelligence, in other words, as it operates on the organic level. . . . . And beyond survival is transfiguration.[94]

In 1957, soon after *Tomorrow* was published, Huxley gave a revealing (but unpublished) interview to the faculty of the UCLA School of Journalism. Questioned as to the effect of blindness on the creative process, Huxley offered a principle which combined his study of physical training (the Bates and Alexander methods), Indian religion, and psychedelics. He called this a "principle of perfect functioning": "In some way you have to combine relaxation with activity: be active but do it without strain."[95] This psychophysical training was nothing foreign, he insisted; tennis pros as well as Bodhisattvas agree on relaxing in order to concentrate.

Then he indulged in another prophecy, citing as its inspiration James's *Varieties of Religious Experience*. Lacking now current expressions such as "new age," Huxley postulated a "new thought movement":

> That hundreds of thousands or millions of people are concerned with this is good. They may not have got hold of the best possible tool but they're certainly using some tool. . . . [There is] a health side of it . . . a way of getting your organism to behave better.[96]

Here, in a few casual words, Huxley projected a generational transformation in the ways people looked not only at the healing process (including the vitamin- and homeopathic-based care he favored) but at the environment, at attitudes toward dying and aging, at American materialism.

Huxley spent the late fifties struggling with how to transfer this principle into fiction.[97] Throughout his other projects of the period—plays, films, lectures—he kept returning to the task, perhaps the hardest fiction he ever wrote, *Island*. He concluded the interview with an illustration of how he wrote:

> My research consists in reading scholarly books, being reminded by passages in them of something written by someone else, or made a note of by myself—which takes me then to other books or my own card indexes, and leads finally to another card, or something dictated on the audograph, or a fully worked out page of writing—sometimes on the theme I have been trying to elucidate, sometimes on something quite different but related, in some subterranean way, to that theme through the trains of association within my own mind.[98]

Huxley's literary reputation ebbed but persisted; in 1955 *The London Magazine* sponsored a critical symposium on his writing. Evelyn Waugh surveyed *Antic Hay*, concluding with regret that Huxley has "travelled far. He has done more than change climate and diet. I miss that [ironic] overtone in his later work." Angus Wilson likewise insisted that the outrageousness of *Crome Yellow* and *Those Barren Leaves* had evaporated. John Wain dismissed the only American work discussed, *After Many a Summer Dies the Swan*, as a "foaming attack."[99] To some British critics, Huxley, their Huxley, seemed to have been swallowed by an odious swamp and replaced by a tall, dotty *poseur*. The tables had turned since World War II: *they* were now the boycotters, and Huxley the Vedantist, the pacifist, the experimenter in psychic and psychoactive phenomena was dismissed.

Even as this symposium took place, a new Huxley emerged on the literary horizon: the committed playwright. Huxley was not new to the stage. He had drafted sketches at Oxford, and, as early as 1920, the part-time theater critic for *The Athenaeum* had crafted two scenarios from which he derived a significant insight: "There is nothing but commercial success that can free one from this deadly hustle. I shall go on producing plays until I get one staged and successful."[100]

Over the years he'd seen friends virtually retire after successful dramas: Robert Nichols, Anita Loos, who earned more from plays than films, John Van Druten, and particularly Isherwood, who reached economic self-sufficiency not from any of his novels or films but from *I Am a Camera.* "You see, he'd been attracted by the money," Matthew explained. "If he had gotten to sell something he wrote directly to the movies, he would have made a lot of money. All he sold were screenplays which they hired him for, *not* the same thing. At this point, he was getting hooked on the idea [of writing plays], not so much for the money, but for the sheer doing of it."[101]

Huxley's first play with a critical (thought not financial) success was probably the 1931 *World of Light.* Despite his many dramatizations of novels and stories—including *Brave New World, Ape and Essence, After Many a Summer Dies the Swan,* "The Gioconda Smile"—only the last, in its British run, rewarded him.

Wendell and he had begun their adaptation of *The Genius and the Goddess* at the end of 1954. For three years, weekly letters passed between the coasts, specifying characterization, staging, cast. High hopes gave way to crestfallen recrimination, and then Huxley's hopes began again. As if one play wasn't enough, Huxley started a musical comedy adaptation of *Brave New World.*

Huxley was forced to write his dramatization as a musical comedy—though the work has only a half-dozen songs, several unsingable and scarcely comic—because RKO still clung to film and TV rights for *Brave New World.* His 104-page script is no more a musical than his earlier novel on *Madame Curie* could be called a treatment. The dramatic techniques Huxley learned in Hollywood improved his pacing and added a staginess but did not fundamentally change his writing; his passing enthusiasms for matters mystical and visionary accomplished that.

Huxley updated *Brave New World* with an H-bomb instead of

the Nine Years War, and he added a mockery of American anticommunism (similar to Chaplin's later *King in New York*):

"He's an individualist" (said of Bernard Marx).

"That's a lie. He's not an Individualist."

"Well, he's certainly a fellow traveler."

His commentary on drugs had expanded, but the original frame of reference—Soma as a numbing narcotic—was unchanged by his subsequent experiences with mescaline. In the New Brave New World,

> *Every day shall end*
> *In global loving and creative dope*
> *Sustained by this enchanting hope*
> *We ply our mops . . . magic pills*
> *They'll make the homeliest female seem resplendent*
> *They'll make the lousiest TV show transcendent.*

Huxley does have a change of heart, however: he doesn't make the Savage commit suicide, his feet turning in a morbid compass. Instead, the Savage goes into exile with his girl: Happily Ever After in the Brave New World.[102]

This manuscript disappeared for many years, following the debacle of *The Genius and the Goddess,* which, when it finally arrived on Broadway, was in an unauthorized version. During out-of-town trial runs, Huxley and Wendell let themselves be pressured into rewriting the script to the producer's whim. Then, new scenes—written by neither Huxley or Wendell—were added for a Philadelphia run. Huxley angrily pulled his name off the script. The resulting mishmash opened on December 10, 1957, and closed five days later.

As the play seemed certain to fizzle, Huxley returned to film. His first project was a documentary, toward the end of 1956. This he hoped would be directed and produced by Fred Zinnemann, director of *High Noon* and *From Here to Eternity*.[103] It seems improbable that the Austrian director would produce a low-budget documentary on overpopulation immediately after the mammoth success of his *Oklahoma!*; but Huxley suffered from the relentless optimism which is one of the occupational hazards of screenwriters. (More puzzling, in fact, was why Huxley hadn't written documentaries earlier, since in 1932 Julian had won an Academy Award for his efforts.) The next documentary which presented itself—a CBS special on psychedelics— he resoundingly refused because of the unwelcome publicity.

Next, at the beginning of 1957, Huxley was approached by United Productions of America (UPA), a cartoon factory which turned out witty, high-quality shorts featuring Gerald McBoing Boing and Mr. Magoo. The studio decided that they wanted a "name" writer, preferably British, to script *Don Quixote* for the grumpy, near blind Mr. Magoo. "The classic tale, long in the public domain, would cost Columbia Pictures nothing for rights," a subproducer later noted in the *Los Angeles Times*. John Collier was first suggested, but no one had heard of him. A wag then offered William Congreve, Richard Sheridan, and Charles Dodgson, but no one had heard of them either. As everyone ran out of ideas, Huxley was contracted for the treatment— in three weeks' time. As one of the very few detailed accounts of Huxley's studio work in the 1950s, the account by fellow writer Dun Roman is worth quoting at length:

"Huxley showed up bright and early the first morning, all smiles and eager to start, and in very short order we became painfully aware that he was on the verge of total blindness. With pale once-blue eyes layered over like milk glass, he groped apologetically about for the first few minutes, stumbling against the furniture and into the walls until he got used to his surroundings, and all the while bubbling over with enthusiasm about what fun we would have rewriting *Don Quixote* for little Mr. What's-his-name, McGrew? McGoogle?"[104] (Apparently no one connected with the project had the courage to inform Huxley that the jokes were to be based on Mr. Magoo's visual handicap.)

Here was an extremely bizarre situation. First of all, why would Huxley perform a literary abortion on Cervantes? Second, why would he do so eagerly, in the company of those so insensitive they assigned him to this make-fun-of-the-handicapped cartoon?

Answers to these questions may lie in what had happened in the film industry by the midfifties. By this point the Hollywood studios were literally on the run—out of the United States to escape guild contracts, out to Wall Street for new capital, out to pasture as back lots were broken up for lucrative suburban developments. As the industry contracted, the remains of the studios were bought by share-holding conglomerates. Hughes sold RKO to General Tire and Rubber Company; the Warner brothers lost control of their studio; MCA bought Universal Pictures. Movies were merchandised just as Sammy Glick had predicted, can after can.

Nineteen fifty-eight brought Hollywood film the worst admissions since 1922; annual attendance dropped steeply, from 90 million a decade before to 39.6 million now.[105]

Many contemporary films contained anti-TV diatribes, such as *The Man in the Gray Flannel Suit,* an anticonformity drama starring Gregory Peck. TV is shown as a loud, glaring presence—one long Western, hypnotizing children. "Don't they have but that one movie?" Peck asks, becoming more militant as the picture ends: "Kick that television in, stomp it, if it gets in the way of the family."

Hollywood was by no means moribund, yet; 1956 saw Raymond Burr fighting Godzilla, and Shakespeare's *Tempest* creatively restaged as science fiction in *Forbidden Planet.* In *Between Heaven and Hell,* World War II still stains the sky, as Technicolor reds and greens evoke the menacing jungles of Guadalcanal and Korea. When a pacifist appears, such as in *East of Eden,* he's subjected to mob violence. There remained a few films for the literate, which is where Huxley and Cervantes came in.

Everyone working on the Magoo project agreed not to embarrass themselves and Huxley by telling him that Magoo was as blind as he was.

"Since the whole venture was doomed from its inception," Roman continued, "we began by reassuring him that in the unusual nature of animation all that was required of us at this early stage was the most loosely elastic of outlines." Then everyone repaired to lunch, and Huxley told anecdotes of studio work in the thirties and forties until they put him in a cab home. Day after day passed in this fashion, until Huxley grew impatient for work; eventually the studio came up with a story line of Magoo on board a bus of tourists catapulted into the seventeenth century, "as far as we could go in keeping Huxley in the dark about Magoo's failing vision." All went along merrily until Huxley's last day, when the front office called: they wanted to see what the team had so far—at 9:00 A.M. the next morning.

Huxley showed up with twenty-five single-spaced pages, offering his work as the team's. He had stayed up half the night dreaming up a busload of characters, "all very British and 1920 in the manner of A. A. Milne. . . . There were chases and fights and uproars, and every frenzied twist and turn of plot he imagined typical of animated films."[106] The author was showing he was a professional.

Unfortunately, Huxley had invented a Pekinese infelicitously named "Poo-poo." He expanded on this character rather than Magoo—about whom he apparently still knew nothing. The script was read aloud and, Dun Roman continued, "by the minute this name was sinking my audience and, I am sorry to say, myself deeper and more irretrievably into rigor mortis. . . . When I had finished reading, hoarse and trembling and wasted, the silence was like thunder. Though it was only a little past 10 that morning, silently they all rose and silently they departed. We summoned Huxley's cab and silently helped him into it.

"Huxley, of course, was paid. But I have often wondered if we did the right thing . . . Might not this gentle, kindly man have just not laughed, 'Magoo blind! Why, I should be delighted to supply him with any number of uproarious situations, and all of them quite at first hand.' ¿Quién sabe?" Such was Huxley's career as a screenwriter in the late fifties.

H̲uxley's friends had wound down or ended their Hollywood careers. Of his circle, only Burgess Meredith and Chaplin were making movies in 1957.

Chaplin's *A King in New York* revolves around a recently deposed king who exiles himself in New York, a city of movie theaters, rock'n'roll clubs, and teenagers in tight sweaters.

Chaplin took on the House Committee on Un-American Activities, which the hapless sovereign appears before because of his political affiliations. Finally, after the king has paid his dues to anticommunism, he is told he's an American success: "You can write your own ticket!"

"I've bought it," the king snaps. "Back to the continent. I'm sitting it out."[107]

Chaplin worried about censorship in America, and correctly so: his film was not shown in the United States until 1973, by which time his anti-anti-Communist humor was dated.

Censorship had been a problem for American film ever since the 1934 founding of the Roman Catholic Legion of Decency to boycott objectionable films. Among their criteria—incorporated into the first Motion Picture Production Code that year—were prohibitions on excessive violence, nudity, and profanity. Kisses could last no more than three seconds; in love scenes, one foot had to remain on the floor at all times. The 1934 *Sex Madness* fared poorly under such scrutiny, with its scenes of a lesbian reaching her hand into her companion's blouse.

As a result, even cartoon vamp Betty Boop cleaned up her act; King Kong relinquished his top side views of Fay Wray as he climbed the Empire State Building. Film-makers who bucked the code usually did so for publicity's sake, with a wink in the direction of code censors. The classic case was the battle over Howard Hughes's 1943 *The Outlaw*, in which Jane Russell bent over a bed and her blouse fluttered open. For two years Hughes fought to reclaim a few seconds' view of Russell's nude upper torso.[108] Joe Breen, Production Code administrator, took his prudery so seriously he actually censored song lyrics in the 1953 film of Anita Loos's *Gentlemen Prefer Blondes*. To partially circumvent this, studios routinely reshot and recut films for European distribution.

A 1955 exposé of sin in movietown, *Hollywood Cesspool*, written by the author of *Sin's Surprise* and *The Blight of Booze* and published by the ominous-sounding Sword of the Lord Publishers, let no one off the hook. Evangelist Robert Sumner's list of "documented" party members included all of Huxley's Hollywood friends: Goddard, Chaplin, Meredith, Welles, and Houseman—alongside Humphry Bogart, Leonard Bernstein, Bette Davis, and Groucho Marx. This was the blacklisting publication *Red Channels* in spangles; somehow the writer forgot to include the documentation of his charges.[109]

"How Red is Hollywood?" Sumner quotes an ambitious Hollywood columnist. "My answer is 'How deep is the ocean, how high the sky?' Hollywood is Stalin's tightest Red fortress in America." To which Sumner appended, "It is impossible to be a 100% American and a devotee of the silver screen." To fundamentalists like this one, modern film was to blame for juvenile delinquency, broken homes, the rise in sex crimes, free love, even nervous disorders.

By the end of the fifties, following his debacle with Magoo and the poor staging of *Genius*, Huxley turned to the lecture podium to support himself. He accepted academic appointments here and there, lecturing at Stanford ("on Creative Writing, whatever that is") and at Santa Barbara's Center for the Study of Democratic Institutions.

With the widespread use of *Brave New World* as a school text, Huxley again counted a small but steady income from his writing. He published popular essays in *The Saturday Evening Post;* the Long Island paper *Newsday* commissioned the series eventually published as *Brave New World Revisited.* The latter became his text on the college lecture circuit across the United States and abroad. The Huxley who spoke at campuses like Fort Lewis State College in Durango, Colorado, had little in common with the timorous, spindly intellectual who had lectured on pacifism twenty-one years earlier. Now he stood straight with a clear, steady voice; he met people on their own terms, not glowering down at them if they said something idiotic. Unfortunately, Huxley hit the campus circuit a few years too soon; the conservative trend in American universities had not yet fallen before the yeasty idealism of the Kennedy and civil rights era.

In Durango, students in cowboy garb watched with growing perplexity as this specter of English gentility read from his notes in the college gym. Students could barely understand his Oxfordian English. As the last light of the afternoon filtered through the gym windows, many of the students left midtalk, their boots clacking on the wooden floor.[110]

Huxley was more in his element that autumn, when he, Stephen Spender, Bertrand Russell, and E. M. Forster had a reunion of sorts in London. Huxley had just come from South America, where he had been greeted as one of England's greatest living authors. The front page of the São Paulo paper had run banner headlines: HUXLEY ARRIVES. He found England old-fashioned after São Paulo ("no skyscrapers in sight") and was amused by the incestuousness of London's literary life, where "Cyril Connolly is being cited as a co-respondent by the man whom *he* cited as a co-respondent last year, the lady having (by force of habit, I suppose) injudiciously slept with her former husband after her second marriage." While Huxley reveled in internecine gossip, it reminded him why he left London following attacks on his pacifism.

Julian had just been knighted; Aldous had likewise been proposed, but Laura felt uncomfortable with the honor: "We led a different life here in California than his brother did. We would go down to the store in shorts, take the garbage in and out. . . . I couldn't see anyone calling me 'Lady Laura.' " Aldous also did not want to detract from Julian's recognition and wrote the Queen politely refusing. He was nonetheless received at Windsor and by the provost at Eton. The honors list, the visiting professorships—Huxley was slowing down to celebrity. In May 1959, he received the Award of Merit for the Novel from the American Academy of Arts and Letters.

The Huxley house atop Deronda Drive in the Hollywood Hills continued a major joy. Laura had outfitted it with dazzlingly white floor tiles and huge windows; Huxley saw visitors (and his work) more clearly.

Gerald Heard would drop by occasionally. He was becoming a guru in his own right, known nationally not only for his Vedantist/psychic/gay writings but as a leader in psychedelic experiments. He gave biweekly audiences in L.A. at the Coronet Theatre on La Cienega. One neophyte recalled: "He was a dramatic speaker leaning out of the shadows or back into them to make a point to the cream of the Hollywood intellectual/psychic community, a hundred of us at a time. Heard's magnetic power was derived from his particularly penetrating eyes; he spoke extemporaneously, without notes; we talked of him as an 'advanced contemplative.' This was after Heard's break with the Vedanta Society which came, I believe, after he witnessed a heterosexual couple meet and fall in love at one of his classes there."[111] Heard's devotees called themselves the Wayfarers and published a newsletter.

In the late fifties, Heard continued to articulate male homosexuality, deeply influencing the founders of the Mattachine Society and Dorr Leg, a founder of the homosexual journal *One* (for which Heard wrote under the pseudonym, D. B. Vest). Heard urged self-sufficient gay commmunities and suggested the term "isophyl" (lover of the same) in place of "homosexual":

> Heard urged gays to go beyond seeking fair treatment from the host majority, to consciousness-raising within our own community. We must not be so lured by acceptance by a dreary, conformist, money-mad society that we sally out in hyper-male tweeds or leather, putting down swishes and drags. Gays need to accept and act out their effeminate urges as well as their need for male display.[112]

Unfortunately for Huxley, this celebrity meant Heard was often absent giving workshops around the country. Huxley still visited Peggy Kiskadden, but she was occupied full-time with nursing Bill, who barely recovered from an operation in February 1958. Pauline and Anita had long since moved to New York, and Grace, mildly horrified at Huxley's abrupt wedding, remained distant. On stops to San Francisco, he would visit Gregory Bateson and Alan Watts, but his circle of intimates had narrowed.

One warm August evening in 1959, while Laura was out or at Ginny's, Huxley was late starting his afternoon walk. Just as the sun dipped into the Pacific, he strayed out on a path by a canyon near his home. Along the fire trail grew prickly pear cactus and sagebrush, fragrant with the warm currents rising from the city. Raptors circled overhead in the gentle wind.

Halfway down the path, he stepped off the edge (or stumbled on a curb); dusk was the worst time for his depth perception. Down he plunged into the cactus and dust, feet first, injuring his back. He lay there in the dark for some time before he could get to his feet and limp home.

In writing to Matthew of his fall, he admitted it gave him considerable pain for three weeks, as his back recovered, but he also took pride in the working of his new principle. "This was so trifling in comparison to what I might have suffered, if I hadn't fallen in the most perfect way imaginable . . . I can only think of the accident with the most profound thankfulness; if ever guardian angels were at hand, it was on that night."[113]

Some thought Laura neglectful, but, other than this incident, Aldous seems to have thrived on his new independence. Working around his disability opened endless exploration. He was more his own man, whether this meant fixing himself a soup he fancied or traveling cross-country on his own.

Despite his fall, Huxley continued his lectures at Berkeley, Arizona, and other campuses the next year. He moved briefly to Topeka, Kansas, as a visiting scholar at the Menninger Foundation, a post which puzzled many, for Menninger was the most distinguished training center for Freudian analysts and Huxley a public opponent of analysis: "Freud's greatest error, it seems to me, was to not have paid sufficient attention to the more than personal not-self. [He] concentrated the therapist's attentions on the self and its [basements full of] rats and black beetles." [114]

"It was around that time that Aldous developed a radiance," his nephew Francis said. "You felt in his presence something—extraordinary." [115] Huxley had relaxed into his own personality; however out of step with his time he might have been, he was sure of himself. "He seemed to radiate charisma," his brother remarked after a visit. [116] Aldous finally returned to his utopian novel, into which he trusted this inner peace.

Progress on the work came at a cost, however, for Huxley was sorely distracted. The calm which had surrounded him burst: Huxley discovered that he too had cancer.

While at the Menninger, Aldous had visited a dentist and asked what could be done about a new growth on his tongue. The dentist tried to scrape it off, according to Laura, thus scattering the malignant cells throughout Huxley's system.

"Shantih"—"The peace which passeth understanding"—with which his friend T. S. Eliot ended *The Waste Land*, was to receive its final test.

ELEVEN

ISLAND

"He calls it dope and feels about it all the disapproval that, by conditioned reflex, the dirty word evokes. We, on the contrary, give the stuff good names—the *moksha*-medicine, the reality revealer, the truth-and-beauty pill. And we know, by direct experience, that the good names are deserved. Whereas our young friend here has no firsthand knowledge of the stuff and can't be persuaded even to give it a try. For him, it's dope and dope is something that, by definition, no decent person ever indulges in."   (1961)

On May 12, 1960, Aldous Huxley lay in a dreary hospital bed in Los Angeles, awaiting a biopsy for a disturbing bump on his tongue. Something hurt when he ate, he had told his doctor, who'd hurriedly booked a hospital room. After a general anesthetic, a team of doctors cut away a sliver of his tongue for testing.

He was wheeled back to his room while the laboratory staff examined the tissue. Laura awaited the verdict in a corridor smelling of disinfectant:

> " 'It is malignant,' the doctor told me. He was an intelligent man, quite young, with ice-blue eyes. 'We have a very good surgeon here; he is a specialist in this type of operation.'
>
> " 'What operation?'
>
> " 'The best thing to do for this malignancy is to cut out one third of the tongue.'

> "Aldous's speech, that perfection of each sound, his love for words, his pleasure in reading poetry aloud! . . . I wanted to strike the man, to shout defiantly . . . but I only murmured: 'But he is a public speaker . . .'
>
> " 'Yes, yes, his speech will be a little impaired, but there are exercises . . .' "[1]

Aldous Huxley currently earned his living as a lecturer. After an operation, he would have spoken as thickly as the Irishman with paraphasia in *Point Counter Point*.[2] Cancer had already taken his mother and Maria; now it had come for him.

Laura worried about being railroaded into a hasty decision. The next day, a surgeon entered the sickroom with a large writing tablet and made a drawing of the tongue; he showed the couple where he proposed to saw. His hands trembled as he talked. After a long silence Aldous said, "We will let you know."

As soon as the doctor left the room, Laura insisted they leave immediately. "You mean escape?" Aldous asked quizzically. In answer, she handed him his clothes. They walked briskly out the door, nurses shouting, "He has not been dismissed! The papers, the signatures . . ."

"Send us the bill at home," Laura answered and spirited him into the elevator.[3]

An hour later they visited prominent cancer researcher Dr. Max Cutler, whom Huxley had last consulted before Maria's death. "I will not consider this type of extensive and mutilating surgery," Aldous told him. "Isn't there something else that can be done?"

"There is only one alternative," Cutler told them: radium needles.[4]

Huxley's choice was not a simple one. Surgery could prolong his life, removing the cancer before it could metastasize. Radium needles might not have the same effect, though they would almost certainly heal his tongue. The clearheaded communicator chose between "perfect functioning" of his speech organs and prolonging his life. The worst part was that there was no way of predicting what might happen: was it worth becoming dumb to extend his life? Which did he prefer, fate seemed to ask: being dead or being handicapped?

$\mathbf{H}$e had so many things to write and say. Only two weeks earlier, he had written to Matthew of lectures slated for Berkeley and Idaho State; he had hoped to rest before lecturing full-time at Dartmouth and at the Massachusetts Institute of Technology that Autumn.[5] Lecturing—so traumatic for Huxley (and Anthony Beavis) at the time of *Eyeless in Gaza*—had become second nature. Its income supplanted screenwriting, a profession drowning in fluff. His Magoo version of *Don Quixote* seemed the height of literacy amidst the recent suburban melodrama—*Gidget* (1959) and *Tammy Tell Me True* (1961), with Miss Teen Queen Sandra Dee.

Contract screenwriting jobs had largely disappeared. In 1945, 490 screenwriters were on studio payrolls; by 1960, less than a tenth remained. In response, the Writers' Guild called a prolonged strike, the first of many for residual royalties from television and video sales.[6]

Foreign films—the words evoke smoldering passion to a generation of filmgoers—had developed regular showcases, such as the Thalia on New York's Upper West Side. By 1960, Italian and French films had cut deeply into Hollywood's box office. American producers offered endless adolescence to the baby-boom generation, thinking them a nation of Gidgets and Mousketeers.

The town of Hollywood was also changing. From the Huxleys' terrace, they looked down on urban blight in the flatlands. Ranch-style developments splintered the carefully planned, eucalyptus-scented alleys of Hollywoodland.

Hollywood's big news of the 1959–1960 season was Smell-o-Vision, which wafted scents matching the action through the air-conditioning vents of the theater. (Perhaps next to arrive would be the feelies Huxley invented for *Brave New World*, in which moviegoers received tactile sensations by holding balls on the arms of their seats.) Unfortunately, the smell of hamburgers and fries lingered as the odor of gunfire filled the hall, creating truly repulsive results. One long-time Hollywood columnist was moved to comment: "First they talked, then they moved, now they smell."[7]

This just about summed up Huxley's current attitude toward his former profession. According to Robert Craft, about the only films

Huxley enjoyed were documentaries, particularly his favorite, *The Sex Life of Lobsters*. Though he had thrown himself into earlier, literary projects such as *Jane Eyre*, he increasingly disliked visiting cinemas, where he was obliged to sit in the first row. "Semi-minus Epsilons," he moaned to Stravinsky, who egged him on. "Inconceivable tripe," Huxley said as he squirmed in his seat.[8] Television little impressed him, though he appeared occasionally on talk shows. His lecturing experience allowed him to deliver on cue, as he did in a teleconference with Jawaharlal Nehru and others on population control.[9] Otherwise, he resented television's inherent reductionism and its inflated salaries: "The writer of the *Beverly Hillbillies* earns more in a week than I do in a year," he told another writer morosely.[10]

In the end, Huxley chose the immediate solution to his disease, radium needles. He would not be speechless in his final years. Perhaps science, Old Artificer, would develop a new cure.

As Maria had earlier, and as Huxley's father had done before that, Aldous refused to let friends and family know his condition. Bill Kiskadden, Dr. Cutler, and Laura knew. He checked into the Good Samaritan Hospital as Mr. Matthew Leonard on May 31, 1960. The treatment passed quickly, the stay was short. Sharp fingers of radiation cauterized his flesh.

The summer Huxley chose not to have an operation on his tongue he spent writing *Island*, a novel which, like *Eyeless in Gaza*, simply would not behave. "After a day or two or three he would say, 'Nothing!—I am stuck,' " Laura recalled. " 'I get these stupid ideas that I cannot do ever anything again.' "[11]

Huxley had struggled with a positive utopia at least since his preface to the reissue of *Brave New World* in 1946. There, haunted by the notion of a sequel, he had speculated on a "Higher Utilitarianism" whose economics were "decentralist and Henry Georgian," with "politics Kropotkinesque and co-operative."[12] Immediately afterward, he had written *Science, Liberty and Peace*, to spell out the organization of such a society. *Ape*, which followed, had been a dystopia (like *Brave New World*).

The first inkling that Huxley would write a utopian novel occurs in a letter to Humphry Osmond the month before he took his first mescaline trip in 1953.[13] Here the novel stalled, as Huxley became absorbed in testing psychedelics and seeing for himself. Yet he needed a sequel to *Brave New World;* the book trailed him, as acclaimed works will. The problem, he had realized, was that "it's always a great deal easier to write about negative than about positive things, easier to criticize negative things than to set up positives."[14]

Accentuating the positive was not a new dilemma for utopians, as Huxley knew. Over the years he had read Wells's *A Modern Utopia* and written prefaces to *Erewhon* and *Looking Backward;* he often referred to Swift's utopian writings and to William Morris's *News from Nowhere.* Other basic works from the American utopian tradition were Hawthorne's *Blithedale Romance* (set partly at Brook Farm), Melville's *Typee,* and Austin Wright's *Islandia.*

Huxley's habit of writing essay in the guise of fiction has been noted by virtually every critic of his work. Over the years, as more of a message made its way into his prose, the battle between exposition and narration had grown pitched. The struggle between ideas and their fictional embodiment had frustrated Huxley to the point where he'd decided he was "congenitally unsuited" to fiction. Huxley's fictional output resembles a bell-shaped curve, tapering off after the late forties. Once he had glimpsed the Perennial Philosophy, perhaps it was more difficult to laugh at human foibles; the species needed a stern schoolmaster more than a satirist, persuasion more than repartee.

Creating a true utopia to balance *Brave New World* returned him to the messy business of sustaining a narrative. Huxley's first more-or-less complete projection of *Island,* "an imaginary society, whose purpose is to get its members to realize their highest potentialities," occurred in a letter in March 1956:

> I shall place the fable, not in the future, but on an island, hypothetical, in the Indian ocean, not far from the Andamans, and inhabited by people who are descended from Buddhist colonists from the mainland, and so know all about Tantra (which is more than I do—but one can do some learning and some pretending!).
>
> To build a bridge between them and us, I postulate an Englishman who made a fortune in the most cynical way in the later days of the east India Company, who came to explore the island and stayed

because he saw, in a kind of psychological conversion, that its people knew most of the answers. He stays, organizes a kind of East-West school of wisdom . . . [including] a sacramental view of sex and other natural functions.[15]

By July he had begun sketches, ruminating still on the project's difficulties, particularly how to personalize its "tantric philosophy and praxis." "I do hope I can bring this off with some measure of success," he closed a letter to Osmond.[16]

This lack of confidence asserted itself as it had in writing *Eyeless in Gaza* and in his first screenplays. Huxley froze when writing himself a new identity—as a pacifist, as a screenwriter, or, now, as a literary guru. "He never had any problem in writing essays or prefaces," Laura pointed out. "That was very easy, and he would enjoy it."[17]

Periodically he encountered snags; he put *Island* aside to write *Brave New World Revisited*. When he returned to it in June 1958, the same literary stage fright remained. "I don't know yet if I have a satisfactory fable, or . . . how reluctant people will be to read material which isn't straight story telling."[18]

He had the summer to recover before moving to Cambridge. Following his radium needle treatments, Huxley arrived at MIT at the end of September, alone. Professor Roy Lamson and his wife Peggy found him an apartment and discussed the series of lectures he was to give entitled *What a Piece of Work Is Man*. In October 1960 1,500 people filled Kresge Auditorium for the first one. Huxley invited students up to his place for a small at-home once a week. Probably the most exciting experience of the term came via a phone call from Dr. Timothy Leary, recently billeted in Harvard's Center for Personality Research.

Leary, a tall, personality-test psychologist, looked eminently professional in gray flannels and crew cut. He had published *The Interpersonal Diagnosis of Personality*, which one psychology journal had heralded as the most important book of the year. As Aldous arrived, Leary was planning experiments with psilocybin, synthesized from the "magic mushroom," *psilocybe cubensis*.

Thus the famous psychedelic research project at Harvard began, on quiet Divinity Alley in Cambridge, where Richard Alpert, Ralph Metzner, Andrew Weil, and others charted the psychoactive effects of marijuana, LSD, and other substances—the first large-scale explorations under prestigious academic auspices. The project was too exciting. The "new kind of microscope" drew a disproportionate number of graduate students (and hence academic envy). Self- and group-use by the experimenters added a fuzzy subjectivity to their work.

Osmond and Huxley dined with Leary. The veteran British mind-researchers found Leary "on the square side," but thought his connections with Harvard added respectability to psychedelics.[19] Thus, almost by chance, Huxley sat in on the creation of the world's first psychedelic curriculum. Around Thanksgiving, the first shipment of psilocybin arrived and everybody at the center, Huxley included, began to trip. Ever the well-read traveling companion, Huxley brought in Théophile Gautier's accounts of the Hashish Club of Paris from the previous century.

Leary brought his magic pills over to Huxley's apartment; they spent three hours listening to Bach, Mozart, African drums, and Ravi Shankar, Aldous cross-legged in lotus position, meditating behind closed eyes.

All at once he turned to Leary: "So you don't know what to do with this bloody philosopher's stone we have stumbled unto?" He reminded the psychologist how in many cultures transcendental substances remain esoteric, out of public sight.

"But society needs this information," Leary remembers having answered.

"These are evolutionary matters; they cannot be rushed. Work privately. Initiate artists, writers, poets, jazz musicians. . . . Your role is quite simple. Become a cheerleader for evolution. That's what I did and my grandfather before me." Now while this syntax doesn't sound like Huxley, the ending does: a warning that managers of minds "from the Vatican to Harvard" have been in the business of channeling consciousness for a long time, "and they are not about to give up their monopoly."[20]

At that time, Leary was also guiding sessions with Allen Ginsberg and Jack Kerouac (who persisted in drinking alcohol while tripping—and is credited with inventing a Beat homily under psilocybin: "Walking on water wasn't made in a day").

Psychedelic research was giving way to a psychedelic movement, and Leary had become its stupefied lightning rod. Robert Graves had experimented more quietly with psychedelics, writing up the experience in *Food for Centaurs* (1960). Fully abreast of this creeping intellectual interest, the CIA had begun its secret experiments with drugs and mind control.

Early experimenters overlooked the adaptability of the experience for diverse audiences, providing entertainment (but not enlightenment) to prominent Washingtonians, including, some said, the Kennedy brothers. A conservative vice president at J. P. Morgan, Gordon Watson, discovered traditional psilocybin use in Mexico. The disassociative but ultimately unifying effects of psilocybin worked equally splendidly on bankers and trainmen: Neal Cassady, the Beats' antihero, called mushrooms "the Rolls-Royce of dope."[21]

In only a few years, the psychedelic movement had swirled beyond the coterie which had furthered its exploration in the fifties. As the man then most publicly associated with mind-expanding chemicals, Huxley tried to dissuade Leary from making psychedelics a mass phenomenon. Huxley and Leary's colleagues at Harvard discussed eliminating nonmedical use, warning that excessive publicity might lead to prohibition.

A generation younger than Huxley but with all the arrogance of a Grandier, Leary underestimated the witch hunting his work would provoke. He brought psychedelics into the Concord State Prison to prove that guided experiments—supplemented by support services after release—could reduce recidivism. He was right, but as word spread and undergraduates queued up for supplies, his resignation from Harvard was virtually assured. Alpert and Leary debated whether mild, disorienting dosages were better than dramatically larger ones. Discussions like these reeked of playing God, a hobby of the so-called psychedelic fringe, the "acid fascists."[22]

Leary, Huxley, and the Harvard crew soon discovered that setting, company, and mood determined whether one emerged from a psychedelic session as a mystic or as a carouser. Psychedelics stimulated twenty-year-old collegians in a distinctly different manner (sexually, politically) from the way they affected sedate middle-aged intellectuals committed to religious study. From psychedelic drugs Huxley had learned the inner strength to feel what he knew, to tear down emotional barriers, to find a new way of seeing. Cary Grant found in LSD a strengthened resolve to limit his drinking;[23] others might encounter only a good time.

Huxley also warned that the drug might become *too* exclusive, as demonstrated by his anger at Beverly Hills psychologists who offered LSD in "therapeutic" sessions at $100 per session. He was caught between "professional" usage and Leary, wafted on the egalitarian tide of his decade. In December, Huxley returned to California.

At night, in the lizard-dry air of the Hollywood Hills, Aldous Huxley took pride in showing visitors how Los Angeles shimmered below his terrace. The house sat on a bluff surrounded by high desert chaparral, the dry brushland which covers vast stretches of the Southwest. Just to the east lay Griffith Park and the Observatory. To the west, the eye swept past downtown city hall, across Santa Monica to the ocean. Below, boulevards stretched into a vast, noisy carpet of lights.

At dusk on a May evening in 1961, the reds and the oranges of the smoggy city drained into the sea. It was a hot day with an even hotter wind. Fire weather.

Aldous was alone in his study, working on *Island*. Laura was running errands, stopping on her way up the hill to feed the cat at Ginny's house. She was in an excellent mood, returning home from seeing a client. As the sunset faded, the hills kept their orange glow. Not until Laura turned into Ginny's driveway did she notice the fire chief's car 500 yards from her own house. In Ginny's backyard, she saw flames racing up from the canyon.

The region where the Huxleys lived belonged to a fire-prone belt which nature probably never intended to be inhabited by humans. In May and June, following periodic droughts, wildfires break out from Montana to Southern California; sometimes as many as a million acres are ablaze. Flames lick the dry edges of California's inland coastal range. After the fires, grasses sprout on the blackened land and the forest is renewed. But humans must interfere with nature: the shrubs that developers plant multiply until the hillsides are covered with tinder.

No one found out what ignited that fire that day: an electric storm's bolt crashing down to dry earth, arson, a spark carried by a Santa Ana wind. "Beyond the trees was a black hillside where the fire had browsed," wrote Ross MacDonald in his classic description of a Los Angeles fire. "The flames that from a distance had looked like artillery flashes were crashing through the thick chaparral like cavalry."[24]

As the fire roared toward her, Laura was immobilized in Ginny's yard "by the wild grace of the flames, by the ever-changing voice of the wind." She stood and watched, then slowly walked into the kitchen to open a tin of food for the cat. She walked past a fur coat, thinking "too hot for that now."[25]

> Somehow I didn't touch anything, although in Ginny's house I should have taken some things that I knew were irreplaceable and also even money—there was some stock, but I didn't do it. . . .
> No, it was very strange, because usually, in emergencies I am quite prompt; and instead I was passive.[26]

In Aldous's room a few hundred yards away, it must have been hot. Before he could have seen flames, he would have heard their sound, like an infernal popcorn popper. A low black cloud seeped into his study, carrying a charred, chemical bite. Still he stayed upstairs. "Aldous might not have realized how far the fire had gone," Peggy Kiskadden reflected.[27]

A neighboring architect ran into Ginny's house. He led Laura back to her car, and she drove home. The fire bloomed in the darkness and lurched unsteadily up the canyon walls, jumping from bush to bush, their tips exploding in flame. Laura found Aldous upstairs in his study without a fire escape. The light must have been marvelous—all the brightness he could ask for, at last.

They moved the car down the hill, past Ginny's house, before Aldous realized how close to incineration their own home was. "The road was already swept by fire. We could not get to our car or walk home the usual way," Laura wrote in *This Timeless Moment*. A stranger drove them back around the hill, where they arrived just as the plants on the terrace burst into flame. Aldous ran upstairs to his study for his manuscript of *Island*, but Laura stayed in the living room, transfixed.

> *Fire is hypnotic, I think. There I was on the top of the hill, and the windows were open and I saw the curtains going towards the fire. The curtains were very light and went through the windows. It was something delightful. . . .*[28]

She was having her own transcendental moment, comparable, perhaps, to Aldous's bright May morning. She walked from one room to another, touching her objects, savoring the cool feel of a glass Steuben owl. The stranger trailed behind her, asking what she wanted removed. Aldous grabbed a few suits; Laura took a dress or two from her closet, as if going away for a weekend.

People gathered outside. Huxley laid down his clothes and manuscript and stood there. Laura's shock must have been catching. Why else stand before a garage full of papers about to burn and not salvage them? He was a professional editor and bibliophile; he knew the worth of literary papers.

Perhaps he couldn't see well enough to act. A reporter from *Time* said he was frantic and had to be restrained; Aldous denied it. Laura said that he reacted with dispassion. Perhaps a part of him wished it all would burn. He may have suspected his cancer had returned.

Laura picked up her 256-year-old Guarnieri violin and walked out the door. Something Aldous cherished remained: a turn-of-the-century, domed chest he had carried everywhere for the last forty years. It contained Maria's letters and journals—thousands of pages of their life together. There was the manuscript of *St. Mawr* which Lawrence had given him, letters from Bertrand Russell. A few months before, he had written to Matthew about shipping him manuscripts for storage. His son had no closet space. The papers curled and burst into ash.

In a tone more wry than desperate, Huxley recalled what happened next: "The gang [of local teenagers] warned me about fifteen minutes before the arrival of the TV camera-trucks which, in turn, were half an hour ahead of the fire-engines that could have saved the house. After the boys had guided me to safety, by the one passable street, I noticed that some familiar faces among them were absent. I said I was concerned about them, but the leader told me not to worry, that they were merely out starting more fires."[29]

The reporters found frightened people on a burned-out hillside; they knew the tall, erect gentleman was a highbrow. He looked the part—withdrawn, ineffective, wringing his hands at the end of his library and fortune. After the flames burned down, Aldous and Laura checked into a hotel at the bottom of the hill.

The next day, they poked through the ashes, accompanied by reporters and curiosity seekers. They found a marble bust of Maria amid the twisted wreckage. Eight chimneys stood in a row, surrounded by the acrid ashes. Gone were his manuscripts, shelves of first editions of his work, the library of a lifetime. Reporters asked if he planned to rebuild, but the writer shook his head; he was still assessing losses. Toting up all that had burned was like going over a supermarket receipt in reverse, where each item discovered was a loss. "HUXLEY TREASURES NOW JUST ASHES" read the day's headline.[30]

Observers reported two different reactions. Some say Huxley's losses devastated him; some say it afforded an unwilling but practical example of nonattachment.

In 1947, Huxley had tried to anticipate his feelings at such a loss in an article entitled "If My Library Burned Tonight": "To enter the shell of a well-loved room and to find it empty except for a thick carpet of ashes that were once one's favorite literature—the very thought of it is depressing."[31]

One of those who found Huxley devastated was his cousin Renée Haynes, who heard about the fire over lunch with him soon afterward at London's Tate Gallery. He asked what she thought he should write next. She came up with an obvious answer: " 'Why not write your life?' His searching eye had a look of despair: 'How could I? All the records were burnt in the fire!' "[32]

Laura remembers him moody and despondent, perhaps also due to a recurrence of pain in his mouth. Jake Zeitlin likewise remembers Huxley as disconsolate, particularly at the loss of out-of-print European and Oriental books. This could also have been Zeitlin's own despondency. A month before, he had been asked to inventory the library for a partial sale. The great book collector waited too long.

Others suggest—and Huxley's own letters tend to authenticate—that he passed his involuntary test of nonattachment. The day after the fire, he wrote Robert Hutchins, ex-president of the Ford Foundation and the man who had first arranged for him to lecture in Santa Barbara:

> It is odd to be starting from scratch at my age—with literally nothing in the way of possessions, books, mementos, letters, diaries. I am evidently intended to learn, a little in advance of the final denudation, that you can't take it with you.[33]

The letter he wrote to his British editor, Ian Parsons, at Chatto & Windus is even less preoccupied: "My house is no more. It went last Friday night in a raging brush fire fanned by a gale, and with it went books, papers, MSS, old letters, etc—all of the accumulations. So now I am preparing to start again from scratch. I saved the MS of *Island* and hope to finish it in the next two or three weeks—tho' at the moment writing seems difficult."[34]

He complained about writing *Island*—but not about the loss of all of his possessions at once. His nephew Siggy, Rose's teenage son, whom he saw regularly, remembers no complaints after the fire. Juliette, in her autobiography, may have the last word: "In one moment his past was destroyed utterly and the future stripped like vacant land. Yet, in the end, it must be seen that although he had to endure many calamities, he achieved a profound serenity of acceptance."[35]

One thing is for certain: the traumatic episode produced passages as emotional as any Huxley had ever written:

> Openness to bliss and understanding was also, he realized, an openness to terror, to total incomprehension. Like some alien creature lodged within his chest and struggling in anguish, his heart started to beat with a violence that made him tremble. (Island, 280)

Aldous and Laura stayed on at the hotel for a week or so, then he moved in with Gerald in Santa Monica. There Huxley finished the last chapter of *Island*, including the blazing, stream-of-other-consciousness passages which culminated his career as a novelist.

The plot of *Island* reads like an updated version of *Lost Horizon*, the film circulating in Huxley's first months in America. Journalist

Will Farnaby (who doubles as private ambassador for an oil million-aire) visits twin islands located somewhere between Ceylon and Sumatra. One was a Westernized oil-producing colony; the other, Pala, a remote Buddhist enclave which refuses industrial development.

In an entry worthy of Candide's descent into El Dorado, Farnaby is shipwrecked in Pala. His healing is superintended by descendants of the wise Raja and the Scottish doctor who set in motion the uto-pian community. In exchange for a year's paid vacation, Farnaby se-cretly begins to sell out Pala to an oil-seeking, Westernized zealot; Huxley's parody of her Crusade of the Spirit shows that the author had not mellowed in his hostility to fundamentalism.

Island was Huxley's *Temptation of the West*, his far-reaching effort to unify Buddhist quietism with Western pragmatism. In direct lineage to Huxley's synthesis of world religions in *The Perennial Philosophy*, the book sways under the weight of his exposition.

In *Island*, Huxley applied an aesthetic similar to Rousseau's in *Emile*; by the end of the sixties, those advocating a warmed-over be-lief in innate goodness would be called "hippies." *Island* is Huxley's proto-hippie book, developing themes of his American years: decen-tralizing institutions and replacing them by cooperatives and com-munes, promoting alternative medicine and education (including med-itation, hypnosis, and mind-expanding drugs), and popularizing environmental balance based on population restraint.

This summation reads like a potpourri, but Huxley was ex-tremely attentive to its balance—for instance, in his handling of drugs. Pala occasionally teaches its children via *moksha*, a substance resem-bling the psilocybin Huxley tried with Leary. Palanese psychedelic experiences are nonrecreational and carefully supervised by teachers. When the castaway journalist undergoes his own psychedelic experi-ence, enjoying it so much he doesn't want to return to earth, he is rebuked by his guide: "Pure Spirit, one hundred percent proof—that's a drink that only the most hardened contemplation guzzlers indulge in. Bodhisattvas dilute their Nirvana with equal parts of love and work" (*Island*, 273).

Huxley never suggested that the insights of mind-expanding drugs were without responsibility or cost; for him they were a tool best used in the context of spiritual discipline—with a competent guide, in a stable surrounding. He was acutely conscious of the difference separating mind-activating drugs (such as mushrooms) and alcohol or cocaine. He had written to Osmond from Peru about cocaine: "a most unsatisfactory and dangerous mind-changing drug—coca—still consumed in great quantities."[36]

Huxley had learned his lesson about publicizing drugs; their use could only be a beginning, he now insisted.

"So why bother to meditate," Farnaby asks his guide after his trip.

" 'You might as well ask, why bother to eat your dinner?'

" 'But, according to you, the *moksha*-medicine is dinner.'

" 'It's a banquet,' she said emphatically. 'And that's precisely why there has to be meditation. You can't have banquets every day. They're too rich and they last too long. Besides, banquets are provided by a caterer; you don't have any part in the preparation of them. For your everyday diet you have to do your own cooking' " (*Island*, 189).

Self-conscious references to illumination stretch across the novel like a welcome-home banner for a football team. For Huxley, sixty-seven, illumination increasingly meant death and liberation; *Island* contains Huxley's *ars moriendi*. Two deaths are contrasted: a composite character of his mother and his wife, under the influence of Western medicine:

> *She was the only person I ever loved, and when I was sixteen she got cancer. Off with the right breast; then, a year later, off with the left. And after that nine months of X-rays and radiation sickness. . . .* (100)

and a Buddhist in Pala:

> *No rhetoric, no tremulos, no self-conscious persona putting on its celebrated imitations of Christ or Goethe or Little Nell. And, of course, no theology, no metaphysics. Just the fact of dying and the fact of the Clear Light. So throw away all your baggage and go forward.* (266)

If the work dwells on the right way to die, it also takes up the right way to heal. Huxley created his own medical specialty, a "neurotheologian": "Somebody who thinks about people, in terms, simultaneously, of the Clear Light of the Void and the vegetative nervous system" (*Island*, 94).

Island ends on a heroic note worthy of the old Quaker hymn

"Amazing Grace": "I once was lost, but now am found/Was blind, but now I see." Like Anthony Beavis in *Eyeless in Gaza*, Farnaby must begin as a louse, "the man who won't take Yes for an answer," before he can, at the end, see with the infernally bright eyes of the convert:

> Little by little his fears had died away; the awareness of this intimate, unexpected, potentially dangerous contact remained. An awareness so acute and, because the eyes were supremely vulnerable, so absorbing that he had nothing to spare for the inner light or the horrors and vulgarities revealed by it. "Pay attention," she whispered. (Island, 287)

Huxley planted weeds and snakes in Eden, however. Just as Farnaby develops compassion, troops from the neighboring island take over Pala and her oil wealth.

Why did Huxley doom his utopia?—to show he was no Pollyanna, perhaps, or to underscore that where peace is concerned, no man is an island.

Eyeless in Gaza and *Island* stand like bookends around Huxley's American years. The differences in the lead characters reveal the distance Huxley had come during that time. Both heroes are flawed by the lack of love against which Huxley's mother warned him, but they arrive at different destinations. Beavis struggles and finds the point of life; Farnaby sees, but only too late to act. While the ending of *Eyeless* is hopeful, a military invasion of Pala provides a more modern triumph to materialism. Another contrast is their national stereotypes. Beavis is the model of a British public-school prig, at least initially. Farnaby is not accidentally American; he speaks the language of Sam Spade "in the best movie tycoon style."[37]

As literature, *Eyeless* surpasses the later work; its snapshot-album format develops more handily than *Island*'s mulish pace. *Eyeless*'s characters are rounded and quirky, whereas the inhabitants of Pala, utopia's baggage carriers, are scantily described.

Finally, *Island*'s tone is pedagogic. This didacticism had crept forward steadily in Huxley's American fiction: Mr. Propter in *After Many a Summer Dies the Swan*, John Barnack in *Time Must Have a Stop*, even the Arch-Vicar in *Ape and Essence*.

This schoolmasterly streak in Huxley's writings was a predictable, though misunderstood, turn for an author descended from George Huxley, senior assistant master of Great Ealing, Arnold of Rugby, and T.H., appointed to the London School Board. Aldous's father, mother, and sister were all schoolmasters.[38]

Huxley's educational ideals centered around his "principle of perfect functioning": "Given mysticism and such psycho-physical techniques as the Bates method and the Alexander method, it is possible to conceive of a totally new kind of education starting at the level of bodily function and going up to the heights of the spirit."[39] Thus, children in *Island* study Buddhism and ecology to develop their sense of belonging on the earth:

> *Which is better: to have Fun with Fungi or to have Idiocy with Ideology, to have Wars because of Words, to have Tomorrow's Misdeeds out of Yesterday's Miscreeds?*[40]

*I*sland became a cookbook for student rebellions of the 1960s. The book was quoted over oatmeal and coffee in college dorms—as were parallel American science fiction novels of the sixties, Robert Heinlein's *Stranger in a Strange Land* and Kurt Vonnegut's *Cat's Cradle.*

Matching the impatience of this new audience, Huxley grew more forceful in condemning the greed of companies polluting America:

> *Forgive them, for they know not what they do. But will there be forgiveness for those who know quite well what they are doing, and how bad it is, but refuse, nonetheless, to stop?*
>
> *Everybody knows (there is no question of, in this case, of extenuating ignorance) that it is sheer folly to cut down forests without replanting. But more money can be made that way, more quickly. Over vast areas of the Earth the lumber industry is indulging in this kind of insane delinquency.*[41]

The serious study of the biosphere remained in its infancy as a science; rarer still were long-range plans for the earth's restoration.[42] Huxley considered the earth's degradation and overpopulation a moral rather than a geopolitical dilemma—the failure of human resolve. Long before Green parties and deep ecologists such as James Lovelock, before ecological activist organizations such as Earth First!, Huxley suggested that without alternative energy—wind and solar—the human-focused use of natural resources would lead to a global cancer as harrowing as his own:

> *For the ecologist, man's inhumanity to Nature deserves almost as strong a condemnation as man's inhumanity to man. Not only is it profoundly wicked, and profoundly stupid, to treat animals as though they were things, it is also wicked and stupid to treat things as though they were mere things. They should be treated as though they were component parts of a living planetary whole, within which human individuals and human societies are tissues and organs of a special kind—sometimes, alas, horribly infected, riddled with proliferating malignancy.*[43]

Huxley turned over his ms. to Harper in the summer of 1961. Cass Canfield thought the book overlong—one of the very few times the editor suggested cuts. Huxley acknowledged that he still hadn't resolved his problems balancing exposition and narration:

> *I know what I want to say clearly enough; the problem is how to embody the ideas. Of course, you can always talk them out in dialogue, but you can't have your characters talking indefinitely without becoming transparent—and tiresome. Then there's always the problem of point of view: who's going to tell the story or live the experiences? I've had a great deal of trouble working out the plot and rearranging sections that I've already written. Now I think I can see my way clear to the end. But I'm afraid it's getting hopelessly long.*[44]

Parsons and Canfield each suggested cuts; Huxley agreed to so many the manuscript was retyped during his visit to England that Autumn.[45] Huxley traveled alone; Laura was home taking care of Ginny, who had a broken collarbone. He circled Europe, speaking in England, Denmark, and France on para- and applied psychology. In Basel, visiting Dr. Albert Hofmann, synthesizer of LSD, Huxley struck friends as frail and gray, more silent than ever. Only when he talked of ideas did his color return and his eyes kindle. Pictures show a man whom nonattachment had made ghostly, fringed with silvery hair.

Laura joined him in July, and they visited her family in Italy and then Switzerland, for Krishnamurti's annual seminar. In October, Huxley returned to California, and corrected the galleys of *Island*. He waited to see what critics and public would think. Laura had moved them both into Virginia Pfeiffer's new house at the top of Mulholland Drive not far from the Hollywood sign. This made a sometimes crowded house—Laura, Ginny, Ginny's two adopted children—and Aldous, who slept in his own bedroom.[46]

On January 22, 1962, Laura guided Huxley on psilocybin. In the course of a trip, she asked him how one prepares for death:

> *Preparation for ultimate death* [he replied] *is to be aware that your highest and most intense form of life is accompanied by, and conditional upon, a series of small deaths all the time. We have to be dying to these obsessive memories.*[47]

Reactions to *Island* were polarized, mostly con. His old friend, Cyril Connolly, began his review in the *Sunday Times* with the phrase, "This is Huxley's most important novel since *Time Must Have a Stop*" (praise tempered by the fact that this was Huxley's *only* full-length novel since *Time*). In *Partisan Review*, Frank Kermode bluntly called it "one of the worst novels ever written." Again, Huxley had failed to anticipate the criticism his American writings would bring down upon his head, like the heaps of coal of biblical times, one of his favorite images of the Bible:

> *Aldous was appalled, I think (and certainly I am), at the fact that what he wrote in* Island *was not taken seriously. It was treated as a work of science fiction, when it was not fiction, because each one of the ways of living he described in* Island *was not a product of his fantasy, but something that had been tried in one place or another.*[48]

"*Island* has had a curiously mixed reception," Huxley wrote to his niece Claire White, "some people enthusiastic, others intensely hostile, nobody, it seems, indifferent. . . . It's with bad sentiments that one makes good novels. Which is why, as a novel, *Island* is so inadequate."[49]

In February, Laura drove him to Berkeley, where he was a full professor of Nothing-in-Particular, as he liked to call it, during one of the busiest springs of his life: in the first three weeks of April alone, he spoke in New York, Boston, Syracuse, Berkeley, Los Angeles, and Oregon.

In Berkeley, he found a graceful university town of 50,000—fringed with uncredentialed intellectuals, street poets, and unfrocked Zen types. Telegraph Avenue, by the campus, boasted Robbie's Cafeteria (where Allen Ginsberg washed dishes), the Café Mediterranean, extracurricular frolic and bookstores for the erudite. In the afternoons, Huxley walked along the quiet boulevards, scented by cherry and plum blossoms. One of the city's intersections, Tom Hayden later declared, was "America's first Liberated Zone."

As he had among the Hollywood expatriates or the psychedelic crew in Cambridge, Huxley entered a vanguard at the right moment. In 1962, Berkeley was an extraordinary university—one of the highest concentrations of Nobel Prize winners in the world, yet a campus where professors led students in breathing exercises on the lawn. There were free clinics and crash pads where travelers could unroll a sleeping bag just for asking. This was pre–Haight-Ashbury, before the Free Speech movement brought troops to the streets, before college students marched for integregation or donned gas masks to fight police.[50]

If some drew their philosophy from Mao and their savings from Daddy, the Berkeley students were nevertheless in a historic struggle. Unfortunately, many lacked historical perspective. A hiatus separated them from earlier revolutionists, who would have passed along their thirties' history but for McCarthyism.

In Berkeley, Huxley drew inspiration from his radio. In bed with the flu, with few visitors, he tuned in KPFA-FM, "precariously supported by the subscriptions of that eccentric minority that like to listen only to what is worth hearing . . . impromptu talks on every conceivable subject from Oriental religion and strontium 90, space exploration, race riots and why Johnny can't read. Rich mixed feeding, he wrote to Laura."[51]

The Pacifica stations (often called "free-speech radio") were one of the few political groups Huxley still supported. The FBI noted this in his file and underlined this excerpt from an interview with Mike Wallace: "Dictators of the future will find if you want to preserve power indefinitely you have to get the people's consent to the rule, and this they will do partly with drugs, as I foresaw in *Brave New World*, and partly by new techniques of propaganda."[52]

From Berkeley, Huxley visited New Mexico, closing a circle in his visit to America.

He urged the scientists at Los Alamos, the same ones he had excoriated in *Ape and Essence,* to explore "that other world of the mind—unmeasurable and unfathomable [and] make bridges from poetry to chemistry to mysticism."[53]

Preaching the vision quest to arms scientists, did he wonder if visions would only improve their bombs? Or did he stand before them like Isaiah and thunder, as he had earlier that summer, against missiles which

> turn at right angles, skim along the ground, shoot perpendicularly up into the air to avoid interception and finally be guided, warhead and all, to whatever orphanage or old people's home may have been selected as the target.
>
> All this concentrated knowledge, genius, hard work and devotion, not to mention all those incalculable billions of dollars, poured forth in the service of vast collective paranoias—and meanwhile our three billions of mainly hungry people are to become six billions in less than forty years and, like parasites, are threatening to destroy their planetary host.[54]

Despite a growing weakness, he decided to lecture in Europe again that autumn; it might be his last visit. Chest colds and bronchitis gave an ashen look to his lined forehead. Old friends were alarmed at his slowness and fragility—particularly since he insisted he was well.

At a parish church in Surrey, the reverend recognized from pictures Sir Julian Huxley, leading his still taller brother. Fifty years ago they had crossed Prior's Field to this spot to mourn at their mother's funeral.[55] The brothers also stopped at Laleham, the house where Aldous was born; the current tenant allowed him to ponder the view from his own nursery. Nightingales had disappeared from the hedgerows, he sadly noted, because the caterpillars they required for food were killed by DDT. Trails he hiked as a boy were overgrown by weeds, after a different pesticide killed the local hares.[56]

He included these discoveries in *Literature and Science,* another excursion into his past, for which he exhumed writings of his great-uncle Matthew Arnold and his grandfather T.H. He finished the short volume in Virginia Pfeiffer's house, where all three still resided. Laura had never found a house that suited her better.[57]

Fire was still on his mind as he finished this extended essay bridging C. P. Snow's famous gap between the two cultures of science and humanities. As an example of individual differences, he wrote: "One member of a group [watching a fire] may feel sexual excitement, another aesthetic pleasure, another horror and yet others human sympathy or inhuman and malicious glee."[58]

At the beginning of January 1963, Aldous Huxley was asked to take over the presidency of a new foundation devoted to the study of psychedelics. He refused:

> *The last thing I want is to create an image of myself as "Mr. LSD"; nor have I the least desire (being without any talent for this kind of thing) to get involved in the politics of psychedelics. . . . I am not a medical man, nor a psycho-therapist, nor a research worker, nor an evangelist; and I am neither an organizer, nor a sitter on committees, nor a forensic orator. I am a man of letters who can work only in solitude, a writer on a great diversity of themes, of which LSD is only one.[59]*

Dr. Timothy Leary's transition from experimenter to experimentee partially explains this withdrawal. Huxley had helped launch a cult, he realized, and it profoundly disturbed him. He was unsure the American public was prepared for LSD.

He had used *Island* to demonstrate how training in nonviolence and mysticism was crucial to learning from psychedelics. His psychedelic experiences had opened more than visual doors, as he wrote to Thomas Merton:

> *[It] helped me to understand many of the obscure utterances to be found in the writings of the mystics, Christian and Oriental. An unspeakable sense of gratitude for the privilege of being born into this universe. . . . A transcendence of the ordinary subject-object relationship. A transcendence of the fear of death. A sense of solidarity with*

the world and its spiritual principle and the conviction that, in spite of
pain, evil and all the rest, everything is somehow all right.

Here, at last, was an answer to the Buddhist equation of sorrow and
the end of sorrow. In addition, the drug wasn't habit-forming:

> *The experience is so transcendently important that it is in no circum-*
> *stances a thing to be entered upon light-heartedly or for enjoyment.*
> *(In some respects, it is not enjoyable; for it entails a temporary death*
> *of the ego, a going-beyond.) . . . A repetition every year, or every six*
> *months, is felt, most often, to be the desirable regimen.*[60]

What Huxley thought mind-altering drugs offered the world is
less clear. Such substances allowed a Bergsonian *élan vital* to flow
through an individual's personality, he had concluded in *The Doors
of Perception*. Whether he believed this experience hastened progress
up the evolutionary ladder—as Gerald suggested and as Aldous had
insisted on first meeting Leary—remains obscure; his letters are contradictory.

Certainly he never intended to dump the stuff into the water
supply. Long before, he had tried to deny a supply to Isherwood,
whom he and Gerald considered unstable. He wrote Leary, insisting
that "LSD and the mushrooms should be used in the context of this
basic Tantrik idea of the yoga of total awareness, leading to enlightenment within the world of everyday experience."[61]

But a guerrilla-activist side to the psychedelic movement had
emerged, with the founding of the Brotherhood of Eternal Love in
Southern California (and the League of Spiritual Discovery on New
York's Lower East Side). Following a psilocybin trip at Leary's house
outside Cambridge, Ginsberg insisted Leary abandon Huxley's plan of
turning on only distinguished artists and authors. Leary remembers,
"Allen, the quintessential egalitarian, wanted everyone to have the
option of taking mind-expanding drugs. It was the fifth freedom—the
right to manage your own nervous system. . . . It was at this moment that we rejected Huxley's elitist perspective and adopted the
American open-to-the-public approach."[62] Together they fomented a
Joshua-like attack on the status quo, using the language of advertising:

> *Listen! Wake up! You are God! You have the divine plan engraved*
> *in cellular script within you. Listen! Take this sacrament! You'll see!*

You'll get the revelations! It will change your life! You'll be reborn! [63]

Such hasty, visceral responses upset Huxley. He had overstated matters, he now realized, on first calling mescaline "the most extraordinary and significant experience available to human beings this side of the Beatific Vision." [64]

An outright split with Leary took place in the spring of 1962. Leary confronted Huxley with why he had never mentioned the sexually stimulating effect of psychoactive drugs: "His immediate reaction was agitation. 'Of course this is true, Timothy, but we've stirred up enough trouble suggesting that drugs can stimulate aesthetic and religious experiences. I strongly urge you not to let the sexual cat out of the bag.' " [65]

Huxley had switched places since he told Anaïs Nin that "other people need drugs and should have them." But he didn't mean many others and he definitely didn't mean everyone. Now he concluded Nin was right when she wrote: "We shared our esoteric experiences. These experiences should have remained esoteric." In one of her last meetings with Huxley, Nin found him sad and lonely, "beautiful physically but again without vibrations and sensory antennae. . . . I had a painful impression of a psychic blindness." [66]

This was an uncharitable position to take on a man who was, it turned out, dying of cancer, the same disease which had killed characters in *Point Counter Point, Swan, Time, Devils*, and *Island*. [67] Huxley returned to this disease as if it were a permanent boarder; he explored so many cures from hypnotism to enemas that he was in effect practicing medicine without a license.

Huxley's pain in swallowing had increased. In April 1963, he visited Dr. Cutler, who told him a gland in his neck had to be removed, immediately, for biopsy. It proved malignant. Other glands were at risk; his whole jaw was affected.

"Cancer isn't always the winner," he answered Cutler. "Perhaps my body is building up its own resistance." Cutler said nothing. "If it isn't, there isn't much we can do about it, is there?" Huxley finished. [68]

In July, he went into the hospital for cobalt treatments. About the only wholly positive development that spring was Matthew's remarriage, for which Aldous flew to New York. Matthew and Ellen had split up in 1959; chagrined, Huxley finally acknowledged his regrets as a parent:

> I know very well what you mean when you talk about dust and aridity and a hard shell that makes communication in or out extremely difficult. It was something that made the first part of our marriage difficult at times, but Coccola was very patient and in the long run I learned to get through the shell and let the dust be irrigated. Unfortunately, when you were a child, I was predominantly in the dust-crust stage, and so, I am afraid, must have been—indeed, know that I was—a pretty bad father.[69]

By now disappointment in Matthew's divorce was forgotten; the family worried what would become of Trev. The weight of being a Huxley—which Matthew gladly dropped in emigrating to the United States—now lay on Trev. Matthew expected him to be the first Huxley Rhodes scholar; instead, Trev would turn and run, refusing to go to college. He eventually moved to Berkeley, took LSD, grew his hair to his waist, and started one of the first businesses selling silk-screened T-shirts—plagued everywhere he went by rumors of his "trippy" grandfather.[70]

Nineteen sixty-three was a painful summer for Huxley. He healed slowly from the cobalt treatments. "Being sick makes me very inarticulate," he wrote Laura, now on tour for her new book, *You Are Not the Target.* "I tend to just creep into a corner and lie down, like a dog, until the thing is over. The little infection is about over now—as for the other thing, let's hope we'll get the better of that, at least for a few years."[71]

He still visited Jake Zeitlin's shop or UCLA on research trips for a new essay, "Shakespeare and Religion," but often he was forced to pause and regain his strength. To the undergraduates who clustered around him, a frail figure resting on a bench, he might have seemed a character from Matthew Arnold:

> They see Tiresias
> Sitting, staff in hand,
> On the warm, grassy

Asopus bank,
His robe drawn over
His old, sightless head,
Revolving inly
The doom of Thebes.[72]

More than a decade earlier, Huxley had quoted Maine de Biran on death: "The most painful manner of dying to oneself is to be left with only so much of a reflective personality as suffices to recognize the successive degradation of those faculties, on account of which one could feel some self-esteem."[73]

Huxley told Laura he hoped to avoid this, yet he had risked this very cancer by not opting for the operation on his tongue.

Across the continent from where Huxley lay abed, a quarter-million people massed in Washington for the largest demonstration since World War II: the March on Washington for Jobs and Freedom. The Reverend Dr. Martin Luther King, Jr., told the cheering crowd that no matter how just their ends, they must shun violence; his text might have come from *Ends and Means*. King's restatement of Gandhian satyagraha must have cheered the ailing writer. Huxley never had given up on pacifism, as the following quotation suggests, and now he was surer than ever what such a movement required:

> *first, a realistic appraisal of the nature of human beings, and second, a repertory of psycho-physical procedures. . . .*
>
> *Otherwise, so it seems to me, a campaign in favour of peace and non-violence has little or no chance. . . . convincing arguments and the moral categorical imperatives will be ignored, if nothing is done at the same time, about the instinctual and emotional factors involved in individual and collective violence.*[74]

B y November, when Huxley did not recover his strength and color, he was hospitalized. Matthew and his new wife, Judy Bordage, flew out from Washington. Aldous asked his son to finish research for an essay, promised to *Show* magazine for November 15. Huxley was behind on a deadline, and both Matthew and Laura helped him with his writing for the first time.

On November 4, Christopher Isherwood visited. He remembers,

I knew that he had cancer and that it was spreading rapidly. Aldous was in obvious discomfort, but there was nothing poignant or desperate in his manner, and he clearly didn't want to talk about death. Not talking about it made me embarrassed, however, and I touched on subject after subject, at random. Each time I did so, Aldous commented acutely, or remembered an appropriate quotation. I came away with the picture of a great noble vessel sinking quietly into the deep; many of its delicate marvelous mechanisms still in perfect order, all its lights still shining.[75]

On November 19, after he'd won an extension on what would be his last article, Huxley told Laura of a strange dream. He was being flown by night in a jet plane: "I came in, in the morning, feeling this strange and wonderful feeling of elation. . . . in some way I was in a position to make an absolute . . . *cosmic* gift to the world. I don't exactly know how—but anyhow in doing this I have been sort of flying around in immense spaces—and I had been looking in at windows and helping people, and that some *vast* act of benevolence was going to be done, in which *I* should have the sort of star role.

"And then people were saying, 'Well, this must be a dress rehearsal really, and we'll get down to the real thing another time.'. . . Then the next night I kept saying 'When do we start?' and people just laughed."[76]

Huxley worried that his dream meant he hadn't managed to overcome his ego, "the most dangerous of errors." When the chance to do his deed for humanity might arrive, he didn't know, but he had already accomplished much: fifty books, a half-dozen plays, nearly a dozen film scripts. Even in his last months, he was negotiating for two more films, one with George Cukor on a pair of spiritualists and an adaptation of an old short story, "The Tillotson Banquet," for television.

In his last days, Huxley fought grogginess to work daily with Laura. Matthew had left, under the impression that his father's condition had stabilized; he was moving to a new job at the National Institute of Mental Health in Washington, D.C. Gerald dropped in every few days, bringing books and sitting silently by his side. Huxley sat up in bed, his gray pallor slowly fading to transparent ivory. From time to time, he would break into a heavy cough when he tried to speak; his words grew fainter, until he spoke to Dr. Cutler in a whisper.

Huxley must have realized his time, finally, had a stop. A stop but not an end, for, as the death scene in *Island* recorded, there was no need for a lugubrious passing.

On November 22, he began losing ground quickly. Laura called Matthew to come, but the airports were jammed. Visitors passed through the sick room: Peggy Kiskadden, Rosalind Rajagopal. Aldous worried over details of his insurance. Laura promised to take care of it. She had just engaged a lawyer to draw up a will.[77] Toward the end, he followed the unusual course he had described in *Island*, taking a psychedelic *in extremis*. Dr. Cutler agreed; it could do no harm.

"Death brings an end to all desire," Isherwood had written. "Worldly wealth is a house built upon the sand, the beautiful body is a decaying bag of filth. The truth is obvious, if we consider it. But we do not wish to consider it. . . So we dismiss our prophets as pessimists, and their teaching as other worldly defeatism. We hurry away with a sigh."[78]

"Aldous asking for the *moksha*-medicine while dying is not only a confirmation of his open-mindedness and courage," Laura asserted, "but as such a last gesture of continuing importance. Such a gesture might be ignorantly misinterpreted, but it is history that Huxleys stop ignorance, before ignorance stops Huxleys."

Laura began whispering to him just as the drug took effect, "Light and free you let go, darling; forward and up. You are going toward the light. . . ."[79] She spoke directly into his ear, asking him at one point if he could still hear her. He squeezed her hand.

Like his reformed heroes in *Eyeless* and *Island*, he prepared himself for that roomful of light—as had Farnaby, who "saw the Suchness of the world and his own being blazing away with the clear light that was also (how obviously now!) compassion—the clear light that, like everyone else, he had always chosen to be blind to, the compassion to which he had always preferred his tortures" (*Island*, 284).

Beavis had also visited this room at the top of the stairs:

From storm to calm and on through yet profounder and intenser peace to the final consummation, the ultimate light that is the source and substance of all things; source of the darkness, the void, the submarine night of living calm; source finally of the waves and the frenzy of the spray—forgotten now. For now there is only the darkness expanding and deepening, deepening into light; there is only this final peace, this consciousness of being no more separate, this illumination.

"It is easy, and you are doing this beautifully and consciously," Laura repeated from *The Tibetan Book of the Dead.* "Forward and up, light and free, forward and up toward the light, into the light, into complete love."

At 5:00 P.M., on November 22, 1963, he died. News of Huxley's passing was buried in a world shattered by the assassination of John F. Kennedy. As the prophet Isaiah declaimed: "The sun shall no more go down/Neither shall the moon withdraw itself/For the Lord shall be thine Everlasting Light/and the Days of thy mourning shall cease."

That evening Eileen Garrett had a dream. Maria Huxley came to her and said, "It is finished. He is sleeping now."[80]

EPILOGUE

 Three years after Huxley's death, Timothy Leary struggled with how to sum up the Huxley legacy:

> *He just wouldn't slide symmetrically into an academic pigeonhole. What shall we call him? Sage? Wise teacher? Calypso guru? Under what index heading do we file the smiling prophet? The nuclear age bodhisattva?*[1]

In an essay published posthumously, "America and the Future," Huxley wrote, "The prophet must make a selection of the facts that are most significant, that will have the greatest effect on the greatest number of future human beings." Huxley's ultimate contribution may well be his cultural criticism and social prophecy, rather than his fiction.

He foresaw a world of "great trusts" taking over newspapers, the cinema, the radio, the phonograph, with the result that "government will tend to be concentrated in the hands of intelligent and active oligarchies . . . owing to the strength of her democratic tradition, America will probably be one of the last countries to change her present form of government. But in the end the change will come."

Huxley also predicted an increase in the middle-class of industrialized nations, accompanied by a progressive rise in mindlessness in popular culture. New technology will only perpetuate this Circean pursuit of leisure, whose side effect will be international cultural homogenization: "One can anticipate a future in which men will be able to travel round the world without finding an idea or a custom different from those with which they are familiar at home."[2]

Another teacher and social critic, Neil Postman, has compared Orwell's predictions in *1984* with Huxley's: "Huxley believed that it is far more likely that the Western democracies will dance and dream themselves into oblivion than march into it, single file and manacled. Huxley grasped, as Orwell did not, that it is not necessary to conceal anything from a public insensible to contradiction and narcoticized by technological diversions."

"Television is the *soma* of Aldous Huxley's *Brave New World*," Robert MacNeil observed. "In the Huxleyan prophecy, Big Brother does not watch us, by his choice. We watch him, by ours."[3] To understand these insights as they apply to our time, it is worth revisiting the places and people of Huxley's American years.

Hollywood today is caught in a modern Zeno's paradox: there's no stepping in the same river twice. Legends of the film colony loom so large they overshadow the creative activity that once occurred here. Hollywood has become so emblematic of the lifestyles of the rich and famous that the Hollywood Chamber of Commerce actually tried to register the city's name as a trademark.

Modern historians and film commentators have thoroughly charted the film industry's decline in artistic standards. As Jack Mathews, film critic, sees the business today:

> The [companies] operate like the toy business—with the need to answer stockholders with quick profits and noticeable, short-term dividends. That means the system is obsessed to the point of fanaticism with hitting commercial home runs, starting with "Jaws," "Superman," "Star Wars," and a few others that have generated countless clones, sequels, and knockoffs. . . .
> Businessmen occupy decision-making roles that should be occupied by artists, filmmakers and those interested more in the creative process than in making money.[4]

That this complaint could have come from Anita Loos a half century earlier doesn't make it less true. Hollywood film always was big business, and railing against the gray-suited locusts who descend every time a conglomerate adds a movie company to its holdings won't solve the industry's problems. Each year the percentage of films managed by M.B.A.'s and lawyers—without training in film or aesthetics—rises precipitously, as does the value of overseas sales.

Today American films gross $2 billion in receipts in the summer alone. Admissions have risen since their decline in the early sixties, with extra yields for the odd picture which attracts viewers over forty.

Though the modern tendency to ignore postteenage viewers has peaked, it remains the most significant difference between the film industry in the thirties and forties and now. As Vincent Canby of the *New York Times* has written:

> *Before World War II, and in the years immediately following (before the advent of television), theatrical movies were the only game in town. The Aldous Huxleys, Scott Fitzgeralds, Dorothy Parkers and William Faulkners, who then slaved in Hollywood for the good money they earned, liked to say they were writing movies for 12-year-olds. . . .*
>
> *Huxley, Fitzgerald, Parker, Faulkner and the rest wouldn't get a chance to turn up their noses at today's Hollywood. Nobody would attempt to hire them. What could Dorothy Parker or Anita Loos add to John Hughes's "Pretty in Pink" that would increase the audience that Mr. Hughes already has sewn up?*[5]

Gone today is the nineteenth-century omnipotence embedded in studio films—where good could be trusted to overcome evil, where boys were boys and wives were wives (unless they were bad). This cozy hegemony has vanished as completely as the studio system where hairdressers, wardrobe, and central casting coexisted under one roof. Though independent film-makers provide valuable independence, the price of decentralization was a loss of quality-control and of the personality each studio brought to its features. Gone, too, is the ultimate repertory system, where actors and writers developed over a career.

Nowhere are these changes clearer than in the recent history of MGM. The ground on which MGM stands became more valuable than its productions or its facilities—and so it was sold to, then by, Ted Turner. MGM's greatest asset was its library of films, a dairy which media entrepreneur Turner now milks for TV, video, and cable sales.

The marble colonnade through which Maria proudly drove her

husband on his first day as a contract writer still stands, but inside Lorimar's sit-coms and teen detective stories hold sway:

> The city that had once been MGM was now virtually a ghost town. In the Seventies, the studio started selling off its acreage and put up its prop and wardrobe department for auction. . . . Next, the company dissolved its distribution networks and started to release through United Artists. In recent years, MGM has gone the Walt Disney route, and instead of making movies, is concentrating on building pleasure palaces for children of all ages, namely its Grand Hotels in Las Vegas and Reno.[6]

The industry's future may be more bleak than even its recent past: "Pretty Soon, All You'll See Are Big Hits in Tiny Theaters," one prominent critic suggested, as "an ever smaller number of films earn an ever larger proportion of total box office receipts."[7] Films not instant hits have a shelf life of weeks—as do mass-market paperbacks in supermarkets. The divestment of theater chains from studios was reversed during the Reagan years; Universal Pictures/MCA alone controls over 1,500 screens across the United States and Canada. As the number of films competing for limited slots in chain-owned theaters steadily increases, the industry more and more resembles A. J. Liebling's famous definition of freedom of the press: it belongs to those who own one.

The sum of all these factors is Hollywood's current processional of sequels and film-by-formula. If a shoe manufacturer commits funds to a movie, its executives want as surefire a return as on a new line of loafers. The next step is the generic film, whose plot elements are so familiar that title, stars, and locale can be selected by column.

One change Aldous and Maria would have applauded is Hollywood's increasingly candid presentation of lesbianism. John Sayles's *Lianna* (1983), *Desert Hearts* (1985), and *Black Widow* (1986) all show the mouth-to-mouth, breast-to-breast kisses which the old code prohibited. In *Black Widow*, a female version of Monsieur Verdoux poisons her husbands' wine. The nurse in the television show "Heartbeat" is the first out-of-the-closet lesbian in an American prime-time, network TV series.[8]

Huxley would also have enjoyed the resurgence of pacifist films, ranging from the unimpressive *Hail, Hero!* (1969) to anti-Vietnam *Hearts and Minds* (1974) to the lightweight sci-fi of John Sayles's overtly pacifist script for *Battle Beyond the Stars* (1980).[9] In *Superman IV* (1987), subtitled *The Quest for Peace*, the all-American superhero finally sets out to end "the folly of our wars."

Between *Lost Horizon* in 1937 and the clichés of Superman a half century later, positive images of peace have been scant. Only in Shangri-la, before World War II, could Americans briefly imagine living in peace—but then only in a valley of the blind where, the saying has it, a one-eyed man is king.

If Huxley were alive today, as the U.S. population surpasses 250 million and the globe pitifully supports its five billion citizens, he would be unsurprised but profoundly distressed. Since he wrote *Science, Liberty and Peace* in 1946, the world has spent $4,000 billion on arms—a sum increasing at a dizzying $800 billion per annum. Guns before food. One in four children of the world goes hungry; one in three cannot read or write.

Today the sum spent educating 1.2 billion children of the developing world just equals the annual budget of the U.S. Air Force.[10] On such an investment, the world's armed powers reap a grim return: in the last ninety years, 78 million have died war-related deaths, a 50 percent increase over the last century—leaving one to wonder if this figure will increase geometrically or arithmetically.

There are more solutions to this population-driven bellicosity than are workable in the present war- and defense-fueled economies of the West: peace conversion where industries and towns phase out military contracts for nonmilitary ones; vast demonstrations, such as those in Europe in the 1980s opposing NATO's deployment of new weapons; teach-ins and peace studies curricula; peace candidates and parties; tax refusers; civil disobedience at Nevada's testing grounds or at Greenham Common, England, where American missiles are stored.

Inner peaceniks find common cause at worldwide meditations for peace.[11] Some vehemently reject the idealism of the sixties, particularly those political theoreticians who in the eighties became anti–New Leftists.[12] Their anti-Soviet positions dovetail with the thoughtful anticommunism Huxley and Russell urged, opposing state centralism and Stalin's mind control. Huxley's antistatism may regain currency, harmonizing as it does with his later explorations of mysticism and spiritualism.

This red-banner generation—which bore the stigma as well as the badge of surviving the sixties—warmed to metaphysical and occult notions. "Beliefs that have existed for a long time on the metaphysical periphery are now becoming very much a part of middle America," commented J. G. Melton, a scholar of American religions, in 1987.[13]

So-called New Age concerns range across a spectrum: from cults like the Church of Scientology or the Unification Church of Reverend Moon to Eastern mysticism and psychotherapy; through self-improvement courses and humane investing; through direct action for ecological or social welfare. Then there are those who worship objects—crystals, pyramids, gods' eyes—and free-thinking pagans, druids, witches, or mediums. [14] What a mighty latitude of psychic preoccupations is America!

Hollywood noted these shifts. *Eyes of Laura Mars* (1978) and *Dune* (1984), among many, casually incorporate telepathy, telekinesis, precognition, and clairvoyance.

The parapsychological increasingly borders the religious. A recent suit against the Church of Scientology revealed the "secret writings" of L. Ron Hubbard, who thought mankind's problems were caused by an evil warlord 75 million years ago, Xemu, who implanted seeds of evil in spirits who hover over humans. (This information was kept from neophytes, elders of the church said, to prevent physical and spiritual harm from its premature understanding.)[15]

Huxley investigated dianetics while writing of the nuns of Loudun: exorcism continues in modern America, three and a half centuries after the travails of Grandier and Father Surin. In 1986, in the town of West Pittston, Pennsylvania, a Catholic bishop appointed a Reverend Alphonsus Trebold as House Exorcist to assist a family whose century-old house made odd noises. Seventy-five percent of those calling a local television poll considered the place haunted by demons.[16]

In 1988, when TV evangelist Jimmy Swaggart lost his ministry because of a taste for the licentious, fellow-preacher Oral Roberts wrote him that his problem was "demons with long fingernails digging in your body." The same month doctor-novelist Michael Crichton wrote of his exorcism from a two-foot-tall devil. In a room full of lighted candles and idols of holy people ranging from Jesus Christ to Swami Muktananda—modern-day non-sectarianism—his unwelcome companion departed. A psychologist commented, "Entities are very big now."[17]

Belief in demons is again mainstream, typical of a nation whose President and First Lady organized affairs of state by astrology.[18] Witches in the U.S. Army petition for dogtags stating their religious preference as "Pagan" or "Wicka"; Henry Luce's Time-Life Books sell millions of volumes of its *Mysteries of the Unknown* series.

Southern California remains a supermarket for every metaphysical urge. The seeker armed with a telephone directory can find high-tech enlightenment—such as spas where a Synchro-Energizer channels one's brain waves with sound, light, or electromagnetic pulsations.

The Synchro-Energizer's promoter, like a modern-day veteran of Huxley's scenario "Success," calls his machine the Buddha in a Can. "It's convenient and it's easy—and it's very American: you pay for it," said the owner of one mind-expansion salon in Marin County, California.[19] Angelinos can buy a clock that rotates through a magnetic field or a mind mirror to reflect one's brain waves—everything needed for the Universe of You. As cartoonist Matt Groening dryly put it, "Two out of three people are enriched after a visit to Akbar and Jeff's Lucky Psychic Hut."

Just over twenty years ago, the Beatles' "Sergeant Pepper's Lonely Hearts Club Band" appeared, the album critics periodically list as the most important rock record of all time. "For the cover, we came up with a list of our heroes," remembered Paul McCartney, "like Oscar Wilde, Marlon Brando, Dylan Thomas, Aldous Huxley, Lenny Bruce. Everyone had their choice. It was really to say who we liked—it was about time we let out the fact that we liked Aldous Huxley. That wasn't the sort of thing we talked about before."[20]

The Beatles weren't the only ones reading Huxley in the sixties. After his death, another generation had discovered him. (Perhaps this was Huxley's problem in keeping his original audience—many of those coming of age after World War I never completely forgave him for embracing a new cohort, as rebellious and superior a generation as they had been.) At the time of "Sergeant Pepper," *Island* had already gone through sixteen printings; then more followed. (*Island* appeared in paper editions as the baby-boom generation entered its teenage years.) The combined Harper *Doors of Perception/Heaven and Hell* went through twenty-three printings from 1963 to 1983.[21] The novelist regained that enviable status of being read under the covers.

What has become of the Cambridge pioneers of psychedelia? Some, like Andrew Weil, continue their research. Richard Alpert went through a few name changes before finding Ram Dass and teaching spiritualism to people dying of AIDS. Leary himself has been through prison, prison escapes, and revolutionary interludes in North Africa. His predictions of the transformational effects of the comet Kahoutek forgotten, Leary today works as a stand-up comic.[22]

On a warm July evening in 1988, Leary and other high-minded dignitaries gathered in the Hollywood Hills, not far from where Huxley lived, at a benefit for the world's first psychedelic library and museum. One of the event's sponsors, Dr. Oscar Janeger, was among the Huxley-Heard coterie. In the late 1950s, he gave LSD to as many as 900 volunteers daily, studying changes in behavior and test performance: "Many of the artists said the experience was worth four years of art school."

Unfortunately, such exuberance suggests that creativity is in the LSD rather than in the LSD taker. Art school is for learning history and techniques; LSD for unleashing such tools. "The use of LSD declined steadily after the late Sixties," the *New York Times* reported. "Too many stories of too many bad trips, some of them fatal, the CIA slipping it to unsuspecting test subjects, and rumors that LSD damaged chromosomes."[23]

Yet interest in psychedelics today exceeds nostalgia, as demonstrated by the continuing popularity of new psychoactive substances, such as MDA and MDMA, colloquially referred to as Ecstasy or Vitamin X.

As Huxley pointed out a quarter century ago, virtually every culture uses intoxicants, most commonly alcohol, caffeine, and nicotine. For Huxley the issue was not drug prohibition, which he thought unlikely, but creative and *responsible* drug use. Huxley urged psychoactive drugs be taken only with an experienced guide, in the context of a long-term, self-help program of mystical awakening.

Huxley's friends from his Hollywood years have survived. Paulette Goddard gave up movies in 1954, with one film, *Time of Indifference*, in 1965. Her last two films were made outside Hollywood, as befits her dissatisfaction with an industry closed to her, Anita, and their friends. Goddard became an expatriate in Gstaad, Switzerland—not far from her former husband, Charlie Chaplin; though, she recalls, they saw little of one another: "We live on different mountains." Remarried to the great German writer Erich Maria Remarque in 1958, Goddard nursed the novelist until his death in 1970, when, Anita Loos wrote, "Romance must have disappeared from her life forever." Some recognize Goddard as she shops Manhattan's Upper East Side, a neighborhood she shares with that retiring actress, Greta Garbo.

The day after Christmas, 1977, Goddard learned of Charlie Chaplin's death. Soon afterward, grave robbers held Chaplin's remains for ransom. When they called Goddard to ask for money, she told them, "So what?" and hung up.[24] Her jewelry and art collection endowed her later years; her Impressionists alone brought 3.1 million dollars at Sotheby's.

As Goddard had tested the waters for a comeback, Chaplin had tried out one of his own: *A Countess from Hong Kong* (1967), starring Marlon Brando and Sophia Loren in roles written thirty years before for Paulette and Gary Cooper. (Chaplin made the film a family affair, featuring his children, Sydney, Geraldine, Josephine, Victoria, and Charles Chaplin.) Though reviewers were generally unsympathetic, his last years were rich with honors: La Légion d'Honneur, a knighthood, an Oscar, festivities at Lincoln Center. In New York, he visited "21" and met a waiter who had attended him in 1952. "I didn't think I'd ever be back, you know," Chaplin told him.[25] In his last years, Chaplin turned to his now institutionalized past, scoring old films. Perhaps if Huxley had lived into his seventies, he, too, might have grown retrospective. Anita certainly did, churning out three volumes of nostalgic essays, photographs, and memoirs. The last of these offers Anita's philosophy of aging, "On Growing Old

Disgracefully": "All that anybody really needs to learn are two short words: Behave Yourself."[26] Anita died on August 18, 1981, two days before the opening of an exhibit at New York's Biltmore Hotel of "Anita Loos and Her Friends."[27]

Orson Welles died in 1985, still trying to fund his *King Lear,* his spirit still alienated from his fleshy colossus.[28] Isherwood followed in 1986. His stay in California had been extraordinarily concentrated—Isherwood once remarked that he had lived in five different places in California and they were all within sight of each other. Don Bachardy remains in their house, and his paintings of Huxley and prominent Californians are prized.

As for the Hubbles, Grace survived Edwin by twenty-seven years, rattling about their enormous house, the image of a frail but distinguished-looking widow. She spent her last decade packing four dozen boxes for a Hubble Collection at the Henry E. Huntington Library in San Marino. Edwin's tangible remains sit only a few hundred yards of exquisite garden from the house he built.

Today, the new, one-of-a-kind Hubble Space Telescope, a $2.3 billion instrument the size of a boxcar, is ready to orbit the earth. This is the most expensive scientific instrument ever devised, one which increases the size of the visible universe 350 times.[29]

Matthew Huxley rarely sees the stars from his house in the woodsy, overgrown corner of Chevy Chase, Maryland, where he's lived for the last twenty-five years. Now retired from the National Institute of Mental Health, he putters in his ground-floor workshop, the legacy of the carpentry classes before his parents removed him to more academic schools. He has remarried twice and maintains his unmistakably British speech and spelling.

Julian died in 1975, only four years before his neglected sister, Margaret. Only six when her mother died and nine at Trev's suicide, Margaret grew up alone after the boys had gone to college. By the time she reached Somerville College (Cambridge), the rootless girl had been shuffled between houses most of her life. Margaret was in many ways the family's true rebel: the only member of her generation to enter teaching; the only one to convert to Christianity; the only one gay. Margaret Huxley's professional, religious, and sexual choices alienated the family, and she was cordially banished. She emigrated to South Africa to teach. Eventually she set up her own school in Bexhill (Sussex), which she shared with her longtime partner, fellow headmistress Cristabel Mumford. She died without receiving the teaching post she wished for at her mother's school.

Laura Huxley, "a sweet-faced woman in her 70s," as the *New York Times* described her, published a memoir in 1968, *This Timeless Moment,* a finely etched portrait of Huxley's last years. Mrs. Huxley includes a sketch from what she remembers as Huxley's last novel.[30]

Today, Laura's attention has turned from therapy (her *You Are Not the Target* was a bestseller) to lobbying for children. In 1978, she set up Our Ultimate Investment, an organization devoted to the health and spiritual nurturing of the unborn. In the eighties, she wrote a children's book, *Oneadayreason to Be Happy,* and *The Child of Your Dreams,* a series of meditations for the pregnant.

The Huxley family has been chronicled masterfully in Ronald W. Clark's *The Huxleys.* Of Julian's sons, Anthony continues his botanical writings and Francis his anthropological research, punctuated by plans for a feature-length film on his uncle. Aldous's grandchildren, Trev and Tessa, both live in Manhattan where Trev has become the first Huxley entrepreneur and Tessa has followed her uncle Anthony's lead into gardening and park administration. After fleeing the intellectual expectations of his family name, Trev expects his children to distinguish themselves intellectually.

Gerald Heard died in 1971, after five invalid years. He was at times lucid in his final coma, giving interviews as a theorist of gay spirituality to a new generation of gay historians.[31] After having dedicated a suite to Aldous Huxley, Stravinsky also died in 1971. His influence on twentieth-century music is undiminished.

After Bill's death, Peggy Kiskadden remains in the Beverly Hills house where she threw her birthday parties for Isherwood and entertained the Huxleys. One son, Derek Bok, is president of Harvard University; another, Ben, settled in the hills overlooking Llano, where he raises wolves.

What about Huxley's L.A.? Could a young writer from Britain, arriving today in Hollywood, follow in his steps?

In the twenty-five years since Huxley's death, Los Angeles County has grown from just over three to eight and a half million people. At the time of Huxley's death, the tallest building in Los Angeles was the twenty-six-story City Hall; the tallest is currently the First Interstate Bank building, sixty-two stories high.[32]

The condoms Aldous once mistook for flowers no longer bloom on Santa Monica's beaches, but the sewage plant about which he wrote his essay, "Hyperion to a Satyr," still throws into the ocean millions of gallons of untreated waste from the Los Angeles basin. Meanwhile, the ocean has receded from Loos's house; at her front door the Pacific Coast Highway booms with traffic.

Santa Monica Canyon's tall palms still wave in the warm breeze, but the canyon's center is filled by a golf course; the farmhouse where Christopher Isherwood lived and the paths where Peter Viertel set his childhood saga, *The Canyon*, now face high-walled, million-dollar mansions. Salka's house on Mabery Road is in the appreciative hands of director Gordon Davidson of the Mark Taper Forum.

The Huxley house in Llano stands virtually unchanged, except for power lines passing from the mountains above Huxley's house down to Saddleback Butte.

The tall tree which shaded the house has been cut down; the irrigation ditch has been moved, and the little orchard Aldous and Maria planted has returned to chaparral. From the front porch, the view remains impressive; on a clear day, the Sierras a hundred miles north and east can be seen. The San Gabriels block much of Los Angeles's smog. Looking down across the Mojave's vast sweep as far as the Sierras, the visitor sees Joshua trees coiled like prize fighters beating at the wind. Trains barrel by toward Palmdale, California's fastest-growing city. The Antelope Valley's population has grown from 15,000, in Huxley's day, to 150,000, a figure expected to double in twenty years.[33]

From the desert basin in Llano, roads rise sharply up to the wooded slopes of Wrightwood, today a land of "snow-play opportunities" where ski rentals abound. The visitor can still find traces of old Wrightwood in the log cabins recessed off the road. Huxley's house, originally fifty feet by thirty feet, has been expanded and remodeled, but it remains shaded, even in summer, by thick woods.

From Wrightwood and Llano, the Huxleys drove down to Trabuco College in the hills above Laguna Beach. On this chilly hilltop, the air has a sweetness not entirely explained by the lingering incense from the monks' meditations. At night, the owls cry as they hunt in inaccessible canyons far below. Coyotes bark and call. The centerpiece of Trabuco is a fountain set amid brick hallways, not far from a domed shrine. The library has an extraordinary collection of out-of-print Huxley and Heard. Works of H. F. Heard, mystery writer, are in a different room from those of Gerald Heard, religious writer.

Among their artifacts is a leather photo album with pictures of Aldous at the construction site in high-waisted flannels, bareheaded, the wind tousling his hair and collar. Besides the photos, all that remains of Huxley is a story the swamis tell of his making breakfast in the old kitchen—laughing at his maladroitness as he cut grapefruits and filled the kitchen with squirts and juice.

Trabuco is no more a city on a hill. It has fallen victim of imperial developers who swallow hillsides in a single gulp. Every afternoon teams of bulldozers in radio contact level the rolling hills of live oak and pine. The doves coo at Trabuco's crest, but its flanks are slated for another 1,500 houses.

In Huxley's futuristic vision of Los Angeles in 2108, he set the headquarters of the Kingdom of Southern California at the Biltmore on L.A.'s Pershing Square—one of the grander hotels at Huxley's arrival in 1937. There Huxley fantasized a communal bread oven fueled by books from the nearby public library. Today, quite a different scene awaits the visitor. The public library is closed, a victim of arson. In Pershing Square, drugs—not psychedelics—pass via the junkie's hot kiss (a small balloonful of heroin, passed lip to lip). The Biltmore still rises majestically from its squalid surroundings.

Its coffee shop (where in Huxley's fantasy cups were fashioned from unearthed skulls) has become a fashionable bar trimmed with black marble. The old lobby, where the Arch-Vicar preached Devolution, houses the cashier's desk.

Across town, hidden under a turning of a freeway, is the Vedanta Society, a shrine incorporated in Angelenos' cultural memory. (In 1987 the *Los Angeles Weekly* cited it as the "best Hindu temple in town.") The green, wooden building where Isherwood bunked has become a gift shop selling volumes he edited and tapes of Gerald Heard's lectures. Eva Herrmann finished her days in a Vedanta monastery outside Santa Barbara.

Today, however, relinquishing concern for one's body is not popular in Hollywood or Beverly Hills, where the annual sum spent on dieting, exercising, and tummy-tucking probably exceeds the cost of erecting a whole new temple. Southern Californians make a fetish of physical perfection. Here, as Isherwood wrote, "the beautiful girls and superb boys in perpetual bloom still ride the foaming breakers. They are not always the same boys, girls, flowers, trees; but that you scarcely notice. Age and death are very discreet here."[34]

A mile or so from the Vedanta Society temple is the drugstore today known as The Rexall Store at Dart Square. Just down the street is Dreamboat Rent-A-Car, with vintage Corvettes and two-seater Thunderbirds, and Cleansville U.S.A., a drive-in dry cleaner with Stars-and-Stripes awning.

Today in The World's Biggest Drug Store, drugs are definitely passé. Look for tank-top formal wear or perhaps an orange, full-length strapless barbecue outfit. Inside, the visitor finds one of those acclimatized playgrounds which cover Southern California. No price tag is too large, no object unpalatable.

In a lower drawer behind the counter near the till is a copy of *Owl Hoots*, the Rexall House organ, dated May 1953. This artifact passes from employee to employee, its curled pages freezing the events on the day Aldous Huxley took mescaline there for the first time.

On a day exactly twenty-five years after Huxley had tripped there, the drugstore was expanding. The walls were torn asunder, berms exposed; wires hung in tangled lines, but no workmen attended—as if the store could, under its own power, extend itself indefinitely, commanding more inventory, adding more shelves and more products until the last customer dropped his or her last dollar into the cash register and departed.

The location for Huxley's epiphany—the book section—has changed; so has publishing in America and Britain. Titles now on display are self-help and impulse moneymakers: *Secretarial Careers Made Simple, Celebrating with Flowers, Wild about Ice Cream*. No old masters remain, nothing but the bustle of stock-taking, stock checkers checking on the checkers, beeping computer registers, displays of $66 teakettles enameled in a horrific purple and yellow.

What remains of the art books—where Huxley learned to see anew? *Draw Fifty Dogs, Draw Fifty Aircraft, Art Dolls.* Almost nothing left of Art—except on a bottom shelf, where a children's book sits, *Marc Chagall.* The younger reader lucky enough to find this next to *Draw Fifty Caterpillars* discovers wisdom truly felt: "As I grow older," Chagall writes, "how ridiculous is everything not achieved with one's own blood and one's own soul, everything not infused with 'love.' "

A few years after Huxley arrived in the United States, he made a surprisingly autobiographical confession. He felt out-of-place everywhere, not just amid the high-pressure salesmanship of Hollywood: "I am an intellectual with a certain gift for literary art, physically delicate, without very strong emotions, not much interested in practical activity and impatient of routine. I am not very sociable and am always glad to return to solitude and the freedom that goes with solitude."[35]

Blindness and childhood tragedies had bred this melancholy. Meditations, self-hypnosis, and writing had helped lighten it, in the course of his twenty-six years in America. Formerly, travel had been what Huxley had used to calm the pounding in his blood. He had circled the globe at thirty-one, pursuing a wanderlust so powerful the world couldn't encompass it. That restlessness had led him to the treeless plain where the road west ends at the ocean—Los Angeles.

At the studios, Huxley's prose had become more visual, faster-paced (particularly in his openings): more cinematic. He acquired a new setting for his essays and for his two California novels, *After Many a Summer Dies the Swan* and *Ape and Essence.* His study of Indian religions and his exposure to an exotic collection of therapies and spiritual enthusiasms hastened the transformation begun at the time of *Eyeless in Gaza.*

Huxley's last decade was his most contradictory one, with moments of illusion painted over with sorrow. He had lost much. His wife died, his only child divorced, his house burned down, taking all his possessions and his past. He discovered he had cancer. Yet this period also brought him first a new way of seeing, through mescaline, then a realization beyond vision of experiences described in Eastern and Western mysticism. He had "stood on the edge of, and peered beyond, the present frontiers of self-knowledge," wrote Isaiah Berlin. He heralded "what will surely be one of the great advances in this and following centuries—the creation of new psycho-physical sciences. . . . he bore the charges [of betraying his original rationalism] with great sweetness and patience."[36]

He lived long enough to finish his utopia—and to see *Island* reviled by those dismayed at open sexuality, communal living, and hallucinogens. Yet by the end of the decade these topics were commonplace.

In the final pages of *Island*, Farnaby reexperiences Huxley's own traumas: "The eyes were supremely vulnerable, so absorbing that he had nothing to spare for the inner light." Huxley's final vulnerability was to join sight and insight, visions and prescience. In America, he had traveled from eyeless to eyeland *(Island)*, the country where even the blind have vision.

At the crisis of *Eyeless in Gaza*, he had described a "world of darkness":

> *with a dim little light here and another there, and between them, invisible, mysterious objects with which at times the beknighted traveller comes into painful contact, but of which he cannot distinguish the form nor function.*[37]

Thirty years later he died, enriched by new facts on which to base a metaphysic, as on the last page of *Island*:

> *The fact that the ground of all being could be totally manifest in a flowering shrub, a human face; the fact that there was a light and this light was also compassion. . . . disregarded in the darkness, the fact of enlightenment remained.*

"At last . . . Aldous Huxley had exorcised the consciousness of the 'Essential Horror' springing from his mother's death, that haunted all his previous novels," George Woodcock wrote in *Dawn and the Darkest Hour*.[38]

If Aldous Huxley had a motto it was *Aún aprendo*, "still learning." His former daughter-in-law, Ellen Hovde, marveled at the way he, like Bernard Shaw, resisted dotage. "As he got older, I think he became more open and more available—rather than closing down and becoming more set in his ways. By the time he died, he was very young."[39]

Today Huxley Street unobtrusively frames one edge of Hollywood, near Griffith Park. Appropriately enough, this street is a road divided, but only one block long.

The bright California sun still dazzles the Beverly and Hollywood hills where Aldous Huxley's community lodged. But the low thunder of traffic on La Cienega and the fumes rising from the streets color the sky an eerie color. Los Angeles has given new meaning to many expressions; "air pollution" is one. The L.A. Police Department's Space Program promises traffic control via satellite. The city's air space is already dotted with helicopters of police and traffic reporters. Blimps and small planes turn and dive in the soupy, brownish-yellow air.

Far below stands the promontory where Aldous and Laura built their house and watched, aghast, as fire swept it away. From these hills Aldous saw the winter sun set across West Hollywood, Beverly Hills, and Santa Monica. The light traced a path from Peggy's house to Gerald's bungalow in the Canyon, past Christopher and Don's place by the sea.

Laura never rebuilt their house atop Deronda Drive. Walking around the site today, one can imagine the flames jumping from one clump of dried wood to the next. A lizard scrabbles out from behind a boulder, hiding from the sun that bleaches Hollywood's hills on a hot August day. Million-dollar houses rise straight up the canyon wall, cantilevered like the New Mexican pueblos Huxley visited a half-century earlier.

The surrounding canyons are filled with cactus, poison oak, and scrub. As one who loved this region, Christopher Isherwood, wrote: "In the first light of dawn, the coyotes can be mistaken for dogs, as they come trotting along the trail in single file, and it is strange and disconcerting to see them suddenly turn and plunge into the undergrowth with the long easy leap of the wild animal."[40] If Huxley's spirit returned, if he passed finally through that room full of light to which he aspired, it lies not in the earth of Surrey where he was born, and where he and Maria are buried, but with the coyotes in those brown hills by the Hollywood sign, gazing down on his adopted city. In the last rays of dusk, as the sun colors the Hollywood hills rust and orange, one may imagine that he waits and watches there, silently laughing.

Notes

ONE

EYELESS IN GAZA

1. Peter Davidson, Secretary of Albany, personal correspondence, June 24, 1987; Sybille Bedford interview, July 10, 1985.

2. Grover Smith, ed., *Letters of Aldous Huxley* (New York: Harper & Row, 1968), pp. 390–92. Russell's glooms often had this effect on Huxley. In a letter to Ottoline Morrell on October 8, 1917, Huxley described a trip to London where he'd found "Eliot and Russell crouching before a dying fire. Long silences were punctuated by Russell saying something characteristic, like 'How much good it would do if one could exterminate the human race.'"

3. Sybille Bedford interview, 1985.

4. Matthew Huxley interview, June 11, 1985. When Huxley came to list the ills of Anthony Beavis in a similar situation they included constipation, eczema, headaches, a sallow skin, and a persistent stoop.

5. E. W. McBride, "Huxley," *Life and Letters* (May 1934), p. 254.

6. Beverly Nichols, *Are They the Same at Home?* (New York: Doran, 1927), p. 136. Another fascinating profile of Huxley in his immediate predepression period is Sewell Stokes's "Aldous Huxley in London," in the BBC's *The Listener* (December 12, 1957).

7. At Oxford, Huxley studied literature, "Greats," which Oscar Wilde extravagantly called "the only sphere of thought where one can be, simultaneously, brilliant and unreasonable, speculative and well-informed, creative, as well as critical, and write with all the passion of youth about the truths which belong to the august serenity of old age" (Steven Marcus, quoting *More Letters of Oscar Wilde* [New York: Vanguard, 1986], in the *New York Times Book Review*.) Wilde could not have composed a better epitaph for Huxley.

8. "Chawdron," in *Twice Seven* (London: The Reprint Society, 1944), p. 346.

9. "Chawdron," in *Twice Seven*, p. 346.

10. T. H. Huxley was the seventh son of a seventh son, which, in Afro-American lore, meant he was destined to great achievement. As T. H. Huxley reflected in 1910, his family was "mostly Iberian mongrels, with a good dash of Norman and a little Saxon."

11. Ronald W. Clark, *The Huxleys* (New York: McGraw-Hill, 1968), p. 140.

12. Julian Huxley, *Memories* (New York: Harper & Row, 1970), p. 70.

13. Juliette Huxley, *Leaves of the Tulip Tree* (London: John Murray, 1986), p. 226.

14. *Antic Hay*, quoted in Clark, *The Huxleys*, p. 141.

15. Julian Huxley, *Memories*, p. 20.

16. Julian Huxley, *Memories*, vol. II (New York: Harper & Row, 1972), p. 96.

17. Aldous's grandfather was every bit as fixated on his mother as Aldous Huxley was: "My love for her was a passion," T.H. wrote. "I have lain awake for hours crying because I had a morbid fear of her death" (Leonard Huxley, *T. H. Huxley, Life and Letters*, vol. I [London: Appleton, 1901]), p. 4.

18. Aldous Huxley to Eddy Sackville-West, March 5, 1934.

19. Lord David Harman, quoted in Sybille Bedford, *Aldous Huxley* (New York: Harper/Knopf, 1973), p. 33.

20. Aldous Huxley interview, in University of California, Los Angeles Library, Special Collections Department, 1957, p. 11: "People who suddenly become totally blind . . . have to accept that they are in a certain sense dead to one life and are starting a new life." This insight corresponds to that of Bavman and Yoder, eds., "Reaction to Loss," in *Adjustment to Blindness—Reviewed* (Springfield, Illinois: C. C. Thomas, 1966).

21. Rosalind Huxley interview, August 8, 1987. The medical records surrounding Huxley's treatment for keratitis at the Institute of Tropical Medicine have been discarded. One story, propounded by Clark, was that a laboratory explosion threw dirt in the air, but Huxley's problem was bacteriological; its most likely origin was an infection spread by sharing a towel.

22. Rosalind Huxley interview, August 8, 1987.

23. Bedford, *Aldous Huxley*, p. 35.

24. "I wrote a novel when I couldn't see," Huxley later affirmed. "Well, I certainly wouldn't have done this if I had been in my right mind or had been in school doing the ordinary things. This certainly pushed my mind in that direction." Interview, UCLA Library, Special Collections Department, 1957, p. 12.

25. Gerald Heard, "The Poignant Prophet," *Kenyon Review* 27 (Winter 1965). A short biographical sketch of Heard is found in J. M. Barrie's "Introduction," to Heard's *Training for the Life of the Spirit* (Blauvelt, New York: Steiner Books, 1975).

26. Clark, *The Huxleys*, p. 227. Russell was himself a contributor to the Eleventh Edition of the *Encyclopaedia Brittanica*.

27. Gerald Heard, *Science in the Making* (London: Faber & Faber, 1935), pp. 160, 25. Heard had an extraordinary talent for a newsy sort of scientific journalism, peppered with phrases such as "The latest findings on the Euphrates show . . ."

28. Smith, *Letters of Aldous Huxley*, p. 392.

29. Julian Huxley, *Memories*, p. 15.

30. Julian Huxley, *Memories*, pp. 54, 153.

31. Julian Huxley, *Memories*, p. 39.

32. Sybille Bedford, Rosalind Bruce Huxley interviews; if the maid had Trev's child, he or she may still be alive and represent an unacknowledged wing of the Huxley family.

33. For accounts of Trev's end, see Julian Huxley, *Memories*, pp. 100–102; Bedford, *Aldous Huxley*, pp. 46–47; Rosalind Huxley interview; and Clark, *The Huxleys*, p. 151.

34. Smith, *Letters of Aldous Huxley*, p. 68.

35. Dennis Gabor, physicist, in *A Memorial Volume, Aldous Huxley*, ed. Julian Huxley (New York: Harper & Row, 1965), p. 20.

36. Matthew Huxley interview.

37. Bedford, *Aldous Huxley*, p. 321.

38. Smith, *Letters of Aldous Huxley*, p. 389.

39. Huxley letter to T. S. Eliot, July 8, 1936; Smith, *Letters of Aldous Huxley*, pp. 405–6.

40. *Proper Studies: The Proper Study of Mankind Is Man*, pp. 211–13. J. B. Priestley eventually wrote *An Inspector Calls*, a popular play whose plot roughly followed Trev Huxley's fate.

41. Juliette Huxley, *Leaves of the Tulip Tree*, p. 32.

42. Juliette Huxley, *Leaves of the Tulip Tree*, pp. 243, 55.

43. *Crome Yellow*, pp. 48–51. This was a parody of Reverend Horne's sermon, *The Significance of Air War* (London: Marshall, Morgan, and Scott, 1916). Other pacifist friends included Siegfried Sassoon and Richard Aldington.

44. Martin Green, *Children of the Sun* (New York: Basic Books, 1976), p. 126.

45. Smith, *Letters of Aldous Huxley*, p. 146.

46. Bertrand Russell, *The Autobiography of Bertrand Russell 1914–1944* (Boston: Little, Brown, 1968), pp. 123–26.

47. C. E. M. Joad, "Aldous Huxley," *The Outline* (July 25, 1936).

48. A few hundred of these bright, glib pieces were scattered about, many out of range of bibliographers. A number of the Hearst pieces are in the collection of the Humanities Research Center at the University of Texas in Austin.

49. "What Gandhi Fails to See," *Vanity Fair* (July 1930), p. 30. This comment, often made of Gandhi at this time, was proven untrue. Gandhi figures prominently in later Huxley works, such as *Ape and Essence*.

50. Smith, *Letters of Aldous Huxley*, p. 375.

51. *The Listener*, November 14, 1935; see also "War and Emotions," *Life and Letters* (April 1934), p. 9.

52. Smith, *Letters of Aldous Huxley*, p. 325. H. G. Wells's wife Jane had a similarly casual attitude to marital infidelity.

53. Wilhelm Reich, *The Mass Psychology of Fascism*, 3rd. ed. (Albion, Calif.: Albion Press, 1970), p. 53.

54. John Middleton Murry, *The Pledge of Peace* (London: Herbert Joseph, 1938), pp. 34–35.

55. Murry, *The Pledge of Peace*.

56. The Peace Pledge Union eventually became the British section of the War Resisters International.

57. Only four years earlier Huxley had written Lady Ottoline Morrell, "I am only a writer, not a speaker, having the greatest dislike of talking in public and never doing so, if I can possibly avoid it" (Letter in the collection of the Humanities Research Center, University of Texas, July 22, 1930).

58. Smith, *Letters of Aldous Huxley*, p. 393.

59. Dennis D. Davis, "Aldous Huxley's Pacifist Work," unpublished monograph in the possession of Matthew Huxley, June 1971.

60. Smith, *Letters of Aldous Huxley*, p. 398.

61. Smith, *Letters of Aldous Huxley*, letter to Victoria Ocampo, November 19, 1935, p. 398 (italics added).

62. Denis Hayes, *Conscription Conflict* (London: Shepard Press, 1939), pp. 370–71. This repudiation of pacifism took place over objections of George Lansbury, another founding member of the Peace Pledge Union.

63. "Vindicator," in *Fascists at Olympia* (London: Left Review/Gollancz, 1935); Robert Skidersky, *Oswald Mosley* (New York: Holt, Rinehart and Winston, 1975). Subsequent descriptions of the Olympia riot are from these sources.

64. Gerald Heard and Aldous Huxley, "The Significance of the New Pacifism: Two Addresses," pamphlet, UCLA Library, Special Collections Department, 1935, p. 3.

65. Heard, "The Significance of the New Pacifism," pp. 5–6.

66. Huxley, "The Significance of the New Pacifism," p. 13.

67. Smith, *Letters of Aldous Huxley*, p. 398.

68. *"1936 . . . PEACE?"* pamphlet, reprinted from the December 31, 1935, edition of the London *Star* by the Friends Peace Committee.

69. David Low, *Autobiography* (New York: Simon and Schuster, 1951).

70. To Leonard Woolf, Huxley fired off a dissenting letter on March 7, 1936: "What the pacifist suggests is the eminently reasonable course of using intelligent generosity to begin with—rather than waiting to use it till the evil act [of war] has been committed" (Smith, p. 401).

71. Maria Huxley to Jeanne Neveux, June 15, 1939. (All correspondence of Maria Huxley, unless otherwise noted, is from the Belgian Royal Library, Musée de La Literature.)

72. Huxley makes the same point in correspondence with his American editor, Cass Canfield. To Joad, Huxley wrote of *Eyeless:* "I'm very glad to know you think the book's all right. I had lost all sense of what it was like" (Smith, *Letters of Aldous Huxley*, p. 404).

73. Cyril Connolly, *Journal and Memoir*, David Pryce-Jones, ed. (New York: Ticknor and Fields, 1984), pp. 276–77.

74. Green, *Children of the Sun*, p. 269.

75. Stephen Spender, *Letters to Christopher*, Lee Bartlett, ed. (Santa Barbara, Calif.: Black Sparrow Press, 1980), p. 120.

76. Spender, *Letters to Christopher*, pp. 120, 138.

77. Cecil Day Lewis, *We're Not Going to Do Nothing* (London: Left Review, 1936), limited edition. Though Brian Howard praised Huxley for making righteousness readable, "that Supreme merit of a writer," in the *New Statesman and Nation*, his was a minority opinion.

78. One virulent attack on Huxley's politics at this time from outside Britain is Dimitri Mirsky, *The Intelligentsia of Great Britain*, Alec Brown, trans. (New York: Covici-Friede, 1935), where Huxley is termed a "decadent sceptic."

79. Peter Stansky and William Abraham, *Orwell: The Transformation* (London: Constable, 1979), p. 185.

80. Stephen Spender, "Open Letter to Aldous Huxley," *Left Review* (June 1936). Alongside Spender's letter, Geoffrey West's ill-tempered review of *Eyeless* in the same issue was mild: "Here were the same evasive, irresponsible, discontented, super sensitive negative beings. . . . Then he puts down his cards. . . . The trouble is that he puts them down too late. The new man walks upon the stage and—curtain!"

81. Smith, *Letters of Aldous Huxley*, p. 411. Even in Sanary, Huxley kept up with British publications, writing several letters to *The Times* on the dangers of war-oriented Collective Security, on the impossibility of "just wars" ("Just Wars," *The Times*, April 30, 1936; see also letters on "Collective Security," September 19, 1936, and on August 28, 1936).

82. A. L. Lloyd, "On Surrealism," *Left Review* (December 1936), pp. 897–98. Louis Aragon's poem *Front Rouge* appeared in 1932–1933; it is translated as *Red Front* by the author in *Gallery Works II*, Holland and Yurechko, eds. (Berkeley, Calif.: Poets' Commune, 1976). Actions against the Surrealists occurred despite the group's having joined the Party *en masse*, publishing such journals as *Clarté* and *Le Surréalisme au service de la révolution*, and despite Aragon's having been formally tried for sedition (the first European poet so chosen) for a poem.

83. "The Pacifist Case," *The Listener*, October 21, 1936, p. 795. At a writers' congress in London that summer, writers called for an anti-Fascist encyclopedia. Huxley began editing and writing a pacifist version.

84. There can be no question that family reputation shadowed Matthew Huxley all his life; the British have a multigeneration literary tradition within select families, such as the Waughs, the Longfords, the Huxleys, and others. Gavin de Beer called

this tendency "Not a dynasty, nor a clan, but an *élite*," in his preface to Clark, *The Huxleys*.

85. Henri Barbusse, "Writing and War," in Joseph North, ed., *New Masses: An Anthology of the Rebel Thirties* (New York: International, 1969), p. 212.

86. Smith, *Letters of Aldous Huxley*, p. 413. Huxley's overt political statements, which might have expanded his apparent commitment to anarchism, are scant; the closest we find to a developed ideology in his writings occurs in the next two volumes he wrote, *Ends and Means* and *After Many a Summer Dies the Swan*.

87. Nancy Cunard, "Authors Take Sides," *Left Review* (June 1937). For background on her survey, which included international figures like Pablo Neruda, Tristan Tzara, and others, see Ann Chisholm, *Nancy Cunard* (New York: Knopf, 1979), p. 241.

88. Heard, "The Poignant Prophet," p. 58.

89. Smith, *Letters of Aldous Huxley*, pp. 409–10. "The character [of Brian Foxe] was, of course, definitely Trev's," Huxley acknowledged. "If I preserved the stammer and insisted on the ascetic obsession, . . . [it was] reproduced entirely in love and in an attempt to understand a character I profoundly admired." This didn't heal the hurt any more than a similar letter to Lady Ottoline had when *Crome Yellow* satirized life at Garsington.

90. C. E. M. Joad, "Aldous Huxley," p. 4.

91. The Oxford peace pledge was actually modeled after a speech of an American minister in 1934 and a similar oath of the American Anti-Conscription League of 1916.

92. Lewis, *We're Not Going to Do Nothing*, p. 25.

93. D. H. Lawrence, *Letters*, Richard Aldington, ed. (New York: Penguin Books), p. 88.

94. Aldous Huxley to art critic Sidney Schiff, unpublished letter, June 21, 1931.

95. Aldous Huxley to Sidney Schiff, unpublished letter, February 19, 1933, just as his writing block began.

96. Smith, *Letters of Aldous Huxley*, p. 409; *Aldous Huxley*, Bedford, p. 337; Matthew Huxley interview, August 18, 1988.

97. *New York Times*, November 28, 1936.

98. Bedford, *Aldous Huxley*, p. 347.

99. Betty Wendell interview, June 2, 1985.

TWO

ENDS AND MEANS

1. Joe Klein, *Woody Guthrie: A Life* (New York: Knopf, 1980), pp. 93–95.

2. Maria Huxley to Jeanne Neveux, March (undated), 1937.

3. Woody Guthrie, *Bound for Glory* (New York: Dutton, 1943), p. 100.

4. Matthew Huxley interview, June 11, 1985.

5. Maria Huxley to Jeanne Neveux, April 30, 1937.

6. Maria Huxley to Jeanne Neveux, April 30, 1937.

7. Maria Huxley to Jeanne Neveux, April 30, 1937.

8. Stephen Spender, *Love-Hate Relations* (New York: Random House, 1974), p. xx. Of course many twentieth-century British writers—from Oscar Wilde to Rupert Brooke—had preceded Huxley and Heard across America.

9. Sean Hignett, *Brett* (New York: Franklin Watts, 1985), p. 171.

10. Matthew Huxley interview, June 11, 1985.

11. Matthew Huxley interview, June 11, 1985.

12. Smith, *Letters of Aldous Huxley* (New York: Harper & Row, 1968), p. 425.

13. Denis Hayes, *Conscription Conflict* (London: Shepard Press, 1939), p. 372.

14. Matthew Huxley interview, June 11, 1985.

15. *D. H. Lawrence: Selected Letters*, Aldous Huxley, ed. (New York: Viking, 1932), p. 22.

16. Keith Sagar, ed., *D. H. Lawrence of New Mexico* (Salt Lake City: Peregrine Smith, 1982), p. 31.

17. Quoted in Sagar, *D. H. Lawrence in New Mexico*, p. viii.

18. *Brave New World*, p. 70.

19. *Brave New World*, p. 70.

20. Robert Lucas, *Frieda Lawrence* (New York: Viking, 1972), p. 253.

21. Lucas, *Frieda Lawrence*, p. 256. Frieda's hopes for Angelo were unrealistic; after her death, he retired to Italy and his first wife.

22. Quote from *St. Mawr*, cited in Sagar, *D. H. Lawrence of New Mexico*, p. 59.

23. Hignett, *Brett*, pp. 118–58 passim.

24. Hignett, *Brett*, p. 171.

25. Strong-willed, highly intelligent, Mabel Dodge even intimidated Lawrence, who refused her deed to the ranch in fear of being indebted. Frieda accepted the ranch in exchange for the handwritten manuscript to *Sons and Lovers*, which Mabel casually traded to her psychiatrist as partial payment for therapy.

26. Lucas, *Frieda Lawrence*, p. 209.

27. Smith, *Letters of Aldous Huxley*, p. 422.

28. Matthew Huxley interview, June 11, 1985.

29. Maria Huxley to Jeanne Neveux, June 21, 1937.

30. Reprinted in Sagar, *D. H. Lawrence in New Mexico*, p. 60. Lawrence gave the original manuscript to the Huxleys; it perished in a terrible fire in 1961.

31. Smith, *Letters of Aldous Huxley*, p. 417.

32. Angus Wilson, "The Naive Emancipator," *Encounter* 5 (July 1950), p. 74.

33. *D. H. Lawrence, Selected Letters*, Aldous Huxley, ed., p. 23.

34. Charles Holmes, *Aldous Huxley and the Way to Reality* (Westport, Conn: Greenwood Press, 1970), p. 119.

35. Gerald Heard, "The Poignant Prophet," *Kenyon Review* (Winter 1965), p. 3.

36. Jenny Wells Vincent interview, September 28, 1985.

37. Maria Huxley to Jeanne Neveux, August 7, 1937.

38. Maria Huxley to Jeanne Neveux, August 20, 1937.

39. Jacob Zeitlin interview, June 1, 1985.

40. Tom Dardis has written useful sketches of the Hollywood periods of these writers in *Some Time in the Sun* (New York: Scribner's, 1976).

41. Jenny Wells Vincent interview, September 28, 1985.

THREE

SUCCESS

1. Margaret (Peggy) Kiskadden interview, May 31, 1985.

2. Matthew Huxley interview, June 11, 1985. (The only child of Aldous Huxley, Matthew is a retired administrator for the National Institute of Mental Health in Washington, D.C.)

3. Maria Huxley to Jeanne Neveux, October (undated), 1937.

4. Sheridan Morley, *Tales from the Hollywood Raj: The British, the Movies, and Tinseltown* (New York: Viking, 1984), p. 135. The son of Robert Morley, Sheridan proved one of the most pungent commentators on the English colony in Hollywood.

5. J. B. Priestley, *Midnight on the Desert* (New York: Harper & Row, 1937), p. 172.

6. Peggy Kiskadden interview, May 31, 1985.

7. Greater London Council, *Blackout to Whitewash: Civil Defense Since 1937* (pamphlet), 1985, p. 1.

8. Quoted in Robert Hewison, *Under Siege: Literary Life in London 1939–45* (London: Quartet Books, 1979), p. 3.

9. Peggy (Bok) Kiskadden interview, May 31, 1985.

10. Peggy Kiskadden interview, May 31, 1985. Serving dinner, Peggy wondered nervously if the Huxleys were vegetarians; she told them to leave the meat if they didn't want it. Everyone, except hearty Matthew, did so—later she discovered that Aldous and Maria had become vegetarians that same night, one of many foods fancies of the Huxleys.

11. Grover Smith, *Letters of Aldous Huxley* (New York: Harper & Row, 1968), p. 71.

12. Peggy Kiskadden interview, May 31, 1985. In a memorial volume *Aldous Huxley*, Julian Huxley ed. (London: Chatto & Windus, 1965), others comment on Huxley's blindness.

13. Larry Ceplair and Steven Englund, *Inquisition in Hollywood: Politics in the Film Community, 1930–1960* (Berkeley: University of California Press, 1983), Appendix 1.

14. Anita Loos, *A Girl Like I* (New York: Viking, 1966), pp. 181–82.

15. Anita Loos, *Kiss Hollywood Good-by* (New York: Viking, 1974), pp. 11–12. See also Gary Carey, *Anita Loos* (New York: Knopf, 1988).

16. Anita Loos, *Fate Keeps on Happening* (New York: Dodd, Mead, 1984), pp. 167–68. Loos kept erratic but fascinating date books, consulted for this work.

17. Anita Loos, *Kiss Hollywood Good-by*, pp. 148–49.

18. Morley, *The Hollywood Raj*, p. 9.

19. Charles Chaplin, *My Autobiography* (New York: Simon and Schuster, 1964), p. 131.

20. Morley, *The Hollywood Raj*, p. 142.

21. Priestley, *Midnight on the Desert*, pp. 173–78. Like most British writers visiting California, Priestley could not get over the sheer expanse of L.A.— as if London weren't vast!

22. P. G. Wodehouse, *Laughing Gas* (London: Penguin, 1957), pp. 26, 98–99. This timeless satirist apparently set very few of his hundred-odd novels in Hollywood, though some, like *Barmy in Wonderland* (London: Pan, 1952), have comic passages reflecting Tinseltown.

23. Morley, *The Hollywood Raj*, pp. 144–45. In Henry King's 1936 film, *Lloyds of London*, diligent British researchers counted ninety-two errors of history, geography, or costume.

24. Morley, *The Hollywood Raj*, p. 125.

25. John Russell Taylor, *Strangers in Paradise: The Hollywood Emigrés, 1933–1950* (London: Faber & Faber, 1983), p. 115.

26. Morley, *The Hollywood Raj*, p. 51.

27. Maria Huxley to Jeanne Neveux, April 30, 1937.

28. Evelyn Waugh, *The Loved One* (Boston: Little, Brown, 1977), originally published in *Horizon* in 1948, p. 5.

29. *After Many a Summer Dies the Swan*, pp. 8–10.

30. This phrase occurs in a letter to Ottoline Morrell, September 11, 1919, in the Collection of the Humanities Research Center, University of Texas.

31. *The Most of S. J. Perelman* (New York: Simon and Schuster, 1957), p. 600.

32. Maria Huxley to Jeanne Neveux, June 1938.

33. Grace Hubble, Journal entry, March 14, 1938, The Hubble Collection, the Henry E. Huntington Library, San Marino, Calif.

34. Budd Schulberg, *What Makes Sammy Run?* (New York: Random House, 1941), p. 42.

35. As one critic astutely commented, "That Huxley should have imagined Hollywood would even touch a manuscript with this kind of subject (when it was clear that only Fascists indulged in propaganda) reveals how little he knew about the industry when he first began working for it" (Peter Firchow, *Aldous Huxley: A Satirist and Novelist* [Minneapolis: University of Minnesota Press, 1972], p. 159). An undated manuscript in UCLA's Special Collections Department, "Music as Propaganda" (probably one of Huxley's pieces from the twenties for the Hearst syndicate) anticipates the "Success" scenario.

36. Maria Huxley to Jeanne Neveux (undated). The scenario "Success" is in Special Collections, Stanford University Library, Palo Alto, California.

37. Jacob Zeitlin interview, June 1, 1985.

38. Christopher Isherwood, *Prater Violet* (New York: Farrar, Straus, 1946), p. 53. In fact, Huxley had come to Hollywood for the same reasons many other writers did, as suggested in William Goldman's *Adventures in the Screen Trade* (New York: Warner Books, 1983).

39. "Two or Three Graces," in *Twice Seven* (London: The Reprint Society, 1944), p. 314.

40. *Jesting Pilate: An Intellectual Holiday* (New York: George Doran, 1926), p. 296.

41. Grover Smith, *Letters of Aldous Huxley* (New York: Harper & Row, 1968), p. 247. The hostility of Huxley's previous comments on America may have caused a cognitive dissonance which deepened his depression.

42. Matthew Arnold, "Civilization in the United States," quoted in Justin Kaplan, *Mr. Clemens and Mark Twain* (New York: Simon and Schuster, 1966), p. 299. De Tocqueville makes a similar point in his writings on America. Huxley's mother bore the Arnold name, and Aldous grew up in (and his essays carry on) this tradition.

43. Quoted in Sybille Bedford, *Aldous Huxley* (New York: Harper/Knopf, 1973), p. 643.

44. Henry Seidel Canby, "Keep the Mind Free," *Saturday Review of Literature*, November 20, 1937, pp. 5–6.

45. Hyman was one of the five "Thalberg Men," line producers, at MGM. For his background, see Thomas Schatz, *The Genius of the System* (New York: Pantheon, 1988), p. 43.

46. Taylor, *Strangers in Paradise*, p. 115.

47. Smith, *Letters of Aldous Huxley*, pp. 427–28. When a full-scale adaptation of *The Forsyte Saga* was finally done for public television, forty years later, it proved an immense Anglo-American hit.

48. Phil Stong, "Writer in Hollywood," *Saturday Review of Literature*, April 10, 1937, p. 14.

49. Smith, *Letters of Aldous Huxley*, p. 424.

50. Grace Hubble, Journal entry, October 17, 1937, The Hubble Collection, Huntington Library. The Loos house still stands, on the Pacific Coast Highway.

51. Grace Hubble, The Hubble Collection, "Characteristics," undated.

52. Aldous Huxley, "Stars and the Man," The Hubble Collection. A novel based on these papers is Tom Bezzi's *Hubble Time* (San Francisco: Mercury House, 1987), which includes Huxley's sketch of Hubble.

53. Jess Stearn, *The Grapevine* (New York: Doubleday, 1964), p. 114.

54. Norman Zierold, *Garbo* (New York: Stein and Day, 1969), p. 108.

55. Zierold, *Garbo*, p. 109.

56. Richard Dyer, *Gays and Film* (New York: Zoetrope, 1984). See also Simon Watney, "Hollywood's Transsexual World," *Screen*, September-October 1982, and Vito

Russo, "Gays in Hollywood," *Village Voice*, June 25, 1979. Vito Russo's *The Celluloid Closet: Homosexuality in the Movies* (New York: Harper & Row, 1981) is useful for sexual role models. The quote about Garbo and Dietrich is from Penny Stallings, *Flesh and Fantasy* (New York: St. Martin's Press, 1978), p. 114.

57. Stearn, *The Grapevine*, p. 112.

58. Archives Bulletin, International Gay and Lesbian Archives, Hollywood, Calif., September 1987.

59. Vito Russo, *The Celluloid Closet*, p. 42. The Hays (later Breen) Office required kisses to end with lips sealed, no more than one and one-half inch of cleavage in close-up, and other bizarre moralisms.

60. Bedford, *Aldous Huxley*, pp. 80–81.

61. Peggy Kiskadden interview, May 31, 1985.

62. Christopher Isherwood interview, June 2, 1985.

63. Christopher Isherwood, *My Guru and His Disciple* (New York: Farrar, Straus and Giroux, 1980), p. 9.

64. Gerald Heard, in his *The Source of Civilization* (New York: Harper & Row, 1937), a companion volume to *Ends and Means*, traced waves of nonviolent consciousness: Buddhism in India, Taoism in China, Gnosticism in Europe, Quaker quietism in the United States; he hoped a similar wave might materialize to stop World War II.

65. Francis Huxley interview, July 8, 1985.

66. Peggy Kiskadden interview, May 31, 1985.

67. Bedford, *Aldous Huxley*, p. 361.

68. Quoted in Ronald W. Clark's *The Huxleys* (New York: McGraw-Hill, 1968), p. 289.

69. Clark, *The Huxleys*, p. 289.

70. In hindsight, Mussolini's appeal to a growing Italian national spirit "which no power on earth can deny" sounds uncannily like statements which either Chamberlain or Stalin could have made.

71. Grace Hubble, The Hubble Collection, June 16, 1938.

72. Maria Huxley to Suzanne Nys, September 25, 1938.

73. Aldous Huxley, Foreword to Alan Hunter, *White Corpuscles in Europe* (Chicago: Willet, Clark, 1939), pp. 1–2.

74. Hewison, *Under Siege*, p. 8.

75. "Mr. Huxley at the Zoo," *New York Times*, October 10, 1937, Sec. XI, p. 5.

76. Philip Scheuer, "Town Called Hollywood," *Los Angeles Times*, December 5, 1937.

77. Maria Huxley to Eddy Sackville-West, December 16, 1937.

78. Nicholas Butler, interview, *New York Times*, October 10, 1937, p. 3. Butler, President of Columbia University, echoed their points when he told the *New York Times*: "The one sure way to keep out of war is to prevent war."

79. *New York Times*, December 12, 1937, p. 45. Strangely enough, despite Huxley's celebrity, the paper did not cover his pacifist lecture.

80. Quoted in Clark, *The Huxleys*, p. 290. *Nature*, which always had insightful comments on the Huxleys, was actually five years ahead in its notice: he was not yet a mystic. Evelyn Waugh, *Essays, Articles, and Reviews of Evelyn Waugh*, ed. Donat Gallagher (London: Metheun, 1983), p. 211.

81. Maria Huxley to Madame Nys, November 6, 1937.

82. Letter in collection of UCLA Library, Special Collections Department, December 10, 1937.

83. Jacob Zeitlin interview, June 1, 1985.

84. Maria Huxley to Jeanne Neveux, April 1938.

85. *After Many a Summer Dies the Swan*, p. 24.

86. Loos, *Kiss Hollywood Good-by*, pp. 56–57.

87. Morley, *The Hollywood Raj*, p. 131.

88. P. G. Wodehouse, quoted in Morley, *The Hollywood Raj*, pp. 86–87.

89. Morley, *The Hollywood Raj*, p. 125.

90. Charles Chaplin, *My Autobiography*, p. 331.

91. "Two or Three Graces," in *Twice Seven*, p. 251.

92. Grace Hubble Travel Diaries, The Hubble Collection, June 7, 1939.

93. Maria Huxley to Grace Hubble, June 28, 1939, The Hubble Collection. Doubtless Grace had little experience with which to answer questions such as this one.

94. Maria Huxley to Jeanne Neveux, May 29, 1938.

95. Smith, *Letters of Aldous Huxley*, p. 440.

96. James K. Lyon, *Brecht in America* (Princeton, N.J.: Princeton University Press, 1980), pp. 3–4.

97. Christopher Hampton, *Tales from Hollywood* (London: Faber & Faber, 1983), p. 54.

FOUR

AFTER MANY A SUMMER DIES THE SWAN

1. Norman Zierold, *Garbo* (New York: Stein and Day, 1969), pp. 107–8.

2. Salka Viertel, *The Kindness of Strangers* (New York: Holt, Rinehart and Winston, 1969), pp. 219–20.

3. Bosley Crowther, *Hollywood Rajah* (New York: Holt, 1960), pp. 141–48.

4. Gary Carey, *All the Stars in Heaven* (New York: Dutton, 1981), pp. 48, 95.

5. Anita Loos, *A Mouse Is Born* (New York: Doubleday, 1951), p. 28.

6. *The Olive Tree and Other Essays*, pp. 38–41; in *Eyeless in Gaza*, Huxley had made another anti-Hollywood crack, lamenting "the pitiable models on which people form themselves. Once it was the Imitation of Christ—now of Hollywood" (p. 326).

7. Grover Smith, *Letters of Aldous Huxley* (New York: Harper & Row, 1969), p. 435.

8. The first quotation is from "The Outlook for American Culture: Some Reflections in a Machine Age," quoted in Peter Firchow, *The End of Utopia* (Lewisburg, Pa.: Bucknell University Press), p. 34; the second is from *Jesting Pilate*, p. 301.

9. Smith, *Letters of Aldous Huxley*, p. 241.

10. Fred Guiles, *Hanging On in Paradise* (New York: McGraw-Hill, 1975), p. 35.

11. Salka Viertel's son Peter wrote a novel describing the canyon in this period, *The Canyon* (New York: Harcourt, 1940).

12. S. N. Behrman, *New York Times*, July 17, 1966. (One historian actually compared this Hollywood influx to that of scholars into Western Europe after the fall of Constantinople in 1453.)

13. John Baxter, *The Hollywood Exiles* (New York: Taplinger, 1976), p. 56.

14. Anthony Heilbut, *Exiled in Paradise* (New York: Viking, 1983), p. 301.

15. Matthew Huxley interview, June 11, 1985.

16. Peggy Kiskadden interview, May 31, 1985.

17. Lionel Rolfe, *Literary L.A.* (San Francisco: Chronicle Books, 1976), p. 36.

18. *The Letters of Thomas Mann: 1889–1955*, ed. and trans. Richard and Clara Winston (New York: Knopf, 1975), p. 183.

19. Smith, *Letters of Aldous Huxley*, p. 375 (letter to Julian Huxley).

20. Maria Huxley to Jeanne Neveux, April 17, 1938.

21. *Ape and Essence*, p. 41.

22. Lowell Bergreen, *James Agee* (New York: Dutton, 1984), p. 364.

23. Lillian Hellman, *Pentimento* (Boston: Little, Brown, 1973), p. 153.

24. James K. Lyon, *Brecht in America* (Princeton, N.J.: Princeton University Press, 1980), p. 239.

25. Maria Huxley to Jeanne Neveux, September 4, 1938.

26. Grace Hubble, Journal entries, April 1, May 11, 1938, The Hubble Collection, The Henry E. Huntington Library, San Marino, Calif.

27. Quoted in Sybille Bedford, *Aldous Huxley* (New York: Knopf, 1973), p. 373.

28. Grace Hubble, The Hubble Collection, April 1, May 11, 1938.

29. George Orwell, *New English Weekly*, May 26, 1938.

30. Baxter, *The Hollywood Exiles*, p. 197. America's neutrality was more widespread and influential than hindsight would suggest; in December 1937, a Democratic congressman had introduced an (unsuccessful) constitutional amendment requiring a national referendum before declaring war, unless the United States were invaded.

31. Sheridan Morley, *Tales from the Hollywood Raj* (New York: Viking, 1984), pp. 139–40.

32. *Ends and Means* was timely, eventually selling twice as much as *Swan* in hardback, and significantly better than *Eyeless*, according to the introduction to Eben Bass's excellent *Aldous Huxley: An Annotated Bibliography of Criticism* (New York: Garland, 1981).

33. Grace Hubble, The Hubble Collection, July 16, 1938.

34. Marie Le Put interview, July 10, 1986.

35. Grace Hubble, The Hubble Collection, April 1, 1938; Maria Huxley to Jeanne Neveux, April 1938.

36. Morley, *The Hollywood Raj*, pp. 125–26. This same provision was discussed in *A Night at the Opera*. Groucho: "A sanity clause! It's in every contract." Chico: "You can't fool me; there ain't no Santa Claus."

37. Joseph Weintraub, ed., *The Wit and Wisdom of Mae West* (New York: Avon, 1967), p. 12.

38. Nathanael West, *The Day of the Locust* (New York: Random House, 1939), p. 95.

39. F. Scott Fitzgerald, *The Last Tycoon* (New York: Scribner's, 1941), p. 57.

40. Crowther, *Hollywood Rajah*, p. 191. The capital-intensive technological changes in film-making invited further manipulation of studio stock, to the point where, in 1929, Louis B. Mayer's feuds with Nicholas Schenck's Loew's Films had Mayer lobbying the White House for an antimonopoly prosecution to wipe out his rival.

41. Fitzgerald, *The Last Tycoon*, p. 21.

42. Thomas Schatz, *The Genius of the System: Hollywood Studio Production 1920–1955* (New York: Pantheon, 1988), pp. 243–49.

43. Carey, *All the Stars in Heaven*, p. xiii.

44. Carey, *All the Stars in Heaven*, p. 209.

45. Anita Loos, *Kiss Hollywood Good-by* (New York: Viking, 1974), p. 119.

46. P. G. Wodehouse, quoted in Morley, *The Hollywood Raj*, pp. 86–87.

47. Baxter, *The Hollywood Exiles*, p. 120.

48. Crowther, *Hollywood Rajah*, p. 179.

49. Huxley had been experimenting with a Hearst-like character and his bubble-headed mistress since his short story "Chawdron," nearly a decade earlier: "If you're totally uneducated and have amassed an enormous fortune by legal swindling, you can afford to believe in the illusoriness of matter, the non-existence of evil, the oneness of all diversity and the spirituality of everything." "Chawdron," in *Twice Seven* (London: The Reprint Society, 1944).

50. West, *The Day of the Locust*, p. 3.

51. "The Most Agreeable Vice," pamphlet privately published by Jake Zeitlin, 1938.

52. Bedford, *Aldous Huxley*, p. 303.

53. Loos, *Kiss Hollywood Good-by*, p. 193.

54. Zierold, *Garbo*, p. 107.

55. Zierold, *Garbo*, p. 91. Irving Thalberg understood Garbo's popularity among women, as a recollection of Salka's on the making of *Queen Christina* shows: "Abruptly he asked if I had seen the German film *Mädchen im Uniform* [which] dealt with a lesbian relationship. Thalberg asked: 'Does not Christina's affection for her lady-in-waiting indicate something like that?' He wanted me to 'keep it in mind,' and perhaps if 'handled with taste it would give us very interesting scenes.' Pleasantly surprised by his broadmindedness, I began to like him very much" (Viertel, *The Kindness of Strangers*, p. 175).

56. Madame Curie treatment, revision of September 22, 1938. MGM producer Bernie Hyman, who wanted a love story, not a science lesson, rejected Huxley's script as "too scientific." See also Virginia Clark, *Aldous Huxley and Film* (Metuchen, N.J.: Scarecrow Press, 1987), pp. 30–36.

57. Smith, *Letters of Aldous Huxley*, p. 437.

58. *New York Times*, November 27, 1938.

59. Viertel, *The Kindness of Strangers*, pp. 222–23.

60. Isherwood, *Down There on a Visit* (New York: Simon and Schuster, 1962), p. 148.

61. Ronald W. Clark, *The Life of Bertrand Russell* (New York: Knopf, 1976), p. 462. In California, the first thing Russell did was to have his children leave England for the U.S.: "The atmosphere of England is now bad enough for young people. Nothing is so depressing as despairing preparations for war which inspires no-one with enthusiasm." See also Feinberg and Krasrils, *Bertrand Russell's America* (London: Allen & Unwin, 1973), pp. 28–32.

62. Guiles, *Hanging On in Paradise*, pp. 17–18.

63. Northrop Frye, "The Great Charlie," *The Canadian Forum* (August 1941), p. 150.

64. Bergreen, *James Agee*, p. 343.

65. Charles Chaplin, *My Autobiography* (New York: Simon and Schuster, 1964), p. 424.

66. Joe Morella and Edward Z. Epstein, *Paulette* (New York: St. Martin's Press, 1985), p. 24.

67. *Swan*, pp. 18, 45. Frank Baldanza, "Huxley and Hearst," *Essays on California Writers* (Bowling Green, O.: Bowling Green University Press, 1978), pp. 39–42. Naturally, not all details correspond. In *Swan*, Hearst's castle is moved closer to L.A.—to Chatsworth, where the Huxleys were now thinking of buying a ranch; the architecture of the house becomes Early English, rather than Spanish; and Hearst didn't make a habit of hiring Spanish Civil War vets. Yet the book does follow known fact, down to the soda fountain in the basement of Davies's home; and Hearst did endow a home for sick children.

68. *Swan* owes a peculiar debt to Lady Ottoline Morrell, who died several months before the book was started: the magnate's household resembles Garsington tethered off California's coastal range, and Huxley borrowed stories of Ottoline's cousin, "the burrowing duke," whose castle had hidden basements and subbasements, for *Swan's* climax.

69. Milton Birnbaum, "Aldous Huxley," in *The Politics of Twentieth-century Novelists*, George Panichos, ed. (New York: Hawthorn, 1971).

70. Thomas Merton, "Huxley's Pantheon," *Catholic World* (November 1940), p. 208. A foreword written at this time for an edition of Gorky's short stories suggests that Huxley grappled with the deficiencies of Propter/Heard's character: "When writers attempt to portray a person who is both virtuous and grown-up, they gen-

erally succeed only in portraying a prig" (London: Jonathan Cape, 1939), p. x.

71. *Swan*'s hero (Propter) is called a "Commie," but in fact he spends his days in Emersonian self-reliance, creating a self-help community modeled after Ralph Borsodi's School of Rational Living in New York, which Huxley had visited the previous year.

72. *Swan*, p. 184. Unfortunately, even the best novelist must take care in renovating earlier successes, and the structure of *Swan*—borrowed from earlier, episodic House Party novels such as *Crome Yellow* and *These Barren Leaves*—sags under the weight of the deeper political philosophy it contains.

   Twenty years earlier, Aldous had confessed to Ottoline that he used the house party as "a simple device for getting together a fantastic symposium" (Sarah Darroch, *Ottoline: The Life of Lady Ottoline Morrell* [New York: Coward McCann, 1975], p. 217).

73. Quoted in Robert Baker, *Darkness at Noon* (Madison: University of Wisconsin Press, 1982), p. 188.

74. Grace Hubble, The Hubble Collection, November 30, 1938.

75. Grace Hubble, The Hubble Collection, Journal, December 24, 1939.

76. In *Swan*, lectures overtake the story; a good forty pages of speechifying could have been dropped. Huxley also indulged his bad habit of improbable interior monologues: Virginia (the Davies character) complains that her patron wants her to "talk like Louisa M. Alcott," an author she could hardly be expected to know. Finally, the author drops several subplots and characters—including Propter, his nonattached hero—without resolution.

77. Smith, *Letters of Aldous Huxley*, p. 439. *They Still Draw Pictures: A Collection of 60 Drawings Made by Spanish Children During the War* (New York: Spanish Children Welfare Association, 1938).

78. "The Farcical History of Richard Greenow," in *Twice Seven* (London: The Reprint Society, 1944), p. 451.

79. Anita Loos, *Fate Keeps on Happening* (New York: Dodd, Mead, 1984), p. 142.

80. Christopher Isherwood interview, June 2, 1985.

81. Christopher Isherwood, *My Guru and His Disciple* (New York: Farrar, Straus and Giroux, 1980), pp. 4–6.

82. Isherwood, *My Guru and His Disciple*, p. 11.

83. Isherwood, *Down There*, p. 191.

84. Maria Huxley to Jeanne Neveux, January 29, 1939.

85. Rosemary Dinnage, *Annie Besant* (New York: Penguin, 1986), p. 90. See also Mary Luyters, *Krishnamurti* (New York: Farrar, Straus and Giroux, 1975).

86. Loos, *Fate Keeps on Happening*, p. 170.

87. Grace Hubble, The Hubble Collection, July 30, 1939.

88. Grace Hubble, The Hubble Collection, June 16, 1939.

89. Smith, *Letters of Aldous Huxley*, p. 437.

90. Smith, *Letters of Aldous Huxley*, p. 445.

91. Smith, *Letters of Aldous Huxley*, p, 245.

92. Maria Huxley to Jeanne Neveux, June 1939. Maria presumably would have been even more shocked if Aldous had included Hearst's widely known pet name for his mistress's genitalia, "Rosebud," the word which echoes through the later Orson Welles–Herman Mankiewicz film, *Citizen Kane*. Huxley actually restrained himself (Barbara Leaming, *Orson Welles* [New York: Viking, 1985], p. 205).

93. Rosalind Huxley interview, August 8, 1987.

94. Aldous Huxley to Flora Strousse, February 19, 1932, in Smith, *Letters of Aldous Huxley*, p. 357.

95. Francis Huxley interview, July 10, 1985.

96. Peggy Kiskadden interview, June 6, 1985.

97. Christopher Isherwood, *Prater Violet* (New York: Farrar, Straus, 1946), p. 33.

98. Grace Hubble, The Hubble Collection, January 8, 1939.

99. Morley, *The Hollywood Raj*, p. 5.

100. Grace Hubble, The Hubble Collection, July 30, 1939.

101. Loos, *Kiss Hollywood Good-by*, pp. 154–55.

102. Grace Hubble, Travel Diaries, The Hubble Collection, July 30, 1939.

103. Maria Huxley to Jeanne Neveux, June 31, 1939.

FIVE

GREY EMINENCE

1. Grace Hubble, The Hubble Collection, August 23, 1939.

2. Maria Huxley to Jeanne Neveux, August 28, 1939.

3. Matthew Huxley interview, June 11, 1985. Huxley probably didn't expect much from his new allies of the Hitler-Stalin pact; he remained as isolated from them as the America Firsters were from Europe.

4. "Blackout to Whitewash: Civil Defence Since 1937," pamphlet printed by Greater London Council, Public Relations Branch, 1984, p. 2.

5. J. B. Priestley, *Midnight on the Desert* (New York: Harper & Row, 1937), pp. 46–47.

6. Kenneth Clark, in *A Memorial Volume, Aldous Huxley*, ed. Julian Huxley (New York: Harper & Row, 1965), p. 15.

7. *The Art of Seeing* (New York: Harper, 1942; reissued, Seattle: Montana Books, 1975), pp. vii–viii.

8. John Keats, *You Might As Well Live* (New York: Simon and Schuster, 1970), pp. 177–78.

9. Ezra Goldman, *The Fifty-Year Decline and Fall of Hollywood* (New York: Simon and Schuster, 1961), p. 171.

10. Aldous Huxley, interviewed in *The New Yorker*, October 25, 1947. Huxley told Douglas Churchill of the *New York Times* that he "found it necessary to broaden Miss Austen's subtle humor so that audiences would know they were viewing a comedy" (March 3, 1940).

11. Christopher Isherwood, *Prater Violet* (New York: Farrar, Straus, 1946), p. 57.

12. Christopher Isherwood, *Down There on a Visit* (New York: Simon and Schuster, 1962), pp. 131, 165.

13. A good overview of Huxley's film career can be found in Virginia Clark, *Aldous Huxley and Film* (Metuchen, N.J.: Scarecrow Press, 1987).

14. Sheridan Morley, *Tales from the Hollywood Raj* (New York: Viking, 1984), p. 162.

15. Morley, *The Hollywood Raj*, p. 165.

16. Morley, *The Hollywood Raj*, p. 182.

17. Christopher Isherwood, *My Guru and His Disciple* (New York: Farrar, Straus and Giroux, 1980), p. 117.

18. Morley, *The Hollywood Raj*, p. 172.

19. Grover Smith, *Letters of Aldous Huxley* (New York: Harper & Row, 1968), p. 70.

20. Sarah Darroch, *Ottoline: The Life of Lady Ottoline Morrell* (New York: Coward-McCann, 1975), p. 128. Ottoline and Huxley shared another parallel attitude to war: neither could bear to read the war news. Each German victory brought a repressed shiver (of despair or guilt) that they could not bring themselves to join the patriotic frenzy.

21. *Grey Eminence*, p. 193.

22. Christopher Isherwood, *A Single Man* (New York: Simon and Schuster, 1964), p. 57.

23. Hugh Kenner, review of G. K. Chesterton, *New York Times Book Review*, February 10, 1987, p. 16.

24. "Cruelty," essay in the collection of the Humanities Research Center, University of Texas, Austin; in the collection of materials which Huxley sent to Hearst's *Journal-American* and other papers.

25. Smith, *Letters of Aldous Huxley*, p. 428.

26. According to a recent survey, at 6'4", Huxley stood above 99.27 percent of Americans (N. R. Kleinfeld, *New York Times*, March 8, 1987), p. 6.

27. *The Art of Seeing*, p. 67.

28. *The Art of Seeing*, p. 7.

29. Sybille Bedford, *Aldous Huxley* (New York: Harper/Knopf, 1973), p. 386.

30. *The Art of Seeing*, p. 96.

31. Letter dated December 1939, at UCLA Library, Special Collections Department.

32. Bosley Crowther, *Hollywood Rajah* (New York: Holt, 1960), pp. 178–83. Frank Baldanza asserts that Hearst did not believe in suing authors (though there is no evidence that Huxley knew this) in "Huxley and Hearst," in *Essays on California Writers* (Bowling Green University Press, Bowling Green, O., 1978), pp. 40–41. Ironically the Hearst corporation's Avon Books kept *Swan* in print for at least seven printings.

33. See summary of reviews in Robert Baker, *Darkness at Noon* (Madison: University of Wisconsin Press, 1982), p. 188. Even in retrospect, *Swan* has been undervalued, with critics calling the novel "inferior to his later novels" and other bad names, as C. S. Ferns noted in *Aldous Huxley: Novelist* (London: The Athlone Press, 1980), p. 163.

34. Juliette Huxley, *Leaves of the Tulip Tree* (London: John Murray, 1986), p. 121.

35. Juliette Huxley, *Leaves of the Tulip Tree*, p. 138.

36. Peggy Kiskadden interview, June 6, 1985.

37. Julian Huxley, *Memories* (New York: Harper & Row, 1970), p. 68.

38. *Time*, March 4, 1940.

39. Julian Huxley, *Memories*, p. 217.

40. Smith, *Letters of Aldous Huxley*, p. 450.

41. Maria Huxley to Jeanne Neveux, February 12, 1940.

42. Smith, *Letters of Aldous Huxley*, p. 454.

43. David Fine, ed., *Los Angeles in Fiction* (Albuquerque: University of New Mexico Press, 1985), p. 172.

44. Harold Nicolson, *The War Years* (New York: Atheneum, 1967), p. 65.

45. Ted Morgan, *Maugham* (New York: Simon and Schuster, 1980), p. 435.

46. Morgan, *Maugham*, p. 435.

47. As quoted in *Maugham*, p. 459; American reviews of *Swan*, such as George Catlin's in the *New York Times* (January 27, 1940), tended to contrast Huxley's esotericisms with Hollywood's mass cultural context.

48. Smith, *Letters of Aldous Huxley*, p. 452.

49. Smith, *Letters of Aldous Huxley*, pp. 451–52. (Like the biography of Catherine of Siena which he had abandoned in favor of writing *Swan*, this untitled fantasy would have been a fascinating addition to his works.)

50. Otto Friedrich, *City of Nets* (New York: Harper & Row, 1986), p. 252.

51. Budd Schulberg, *What Makes Sammy Run?* (New York: Random House, 1941), pp. 222–23.

52. Kenneth Anger, *Hollywood Babylon II* (New York: Dutton, 1984), p. 99. The first explanation comes from this improbable book: "It is an unpleasant truth that

for many people war is an aphrodisiac. America was under the spell of Mars."

A second hypothesis has the Hollywood studios sympathetic, remaining neutral only to honor government policy: "By 1940 Hollywood could no longer ignore the fact that thousands of men and women were dying when a word from the more influential members of the film community could save them," John Baxter wrote in *The Hollywood Exiles* (New York: Taplinger, 1976), p. 201.

A third way of reading this period has industry executives cravenly deleting Jewish-sounding names from credits until war was declared. Only then did the studios rush around to cash in on a good anti-Nazi story.

53. Quoted in J. R. Taylor, *Strangers in Paradise: The Hollywood Emigrés, 1933–1950* (London: Faber & Faber, 1983), p. 145.

54. Bruce Cook, *Brecht in Exile* (New York: Holt, Rinehart and Winston, 1983), p. 58.

55. Robert Craft, *Chronicle of a Friendship* (New York: Knopf, 1973); Stravinsky in exile is given a cameo in the 1988 film *Bird*.

56. Ronald W. Clark, *The Life of Bertrand Russell* (New York: Knopf, 1976), p. 467.

57. Clark, *Bertrand Russell*, p. 471.

58. Bertrand Russell, *The Autobiography of Bertrand Russell 1914–1944* (Boston: Little, Brown, 1968), p. 360.

59. Smith, *Letters of Aldous Huxley*, p. 454.

60. Quoted in Baxter, *The Hollywood Exiles*, p. 202.

61. Barbara Leaming, *Orson Welles* (New York: Viking, 1985), p. 209.

62. Edwin Robertson, *The Way to Freedom* (New York: Harper & Row, 1966), p. 246.

63. Maria Huxley to Eddy Sackville-West, October 7, 1940, letter in the possession of Matthew Huxley.

64. Francis Partridge, *A Pacifist's War* (London: Robin Clark, 1985), p. 34.

65. Partridge, *A Pacifist's War*, p. 86.

66. Smith, *Letters of Aldous Huxley*, p. 433.

67. Anita Loos, *Fate Keeps on Happening* (New York: Dodd, Mead, 1984), p. 171.

68. Colin Shindler, *Hollywood Goes to War* (London: Routledge & Kegan Paul, 1979), p. 24.

69. The history of the Peace Pledge Union is described in J. M. Murry's *The Pledge of Peace* (London: Cape, 1938).

70. Smith, *Letters of Aldous Huxley*, p. 455.

71. Grace Hubble, The Hubble Collection, December 3, 1939.

72. Maria Huxley to Jeanne Neveux, January 19, 1940.

73. Isherwood, *My Guru and His Disciple*, p. 50.

74. *Writers at Work: The Paris Review Interviews*, 6th series, George Plimpton, ed. (New York: Viking, 1984), p. 112.

75. Grace Hubble, The Hubble Collection, April 1940.

76. Grace Hubble, The Hubble Collection, July 3, 1940.

77. As quoted in Bedford, *Aldous Huxley*, p. 406.

78. Morley, *The Hollywood Raj*, p. 177.

79. Bedford, *Aldous Huxley*, pp. 405–6.

80. Bedford, *Aldous Huxley*, p. 405.

81. Probably the reason Huxley considered adapting *Lady Chatterley's Lover* for the screen now was that Frieda Lawrence had asked him to help with a stage adaptation, for which Huxley recommended Isherwood; the film wasn't made until 1981, directed by Just Jaecken and written by Christopher Wickins.

82. "Chawdron," in *Twice Seven* (London: The Reprint Society, 1944), p. 319. This story of a biographer may contain the earliest sketches for *Swan*, complete with an

aging tycoon who falls in love with a spiritual but unsophisticated artist and an explanation of the word "propter."

83. Smith, *Letters of Aldous Huxley*, p. 462.

84. Smith, *Letters of Aldous Huxley*, p. 444.

85. Smith, *Letters of Aldous Huxley*, p. 461.

86. Grace Hubble, The Hubble Collection, September 29, 1940.

87. Grace Hubble, The Hubble Collection, May 25, 1941.

88. Mary Anita Loos interview, July 10, 1986.

89. Smith, *Letters of Aldous Huxley*, p. 464.

90. Grace Hubble, The Hubble Collection, August 23, 1940.

91. Maria Huxley to Jeanne Neveux, March 25, 1940.

92. Charlie Chaplin, Jr., *My Father, Charlie Chaplin* (New York: Random House, 1960), pp. 227–28. Goddard was already struggling out from under Chaplin's shadow; in 1940, she appeared in four films.

93. David Robinson, *Chaplin: His Life and Art* (New York: McGraw-Hill, 1985), pp. 489–96. Like Huxley and Bertrand Russell, Chaplin disliked Stalin and detested the Soviet-German nonaggression pact.

94. Robinson, *Chaplin*, p. 506.

95. Smith, *Letters of Aldous Huxley*, p. 464. Several critics have suggested *Grey Eminence* as the work in which Huxley's disaffection with politics was most clearly outlined; see Charles M. Holmes, *Aldous Huxley and the Way to Reality* (Bloomington: Indiana University Press, 1970), p. 129.

96. Christopher Isherwood, *The World in the Evening* (New York: Random House, 1954), p. 11.

97. *Time Capsule 1940* (New York: Time-Life Books, 1968), pp. 192–93.

98. Christopher Isherwood interview, June 2, 1985.

99. Quoted in Shindler, *Hollywood Goes to War*, p. 13.

100. In this context must be placed a Christmas play Huxley wrote for an NBC radio production with Spencer Tracy and Bette Davis, "Christmas Greetings to Great Britain" (Boston: David Godine, 1972). Huxley's sketch shares motifs with Dickens's *A Christmas Carol*.

101. Maria Huxley to Rose D'Haulleville, March 13, 1941.

102. Norman Zierold, *Garbo* (New York: Stein and Day, 1969), pp. 126–27.

103. Mercedes De Acosta, *Here Lies the Heart* (New York: Reynal, 1960), p. 261.

104. Anita Loos, *Kiss Hollywood Good-by* (New York: Viking, 1974), pp. 55–56.

105. Grace Hubble, The Hubble Collection, January 25, 1940.

106. Smith, *Letters of Aldous Huxley*, p. 451.

SIX

THE PERENNIAL PHILOSOPHY

1. Julian Huxley, *Memories* (New York: Harper & Row, 1970), p. 257. At the very moment Julian promoted U.S. support of Britain, he was losing his job as director of the London Zoo.

2. Benjamin Bok interview, June 14, 1985.

3. Grace Hubble, The Hubble Collection, December 7, 1941.

4. Quoted in Sheridan Morley, *Tales from the Hollywood Raj* (New York: Viking, 1984), p. 77.

5. John Berger interview, *In These Times*, May 21, 1980, p. 14.

6. Smith, *Letters of Aldous Huxley*, pp. 474–75. This is one of several dozen occasions where Huxley's spiritual crises resulted in new physical ailments.

7. Grace Hubble, *The Hubble Collection*, August 28, 1941.

8. Juliette Huxley interview, June 24, 1985.

9. "Ozymandias, The Utopia That Failed," in *Tomorrow and Tomorrow and Tomorrow and Other Essays*, p. 86.

10. "Ozymandias," p. 100.

11. *Tomorrow and Tomorrow and Tomorrow*, p. 71.

12. Grover Smith, *Letters of Aldous Huxley* (New York: Harper & Row, 1968), p. 483.

13. Maria Huxley to Grace Hubble, *The Hubble Collection*, April 20, 1942.

14. Eugen Herrigel, *Zen in the Art of Archery*, R. C. Hull, trans. (New York: Pantheon, 1953), p. 39.

15. Smith, *Letters of Aldous Huxley*, p. 406.

16. *Grey Eminence*, p. 285.

17. Like Huxley, Allen's filmed persona is haunted by human misery and the uncertainty of God's existence. Why so much human suffering, he asks, turning his loaded pensiveness into a New Age gag. In *Stardust Memories*, Allen even has a psychiatrist name his obsession "Ozymandias Melancholia," a faulty denial mechanism.

18. *Grey Eminence*, p. 175.

19. *Grey Eminence*, p. 89.

20. Smith, *Letters of Aldous Huxley*, p. 431. This feared breakdown, discussed in a letter to Gordon Sewell on December 31, 1937, was written following Huxley's depression on arriving in Hollywood and just as he decided to move to California for good.

21. Christopher Isherwood, *Prater Violet* (New York: Farrar, Straus, 1946), p. 100.

22. *Grey Eminence*, p. 285.

23. Founding documents for Trabuco College, Vedanta Society of Southern California. The three pillars of Heard's credo were *research* (into "psycho-physical methods of development," such as the exercises of Bates and Alexander), *experiment* (meditation and other spiritual exercises), and *practice* (a cooperative farm).

24. Richard Chase, "Yogi-Bogey," *Partisan Review* (May 1942), p. 262.

25. William Tyndall, "The Trouble with Aldous Huxley," *American Scholar* (October 11, 1942), p. 459.

26. Maria Huxley to Grace Hubble, *The Hubble Collection*, January 9, 1944.

27. Mercedes De Acosta, *Here Lies the Heart* (New York: Reynal, 1960), pp. 228–29.

28. Norman Zierold, *Garbo* (New York: Stein and Day, 1969), p. 118.

29. Vito Russo, *The Celluloid Closet: Homosexuality in the Movies* (New York: Harper & Row, 1981), p. 44. Actually, Hollywood portrayals of tomboys (and lesbianism in general) was "an exotic and often fascinating extension of the male myth. . . . True lesbianism, relationships defined by and in terms of women's needs and desires, was not contemplated. In the popular arts especially, such women were simply perceived to be 'like men' and they conjured up a far more appealing androgyny than did male sissies" (p. 5).

30. De Acosta, *Here Lies the Heart*, p. 304.

31. Charles Chaplin, *My Autobiography* (New York: Simon and Schuster, 1964), p. 391.

32. *The Art of Seeing*, p. viii.

33. Smith, *Letters of Aldous Huxley*, p. 473.

34. *After Many a Summer Dies the Swan*, p. 139.

35. Maria Huxley, quoted in Sybille Bedford, *Aldous Huxley*, p. 422.

36. *Leda* (New York: Doran, 1922), p. 24.

37. *Brief Candles*, p. 247.

38. Aldous Huxley to Sybille Bedford, in Smith, *Letters of Aldous Huxley*, p. 476.

39. Smith, *Letters of Aldous Huxley*, p. 521.

40. Bedford, *Aldous Huxley*, p. 415.

41. George Grossmith, as quoted in Morley, *The Hollywood Raj*, p. 102; another sketch of conditions at Fox in the early forties is in Joseph Schrank, "Facing Zanuck," *American Heritage* (December 1983).

42. Irving Hoffman summed up critical response to *Jane Eyre* in the *Hollywood Reporter*, February 18, 1944; Huxley was interviewed on his role in the film on December 30, 1942, in the *New York Times*.

43. Anita Loos, *Fate Keeps on Happening* (New York: Dodd, Mead, 1984), p. 168.

44. Anita Loos, *A Girl Like I* (New York: Viking, 1966), p. 184.

45. Anita Loos, *Kiss Hollywood Good-by* (New York: Viking, 1974), pp. 175–76. Selznick, it must be said, was having personal difficulties which affected his behavior on the set of *Jane Eyre*; he fell into a period of heavy gambling and drinking— swallowing enough Benzedrine to make a speed freak taciturn in comparison. The death of his brother Myron in 1944 only accentuated his self-destructive tendencies.

46. John Baxter, *The Hollywood Exiles* (New York: Taplinger, 1976), p. 159.

47. Gary Carey, *All the Stars in Heaven* (New York: Dutton, 1981), p. 29.

48. Grace Hubble, The Hubble Collection, January 20, 1942.

49. Lillian Schlissel, *Conscience in America* (New York: Dutton, 1968), p. 17; Helen Michael Kowski, "The Roots of American Nonviolence," in *The Power of the People*, R. Cooner and H. Michael Kowski, eds. (Philadelphia: New Society, 1981), pp. 17– 24.

50. Harold Story, UCLA Oral History Collection, Los Angeles, Calif.; Norman Thomas, *Conscientious Objectors in America* (New York: Heubsch, 1935), p. 46.

51. Welles dominated the production, according to Virginia Clark's *Aldous Huxley and Film* (Metuchen, N.J.: Scarecrow Press, 1987), p. 51. For critical studies of *Jane Eyre*, see *Journal of Popular Film* 6, no. 1 (1978) and *Literature Film Quarterly* 3, no. 2 (1975). See also Huxley's interview with the *New York Times*, December 30, 1942.

52. Christopher Isherwood interview, June 2, 1985.

53. Salka Viertel, *The Kindness of Strangers* (New York: Holt, Rinehart and Winston, 1969), p. 261.

54. Quoted in Bruce Cook, *Brecht in Exile* (New York: Holt, Rinehart and Winston, 1983), p. 72.

55. Colin Shindler, *Hollywood Goes to War* (London: Routledge, Kegan Paul, 1979), p. 52.

56. Carey, *All the Stars in Heaven*, p. 255.

57. John Russell Taylor, *Hollywood Forties* (New York: Gallery Books, 1985), pp. 22–23. In the words of film historian Taylor, "The war in Europe was simpler to portray: lots of spies and secret service, suave sinister Nazis and brave Europeans fighting them."

58. Ezra Goldman, *The Fifty-Year Decline and Fall of Hollywood* (New York: Simon and Schuster, 1961), p. 66.

59. Christopher Isherwood, *My Guru and His Disciple* (New York: Farrar, Straus and Giroux, 1980), p. 130.

60. "Distractions I," in *Vedanta for the Western World*, Christopher Isherwood, ed. (Vedanta Press: Vedanta Society of Southern California, 1945), pp. 126–27.

61. Smith, *Letters of Aldous Huxley*, p. 482.

62. Maria Huxley to Grace Hubble, The Hubble Collection, April 10, 1943.

63. Mary Anita Loos interview, July 10, 1986.

64. Loos, *Kiss Hollywood Good-by*, p. 149.

65. Grace Hubble, The Hubble Collection, November 4, 1942; Grace's response to Edwin is from an attached manuscript, "The Missing Years."

66. Gerald Heard, *Pain, Sex, and Time* (New York: Harper's, 1939), pp. 299, 185.

67. Smith, *Letters of Aldous Huxley*, p. 430; in a letter to J. B. Priestley, December 17, 1937.

68. De Acosta, *Here Lies the Heart*, p. 322.

69. Quoted in Morley, *The Hollywood Raj*, p. 176.

70. G. C. Field, *Pacifism and Conscientious Objection* (Cambridge, Eng.: Cambridge University Press, 1945). Huxley's relationship to Hinduism caused contradictions in his pacifism; on the one hand, the *Bhagavad-Gita* includes lines like "Evil they may be/Worst of the wicked/Yet if we kill them/Our sin is greater." On the other hand, in the same volume Krishna teaches that nothing, including war, affects human divinity; in fact, soldiering is offered as one path to enlightenment.

71. Martin Green, *Gandhi and Tolstoy* (New York: Basic Books, 1983), pp. 238–39.

72. Niccolò Tucci, *The Power of the People* (Philadelphia: New Society, 1987), Cooney and Michalowski eds., text by Marty Jezer, pp. 91–94. Many pacifists, such as Jessie Hughan, in *Pacifism and Invasion*, cannot avow any final step to violence, however justifiable philosophically; Hughan thus outlined plans for nonviolent resistance to Hitler, along the lines of Norwegian and Danish pacifists under Nazi occupation.

73. George Orwell, *Letters and Reviews* (London: Secker and Warburg, 1968), p. 63. Orwell overstates matters. Huxley had dwelled on human perfectibility since *Ends and Means*; the problem was the method and the mass will.

74. Smith, *Letters of Aldous Huxley*, p. 462.

75. Again, Heard and Huxley reworked the same theme at the same time, though there is no telling who hit on the idea first. The same months Aldous was writing the posthumous sequence of Uncle Eustace in *Time*, Gerald worked on "The Rousing of Mr. Brodegar," in *The Great Fog* (New York: Vanguard, 1944), an account of a man who discovers his own death, in bed alone. Both writers were preoccupied with the moment of passage: when, precisely, does one realize death?

76. *Time Must Have a Stop*, p. 295. If Huxley had looked at war from a more anthropological viewpoint, he might have concluded, with Margaret Mead, that "social measures for the prevention of warfare might include ways of modifying the gene pool or radical changes in diet" (Margaret Mead, "Alternatives to War," in Fried, Harris, and Murphy, eds., *War: The Anthropology of Armed Conflict* [New York: Museum Press, 1968], p. 219).

77. *Time Must Have a Stop*, p. 295.

78. *The Art of Seeing*, p. 16.

79. *The Perennial Philosophy*, p. 105.

80. *Crome Yellow*, p. 34.

81. Christopher Isherwood, *Down There on a Visit* (London: Methuen, 1962), p. 248. Isherwood has divided his reminiscences of the war period into fiction *(Down There)* and autobiography *(My Guru and His Disciple)*; material here is drawn from both sources and from an interview with the author. This same macabre postwar mood of Hollywood appears in Budd Schulberg's *What Makes Sammy Run?* (New York: Random House, 1941): "All along the sidewalk were little knots of pool-room characters. . . . There was something savage and tense about that street. Autograph hunters prowled it, and ambitious young ladies in fancy hair-dos and slacks" (p. 213).

82. Bedford, *Aldous Huxley*, p. 437.

83. Isherwood, *My Guru and His Disciple*, p. 51.

84. Christopher Isherwood interview, June 2, 1985. As early as 1920, in *Leda*, Huxley had contemplated a similar notion in his poem "The Birth of God": "And the void was filled by a rushing wind/And he breathed a sense of something friendly and near/And in privation the life of God began."

85. "Introduction," *Bhagavad-Gita*, trans. Prabhavananda and Isherwood (New York: New American Library, 1944).

86. See, for example, *The Oxford Book of English Mystical Verse*, Nicholson and Lee, eds. (Oxford, Eng.: Clarendon Press, 1917).

87. Ronald W. Clark, *The Huxleys* (New York: McGraw-Hill, 1968), p. 302.

88. "Introduction," *Bhagavad-Gita*, p. 22. Huxley's contribution dates from the midforties.

89. Erwin Schrödinger, *What Is Life?* (New York: Doubleday, 1956), p. 88.

90. W. Somerset Maugham, *Introduction to Modern English and American Literature* (Philadelphia: Blakiston, 1944), p. 336.

91. Maria Huxley to Jeanne Neveux, May 1, 1945.

92. Christopher Isherwood interview, June 2, 1985.

93. Bedford, *Aldous Huxley*, p. 442.

94. *Grey Eminence*, p. 175.

95. *Jacob's Hands* is the story of a ranch hand (similar to one in Llano) skilled at healing animals who tried his skills on humans. Blocked by studio fears of retaliation by the American Medical Association, the project was abandoned, according to Isherwood in Gilbert Adair's "Isherwood in Hollywood," *Sight and Sound* (Winter 1976), p. 25. Brian Finney, in *Christopher Isherwood* (London: Faber & Faber, 1979), says the script was later telecast in the United States; no extant copies of the original screenplay were found.

96. Aldous Huxley to Matthew Huxley, April 21, 1944.

97. *Tomorrow and Tomorrow and Tomorrow*, pp. 101–2.

98. *The Crows of Pearblossom* (New York: Random House, 1967). The work was written at Llano in December 1944.

99. Aldous Huxley to Matthew Huxley, July 22, 1944. One thing Huxley tried to pass along to his son was the discipline necessary to achievement in writing, illustrating this with examples of how he compiled *The Perennial Philosophy*: the hundreds of note cards in various files, notes by selection and author, a précis, and a critique for each selection.

100. Susan Squire, "Shock Therapy's Return to Respectability," *The New York Times Magazine*, November 22, 1987.

101. Julian Huxley, *Memories*, pp. 279–80. Julian wasn't the only family member affected by the German bombing; Aunts Ethel and Nettie, T.H.'s two surviving daughters, likewise became ill. The Huxley family was as a whole deeply involved in World War II: Thomas Eckersley developed sophisticated radar to locate submarines; another cousin was chief censor for the BBC (and as such, might have resented, if not suppressed, Huxley's earlier antiwar writings).

102. Loos, *Fate Keeps on Happening*, p. 216.

103. Though few noticed at that time, works like *The Art of Seeing* and *The Perennial Philosophy* paralleled the mood of Huxley's British contemporaries, for whom "the political commitment of the thirties was replaced during the course of the war by a call for a return to 'personal values'" (Robert Hewison, *Under Siege* [London: Quartet Books, 1979], p. 72). In Britain, outside active duty, writers' sacrifices involved far less: shortages of paper and unsatisfying desk jobs. Meanwhile, crowds slept in the Underground, the awful smell of a city in smoking ruins biting at their nostrils.

104. Niccolò Tucci, *The Power of the People*, p. 91.

105. Smith, *Letters of Aldous Huxley*, p. 513.

106. Albert Camus, *The Myth of Sisyphus*, trans. Justin O'Brien (New York: Knopf, 1955), p. 91.

107. *Swan*, p. 137.

108. George Woodcock, *Dawn and the Darkest Hour* (New York: Viking, 1972). The

Saturday Review of Literature, September 2, 1944, excoriated Huxley for his "abdication of a fine intelligence":

His abdication is only one among many. Few have gone as far as he in flight from the world, but there are numbers who are fleeing.

Huxley's cousin Laurence Collier made a similar critique in his *Flight from Conflict* (London: C. A. Watts, 1944).

109. Smith, *Letters of Aldous Huxley*, p. 525. This is only one of the dozens of examples where Huxley, contrary to claims that he did not read critics, followed their treatment of his work.

110. H. G. Wells, *The Door in the Wall* (Boston: David Godine, 1980). John Fowles, in *Daniel Martin* (New York: New American Library, 1977), p. 290, traces this "hidden garden" motif in English mysticism to Samuel Palmer, the painter:

A place outside the normal world, intensely private and enclosed, intensely green and fertile, numinous, haunted and haunting, dominated by a sense of magic that is also a sense of a mysterious yet profound parity in all existence [recurring] from the sublimities of the Garden of Eden and the Forest of Arden to the 1930s hokum of James Hilton's Shangri-La.

SEVEN

APE AND ESSENCE

1. S. J. Perelman had a similar scriptwriter's nightmare, "huge piles of burning motion-picture scripts lit up the sky. The crisp tang of frying writers and directors whetted my appetite" *(The Most of S. J. Perelman* [New York: Simon and Schuster, 1957], p. 47).

2. Bedford, *Aldous Huxley*, pp. 435–36.

3. Bedford, *Aldous Huxley*, p. 453.

4. *Time Must Have a Stop*, pp. 305–6.

5. From the film *Crossfire*, 1947, directed by Edward Dmytryk.

6. Quoted in Robert Hewison, *Under Siege: Literary Life in London 1939–45* (London: Quartet Books, 1977), pp. 170–71.

7. Quoted in Colin Shindler, *Hollywood Goes to War* (London: Routledge, Kegan Paul, 1979), p. 104.

8. Smith, *Letters of Aldous Huxley*, p. 503.

9. *The Perennial Philosophy*, p. 107.

10. Gerald Heard, "The Poignant Prophet," *Kenyon Review* 27 (Winter 1965), pp. 49–79.

11. *The Perennial Philosophy*, p. 94.

12. In Morris's collected letters, 1888, he stated, "I have an Englishman's wholesome horror of government interference and centralization," quoted by Peter Stansky in a review, *New York Times Book Review*, April 17, 1988, p. 14.

13. *Science, Liberty and Peace* (London: Fellowship of Reconciliation/Harper's, 1946), p. 61.

14. The social prophecy of *Science, Liberty and Peace* parallels Jack London's in *The Valley of the Moon* (1913) and *The Little Lady of the Big House*—except for London's half-digested social Darwinism of Herbert Spencer. London and Huxley came to similar conclusions about decentralization and the social responsibilities of scientists.

15. Peter Thody, *Aldous Huxley: A Biographical Introduction* (New York: Scribner's, 1973), p. 108.

16. Quoted in Charles Rolo, "Aldous Huxley," *Atlantic Monthly* (August 1947).

Scholars in the 1940s had as much trouble tracing the turns in Huxley's career as rock critics did with Bob Dylan in the sixties and seventies.

17. Jerome Meckier, "Mysticism or Misty Schism?" in *British Studies Monitor* 5 (Fall 1974): 3–35. Meckier is a leading critic of Huxley. See also *Time*, October 1, 1945.

18. Edmund Wilson, *The New Yorker*, September 2, 1944, pp. 64–66. In files now housed at the Library of Congress, an outside reader for *The American Scholar* confessed: "I must say if this article [an excerpt from *Time*] was sent in without a name I should have called it bosh. I still think it's bosh, but it has a certain historical value" ("Eternity and Time," *American Scholar*, July 1945).

19. *Variety*, February 2, 1944; *Jane Eyre*'s problem, from *Variety*'s standpoint, was its original plot: "The original story was as pat as all that."

20. Smith, *Letters of Aldous Huxley*, p. 534.

21. *Brave New World*, Preface (New York: Harper's, 1946, new edition), p. xiii. The persistent (and temporary) optimism of this preface matched that of *Science, Liberty and Peace*.

22. David Caute, *The Great Fear: The Anti-Communist Purge under Truman and Eisenhower* (New York: Simon and Schuster, 1978), pp. 488–89.

23. Matthew Huxley to Sophie Moulaert, September 12, 1945.

24. Alvah Bessie, *Inquisition in Eden* (New York: Macmillan, 1965), pp. 154–56.

25. Jake Zeitlin interview, June 1, 1985.

26. Smith, *Letters of Aldous Huxley*, p. 536; Matthew Huxley interview, June 11, 1985; Otto Friedrich, *City of Nets* (New York: Harper & Row, 1986), pp. 246–49.

27. Smith, *Letters of Aldous Huxley*, p. 537.

28. Script dated December 5, 1945, "and supplemental materials" in possession of the Walt Disney Studios.

29. Friedrich, *City of Nets*, p. 187.

30. Billy Wilder once joined Walter Reisch, scenarist of *Ninotchka*, in asking Garbo who she wanted to play:

> "A male clown," she answered, to their distress. "Under the makeup and the silk pants, the clown is a woman. And all the admiring girls in the audience who write him letters are wondering why he does not respond. They cannot understand."

Norman Zierold, *Garbo* (New York: Stein and Day, 1969), pp. 99–100.

31. Zierold, *Garbo*, p. 130.

32. NBC's three-hour *Brave New World* miniseries aired in March 1980, originally produced by University Television in 1978. The *Los Angeles Herald* in a classic film-industry bromide wrote "Many of Huxley's ideas survive in this version" (March 7, 1980).

33. Christopher Isherwood, "Los Angeles," *Horizon*, nos. 93–94 (October 1947). History proved Isherwood wrong, though a backlash against today's Hollywood teens-at-the-mall films might yet validate his prediction.

34. Smith, *Letters of Aldous Huxley*, p. 566. "The Gioconda Smile" was based on the 1920 Greenwood murder case in London.

35. Smith, *Letters of Aldous Huxley*, pp. 550–51.

36. Shindler, *Hollywood Goes to War*, p. 97.

37. P. G. Wodehouse, *Barmy in Wonderland* (London: Pan, 1952), p. 39.

38. Hortense Powdermaker, *Hollywood: the Dream Factory* (Boston: Little, Brown, 1950), p. 22.

39. Sheridan Morley, *Tales from the Hollywood Raj* (New York: Viking, 1983), p. 3.

40. Morley, *The Hollywood Raj*, p. 210.

41. From Katia Mann's *Unwritten Memories*, trans. Hunter and Hildegarde Han-

num, ed. Elizabeth Plessen and Michael Mann (New York: Knopf, 1975), p. 128.

42. In *Reply Paid,* Heard's detective character becomes a free-lance cryptographer in L.A. (Denial plays a major role in Heard's fiction: Heard doesn't mention what other cryptographers were doing in 1942. Nor do his mysteries have a romantic angle; unable to portray a homosexual romance, Heard included none at all.)

43. The Hubble Collection, The Huntington Library.

44. Donald Watt, *Aldous Huxley: The Critical Heritage* (London: Routledge & Kegan Paul, 1975), p. 345. Despite Mann's harsh words, he continued to respect Huxley's writing; in a letter written before returning from his 1949 visit, Mann included "a good many of things by Huxley" in his list of works unsurpassed by the next generation (*The Letters of Thomas Mann,* ed. and trans. R. and C. Winston [New York: Knopf, 1971]), p. 416.

45. Smith, *Letters of Aldous Huxley,* p. 572.

46. Smith, *Letters of Aldous Huxley,* p. 566.

47. Smith, *Letters of Aldous Huxley,* p. 572.

48. Smith, *Letters of Aldous Huxley,* p. 576; *Time,* February 9, 1947.

49. Doug McClelland, *Hollywood on Hollywood* (London: Faber & Faber, 1985), p. 244.

50. Christopher Hampton, *Tales from Hollywood* (London: Faber & Faber, 1983), p. 85.

51. *Grey Eminence,* p. 30.

52. *Grey Eminence,* p. 286.

53. *Time Must Have a Stop,* p. 300.

54. Gerald Heard, "Dromenon," in *The Great Fog* (New York: Vanguard, 1944), pp. 178–79, 186.

55. Matthew Huxley interview, June 11, 1985.

56. Edmund Wilson, "Aldous Huxley in the World Beyond Time," *The New Yorker,* September 2, 1944, p. 65.

57. Bedford, *Aldous Huxley,* p. 469.

58. Smith, *Letters of Aldous Huxley,* p. 565.

59. Bedford, *Aldous Huxley,* p. 464.

60. Matthew Huxley to Sophie Moulaert, September 12, 1945.

61. Salka Viertel, *The Kindness of Strangers* (New York: Holt, Rinehart & Winston, 1969), p. 298.

62. Bedford, *Aldous Huxley,* 458–65.

63. These revealing letters are reprinted in Bedford, *Aldous Huxley,* pp. 477–79.

64. Smith, *Letters of Aldous Huxley,* pp. 548, 561–62, 565, 567. These letters suggest that he never decided if this work should take the form of fiction or biography, which may have been the reason for the project's downfall.

65. Smith, *Letters of Aldous Huxley,* p. 569.

66. Smith, *Letters of Aldous Huxley,* p. 600.

67. Nathanael West, *The Day of the Locust* (New York: Time-Life, 1965), p. 78.

68. David Fine, "Introduction," in *Los Angeles in Fiction* (Albuquerque: University of New Mexico Press, 1984), p. 140.

69. Smith, *Letters of Aldous Huxley,* p. 546.

70. *Ape and Essence,* p. 67. Huxley apparently scouted the locations at the L.A. Biltmore when his sister-in-law, Suzanne Nicolas, held an exhibition of sculpture there in the fall of 1946.

71. Smith, *Letters of Aldous Huxley,* p. 528.

72. Grace Hubble, The Hubble Collection, undated.

73. *Ape and Essence,* p. 92. In a long essay written at the same time, Huxley revealed another key source for this work, his former teacher J. B. S. Haldane: "If a

tenth of a society's members were affected by gamma radiation . . . the species would be doomed . . . because of some unfortunate little accident . . . men of the 50th century may face hare-lipped imbeciles" ("Double Crisis," *World Review*, December 1948, p. 36). *Ape* can be read as a mirror-image of T. H. Huxley's essay, "On the Relations of Man to the Lower Animals," in *Man's Place in Nature* (New York: Appleton, 1898).

74. From Dennis Gabor's contribution to *A Memorial Volume, Aldous Huxley*, Julian Huxley, ed.(New York: Harper & Row, 1965).

75. George Woodcock notes these points in his excellent *Dawn and the Darkest Hour* (New York: Viking 1972), pp. 255–62. There are major differences between attitudes to science in Huxley's two California novels: in *Swan*, experiments on apes and carp promised immortality; in *Ape*, the Satanic Scientific Investigator forces Einstein to unleash a plague on the earth.

76. Hermann Bowersox, "Aldous Huxley: The Defeat of Youth" (Ph.D. diss. University of Chicago, 1946). This is one of approximately two dozen dissertations on Huxley at American universities. See Eben Bass, *Aldous Huxley: An Annotated Bibliography of Criticism* (New York: Garland, 1981).

77. The parallels between *Ape and Essence* and *Things to Come* are previously noted in Virginia Clark, *Aldous Huxley and Film* (Metuchen, N.J.: Scarecrow Press, 1987), and Tom Dardis, *Some Time in the Sun* (New York: Scribner's, 1976).

78. Robert Philmus, *Into the Unknown* (Berkeley: University of California Press, 1970, second edition, 1982), p. 2. For a survey of other novels of apocalypse, see Michael Dorris and Louise Erdrich, "Bangs and Whimpers," *New York Times Book Review*, March 13, 1988.

79. Robert Heinlein, *Assignment in Eternity* (New York: Signet, 1963), p. 152. In "Lost Legacy," written the same year as *Ape*, Heinlein recycled Huxley's notion of genetic engineering, even down to creating classes of workers biologically "suited" to their work tasks. The hero, one Philip Huxley, suffers much of Aldous's postwar disaffection: "Any attempt to place the essentials of the ancient knowledge in the hands of the common people is met by a determined, organized effort to prevent it, and to destroy, or disable the one who tries it." Heinlein insists that after man decimates the planet, apes would re-begin evolution.

80. Maria Huxley to Rosalind Rajagopal, in Bedford, *Aldous Huxley*, p. 78.

81. "Talk of the Town," *New Yorker*, October 25, 1947.

82. "A Note on Gandhi," *Vedanta and the West* (April–May 1948), p. 66.

83. Claire Nicolas, "Aldous Huxley," *Vogue* (August 1947). She sent the manuscript to Aldous for comment and he rewrote two paragraphs.

84. *Variety*'s Christmas week review of *A Woman's Vengeance* was little kinder by being backhanded: "Huxley's philosophical platitudes do not bore because of capable handling by players and directors."

85. Quoted in David Robinson, *Chaplin* (New York: McGraw-Hill, 1985), p. 529. In *Verdoux*, Chaplin equated Nazi mass murders and those of war munitioneers, the sort of brilliant equivalence Martin Luther King Jr. would make in 1965 between civil rights and the war in Vietnam.

86. Chaplin, *My Autobiography* (New York: Simon and Schuster, 1964), pp. 488–93; David Robinson, *Chaplin*, pp. 538–43.

87. Bedford, *Aldous Huxley*, p. 483.

88. Friedrich, *City of Nets*, p. 330.

89. Laura Archera Huxley, *This Timeless Moment* (New York: Farrar, Straus & Giroux, 1968), pp. 1–4.

90. Burgess Meredith interview, August 7, 1986. Meredith was at that time finishing *Mine Own Executioner*, about an unlicensed analyst working with hypnosis. He and Huxley discussed a documentary on hypnosis.

91. Smith, *Letters of Aldous Huxley*, p. 636.

92. Susan Sontag, "Pilgrimage," *New Yorker*, December 21, 1987, p. 41.

93. Quoted in Bedford, *Aldous Huxley*, p. 481.

94. Huxley's predictions of the danger of nuclear power occurred even before the "Our Friend The Atom" campaign of the late forties and fifties documented in the award-winning 1982 film *Atomic Café*.

95. Bedford, *Aldous Huxley*, p. 485.

96. Isherwood, "Los Angeles," *Horizon*, nos. 93–94 (October 1947). This double issue on the arts, film, and literature of America was one of Cyril Connolly's best and included Ralph Ellison, Donald Windham, John Berryman, Walker Evans, and Marshall McLuhan, a stellar number of a stellar publication.

EIGHT

THE DEVILS OF LOUDUN

1. Smith, *Letters of Aldous Huxley*, p. 541.

2. Christopher Isherwood, "Coming to London," in *Exhumations* (New York: Simon and Schuster, 1966), p. 155.

3. Christopher Isherwood interview, June 11, 1985.

4. D. H. Lawrence, "Things," in *The Lovely Lady* (New York: Penguin, 1946), p. 134.

5. "The Double Crisis," *World Review* (December 1948), pp. 33–38.

6. Smith, *Letters of Aldous Huxley*, p. 507.

7. *America and the Future* (New York: Pemberton Press, 1970), p. 2. Beyond the extrapolators of trends, such as Huxley, are those with prevision, able to imagine the future so clearly that it can be seen. Nostradamus's *Centuries* are a famous example. Hollywood has often filmed his predictions: for example, *Nostradamus Says So!*, an MGM serial of the forties, and the docudrama *Nostradamus* (1984) narrated by Orson Welles. Huxley mentions in his letters one of the most famous of Nostradamus's predictions—a world war at the end of the twentieth century.

8. Smith, *Letters of Aldous Huxley*, p. 604.

9. Smith, *Letters of Aldous Huxley*, p. 604.

10. Anthony West, "Post-Atomic Sex," *New Statesman and Nation*, March 5, 1949, p. 233.

11. George Orwell, as quoted in Donald Watt, *Aldous Huxley: The Critical Heritage* (London: Routledge, Kegan Paul, 1975), p. 334.

12. Alice Morris, "Mr. Huxley Holds That Man Is As Yet Many Monkeys," *New York Times Book Review*, August 22, 1948, p. 5.

13. Sybille Bedford interview, July 10, 1985.

14. Quoted in Sybille Bedford, *Aldous Huxley* (New York: Harper/Knopf, 1973), p. 497.

15. Smith, *Letters of Aldous Huxley*, p. 591.

16. Grace Hubble, The Hubble Collection, February 9, 1949.

17. Background to the House Committee on Un-American Activities in Hollywood can be found in David Caute, *The Great Fear* (New York: Simon and Schuster, 1978), and Stefan Kanfer, *A Journal of the Plague Years* (New York: Atheneum, 1973). The survey on alleged Communist involvement is from John Cogley, *Report on Blacklisting* (New York: Fund for the Republic, 1956).

18. Grace Hubble, The Hubble Collection, February 10, 1949.

19. The project, encouraged by John Huston, was a farce set in South America, *Below the Equator*. Like their earlier, ill-fated *Jacob's Hands*, their treatment produced no major interest.

20. Ezra Goodman, *The Fifty-Year Decline and Fall of Hollywood* (New York: Simon and Schuster, 1961), p. 378.

21. Quoted in John Baxter, *The Hollywood Exiles* (New York: Taplinger, 1976), p. 220.

22. Robert Craft, "With Aldous Huxley," *Encounter* 25 (November 1965), p. 10.

23. "A Conversation with Stravinsky," typescript in possession of Matthew Huxley.

24. Craft, "With Aldous Huxley," p. 12.

25. Brian Finney, *Christopher Isherwood: A Critical Biography* (London: Faber & Faber, 1979), p. 206.

26. Christopher Isherwood, "Los Angeles," *Horizon*, nos. 93–94 (October 1947), p. 146.

27. Maria Huxley to Jeanne Neveux, June 5, 1949.

28. "Variations on a Philosopher," Bernard Bergonzi, ed., *Great Short Works of Aldous Huxley* (New York: Harper/Perennial, 1969), p. 416. Huxley includes a telling digression on decentralization: "every grant of authority should be hedged about with effective reservations; political, economic, and religious organizations should be small and co-operative . . . the centralization of economic and political power should be avoided at all costs."

29. Bernard Bergonzi, Preface to *Great Short Works of Aldous Huxley*; André Maurois, *Aldous Huxley 1894–1963* (New York: Harper & Row, 1965); Milton Birnbaum, *Aldous Huxley's Quest for Values* (Knoxville: University of Tennessee Press, 1971).

30. George Woodcock, *Dawn and the Darkest Hour* (New York: Viking, 1972), p. 267.

31. "Variations on a Philosopher," p. 461.

32. Burgess Meredith interview, August 7, 1986. (Meredith claims he was responsible for introducing Huxley to hypnosis.) Aldous, Burgess, and Paulette had planned a film on hypnosis across the ages, with contemporary demonstrations.

33. "Variations on a Philosopher," p. 463. As a biographer, Huxley occasionally overextended his imaginative powers. In *Grey Eminence*, he had described the expression on a magistrate greeting Père Joseph. In the essay on Biran, he conveys purported states of mind of party-goers observing the deputy.

34. Samuel Clemens, *The Autobiography of Mark Twain*, Charles Neider, ed. (New York: Harper/Perennial, 1966), pp. 54–59.

35. *Abbott and Costello Meet the Invisible Man*, Universal, 1951.

36. Laura Huxley interview, April 14, 1987; Milton Ericson, "A Special Inquiry with Aldous Huxley," *American Journal of Clinical Hypnosis* 8 (1965), pp. 14–33.

37. "Variations on a Philosopher," pp. 463, 471. When Huxley tried to publish this biography separately, the work was turned down as overlong by *The American Scholar*. Correspondence at the Library of Congress (August 18, 1949, Beulah Hagen to Aldous Huxley).

38. Anita Loos, *Kiss Hollywood Good-by* (New York: Viking, 1974), p. 145.

39. "Variations on a Philosopher," p. 438.

40. *In These Times*, May 21, 1980.

41. Caute, *The Great Fear*, p. 501.

42. *Time Capsule 1950* (New York: Time-Life Books, 1967), p. 49. Typical of the era is the following quote from *Time*: "For years, squatting behind the rock of the First Amendment, U.S. Communists had screamed their denunciations and thumbed their noses at U.S. democracy."

43. Alvah Bessie, *Inquisition in Eden* (New York: Macmillan, 1965), p. 265.

44. Quoted in Caute, *The Great Fear*, p. 516.

45. David Robinson, *Chaplin: His Life and Art*, Appendix IX: "The FBI V. Chaplin" (New York: McGraw-Hill, 1985).

46. Stephen Spender, *New York Times Book Review*, April 30, 1950, p. 5.

47. Harvey Breit, "Talk with Aldous Huxley," *New York Times Book Review*, May 21, 1950, p. 28.

48. Documents released to the author under the Freedom of Information Act.

49. Juliette Huxley, *Leaves of the Tulip Tree* (London: John Murray, 1986).

50. Smith, *Letters of Aldous Huxley*, p. 629. At the time Isherwood and Huxley were cowriting their never produced screenplay *Below the Equator;* all that is left of it may be their correspondence.

51. Smith, *Letters of Aldous Huxley*, p. 632.

52. Quoted in Bedford, *Aldous Huxley*, p. 514.

53. Smith, *Letters of Aldous Huxley*, p. 480.

54. Arthur Miller, *The Crucible* (New York: Penguin, 1976), p. 34.

55. Miller, *The Crucible*, p. 6. Miller's play treats distinctly New England themes: the virgin forest ("the best place on earth not paying homage to God") and small-town provincialism. For his efforts, Miller found the anti-Red noose tightening around his neck (provoked by his earlier and more explicit anti-HUAC play, *You're Next*).

56. Craft, "With Aldous Huxley," 1965, p. 12.

57. R. H. Robbins, *Encyclopedia of Witchcraft and Demonology*, Introduction (New York: Crown, 1959), p. 7.

58. Quoted in Caute, *The Great Fear*, p. 502.

59. The last such proceedings apparently occurred in Scotland in 1707, according to the entry "Witchcraft," in *The New Columbia Encyclopedia* (New York: Columbia University Press, 1975).

60. Julian Huxley, *Memories* (New York: Harper & Row, 1970), pp. 175–76.

61. Robbins, *Encyclopedia of Witchcaft and Demonology*, p. 15.

62. Smith, *Letters of Aldous Huxley*, p. 480.

63. Quoted in Woodcock, *Dawn and the Darkest Hour*, p. 103.

64. Maria Huxley to Matthew, April 4, 1951.

65. Matthew Huxley interview, June 11, 1985.

66. Quoted in Bedford, *Aldous Huxley*, p. 518.

67. Francis Thompson, *Highland Smugglers: Second Sight and Superstitions* (New-tongrange, Scotland: privately published, 1980), p. 14.

68. Renée Haynes, *The Hidden Springs: An Inquiry into Extra-Sensory Perception* (New York: Devin-Adair, 1961), p. 16.

69. Jules Romains, *Eyeless Sight* (Secaucus, N.J.: Citadel, 1978; 1st ed., 1921). In the 1960s, a Dr. Vichit in Thailand found these abilities were susceptible to training, particularly among four- to eight-year-olds. A century ago, F. W. H. Myers had encountered many instances of individuals—almost always blind—who accurately guessed color with their fingers. (After Romains's book originally appeared, the great novelist was ridiculed to the point where he left science altogether, but the phenomenon did not disappear after his humiliation.)

70. Quoted in Bedford, *Aldous Huxley*, p. 518.

71. Quoted in Bedford, *Aldous Huxley*, p. 521.

72. Peggy Kiskadden interview, August 13, 1985.

NINE

THE DOORS OF PERCEPTION

1. Juliette Huxley, *Leaves of the Tulip Tree* (London: John Murray, 1986), p. 229.

2. Marie Le Put interview, July 10, 1986.

3. Smith, *Letters of Aldous Huxley*, p. 639.

4. Smith, *Letters of Aldous Huxley*, p. 634.

5. Smith, *Letters of Aldous Huxley*, p. 87.

6. Smith, *Letters of Aldous Huxley*, p. 383.

7. Smith, *Letters of Aldous Huxley*, pp. 484–85. Huxley accompanied this acknowledgment of Old Testament marvels with an injunction not to stress "powers, personal advantages and future time [rather than] where all the great spiritual leaders have insisted that it should be placed, on eternity, abandonment to the will of God and humility."

8. *What Vedanta Means to Me: A Symposium*, ed. John Yale (New York: Rider and Company, 1951), pp. 29–30.

9. *Eyeless in Gaza*, p. 9.

10. William James, "What Psychical Research Has Accomplished," in Jeffrey Mishlove, *The Roots of Consciousness* (New York: Random House Bookworks, 1975), p. 96.

11. Mishlove, *The Roots of Consciousness*, p. 82.

12. William James, "What Psychical Research Has Accomplished," p. 102; Leonard Huxley, *Life and Letters of T. H. Huxley*, vol. I (London: Appleton, 1901), pp. 451–52; Gerald Myer, *William James* (New Haven: Yale, 1988), p. 10.

13. Smith, *Letters of Aldous Huxley*, p. 642. At times, Huxley blamed humanity's self-defeating streak on diabolical possession.

14. On this ramble, Huxley told Craft of the ether addiction of T. S. Eliot's wife, Vivienne: "the house smelled like a hospital. All that dust and despair in Eliot's poetry is to be traced to this fact" (Robert Craft, "With Aldous Huxley" *Encounter* 25 [November 1965], p. 14).

15. Christopher Isherwood, "Los Angeles," *Horizon*, nos. 93–94 (October 1947), p. 144.

16. Christopher Isherwood, *My Guru and His Disciple* (New York: Farrar, Straus & Giroux, 1980), p. 201.

17. Isherwood, *My Guru and His Disciple*, pp. 201–202.

18. Jonathan Fryer, *Christopher Isherwood* (Los Angeles: Times Mirror/New English Library, 1977), p. 238.

19. Among the sins Viertel had to justify was her support of Hanns Eisler and the causes she had championed in thirty years of activism in Hollywood: the Civil Rights Congress, the Stockholm Peace Petition, the Hollywood Ten and Spanish refugee committees. See Salka Viertel, *The Kindness of Strangers* (New York: Holt, Rinehart and Winston, 1969), pp. 324–34.

20. David Robinson, *Charles Chaplin: His Life and Art* (New York: McGraw-Hill, 1985), p. 576.

21. Robinson, *Chaplin*, pp. 572–81. According to FBI documents released to Robinson under the Freedom of Information Act, the U.S. Immigration and Naturalization Service "stated bluntly that the INS did not have sufficient evidence to exclude Chaplin from the U.S. if he attempts to reenter." The Attorney General was not only vague, he was bluffing.

22. Larry Ceplair and Steven Englund, *Inquisition in Hollywood: Politics in the Film Community, 1930–1960* (Berkeley: University of California Press, 1983), p. 376.

23. Ceplair and Englund, *Inquisition in Hollywood*, p. 388.

24. Quoted in the *New York Times*, June 9, 1988.

25. Ceplair and Englund, *Inquisition in Hollywood*, pp. 373–91.

26. *Saturday Review*, April 12, 1952, p. 3.

27. *Prelude to Fame* was released in November 1950, the first film of Huxley's work to be made without his involvement. It was directed by Fergus McDonel and starred Jeremy Spenser as the child. The *New York Times* reviewer said its "strength lies in sensitive characterization and intelligent use of the classics," which Huxley might

have taken to his credit if he had not been so disappointed about being left out of the project.

28. Aldous Huxley to Gabriel Pascal, December 16, 1951.

29. Smith, *Letters of Aldous Huxley*, pp. 644–45.

30. Aldous Huxley to Gabriel Pascal, December 16, 1951.

31. Aldous Huxley to Matthew Huxley, June 20, 1952.

32. Frank Capra, *The Name Above the Title* (New York: Macmillan, 1971), p. 441.

33. Smith, *Letters of Aldous Huxley*, p. 663.

34. Capra, *The Name Above the Title*, p. 443.

35. Smith, *Letters of Aldous Huxley*, p. 641. Given the virulence of the anti-Communist disease in 1952, probably the only Golden Age Americans look back to in that year is the emergence of rock and roll.

36. Laura Archera Huxley, *This Timeless Moment* (New York: Farrar, Straus & Giroux, 1968), pp. 7–9.

37. Grace Hubble, The Hubble Collection, February 25, 1953.

38. Laurence Collier, interview with Sybille Bedford, quoted in Bedford, *Aldous Huxley* (New York: Knopf, 1975), p. 154.

39. Gervas Huxley, quoted in Bedford, *Aldous Huxley*, p. 14.

40. Smith, *Letters of Aldous Huxley*, p. 634.

41. Bedford, *Aldous Huxley*, p. 523.

42. Smith, *Letters of Aldous Huxley*, p. 650.

43. Smith, *Letters of Aldous Huxley*, p. 647, dated July 1952, to an unidentified correspondent (probably Stravinsky).

44. Bedford, *Aldous Huxley*, p. 523. Huxley would begin *Island* with this procedure: a girl helps a plane-wrecked reporter "talk out [the trauma] several times until there is no further emotional attachment to it."

45. Smith, *Letters of Aldous Huxley*, p. 649.

46. Laura Archera Huxley, *This Timeless Moment*, p. 14.

47. Smith, *Letters of Aldous Huxley*, p. 542. Asked about prophecy by a German futurologist, Huxley responded that while we teach futurology, we must also add "eternitology" to the curriculum.

48. Smith, *Letters of Aldous Huxley*, p. 530.

49. Smith, *Letters of Aldous Huxley*, p. 657.

50. Bedford, *Aldous Huxley*, p. 471.

51. "Whenever things become very, very dark," Loos wrote, "I try to concentrate on the religion of a friend of mine who is a big man at the Studio . . . on the Great Divine Order" (*A Mouse Is Born* [New York: Doubleday, 1951], p. 24).

52. Bedford, *Aldous Huxley*, p. 510.

53. On this occasion, Meredith remembers how Dr. Milton Erickson—as famous a hypnotist as Eileen Garrett was a medium—had his subject entranced. "He asked him to row back and forth in time. 'I want you to look around and find what date it is.' '1952,' the subject answered. 'And what's on the front page?' 'Nothing much except that President Wallace has been assassinated.' " Burgess Meredith interview, August 7, 1986.

54. Eileen J. Garrett, *Many Voices: The Autobiography of a Medium* (New York: Putnam, 1968), p. 198.

55. Jim Kepner, Director of International Gay and Lesbian Archives, interview May 1988.

56. Armistead Maupin, "The First Couple," *San Francisco Examiner*, August 18, 1985, p. 10.

57. Christopher Isherwood, interview with John Lee, *Christopher Street* 10, no. 4 (no date, 1987), pp. 54–55.

58. Isherwood, *My Guru and His Disciple*, pp. 209–10.

59. *The Devils of Loudon* (New York: Harper & Row, 1952), p. 111.

60. Angus Wilson, "Mr. Huxley's Split Mind," *New Statesman and Nation*, November 1, 1952.

61. (With Stuart Gilbert), "Joyce the Artificer," pamphlet in the British Museum, London, 1952.

62. Undated letter in the possession of Matthew Huxley (1952).

63. Francis Huxley interview, July 10, 1985.

64. Humphry Osmond, "May Morning in Hollywood," in *Moksha: Writing on Psychedelics and the Visionary Experience (1931–1963)*, ed., Michael Horowitz and Cynthia Palmer (New York: Stonehill, 1977).

65. Osmond, "May Morning," p. 35.

66. Andrew Weil and Winifred Rosen, *Chocolate to Morphine* (Boston: Houghton Mifflin, 1983), p. 107.

67. Jay Stevens, *Storming Heaven: LSD and the American Dream* (Boston: Atlantic Monthly Press, 1987), p. 11; Aronson and Osmond, *Psychedelics* (N.Y.: Doubleday/ Anchor, 1970), p. 23.

68. Quoted in Stevens, *Storming Heaven*, p. 7.

69. *Brief Candles*, "After the Fireworks," p. 246.

70. Huxley, "Wanted, A New Pleasure," in *Moksha*, p. 9. In an essay on drugs in the works of Huxley and Arthur Koestler, Arthur Gilbert postulated a name for Huxley's ideal drug, Huxene, which he called a "pop nirvana . . . transcend with Huxley on Tuesday with Huxene," in "Pills and the Perfectibility of Man," *Virginia Quarterly* 45 (Spring 1969), pp. 315–28.

71. *The Perennial Philosophy*, p. 107.

72. Thomas Henry Huxley, *Autobiography* (Oxford: Oxford University Press, 1983), ed. Gavin de Beer, p. 109.

73. *Devils*, p. 324.

74. Betty Wendell interview, June 2, 1985.

75. Gerald Heard, "Dromenon," in *The Great Fog* (New York: Vanguard, 1944), p. 198.

76. Betty Wendell interview, June 2, 1985.

77. Stefan Kanfer, *A Journal of the Plague Years* (New York: Atheneum, 1973), pp. 197–99.

78. David Dunaway, *How Can I Keep From Singing: Pete Seeger* (New York: McGraw-Hill, 1981) (London: Harrap, 1985), p. 153.

79. John Wexley, *The Trial of Julius and Ethel Rosenberg* (New York: Cameron and Kahn, 1955), p. 607.

80. David Caute, *The Great Fear* (New York: Simon and Schuster, 1978), p. 505.

81. Kanfer, *The Plague Years*, p. 204.

82. Ezra Goldman, *The Fifty-Year Decline and Fall of Hollywood* (New York: Simon and Schuster, 1961), pp. 391–94. Another Hollywood drugstore, Turner's, specialized in delivering money.

83. *Owl Hoots*, May 1953, p. 14.

84. Francis Huxley interview, July 10, 1985.

85. Renée Haynes, *The Hidden Springs* (New York: Devin-Adair, 1961), p. 76.

86. Bergonzi, *Great Short Works*, p. 450. When Hollywood finally filmed peyote hallucinations, in Cheech and Chong's *Things Are Tough All Over* (1982), the best it could come up with was snakes and belly dancers.

87. *Doors*, pp. 56–57. Dr. Humphry Osmond understood this fit of paranoia; he

himself had taken a dose of a chemical similar to adrenochrome and wandered around his hospital for hours, staring at menacing cracks in the floor.

88. Smith, *Letters of Aldous Huxley*, p. 603.

89. Juliette Huxley, *Leaves of the Tulip Tree*, p. 225.

90. Nathanael West, *The Day of the Locust* (New York: Random House, 1939), p. 133.

91. William James, *The Varieties of Religious Experience*, p. 388.

TEN

HEAVEN AND HELL

1. D. S. Maini, *Indian Review* (July 1953), p. 294.

2. Alistair Sutherland, "Aldous Huxley's Mind At Large," *The Twentieth Century*, no. 155 (May 1954), pp. 446–47; R. C. Zaehner, "The Menace of Mescalin," *Blackfriars*, no. 412 (July 1954), p. 323.

3. Dr. Humphry Osmond, "Peeping Tom and Doubting Thomas," *The Twentieth Century*, no. 155 (June 1954), p. 522.

4. Betty Wendell interview, June 2, 1985.

5. Peggy Kiskadden interview, June 3, 1985.

6. Jake Zeitlin interview, August 7, 1986.

7. Thomas Mann, letter to Ida Hertz, March 21, 1954, quoted in Watt, *The Critical Heritage*, pp. 394–95.

8. *New Yorker*, March 12, 1954. The *New Yorker's* critic rejected Huxley's use of capital letters as undermining his down-to-earth setting.

9. Grover Smith, *Letters of Aldous Huxley* (New York: Harper & Row, 1968), pp. 700, 715.

10. *Doors*, p. 78.

11. Sybille Bedford, *Aldous Huxley* (New York: Knopf, 1973), p. 525.

12. Smith, *Letters of Aldous Huxley*, p. 643.

13. Peggy Kiskadden interview, May 31, 1986.

14. Marie Le Put interview, July 10, 1986.

15. The Hubble Collection, Aldous Huxley to Grace Hubble, September 30, 1953.

16. Bedford, *Aldous Huxley*, p. 545.

17. Edward Abbey, *The Brave Cowboy* (New York: Dodd, Mead, 1956), p. 105. Abbey's novel of draft resistance was a decade ahead of its time.

18. Note, however, that Huxley endorsed the Buddhist Eight-fold Path which, among other injunctions, prohibits the manufacture and use of arms.

19. Betty Wendell, essay in the possession of Sybille Bedford.

20. Unpublished document in possession of the U.S. Immigration and Naturalization Service, 1953.

21. Declassified hearing results, U.S. Immigration and Naturalization Service, Barney Potratz, hearing officer.

22. Aldous Huxley to Matthew Huxley, January 20, 1954.

23. Smith, *Letters of Aldous Huxley*, pp. 830–31. *The Genius and the Goddess* has been misinterpreted as autobiographical; in these letters Huxley makes explicit the qualities which attracted (and repelled) him to Frieda Lawrence.

24. Maria Huxley to Elsie Murrell, quoted in Bedford, *Aldous Huxley*, 570.

25. Renée Haynes, "Aldous Huxley," *New Blackfriars* (November 1964), p. 100.

26. Bedford, *Aldous Huxley*, p. 564.

27. Juliette Huxley interview, July 5, 1985.

28. Juliette Huxley interview, July 5, 1985.

29. *The Genius and the Goddess,* in *Great Short Works,* p. 318. George Woodcock, in *Dawn and the Darkest Hour* (New York: Viking, 1972), has commented on the sadomasochistic references in this work, particularly recurring book titles such as *Miss Floggy's Boarding School.* Orwell had already noted this tendency in Huxley at the time of *Ape and Essence.*

30. "Variations on a Philosopher," in *Great Short Works of Aldous Huxley* (New York: Harper/Perennial, 1969), p. 435. Searching for autobiography in a subject's biography of others requires some justification. Huxley chose his subjects with extreme care and the timing of their dilemmas—Father Joseph in 1940, Maine de Biran in 1951—provide a fascinating gloss for how Huxley mined his life for his nonfiction. Huxley frequently quotes the biographical writings of his own subjects, where available.

31. "Variations on a Philosopher," p. 439. No better guide exists to Huxley's fate after his wife's death than his projection in the Biran biography; thus do biographers find their own troubles in the life of another.

32. William James, "What Psychical Research Has Accomplished," in Jeffrey Mishlove, ed., *The Roots of Consciousness* (New York: Random House/Bookworks, 1975), p. 104.

33. Robert Heinlein, *Assignment in Eternity* (New York: Signet, 1963), p. 46.

34. Norman Mailer, *The Deer Park* (New York: Putnam, 1954), p. 150.

35. Mailer, *The Deer Park,* p. 270.

36. Vito Russo, *The Celluloid Closet* (New York: Harper & Row, 1981), p. 107.

37. Amos Vogel, *Film as a Subversive Art* (New York: Random House, 1974), p. 235.

38. Russo, *The Celluloid Closet,* p. 112.

39. Brian Finney, *Christopher Isherwood* (London: Faber & Faber, 1979), p. 223.

40. Christopher Isherwood, *My Guru and His Disciple* (New York: Farrar, Straus & Giroux, 1980), pp. 211–12.

41. Isherwood, *My Guru and His Disciple,* p. 212.

42. Smith, *Letters of Aldous Huxley,* p. 720. For five hours Huxley experienced "luminous illustrations of the Christian saying, 'Judge not that ye be not judged,' and the Buddhist saying, 'To set up what you like against what you dislike, this is the disease of the mind.' "

43. Smith, *Letters of Aldous Huxley,* p. 723.

44. Smith, *Letters of Aldous Huxley,* pp. 725–26. As Huxley poured his premature grief over losing Maria into his writing, he concocted a role reversal for *The Genius and the Goddess:* the great man is ill and his wife successfully revives him.

45. Peggy Kiskadden interview, May 31, 1985. A number of Maria's friends assert that just before she died, she said aloud, "Don't let her get Aldous." But to whom Maria referred, among the many women consoling Aldous at this time, is unknown.

46. Smith, *Letters of Aldous Huxley,* p. 712. Huxley had actually pursued this subject even *before* he took mescaline, in a letter dated April 10, 1953: "Disease, mescaline, emotional shock, aesthetic experience and mystical enlightenment have the power, each in its different way and in varying degrees, to inhibit the functions of the normal self and its ordinary brain activity, thus permitting the 'other world' to rise into consciousness" (Smith, *Letters of Aldous Huxley,* p. 688).

47. *Writers at Work: The Paris Review Interviews,* 2nd series, ed. Malcolm Cowley (New York: Viking, 1963), p. 204.

48. Smith, *Letters of Aldous Huxley,* p. 699.

49. *Tomorrow and Tomorrow and Tomorrow,* p. 102.

50. Smith, *Letters of Aldous Huxley,* pp. 735–37. Rose, Maria's sister, drove in from the desert to pick up their mother; she received a speeding ticket in Beverly Hills and both thus missed Maria's actual death.

51. *The Tibetan Book of the Dead,* ed. W. Y. Evans-Wentz (New York: Oxford

University Press, 1960), p. xv. Allen Ginsberg, in an interview with the author on July 2, 1988, pointed out that the Evans-Wentz translation was flawed in several key terms: "Maria may still be up there."

52. Matthew Huxley interview, June 11, 1985.

53. *Ape and Essence*, p. 152. After this bit of Shelley, Huxley added a poignant exchange: "He must have been a very sad man." "Perhaps not quite so sad as you imagine."

54. Marie Le Put interview.

55. Aldous Huxley to Claire White, April 7, 1955.

56. Rose D'Haulleville Nys interview, August 11, 1985.

57. Rose D'Haulleville Nys interview, August 11, 1985. On the trip east with Rose, Huxley wrote his secretary for addresses he had left behind; significantly, among the requests for Peggy, Gerald, and Betty was "Archera," one of those who had silently eaten the dinners the cook had left behind.

58. Bedford, *Aldous Huxley*, p. 589. Huxley was so committed to restructuring personality through meditation and hypnosis that he loved to poke fun at those who went at the task with a couch.

59. Juliette Huxley, *Leaves of the Tulip Tree* (London: John Murray, 1986), pp. 230 –31.

60. Eileen Garrett, *Many Voices* (New York: Putnam, 1968), p. 171.

61. William James, "What Psychical Research Has Accomplished," p. 100.

62. *Heaven and Hell*, pp. 139–40. The empirical, agnostic, scientific cast of his public assertion of mediumship parallels the thinking of Erwin Schrödinger in 1944 in *What Is Life?*, where he insists scientists "must be prepared to find [living matter] working in a manner that cannot be reduced to the ordinary laws of physics."

63. To Grace Hubble, The Hubble Collection, July 1955, n.d.

64. Ronald W. Clark, *The Huxleys* (New York: McGraw-Hill, 1968), p. 340.

65. Mark Trevenen Huxley interview, July 12, 1985.

66. Ellen Hovde interview, June 10, 1985.

67. Ellen Hovde interview, June 10, 1985. Huxley first took LSD on December 22, 1955, after his summer in Connecticut.

68. *Heaven and Hell*, p. 112. A fascinating parallel exists between *Heaven* and a passage in Heard's story "Dromenon," where amidst his moments of satori Heard reported an "awful spasm" of feeling lost between "the small weary words, Heaven and Hell."

69. Anaïs Nin, *The Diary of Anaïs Nin* (New York: Harcourt, Brace & World, 1966), vol. 6, p. 131.

70. Laura Archera Huxley interview, August 12, 1985.

71. J. E. Brown, "Mysticism within Native American Traditions," in Richard Woods, ed., *Understanding Mysticism* (New York: Doubleday/Image, 1980), p. 206.

72. Quoted by W. E. Hocking, "Mysticism as seen through its Psychology," in *Understanding Mysticism*, p. 228.

73. Peggy Kiskadden interview, May 20, 1988. Non-drug-induced transcendence may be easier to carry forward into daily life, often as a unitary "nature mysticism" many experience in communion with the outdoors.

74. In the pages of the BBC's *The Listener*, Zaehner reported taking mescaline in Christ Church, Oxford, where he had an unwelcomingly hilarious time, a mirror-opposite trip from Huxley's in *Doors*: "I refused, when under the influence of the drug, to look at any picture which had religious significance" (R. C. Zaehner, "Mescalin and Mr. Aldous Huxley," *The Listener*, April 26, 1956).

75. Renée Haynes, *The Hidden Springs* (New York: Devin-Adair, 1961), p. 105.

76. Heinlein, *Assignment in Eternity* (New York: New American Library, 1953), p. 46.

77. Smith, *Letters of Aldous Huxley*, p. 802.

78. Smith, *Letters of Aldous Huxley*, p. 801.

79. See Jerry Mander, *Four Arguments for the Elimination of Television* (New York: Morrow, 1980).

80. Smith, *Letters of Aldous Huxley*, p. 769.

81. Laura Huxley, "Disregarded in the Darkness," in *Moksha: Writings on Psychedelics and the Visionary Experience (1931–1963)*, eds., Horowitz and Palmer (New York: Stonehill, 1977), p. 77.

82. Bedford, *Aldous Huxley*, p. 613.

83. Smith, *Letters of Aldous Huxley*, p. 794. Aldous Huxley to Matthew Huxley, March 19, 1956. The Huxley family had a history of hasty remarriages, extending three generations. Leonard passed the news of his remarriage inadvertently to his three sons; Julian likewise surprised his father unpleasantly with his intention to marry Juliette; and Matthew Huxley, at his third marriage, didn't include his children. Laura Huxley says that she wrote only one person, her father, of the wedding but subsequently lost the letter. One old friend of Huxley opposed to Laura suggested the idea of marriage arrived during a drug trip.

84. Aldous Huxley to Peggy Kiskadden, March 19, 1956.

85. Gary Carey, Loos's biographer, in personal communication.

86. Smith, *Letters of Aldous Huxley*, p. 800.

87. Huxley rented a bungalow in the university town of Isla Vista, on Camino del Playa overlooking the ocean, where he reputedly took mescaline with faculty and students.

88. Francis Huxley interview, July 10, 1985. Huxley was not the first man in Hollywood to marry two women who preferred women; Rudy Valentino married both Jean Acker and Natacha Rambova in marriages of convenience.

89. John Atkins, *Aldous Huxley*, revised ed. (London: Calder and Boyers, 1967), p. xi.

90. Smith, *Letters of Aldous Huxley*, p. 651. Given his love of travel in the American West, it's surprising that Huxley delayed as long as he did before writing it up in nonfiction.

91. Richard Lewinsohn, *Science, Prophecy, and Prediction* (New York: Harper & Row, 1961), pp. 40–42.

92. *Tomorrow and Tomorrow and Tomorrow*, p. 141.

93. Jacques Barzun, "The Anti-Modern Essays of Aldous Huxley," in *Aldous Huxley*, ed. Robert Kuehn (Englewood Cliffs, N.J.: Prentice-Hall, 1974), pp. 51–55.

94. *Tomorrow and Tomorrow and Tomorrow*, pp. 74–75, 82–83.

95. Interview in the possession of UCLA Library, Special Collections Department, March 18, 1957.

96. UCLA interview, March 18, 1957. Huxley had complained about the lack of a "correlating principle" unifying physical and spiritual training as far back as January 9, 1940, in a letter to Eddy Sackville-West (in possession of Matthew Huxley).

97. UCLA interview, March 18, 1957. "Voices," one of the last stories he published, just as *The Genius and the Goddess* appeared, was for *The Atlantic*. Set in Santa Barbara, where he now lectured, his subject was a mischievous coed who inadvertently became possessed by the devil—Huxley at his most macabre. If this was the fictive impulse he contained, perhaps it was just as well he waited until *Island* to release it.

98. Smith, *Letters of Aldous Huxley*, p. 680.

99. Symposium papers included in Kuehn, ed., *Aldous Huxley*, pp. 18–33; at the same time, this *ubi sunt* was echoed by V. S. Pritchett in the *New York Times*: "His savagery, his horror, his misanthropy, and his satire belong to literature; the mellower pages of his later work, I think, do not" (August 26, 1955).

100. Smith, *Letters of Aldous Huxley*, p. 171.

101. Matthew Huxley interview, June 11, 1985.

102. Transcript in possession of Matthew Huxley, undated. In the spring of 1957, Huxley offered this project to Stravinsky, via Robert Craft, then to Leonard Bernstein. Both rejected it. Smith, *Letters of Aldous Huxley*, pp. 820–21.

103. Aldous Huxley to Matthew Huxley, September 30, 1956; see also the letter to Julian Huxley, August 30, 1956. Apparently Huxley hoped that the Ford Foundation's interest in overpopulation would help persuade the motorcar company to underwrite expenses.

104. Dun Roman, "Magoo by Huxley: A Tale of Movie Myopia," *Los Angeles Times*, January 30, 1977, p. 3.

105. John Baxter, *Sixty Years of Hollywood* (New York: A. S. Barnes, 1973), p. 190.

106. Roman, "Magoo by Huxley," p. 3.

107. The film is far more sophisticated than its casual reviews let on: "It is not the Chaplin of old but just old Chaplin, and too much of him." Martin and Potter, *Video Movie Guide 1988* (New York: Bantam, 1988), p. 364.

108. This battle was described in the 1987 film *Hollywood Uncensored.*

109. Robert Sumner, *Hollywood Cesspool* (Murfreesboro, Tenn.: Sword of the Lord, 1955).

110. Interview with a Fort Collins alumnus, Cheri Pann, December 25, 1986.

111. Michael Fles was one of the Wayfarers in the midfifties; personal communication to the author, June 18, 1988.

112. Jim Kepner, Gay Alliance Newsletter, October 1971.

113. Smith, *Letters of Aldous Huxley*, p. 875.

114. Aldous Huxley, July 21, 1952 (addressee unknown); see also Smith, *Letters of Aldous Huxley*, p. 647.

115. Francis Huxley interview, July 10, 1985.

116. Julian Huxley, *Memories*, vol. II (New York: Harper & Row, 1972), p. 176.

ELEVEN

ISLAND

1. Laura Archera Huxley, *This Timeless Moment* (New York: Farrar, Straus & Giroux, 1968), p. 87.

2. *Point Counter Point*, p. 391.

3. Laura Achera Huxley, *This Timeless Moment*, p. 88.

4. Dr. Max Cutler, in *A Memorial Volume, Aldous Huxley*, ed. Julian Huxley (New York: Harper & Row, 1965), p. 125.

5. Smith, *Letters of Aldous Huxley* (New York: Harper & Row, 1968), p. 889.

6. John Baxter, *Sixty Years of Hollywood* (New York: A. S. Barnes, 1973), p. 199.

7. Ezra Goldman, *The Fifty-Year Decline and Fall of Hollywood* (New York: Simon and Schuster, 1961), p. 436.

8. Robert Craft, "With Aldous Huxley," *Encounter* 25 (November 1965), p. 15.

9. Transcription in the collection of the Museum of Broadcasting, New York.

10. Patrick Faulk, "Aldous Huxley," *Horizon* (May 1980), p. 70.

11. Laura Huxley interview, June 1, 1985.

12. *Brave New World*, rev. ed. (New York: Harper & Row, 1946), p. xiii. Huxley made his long gestation period for *Island* explicit in *Writers at Work: The Paris Review Interviews*, 2nd series (New York: Viking, 1963), p. 199.

13. Smith, *Letters of Aldous Huxley*, p. 668. The priorities of the chaotic mix which

would become *Island* apparently began with an educational theory, this letter suggests.

14. Interview with Aldous Huxley in the UCLA Library, Special Collections Department, March 18, 1957. E. M. Forster has pointed out the parameters of prophetic fiction: "It demands friction and the absence of a sense of humour. . . . It is spasmodically realistic . . . its force is towards unity." *Aspects of the Novel* (New York: Harcourt, Brace, 1954), p. 130.

15. Smith, *Letters of Aldous Huxley*, pp. 791–92.

16. Smith, *Letters of Aldous Huxley*, p. 803.

17. Laura Huxley interview, June 1, 1985.

18. Smith, *Letters of Aldous Huxley*, p. 850.

19. Timothy Leary, *Flashbacks* (Boston: Tarcher Books, 1983), p. 379.

20. Leary, *Flashbacks*, pp. 43–44. One of the obscure sides to Huxley's involvement in psychedelics has been the actual number of drug sessions in which he participated. Laura asserts this was no more than a dozen; Sybille Bedford echoes this figure, warning of many people who claim to have taken drugs with Huxley. Given his proximity to active researchers such as Puharich, Osmond, and Leary, however, the number of sessions may be at least double this number, spread out over the decade 1953–1963.

21. Leary, *Flashbacks*, p. 55.

22. Musician Mel Lyman, of the Jim Kweskin Jug Band, was one accused of massaging minds under extrapowerful jolts of LSD, at his Boston commune (David Dalton, *Mind Fuckers* [San Francisco: Straight Arrow, 1971]).

23. Interview with Dyan Cannon, Cary Grant's ex-wife, *New York Times*, July 22, 1973.

24. Ross MacDonald, *The Underground Man* (New York: Bantam, 1972), p. 32.

25. Laura Archera Huxley, *This Timeless Moment*, p. 71.

26. Laura Huxley interview, June 1, 1985.

27. Peggy Kiskadden interview, August 8, 1988.

28. Laura Huxley interview, June 1, 1985.

29. Craft, "With Aldous Huxley," p. 16.

30. *Los Angeles Examiner*, May 14, 1961.

31. "If My Library Burned Tonight," *Vogue* (November 1947). His replacements show the authors to whom he was most indebted: Shakespeare, Chaucer, Homer, Dante, Yeats, Donne, Wordsworth, Baudelaire, Rimbaud, and Mallarmé, among others.

32. Juliette Huxley, *Leaves of the Tulip Tree* (London: John Murray, 1986), p. 233.

33. Smith, *Letters of Aldous Huxley*, p. 912.

34. Smith, *Letters of Aldous Huxley*, p. 911.

35. Juliette Huxley, *Leaves of the Tulip Tree*, p. 227.

36. Smith, *Letters of Aldous Huxley*, p. 853. Huxley never publicly reported experimenting with marijuana and hashish; the passing references in *Doors* and *Devils* suggest only book knowledge of their effects.

37. *Eyeless in Gaza*, p. 42. A Good Doctor appears in both works—Dr. Miller, who heals Beavis's friend and teaches him alternatives to pill-oriented medicine; in *Island*, this character becomes McPhail, who heals by mesmerism.

38. Huxley's first major statement on education dated from a 1929 preface where he wrote of "an entirely new system of training which may one day be discovered" (J. H. Burns, *A Vision of Education* [London: Williamson and Norgate, 1929], preface).

Many of *Island*'s ideas of spiritual education are traceable to the writings of Krishnamurti, particularly *Education and the Significance of Life* (London: Gollancz, 1969).

39. Smith, *Letters of Aldous Huxley*, pp. 473–74.

40. Huxley, "Culture and the Individual," in *Moksha: Writings on Psychedelics and the Visionary Experience (1931–1963)*, ed. Horowitz and Palmer (New York: Stonehill, 1977), pp. 253, 255.

41. Aldous Huxley, Foreword, in S. Charters, *Man on Earth* (Sausalito, Calif.: Contact, 1962), pp. vii, xi.

42. In this context, see John Berger, *Restoring the Earth* (New York: Knopf, 1987).

43. *Literature and Science*, pp. 109–110.

44. *Writers at Work: The Paris Review Interviews*, 2nd series, ed. Malcolm Cowley (New York: Viking, 1963), p. 199.

45. Professor Nugel of the University of Münster is currently writing on Huxley's revisions and deletions in the manuscript of *Island*. Harper's Huxley files are in the UCLA Library, Special Collections Department. The major cuts suggested were in the Raja's *Notes on What's What*.

46. At one point Laura had suggested a divorce, saying she was not the sort who married (Laura Archera Huxley, *This Timeless Moment*, p. 119).

47. Laura Archera Huxley, *This Timeless Moment*, p. 182.

48. Laura Archera Huxley, *This Timeless Moment*, p. 308.

49. *Aldous Huxley: The Critical Heritage*, ed. Donald Watt (London: Routledge & Kegan Paul, 1975), p. 453; to Claire White, July 10, 1962.

50. In Huxley's time, confrontations with authority had already begun in the Bay Area. In May 1959, Berkeley students were dragged down a flight of stairs, hit with water cannons, and clubbed for protesting HUAC hearings in San Francisco, an event Abbie Hoffman characterized as the first confrontation of the sixties, "when a generation had cast its spirit into the crucible of resistance." Lynda Obst, ed., *The Sixties* (New York: Rolling Stone, 1977), p. 24.

51. Laura Archera Huxley, *This Timeless Moment*, p. 193. KPFA survives, precariously, as one of America's maverick noncommercial radio stations.

52. "Aldous Huxley on Thought Control," *The Listener*, September 11, 1958; Wallace interviewed Huxley for his ABC program, "Mike Wallace Interviews."

53. Laura Archera Huxley, *This Timeless Moment*, p. 200.

54. Smith, *Letters of Aldous Huxley*, p. 936.

55. Ronald W. Clark, *The Huxleys* (New York: McGraw-Hill, 1968), pp. 1–2.

56. "Achieving a Perspective on the Technological Order," in *Technology and Culture*, ed. Kranzberg and Davenport (New York: New American Library, 1972), pp. 125–27.

57. "He was docile, he would have done what I wanted," she told Sybille Bedford, "but the homes we saw were so unlike my dream" (Bedford, *Aldous Huxley* [New York: Knopf, 1973], p. 707).

58. *Literature and Science*, p. 4.

59. Laura Archera Huxley, *This Timeless Moment*, pp. 137–38.

60. Smith, *Letters of Aldous Huxley*, pp. 863–64.

61. Smith, *Letters of Aldous Huxley*, p. 929.

62. Quoted in Jay Stevens, *Storming Heaven* (Boston: Atlantic Monthly Press, 1987), p. 146.

63. Stevens, *Storming Heaven*, p. 133.

64. Smith, *Letters of Aldous Huxley*, p. 678.

65. Timothy Leary, *Flashbacks*, p. 114. Leary's reports of Huxley's remarks often don't quite sound like Huxley.

66. Anaïs Nin, *The Diary of Anaïs Nin*, vol. 6 (New York: Harcourt, Brace & World, 1966), pp. 333–337.

67. Paulette Conrad-Bruat, *A Frenchwoman Looks at Aldous Huxley,* in British Museum Collection, p. 177.

68. Dr. Max Cutler, *A Memorial Volume,* p. 126.

69. Smith, *Letters of Aldous Huxley,* p. 861.

70. Trev Huxley interview, July 12, 1985.

71. Laura Archera Huxley, *This Timeless Moment,* p. 122.

72. Matthew Arnold, "The Strayed Reveller," in *Poetry and Criticism of Matthew Arnold,* ed. A. Dwight Culler (Boston: Houghton Mifflin, 1961), pp. 11–12.

73. "Variations," in *Great Short Works,* p. 422.

74. Smith, *Letters of Aldous Huxley,* p. 923. Sybille Bedford, in a letter to the author, remembered a 1954 conversation in which Huxley favored a nuclear deterrence.

75. Christopher Isherwood, *My Guru and His Disciple* (New York: Farrar, Straus & Giroux, 1980), p. 259.

76. Laura Archera Huxley, *This Timeless Moment,* pp. 266–68.

77. See Laura's discussion in *This Timeless Moment,* p. 301. The will entitled almost all his estate to her, including the lion's share of his royalties.

78. *Vedanta for the Western World,* ed. Christopher Isherwood (Hollywood, Calif.: Vedanta Press, 1945), p. 3.

79. Laura Archera Huxley, *This Timeless Moment,* pp. 308, 307.

80. Eileen Garrett, *Many Voices* (New York: Putnam, 1968), p. 172.

EPILOGUE

1. Timothy Leary, *The Politics of Ecstasy* (London: Granada Publishing Ltd., 1970), p. 252.

2. *America and the Future* (Austin, TX: Pemberton Books, 1970); all quotes in this passage are from this obscure but provocative essay, probably an updated version of his 1927 essay on America for *Harper's.*

3. Neil Postman, *Amusing Ourselves to Death* (New York: Penguin, 1985), pp. 111, 155.

4. Jack Mathews, interview in Daniel B. Wood, "Films' Commercial, Artistic Concerns at Odds," *Albuquerque Journal,* Dec. 18, 1987.

5. Vincent Canby, "Missing—Grown-Up Romance," *New York Times,* June 29, 1986.

6. Gary Carey, *All the Stars in Heaven* (New York: Dutton, 1981), p. 304.

7. Vincent Canby, "Pretty Soon, All You'll See Are Big Hits in Tiny Theatres," *New York Times,* January 25, 1987.

8. As straightforward depictions of alternate sexual identities increase, groups challenging gay stereotypes in mass media, such as the Gay and Lesbian Alliance against Defamation (GLAAD), have risen to prominence. American film has progressed significantly from *Sex Madness* (1934), in which homosexuals went insane, quietly, from their affliction.

9. In *Battle Beyond the Stars,* an ecologically devastated earth develops cancer. A mystic, "guided by the Varda [sic]," helps save the planet while counseling against taking life.

10. Ruth L. Sivard, *World Military and Social Expenditures 1985* (Washington, D.C.: World Priorities, 1986).

11. Susan Faludi, "Inner Peaceniks," *Mother Jones* (April 1987). Members of Beyond War (devoted to ending war by "changing the way we think") recite an anti-conflict pledge. Yet such good-hearted organizations may emphasize awareness over structural change, which leads to paradox. A few Beyond War members hold Peace

Teas in the evenings after returning from jobs with defense contractors.

12. Todd Gitlin and Michael Kazin, "Second Thoughts," *Tikkun* 3 (January 1988).

13. Fergus Borgdewich, "Colorado's Thriving Cults," *New York Times Magazine*, May 1, 1988.

14. Borgdewich, "Colorado's Thriving Cults."

15. "Scientologists Mob Courthouse Over Records," *Los Angeles Times*, November 5, 1985.

16. "Ghost Story," *Orlando Sentinel*, August 29, 1986.

17. Michael Crichton, "My Journey into the Twilight Zone," *Esquire* (May 1988), p. 105.

18. Today at least 5,000 full-time professional astrologers in the United States command $35 million a year from private readings; 92 percent of U.S. daily newspapers carry horoscopes—up from 78 percent of papers in 1979 ("Seeing Dollar Signs in Searching the Stars," *New York Times*, May 15, 1988).

19. Alan Gathright, "Machine Being Used to Exercise the Brain," Knight-Ridder, January 19, 1988.

20. Lee Mitgang, "It Was Twenty Years Ago Today . . . ," Associated Press wire, *Albuquerque Journal*, June 1, 1987.

21. Hollywood correspondingly underwent a mind-expanding period, including Peter Fonda's *The Trip* (1967) and Dennis Hopper's *Easy Rider* (1969), sequences in Stanley Donen's *Arabesque* (1966). In *Seconds* (1966), John Frankenheimer offers a look into the Summer of Love and psychedelics.

22. *Boston Globe*, January 20, 1988.

23. Ann Fleming, "A Mecca for Psychedelic Pilgrims," *New York Times*, August 10, 1988. Researcher Terence McKenna refutes such myths.

24. Joe Morella and Edward Epstein, *Paulette* (New York: St. Martin's Press, 1985), pp. 216–17.

25. David Robinson, *Chaplin* (New York: McGraw-Hill, 1985), p. 622.

26. Gary Carey, *Anita Loos* (New York: Knopf, 1988), p. 315.

27. Carey, *Anita Loos*, p. 313.

28. Barbara Leaming, *Orson Welles* (New York: Viking, 1985), pp. 613–16.

29. Max Turner, "Late for the Sky," *American Way* (October 1988). The Hubble Telescope has a wide-field planetary camera and a high-speed photometer to detect rapidly pulsating stars. It must give the Hubbles' cat, Copernicus, good company on dark and starry nights.

30. Laura Archera Huxley, "Oh, What Am I? Tell Me, What Am I?" in *This Timeless Moment*, pp. 205–38. Judging from its style, this work would have been an utter throwback to Huxley's earlier *comédie de moeurs*. Its lack of introspection and moral didacticism make it conceivable that Huxley may have rewritten or exhumed this from an earlier period.

31. Jim Kepner wrote a memorial of Gerald Heard, *Gay Alliance Newsletter* (October 1971).

32. *Los Angeles Times Magazine*, April 3, 1988, p. 7.

33. David Farrell, "Preservationists Rally Round the Joshua Tree," *Los Angeles Times*, March 4, 1988.

34. Christopher Isherwood, "Los Angeles," *Horizon*, nos. 93–94 (October 1947), p. 146. This key essay is reprinted in his *Exhumations*.

35. Smith, *Letters of Aldous Huxley*, p. 473.

36. Isaiah Berlin in *A Memorial Volume, Aldous Huxley*, ed. Julian Huxley (New York: Harper & Row, 1965), p. 149.

37. *Beyond the Mexique Bay*, p. 255.

38. George Woodcock, *Dawn and the Darkest Hour* (New York: Viking, 1972), p. 41.

39. Ellen Hovde interview, June 10, 1985.

40. Isherwood, "Los Angeles," p. 143.

A Note on
Sources

In the nearly seventy years since Aldous Huxley became well-known, his writing has received extraordinarily close and sophisticated attention. The sheer volume of Huxley studies over the last seven decades has generated bibliographies of bibliographies, the best of which is Eben Bass's *Annotated Bibliography* (listed in the Selective Bibliography that follows). This excellent work lists twelve bibliographies on Huxley, including two full-length works and over three dozen dissertations from around the world. Donald Watt's anthology of critical essays and reviews on Huxley is also an invaluable beginning.

Huxley never published an autobiography; he documented his personal life narrowly in nonfiction (particularly in *Ends and Means, The Art of Seeing, The Perennial Philosophy*, and *Tomorrow and Tomorrow and Tomorrow*) and in his letters. Yet his fiction contains many references that were sufficiently autobiographical to disturb his family and friends. (Among the most notable incidents were the death of the young child in *Point Counter Point*, which gravely upset Maria Huxley; the backdrops and conversations at Philip and Ottoline Morrell's estate Garsington that appeared in *Crome Yellow* and that Ottoline never forgave Huxley for publishing; and the portraits of Huxley's father and brother in his most autobiographical novel, *Eyeless in Gaza*, which prompted irritated letters from members of his family. According to Huxley's second wife, Laura Archera Huxley, passages from *Island* are closely drawn from Huxley's experiences under the influence of psychedelics.)

Literary biographers, chary of autobiographical fallacy, approach such parallels between fictional characters and events in the life of the author with great wariness. Biographers often turn to the work to inform the life, particularly when, as in the case of Huxley, autobiographical papers are destroyed. Huxley's tragic fire of 1961—when his manuscripts, journals, and letters vanished—is a principal reason why so few studies of Huxley are truly biographical. Major Huxley critics such as Baker,

Birnbaum, Bowering, Ferns, Firchow, Holmes, May, Meckier, Thody, Watts, and Woodcock have written critical/intellectual histories of the author. With a new generation of Huxley scholars, I challenge the widely accepted notion that Huxley's American period was a retreat into obscurantism.

While the critical literature on Huxley is enormous, the biographical is scant. Only Atkins, Clark, and Bedford have given prominence to Huxley's life. Atkins originally wrote before Huxley's death, and Clark's work is a family history. This leaves Bedford (who never fully acknowledged her role in Maria and Aldous Huxley's life) as the sole comprehensive biographer.

Huxley's life shows a dramatic shift in direction and emphasis in its second portion. As the Bedford work opens, Huxley's readers "waited with growing anticipation to see where Huxley would turn next," Watt writes in his introduction, quoting one of Huxley's contemporaries: "What course Mr. Huxley's destiny will now assume is one of the most interesting literary problems of the present decade." As in Justin Kaplan's *Mr. Clemens and Mark Twain*, Huxley's life is here joined in its second half, with his English years interpolated into the narrative of his American period.

A number of Huxley's associates, including Mann, Brecht, and Stravinsky, have had studies of their Hollywood periods. Other major works explore the general situation of English and European exiles to California (Taylor's *Strangers in Paradise*, Morley's *Tales of the Hollywood Raj*, Heilbut's *Exiles in Paradise*, and Baxter's *Hollywood Exiles*). Dardis, in his study of Faulkner, Fitzgerald, Huxley, and West, has outlined Huxley's American years. I use the word "Hollywood" as anthropologist Hortense Powdermaker does, "not an exact geographical district [but] wherever people connected with the movies live and work," and to refer to the (once) studio-dominated mainstream American film industry.

Over the last five years, I have consulted the works cited above and the research holdings on Aldous Huxley at the New York Public Library (Berg Collection), at the University of California at Los Angeles Library's Special Collections department, at the Huntington Library (which holds the papers of Edwin and Grace Hubble), at the University of Texas's Humanities Research Center, and at the British Library. The most comprehensive collection of biographical information on Huxley is the three-thousand-odd letters of Maria Nys Huxley to her sisters (in French), housed in the Museum of Literature, Belgian Royal Library, Brussels, Belgium.

I have also reviewed letters and manuscripts on Huxley's American years in private collections, including those of Margaret (Peggy) Kiskadden, Matthew Huxley, Laura Huxley, Betty Wendell, Mary Anita Loos, and Jacob Zeitlin.

The enormous imbalance between criticism and biography caused by the unavailability of personal sources on Huxley's life led me to rely on contemporary reminiscence (oral history). As Huxley's life receded in time, many of his associates and family have been willing to discuss his life candidly for the first time.

In these interviews my basic approach has been oral historiography, the tape-recorded recollections of eye witnesses to historically significant events. By checking the reliability and validity of oral sources against existing print sources and against each other, the researcher triangulates toward a larger, ideally objective, truth. Huxley's American period provides a classic test of this method, described in greater detail in Dunaway and Baum's *Oral History: An Interdisciplinary Anthology*. The most extensive of these interviews were tape-recorded, transcribed, and reviewed by the narrators, in standard oral history procedure.

The fusion of written sources and interviews has been called "oral biography," a genre that may possess advantages over works limited to written sources: interview sessions expose new collections of documents, including letters and photographs; interviews cover a full range of the subject's life, not just periods of public activity; the sources themselves are available for cross-examination and correction of the record; and, finally, orally sourced biography has an authenticity based on the triangular collaboration between the biographer, the sources, and occasionally, though not in this instance, the subject.

The problems of using interviews as a historical source transcend the homily that just telling something aloud does not make it true. Both the "halo effect," as sociologists call the desire of narrators to meet the expectations of interviewers, and the role of verbal performance must be factored into any assessment of oral sources.

Oral accounts mediate between previous life events and an interviewer's contemporary, research-based frame of reference. Because collecting oral sources for biographical research involves eliciting narration, aesthetic formulae and discourse rules of storytelling skew the information received in sometimes subtle ways. The narrator configures actual events into a symbolic representation of personal mythology, often based on hindsight and readings of subsequently written history. Factors affecting oral performance of personalized historical narratives—audiences historical and immediate, self-justification and catharsis, to name but a few—cannot be ignored. Many interviews inevitably yield "set pieces," rehearsed anecdotes of the past which are more prone to story than to history.

The transcripts of my interviews are deposited at the Huntington Library in San Marino, California; excerpts will appear as *Aldous Huxley Recollected* (Berkeley: University of California Press, 1991). In all, I conducted nearly a hundred interviews about Huxley's life. Of these, the tape-recorded interviews, and their dates, are found in the following list:

Rose D'Haulleville Nys	August 11, 1985	sister-in-law
Sidney Field	August 12, 1985	friend
Dorris Halsey	August 12, 1985	agent
Ellen Hovde	June 10, 1985 March 20, 1986	daughter-in-law
Francis Huxley	July 10, 1985	nephew
Juliette Huxley	July 5, 1985	sister-in-law
Laura Huxley	June 1, 3, 1985 August 12, 1985	widow
Matthew Huxley	March 18, 19, June 11, 1985 August 18, 1988	son
Tessa Huxley	June 13, 1985	granddaughter
Trevenen Huxley	July 12, 1985	grandson
Christopher Isherwood	June 2, 1985	fellow author
Margaret (Peggy) Kiskadden	May 31, June 3, August 13, 1985	friend
Marie Le Put	July 10, 1986	cook
Mary Anita Loos	July 10, 1986	friend
Burgess Meredith	August 7, 1986	friend

Jeanne Neveux	July 8, 1985	sister-in-law
Sylvia O'Neill	June 21, 1985	niece
Lawrence Powell	December 8, 1985	librarian
Rosalind Rajagopal	August 14, 1985	friend
Betty Wendell	June 2, 1985	fellow author
Claire White	June 14, 1985	niece
Jacob Zeitlin	June 1, 1985	friend, bookseller
	August 7, 1986	

Critical Bibliography

Atkins, John. *Aldous Huxley*. London: Orion, 1953, revised edition, 1968.

Baker, Robert S. *The Dark Historic Page*. Madison: University of Wisconsin Press, 1982.

Bass, Eben. *Annotated Bibliography*. New York: Garland, 1981.

Baxter, John. *Hollywood Exiles*. New York: Taplinger Publishing Co., 1976.

Bedford, Sybille. *Aldous Huxley*. New York: Harper/Knopf, 1973.

Bowering, Peter. *Aldous Huxley: A Study of the Major Novels*. New York: Oxford University Press, 1969.

Clark, Ronald. *The Huxleys*. New York: McGraw-Hill, 1968.

Dardis, Tom. *Some Time in the Sun*. New York: Scribners, 1976.

Dunaway, David and Willa Baum. *Oral History*. Nashville: AASLH, 1984.

Ferns, C. S. *Aldous Huxley, Novelist*. London: Athlone, 1980.

Firchow, Peter. *Aldous Huxley: Satirist and Novelist*. Minneapolis: University of Minnesota Press, 1972.

Heilbut, Anthony. *Exiled in Paradise*. New York: Viking, 1983.

Holmes, Charles. *Aldous Huxley and the Way to Reality*. Westport: Greenwood, 1970.

Lyon, James. *Brecht in America*. Princeton: Princeton University Press, 1980.

Meckier, Jerome. *Aldous Huxley: Satire and Structure*. New York: Barnes and Noble, 1969.

Morley, Sheridan. *Tales from the Hollywood Raj*. London: Weidenfeld, 1983.

Nance, Guinevera. *Aldous Huxley*. New York: Continuum, 1988.

Powdermaker, Hortense. *Hollywood: The Dream Factory*. Boston: Little, Brown, 1950.

Taylor, John Russell. *Strangers in Paradise*. New York: Holt, Rinehart, and Winston, 1983.

Thody, Philip. *Aldous Huxley: A Biographical Introduction*. New York: Scribners, 1973.

Watt, Donald. *Aldous Huxley: The Critical Heritage*. London: Routledge & Kegan Paul, 1975.

Watts, Harold. *Aldous Huxley*. New York: Twayne, 1969.

Woodcock, George. *Dawn and the Darkest Hour*. New York: Viking, 1971.

Books by Aldous Huxley

This listing is of works by Huxley referred to in the text and does not include anthologies, one-act plays, dramatic adaptations, selected works, and reprint editions. If only one publication date appears for a book published both in the United States and the United Kingdom, then those editions occurred in the same year.

An *asterisk** indicates a book first published in the United States. British titles that differ from American titles of the same book are in parentheses. All page number references to the works of Aldous Huxley in *Huxley in Hollywood* are from the first American edition of the work.

1916   *The Burning Wheel*
      B.H. BLACKWELL, U.K.

1917   *Jonah*
      HOLYWELL PRESS, U.K.

1918   *The Defeat of Youth*
      LONGMANS, GREEN, U.S.; B.H. BLACKWELL, U.K.

1920   *Leda*
      DORAN, U.S.; CHATTO & WINDUS, U.K.

1920   *Limbo*
      DORAN, U.S.; CHATTO & WINDUS, U.K.

1921   *Crome Yellow*
      CHATTO & WINDUS, U.K.

1922   *Crome Yellow*
      DORAN, U.S.

1922   *Mortal Coils*
      DORAN, U.S.; CHATTO & WINDUS, U.K.

1923 *On the Margin*
      DORAN, U.S.; CHATTO & WINDUS, U.K.
1923 *Antic Hay*
      DORAN, U.S.; CHATTO & WINDUS, U.K.
1924 *Young Archimedes (Little Mexican)*
      DORAN, U.S.; CHATTO & WINDUS, U.K.
1925 *Those Barren Leaves*
      DORAN, U.S.; CHATTO & WINDUS, U.K.
1925 *Along the Road*
      DORAN, U.S.; CHATTO & WINDUS, U.K.
1926 *Two or Three Graces*
      DORAN, U.S.; CHATTO & WINDUS, U.K.
1926 *Jesting Pilate*
      DORAN, U.S.; CHATTO & WINDUS, U.K.
1926 *Essays New and Old*
      CHATTO & WINDUS, U.K.
1927 *Essays New and Old*
      DORAN, U.S.
1927 *Proper Studies*
      CHATTO & WINDUS, U.K.
1928 *Proper Studies*
      DOUBLEDAY, DORAN & CO., U.S.
1928 *Point Counter Point*
      DOUBLEDAY, DORAN, U.S.; CHATTO & WINDUS, U.K.
1929 *Do What You Will*
      DOUBLEDAY, DORAN, U.S.; CHATTO & WINDUS, U.K.
1929 *Arabia Infelix*
      FOUNTAIN PRESS, U.S.; CHATTO & WINDUS, U.K.
1930 *Brief Candles.*
      DOUBLEDAY, DORAN, U.S.; CHATTO & WINDUS, U.K.
1930 *Vulgarity in Literature*
      CHATTO & WINDUS, U.K.
1931 *The World of Light*
      DOUBLEDAY, DORAN, U.S.; CHATTO & WINDUS, U.K.
1931 *The Cicadas*
      DOUBLEDAY, DORAN, U.S.; CHATTO & WINDUS, U.K.
1931 *Music at Night*
      DOUBLEDAY, DORAN, U.S.; CHATTO & WINDUS, U.K.
1932 *Brave New World*
      HARPER & BROTHERS, U.S.; CHATTO & WINDUS, U.K.
1932 *Texts and Pretexts*
      CHATTO AND WINDUS, U.K.
1933 *Texts and Pretexts*
      HARPER & BROTHERS, U.S.
1934 *Beyond the Mexique Bay*
      HARPER & BROTHERS, U.S.; CHATTO & WINDUS, U.K.
1936 *Eyeless in Gaza*
      HARPER & BROTHERS, U.S.; CHATTO & WINDUS, U.K.

1936   *What Are You Going to Do About It?*
      HARPER & BROTHERS, U.S.

1936   The Olive Tree
      CHATTO & WINDUS, U.K.

1937   The Olive Tree
      HARPER & BROTHERS, U.S.

1937   An Encyclopedia of Pacifism
      HARPER & BROTHERS, U.S.; CHATTO & WINDUS, U.K.

1937   Ends and Means
      HARPER & BROTHERS, U.S.; CHATTO & WINDUS, U.K.

1939   After Many a Summer Dies the Swan (After Many a Summer)
      HARPER & BROTHERS, U.S.; CHATTO & WINDUS, U.K.

1941   Grey Eminence
      HARPER & BROTHERS, U.S.; CHATTO & WINDUS, U.K.

1942   *The Art of Seeing
      HARPER & BROTHERS, U.S.

1943   The Art of Seeing
      CHATTO & WINDUS, U.K.

1944   *Time Must Have a Stop
      HARPER & BROTHERS, U.S.

1945   Time Must Have a Stop
      CHATTO & WINDUS, U.K.

1945   *The Perennial Philosophy
      HARPER & BROTHERS, U.S.

1946   The Perennial Philosophy
      CHATTO & WINDUS, U.K.

1946   Science, Liberty and Peace
      HARPER & BROTHERS, U.S.; CHATTO & WINDUS, U.K.

1948   The Gioconda Smile
      HARPER & BROTHERS, U.S.; CHATTO & WINDUS, U.K.

1948   *Ape and Essence
      HARPER & BROTHERS, U.S.

1949   Ape and Essence
      CHATTO & WINDUS, U.K.

1950   Themes and Variations
      HARPER & BROTHERS, U.S.; CHATTO & WINDUS, U.K.

1952   The Devils of Loudun
      HARPER & BROTHERS, U.S.; CHATTO & WINDUS, U.K.

1954   The Doors of Perception
      HARPER & BROTHERS, U.S.; CHATTO & WINDUS, U.K.

1955   The Genius and the Goddess
      HARPER & BROTHERS, U.S.; CHATTO & WINDUS, U.K.

1956   Heaven and Hell
      HARPER & BROTHERS, U.S.; CHATTO & WINDUS, U.K.

1956   Tomorrow and Tomorrow and Tomorrow (Adonis and Alphabet)
      HARPER & BROTHERS, U.S.; CHATTO & WINDUS, U.K.

1958   Brave New World Revisited
      HARPER & BROTHERS, U.S.; CHATTO & WINDUS, U.K.

1960   *On Art and Artists*
        HARPER & BROTHERS, U.S.
1962   *Island*
        HARPER & ROW, U.S.; CHATTO & WINDUS, U.K.
1963   *Literature and Science*
        HARPER & ROW, U.S.; CHATTO & WINDUS, U.K.
1967   *The Crows of Pearblossom*
        RANDOM HOUSE, U.S.

Filmography

Madame Curie, Metro-Goldwyn-Mayer, 1938 (released 1943)
(Aldous Huxley's 1938 treatment is uncredited.)

Screenplay:	Paul Osborn and Paul H. Rameau
Source:	*Madame Curie* (1937) by Eve Curie
Director:	Mervyn LeRoy
Producer:	Sidney Franklin
Film editor:	Harold F. Kress
Principal players:	Greer Garson (Mme. Curie)
	Walter Pidgeon (Pierre Curie)
	C. Aubrey Smith (Lord Kalvin)

Pride and Prejudice, Metro-Goldwyn-Mayer, 1940

Screen play:	Aldous Huxley and Jane Murfin
Source:	novel by Jane Austen
	(dramatization by Helen Jerome)
Director:	Robert Z. Leonard
Producer:	Hunt Stromberg
Film editor:	Robert J. Kern
Principal players:	Edward Ashley (Mr. Wickham)
	Greer Garson (Elizabeth Bennet)
	Maureen O'Sullivan (Jane Bennet)
	Ann Rutherford (Lydia Bennet)
	Laurence Olivier (Mr. Darcy)

Jane Eyre, Twentieth Century-Fox, 1944

Screenplay:	Aldous Huxley, Robert Stevenson, and John Houseman

Source:	novel by Charlotte Brontë
Director:	Robert Stevenson
Producer:	William Goetz
Film editor:	Walter Thompson
Principal players:	Orson Welles (Edward Rochester)
	Joan Fontaine (Jane Eyre)
	Margaret O'Brien (Adele Varens)
	Elizabeth Taylor (Helen Burns)
	Agnes Moorehead (Mrs. Read)

A Woman's Vengeance, Universal-International, 1948

Screenplay:	Aldous Huxley
Source:	"The Gioconda Smile" (1922), a story by Aldous Huxley
Director:	Zoltán Korda
Producer:	Zoltán Korda
Music:	Miklos Rozsa
Film editor:	Jack Wheeler
Principal players:	Charles Boyer (Henry Maurier)
	Jessica Tandy (Janet Spence)
	Sir Cedric Hardwicke (Dr. Libbard)

Alice in Wonderland, RKO, 1951 (animation)
(Huxley's contribution was uncredited.)

Screenplay:	Aldous Huxley, a dozen others
Source:	novel by Lewis Carroll (Charles Dodgson)
Director:	Clyde Geronomi, Hamilton Luske,
	Wilfred Jackson
Producer:	Walt Disney
Voices:	Katherine Beaumont (Alice)
	Ed Wynn (Mad Hatter)
	Sterling Holloway (Cheshire Cat)
	Jerry Colonna (March Hare)

Acknowledgments

Books including oral sources owe a particular debt to those agreeing to be interviewed, an often exhausting process; as one narrator joked to me, "Those of us who lived through history are condemned to repeat it."

Thus my first thanks are to those who agreed to be tape-recorded for this project (a list appears in A Note on Sources). I am also grateful to others who agreed to shorter talks: Sybille Bedford, Isaiah Berlin, Benjamin Bok, Gary Carey, Ronald Clark, Allen Ginsberg, Andrew Huxley, Rosalind Huxley, Jim Kepner, Cheri Pann, Jerry Vincent, and Siggy Wessberg.

Several fine libraries assisted me, including grants-in-aid from the Huntington Library (Martin Ridge, Dan Woodward, Sue Hodson and the staff of Readers' Services); the Herrick Library of the Academy of Motion Picture Arts and Sciences (David Marsh); the Humanities Research Center at the University of Texas; the Special Collections Departments of the UCLA Library (Jeffrey Rankin) and of Stanford University (Margaret Kimball); the Museum of Literature at the Belgian Royal Library (Jan Rubes); the British Library; the Hearst Archives at San Simeon courtesy of the California Department of Parks and Recreation (Robert Pavlik); and the Reference and Interlibrary Loan Departments of the University of New Mexico Library.

Two film companies allowed me to consult Huxley's film scripts: Turner Entertainment (Marian Kidd), Walt Disney Productions (Robin Russell). The Vedanta Society of Southern California and the Ramakrishna Mission allowed me access to their grounds.

Many colleagues at the University of New Mexico have been supportive of my work, particularly F. Chris Garcia, Hobson Wildenthal, Lee Bartlett, Rudolfo Anaya, Hugh Witemeyer, Ira Jaffee, Floyd Williams, and Paul Davis. Professor Nugel of the University of Munster shared his research.

Many associates assisted me in my research and interviews: Victoria Bergvall, C. C. Campbell, Becky Chisman, Juliette Cunico, Lisa Hilber, Carolynne White, Rebecca Zerger; others assisted by reading drafts: John Berger, Steven Mayer, Russell Goodman, Loretta Barrett, Nancy Guinn. Countless other friends discussed the project in various stages: to all my heartfelt gratitude.

Simultaneous Anglo-American publication poses particular challenges; were it not for my superb editors, Simon Michael Bessie at Harper (and Amy Gash) and Liz Calder at Bloomsbury (and Ruth Logan), I would surely have foundered mid-Atlantic. I also thank my agents Perry Knowlton and Andrew Best of Curtis Brown. My particular thanks are to my family: Lillian and Bob Ross, Philip Dunaway, Nina Wallerstein, and Alexander Wallerstein Dunaway.

INDEX

Films are printed in boldface type.

Hollywood (*continued*)
  Ape and Essence on, 218–222
  British colony in, 61–63, 127–129, 210–211
  CSU strike, 204
  German refugee community in, 83–84, 119, 145, 210–211
  movie censorship, 212, 342–343
  television's impact on, 240–241
  World War II movies, 179–180
  see also names of specific actors, films, studios, writers
Hollywood Ten, 204, 239, 248, 291
Horizon (publication), 24
House Committee on Un-American Activities. *See* Un-American Activities, House Committee on
House on 92nd Street, The, 209
Houseman, John, 176
Hovde, Ellen. *See* Huxley, Ellen Hovde
Howard, Brian, 24–25
HUAC. *See* Un-American Activities, House Committee on
Hubbard, Al, 315, 317
Hubbard, L. Ron, 278, 279, 280, 382
Hubble, Edwin, 69–70, 104, 147, 149, 160, 182, 211–212, 226, 247, 304–305, 386
Hubble, Grace Burke, 69–70, 74, 75, 81–83, 93, 95, 104, 109, 114–116, 119, 120, 134, 144, 148, 149, 154, 176, 182, 239–240, 283, 386
Hutchins, Robert M., 277
Huxley, Aldous
  allergy, 196–197, 216
  American citizenship, 305–308
  on anarchism, 28
  anticommunism and antistatism, 17, 23, 47, 381
  anti-Semitism, allegations against, 130
  appearance, 1, 33, 60–61, 184, 226, 285, 309, 365, 368
  arrival in California, 54–61, 63
  back injury, 13, 346–347
  blindness, *see* vision impairment
  bronchitis, 80, 114–115, 164, 224, 238, 368
  Buddhism experiences, 132, 194, 200, 318
  cancer, 347, 348–349, 353, 371–373
  children's story, 190
  cocaine, 362
  conscientious objection, 15, 306, *see also* Pacifism
  death, 373–376
  death of wife Maria, 318–320
  depressions, 11, 63, 64, 66, 124, 139–140, 141, 153, 160, 164, 167, 199, 201, 214–215, 224, 227, 244, 359

Huxley, Aldous (*continued*)
  driver's license, 190
  ecological views, 200, 335–336, 364–365
  education, Eton, 3, 4, 8, 15, 28, 168
  education, Oxford, 4, 9, 12, 28, 59, 129, 168
  European trips, 233–237, 251–252, 308–309
  fame in United States, 36, 225–226
  family background, 3–6, 11–12, 28
  film projects, 339–341
  on film writing, 177–178
  financial problems, 51, 52, 139–140, 141, 158
  friends' epilogues, 385–386
  grief over wife's death, 310, 318–320, 322
  Heard friendship, *see* Heard, Gerald
  Hollywood's attraction for, 51, 52
  house fire, 356–360, 369
  and hypnosis, 244–246, 264, 277, 279–281, 318
  influenza bouts, 255, 258, 367
  insomnia, 2, 11, 262, 279–280
  intestinal disorder, 14, 18
  lecturing activities, 192, 307, 332, 334, 347, 349, 350, 353, 367
  literary reputation, 3, 36, 337
  Llano del Rio ranch, 161–168, 175–176, 180–185, 189–191, 196–197, 215, 216, 218, 388
  loyalty issues, 270, 272
  marriages, 2, 3, 332–333, *see also* Huxley, Laura Archera; Huxley, Maria
  meditation, 14, 168–169, 279
  mescaline experiences, 285–303, 312, 314, 317, 322, 331–332, 339, 352, 371
  pacifism, *see* Pacifism
  parapsychology interests, *see* Parapsychology
  as parent, 191
  personality and outlook, 14, 173, 198–201, 294–295
  press publicity, 226
  prophecies, 199–201, 235–236, 334–337, 377–378
  psychedelic drug use, 327–329, 352–356, 361–362, 369–371, 375
  psychedelic research projects, 353–356, 369–371
  sexuality, views on, 117–118, 181–182
  and son's family, 323–324, 372
  in Southwest, 33–53 *passim*
  spiritual search, 14, 167–171, 173–175, 187–188, 201, 258, 279–281, 307, 316–318, 327–328, 381
  and television, 274–275

World War II
    British expatriates and, 127–129
    end of, 197–201
    movies about, 179–180
    reactions to, 89–90, 119, 127–129, 145–
        147, 150, 192–193
    see also Munich crisis (1938); Pacifism; Pearl
        Harbor

Yoga, 243, 244
You Are Not the Target (L. A. Huxley), 372, 387
"Young Archimedes," 252, 273

Zaehner, R. C., 329, 428
Zeitlin, Jake, 51–57, 62–65, 73, 78, 79, 110,
    126, 254, 336, 359
Zinnemann, Fred, 339

About the Author

David King Dunaway was born and raised in Greenwich Village in New York City. He attended the University of Aix-en-Provence, France, and the University of Wisconsin, with graduate training at the University of California Berkeley, where he received Berkeley's first Ph.D. in American Studies. At the University of New Mexico, Dr. Dunaway teaches biography and oral history and he has served as a Fulbright Senior Lecturer at the University of Nairobi and the University of Copenhagen.

His biography of Pete Seeger, *How Can I Keep From Singing*, won the American Society of Composers, Authors, and Publishers' Deems Taylor Award for excellence in writing about American music. The book appeared in Japanese, Spanish, and English editions. He is coeditor of *Oral History: An Interdisciplinary Anthology* and a consultant to UNESCO. His articles about American culture have appeared in publications ranging from *The Virginia Quarterly* to the *New York Times*.